The Handbook of FORENSIC SEXOLOGY

The Handbook of FORENSIC SEXOLOGY

BIOMEDICAL & CRIMINOLOGICAL PERSPECTIVES

Edited by

James J. Krivacska, Psy.D.
& John Money, Ph.D.

Prometheus Books
59 John Glenn Drive
Amherst, NewYork 14228-2197

Published 1994 by Prometheus Books

 Inquiries should be addressed to Prometheus Books, 59 John Glenn Drive, Amherst, New York 14228-2197, 716-691-0133 / FAX: 716-691-0137.

98 97 96 95 94 5 4 3 2 1

Library of Congress Cataloging-in-Publication Data

The handbook of forensic sexology : biomedical and criminological perspectives / edited by James J. Krivacska and John Money.

p. cm. — (New concepts in human sexuality series)

Includes bibliographical references and index.

ISBN 978-1-87975-883-7

1. Sex crimes. 2. Sex crimes—Investigation. 3. Sexology—Research. 4. Forensic sciences. I. Krivacska, James J. II. Money, John, 1921- . III. Title: Forensic sexology. IV. Series.

HV6556.H36 1994

363.2'5953—dc20 94-8451

CIP

To the memory of Herman Musaph
1915–1992
Leading Dutch Sexologist of the Post-War Generation
and Series Editor of
the *Handbook of Sexology,* Volumes 1–7

Contents

List of Contributors

Lauren R. Boglioli, M.D.
Resident
Lenox Hill Hospital
Department of Medicine
100 East 77th St.
New York, NY 10021, USA

F. M. Christensen, Ph.D.
Professor of Philosophy
University of Alberta-Edmonton
Dept of Philosophy, Faculty of Arts
4-108 Humanities Centre
Edmonton T6G 2E5, Canada

Eli Coleman, Ph.D.
Program in Human Sexuality
Department of Family Practice & Community Health
University of Minnesota
1300 South 2nd St.—Suite 180
Minneapolis, MN 55454, USA

Lee Coleman, M.D.
Center for the Study of Psychiatric Testimony
1889 Yosemite Road
Berkeley, CA 94707, USA

S. Margretta Dwyer, M.A.
Program in Human Sexuality
Department of Family Practice & Community Health
University of Minnesota
1300 South 2nd St.—Suite 180
Minneapolis, MN 55454, USA

Jay Feierman, M.D.
Clinical Professor
Department of Psychiatry
University of New Mexico School of Medicine
Presbyterian Behavioral Medicine Center
1325 Wyoming Boulevard NE
Presbyterian Healthcare Services
Albuquerque, NM 87112, USA

L. J. G. Gooren, M.D., Ph.D.
Professor of Transsexology
Dept. of Edocrinology/Andrology
Free University Hospital
P.O. Box 7057
1007 MB Amsterdam, The Netherlands

Richard Green, M.D., J.D.
Professor of Psychiatry
University of California, Los Angeles
Neuropsychiatric Institute and Hospital
Center for the Health Sciences
760 Westwood Plaza
Los Angeles, CA 90024-1759, USA

Steven J. Hucker, M.B., B.S., F.R.C.P. (C), F.R.C. Psych.
Professor and Chairman
Division of Forensic and Correctional Psychiatry
Queen's University
Kingston, Ontario K7L 3N6, Canada

James J. Krivacska, Psy.D.
Professional Evaluation Services
29 Elm Place
Milltown, NJ 08850, USA

Ron Langevin, Ph.D.
Associate Professor of Psychiatry
Clarke Institute of Psychiatry
Director, Juniper Associates Services
5353 Dundas St., West, Suite 200
Etobicoke, Ontario M9B 6H8, Canada

Nancy Lee
16 Havertown Rd.
Newark, DE 19713, USA

Gregory K. Lehne, Ph.D.
Assistant Professor of Medical Psychology
The Johns Hopkins University and Hospital
4419 Falls Road at Cold Spring Lane
Baltimore, MD 21211-1226, USA

Jean-Ric Meller
6231 Branting St.
San Diego, CA 92122, USA

Philip Meredith, D. Phil.
Senior Research Fellow in Surgical Audit
Royal College of Surgeons of England
Ivy Cottage, West Hoathly
West Sussex, RH19 4QG, England

Jerome G. Miller, Ph.D.
National Center on Institutions and Alternatives
635 Slaters Lane, Suite G-100
Alexandria, VA 22314, USA

John Money, Ph.D.
Emeritus Professor of Medical Psychology and Pediatrics
Psychohormonal Research Unit
The Johns Hopkins University and Hospital
Suite LL 20—Old Town Office Center
1235 East Monument St.
Baltimore, MD 21202-5327, USA

Donald L. Mosher, Ph.D.
The College of Liberal Arts and Sciences
The University of Connecticut
Box U-20, Room 107
406 Babbidge Rd.
Storrs, CN 06269-1020, USA

Herman Musaph, M.D.
Emeritus Professor of Sexology
University of Utrecht
The Netherlands
(deceased)

Joan A. Nelson, Ed.D.
P.O. Box 2232
San Rafael, CA 94979, USA

Paul Okami, Ph.D.
Department of Psychology
University of California
Los Angeles, CA 90024-1563, USA

Fang-fu Ruan, M.D., Ph.D.
P.O. Box 4941
Burlingame, CA 94011-4941, USA

Peter M. Sheridan
Ph.D. Cand. in Psychology
Impulsivity Programme
Clarke Institute of Psychiatry
University of Toronto
250 College St.
Toronto, Ontario M5T 1R8, Canada

H. N. Sno, M.D., Ph.D.
Academic Medical Center
Psychiatric Outpatient Clinic
Meibergdreef 9
1005 AZ Amsterdam, The Netherlands

Charlene Steen, Ph.D., J.D.
1835 First St.
Napa, CA 94559, USA

Mark L. Taff, M.D.
Forensic Pathologist
511 Hempstead Ave., Suite 2
West Hempstead, NY 11552, USA

A. A. Tkachenko, M.D.
Senior Research Assistant
Institute of General and Forensic Psychiatry
Kropotkynsky per., 23, 119034
Moscow, Russia

Ralph Underwager, Ph.D.
Institute for Psychological Therapies
13200 Cannon City Blvd.
Northfield, MN 55057-4405, USA

Frans A. van der Reijt, J.D.
President of the Dutch Gender Foundation
Sullivandreef 19
5012 AM Tilburg, The Netherlands

Jeffrey S. Victor, Ph.D.
Professor, Department of Sociology
State University of New York
Jamestown Community College
30 Hillcrest Ave.
Jamestown, NY 14701, USA

Hollida Wakefield, M.A.
Institute for Psychological Therapies
13200 Cannon City Blvd.
Northfield, MN 55057-4405, USA

Preface

James J. Krivacska

Since the 1600s science has sought to replace religion as the purveyor of truth and knowledge within a progressive world. In the matter of sexology, however, early twentieth-century science often gave its imprimatur to religiously inspired moral dogma, which it then sought to confirm through verification of sensory experiences.

After Karl Popper's mid-century proposal, relative to a philosophy of science, that truth and knowledge can never be verified through inductive reasoning alone, the most that science could hope for was to determine an approximation of reality by way of falsification (Popper 1959). Science subsequently saw its role as that of the skeptical observer of phenomena, seeking always to disprove its own theories through experiment and observation. Science during this period became more humble about its ability accurately to observe and explain reality, and more cautious in its presumption of knowledge.

In the 1980s, the social sciences, including sexology, saw a retrenchment from its earlier position wherein science, while no longer necessarily serving as validator of religious dogma, was still being used to support, rationalize, and justify sociopolitical "correctness," much of which was based on the religious dogma of the last half millennium. While science, then, has never been wholly objective, it has, for the better part of this century, disciplined itself with a process that offers the best hope of furthering knowledge and understanding of the human condition. As I. L. Reiss (1993: 5) puts it:

> No other way of gaining knowledge about the world is as rigorous and precise or as demanding of relevant evidence. Moreover, scientific results require validity, reliability, peer review, publication of results, disciplined

inquiry, careful logic and reasonable conclusions. In short, scientific inquiry provides a systematic and valuable way of understanding.

The science of sexology, from the perspective of social policy and legal systems, offers the best available vehicle within legal systems for making rational decisions that are most likely to be consistent with "reality."

This volume seeks to aid in that process by providing a dialogue based not on sociopolitical dogma, but on a process of investigation, critique, analysis, and systematic research. Sociopolitical systems are increasingly looking to science to support prescribed and predetermined agendas, rather than to help establish those agendas. We serve neither the long-term interests of scientific endeavor nor those of society by supporting dogmatism. Rather, we look to educate and instill discipline within ourselves, first by the manner in which we conduct our science, and second in the way we use what has been acquired to foster and promote public policy and legal reform that will ultimately further societal interests.

Part of this process is both the self-recognition and the promotion of a public view of science and the acquisition of knowledge as an evolutionary, rather than a static process. Too frequently, science is presented in public forums and utilized by those with sociopolitical purposes as the absolute determiner of reality—but only when science is consistent with the previously established belief system of the group seeking to use it. In other words, science is used adversarially, not impartially.

When sexological science becomes absolutist and inflexible, its credibility is damaged. Too frequently, that inflexibility is challenged by conflicting information; moreover, when sexologists fail to revise their theories, their science is at risk of being replaced by populist theories and of losing credibility as a whole.

Scientific objectivity, rather than presenting a monolithic representation of the true reality of sex, gives a constantly evolving conceptualization of sexological events and phenomena that best represent the understanding of reality at a given moment, but subject to revision with further data.

What legal systems have to gain from sexology is, first, that of all the systems for gathering sexual knowledge, scientific sexology is the best and most reliable, and, second, that despite its lofty superiority, it is subject to evolution and even, at times, radical change. However, this process of evolution and change is not one we fear, but one we welcome and pursue.

In the present day and age, forensic sexology finds itself pretty much in the position of the woodcutter who finds the trees but can't see the forest. Then, when he discovers what he deems to be the forest, it turns out to be only a segment of the forest—a stand of only one species of trees, a patch of evergreens, or a deciduous grove.

In the present volume, this metaphor signifies that the various contributors to this volume do not view either the forest or the trees of forensic sexology from the same vantage point. In other words, they do not share in their entirety the epistemology, principles, and concepts of sexology in general, and hence of forensic sexology in particular. Thus, in the ensuing chapters, the divergences as well as the correspondences constitute a fair representation of the way things are. We hope that realism is more to be preferred by the reader than a false image of uniformity.

REFERENCES

Popper, K. (1959). *The Logic of Scientific Discovery.* London: Hutchinson.

Reiss, I. L. (1993). "The Future of Sex Research and the Meaning of Science." *The Journal of Sex Research* 30: 3–11.

Prologue

John Money

NORMAL: IDEOLOGICAL VERSUS STATISTICAL

There is a metaphorical seismic fault along which lies, on one side, the very ancient upheaval of the rocks of forensic sexosophy and, on the other, the very recently laid-down deposits of forensic sexology. The first major movement along the fault that began shifting forensic sexology away from forensic sexosophy was registered in 1885, the year that saw the publication of Richard von Krafft-Ebing's *Psychopathia Sexualis* (12th English ed., 1931). This is the book that conventionally marks the separation of sexology as a new science of sex from its provenance in sexosophy, the philosophy and theology of sex.

In sexosophy, the criterion of "normal" is ideological, and to be normal is to qualify as ideologically perfect or ideal. The standard of perfection is not absolute but relative: It varies according to time and place, historically and transculturally; it is set by the authority of those who possess the power to threaten and enforce punishment for disobedience and nonconformity. Thus, to be ideologically "normal" means to be not punitively threatened but approved of.

In sexology, the meaning of "normal" is mathematical and statistical. It means being average or, like the majority of people, in the middle range, not at either extreme. Being normal in genital anatomy means being neither minute nor massive, but somewhere between both extremes. Being statistically normal or average is, in itself, neither good nor bad, but just ordinary or typical. Thus, when there is an epidemic of an STD (sexually transmitted disease) it may be the norm to come down with an infection, although it is not good to do so. Conversely, if it becomes the norm for teenagers and young adults to use condoms for at least partial protection against HIV infection and AIDS, that is good by most people's reckoning.

CRIMINAL VERSUS PATHOLOGICAL

Historically, Krafft-Ebing symbolizes the beginnings of a still ongoing social policy whereby ideologically prohibited and aberrant sexual practices are recognized not only as criminal but also as pathological. He claimed forensic sexology as the future intellectual property of medicine and science, not of juridical and religious dogma.

In forensic sexology, over the course of the twentieth century, sexual emancipation has been stepwise, from criminalization to pathologization to toleration. This stepwise sequence is exemplified in historical instances of the decriminalization of fellation, cunnilinction, anal copulation, contraception, prostitution, homosexuality, and some categories of visual and literary erotica and pornography.

The stepwise transition from pathologization to toleration has often faltered and has also been transculturally divergent: witness such examples as mild and consensual sadomasochism; cross-species sex; and erotic exposure and viewing of the genitalia, solo or while engaging in sexual intercourse, as a form of consensual theatrical entertainment.

In the case of those sexual practices that the law currently classifies as deviant or perverted, the step from criminalization to pathologization has, if not completely stalled, then hardly begun. Deviance and perversion are terms that still appear in forensic sexological usage, but they are giving way to the less pejorative term of paraphilia (from Greek, *para,* amiss or altered + *philia,* love).

The formal definition of paraphilia is as follows.

> **Paraphilia:** a condition occurring in men and women of being compulsively responsive to and obligatorily dependent on an unusual and personally or socially unacceptable stimulus, perceived or in the ideation and imagery of fantasy, for optimal initiation and maintenance of sexuoerotic arousal and the facilitation or attainment of orgasm. Paraphilic imagery may be replayed in fantasy during solo masturbation or intercourse with a partner. Its antonym is normophilia. (Money 1988)

The official list of the paraphilias is published in the American Psychiatric Association's *Diagnostic and Statistical Manual of Mental Disorders,* third edition, revised (*DSM-III-R*).[1] Eight paraphilias are named and specified in detail in *DSM-III-R*: exhibitionism, fetishism, frotteurism (sexual excitement produced by rubbing against someone), pedophilia, sexual masochism, sexual sadism, transvestic fetishism (cross-dressing), and voyeurism. These eight paraphilias are the same as those that are classified in law as perverted criminal practices. Most of the thirty-odd noncriminal paraphilias (listed and defined in Money 1986; 1988) are classified in *DSM-III-R* as "Not Otherwise Specified," a category in which seven examples are enumerated by name only: telephone scatologia, necrophilia, partialism, zoophilia, coprophilia, klismaphilia, and urophilia. Paraphilic rape (raptophilia) is not identified as a syndrome, nor is paraphilic lust murder (erotophonophilia), single or serial. Both of these two paraphilias are subsumed under sexual sadism.

Paraphilic rape and lust murder are extreme examples of paraphilias that confront society with the vexed question of where to draw the line between individual and societal sexual rights. The touchstone criterion of consensual agreement between adults is satisfying for a multitude of cases, but not for all. For example, consenting adults, men and women, some HIV positive and some HIV negative, may reciprocally agree to participate in a group sex scene; but their consent does not cancel their transmission of the virus and its epidemic spread, which is a societal concern.

There is a principle to apply to this dilemma, namely, that it is not possible to achieve fully informed, mutual consent unless the outcome can be predicated at the outset. In the HIV example above, none of the consenting adults can fully foresee what will be the long-term infectious outcome, and how many other members of society will ultimately pay the price of infection as a sequel to their engagement in epidemic-spreading behavior.

Foresight is not the same as prophecy. No outcome of anything can be foreseen with absolute prophetic or clairvoyant certainty. To foresee the outcome of something is to predict the chances of its occurrence with a greater or lesser degree of confidence according to the statistics of the laws of chance. The range of predictability is from extremely likely to extremely unlikely. To use the HIV-AIDS example again: Two young people mutually consent to have sexual intercourse. Neither has ever been tested for HIV. Thus, they give their mutual consent not to the risk of knowingly exposing one or the other to the virus, but to the risk of assuming that both are virus-free, which may be extremely unlikely, extremely likely, or at some degree in between.

Another example applies to rape: being unable to foresee that a walk to the parking lot will be cut short by abduction and violently coerced sexual intercourse, one cannot consent to being raped, and so the rapist forfeits his own rights to those of society.

In the case of paraphilically violent rape or lust murder, society exercises its rights irrespective of extenuating circumstances—brain disease or toxicity, for example—consideration of which comes later when deciding how further to intervene. In response to paraphilias, for centuries society's only form of intervention has been through the criminal justice system of incarceration and punishment. Society is so wedded to the criminalization of paraphilic behavior that rather than expedite, it hinders their pathologization, and so impedes the medical and scientific possibility of discovering their cause and cure—a policy which is the equivalent of cutting off one's nose to spite one's face.

This policy is deeply entrenched in ancient religious and moral dogmas of personal responsibility for, and voluntary choice of, sexual righteousness versus sexual transgression. Its corollary is the dogma of vengeance and retribution for the sin of sexual transgression. Transgressions are against rules, no matter how arbitrary, that themselves constitute a large part of all sexosophies. There is no guarantee in the formulations of any sexosophy that its rules will be rational or consistent, and very often they are not.

From Krafft-Ebing's time at the end of the nineteenth century to the present, one of the legacies of the dogma of vengeance and retribution has been an antithetical relationship between the criminal justice and the biomedical scientific systems with respect to forensic sexology. Criminal justice equates biomedical science with being soft on sexual crime. Thus prejudice puts a winter freeze on biomedical research into the etiology, treatment, and, above all, the developmental prevention, from infancy onward, of syndromes of sex-offending. The paradox of the dogma of vengeance and retribution is that, by having no effective power of prevention, it fails to protect society against a progressive escalation of sexual pathology from each generation to the next.

NATURE/NURTURE REDACTED

A second legacy of the dogma of vengeance and retribution, also from Krafft-Ebing's time to the present, has been a dichotomous relationship between reform and research in sexology. Impatient with the slow process of sex research, sex reformers jettisoned worn-out doctrines from the past and replaced them with trendy new ones that were more fashionable than scientific. The new doctrines were engines of moral and political change. Social eugenics, for example, promised at the end of the nineteenth century to engineer the evolutionary purity of the race. It ended up in disgrace half a century later in the moral depravity of Hitler's Holocaust. Planned parenthood, by contrast, in the same era showed that the outcome of reformist zeal may be, dispute notwithstanding, positively commended.

The divergence between sex reformers and sex research continues to bedevil forensic sexology, and nowhere more conspicuously than in doctrinal competition regarding the efficacy of sex education for youth, and of therapeutic intervention for sex offenders and other paraphiles. The major divergence is the one that has rekindled the nature versus nurture debate as the polemics of biological essentialism versus social constructionism. Constructionism is both deconstructive and reconstructive. For example, rape and child abuse have been deconstructed as manifestations of sex, and reconstructed as manifestations of violence and power. Gender and erotic orientation have been deconstructed so as to be devoid of any manifestations attributable to biology, and reconstructed so as to be manifestations of learned social stereotypes, exclusively.

There is a third legacy of the dogma of vengeance and retribution, namely, assimilation of the age-old religious and legal disciplinary paradigm of reward and punishment into the academic paradigm of approach/avoidance learning. Reissued under the name of behavior modification, the latter has become assimilated into forensic sexology by way of psychiatry. Variously adapted, behavior modification is applied as, ostensibly, a method of socially reconstructing sex offenders.

In the treatment of sex offending and other paraphilias, behavior modification has met with greatest popularity in those healthcare professions that are not licensed by the state to prescribe medications and carry out invasive medical procedures. If they are licensed at all, it is to provide only the services of talking treatment. This legal restriction accentuates the dichotomy between the theory and practice of biomedical science and therapy, on the one hand, and social constructionist science and therapy, on the other.

Scholarly dispute that revolves around this dichotomy constitutes a rehash of the body/mind conundrum. It fails to recognize the now rapidly accumulating data on the molecular biology of learning and remembering in the brain. Take away the brain, and there is absolutely no social construction of anything. The great challenge to forensic sexology is not whether, in the final analysis, sexopathology exists in the brain and nervous system or someplace else (the soul? the spirit? the psyche? the astral body?). No, the challenge is to discover where in the brain sexopathology exists, when and how it gets in there, and how immutably it gets stuck there. From conception through maturity, hormones and other neurochemistries that enter into the development and functioning of the sexual brain by way of the bloodstream are not intrinsically more powerful or important than are sensory stimuli and signals that enter the brain by way of the eyes, ears, nose, skin, and taste. Even the genome itself is not an absolute dictator, for it cannot unfold and reveal itself, except in interaction with its environment, inside as well as outside the cell.

VICTIMOLOGY

In addition to these three legacies of the dogma of vengeance and retribution there exists another dogma, namely that of supernatural sexual evil. Thought to have disappeared after the Inquisition and the Salem witch trials, it has now returned to haunt sexology at the end of the twentieth century. Supernatural sexual evil is the welcome guest of *fin de siècle* religious fundamentalism, juridical antisexualism, political androphobia, and professional victimology. The new professional specialty of victimology became established after pediatrics rediscovered the battered child syndrome in the 1960s (Kempe et al. 1962) and state legislatures passed child protection laws. The professed mission, or crusade, of victimology is one of social reform: to protect children exposed at home to violent cruelty, abusive punishment, and criminal neglect. In court, it is difficult to challenge the sanctity of the family and the right of parents to administer corporal punishment. It is not difficult, on the other hand, to get convictions when the charges are of sexual abuse, especially incest. As a consequence, victimology has veered away from nonsexual violence and cruelty, and has become a crusade for sexual reform—a crusade of healthcare professionals acting as undercover agents for the criminal justice system and dedicated to eradicating the sexual abuse and molestation of children, as well as the rape of females, young or old.

In cases of false accusation or of insufficiency of evidence, in order to obtain a prosecution, interrogation of the alleged victim has been conducted in such a way as to evoke the phenomenon of *pseudologia fantastica,* that is, a fictional or fantastically pseudological account of abuse. A skillful serial interrogation is readily able to evoke elaborate accounts of ritual sexual abuse, human sacrifice, and even cannibalism, conducted in the ceremonial secrecy of a satanic cult, all of which are false.

Dissemination of such fantastical information in the electronic and print media allows it to be assimilated by an enormously large audience of children and adults, nationally and internationally. By a process of social contagion, some members of this audience, young and old alike, will have the mental experience of *pseudologia fantastica* themselves, with or without being interrogated. Some will initiate retrospective charges against even their own parents, accusing them of a history of infant and child sexual molestation. Their phantasmagorias might be, as they have been in the past, accepted as factual history by victimologists who are trained as social workers, police officers, prosecuting attorneys, psychologists, and physicians.

In the theory of victimology, clients or patients are classified as either victims or perpetrators. The theory to explain victimhood is explicitly a revival of Freud's 1895–96 theory (now discredited) of the origin of hysteria or hysterical psychoneurosis (Breuer and Freud 1895; Freud, in Masson 1985), popularly known as his seduction theory. Seduction theory attributed neurotic symptoms at any age to the trauma of sexual abuse earlier in life, especially within the family in childhood. In today's victimology usage, sexual trauma is defined inclusively, and is not age-restricted. It comprises not only child molestation but rape and any kind of sex-related experience, including noncoercive affectionate caressing or touching, that a person subjectively interprets to have been offensive.

The theoretical locus of victimology is far removed from orthodox psychoanalysis. It is situated instead in the rival battlefield model of what in World War I was called shell shock, a term subsequently changed to war neurosis or combat fatigue, and most recently to post-traumatic stress disorder. Insofar as the etiological connection between trauma and disorder is not always self-evident, there has been in victimology a return to the concepts of dissociation and dissociative or multiple personality, originally formulated by the psychologists Pierre Janet (1859–1947) and Morton Prince (1854–1929). It is a fixed principle of victimology, though not an essential principle of dissociation, that a long dormant alternative personality or "alter" (i.e., "other") may be conjured up, possibly under hypnosis or coerced suggestibility. This *alter* is the personality that, manifesting *pseudologia fantastica,* recognizes a history of fictional sexual abuse which is not recalled by the other personality or personalities, where it is ostensibly "in denial."

For those whom it calls perpetrators, victimology has no theoretical explanation of perpetratorship, other than to fall back on prescientific moral, legal, and religious explanations. These are explanations that rest ultimately on ideas of voluntary depravity, possibly in combination with social contagion (for example, from contact with pornography), and possibly under the disinhibiting influence of alcohol or drugs. Victimology theory closes the door upon biomedical scientific explanations of sexopathology, even in such cases as those attributable to intracranial injury or tumor, brain cell degeneration, atypical epileptiform seizures, and so on.

Victimology's greatest theoretical threat to scientific forensic sexology is not, however, its neglect of biomedical explanations and its espousal of sexual reform, but its active policy of promulgating occult explanations attributed to Satanism. Satanic explanations not so long ago might have been written off as the folly of a few crackpots, but no longer. The myth of Satanism has today infected too large a public, and has coopted too many people with authority and power in the criminal justice system. Satanism impedes the growth of scientific forensic sexology. It depletes the resources available for basic research into the origin and prevention of the paraphilias and related disorders. In the place of the science of sex, it substitutes a sexosophy of the occult.

NOTE

1. As of April 1994, The American Psychiatric Association's *Diagnostic and Statistical Manual of Mental Disorders,* 3rd ed., revised (*DSM-III-R*), 1987, has been superseded by: American Psychiatric Association (1994). *Diagnostic and Statistical Manual of Mental Disorders.* 4th ed. Washington, D.C.: American Psychiatric Press.

REFERENCES

Breuer, J., and Freud, S. (1895). *Studien über Hysterie.* Leipzig and Vienna: Franz Deuticke, 1895. Also in *The Standard Edition of the Complete Psychological Works of Sigmund Freud* (trans. J. Strachey, with A. Freud). Vol. 2. London: Hogarth Press and the Institute of Psycho-analysis, 1955.

Kempe, C. H.; Silverman, F. N.; Steele, B. F.; Droegemueller, W.; and Silver, H. K. (1962). "The Battered-Child Syndrome." *Journal of the American Medical Association* 181: 17–24.

Krafft-Ebing, R. von. (1931). *Psychopathia Sexualis with Special Reference to the Antipathic Sexual Instinct: A Medico-Forensic Study.* (Authorized English adaptation of the twelfth German edition, by F. J. Rebman.) Chicago: Logan Brothers.

Masson, J. M. (1985). *The Assault on Truth: Freud's Suppression of the Seduction Theory.* New York: Penguin.

Money, J. (1986). *Lovemaps: Clinical Concepts of Sexual/Erotic Health and Pathology, Paraphilia, and Gender Transposition in Childhood, Adolescence, and Maturity.* New York: Irvington.

———. (1988). *Gay, Straight, and In-Between: The Sexology of Erotic Orientation.* New York: Oxford University Press.

Part One

Sexology and Criminology

Introduction

There exists at the conjunction of sexology and forensics a core of sexual behavior and activity which, according to current societal norms and criteria, is deviant or against the interests of society on either moral or political grounds. This first section examines a diverse range of sexual behavior, orientation, and desire from an etiologic and phenomenological perspective so as to better understand the nature and the role they play in the lives of those predisposed to them. Ultimately, it is hoped that this understanding will come to underlie a rational and reasoned response by society to affected individuals. Divergent viewpoints are represented, some overlapping and some incompatible, even highly incompatible—which is an accurate representation of contemporary sexology.

Richard Green leads this section with a brief review of the history of sodomy laws in contemporary civilization, with a particular emphasis on this past half century. Green's chapter engenders some optimism that current judicial trends are moving toward recognition of the right to privacy in matters relating to consensual sexual activities between adults. Contemporary Western society's probably most despised sex offender, the child molester, is the subject of Jay R. Feierman's chapter on pedophilia. Recognizing that prevention is best conceptualized when founded upon a solid understanding of etiology, Feierman summarizes and critiques the current state of knowledge of pedophilia, as well as outlining some of his research and his biosocial theoretical model.

Joan A. Nelson and Jean-Ric Meller's chapter forthrightly challenges currently held assumptions about the adverse interpersonal and sexological sequelae of incest between consenting adult partners. They propose legal modifications which, while not unduly restricting consensual adult sexual relationships, provide appropriate protection of minors from intergenerational incest.

Peter M. Sheridan and Steven Hucker's chapter on rape and sadomasochistic paraphilia reflects a current trend being pursued by some in the field of forensic sexology to deemphasize the forensic application of sexologic science in favor of a simplistic model of behavioral choices or preferences as the underlying cause of paraphilia. The authors refer to the preference of the rapist for violent sexual assault or coercive sex as if it were equivalent to the choice of an item from a menu or a style of clothing.

This simplistic model obviates the need for any further research as to causality, for it declares rape to be the result of free will. By enlarging the definition of rape, it also allows for far too many men to be accused falsely of rape. When rape can mean anything from forced vaginal penetration on a woman by an unknown assailant to lack of explicit consent to engage in sexual intercourse between a married couple, the term loses its power to discriminate, describe, and define behavior. This is medical science held hostage to criminological dogma.

Ron Langevin's chapter on exhibitionism and voyeurism and Lauren R. Bogliani and Mark L. Taff's chapter on autoasphyxiation strive to reframe professional understanding of these paraphilias from a criminological to a mental health perspective. In this context, a rational and potentially more successful strategy for paraphilic intervention and prevention may be sought.

Louis Gooren and Frans van der Reijt's chapter on transsexualism and sex reassignment, and Nancy Lee's survey of the world of the prostitute provide a strong case for delimiting the role of the law and legal systems as applied to issues of fundamental biological and physiological process, as well as to issues of consensual sexual behavior and quality of life.

Herman Musaph's chapter reflects his initial analysis of the issue of sexual harassment, which was not completed prior to his untimely death in November 1992. His chapter is presented here, in part, as an illustration of how the Netherlands, a culture considerably more liberal and progressive relative to sexuality than that of North America and much of Europe, is responding to the contemporary sexual issue of sexual harassment. Musaph's discussion of sexual harassment is primarily directed toward overt actions of a sexual nature (involving either direct physical contact or an unambiguous sexual proposition) between two individuals, one of whom holds power over the other by virtue of a work or school relationship, or within the context of a therapist/client relationship. This is in sharp contrast to the rapidly expanding view of sexual harassment in the United States, where harassment has become an overly inclusive category for any unwanted or unwelcome gesture, glance, comment, or physical approach regardless of the relative status of the participants. The differences between these two perceptions of what constitutes sexual harassment may be representative of a pervasive difference in how sexuality is viewed in the two cultures.

Together, the chapters of Part One lay the essential groundwork for understanding in Part Two how to respond to and intervene with both the initiator and the target of sex offending and/or paraphilic behavior, as well as for conceptualizing in Part Three how society needs to reformulate and restructure its views of sexuality and paraphilia. Absent this understanding, efforts at prevention and intervention readily fall victim to the winds of societal discontent or the righteous moralizing of those whose understanding of mental health and functioning is constrained by dichotomous conceptualizations of "good" and "evil" intent.

1

Sodomy Laws

Richard Green

INTRODUCTION

When a sexual act is designated by a term deriving from a biblical city's destruction by the wrath of God (Gen. 19:24), clearly the act is not held in high regard. So offensive is the act that legislators have been unable to put the term to pen in prohibitory laws. Sodomy is the "abominable and detestable crime against nature," or "a crime not fit to be named among Christians." But, irrespective of the social condemnation evoked by sodomy, as with all sexual acts it is behavior typically conducted in private. Thus it could find sanctuary under an overarching legal principle, the right to privacy.

SEXUAL PRIVACY

The controversy over whether there is a constitutionally based right to privacy in American law was headlined during the televised hearings on the nomination of Judge Robert Bork to the Supreme Court. He argued that there was not. Other legal scholars countered with reference to a series of cases marking zones of sexuality that have been protected from governmental regulation.

From the constitutional law perspective, a source of this dispute is that the United States Constitution makes no mention of sex, nor of privacy. However, amendments to the Constitution that protect against deprivation of "life, liberty, or property, without due process of law," "[or assure] to any person . . . the equal protection of the laws" have been interpreted to create dominions of sexual privacy (United States Constitution, Amendments V, IV).

Condemnation and Control of Homosexuality: Religious and Moral Bases

Christianity's preoccupation with the unnaturalness of sodomy derives from St. Augustine's contention that the otherwise shameful "genital commotion," his tumultuous depiction of sexual conduct, is appropriate only for marital procreation (Augustine 1950). Similarly, St. Thomas Aquinas argued that homosexual acts were unnatural and immoral, for God's given sexuality was to be used only for reproduction (Aquinas 1946).

Against this religiously based restrictive standard, John Stuart Mill staked out the modern libertarian argument for sexual privacy. In 1859 he argued that society has jurisdiction over a person's conduct only when it prejudicially affects the interests of others. No one has the right to say to another adult "that he shall not do with his life for his own benefit what he chooses to do with it" (Mill 1859).

Mill's contemporary critic, Sir James Stephen, objected: "How can the State or the public be competent to determine any question whatever if it is not competent to decide that gross vice is a bad thing?" To enforce moral behavior "[Society has at its disposal two great instruments . . . law and public opinion" (Stephen 1873).

A century later, the English legal scholar Lord Devlin argued that society has the right to legislate against immorality and that immorality is what the public or the "man in the street" reacts to with "intolerance, indignation, and disgust." For Devlin, a collection of individuals does not make a society; rather, it is the shared morality that defines society. Because vice is subversive to that society, it ought to be eradicated in the same manner as treason. Devlin saw homosexuality as analogous to treason since both were destructive of the stable fabric of society (Devlin 1965). In his debate with Devlin, Professor J. Hart objected to the concept of society as a "seamless web" that will disintegrate "unless all its emphatic vetoes are enforced by law." For Hart, the risk of democratic rule by the majority lay in telling the man in the street that if "he feels sick enough about what other persons do in private to demand its suppression by law, no theoretical criticism can be made of his demand" (Hart 1961).

Shall/should/can a nation set legal standards for morality? Dean Rostow wrote: "Men often say that one cannot legislate morality. I should say that we legislate hardly anything else" (Rostow 1960).

PROTECTED RIGHTS UNDER AMERICAN LAW

"Fundamental rights" receive special protection in American constitutional law. When a right is declared fundamental, a law may curtail it only to serve a compelling state interest. Further, the law must be the most narrowly drawn, such that the state interest is served with surgical precision.

With sexuality, the United States Supreme Court has defined few fundamental rights. In 1942, the Court struck down a law mandating sterilization for men after a third conviction for "moral turpitude." It wrote:

> We are dealing here with legislation which involves one of the basic civil rights of man. Marriage and procreation are fundamental to the very existence and survival of the race. (Without them a person) is forever deprived of a basic liberty. (*Skinner* v. *Oklahoma,* 1942)

The Court decision typically cited as laying the foundation for the contemporary sexual privacy argument is the contraception case decided in 1965. A Connecticut law criminalized the use of contraceptives by married partners. In striking down the statute, the Court held that the use of contraceptives to prevent pregnancy was a private decision. They ruled:

> [C]oncern[ing] a relationship lying within the zone of privacy created by several fundamental constitutional guarantees . . . a law . . . forbidding the use of contraceptives . . . seeks to achieve its goal by means having a maximum destructive impact upon that relationship. (*Griswold* v. *Connecticut,* 1965)

The right to possess adult obscene materials (not child pornography) in one's home was held a protected right in 1969. It was founded on the "right to be free, except in very limited circumstances, from unwarranted governmental intrusion into one's privacy" (*Stanley* v. *Georgia,* 1969).

The right of an *unmarried* person to use contraceptives was declared in 1972:

> If the right of privacy means anything, it is the right of the individual, married or single, to be free from unwarranted governmental intrusion into matters so fundamentally affecting a person as the decision whether to bear or beget a child. (*Eisenstadt* v. *Baird,* 1972).

The right to abortion was held fundamental in 1973 in part because otherwise "the detriment that the state would impose upon the pregnant woman by denying this choice altogether is apparent [and profound]" (*Roe* v. *Wade,* 1973).

Marriage (between [only] two persons of the opposite sex) was held to be a protected right in 1978.

> The right to marry is of fundamental importance. (The Connecticut contraceptive case and others) established that the right to marry is part of the fundamental "right of privacy" implicit in (the) Due Process Clause (of the Constitution). (*Zablocki* v. *Redhail,* 1978)

ENGLISH HISTORY AND LAW

The earliest English law book dealing with homosexual acts, written in about 1300, combined sodomy with other prejudices of the time: "Those [i.e., Christians] who have connections with Jews or Jewesses or are guilty of bestiality or sodomy shall be buried alive in the ground" (Crompton 1978). With the abolition of secular courts, England enacted its sodomy statute in 1533, with the punishment being death. The religious base for capital punishment was that, as put by the legal scholar Sir William Blackstone in his famed commentaries, "The express law of God determines [sodomy] to be capital . . . we have a single instance . . . the destruction of two cities by fire from heaven" (Blackstone 1797). Over eighty men were executed for sodomy in England between 1800 and 1835, usually by hanging. "In 1859 more men were sentenced to death for consenting sexual acts with men than for killing them" (Crane, undated).

England abolished the death penalty for sodomy in 1861, but prison sentences continued. In a notorious trial, the celebrated writer Oscar Wilde was sentenced to two years' imprisonment in 1895 for a homosexual relationship with Lord Alfred Douglas. Wilde had been called a sodomite by Douglas' father and sued for defamation, which resulted in a countersuit and Wilde's downfall.

The principal modern reform regulating homosexual conduct in England derived from the 1957 Wolfenden Report. It concluded that consenting adult male homosexual acts in private should not be criminalized. (No laws regulated lesbianism. This because in 1921 the House of Lords rejected a bill that would have criminalized female homosexual acts. One reason given was that the law would have introduced the concept of lesbianism "to the notice of women who have never heard of it, never thought of it, never dreamed of it.") (Weeks 1971).

A decade passed before the Wolfenden recommendations were approved by Parliament. However, the Sexual Offences Act of 1967 continued discrimination against homosexuals. The age of consent for same-sex acts was twenty-one, whereas for opposite-sex acts it was sixteen. Public displays of homosexual conduct were prosecuted vigorously, and the penalty for "gross indecency" (acts that did not include anal intercourse) with a male under 21 was increased from two to five years in prison. Convictions for "homosexual offenses" quadrupled in England and Wales between 1967 and 1979. (Home Office 1979).

SODOMY AND AMERICAN HISTORY

When the Bill of Rights to the American Constitution was ratified by the thirteen states in 1791, sodomy was a crime in all thirteen. These included laws deriving from 1672 in Connecticut; 1719 in Delaware; 1784 in Georgia (under the English Common Law); 1776 in Maryland; 1785 in Massachusetts (under the English Common Law); 1718 in New Hampshire; under the common law in New Jersey, and then under statute in 1796; 1787 in New York; under the English Statute of Henry III in North Carolina; 1790 in Pennsylvania; 1662 in Rhode Island; 1790 in South Carolina; and 1776 in Virginia (under the common law) (*Bowers* v. *Hardwick,* 1986).

In Colonial America, the crime against nature "was a capital offense" (invoking the death penalty). Under the Virginia statute of 1792 ". . . if any do commit the detestable and abominable vice of Buggery . . . he or she so offending, shall be adjudged a felon, and shall suffer death, as in case of felony, without benefit of clergy" (Richmond 1803). Further condemnation is found in a 1774 Virginia writing:

> Buggery is a detestable and abominable sin, among Christians not to be named, committed by carnal knowledge, against the Ordinance of the Creator. . . . Buggery committed with Mankind, or Beast, is made Felony without Benefit of Clergy (a capital offense). . . . (Starke 1774)

The wording of criminal indictments for buggery informs of the religious base of horror: The perpetrator

> [n]ot having the fear of God before his eyes, nor regarding the order of nature, but being moved and seduced by the instigation of the devil . . . did commit that detestable and abominable crime of buggery (not to be named amongst Christians) to the great displeasure of Almighty God. . . . (Hening 1795)

Thomas Jefferson, revered Virginia advocate of civil liberties, argued for the abolition of the death penalty for sodomy. In its place, he encouraged castration (Boyd 1950). In 1800, Virginia repealed the death penalty (for non-slaves only) and substituted a prison term of one to ten years (Oaks 1980). By then, one person had been executed (in 1625) (Crompton 1976).

Reform in the United States has been slow. Until 1961 every state continued to criminalize homosexual behavior. The learned American Law Institute formulated a Model Penal Code in the late 1950s and early 1960s (American Law Institute 1962), which advocated decriminalizing private, noncommercial, consenting sexual behavior. In 1961, Illinois adopted the Code and became the first state to abolish its sodomy laws. Yet, in 1993, nearly half the states still maintained statutes criminalizing homosexual acts between consenting adults in private.

AMERICAN STATE CASES

In American law, individual states can grant more liberties to the person than available under the federal constitution. Some state constitutions have specifically incorporated a right to privacy. When such a right is absent from a constitution, the state court may read the right into it, perhaps by inferring it from prior federal constitutional law cases.

New Jersey declared its sodomy law unconstitutional in 1978. The decision was based on an earlier case finding the state's fornication statute (prohibiting consenting unmarried heterosexual intercourse) unconstitutional (*State* v. *Cuiffini,* 1978).

The Pennsylvania statute prohibiting "deviate sexual intercourse," or sexual intercourse by mouth or anus between persons who are not husband and wife, was litigated in 1980. Unmarried heterosexual men and women challenged the law although it applied to homosexual persons as well. The court held that the proper role of the state in regulating sexual conduct was confined to

> protecting the public from inadvertent offensive displays of sexual behavior, in preventing people from being forced against their will to submit to sexual contact, in protecting minors from being sexually used by adults, and in eliminating cruelty to animals. (*Commonwealth* v. *Bonadio,* 1980).

Virginia maintained its high profile in fighting sodomy with a landmark 1975–1976 case. A three-judge federal court upheld the Virginia statute penalizing this "crime against nature" when committed by adults in private. The United States Supreme Court affirmed the lower court ruling without writing an opinion (*Doe* v. *Commonwealth's Attorney,* 1976). As described below, substantial debate followed over the precedential significance of the Court's silent affirmance.

New York State held its sodomy statute unconstitutional in 1980 (*People* v. *Onofre,* 1980). Persons bringing the case included a homosexual man admitting deviate sexual intercourse in his home, two homosexual men convicted of oral sodomy in a parked car, and a woman (Ms. Sweat) convicted of performing fellatio in a truck. On initial appeal, the first man's conviction was overturned as unconstitutional but the latter two were affirmed. However, the court of appeal held that because all the forbidden activities could occur in noncommercial cloistered settings, and the law permits such conduct for married partners, the statute violated both the right of privacy and the right to equal protection as guaranteed by the U.S. Constitution. The "moral enforcing intent" of the law was insufficient justification because one of the earlier federal contraception cases stated that what is considered "inimical to public morality" was an insufficient basis for sustaining a law affecting private behavior. The line of cases invoked by New York to nullify the sodomy statute was the federal sex and privacy cases prior to the *Hardwick* case (discussed below). Although New York's inference that homosexual conduct was a logical extension of these pre-*Hardwick* cases was not subsequently endorsed by the Supreme Court, the New York law has not been reinstated.

Texas has had an imposing series of sodomy statutes. The first, adopted in 1860, provided that "Whoever commits with mankind or beast, the abominable and detestable crime against nature shall be confined in the penitentiary for not less than five nor more than fifteen years" (Texas Penal Code, Article 342). Sodomy did not include oral-genital sex for 83 years, but in 1943, the statute was revised to prohibit oral or anal sex, regardless of the marital status of participants. Conviction carried an imprisonment of two to fifteen years. In 1970, that law was declared unconstitutional because it prohibited private consensual sex acts of married couples, violating their right of privacy, but the Texas Court of Criminal Appeals refused to follow the decision, arguing in part that it was inappropriately decided by a federal, not a state court. In 1974, the law was revised, removing penalties for heterosexual sodomy but continuing to criminalize homosexual oral or anal sex (deviate sexual intercourse). The crime became a misdemeanor punishable by a fine. The definition of deviate sexual intercourse was amended in 1981 to prohibit "the penetration of the genitals or the anus of another with an object." (See history in *Baker* v. *Wade,* 1982).

In 1982, a federal trial court held the Texas statute proscribing "deviate sexual intercourse between individuals of the same sex" unconstitutional as it violated both the right of privacy and the right to equal protection of law (heterosexual deviate intercourse was not criminalized). For the court widespread public distaste over a sexual act was not a "legitimate state interest to deny privacy or equal protection." The court did not see the summary Supreme Court affirmance of the Virginia case as controlling because the issues in the two cases might not have been identical. Further, in a case decided after the Virginia one, concerned with the sexual right of privacy inherent in contraceptive use, a majority of Supreme Court Justices noted that the Court had not yet "definitively answered the difficult question whether and to what extent the Constitution prohibits state statutes regulating [private consensual sexual] behavior among adults" (*Carey* v. *Population Services,* 1977).

Following this decision, one local Texas district attorney, a member of the class of defendants (containing all Texas state attorneys) in the earlier suit, sought to appeal the decision. His intervention followed the refusal by the Texas Attorney General to appeal. A three-judge federal panel rejected his demand; however, a full complement of the federal court held that the district attorney did have that right. Moreover, this court held that the Virginia sodomy case, summarily affirmed by the Supreme Court, did control the Texas case. Consequently, the right of privacy argument was rejected. The appellate court also held that the statute did not deprive homosexuals of equal protection under the law. Homosexuals, to the court, did not constitute a class to receive heightened scrutiny when affected by discriminating laws.

> In view of the strong objection to homosexual conduct, which has prevailed in Western culture for the past seven centuries, we cannot say that [this law] is not related to the pursuit of implementing morality, a permissible state goal.

The vote to reverse the prior court decision was a remarkable 9–7 (*Baker* v. *Wade,* 1987)

A renewed attack on the sodomy statute was launched by the Texas Human Rights Foundation (*State* v. *Morales,* 1992), which argued that prohibiting same-sex intercourse violated the Texas Constitutional right of privacy. Although the governor and attorney general of Texas stated their opposition to the law, the state defended the case to create a legally binding precedent. The Texas Court of Appeals ruled unanimously that the statute was unconstitutional. The Texas Supreme Court found that several Texas Bill of Rights provisions establish collectively a right of privacy: "[We] can think of nothing more fundamentally private and deserving of protection than sexual behavior between consenting adults in private. . . ." The state's justification for the law, "The implementation of public morality," was insufficient, indeed irrelevant. A public health rationale was rejected because the state permitted heterosexuals to engage in the same conduct.

In 1992, the Kentucky sodomy statute was struck down (*Commonwealth* v. *Wasson,* 1992). In doing so, the State Supreme Court, by a 4–3 decision, looked to the Kentucky Constitution and the common law when that constitution was adopted. The 1891 constitution referred to "positive liberty" and required an affirmative duty to protect individual liberties: "The theory of [Kentucky's] government is to allow the largest liberty to the individual commensurate with the public safety. . . ." Equal protection guarantees were also invoked. Homosexuals are "a separate and identifiable class . . . [and] no class of persons can be discriminated against under the Kentucky Constitution." The Texas Constitution (Section 3) states, "[A]ll men, when they form a social compact, are equal." The dissent relied on a 1909 case where the state Supreme Court declared that oral sex is "as much a crime against nature" as sodomy. They also stressed that Kentucky had a criminal sodomy statute in effect at the time the 1891 constitution was adopted. However, the 1860 sodomy law in effect in 1891 only prohibited anal intercourse and applied equally to same- or opposite-sex conduct. The extension to oral sex and then only to same-sex acts introduced new issues. The Kentucky Supreme Court is the highest state court to extend sexual privacy protection to sodomy after the federal *Hardwick* case (discussed below).

FEDERAL CASES

The ultimate sodomy case to reach the U.S. Supreme Court began in 1982, when Michael Hardwick was arrested in his bedroom for sodomy with another male. He was jailed and brought before an Atlanta court. Although the District Attorney's office elected not to present the case to the grand jury, Hardwick filed suit asking a federal court to declare the sodomy statute unconstitutional. He was joined by a married couple who sued for their right to engage in sodomy. The trial court dismissed the couple's suit, holding that they did not have standing to sue because they were not threatened with arrest. The court also held that Hardwick was foreclosed from relief in consequence of the summarily affirmed Virginia case. The appellate court overruled the decision on Hardwick; it held that the Virginia case was not decided squarely on the constitutionality of a sodomy statute and that subsequent sexual privacy cases undermined its precedential value. The court's holding focused on the standard of judicial review to be accorded Hardwick's claim. It found that private sexual behavior of the type engaged in by him was a *fundamental* right. "[It is] quintessentially private and lies at the heart of an intimate association beyond the proper reach of state regulation" (760 F. 2d 1212). As such, for the right to be compromised, the state must demonstrate a compelling interest behind its penalizing law.

The appeal by the State of Georgia was decided by the U.S. Supreme Court in 1986. A succinct ruling delivered by Justice White, and endorsed by Justices Burger, Powell, Rehnquist, and O'Connor, found no link between prior sexual privacy cases and homosexuality. The court's previously declared fundamental rights were those "implicit in the concept of ordered liberty," such that "neither liberty nor justice would exist if [they] were sacrificed," or, the protected right was a liberty "deeply rooted in this Nation's history or tradition." The majority pointed to the "ancient roots" of proscriptions against sodomy, and stressed that in 1868 when the Fourteenth Amendment was ratified (the springboard for privacy rights and equal protection under law), 32 of 37 states criminalized sodomy. "Against this background, to claim that a right to engage in such conduct is 'deeply rooted in this Nation's history and tradition' . . . is, at best, facetious" (478 U.S. 193). A *rational* basis existed for the law (a compelling one no longer being needed because the right was not fundamental). That basis was the people of Georgia's belief that homosexual sodomy is immoral. The concurrence by Chief Justice Burger emphasized the historic origins of the anti-sodomy stance. It was "firmly rooted in Judaeo-Christian moral and ethical standards," and designated by the English law scholar Blackstone as a "disgrace to human nature" and "a crime not fit to be named." In the Chief Justice's view, "to hold that the act of homosexual sodomy is somehow protected as a fundamental right would be to cast aside millennia of moral teaching" (478 U.S. 196).

The ringing dissent by Justice Blackmun, joined by Justices Stevens, Marshall, and Brennan, refocused the case from that of the majority. The case was not about a fundamental right to engage in sodomy. It was about the "most comprehensive of rights and the right most valued by civilized men," namely "the right to 'be let alone' " (478 U.S. 198). To the dissent:

> Our cases long have recognized that the Constitution embodies a promise that a certain private sphere of individual liberty will be kept largely beyond the reach of government. . . . Only the most willful blindness could obscure the fact that sexual intimacy is a "sensitive, key relationship of human existence. . . ." (478 U.S. 205).

ARE THESE CASES "ACADEMIC"?

An argument against challenging sodomy statutes is their rare enforcement. But in addition to selective enforcement, another form of discrimination, and the disrespect for law when laws go unenforced, this argument fails to address three issues: (1) the psychological impact of anti-homosexual laws on homosexuals; (2) the attitudinal affect of anti-homosexual laws on heterosexuals; and (3) the manner in which anti-sodomy criminal laws can be used in civil law matters.

Sexual identity, encompassing sexual orientation, is a fundamental feature of personhood. When that pattern of intimate expression is stigmatized by the individual's society as warranting criminal sanction, it traumatizes self-worth and scars self-image. A multinational research study concluded: "The most universal . . . effect of legal repression is to symbolize society's rejection of the homosexual. This rejection seems to be a major source of the homosexual's problems" (Weinberg & Williams 1974).

Homosexuals remain a disapproved minority, subject to prejudicial stereotypes and violence from heterosexuals. Preserving laws criminalizing homosexual conduct provides a basis for anti-homosexual bias.

Anti-homosexual laws perpetuate civil legal discrimination. In controversies over employment or parental rights, that a person's sexual conduct is criminal in consequence of sodomy statutes has been invoked as justification for denying equal treatment. The most recent Texas case described above was invoked by that state's Supreme Court in 1993. It denied review of a case in which the Texas Court of Appeals held that because the state sodomy law had been held unconstitutional, a police department could not use a Texan's homosexuality as a pretext to avoid hiring an otherwise qualified job applicant (*England* v. *State of Texas,* 1993).

EUROPEAN LAW

Several European nations have consented to jurisdiction by the European Convention on Human Rights and the European Court of Human Rights. While individual applicants do not bring a complaint to the Court, they can be heard by the Commission that has authority to bring the case to the Court. (European Convention, 1963). Article 8 of the European Convention of Human Rights specifies that everyone has the right to respect for his private and family life, home, and correspondence.

The first attempt to challenge sodomy laws before the European Commission failed. In 1960, a German argued that his country's Penal Code criminalizing homosexual acts violated his private life (Application No. 530 159, European Convention on Human Rights, 1960). The Commission held that the law was justified to protect public morals.

Another German challenged the statute prohibiting homosexual acts with persons under twenty-one. (*X* v. *Federal Republic of Germany,* 1976). The Commission deferred to the national interest in protecting children and adolescents. In 1977, a similar case from the United Kingdom challenging the age of consent law (twenty-one versus sixteen for heterosexuals) also failed. (European Convention, Application 27215/75, 1980).

A landmark 1981 case before the Court was *Dudgeon.* There the law in Northern Ireland making sodomy between consenting males a criminal offense was challenged (*Dudgeon,* 1981). Although recognizing the moral climate of Northern Ireland as anti-homosexual, the Court gave priority to the private expression of human sexuality.

> . . . [T]the moral attitudes towards male homosexuality in Northern Ireland and the concern that any relaxation in the law would tend to erode existing moral standards cannot . . . warrant interfering with the applicant's private life to such an extent.

Northern Ireland law was brought in line with the rest of the United Kingdom.

In 1988 a case from Ireland challenged the continuing sodomy law in that nation (*Norris,* 1988). Ireland argued that the litigant had never been prosecuted and so could not claim to be a victim. However, the court held that in the absence of a stated policy of nonenforcement, the threat of possible enforcement had a detrimental psychological impact.[1]

Europeans continue to obtain legal relief in the European Court. In 1993 the Court of Human Rights ruled 8–1 that the sodomy law of Cyprus also violated the right to privacy (*Modinos* v. *Cyprus,* 1993).

HETEROSEXUAL SODOMY AND AMERICAN LAW

In deciding that American states could criminalize homosexual sodomy, the Supreme Court in *Hardwick* (1986) decided not to determine whether states could criminalize heterosexual sodomy. Only Justice Stevens stated that such a prohibition would be unconstitutional: "Our prior cases . . . establish that a state may not prohibit sodomy within 'the sacred precincts of marital bedrooms,' or indeed between unmarried heterosexual adults" (478 U.S. 186).

Not all states agree, however. A New Mexico court reversed a conviction for heterosexual sodomy in 1975 but an appellate court reinstated conviction. Their reasoning was that the case did not engage the protected rights of marital privacy or the nurturing of family life (*State* v. *Eliot,* 1976).

An Arizona court held that a conviction for heterosexual fellatio violated the right of privacy, but the appellate court reversed the decision because the state may "regulate sexual misconduct in its rightful concern for the moral welfare of the people" (*State* v. *Callaway,* 1975).

North Carolina upheld a 1979 conviction for the "crime against nature," here heterosexual fellatio. Conceding that married persons might not be prosecutable, unmarried persons could be, because laws such as fornication, affecting only the unmarried, had been viable in that state since 1805.

Rhode Island upheld a conviction for "committing an abominable and detestable crime against nature" in 1980. This was anal intercourse between an unmarried heterosexual couple. The court's reasoning was that child bearing was not involved and that the Supreme Court had upheld anti-homosexual sodomy laws. Thus, the right of privacy did not extend to "private unnatural copulation between unmarried adults" (*State* v. *Santos,* 1980).

Heterosexual fellatio, even when consensual, can result in imprisonment. A North Carolina man was given a ten-year sentence (*State* v. *Frye,* 1989). His petition to a federal court of appeals was denied because under *Hardwick* he was not convicted for engaging in constitutionally protected conduct. The court may have misapplied Justice Steven's dissent in *Hardwick,* when it stressed that Stevens opined that "the rationale of the court's opinion applies equally to the prohibited conduct (oral or anal sex) regardless of whether the parties who engage in it . . . are of the same or different sexes." As previously noted, in arguing that the prohibition against homosexual sodomy was unconstitutional, Justice Stevens wrote: "Our prior cases (on sexual privacy) . . . establish that a state may not prohibit sodomy within 'the sacred precincts of marital bedrooms,' or, indeed, between unmarried heterosexual adults" (478 U.S. 218).

CONCLUSION

Examples from history, jurisprudential analysis, the teachings of philosophy, the data of behavioral science, and common sense substantiate the words written in dissent by Justice Blackmun of the United States Supreme Court in *Hardwick*:

> [D]epriving individuals of the right to choose for themselves how to conduct their intimate relationships poses a far greater threat to the values most deeply rooted in our Nation's history than tolerance of nonconformity could ever do. . . . The fact that individuals define themselves in a significant way through their intimate sexual relationships with others suggests, in a nation as diverse as ours, that there may be many "right" ways of conducting those relationships. . . . [W]hat the Court . . . has refused to recognize is the fundamental interest all individuals have in controlling the nature of their intimate associations. . . . [T]he issue raised by this case touches the heart of what makes individuals what they are. (478 U.S. 205, 213)

This expressed Blackmun's hope for an early reversal of *Hardwick* that would forbid the criminalization of private, consenual homosexual behavior. But for now, protecting privacy is embraced only by some individual state legislatures and courts of the United States, and by the emergent community of the European states.

NOTE

1. Appreciation is expressed to Ms. Sandra Rodriguez for material gathered in "Sodomy Statutes and the Right to Privacy according to International Human Rights Instruments," unpublished.

REFERENCES

American Law Institute (1962). Model Penal Code. Section 213.2. (Proposed Official Draft).

Aquinas, Thomas, Saint (1946). *On the Truth of the Catholic Faith.* (*Summa contra gentiles*). Bourke, trans.

Augustine, Saint (1950). *The City of God.* Marcus Dods, trans.

Baker v. *Wade,* 553 F. Supp. 1121 (1982).

Baker v. *Wade,* 769 F. 2d 289 (1985).

Blackstone, W. (1797). *Commentaries.*

Bowers v. *Hardwick,* 478 U.S. 186 (1986).

Boyd, J., ed. (1950). *The Papers of Thomas Jefferson.* Vol. 2, p. 325; cited by Oaks, p. 39. Princeton: Princeton University Press, 1950–.

Carey v. *Population Services International,* 431, U.S. 67 (1977).

Commonwealth v. *Bonadio,* 490 Pa. 91 (1980).

Commonwealth v. *Wasson,* No. 90-SC-558-TG (September 24, 1992).

Crane, P. (undated). *Gays and the Law.* London: Pluto Press.

Crompton, L. (1976). "Homosexuals and the Death Penalty in Colonial America." *Journal of Homosexuality* 1: 277–93.

——— (1978). "Gay Genocide from Leviticus to Hitler." In *The Gay Academic,* quoted in Crane, p. 11. Palm Springs: Etc.

Devlin, P. (1965). "Morals and the Criminal Law." In *The Enforcement of Morals,* pp. 14, 17, 22. Oxford: Oxford University Press.

Doe v. *Commonwealth's Attorney,* 425 U.S. 901 (1976), *aff'd without opinion,* 403 F. Supp. 1199 (E.D. Va. 1975) (Three-judge court).

Dudgeon Case, European Court of Human Rights, October 22, 1981.

Eisenstadt v. *Baird,* 405 U.S. 483 (1972).

England v. *State of Texas,* 846 S.W. 2d 957 (1993), relying on *State* v. *Morales,* 826 S.W. 2d 201 (1992).

European Convention on Human Rights Manual (1963), pp. 97–122.

Griswold v. *Connecticut,* 381 U.S. 479 (1965).

Hart, H. L. A. (1961). "Immorality and Treason." In L. Blom-Cooper (ed.), *The Law as Literature.* London: The Bodley Head.

Hening, W. (1795). *The New Virginia Justice,* pp. 93–94, quoted in Oaks, p. 38. Richmond, Va.

Home Office (1979). *Sexual Offences, Consent and Sentencing,* cited in Crane, p. 14. London: Her Majesty's Stationery Office.

Mill, John Stuart (1859). *On Liberty.* E. Rapaport, ed. Indianapolis: Hackett (1978).

Modinos v. *Cyprus,* 1993. Reported in *Lesbian/Gay Law Notes* (1993), p. 42.

Oaks, R. (1980). "Perceptions of Homosexuality by Justices of the Peace in Colonial America." In D. Knutson, ed., *Homosexuality and the Law.* New York: Haworth Press.

People v. *Onofre,* 415 N.E. 2d 936 (N.Y. 1980).

Richmond (1803). "A Collection of All Such Acts of the General Assembly of Virginia . . . Now in Force" (1803), p. 179, quoted in Oaks, p. 38.

Roe v. *Wade,* 410 U.S. 113 (1973).

Rostow, E. (1960). "The Enforcement of Morals." *Cambridge Law Journal* 174: 197.

Skinner v. *Oklahoma,* 316 U.S. 535 (1942).

Stanley v. *Georgia,* 394 U.S. 546 (1969).

Starke, R. (1774). *The Office and Authority of a Justice of the Peace.* (Williamsburg, 1774), p. 61, quoted in Oaks, p. 37.

State v. *Bateman,* 540 P. 2d 732 (Ariz. 1975), *vacated, State* v. *Bateman,* 547 P. 2d 6 (Ariz. 1976) *cert. denied,* 429 U.S. 864 (1977).

State v. *Callaway,* 542 P. 2d 1147 (Ariz. 1975).

State v. *Cuiffini,* 164 N.J. Super. 145 App. Div. (1978).

State v. *Eliot,* 539 P. 2d 207 (N.M. 1975), *reversed,* 551 P. 2d 1352 (N.M. 1976).

State v. *Frye,* 384 S.E. 2d 542 (N.C.1989), *cert. denied,* 495 U.S. 920 (1990).

State v. *Morales,* 826 S.W. 2d 201 (Texas, 1992).

State v. *Santos,* 413 A. 2d 58 (R.I.1980).

Stephen, J. (1873). *Liberty, Equality, Fraternity,* pp. 125, 146. London: Smith Elder.

Weeks, J. (1971). *Coming Out: Homosexual Politics in Britain.* London: Quartet, quoting the House of Lords debate, 1921.

Weinberg, M., and Williams, C. (1974). *Male Homosexuals: Their Problems and Adaptations.* New York: Oxford University Press.

X v. *Federal Republic of Germany* (1976), European Convention on Human Rights.

Zablocki v. *Redhail,* 434 U.S. 374 (1978).

2

Pedophilia: Paraphilic Attraction to Children

Jay R. Feierman

INTRODUCTION

Gender, Age, and Hierarchical Role Relationship

If one were to examine the major attributes used by vertebrate males in choosing a conceptive sexual partner, once sexual receptivity had been signaled by the other individual, gender, age, and hierarchical role relationship (i.e., equal, dominant, or submissive to self) would be the three attributes most commonly chosen. The average adult vertebrate male is sexually attracted to individuals more feminine, younger, and more hierarchically submissive than himself. In contrast the average adult vertebrate female is sexually attracted to individuals more masculine, older, and more dominant than herself. In many vertebrate females, resource accrual ability (i.e., the ability to acquire resources desired by the female, such as food and shelter) is an additional attribute of appeal in a sexual partner. In both vertebrate males and females, health and vitality as well as average morphology (to be explained), anthropomorphically called "physical attractiveness," is the final major attribute by which a conceptive sexual partner is chosen (Daly & Wilson 1978; Symons 1979; Wickler 1973).

Making generalizations at the broad level of Subphyla (Vertebrata), as was done above, is possible only for traits that are very old. The traits that underlie the mechanisms of vertebrate sexual attraction are indeed very old, being first identifiable in species as primitive as teleost (bony) fish. Therefore, explanations of why gender, age, and hierarchical role relationship are so important in human sexuality are based upon the earliest origins of vertebrate sexuality. Added to this older form of sexuality is a more recently appearing, affiliative sexuality, which evolved independently from reptiles in avian as well as our own mammalian and primate ancestors (Eibl-Eibesfeldt 1974). These ancient vertebrate relationships among gender, age, and hierarchical role relationship still hold true in our modern sexual lives in spite of our more recent awareness of the need for nonhierarchical social equality for all persons (i.e., social justice) in the nonsexual areas of our lives (Medicus & Hopf 1990).

In this chapter, in which pedophilia is developed as a paraphilic attraction to children, the gender terms "masculine" and "feminine" play a central role. They are defined as follows: Any attribute that is present in both biological sexes but in which the distribution is skewed so as to be more common in one biological sex than the other is called either "masculine" or "feminine" depending upon the biological sex in which the attribute is more common. It does not matter if the skewing is mainly the result of genetic/biological factors (e.g., aggressivity) or of cultural factors (e.g., wearing a dress). The terms "male" and "female," in addition to being used for the two biological sexes, are also used for traits that are limited exclusively to one or the other sex (e.g., "penis" is a male attribute and "uterus" is a female attribute).

At the most general biosocial level, pedophilia can be partially understood as follows: Assuming that the average adult vertebrate male is sexually attracted to individuals more feminine, younger, and more submissive than himself, it is reasonable to assume that there are biosocial regulatory mechanisms underlying these processes. In all biological processes, there are variations around means or central tendencies. As a result of inevitable biological variation, there will be some adult males who will be sexually attracted to individuals who are more or less feminine than average, more or less youthful than average, and more or less submissive than average. When such proclivities exist to only a minor degree, they often go unnoticed; when, however, they exist to a marked degree, they are noticed as well as labeled.

The term "pedophile" is the label given to adult human males who fall within the category of adult men who are preferentially sexually attracted to (juvenile) individuals considerably younger than themselves. The true definition of *pedophilia* is "sexual attraction to prepubertal persons." There is another term, *ephebophilia,* which means "sexual attraction to pubescent persons." The lay media often use the term pedophilia to mean sexual attraction to any legally underaged person and the term "pedophile" for an adult male with such a proclivity. The correct (legal) term for the actual pedo- or ephebosexual behavior is "statutory rape." With very young children, e.g., age twelve and under, where the issue of "consent" is not even considered, terms such as "rape of a child" are used.

Pedo- and ephebophilia are examples of *paraphilias.* A paraphilia is

> a condition occurring in men and women of being compulsively responsive to and obligatively dependent upon an unusual and personally or socially unacceptable stimulus, perceived or in the imagery of fantasy, for optimal initiation and maintenance of erotosexual arousal and the facilitation or attainment of orgasm. (Money 1986: 267)

The sexes of persons to whom male pedophiles and ephebophiles are attracted can be "same sex" or "opposite sex." Synonyms are "androphilic" and "gynephilic." These words (same sex, or androphilic, versus opposite sex, or gynephilic) are preferable to the terms "homosexual" and "heterosexual" in the view of this author, because there is no word corresponding to "pedophile" or to "ephebophile" for persons who are sexually attracted to mature adults of either biological sex, although the term "adultophile," in quotation marks, can be used. Because of this quandary, to call pedophiles who are sexually attracted to little boys "homosexuals" creates two problems. First, many such men actually have as much in common with heterosexual "adultophiles" as they do with homosexual "adultophiles." For example, pedo- and ephebophiles as well as heterosexual "adultophiles" generally are sexually attracted to individuals younger and more feminine than themselves. Even a pubescent boy is more "feminine" than almost any adult male. Second, politically, homosexual persons have enough social prejudice directed toward them (i.e., "homophobia") without the additional attribute through word association of "child molester." Homosexual "adultophiles" are no more interested sexually in little boys (minor males) than heterosexual "adultophiles" are interested sexually in little girls (minor females). In fact, there is some suggestion, based on plethysmograph data (see below), that heterosexual "adultophiles" may be more aroused by minor females than homosexual "adultophiles" are aroused by minor males. Both minor and adult females are soft, smooth, and hairless. Minor males are also soft, smooth, and hairless, but adult males are (potentially) hard, rough, and hairy.

A case can be made that this argument is not compatible with the "male homosexual subculture," a segment of which idolizes or celebrates male youth, with portrayals of late adolescents with little body hair, smaller stature, and submissive capacity that are quite common in their pornography. As will be developed later in this chapter, this segment represents androphilic ephebophiles, and it is a misnomer to call them homosexual "adultophiles." For reasons that will be explained later in the chapter under the section "Testing of the Model," there should be more adult males in the general population who are attracted to pubescent males (i.e., ephebophiles) than to more physically mature men (i.e., homosexual "adultophiles").

Pedophilia within a Biosocial Perspective: Sexuality in the Context of Natural Selection

Although Charles Darwin made a convincing argument that the anatomical forms of life evolved by natural selection, it was not until almost a century later that three ethologists—Konrad Lorenz, Niko Tinbergen, and Karl von Frisch—demonstrated that behavior also evolved by natural selection. The biosocial perspective within which this chapter is framed derives from their pioneering work and assumes that human sexual behavior, both normative and variant, also evolved in the context of natural selection. Darwinian evolutionary theory is a powerful paradigm with which to understand any behavior. It is particularly applicable to the understanding of sexual behavior, because differential reproduction is the driving force of evolution by natural selection. Any view of human sexual behavior in general, and pedosexual behavior in particular, that does not consider these biological factors, therefore, is incomplete.

One of the dogmas of behavioral biology (ethology) is that *phylogenetic adaptations* determine behavior in a definable manner (Eibl-Eibesfeldt 1975). In behavioral biology, a phylogenetic adaptation is a *coordinated motor pattern* that was selected by natural selection because individuals who had the ability to express this motor pattern outreproduced those individuals who did not. Coordinated motor patterns fall somewhere between simple reflexes (e.g., a knee jerk) and goal-oriented behaviors (e.g., courtship). However, species atypical, or variant, behavior, such as pedosexual behavior, poses a special problem. It cannot be assumed that any behavior expressed by any member of a species necessarily is (or even was) adaptive. The term "adaptive" means "facilitating getting one's genes into the next generation, irrespective of which close biological relative's genitals actually make the transfer." An "adaptation" is an adaptive trait.

Appreciate, however, that under natural conditions individual learning almost always leads to the adaptive modification of behavior (Lorenz 1981). There are exceptions to this rule, especially in some areas of human sexuality, where learning plays a role in the expression of atypical sexual behavior. Learning appears to influence the individual idiosyncracies so characteristic of the sexual appetite of the human male. Species atypical behavior, such as the particular sexual acting out of one human male's pedophilia, irrespective of the degree to which components of it are innate or individually learned, is difficult to conceptualize as an adaptation within the context of behavioral biology. It is for this reason that pedophilia appears to have evolved *in the context of* natural selection, rather than *by* natural selection. There are several mechanisms by which the genetic components of behavioral traits can be influenced by natural selection without being directly selected. These mechanisms are technically known as heterozygote advantage, balanced polymorphism, genetic drift, and by-product of selection.

About twenty years ago the American Psychiatric and American Psychological associations both took positions that (adult-adult) homosexuality is not a mental disorder but rather a normal variation of human sexual behavior within the dimension of gender. If one extends this reasoning within the dimension of age to pedosexual behavior (the acting out of pedophilia), the disease/non-disease analogy does not hold. The same two organizations consider pedophilia-motivated pedophilic behavior a mental disorder. It should be appreciated that the decision to consider variant gender orientation (a gender transposition) a *normal variation* and variant age orientation (a paraphilia) a *psychiatric disorder* was not made on strictly scientific grounds. Science is not performed in a sociopolitical vacuum. Consenting adult-adult homosexual behavior is now decriminalized in most jurisdictions, as long as it is done in private. Adult-child sexual behavior is criminal in most jurisdictions, irrespective of privacy and consent and irrespective of the degree to which the capacity for consent could be present. The reader should not misinterpret the above as implying that the author believes that adult-adult homosexuality should be re-"pathologized." Rather, the point is that pedophilia is (rightly) "pathologized" on the basis of value judgments rather than on strictly scientific criteria.

The above discussion points out how law as well as culturally and temporally dependent value judgments influence scientific taxonomy. It is, therefore, important for behavioral scientists studying phenomena, such as variant age and gender orientations, to construct scientific taxonomies that are as free as possible from known legalistic and value judgment influences.

Under the current taxonomies, homosexuality is considered a "gender transposition," a category that it shares with transsexualism and transvestism. Interestingly, transsexualism and transvestism are still considered psychiatric disorders. There sometimes are interesting legal ramifications to transsexualism and transvestism when they are carried out in public in some jurisdictions, although in private neither is illegal in any way. Pedophilia, on the other hand, is considered a "paraphilia," a category that includes some forty or so other oddities or "perversions," as they are called in the vernacular (Money 1986). Many of the paraphilias are illegal—e.g., biastophilia (a fondness for rape), exhibitionism, and frotteurism—whereas others are simply curiosities, e.g., acrotomophilia (an erotic fixation on amputees), coprophilia (an erotic fixation on feces), and gerontophilia (sexual attraction to elderly people). The term "paraphilia" has been already defined.

The biosocial perspective of pedophilia to be developed in this chapter breaks somewhat from sexological tradition in that the perspective conceptualizes both variant age and gender orientations within a common framework.

That is, it creates a common framework in which gender transpositions and (at least some) paraphilias can be conceptualized. The author is not making the argument that taxonomic parity implies legal or moral parity. In variant age orientation, there is almost always a large power and dominance difference between the two interactants. In such instances, the more dominant individual has proportionally more legal and moral responsibility for the interaction. Also, consent is an understood precondition for any morally sanctioned sexual interaction. With variant age orientation interactions, even the most diehard pedophile would admit that there is an age beneath which one of the interactants is incapable of giving consent.

Normophilic and Paraphilic Categories

One way to conceptualize a paraphilia, alluded to in the opening section of this chapter, is to consider it too much or too little of what in moderation is either normative or adaptive. Psychiatric taxonomies have been developed around such a schema (Dienske et al. 1987). Many paraphilias can be so conceptualized: e.g., pedophilia and gerontophilia. Some paraphilias, however, such as acrotomophilia (sexual attraction to amputees) are difficult to conceptualize as too much or too little of something that in moderation would be normative and/or adaptive. In particular, pedophilia has more in common with the other paraphilias than it does with the gender transpositions. Individuals can and often do have multiplex or compound paraphilias (Abel 1991a; Abel et al. 1987), suggesting that the vulnerability to paraphilias in general and the particular type of paraphilia expressed may be controlled by different biosocial mechanisms. The gender transpositions (homosexuality, transvestism, and transsexualism) also are not mutually exclusive. In addition, different paraphilias can be present in persons with or without a gender transposition, (e.g., a transvestophile can be a heterosexual or homosexual "adultophile").

Pedophilia within the Context of Paraphilic Categories

Paraphilias can be divided into two general categories: type paraphilias and size paraphilias. This classification is admittedly arbitrary and not mutually exclusive. It is a clinically useful typology, however. Type paraphilias are sexual attractions to structural attributes that are *qualitatively* distinguishable. Size paraphilias are sexual attractions to attributes that are *quantitatively* distinguishable. Before an elaboration on type and size paraphilias, the male sex bias as well as other classifications of the paraphilias will be discussed briefly.

There are sex biases found for all the paraphilias. Males are much more prone to paraphilias than are females. Something about this bias must be understood in order for pedophilia to be comprehended. There are several explanations at two different levels for the male bias. At the *proximate* level, since all brains start out *in utero* unmasculinized and feminized, male brains need to be hormonalized to a greater extent than female brains. With more hormonalization there is more opportunity for variation. Also, males have only one sex chromosome while females have two. It is harder to regulate physiological processes with fewer than with more chromosomal (genomic) regulators. There is more variance in males than in females in almost anything measured (Harrison et al. 1977). At the *ultimate* level, there are two explanations. First, males have more gametes (germ cells) than females and therefore, with more "ammunition," can afford to be more careless with their "aim." Second, as will be subsequently shown in the development of the two-dimensional neurohormonal model, the "lovemap" of males is stored more on the basis of structural attributes than is the lovemap of females. Therefore, it is easier for the average male than for the average female to have a variety of previously neutral structural objects conditioned to sexually evocative status and for sexually evocative attributes for some males to become even more evocative with extremes of size.

There are other classifications of the paraphilias, most notably that of Money (1986). This classification relates paraphilias to one of six "grand stratagems": (1) sacrificial/expiatory; (2) marauding/predation; (3) mercantile/venal; (4) fetishistic/talismanic; (5) eligibilic/stigmatic; and (6) solicitational/allurative. Within this classification, which is conceptually complex, pedophilia is within the context of an eligibilic/stigmatic stratagem.

Pedophilia as a Type and Size Paraphilia

There are two basic differences of erotosexual importance between adults, on the one hand, and children and adolescents, on the other. There are qualitative structural differences in the appearance of a child and an adolescent when compared to an adult, with the differences being greater in males than in females, as previously discussed. There are also quantitative size differences. *Type paraphilias* are sexual attractions to specific structural characteristics. Because of the highly discriminable budding stages of puberty (see Table 1), pubescent persons are particularly vulnerable to becoming the object of desire of ephebophiles with type paraphilias. There are subtle but identifiable differences in both genital and breast structure during the stages of pubertal development.

Size paraphilias are the attractions to attributes that are either larger or smaller than average size. One of the more interesting findings to come out of ethology is that natural selection, acting on individuals, indirectly configures human populations so that "average is beautiful" for the average person in regard to structural *shape*. Said slightly differently, most persons find attributes of average structural shapes the most appealing (Eibl-Eibesfeldt 1988). The

Table 1
Tanner Stages of Male and Female Sexual Maturity
(adapted from several sources)

BOYS				GIRLS		
Stage	**Pubic hair**	**Penis**	**Testes**	**Stage**	**Pubic hair**	**Breasts**
1	None	Preadolescent	Preadolescent	1	None	Preadolescent
2	Scanty, long, slightly pigmented	Slight enlargement	Enlarged scrotum, pink, texture altered	2	Sparse, lightly pigmented, straight; medial border of labia	Breast and papilla elevated as small mound; areolar diameter increased
3	Darker, starts to curl, small amount	Penis longer	Larger	3	Darker, beginning to curl, increased amount	Breast and areola enlarged, no contour separation
4	Resembles adult type but less in quantity; course, curly	Larger, glans and breadth increase in size	Larger; scrotum darker	4	Course, curly, abundant, but amount less than in adult	Areola and papilla form secondary mound
5	Adult distribution, spread to medial surface of thighs	Adult	Adult	5	Adult feminine triangle, spread to medial surface of thighs	Mature, nipple projects, areola part of general breast contour

proximate mechanism of attraction to health and vitality may also work through this type of normative selection for average-shaped attributes. This does not appear to be the proximate mechanism for attraction to more or less than average size, however. Size attractions are always to relative size, such as the relative size of the head to the size of the body. Most adult humans find juvenile mammals "cute" because of their relatively large head-to-body ratios. Also, as will be discussed further and as first pointed out by Desmond Morris (1982), submissiveness and smallness are almost synonymous.

In the two-dimensional neurohormonal model to be developed, the predisposition toward developing size paraphilias increases with the degree of variation from the mean of brain masculinization. Individuals in the "tails" of the distribution, i.e., with significantly more or less than average brain masculinization, would be more prone to developing size paraphilias than individuals with an average amount of brain masculinization. In the model, adult males with less than average brain masculinization would be sexually

Table 2
Attribution of Characteristics to Brain Masculinization and Brain Defeminization. A Theoretical Proposition. (Adapted from Feierman, 1990a)

BRAIN MASCULINIZATION	BRAIN DEFEMINIZATION
Proceptive searching (versus display) behavior	Low frequency of feminine (effeminate) mannerisms in self
Mounting-inserting/active role preferred	High visual attraction to feminine mannerisms in others
Aggressive mood in self, compatible with sexual mood in self	Lovemap stored in the brain mainly on the basis of structure
Fear mood in self incompatible with sexual mood in self	Neutral objects easily sexually conditioned
Sexual attraction to submissive/diminutive attributes in others	High vulnerability to conditioned sexual attractions, (i.e., fetishes).

attracted to larger than average attributes (e.g., large penises in homosexual "adultophiles" and large breasts in heterosexual "adultophilies"). In the model, adult males with more than average brain masculinization would be sexually attracted to smaller than average attributes (e.g., small penises and small breasts) (see Table 2). In the model, the determination of andro- versus gynephilic pedo- and ephebophilia would be the degree of defeminization (see Figure 1).

THE DEVELOPMENT OF PEDOPHILIA

The Biosocial Perspective

It is often possible for some aspects of human social behavior, such as the sex and age composition of social groups, to be understood within the context of primate socioecology (Smuts et al. 1986). Behaviors that are species typical and can be observed fairly easily across species are most amenable to this type of broad analysis. Pedosexual behavior, one of the outward manifestations of pedophilia, has some unique problems, however, for this type of analysis.

One major problem, for reasons already given, is that there is no convincing evidence that exclusive and fixated pedosexual behavior, as it occurs among both industrialized and nonindustrialized contemporary humans, is in any way adaptive. Behavior at the socioecological level should be adaptive to be applicable to this type of etiological analysis. Although there are some theoretically

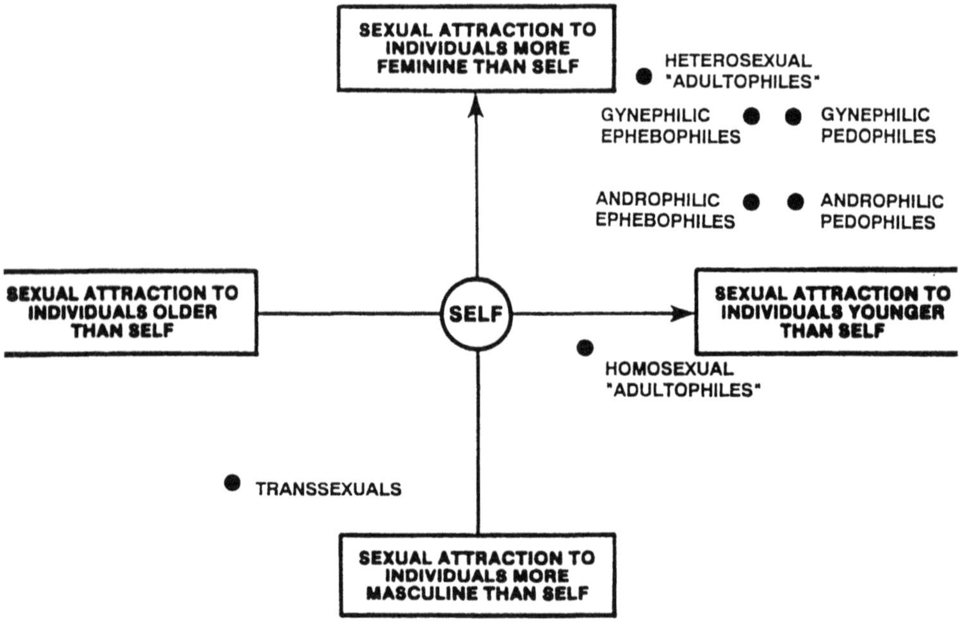

Figure 1. The two-dimensional model of age and gender orientations. Individual adult males are put into the two-dimensional matrix based on the degree to which they are sexually attracted to individuals more or less youthful than themselves (x-axis) and more or less feminine than themselves (y-axis). It is proposed in the two-dimensional model that the East-pointing arrow represents "degree of brain masculinization" and that the North-pointing arrow represents "degree of brain defeminization." Both male and female brains start out *in utero* unmasculinized and feminized. There is variation both between and within the two biological sexes in the degree to which their brains are masculinized and defeminized. This model should be viewed only as a theoretical proposition. (Adapted from Feierman 1990a.)

possible instances in which pedosexual behaviors could possibly be adaptive, except in the case of subhuman primates, these instances seem contrived (Feierman 1990a; Taub 1990). A second problem is that preferential pedosexual behavior is not a species typical behavior in any species, including humans. Because of its rarity, human pedosexual behavior would probably not even be observed or commented upon by an outside observer. Nevertheless, perhaps because we know our own species relatively well, preferential pedosexual behavior in a small percentage of adult human males is common enough to be considered a species characteristic variant, or atypical, behavior in humans. Surprisingly, the prevalence, or population frequency, of pedophilia is not known.

It is unknown whether *preferential* pedosexual behavior occurs infrequently in the occasional nonhuman primate individual in nature. What is known from observing nonhuman primates is that bouts of pedosexual behavior are quite common among many adult individuals in a variety of primate species. Most often the behavior consists of adult *females* tolerating sexual play with them by juvenile males (Anderson & Bielert 1990). However, pedosexual behavior does not appear to be a preferred type of sexual behavior for any adult male as it is in human pedophiles. In some species, such as bonobos (the pygmy chimpanzee) (de Waal 1990), sexual behavior is used for tension regulation and appeasement among all age and sex combinations. Again, this use of pedosexual behavior appears to serve a quite different function than it does in human pedophilia. This finding should not be surprising, since coordinated motor patterns, the units of behavioral evolution, often acquire different functions in closely related species.

Coordinated motor patterns, the biosocial level at which human pedosexual behavior can best be analyzed, are for present purposes said to constitute three components of sexual behavior: proceptive, receptive, and conceptive. Within a biosocial/ethological perspective, *proceptive* behavior can be defined as that behavior exhibited by one individual directed toward a second individual when there is not yet a commitment for a sexual interaction on the part of the second individual, or else in preparation for it. *Receptive* behavior is nonovertly sexual behavior between two individuals when there already is an ongoing conceptive sexual relationship. *Conceptive* behavior is behavior that under certain conditions can lead to conception. Conceptive behavior does not have to lead to conception, however. It is associated with direct genital stimulation, anterior-posterior "humping" (pelvic thrusting) movements, and potentially, orgasm and/or ejaculation between individuals of varying genders and ages. There is variability both between the two biological sexes and within each biological sex in the three components (proceptive, receptive, and conceptive) of sexual behavior. It is in proceptive behavior, however, that one finds the greatest difference between the two biological sexes.

There also is a biosocial relationship between reproductive behavior and sexual behavior that is useful to the understanding of pedophilia. There are nonreproductive sexual behaviors, such as masturbation and fondling, as well as nonsexual reproductive behaviors. Reproductive behavior has three components: mating effort, parturition, and parental care. Some of the coordinated motor patterns involved in both mating effort and parental care are part of the human pedosexual repertoire. These motor patterns will be discussed under mating effort and parental care. In adult heterosexual women, the facial motor patterns (i.e., affect-displaying muscular movements) as well as vocalizations are very similar during parturition and the conceptive component of mating effort. The vocalizations (high-pitched "yelping") act as sexual releasers to heterosexual but not to homosexual "adultophile" males. Their effects on androphilic as well as gynephilic pedo- and ephebophiles are not known.

Mating Effort

Proceptively, most mammalian males search and most mammalian females display. Adult male expressions of pedo- and ephebosexual behavior involve proceptive searching behavior, which is very similar to the more usual adult male searching behavior involved in looking for an age appropriate adult female. One difference is the location (a.k.a. context/domain) of the searching. Pedo- and ephebophiles will naturally concentrate their searching to areas where children and adolescents congregate. Often, pedo- and ephebophiles become friendly with families with children, befriend wayward youth, and join volunteer or youth organizations to gain access to children and adolescents. *Receptively,* the behavior of a pedo- or ephebophile with a child or an adolescent looks similar to the relationship between any adult and juvenile where there is an affiliative bond. There are some differences, however, which can be noticed by the careful observer. Affiliative receptive affection in courtship tends to escalate by caressing more intimate areas of the partner over time. Non-(sexually) receptive affection in the context of true parental care does not escalate in this manner. *Conceptively,* much pedosexual behavior consists of the adult fondling the child. Occasionally the adult coerces the child to reciprocate. With adolescents there is more often mutual genital activity, which includes mutual masturbation and oral-genital, genital-genital, and genital-anal sexual contact.

Parental Care

It is in the parental care component of reproductive behavior that the boundaries become most blurred between appropriate parental care and eroticized pedophilia. Parental care includes nurturing, grooming, feeding, and protecting.

Because the average adult male uses the provisioning component (which is phylogenetically derived from parental care) as part of his courtship of an age appropriate female, there is a certain degree of "functional proximity" between the moods and coordinated motor patterns involved in parenting and courting. "Functional proximity" is an ethological concept that means two moods (e.g., sexual and provisioning) can easily occur together or in rapid succession. (Ethologically, "mood" is a *specific* internal readiness to act.) This similarity between sexual and provisioning moods is found to a much lesser degree in human females and also accounts for why the proclivity toward pedosexual behavior is so much more an adult male than an adult female phenomenon.

The Two-Dimensional Neurohormonal Model of Pedophilia

The two-dimensional neurohormonal model of age and gender orientations into which ephebo- and pedophilia can be placed (Feierman 1990a) was developed as a first-order approximation of preliminary data. The model is constructed in two dimensions: masculinization and defeminization. In the area of the gender transpositions, the argument has already been made (Pillard & Weinrich 1987) that a two-dimensional model of gender attributes better accommodates the data than does a one-dimensional model. The particular datum that the two-dimensional model better accommodates is that homosexual "adultophile" males like to both insert and receive the penis, which is difficult to accommodate along a one-dimensional axis with masculinity (insert the penis) at one end and femininity (receive the penis) at the other. This two-dimensional model, called "the periodic table model of the gender transpositions" when first proposed by Pillard and Weinrich (1987), can also be extended to variant age orientations with some modifications. Androgens and their metabolites, infusing through the developing fetus during the last trimester of pregnancy and the immediate neonatal period, are believed to underlie the masculinization and defeminization processes of the brain.

In the two-dimensional model of age and gender orientations, individual adult males are first put onto a two-dimensional matrix based on the degree to which they are sexually attracted to individuals more or less youthful than themselves (x-axis) and more or less feminine than they are (y-axis). The term "feminine," as it is used in the model, is defined in the first section of this chapter (see Figure 1). The two axes are then renamed "degree of brain masculinization" (x-axis) and "degree of brain defeminization" (y-axis). In the model, the etiological attribution of masculine gender characteristics to brain masculinization and of feminine gender characteristics to brain feminization are also first-order approximations derived from a variety of sources. They should be viewed as working hypotheses, i.e., a model only, to be validated or refuted and certainly modified by future empirical research (see Table 2).

One of the new additions to the two-dimensional neurohormonal model, which is shown in Table 2, is that brain masculinization has been endowed with the additional characteristic, "sexual attraction to individuals more submissive than self." It should be appreciated that hierarchical role (equal, dominant, or submissive to self) is a major attribute to which individuals are attracted when searching for a mate. The phylogenetic origins of this relationship have already been discussed. It may be that "younger than self" is simply an intervening variable and that "more submissive than self" is the more important, or primary, variable. The relationships between submissive, small, and young have also been discussed previously. Interestingly, although the proclivity to "feminine" movements in the model is dependent on androgen and its metabolites through *in utero* brain hormonal organization, the expression of human "feminine" proceptive movements may be estrogen dependent at least to some degree. In human females, such behavior is rarely seen before puberty and virtually disappears after menopause. Lordosis (sexual crouching or presenting) in mammalian female quadrupeds has been shown to be estrogen-dependent.

Testing of the Model

The two-dimensional neurohormonal model makes several counterintuitive predictions about the relative population frequencies of persons with differing age and gender orientations. Based on the expected relative population frequencies on the masculinization (x) axis and the defeminization (y) axis, it is counterintuitively predicted that there should be more adult males in the general human population who are sexually attracted to minor (juvenile) males than to adult males. This is empirically testable through penile plethysmography* or less invasive attention measures on a *nonselected* general population of adult males.

The Developmental Arrest Model of Pedophilia

One of the more popular folk psychologies about pedophilia is that it represents a developmental arrest on the age axis. There is a similar folk psychology on the gender axis regarding the development of adult-adult homosexuality. "Developmental arrest" is a reasonable hypothesis inasmuch as there is a large literature in child development that supports periods of juvenile sexual rehearsal play as part of normative child development. The problem with the developmental arrest model is that it is difficult to disprove. Juvenile sexual rehearsal

*I.e., measuring and recording changes in the size of the penis. See subsection "Penile Plethysmography" below.

play is so common. Depth psychologies (e.g., Freudian, Jungian) seem particularly fond of developmental arrest models, perhaps because of their relative irrefutability.

Learning Theory Models of Pedophilia

There are a variety of learning theories on the development of variant age orientation. Learning theory models are particularly attractive to behaviorists, social constructionists, and *tabula rasa* enthusiasts. Learning has two aspects in relation to variant age orientation: critical period learning (imprinting) and the modification of adult sexual behavior by learning. Critical periods are present in the development of erotosexual preferences in precocial birds and rodents, as determined by cross-fostering experiments (D'Udine 1990). Critical period learning plays some part in human erotosexual preferences, as evidenced by the attachment of an aging male fetishist to female undergarments that were fashionable in his youth. Also, contextual conditioning plays an important role in all adult human sexual behavior. The sexual aspects of such contexts are certainly learned during both childhood and adulthood, with childhood contexts more resistant to deeroticization (i.e., "unlearning") than the adult contexts. The question is whether or not learning, either critical period or adult, does more than fine tune the erotosexual preference mechanisms. The two-dimensional neurohormonal model could, for example, bias age and gender orientation toward general classes of individuals, and individual learning could bias orientations toward specific idiosyncrasies within the general classes.

The "abused/abuser hypothesis," which perhaps should be renamed "the master's myth" because of its uncritical acceptance by so many master's level psychotherapists, is an example of a learning theory model gone awry. The best one can say about the abused/abuser hypothesis is as follows: Having been sexually abused as a child is neither a necessary nor a sufficient determinant of a previously sexually abused child's becoming an adult sexual abuser of children. Nevertheless, there appears to be a weak correlation between being sexually abused as a child and again as an adult. No causal relationship can be concluded from a mere correlation, however (Garland & Dougher 1990). Most of the myriad adult psychopathologies attributed to the sequelae of previous childhood sexual contact with an adult are without scientific bases.

Opponent process learning, the process by which the opposite is learned, has also been suggested as an intervening mechanism. One version of opponent process learing is that if a child has a sexual experience with an adult that is unpleasant and aversive, or if the consequences are traumatizing, then subsequently the only way to become sexually aroused as an adult may be by repeating adult-child sexual encounters. They are then not negative and unpleasant but positive and pleasant, even despite the risk of arrest and imprisonment. As a mechanism for the expression of pedophilia, opponent process is difficult to disprove systematically and experimentally. For that reason, it has limited scientific usefulness (Money 1990).

Last is the social constructionist view (Dickemann 1992; Feierman 1992). This view has developed mainly to accommodate variant gender orientation and appears to be as much a defensive political position of questionable effectiveness as it is a scientific hypothesis. Nevertheless, by analogy, there is no reason why the argument should not be extended to variant age orientation. Social constructionism argues that categories, such as "homosexual" or "pedophile," are products of social construction. They argue that behavior rather than individuals should be labeled. They also argue that the attributes of the individual to whom one wants to relate sexually are willingly chosen. The model is very popular within certain paradigmatically entrenched sectors of the social sciences as well as within certain sectors of the lesbian and gay communities. However, trying to understand pedophilia as a social construction, totally devoid of the influence of behavioral biology, requires more of a commitment to ideology than to knowledge.

CATEGORIZATION OF PEDOPHILES

Groth's Classification

The most widely quoted categorization of pedophiles is that of Groth, Hobson, and Gary (1982). Within this categorization there are two types: *regressed* and *fixated*. Regressed pedophiles (and regressed ephebophiles) are persons who are not exclusively fixated on children and adolescents as sexual partners. Such persons can inadvertently, for a variety of extenuating circumstances, become sexually involved with a child or an adolescent. Examples might include a stepfather who moves into a house with a 14-year-old girl who is the daughter of the woman he marries. The intimacy created by his parental relationship with her might become sexualized. Neither she nor he is protected by the usual biosocial mechanisms (i.e., the Westermarck effect [Westermarck 1891]) that usually keep biological fathers and their daughters from sexually interacting with each other. Another example is any situation that creates a degree of intimacy between an adult male and a juvenile when the usual channels for sexual expression for the adult male are not available. Last, various extenuating circumstances, such as the effect of alcohol or dementia, can broaden the range of stimuli capable of eliciting sexual arousal in an adult male. In such circumstances, a demented adult male may become sexual with a child or an adolescent.

Groth et al.'s (1982) "fixated" pedophile is what most people mean by the term "pedophile" when the term is used without qualification. A fixated pedophile is an adult male who is preferentially sexually attracted to prepubertal persons. (Fixated ephebophile is the corresponding term for preferential sexual attraction to pubescent adolescents.) It is important to specify how preferential sexual attraction is determined or defined. There are a variety of methods: historical (arrest) record, allegations of others, penile plethysmography, attention measurement, and verbal self-report.

Penile Plethysmography

It is important to appreciate that when the object of one's sexual attraction is considered illegal, immoral, or both, verbal self-report is the least valid method to determine the attributes of individuals toward whom one is preferentially sexually attracted. Historical arrest record is useful only if it consists of repeated arrests, inasmuch as arrested individuals will often deny that a child or an adolescent is their preferred sexual partner after a first arrest. The same holds true with allegations of others. Penile plethysmography is a valuable assessment tool. It can determine whether the accused individual shows more sexual arousal (penile tumescence) to visual or auditory images of children and adolescents than to "age appropriate adults." There also are less invasive, indirect measures of attention that can be used as a measure of sexual interest (Abel 1991b; Rosenzweig 1942). Neither the penile plethysmograph nor the less invasive attention measures can ever determine whether a particular sexual act occurred (i.e., neither can be used to determine guilt or innocence in criminal proceedings). They can, however, be used to influence professional opinion (medical/psychological) as to the likelihood that a particular criminal act might or might not have occurred. Whereas in criminal proceedings in the United States such increased likelihood is unlikely to be conclusive beyond a reasonable doubt, in civil proceedings, where the issue rests on a preponderance of the evidence, the outcome of such tests may be more influential.

Over-Dominant versus Low-Status Classification of Pedophiles

Another classification of (fixated) pedophiles, which derives from the two-dimensional neurohormonal model, is the *over-dominant* pedophile versus the *low-status* pedophile. Within this classification there are two possible conditions that could theoretically lead to the expression of pedophilia-motivated pedosexual behavior. (These two conditions suggest heterogeneity to Groth et al.'s [1982] category of "fixated pedophile.") One condition is whether an over-dominant adult male is highly aroused by diminutive/submissive attributes in others. The other condition is whether the adult male is of low social status.

In the latter case, because of the male's lower social status, age appropriate females might not display enough feminine (submissive) motor patterns to evoke sexual attraction to them. Children and adolescents, however, because they are naturally submissive to almost all adults, would display these submissive motor patterns even to a low-status male.

Theoretically, if an adult male loses a symbolic or real agonistic encounter with another adult male or loses accrued or potential resources, the losing adult male would drop in social status. Such a drop would make age appropriate females who knew this adult male relate differently to him. They would exhibit fewer proceptive, "feminine" displays to him. Such a male may, therefore, interact with juveniles to receive the submissive releasing stimuli from them that evoke his own sexual interest. Change in social status (lowering) should, therefore, be investigated as a possible mitigating circumstance in what Groth et al. (1982) would call "regressed pedophilia." Appreciate the importance of these proceptive, feminine/submissive displays in the female-evoked sexual behavior of the average adult male. Human adult females exhibit more "female choice" over which male inseminates them than any other primate female. One way they accomplish this selectivity is through their proceptive signaling of receptivity through very directionally oriented behavioral proception, rather than through a nondirected, airborne pheromone or fixed signal, either anatomical or by means of clothing or adornment.

Polymorphous Perverse Category of Pedophiles

A third categorization of pedophiles, apart from the fixated/regressed and over-dominant/low-status, is the *polymorphous perverse* type. There are two types of individuals who could fall within the polymorphous perverse category. To understand them one must understand the pattern of development of so-called sexual object choice. It is well known from the penile plethysmograph literature that adolescent males are much less specific in the stimuli that are capable of eliciting sexual arousal in them than are adult males. Also, adolescent males will "experiment" with a variety of sexual objects much more than will the average adult male. Therefore, some adolescent males will sexually interact with children during their own adolescence and not have children be their primary objects of sexual attraction as they become adults. These adolescents are the first type that could be included in the polymorphous perverse category. The second type is adults who do not follow the typical pattern in narrowing their sexual preferences as they age. These adults are appropriately called polymorphously perverse during adulthood, inasmuch as a variety of individuals are capable of eliciting sexual arousal with them. Certain personality disordered males (mainly in "CLUSTER B" in the classification of *The Diagnostic and Statistical Manual of Mental Disorders,* 3rd edition, revised [*DSM-III-R,* American Psychiatric Association, 1987]) with poor identity of self, and, therefore, poor identity of whom the self finds erotosexually appealing, can be polymorphously perverse in their sexual orientation. More empirical research is needed in this area to better delineate the relationship between personality traits and the range of adult sexual object choice.

THEORIES OF CHILD SEXUAL ABUSE

Relationship to Pedophilia

It is very important to keep separate the concepts of "pedophilia" and "child sexual abuse." As previously stated, "pedophilia" means the erotic love of children, and a person with such a proclivity is called a pedophile. "Child sexual abuse" means the harm of children through sexual means. Technically, pedophilia is not even a behavior. It is an emotional feeling or a desire for an erotosexual relationship with a child. The term for the acting out of pedophilic desires is "pedosexual behavior," although not all pedosexual behavior is expressed by pedophiles. Whether or not an adult's pedosexual behavior is child sexual abuse depends on the effects of the behavior on the child. Effects means the immediate effects as well as the long-term effects. One can not necessarily assume that any sexual contact between an adult and a child or an adolescent is harmful. As an example, a sexual contact between a 14-year-old boy and a 35-year-old woman may have no immediate or long-term deleterious effects on the boy. In fact, it may have a beneficial effect, defining beneficial in a variety of ways. More controversial would be a sexual relationship between a 14-year-old boy and a 25-year-old man. Such relationships have mixed outcomes, both immediately and over time. Selective reviews of the literature can support both good (Okami 1991; Sandfort, Brongersma, & van Naerssen 1991) and deleterious (A. W. Burgess et al. 1978; Faller 1988; Finkelhor 1984; Marshall, Laws, & Barbaree 1990) outcomes. In reality, most of the conclusions about the long-term effects of adult/child-adolescent sexual contact are premature in that there are a variety of methodological problems in trying to draw scientific conclusions from nonassigned "experiments of nature" (Kilpatrick 1987). Somewhat less ambiguous are the various long-term effects on the less dominant party of sexual relationships that violate role-related and professional boundaries. Damaging effects, other than feelings of distrust of authority figures and of having been exploited, although claimed, are difficult to prove for a particular exploited individual (Fortune 1989; Rutter 1989).

The effects of sexual contact between a 14-year-old girl and a 35-year-old man also can have mixed outcomes and are strongly influenced by the cultural context in which the relationship occurs. In many societies, such contacts in the context of marriage are quite normative. There is little known about the outcomes of sexual relationships between 14-year-old girls and 35-year-old women. All of these examples are given, however, to point out the dangers of broad generalizations about the effects, both immediate and long term, of sexual relationships between adults and children or adolescents.

There are societies in the world, such as are found in Melanesia, where sexual relationships between young adult males and prepubescent males are both culturally sanctioned and normative (Herdt 1981, 1984). Specifically, in these societies prepubescent males fellate young adult males in a ritualized manner. When these prepubescent males reach young adulthood, the roles are reversed, and they become the recipients of fellatio by the younger cohort of preadolescents.

Throughout both Western (Dover 1978) and Eastern (Saikaku 1990) history there have been times in which adult males customarily related sexually to both adult women and pubescent boys. In ancient Greece such behavior was considered normative and was socially sanctioned between adult male tutors and their young male students. In the East, Samurai warriors also had young male lovers. The history of intergenerational, same-sex sexual behavior between mentor and younger student can be traced from the Middle Ages (Quinn 1989; Sherr 1991) to the present in the industrial West (Feierman 1991a, 1991b; *National Catholic Reporter,* many issues 1990–present). Also in disadvantaged urban settings, young males of lower socioeconomic status are often sponsored by more affluent adult males who act as their patrons in return for sexual favors (Reeves 1981).

With all the above having been said, which should help to separate adult/child-adolescent sexual behavior from genuine child sexual abuse, there are models of child sexual abuse *per se.* One of the most widely quoted models is that of Finkelhor (1984). Finkelhor's model is not one of pedophilia, however. According to the Finklehor model, child sexual abuse occurs when four preconditions are met: motivation to sexually abuse; weakening of internal inhibitors; weakening of external inhibitors; and decreased resistance by the child. Finklehor's model seems intuitively useful. It is difficult to use as a scientific model because of the difficulty in quantifying the variables. Nevertheless, the model has been helpful to social workers and other clinicians who deal with child sexual abuse on a practical level.

Child Pornography

More controversial is the role of child pornography in the determination or cause of child sexual abuse. For the same reasons that there are correlations between adult female pornography and heterosexual "adultophilia" and between adult male pornography and homosexual "adultophilia," there also is a direct correlation between child pornography and pedophilia. This is not the same thing, however, as saying that there is a direct correlation between child sexual abuse and child pornography. From a scientific perspective, a correlation is not a cause-and-effect relationship. Pedophiles are notorious collectors of child pornography, but whether possessing child pornography increases or decreases the likelihood of a pedophile's acting out pedosexual behavior is not known. Theoretically, one can argue both sides. It is unlikely, however, that showing a non-pedophile examples of child pornography would create the desire or the likelihood of pedosexual behavior or child sexual abuse. The relationship between pornography and child sexual abuse has been studied empirically over the past several years. Most of the measures have been indirect, not measuring child sexual abuse per se but, rather, some other index, such as reporting or incarceration rates. Most empirical studies have dealt with violent sexual crimes, such as rape, although some have addressed specifically the relationship between pornography and child sexual abuse (Goldstein et al. 1974; Marshall 1988; Tate 1990).

Homosexual Recruitment

Another folk theory of the cause of both pedophilia and child sexual abuse is the "homosexual recruitment" notion, wherein an adult homosexual male "recruits" a young male into the homosexual lifestyle. When that young male grows up to be an adult, he in turn recruits members of the younger generation. This notion has several flaws, the main flaw being the assumption that the average homosexual "adultophile" is sexually attracted to or interested in young male children. By definition, a homosexual "adultophile" is an adult male who is sexually attracted to other adult males. The attributes of masculinity (e.g., strength, dominance, hairiness), are what are sexually attractive. The attributes of a male child (e.g., small, weak, hairless, smooth, submissive), have almost no sexual appeal for the homosexual "adultophile."

The Sequelae of Pedosexual Behavior

It is unlikely that an unwanted sexual experience with an adult male will cause a child or pubescent male who is not biologically predisposed to becoming a pedo- or ephebophile to seek out other children or pubescent males for sexual gratification when the former child or pubescent male is himself an adult. This has been discussed already under the "abused/abuser hypothesis." Previous childhood sexual victimization is neither a necessary nor a sufficient determinant of pedophilia expressed during adulthood. If *in utero* brain hormonalization is one of the determinants of adult age and gender orientations, then these factors are already present in a child or pubescent boy who was engaging in sexual behavior with an adult male. Some children and pubescent boys who do engage in such behaviors may themselves be predisposed to it. Such a statement is in contrast to victimological theory, where the younger participant is always seen as a totally passive recipient of the adult male's targeted "sexual aggression." The assumption that any sexual behavior between an adult and a child or an adolescent is motivated by aggression also is unwarranted, although there is most certainly a relationship between sex, aggression, and hierarchical role in the vertebrate brain, as was discussed in the opening paragraphs of this chapter.

The above statement should not be interpreted as implying that young boys are ever morally responsible for sexual interactions with adult males. In dyadic sexual interactions, the person with the higher status needs to take proportionally more responsibility for the interaction. However, some of the mixed outcomes of adult male/pubescent male sexual interactions may relate to this factor. A pubescent male who grows up to be either a homosexual "adultophile" or an androphilic pedo- or ephebophile may have very different feelings about his childhood or adolescent sexual experience with an adult male than a male who grows up to be a heterosexual "adultophile." In contrast to the mixed-outcome literature on males, published outcome data on the interaction of young girls with adult males outside the context of marriage are definitely skewed toward reporting negative outcomes.

Within the field of biosocial anthropology, there is an emerging literature on child abuse (Daly & Wilson 1985; Gelles & Lancaster 1987; Hrdy 1979; Lenington 1981; Lightcap et al. 1982). Such a literature differs considerably from much of the current literature on child sexual abuse emanating from the social sciences. One of the main ways in which these two literatures differ is the emphasis on and systematic measurement of sequelae as a function of reduced (reproductive) fitness in the former literature compared to the latter. As has previously been pointed out, analysis of human pedophilia has not to date been possible at the socioecological level of goal-oriented behaviors, which has proved useful for understanding child abuse and neglect in the studies cited above (Feierman 1990b).

LEGALISTIC IMPLICATIONS

The Relationship between "Normal," "Natural," "Moral," and "Legal"

It is important to keep separate the concepts of "normal," "natural," "moral," and "legal" in relationship to both pedophilia and pedosexual behavior. The most basic distinction is that pedophilia *per se,* irrespective of the degree to which it is a capacity-diminishing psychiatric disorder, is not illegal in any jurisdiction. Pedosexual behavior is illegal in most jurisdictions, but not all pedosexual behavior is carried out by pedophiles. Child sexual abuse, irrespective of its relationship to pedophilia and pedosexual behavior, should be immoral in any society's value system, although it is possible that such abuse may technically not be illegal and in some societies not be considered even immoral (e.g., clitoridectomy in some East African societies).

The concept of "normal" has two meanings: that which is common (statistically) and that which ought to be. One must be clear which meaning one intends when using the word. The concept of "natural" has two meanings. The first relates to the observation of naturalists; the second is rooted in the theological concept of natural law, in which function is thought to follow from form (which is biologically backwards!) and in which variance is not considered. The concept of "moral" implies that which ought to be, based upon some nonarbitrary system of making such a determination. The concept of "legal" also implies that which ought to be, although in this case the determination is based upon specific, nonsystematic, and seemingly arbitrary guidelines called laws. There are instances where what is normal is natural is moral is legal, i.e., sexual intercourse between a legally married adult man and woman. There also are combinations that are not so congruent.

One of the most important considerations within the concept of "normal" is the appreciation that even within the meaning, "that which is common," there is a range to commonality. Almost anything that is measured biologically produces variation around a mean. As previously stated, males vary more than females on almost any measurable trait. Because of this inevitable variability, the concept of "common" implies a certain degree of variation around the mean. For example, if the average adult male in a society is a certain height, males who are 10 percent taller or 10 percent shorter than the population mean would still be considered of "normal" height. The same type of reasoning can be applied to sexual behaviors in the area of frequency, as in the frequency of orgasms (total sexual outlet) for persons at various stages of the life cycle (Kinsey et al. 1948).

Continuous versus Discontinuous Distributions

When a variation does not appear to be part of a continuous distribution, it is harder to apply statistical reasoning to the concept of normalcy. To argue by analogy, some persons believe that adult-adult homosexuality is a qualitatively unique trait rather than a quantitative variation from a central tendency. This is not correct, however. Humans vary on the trait "same-sex affiliation," with some adult males at one extreme being intolerant and aggressive toward other males. On the other extreme, there are males with more than average "same-sex affiliation" who show very little intolerance and aggressivity toward their fellow man. It should be appreciated that humans are one of the few primate species in which nonrelated adult males can tolerate one another's presence without fighting. A 10 percent "homosexuality rate" among adult males may be the trade-off for such toleration, which is a "balanced polymorphism" hypothesis of homosexuality. That which is called "male homosexuality" may simply be one end (or tail) of the distribution of the trait "same-sex affiliation."

The argument that pedophilia is also a quantitative deviation from a statistical norm is easier to make. Adult males are selected individually (by natural selection) so that, as a result of individual selection, the average adult male is sexually attracted to the attributes of nubile females. Whatever the proximate mechanisms might be that lead to this predilection, it is not difficult to imagine that because of inevitable biological variation, there will be some males who are sexually attracted to the attributes of individuals who are older or who are younger than nubile-aged persons, as previously intimated in the beginning of this chapter. One of the values of the two-dimensional neuro-hormonal model of pedophilia from a heuristic perspective is that it puts both variant age and variant gender orientations as quantitative variations of means or central tendencies of hormonalization 4round heterosexual "adultophiles," whose objects of erotosexual desires are nubile females. That is, it frames pedophilia within a continuous distribution.

PEDOPHILIA, EPHEBOPHILIA, PSYCHIATRIC DISORDERS, AND DIMINISHED CAPACITY

As of *DSM-III-R* (American Psychiatric Association, 1987) as well as the emerging version of *The Diagnostic and Statistical Manual of Mental Disorders* (4th ed.) *Options Book* (*DSM-IV*) (American Psychiatric Association, 1991), pedophilia (302.20) is considered a psychiatric disorder, and ephebophilia is not. Pedophilia is defined specifically as follows:

> A. Over a period of at least six months, recurrent intense sexual urges and sexually arousing fantasies involving sexual activity with a prepubescent child or children (generally age thirteen or younger).
>
> B. The person has acted on these urges, or is markedly distressed by them.
>
> C. The person is at least sixteen years old and at least five years older than the child or children in A.

DSM-III-R further stipulates the exclusion of an ongoing sexual relationship between a late adolescent and a twelve- or thirteen-year-old. It also requires specification of whether the relationship is of the same sex, opposite sex, or same and opposite sex; if limited to incest; and if exclusive in type (attraction only to children) or nonexclusive in type.

Since sexual attraction to a legally underaged pubescent person (e.g., ages twelve to sixteen) is not considered a *DSM-III-R* (American Psychiatric Association, 1987) psychiatric disorder, there is really no clinical-legal basis for invoking the concept of diminished capacity for ephebosexual behavior. Is the implication that sexual attraction to pubescent persons is "normal" although illegal? Many anthropologists would argue, "yes" (Symons 1989).

But what about acted out pedosexual behavior with a prepubertal nine-year-old boy? Since the person may be a pedophile and pedophilia is a diagnosable psychiatric disorder, can one invoke diminished capacity as a legal defense? Since not all perpetrators of pedosexual behavior are pedophiles, it would be important to establish whether the alleged offender is indeed a pedophile. The best way to determine this is with a penile plethysmograph test (Freund 1981). Assuming that the penile plethysmograph shows unequivocally that the defendant is maximally sexually aroused (i.e., has the greatest penile tumescence) to stimuli containing nine-year-old boys, what is the implication? Such a physiological finding would indicate that the person is more likely to repeat the act than someone not showing such a response, and that there is bona fide effective treatment available to lessen the probability that another such act will be committed. But what about diminished capacity? Could or should the person be found innocent, be found guilty but mentally ill, or be charged with a lesser offense because of being diagnosed as a pedophile?

There is no simple answer to the above question, although this author prefers "guilty but mentally ill" for "plethysmograph positive" pedophiles in jurisdictions where such a concept exists. An analogy with alcoholism, a *DSM-III-R* (American Psychiatric Association, 1987) psychoactive substance abuse diagnosis, can be made. Some persons do not have the capacity to moderate their use of alcohol and are, therefore, called "alcoholics." Alcoholics are responsible for a proportionally larger number of alcohol-related crimes than are nonalcoholics (e.g., driving while intoxicated, vehicular homicide). This author knows of no jurisdiction where someone's capacity is diminished for a criminal act committed under the influence of alcohol because they are an alcoholic rather than a one-time intoxicated person. However, being intoxicated is often considered a state of diminished capacity as, for example, in premeditated homicide. Are the sexual urges of a pedophile similar enough to the effects of alcohol to make pedophilia a basis for diminishing someone's capacity for a sexual offense? The alcohol consumer voluntarily consumes the first drink of alcohol, but the pedophile feels the urge to be sexual with a child through no act of volition. This author does not know the answer to this question, although extending the argument to violent sex crimes, such as criminal sexual penetration (forced rape), considerably diminishes the appeal of the analogy.

One approach is to hold all men responsible for their expressions of aggressivity and sexuality, without exception. Human behavioral biologists have repeatedly emphasized that biology is not destiny. Predispositions, desires, and urges to everything from aggression to sexual offending do not require or mandate the person to act. There are ways of learning to control behaviors that are considered socially unacceptable, and it is the responsibility of all persons to avail themselves of whatever means are necessary to conduct their behavior within the confines of the law. Persons who have diagnosable psychiatric disorders, such as alcoholism and pedophilia, should probably have the right to receive treatment during their periods of incarceration rather than simply serving time. This would address the issue of diminished capacity from a therapeutic perspective without endangering the well-being of society. It is well known that pedophiles rarely avail themselves of treatment before they are apprehended for sexual offending. Society's attitude toward pedophilia is at least partially responsible for this dilemma.

INFORMED CONSENT

From a broad perspective in regard to the legal implications surrounding pedo- and ephebophilia is the concept of informed consent. It is a fairly well accepted belief that for sexual behavior between any two persons to fall within the realm of being moral, there must be consent by both parties. In regard especially to pedophilia, there must be an age beneath which an individual is not competent to give consent. Also, consent itself is problematic in the area of interpersonal sexuality. Often individuals give mixed messages, such as saying no verbally but continuing to do the very thing their words say they don't want to do. Ambiguity is one of the hallmarks of courtship signals, as evidenced by the dual messages in displays of "coyness." These ambiguous messages contain an element of teasing, which forms part of the courtship ritual in a variety of species, including our own. Beneath a certain age, however, the concept of "consent" is not even applicable.

In the opinion of this author, the issue of the age at which consent is possible should be based on society's first priority to protect the younger and more vulnerable interactant rather than on society's providing certain adult males with the opportunity for the expression of their pedophilia. There is a political movement that supports "sexual rights of minors." Most of the impetus for this movement comes from adult pedophiles who use the civil rights of minors to try to liberalize the age-of-consent laws. Age of consent varies considerably across jurisdictions. Dienske (1990) sums up the issue as follows: "In the absence of solid knowledge about possible functions of pedophilia and pedosexual behavior in humans, reasonable standards of social control are both necessary and required" (p. 335).

TREATMENT

In many jurisdictions, correctional systems have three functions: protection, punishment, and deterrence. When pedophilic sex offenders are institutionalized, society is protected during their period of institutionalization. Punishment has a rather steep extinction curve, however. Within several years after being punished, such negative reinforcement has a rather negligible effect in reducing recidivism. The fear of punishment, i.e., the deterrent value of knowing about other persons' misfortunes after getting caught, also has a negligible effect on reducing sex offenses.

As long as sex offenders are institutionalized, it makes absolutely no sense not to treat them during this period. There now are both theoretical rationales and empirically proven efficacious treatments, both behavioral and hormonal, for pedophilic sex offenders (Abel et al. 1984; Knopp 1984; Laws 1989). The recidivism rates for treated sex offenders (ca. 10–30 percent) are considerably improved over nontreated sex offenders (ca. 60–80 percent). This author is not making the argument that sex offenders should be treated rather than institutionalized. The argument is that if child sex offenders who are plethysmograph-validated pedophiles are institutionalized, this is a potentially ideal time for them to be treated. Even the economics of such treatment over simple institutionalization over the lifetime of the offender are compelling reasons to treat rather than simply institutionalize.

Since the early 1950s, with the introduction of effective antipsychotic medications in the industrialized world, the large governmental psychiatric hospitals have had dwindling numbers of long-term mentally ill (mainly schizophrenic) patients. As a result, most jurisdictions have large psychiatric hospitals that are empty or nearly so. Such institutions could serve as secure treatment centers for sex offenders, who could then be segregated from the general prison populations.

CONCLUSIONS

This chapter has discussed pedophilia and its companion term, ephebophilia, as paraphilic attraction to children and to pubescent persons. In presenting this discussion, some general background material about paraphilias in general was developed, and pedo- and ephebophilia were put within this framework. Various models of pedophilia were discussed, from the two-dimensional neurohormonal model to the developmental arrest, opponent process learning, and social constructionism models. Pedophilia was categorized according to Groth et al.'s (1982) fixed and regressed subtypes and also by the over-dominant and low-status subtypes. Pedo- and ephebophilia were discussed in relationship to child sexual abuse. Various theories of child sexual abuse were discussed. Some legalistic implications of all of the above were covered. The chapter ended with the recommendation that pedo- and ephebophiles should be treated during periods of institutionalization in facilities separate from the general prison population.

REFERENCES

Abel, G. G. (1991a, May). "Percentage of Cross Diagnosis by Paraphilia." Paper presented at the meeting of the American Psychiatric Association, New Orleans, La.

——— (1991b, September). "A Nonevasive Assessment to Identify Pedophiles Attempting to Join Volunteer Organizations." Paper presented at the 2nd International Conference on the Treatment of Sex Offenders, Minneapolis, Minn.

Abel, G. G.; Becker, J. V.; Cunningham-Rather, J.; Rouleau, J. L.; Kaplan, M.; and Reich, J. (1984). *The Treatment of Child Molesters.* Private printing. (Available from Gene G. Abel, M.D., The Behavioral Medicine Institute of Atlanta, Pace Pavilion, 3193 Howell Mill Rd., N. W., Suite 202, Atlanta, Ga. 30327.)

Abel, G. G.; Becker, J. V.; Mittelman, M.; Cunningham-Rather, J.; Rouleau, J. L.; and Murphy, W. D. (1987). "Self-Reported Sex Crimes of Nonincarcerated Paraphiliacs." *Journal of Interpersonal Violence* 2: 3–25.

American Psychiatric Association. (1987). *Diagnostic and Statistical Manual of Mental Disorders.* 3rd ed., rev. Washington, D.C.: American Psychiatric Association Press.

——— (1991). *Diagnostic and Statistical Manual of Mental Disorders.* 4th ed. *Options Book,* September 1, 1991, Task Force on *DSM-IV.* Washington, D.C.: American Psychiatric Association Press. (Limited circulation. Available from American Psychiatric Association.)

Anderson, C. M., and Bielert, C. (1990). "Adolescent/Adult Copulatory Behavior in Nonhuman Primates." In J. R. Feierman, ed., *Pedophilia: Biosocial Dimensions,* pp. 176–200. New York: Springer-Verlag.

Burgess, A. W.: Groth, A. N.: Holmstrom, L. L.: and Sgroi, S. M. (1978). *Sexual Assault of Children and Adolescents.* Lexington, Mass.: Lexington Books.

Daly, M., and Wilson, M. (1978). *Sex, Evolution, and Behavior.* North Scituate, Mass.: Duxbury Publishers.

———. (1985). "Child Abuse and Other Risks of Not Living with Both Parents." *Ethology and Sociobiology* 6: 197–210.

De Waal, F. B. M. (1990). "Sociosexual Behavior Used for Tension Regulation in All Age and Sex Combinations among Bonobos." In J. R. Feierman, ed., *Pedophilia: Biosocial Dimensions,* pp. 378–93. New York: Springer-Verlag.

Dickemann, M. (1992). "Phylogenetic Fallacies and Sexual Oppression" (Review of *Pedophilia: Biosocial Dimensions*). *Human Nature* 3: 71–87.

Dienske, H. (1990). "The Concept of Function in the Behavioral Sciences with Specific Reference to Pedophilia and Pedosexual Behavior: A Biophilosophical Perspective." In J. R. Feierman, ed., *Pedophilia: Biosocial Dimensions,* pp. 324–37. New York: Springer-Verlag.

Dienske, H.: Sanders-Woudstra, J. A. R.; and de Jonge, G. A. (1987). "A Biologically Meaningful Classification in Child Psychiatry That Is Based upon Ethological Methods." *Ethology and Sociobiology* 8, no. 3 suppl.: 27S–45S.

Dover, K. J. (1978). *Greek Homosexuality.* Cambridge, Mass.: Harvard University Press.

D'Udine, B. (1990). "The Modification of Sexual Behavior through Imprinting: A Rodent Model." In J. R. Feierman, ed., *Pedophilia: Biosocial Dimensions,* pp. 221–41. New York: Springer-Verlag.

Eibl-Eibesfeldt, I. (1974). *Love and Hate: The Natural History of Behavior Patterns.* New York: Schocken Books.

——— (1975). *Ethology: The Biology of Behavior.* 2nd ed. New York: Holt, Rinehart & Winston.

——— (1988). "The Biological Foundations of Aesthetics." In I. Rentschler, B. Herzberger, and D. Epstein, eds., *Beauty and the Brain: Biological Aspects of Aesthetics.* Basle: Birkauser Verlag.

Faller, K. G. (1988). *Child Sexual Abuse: An Interdisciplinary Manual for Diagnosis, Case Management, and Treatment.* New York: Columbia University Press.

Feierman, J. R. (1990a). "A Biosocial Overview of Adult Human Sexual Behavior with Children and Adolescents." In J. R. Feierman, ed., *Pedophilia: Biosocial Dimensions,* pp. 8–68. New York: Springer-Verlag.

——— (1991a, June). "Ethological Predictors of Sexual Impropriety with Parishioners in Catholic Priests: The Influence of Age and Gender Orientations on the Allurement of Submissive Behavior in Different Contexts." Paper presented at the 10th World Congress of Sexology, Amsterdam, The Netherlands.

——— (1991b, September). "A Two-Dimensional Biosocial Model of Age and Gender Orientations: Applications to the Evaluation and Treatment of Pedophilic Sex Offenders and Data Collected on 500 Priests." Plenary lecture presented at the 2nd International Conference on the Treatment of Sex Offenders, University of Minnesota, Minneapolis, Minn.

——— (1992). "The Ethology of Variant Sexology" (a response to Mildred Dickemann's review of *Pedophilia: Biosocial Dimensions*). *Human Nature* 3: 279–97.

———, ed. (1990b). *Pedophilia: Biosocial Dimensions.* New York: Springer-Verlag.

Finkelhor, D. (1984). *Child Sexual Abuse: New Theory and Research.* New York: The Free Press.

Fortune, M. M. (1989). *Is Nothing Sacred: When Sex Invades the Pastoral Relationship.* New York: Harper & Row.

Freund, K. (1981). "Assessment of Pedophilia." In M. Cook and K. Howells, eds., *Adult Sexual Interest in Children,* pp. 139–79. London: Academic Press.

Garland, R. J., and Dougher, M. J. (1990). "The Abused/Abuser Hypothesis of Child Sexual Abuse: A Critical Review of Theory and Research." In J. R. Feierman, ed., *Pedophilia: Biosocial Dimensions,* pp. 488–509. New York: Springer-Verlag.

Gelles, R. J., and Lancaster, J. B. (1987). *Child Abuse and Neglect.* New York: Aldine de Gruyter.

Goldstein, M. J.; Kant, H. S.; and Hartman, J. J. (1974). *Pornography and Sexual Deviance.* Berkeley: University of California Press.

Groth, A. N.; Hobson, W.; and Gary, W. (1982). "The Child Molester: Clinical Observations." In J. Conte and D. Shore, eds., *Social Work and Child Sexual Abuse,* pp. 129–44. New York: Haworth.

Hardy, S. B. (1979). "Infanticide among Animals: A Review, Classification, and Examination of the Implications for the Reproductive Strategies of Females." *Ethology and Sociobiology* 1: 13–40.

Harrison, G. A.; Weiner, J. S.; Tanner, J. M.; and Barnicot, N. A. (1977). *Human Biology: An Introduction to Human Evolution, Variation, Growth, and Ecology.* 2nd ed. Oxford: Oxford University Press.

Herdt, G. H. (1981). *Guardians of the Flutes: Idioms of Masculinity. A Study of Ritualized Homosexual Behavior.* New York: McGraw-Hill.

———, ed. (1984). *Ritualized Homosexuality in Melanesia.* Berkeley: University of California Press.

Kilpatrick, A. C. (1987). "Childhood Sexual Experiences: Problems and Issues in Studying Long-Range Effects." *The Journal of Sex Research* 23: 173–96.

Kinsey, A. C.; Pomeroy, W. B.; and Martin, C. E. (1948). *Sexual Behavior in the Human Male.* Philadelphia: W. B. Saunders.

Knopp, F. H. (1984). *Retraining Adult Sex Offenders: Methods and Models.* Orwell, Vt.: Safer Society Press.

Laws, D. R. (1989). *Relapse Prevention with Sex Offenders.* New York: Guilford Press.

Lenington, S. (1981). "Child Abuse: The Limits of Sociobiology." *Ethology and Sociobiology* 2: 17–30.

Lightcap, J. L.; Kurland, J. A.; and Burgess, R. L. (1982). "Child Abuse: A Test of Some Predictions from Evolutionary Theory." *Ethology and Sociobiology* 3: 61–68.

Lorenz, K. Z. (1981). *The Foundations of Ethology.* New York: Springer-Verlag.

Marshall, W. L. (1988). "The Use of Explicit Sexual Stimuli by Rapists, Child Molesters and Nonoffender Males." *Journal of Sex Research* 25: 267–88.

Marshall, W. L.; Laws, D. R.; and Barbaree, H. E. (1990). *Handbook of Sexual Assault: Issues, Theories, and Treatment of the Offender.* New York: Plenum Press.

Medicus, G., and Hopf, S. (1990). "The Phylogeny of Male/Female Differences in Sexual Behavior." In J. R. Feierman, ed., *Pedophilia: Biosocial Dimensions,* pp. 122–49. New York: Springer-Verlag.

Money, J. (1986). *Lovemaps: Clinical Concepts of Sexual/Erotic Health and Pathology,*

Paraphilia, and Gender Transposition in Childhood, Adolescence, and Maturity. New York: Irvington Publishers.

——— (1990). "Pedophilia: A Specific Instance of New phylism Theory as Applied to Paraphilic Lovemaps." In J. R. Feierman, ed., *Pedophilia: Biosocial dimensions,* pp. 445–63. New York: Springer-Verlag.

Morris, D. (1982). "Submissive Behavior: How We Appease Our Critics or Attackers." In *The Pocket Guide to Manwatching,* pp. 217–28. London: Triad Panther. National Catholic Reporter (Independent Catholic News Weekly). (ISSN 0027-8939). Many issues published between 1990 and the present. Kansas City, Mo.: National Catholic Reporter Publishing Co.

Okami, P. (1991). "Self-Reports of 'Positive' Childhood and Adolescent Sexual Contacts with Older Persons: An Exploratory Study." *Archives of Sexual Behavior* 20: 437–58.

Pillard, R. C., and Weinrich, J. D. (1987). "The Periodic Table Model of the Gender Transpositions: Part I. A Theory Based on Masculinization and Defeminization of the Brain." *Journal of Sex Research* 23: 425–54.

Quinn, P. A. (1989). *Better than the Sons of Kings: Boys and Monks in the Early Middle Ages.* New York: Peter Lang.

Reeves, T. (1981). "Loving Boys." In D. Tsang, ed., *The Age Taboo: Gay Male Sexuality, Power, and Consent,* pp. 25–37. Boston: Alyson Publications.

Rosenzweig, S. (1942). "The Photoscope as an Objective Device for Evaluating Sexual Interest." *Psychosomatic Medicine* 4: 150–58.

Rutter, P. (1989). *Sex in the Forbidden Zone: When Men in Power—Therapists, Doctors, Clergy, Teachers, and Others—Betray Women's Trust.* Los Angeles: Jeremy P. Tarcher.

Saikaku, I. (1990). *The Great Mirror of Male Love,* translated wtih an introduction by P. G. Schalow. Stanford: Stanford University Press. (Originally published in 1687.)

Sandfort, T.; Brongersma, E.; and van Naerssen, A., eds. (1991). "Male Intergenerational Intimacy: Historical, Socio-Psychological, and Legal Perspectives." *Journal of Homosexuality* 20, nos. 1–2: 1–325.

Sherr, R. (1991). "A Canon, a Choirboy, and Homosexuality in Late-Sixteenth-Century Italy: A Case Study." *Journal of Homosexuality* 21: 1–22.

Smuts, B. B.; Cheney, D. L.; Seyfarth, R. M.; Wrangham, R. W.; and Struhsaker, T. T. (1986). *Primate Societies.* Chicago: The University of Chicago Press.

Symons, D. (1979). *The Evolution of Human Sexuality.* New York: Oxford University Press.

——— (1989). "The Psychology of Human Mate Preferences." *Behavioral and Brain Sciences* 12: 34–35.

Tate, T. (1990). *Child Pornography: An Investigation.* London: Methuen.

Taub, D. M. (1990). "The Functions of Primate Paternalism." In J. R. Feierman, ed., *Pedophilia: Biosocial Dimensions,* pp. 338–77. New York: Springer-Verlag.

Westermarck, E. (1891). *The History of Human Marriage.* New York: Macmillan.

Wickler, W. (1973). *The Sexual Code.* Garden City, N.Y.: Anchor Books.

3

Incest Taboo and Sexual Abuse

Joan A. Nelson and Jean-Ric Meller

Children of a future age
Reading this indignant page
Know that in a former time
Love, sweet love, was thought a crime.
—William Blake, "A Little Girl Lost"

INTRODUCTION

Incest laws may have been originally designed to create social stability and to prevent inbreeding. Today they are used more for prevention and punishment of abuses of power. Due to this alteration of goals, children may be inadequately protected against abuse while being denied healthy sexual development and normal familial affection. This article presents a brief but comprehensive background for an objective legal policy that could minimize the artificial creation of victims and perpetrators, and create a social environment less likely to turn children into future abusers.

In this article, the term "abuse" will denote harmful use of power through control by physical or emotional manipulation. The term "incest" will signify sexual activity between individuals closely related by kinship. Incest is also distinct from endogamy/exogamy, which relate to marriage, and from inbreeding, which focuses on procreation.

FOUNDATIONS OF INCEST LAWS

Today's incest laws, indeed all sex-related laws, are derived from ancient mores, which include strong incest taboos. Because of the intensity of these taboos and the continued existence of some of them today, it is important to maintain a perspective on past and current opinions about the taboos' origins and their unquestioned acceptance. When speaking of incest taboos, it is all too tempting to lump them together, and to misuse the adjective "universal." When sociologists speak of the "universality of the taboo," they mean that in one way or another, most human groups have practiced some restriction on sexual relations between parents and children or between siblings.

What is not universal is the definition of which other relationships constitute incest. Interdictions related to in-laws, cousins, godparents, and step-siblings vary widely among cultures. For the African Bohindu, for example (Westermarck 1889), all children born the same day in the same village were twins and could not marry. For the Navajo Indians, marriage interdictions extend to all the members of the mother's or the father's clan (Diamond 1992). In some cultures, a man could not marry his widowed sister-in-law. In others, such a marriage was not only permitted but compulsory if she was without children. "Her husband's brother must come to her, and, exercising his levirate, make her his wife" (Deut. 25:5). In many cultures it was common for half-brothers and half-sisters to marry. At least 96 different societies have been counted where some form of sexual activity has been allowed among family members (Fox 1980).

Even in the presence of a "universal" core taboo, there have been many exceptions. In Persia of 600 B.C., the Zoroastrians encouraged marriage between parents and children and between brothers and sisters (Duschesne-Guillemin 1966; Bullough 1976). In ancient Egypt, brother-sister marriage was the norm for the royal family, and at times for the population at large. In the Greek-Egyptian city of Arsinoe, two thirds of recorded marriages during the second century A.D. were between siblings (Middleton 1962). For the Hindu-Sakta sect in India incest was a higher grade of sexual intercourse leading to religious perfection (Justice & Justice 1979). The Mbuti pygmies do not even have a concept for incest (Diamond 1992). More recently, even into the present century, among American Mormons incest was preferred to marriage outside the church.

Also in question is the supposed universality of the "horror of incest." After reviewing the cultural background of a great many human groups from Africa to native America to China, Fox concludes that there is nothing particularly universal about the way incest is viewed. "In some cultures there may indeed be horror; but in others there is mere embarrassment, in still others indifference, and in certain few there may be positive encouragement" (Fox 1980: 6).

From traditional folklore to modern psychoanalysis, theories on the origins and functions of the incest taboo rival each other in complexity and cannot be proven. Moreover, they apply mostly to endogamy or inbreeding, not to sexual activity per se. It is impossible to describe the many complicated theories without some oversimplification. Nevertheless, this section attempts to minimize distortion by summarizing answers to the two main questions: (1) Is avoidance of incest biologically or culturally determined? (2) What purpose does it serve?

Discussion of taboo origins divides theorists into the nature versus nurture schools. The Instinctive Avoidance theory, originally proposed by Edward Westermarck, is still held by some modern anthropologists and sociologists such as Norbert Bischof. (It is ingeniously reconciled with Freudian theory by Robin Fox in *The Red Lamp of Incest.*) From the view of instinctive avoidance, there is a natural, genetically programmed sexual avoidance, not between blood-related individuals, but between "persons living closely together from childhood" (Westermarck 1889). Brothers and sisters, blood related, adopted or simply raised together, will naturally tend to look elsewhere for sexual expression. For example, Spiro (1958) showed that in Israel, boys and girls raised together in a collective environment (kibbutz) tended to look outside their circle for sexual partners. However, the theory goes on, this natural avoidance instinct is not an absolute. It is a statistical truth, a "norm," felt by most people but not all of them, and not all of the time.

Under this theory, the incest taboo is an expression of uneasiness, discomfort, disapproval by the majority of a behavior in which only a minority would naturally engage. At its root, it is nothing more than a prejudice, a fear of the different. The disapproval is then reinforced by the necessity to prove to oneself and to society that one is exempt from any such tendencies. Depending on the particular society, the reaction of the individual to the discovery of a transgression can vary from mere embarrassment to total humiliation, and the sanction of the group can take many forms, from public ridicule to the death penalty (Fox 1980).

By contrast, the theories held by Freud, Levi-Strauss, Jung, Parsons and many others have suggested that our basic animal instincts would inevitably lead us to incest, if it weren't for strong learned negative sanctions against this behavior. In this context, the taboo is what keeps us from engaging in a behavior that would wreak havoc in family-based societies.

These theories attempt to explain, first, the negative consequences that would ensue without the ban, and second, how the ban originated against the supposed background of a natural tendency to consummate incest.

Speculation on the purpose of prohibiting incest falls into two categories, biological and sociological. The biological argument concerns procreation. It asserts that inbreeding can promote the manifestation of harmful recessive genetic traits that lead to racial degeneracy (Westermarck 1889; Lenz 1962).

Thus, societies that bred only with blood relatives may have existed but they have been weeded out by virtue of their own inherited weaknesses. Scientists now argue that one would need *total,* not just occasional, inbreeding to produce this result. As a matter of fact, even *mostly* incestuous societies wouldn't be affected. "No matter how high the inbreeding load may become in a small population, one or two bouts of outbreeding every few generations would rapidly offset this and reintroduce variation" (Fox 1980: 10). Livingstone (1969) found by mathematical modeling that "inbreeding does not increase the death rate from homozygosity [duplication of genes], but rather decreases the frequencies of deleterious genes" and concludes, "inbreeding among the early hominids would be both highly probable and not dysfunctional from the point of view of the population, and the origins of incest [taboos] and exogamy must be sought elsewhere" (p. 46).

The sociological arguments subdivide into three main groups, with only the last two addressing the issue of incest per se. The first and most popular argument is about exogamy. It views wives as valuable possessions and the exchange of women among family groups as a trade that builds alliances and wider social ties. Without these ties, families would stay in constant conflict with each other. It would also be difficult to build larger social structures against the background of isolated, ingrown nuclear families (Murdock 1949; Levi-Strauss 1970).

The second argument, proposed by Parsons (1954) holds incest taboos as a barrier to regression and infantilism. It suggests that in an incestuous society, "people would become fixated on their primary sex choices, [their] parents, and never want sex outside the family" (Fox 1980: 9). The incest prohibition is what gives the individual "enough courage to turn his back on the shelter of his family circle, which would tend to keep him infantile, and stand on his own two feet" (Bischof 1972: 13).

The third group of arguments, held by Freud (1924), Malinowsky (1931), and Seligman (1950), among others, is that sexual promiscuity within the nuclear family would create jealousy and fights. Mostly formulated under a patriarchal societal model, this theory views women as sex objects to be coveted. "The incest prohibitions lessen the grave source of friction . . . due to sexual jealousy and competition between father and son for the possession of the females of the two generations" (Seligman 1950: 307). From a feminist perspective, this theory could explain why there is relatively little mother-son incest while father-daughter incest is more prevalent. A man could control access to his wife since she "belongs" to him. His daughter also "belongs" to him and can be treated as his sexual property, as long as the premium placed on her virginity isn't too high. Indeed, father-daughter incest has been condoned under this view, where rape was seen as a crime against the "property" of a man. Father-daughter incest, perpetrated against one's own property, couldn't be too serious.

Although explanations of incest taboos are plentiful, most are extremely complex, and none is totally satisfactory. First of all there is little which is truly "universal" in the treatment of incest in human groups. Second, the incest "horror" is, at best, a dubious concept. Third, arguments relevant to marriage and procreation are overused in an attempt to explain a sexual prohibition. Fourth, if any of the proposed theories actually explains the origins of historic taboos, virtually none of them would apply to a modern society. Today, sex is generally separate from procreation; social structures do not depend on alliances with in-laws; women are no longer regarded as possessions (or we say that they should not be).

It is tempting to join James Ramey (1979) or Henderson (1983: 35) in asking, "If the taboo were to attenuate . . . as did the taboo against masturbation, would incest be psychologically noxious, or even of any psychological interest?" We might even conclude, as did Yehudi Cohen (1964), that the taboo may be nothing more than "a holdover of primitive need to form personal alliances."

However, we cannot endorse such thinking without a thorough inquiry into the individual psychological consequences of incestuous behaviors and early sexual experiences.

INCEST AND CHILD ABUSE LAWS

The acceptance of nonincestuous ephebophilia in ancient Greece is well known (Bullough 1976). The attitude toward incest, however, was marked with significant change during that period, as is revealed by the evolution of the legend of Oedipus. In the original account, written in the ninth century B.C. by Homer, after marrying his mother and inadvertently killing his father, Oedipus lived on as a ruler of Thebes, and was eventually killed in combat and buried in honor in his own country (Kanzer 1964). Four hundred years later, the moral climate had changed, when Sophocles wrote the famous play in which Oedipus died miserably, after blinding and exiling himself for his crime.

In the Bible, the Old Testament provides a precise set of rules defining all kin relationships within which one can or cannot marry. It was considered a grave offense to have sexual relations with one of the forbidden relatives (Lev. 18:6–18). Death by burning was the sentence for intercourse with a mother and her daughter, public execution for sibling incest (Kling 1965).

At the same time, according to the Talmud, at the age of "three years and one day," a female child could be legally betrothed by sexual intercourse with her father's permission. Although intercourse with a child younger than three was not valid as a commitment to marriage, it was not illegal (Rush

1980). Under Christianity the three-year limit was extended to seven years. However, intercourse with a younger child remained inconsequential. In England, it was not until 1576 that a law was passed protecting girls under ten from forcible rape. Even then, the crime wasn't regarded as serious (Kilpatrick 1992).

The legal shift to adult-child sexuality as a problem seems to have begun in eighteenth- and nineteenth-century America. During that time, the villain was neither incest nor child abuse, but sexual expression in general. Under the so-called Puritan ethic, children were seen as undisciplined animals who needed protection, not against outside abuse, but against their own sexual instincts. Children were sexual in nature, and if not kept in check, would indulge in masturbation, which was held responsible for almost every child disease, mental illness or social problem known at the time. "The fear was that masturbation in boys caused insanity and early death and that girls would become nymphomaniacs or prostitutes" (Kilpatrick 1992: 9). The sexual repression that ensued was sometimes brutal. Schultz (1980) described a range of practices, from strapping hands to bedsides to removal of the clitoris without anesthesia, all designed to protect children against themselves "for their own good."

Humorists today make jokes about still-existing laws against kissing on Sunday, or against any sexual expression other than marital missionary intercourse in the dark. These Puritan ethic laws, though seldom enforced, actually remain on the books, side by side with incest laws that were formulated long before child abuse was recognized as a problem. Incest laws were not intended to protect anyone from any form of abuse. Unfortunately, in the struggle to define the new concept of child sexual abuse without a traditional legal or social background, the temptation has been great to use incest laws to protect children. This is one of the reasons the concepts have been so confused.

INCEST BETWEEN CONSENTING ADULTS

In some cases, prosecution under current incest laws sentences people to long jail terms. More often, consenting adults participating in incest receive suspended sentences.

In such countries as France and Japan, adult incest is not a crime. In 1976, Sweden came close to passing a law making it legal to marry a sibling (Engstrom 1976). In the United States, although such cases are rare, consenting adult incest is still considered criminal. Marriage, if it occurs, is declared void. Children of the relationship are illegitimate, and the principals are subject to imprisonment.

For example, in April 1977, Victoria Pittorino and David Goddu, both in their twenties, met, fell in love and were married in June. When it was discovered that they were in fact siblings separated at birth and raised in different families, Massachusetts Judge Frances Lappin annulled the marriage. The law that was invoked dated back to 1695 and could have been used to incarcerate them for up to twenty years. Instead they were put on probation, and permitted to live together as long as they did not "commit incest."

In the same year, a twenty-year-old Marine, Christopher Lillie, married his mother, Jean Marie Lillie, forty-two, when they were finally united after he had grown up in a foster home. On January 7, 1980, Judge J. M. H. Willis of Stafford County, Virginia, sentenced them both to five years in prison but suspended the terms on condition of ten years of "good behavior." They were ordered not to meet or communicate with each other during that time.

What possible purpose do these laws serve in a modern society? As Victoria Pittorino says, "You know, it's weird, because they want to put you in jail for being in love. Like, love is against the law" (*San Francisco Chronicle,* 1980).

Incest laws also lack uniformity. Marriage with a first cousin, for instance, is legal in only two-thirds of the United States. In Rhode Island it is only permitted for Jews.

CHILDREN AND EARLY SEXUAL EXPERIENCE

Now that sexual behavior between adults and children is legally prosecuted, blood kinship per se is no longer a reasonable criterion for defining a sex crime. The kind of relatedness that matters in sexual relationships is the relationship of power that applies between children and authority or caregiving figures. It is generally agreed that a significant age difference in and of itself creates such a power differential that a consensual, nonexploitative sexualized relationship between adult and child is a contradiction in terms. Such a relationship is now viewed as necessarily harmful regardless of the circumstances.

In order to approach this modern concern with sensitivity, understanding and honesty, legal and social policy makers need to understand the nature of child sexuality in general. We know that the concept of a presexual stage of development is a fallacy. "Children are sexual—only when we accept this fact can we understand our children's normal development" (Goldman 1982: 3). Ignoring this simple fact can have harmful consequences. According to Mary Calderone:

> By denying their child's eroticism, parents rob him or her of an absolutely crucial component of what should be a developing sense of identity and

> self-esteem. The true innocence of childhood is what we destroy or warp by denying sexual pleasure or punishing it or calling it bad, and especially by labeling it as sinful. (1983)

She adds that this very behavior is what creates sexually dysfunctional adults and results in an increasing need for sex therapists:

> And of course, we see such sexual variations as fetishism, exhibitionism, nonorgasmia, premature ejaculation, impotence, sadomasochism, child abuse, and rape. In other words, we are a society of sexual cripples. (1983: p. 529)

Clinical research on the effects of early sexual experiences reveals great diversity. The effects range from very harmful to neutral and, in some cases, beneficial. A groundbreaking analysis by Dr. Allie Kilpatrick, from the University of Georgia (1992) sheds light on the subject. In a study of 501 women in the South East of the United States, she examines the correlation between early sexual experience and adult functioning. The study details the type of sexual experience, the age of the participants, their relationship, who initiated the encounter, the presence of coercion, and several other factors. The study then proceeds to record the subjects' reaction to the event at that time, from very pleasant to very unpleasant, and to measure the level of functioning as an adult according to the standard Hudson Scales, which grade such factors as self-esteem, contentment, marital satisfaction, sexual satisfaction and family relations.

The study finds no correlation between the presence of early sexual experience and adult functioning along any of the measured criteria. Most subjects actually reported such early experiences as pleasurable, except when a high degree of coercion was present. It finds no difference caused by the sexual partner's role definition (relative versus nonrelative, older versus younger) except, again, in cases when force or high pressure was involved.

This study questions the frequent assumption that adult/child sex is by nature abusive and harmful.

> To assume that violations of social norms lead to harm for the child or adolescent without data with which to confirm the assumption is not scientifically sound. The fundamental question concerning the definition of abuse, therefore, becomes: What has been harmed, the child or the moral code? . . . One should not assume that harm has been done or make inappropriate assertions. (Kilpatrick 1992: 35)

Kilpatrick found no more negative consequences in cases of incest than in early sexual experiences in general. She concludes, "the concept of a *child sexual abuse syndrome* that has commonly appeared in clinical literature is not supported scientifically, and the dangers of using the concept are substantial" (p. 118). To many researchers, this isn't a surprise. John Money remarked in 1980 that a childhood sexual experience need not affect the child adversely (Williams & Money 1980). Why then, are child sexual experiences (no matter what the age or relationship of the partner) so often considered harmful?

A partial answer is suggested by Schultz (1973):

> By far the greatest potential damage to the child's personality is caused by society and the victim's parents, as a result of: (1) the need to use the victim to prosecute the offender, and (2) the need of parents to prove to themselves, family, neighborhood and society that the victim was free of voluntary participation and that they were not failures as parents. . . . It isn't the sexual assault that usually creates trauma, but the parent's behavior upon its discovery, and the effect on the child. (p. 150)

This is reinforced by Gibbons (1963), who found in a study of parental behavior after discovery of sex offense that "26 percent of the parents engaged in behavior that aggravated the sex-offense situation or exploited the child's situation for social benefit" (p. 150).

Many other researchers concur (Bender & Blau 1935; Brunold 1964; Burgess & Holstrom 1974; Conte et al. 1989; De Francis 1969; Justice & Justice 1979; Mann & Gaynor 1980; Margolin 1986; Summit & Kryso 1978; Weitzel et al. 1978). They cite the imposed secrecy during the sexual encounter, the effects of disclosure, the climate of the environmental response, and the emphasis on prosecution of the offender as major causes for damage.

Given this information, the logical question follows: If some noncoercive sexual relationships were to be decriminalized, would they become harmless? So far there are some positive, but by no means definitive, reports from Sweden, Switzerland, Holland and Belgium, where sex crimes laws are significantly less restrictive than in United States. In these countries, for example, sex between two people older than twelve is legal if there are fewer than three years of age difference between them, or if they are both over sixteen.

Children and Incest

A great number of clinical studies have reported harmful effects of the type of child sexual abuse currently referred to as "incest" (Benward & Densen-Gerber 1975; Browning & Boatman 1977; Cleveland 1986; Jackson et al. 1990; Justice & Justice 1979; Kubo 1959; Lukianowicz 1972; Medlicott 1967; Meiselman 1978; Molnar & Cameron 1975; Rosenfeld et al. 1977; Sloane

& Karpinsky 1942; Weinberg 1955). These studies tend to show poor functioning in adult sexuality, emotional responses, social adjustments and self-esteem. Most of these studies, however, suffer from a number of serious shortcomings that mostly invalidate the findings. They are generally conducted on biased samples, taken from clinical or offender populations. Violence, alcoholism, physical and mental abuse are often present. Furthermore, the effects of discovery, investigation and prosecution are not separated from the effects of the sexual behavior itself.

Aware of such biases, Yates (1982) remarks:

> . . . almost all the youngsters in these studies were identified by the courts. . . . In addition, families . . . are marked by alcoholism, . . . mental disorder, and other social problems; the children have often been neglected or physically abused. . . . Thus a causal relationship between sexual misuse and emotional damage cannot automatically be assumed. (p. 483)

Weitzel et al. (1978) notice that, "None of the studies reviewed by us contained an appropriate control group. Thus, the effect of incest on the lives of children is presently unknown" (p. 128). Henderson (1983) agrees:

> The frequent working assumption that incestuous experience is always harmful does not rest on valid scientific evidence. . . . The absence of well-controlled studies makes it difficult or impossible to separate the effect of incest from that of other variables highly correlated with developmental trauma, such as low level of parental education, low family income, poor child-rearing practices and high degree of family disorganization. (pp. 34, 38)

Leslie Margolin (1986) concurs:

> Each case came to the attention of the investigator either because the subject or one of his parents was involved in psychiatric treatment or had run into difficulties with the law. Thus, the cases are heavily weighted toward those who are having severe problems with their lives. (p. 107)

A few exploratory studies, although based on limited samples, have evoked some consistently interesting comments on the part of the researchers. As early as 1937, Bender reported that incestuous daughters are found to be generally free of guilt feelings until they are exposed to censure from parents or authorities. Kaufman et al. (1954) observed that guilt seemed to be connected to the disruption of the home rather than to the act of incest itself. LaBarbera et al. (1980) remarked that factors related to the makeup of the incestuous family rather than the sexual behavior are the most pathogenic. Weitzel et al. (1978) found that, "Many children do not seem to regard the experience of incest as highly unpleasant or traumatic, but describe it rather in a benign and matter-of-fact way" (p. 128). Henderson (1983) concluded, "If the parents are able to treat the incestuous disclosure matter-of-factly without too much guilt, the child will do likewise" (p. 37). In the traumatic cases, he speculated that, "It is at least a possibility . . . that the intense personal pain preceded the incestuous interaction and was in part its motive rather than its consequence" (p. 34). Margolin (1986) concluded that, "The primary harm resulting from incest is not the sex act itself, but the child's belief that this form of sexuality is inappropriate and exploitative" (p. 113).

According to these studies, it seems that most of the negative effects reported could be attributed to other family factors such as violence, alcoholism, or criminality; to the reaction of society upon discovery of incest; to the belief that the act is "wrong"; or to trauma caused by prosecution. Money explains:

> For the young participant in incest, it may very well be that the burden of secrecy and deceit takes a heavier toll than does the sexual-erotic experience itself. When the genuine pair-bonding of erotic love has existed between the two partners in incest, then the discovery and disbanding of their partnership, not the partnership itself, may be the source of trauma. Such a psychologic reality, however, bears no weight with the law. The incest taboo is so strong that those who break it must be either secretive or boastful as deviants. Being a sexual deviant is like being a religious deviant in a one-religion society. It is too difficult for most people to cope with. (Williams & Money 1980: 412)

One specific consequence, however, appears to be consistent. Bender and Blau (1937), Rogers and Weiss (1953), Krieger et al. (1980) and Yates (1982) all reported an early awareness of sexual and erotic identity in incest participants. Yates, in particular, found that children with an incestuous background did develop an early erotic response which typically caused problems in foster families:

> The foster parent who accepts an incestuous child into his or her home usually expects to receive and nourish a victim emotionally crippled by an atrocity. When the child's carnal bent becomes an inescapable reality, the [foster] parent first denies any active intent. The child is a puppet, manipulated in absentia by the evil parent. He or she "can't get out of the habit," is still infected by the earlier experience. . . . Then the child becomes an alien, a tainted being not like the foster family and therefore not belonging in their home. Insult follows injury as one foster placement follows another. The incestuous child in foster placement comes to understand that acceptance depends on conforming to the role of the victim. This is heavily reinforced by court proceedings and the attitude of helpful adults, including social workers,

> foster parents, and therapists. Erotic responsiveness is scarcely the prerogative of a victim. To be honest with others is to brook rejection. (p. 484)

Most experts, if asked, agree that society's condemnation of sexual behaviors, fantasies, or feelings in children is a major factor in the harmful guilt and shame experienced by children with incest experience. Some researchers even report positive outcomes despite the apparent condemnation and victimization. Rascovsky and Rascovsky (1950) conclude, in a small clinical study, that incestuous acts diminish the person's chance of psychosis and allow for a better adjustment to the real world. Finkelhor (1980) presents an extensive survey of 796 undergraduates at six New England colleges and universities, and finds that 15 percent of the females and 10 percent of the males report some type of sexual experience involving a sibling. About one-third of the experiences were reported as positive by the participants. These appeared to be vehicles of positive sexual development for women, who give evidence in adulthood of higher sexual self-esteem.

Many people have some difficulty accepting these findings which question a well-established victim/perpetrator model. Kilpatrick (1992) concludes: "They do not want to hear about positive reactions to early sexual experiences. They do not want their preconceived notions that all early sexual experiences are harmful to be challenged. They especially do not want to hear of incestuous experiences that do not cause irreparable harm" (p. xviii).

CHILDREN AND ABUSE

Criminal justice and child protection service professionals have little time or training for sorting out how much damage was caused by secrecy, deceit and shame as opposed to how much of the harm was produced by a sexual-erotic experience itself. As a consequence, incest as a crime has been defined solely on the sexual acts performed. Such a formulation is problematic for several reasons.

First, the act needs to be considered within cultural contexts. Among some traditional peoples, adults masturbate their children of both sexes in order to pacify them. The Sambia of New Guinea believe it is vital for prepubescent boys to ingest male semen every day, and it is the moral obligation of older boys to provide it to them (Herdt, quoted in Money 1991). In traditional Hawaii and Samoa, it was the duty of adults to initiate prepubescent children into sex. "For adults not to have given such education would have been unthinkable" (Diamond 1990: 434). Such acts, integrated into a cultural heritage and regarded as normal, do not bring on negative judgment. In a culturally pluralistic society, certain acts within cultural or ethnic communities may be normalized.

A second problem with an acts-based definition of incest and sexual abuse arises through the conflicting and confusing definitions used in modern studies. In the past decade statistics on child sexual abuse have climbed alarmingly. Some studies have claimed that as many as 62 percent of all American females have suffered from childhood sexual abuse (Peters et al. 1986, Table 1.2: 20–21). There is confusion as to whether the numbers represent an increased incidence of abuse or of its reporting. Incest, now viewed a form of abuse, has seen its original characterization as vaginal sexual intercourse expanded to include many other acts. Says Joel Best (1990), "claimsmakers typified the problem with horrific examples (small children repeatedly forced to have sex, or former victims who continued to suffer as adults) while defining the problem in much broader terms" (p. 71). Such broadening must be particularly confusing to beaten, raped, tortured, starved or otherwise severely abused children who find themselves thrown into the same category with children who reportedly had their genitals fondled. Sgroi (1982) and Ingersoll and Patton (1990) even see "incest" as: "The adult is nude in the presence of one or more nonspousal family members," or "The adult disrobes in the presence of one or more children," or "The adult is unnecessarily present when the child is nude," or "The adult kisses the child in a way that is uncomfortable for the child" (p. 12).

A third consequence is the climate of mistrust such a trend can create in otherwise perfectly healthy families. To inherited taboos are now added fears of legal consequences. Parents become cautious over showing any affection that could be misinterpreted. They also feel less and less comfortable bringing up sexual issues in general. The result is a general withholding of both needed sexual education and healthy family affection. Consequences for the children are real.

> There is cumulative clinical and experimental evidence to indicate that neglect of children's developmental sexuality paves the way, by default, for the development, in large degree, if not in toto, of the . . . so-called "perversions" of adolescence and adulthood; and also for a major proportion of the sexual hypofunctions of adulthood, among which are erotic apathy, impotence and lubricatory failure, premature ejaculation and vaginismus, anorgasmia, erotic pain, and erotic anesthesia. (Williams & Money 1980: 413)

Beyond the problem of a definition of incest is the question of the reliability of substantiating claims of abuse, particularly when the accusation does not directly originate with the child. Richard A. Gardner, a psychiatric expert on child abuse cases, shows that a significant proportion of claims proffered in the context of child custody disputes are fabricated. He likens the phenomenon to the Salem witch trials. Many of the unjustly accused have served time for acts they never committed (Gardner 1991).

When a new concept emerges, it is easy to include deep-rooted past assumptions in the rhetoric. Armed with best intentions, child rights advocates have nowhere to turn but to prevailing ideologies. For some it is the remnants of the puritanical rejection of all forms of sensual enjoyment. For others it is a false interpretation of feminism that sees male sexuality as the ultimate enemy (Money 1991). Regardless of origins, the impact has been felt socially and legally. The Child Protection Act of 1984, for example, is worded so loosely as to allow prosecution as an illegal act for the photographing of nude children in the bathtub by parents or the documenting of normal child sexual play by researchers (Money 1985). Parents have been prosecuted for letting their children look at *Playboy* magazine, photographers for filming families at nude resorts.

RECOMMENDATIONS

It is often said that the rate of change in our society is increasing exponentially and that, in the next few decades, we can expect as profound a transformation of society as has taken place, perhaps, since the beginning of the incest taboo. So far, an abuse-free society exists only in the minds of utopian writers, such as Aldous Huxley (1962), Robert Heinlein (1973), Theodore Sturgeon (1967) and John Varley (1974). They speculate about advanced societies where fear-based taboos and laws have disappeared. Clothes are worn only for protection and adornment. Sex is openly discussed and shared. Enlightened, sex-positive child-rearing practices prepare children for responsible sexuality.

In these visions, children have the capacity to consent to appropriate affection and lovemaking because they are informed and educated. They receive plenty of love that is not conditional upon sex, and take responsibility for their physical, psychological, legal and moral rights to nurture and be nurtured. Sex with an adult is not associated with fear, deprivation or manipulation. It is a socially acceptable opportunity to learn from a more knowledgeable person, to explore new horizons and to grow as a fully expressed, healthy, functional human being. In these fictional accounts, child abuse is unthinkable, because fulfilled children grow into responsible, loving, nurturing adults. Today it is an open question as to whether such a transformation of society is possible.

In judging what is still regarded as a criminal act, the ultimate criterion remains the spirit, not the letter, of the law. The intent of the law is to mitigate, not to exacerbate, extremes of personal judgment. In the spirit of the common good, it is important not to sacrifice healthy sexual development in the name of child protection. With an eye toward uniformity in all jurisdictions, some practical recommendations follow.

Vocabulary

Use of noncondemnatory terms can do much to reduce the tendency to rush to judgment and the drawing of premature conclusions. In particular, professionals should: reserve the term "incest" to mean coitus between blood-related persons for whom marriage is prohibited; use the words "molestation" or "rape" only if and when it is determined that coercion was present; replace the word "abuse" with "experience," "incident," or "liaison" until it is decided that the episode was indeed harmful; and replace the words "victim" and "perpetrator" with "participant" or "partner" until damage is clearly established.

Recognizing Child Abuse

Since abuse cannot be defined by acts alone, justice necessitates a case-by-case search to establish power imbalances, the context and spirit of the interaction, and the actual harm done. To paraphrase Dr. Kilpatrick, the fundamental question will be: What has been harmed—the child or the social code?

Caution in Claiming Causes

It is too easy to blame sex for harm that is actually caused by toxic psychosocial environments, secrecy, fear of discovery, and societal response to actual discovery. Sorting out the degree of relevance of each factor will not always be possible, but being sensitive to the issue will help avoid jumping to rash conclusions.

Bias of Social Workers

Gardner (1991) showed that many professional "validators" are attracted to child abuse cases either because of their own background as molested children or because they themselves have hidden pedophile tendencies which they need to deny. Although such is not always the case, professionals must be aware that their own and others' opinions may be tinged by conscious or unconscious psychological substitution mechanisms such as revenge or displacement of blame. A background check on the professionals involved in the case may identify potential bias (Gardner 1991).

Bias of Therapists

In addition to these types of bias, some therapists might have an interest in reinforcing the victim/perpetrator model in their patients. Tavris (1993) denounces "the incest-survivor machine," a multi-million dollar industry built around the new concept of child abuse. "The problem is not with the advice they offer to victims, but with their effort to *create* victims, to expand the market that can then be treated with therapy and self-help books" (p. 16). In this case, checking into the degree of "specialization" of the therapist may identify conflicts of interest.

False Accusations

Gardner (1991) showed that many child abuse cases were fabricated. Some claim as many as 60 percent of all child abuse reports are unfounded or false, and 80 percent in the context of child custody disputes.[1] Children can and do make false reports for many reasons. Some reports represent deliberate and malicious intent; most are unintentionally created by frightened parents or over-zealous professionals. It should be remembered that conviction under criminal law requires proof beyond reasonable doubt and cannot rely solely on the allegations of a participant.

Distinguishing Thoughts from Actions

Legal and other professionals cannot deny human nature. At every stage of an investigation, it should be remembered that incestuous *thoughts and feelings* are natural and normal. Pedophilia is a common fantasy. It is only acting on these fantasies that is regarded as reprehensible.

Peer Incest

Incest laws that punish on the basis of blood kinship or affinity (detailed in the appendix) are no longer relevant and cannot be enforced to their fullest extent. Thus, they can only undermine the credibility of the legal system, and an effort should be made to remove them from the books as soon as possible.

Intergenerational Incest

Children are best protected by child abuse laws. Using ancient incest laws for child protection distorts the issue. Reasonable child abuse laws, fully enforced, can provide the protection children need in the spirit in which they need it.

Age of Consent

Recent rises in ages of sexual consent have made into felonies, at the ages of sixteen and seventeen, liaisons that were once permitted with people aged twelve and thirteen. Abuse can no more be determined by age alone than by acts alone. Although age can be a valuable guideline, maturity of the participants, context of the relationship and actual harm done should be the primary focus of the investigation.

Prevention Programs

While some sexual abuse prevention programs offer healthy information that promotes responsibility, others instill fear in children and can induce undue suspicion toward family members. The tension, anxiety and confusion that may result can be harmful. Public policy should make it a goal to control behavioral impulses through information and understanding, not fear and indoctrination.

Civil Remedies

In cases of abuse, many victims don't want their abusers in jail. Some want financial restitution for their therapy and for other consequences of abuse. Others just want a written apology or a court order compelling the abuser to get therapy. In such cases, civil remedies give victims a chance to tell their story in court and to be awarded punitive damages for the pain and injury suffered. For many victims, just lodging the complaint gives them a sense of empowerment that helps them heal.

Mandatory Disclosure Laws

When a child (frequently an adolescent girl) reveals during counseling that she has a history of incest, the therapist is often caught in a bind. Many adolescents may not want a report, especially if the incest not currently ongoing. They recognize the trauma such a report will create for themselves and their family, trauma which may far exceed that caused by the sexual contact. Reporting of such abuse by a counselor, when against the wishes of the client, may serve as a secondary trauma, another violation of trust, and another situation in which an adult has exerted power over the life of the adolescent when she is struggling to regain control over her own existence. The reporting laws should give counselors and therapists more flexibility in making decisions and designing solutions that will maximize positive outcomes for the child and minimize such negative consequences.

CONCLUSION

The social issues behind child abuse go far beyond the realm of law enforcement. "Elimination of the problem of sexual child abuse will require a knowledge of the developmental etiology of abuse in those children who grow up to become abusers. Attainment of that knowledge is predicated on medical and scientific sexological research, and on the study of abusiveness as pathology, not solely as crime" (Money 1991: 43). In the short run, it is important to keep in mind the distinctions between incest and child abuse, and to avoid in either case adding to the trauma already present for the participants.

APPENDIX: INCEST LAWS

Aspects of Statutory Definitions of Incest[2]

Blood Kinship

Blood relationship is a prerequisite for prosecution of incest only in California, the District of Columbia, Florida, Hawaii, Indiana, Kansas, Louisiana, Maryland, Minnesota, Nevada, New Mexico, New York, and North Dakota.

Vaginal Penetration

Some states deem vaginal penetration necessary in order for incest to have occurred: Alabama, Alaska, Arizona, Arkansas, California, Delaware, the District of Columbia, Florida, Georgia, Hawaii, Idaho, Indiana, Kentucky, Louisiana, Maryland, Massachusetts, Minnesota, Mississippi, Missouri, New Hampshire, Nevada, New Mexico, North Carolina, Oklahoma, Utah, and West Virginia.

Penalties

Indiana

Incest is punishable by imprisonment of up to 18 months, plus or minus time for aggravating or mitigating circumstances, and a fine of less than $1,000.

Delaware

Incest is punishable by imprisonment of up to 2 years, and a fine of not more than $1,000.

Illinois

Incest is punishable by imprisonment of 4 to 15 years.

Kansas

Incest is punishable by imprisonment of 2 to 10 years.

Louisiana

Uncle-niece and aunt-nephew incest are punishable by imprisonment of up to 5 years, all other incest by 5 years and up.

Alaska, Arizona, California, Florida, Hawaii, Iowa, Missouri, New Mexico, New York, North Dakota, Oregon, South Dakota, Utah, Wyoming

Imprisonment of up to 5 years.

Alabama, Arkansas, Colorado, the District of Columbia, Georgia, Idaho, Kentucky, Maryland, Massachusetts, Minnesota, Mississippi, Montana, Nebraska, Nevada, New Hampshire, North Carolina, Oklahoma, Pennsylvania, Tennessee, Texas, Washington, West Virginia, Wisconsin

Imprisonment of 5 years and up.

South Carolina

Incest is punishable by imprisonment of 10 years and up.

NOTES

1. Victims of Child Abuse Laws (VOCAL), P.O. Box 20074, Castro Valley, Calif. 94546.

2. There are no incest statutes in the states of Connecticut, Maine, Michigan, New Jersey, Ohio, Rhode Island, Vermont or Virginia. In these states, incest cases are prosecuted under other sexual abuse statutes, which often carry a higher penalty.

REFERENCES

Bender, L., and Blau, A. (1937). "The Reaction of Children to Sexual Relations with Adults." *American Journal of Orthopsychiatry* 7: 500–518.

Benward J., and Densen-Gerber, J. D. (1975). "Incest as a Causative Factor in Antisocial Behavior: An Exploratory Study." *Contemporary Drug Problems* 4: 323–40.

Best, J. (1990). *Threatened Children.* Chicago: The University of Chicago Press

Bischof, N. (1972). "The Biological Foundations of the Incest Taboo." *Social Science Information* 11, no. 6: 7–36.

Browning, D. H., and Boatman, B. (1977). "Incest: Children at Risk." *American Journal of Psychiatry* 134: 169–72.

Brunold, H. (1964, Jan./Feb.). "Observations after Sexual Traumata Suffered in Childhood." *Excerpta Criminologia.* Lisse, The Netherlands: Swetz and Fzitlinger, B.V.

Bullough, Vern L. (1976). *Sexual Variance in Society and History.* New York: Wiley.

Burgess, A. W., and Holstrom, L. L. (1974). *Rape! Victims of Crisis.* New York: Brady.

Calderone, M. S. (1983). "On the Possible Prevention of Sexual Problems in Adolescence." *Hospital and Community Psychiatry* 34: 528–30.

Cleveland, D. (1986). *Incest: The Story of Three Women.* Boston: Heath.

Cohen, Y. (1964). *The Transition from Childhood to Adolescence.* Chicago: Aldine.

Conte, J.; Briere, J.; and Sexton, D. (1989, Aug.). *Mediators of Long-Term Symptomology in Women Molested as Children.* Convention of the American Psychological Association, New Orleans, La.

De Francis, V. (1969). *Protecting the Child Victim of Sex Crimes Committed by Adults.* Denver, Colo.: Children's Division, American Humane Association.

Diamond, M. (1990). "Selected Cross-Generational Sexual Behavior in Traditional Hawai'i: A Sexological Ethnography." In J. Feierman, ed., *Pedophilia: Biosocial Dimensions.* New York: Springer-Verlag.

——— (1992). *Sexwatching.* Honolulu: Prion Press.

Duschesne-Guillemin, J. (1966). *Symbols and Values in Zoroastrianism,* pp. 149–50. New York: Harper & Row.

Engstrom, L. G. (1976). "New Penal Provisions on Sexual Offenses Proposed in Sweden." *Current Sweden* 118.

Finkelhor, D. (1980). "Sex among Siblings, A Survey on Prevalence, Variety, and Effects." *Archives of Sexual Behavior* 9: 171–94.

Fox, R. (1980). *The Red Lamp of Incest.* New York: E. P. Dutton.
Freud, S. (1924). *Totem und Tabu. Gesammelte Shriften,* vol. 10. Leipzig-Zurich: Internationaler Psychoanalytischer Verlag.
Gardner, Richard A. (1991). *Sex Abuse Hysteria.* Crestkill, N.J.: Creative Therapeutics.
Gibbons, T. C. N., and Prince, J. (1963). *Child Victims of Sex Offenses.* London: Institute for the Study and Treatment of Delinquency.
Goldman, R., and Goldman, J. (1982). *Children's Sexual Thinking: A Comparative Study of Children Aged 5 to 15 Years in Australia, North America, Britain & Sweden.* Boston: Routledge & K. Paul.
Heinlein, R. A. (1973). *Time Enough for Love.* New York: Putnam.
Henderson, J. (1983). "Is Incest Harmful?" *Canadian Journal of Psychiatry* 28: 34–40.
Huxley, A. (1962). *Island.* New York: Harper.
Ingersoll, S. L., and Patton, S. O. (1990). *Treating Perpetrators of Sexual Abuse.* Lexington, Mass.: Lexington Books.
International Symposium on Childhood and Sexuality. Montreal: Éditions Études Vivantes.
Jackson, J. L.; Calhoun, K. S.; Amick, A. E.; Maddever, H. M.; and Habif, V. L. (1990). "Young Adult Women Who Experienced Childhood Intrafamilial Sexual Abuse: Subsequent Adjustment." *Archives of Sexual Behavior* 19: 211–21.
Justice, B., and Justice, R. (1979). *The Broken Taboo.* New York: Human Sciences Press.
Kanzer, M. (1964). "On Interpreting the Oedipus Plays." In G. H. Pollock and J. M. Ross, eds., *The Oedipus papers.* Madison, Conn.: International Universities Press.
Kaufman, I.; Peck, A. L.; and Tagiori, C. K. (1954). "The Family Constellation and Overt Incestuous Relations between Father and Daughter." *American Journal of Orthopsychiatry* 24: 266–79.
Kilpatrick, A. C. (1992). *Long-Range Effects of Child and Adolescent Sexual Experiences.* Hillsdale, N.J.: Lawrence Erlbaum.
Kling, S. G. (1965). *Sexual Behavior and the Law.* New York: Random House.
Krieger, M. J.; Rosenfeld, A. A.; Gordon, A.; and Bennett, M. (1980). "Problems in the Psychotherapy of Children with Histories of Incest." *American Journal of Psychotherapy* 34: 81–88.
Kubo, S. (1959). "Researches and Studies on Incest in Japan." *Hiroshima Journal of Medical Sciences* 8: 99–159.
LaBarbera, J. D.; Martin, J. F.; and Dozier, J. E. (1980). "Child Psychiatrist's View of Father-Daughter Incest." *Child Abuse & Neglect* 4: 147–51.
Lenz, W. (1962). *Grundlagender genetischen Beratung. Erblische Stoffwechselkrankheiten.* Munich: Urban Schwartzenberg.
Lévi-Strauss, C. (1970). *The Elementary Structures of Kinship.* Oxford: Alden Press.
Livingstone, F. B. (1969). "Genetics, Ecology, and the Origins of Incest and Exogamy." *Current Anthropology* 10: 45–61.
Lukianowicz, N. (1972). "Incest." *British Journal of Psychiatry* 120: 301–313.
Malinowsky, B. (1927). *Sex and Repression in Savage Society.* London: Kegan Paul.
——— (1931). "Culture." In *Encyclopedia of the Social Sciences* 4: 621–46. London: McMillan.

Mann, E. M., and Gaynor, D. A. (1980). "Emotional Reactions and Treatment of Sexually Abused Children, Adolescents, and their Parents." In *The Child in His Family.* Vol. 6 of *Preventive Child Psychiatry in Age of Transitions,* pp. 409–420. New York: Wiley.

Margolin, L. (1986). "The Effect of Mother-Son Incest." *Lifestyles: A Journal of Changing Patterns:* 104–114.

Masters, R. E. L. (1963). *Patterns of Incest.* New York: Julian Press.

Medlicott, R. W. (1967). "Parent-Child Incest." *Australia and New Zealand Journal of Psychiatry* 1: 180–87.

Meiselman, K. C. (1978). *Incest: A Psychological Study of Causes and Effects and Treatment Recommendations.* San Francisco: Jossey-Bass.

Middleton, R. (1962). "Brother-Sister and Father-Daughter Marriage in Ancient Egypt." *American Sociological Review* 27, no. 5: 603–611.

Molnar, G., and Cameron, P. (1975). "Incest Syndromes: Observations in a General Hospital Psychiatric Unit." *Canadian Psychiatric Association Journal* 20: 373–77.

Money, J. (1985). "The Conceptual Neutering of Gender and the Criminalization of Sex." *Archives of Sexual Behavior* 14: 279–90.

——— (1988). "Commentary: Current Status of Sex Research." *Journal of Psychology and Human Sexuality* 1: 5–15.

——— (1991). "Semen-Conservation Theory vs. Semen-Investment Theory, Antisexualism, and the Return of Freud's Seduction Theory." *Journal of Psychology & Human Sexuality* 4, no. 4: 31–45.

Murdock, G. P. (1949). *Social Structure.* New York: Macmillan.

Parsons, T. (1954). "The Incest Taboo in Relation to Social Structure and the Socialization of the Child." *British Journal of Sexology* 5: 101–117.

Peters, S. D.; Wyatt, G. E.; and Finkelhor, D. (1986). "Prevalence." In D. Finkelhor, ed., *A Source Book on Sexual Child Abuse,* pp. 75–93. Beverly Hills, Calif.: Sage.

Ramey, J. W. (1979). "Dealing with the Last Taboo." *SIECUS Report* 7.

Rascovsky, M. W., and Rascovsky, A. (1950). "On Consummated Incest." *International Journal of Psychoanalysis* 31: 42–47.

Rogers, E., and Weiss, J. (1953). "Study of Sex Crimes against Children." In *California Sexual Deviation Research.* Langley Porter.

Rosenfeld, A., et al. (1977). "Incest and Sexual Abuse of Children. *Journal of the American Academy of Child Psychiatry* 16: 327–39.

Rush, F. (1980). *The Best-Kept Secret: Sexual Abuse of Children.* Englewood Cliffs, N.J.: Prentice-Hall.

San Francisco Chronicle, January 10, 1980, p. 5.

Schultz, L. G. (1973). "The Child Sex Victim: Social, Psychological and Legal Perspectives." *Child Welfare* 52: 148–49.

———. (1980). "The Sexual Abuse of Children and Minors: A Short History of Legal Control Efforts." In L. G. Schultz, ed., *The Sexual Victimology of Youth.* Springfield, Ill.: Charles C Thomas.

Seligman, B. Z. (1950). "The Problem of Incest and Exogamy: A Restatement." *American Anthropologist* 52: 305–316.

Sgroi, S. M. (1982). *Handbook of Clinical Intervention in Child Sexual Abuse.* Lexington, Mass.: D. C. Heath & Co.

Sloane, P., and Karpinsky, E. (1942). "Effects of Incest on the Participants." *American Journal of Orthopsychiatry* 12: 666–73.

Summit, R., and Kryso, J. (1978). "Sexual Abuse of Children: A Clinical Spectrum." *American Journal of Orthopsychiatry* 28: 237–51.

Spiro, M. E. (1958). *Children of the Kibbutz.* Cambridge, Mass.: Harvard University Press.

Sturgeon, T. (1967). "If All Men Were Brothers, Would You Let One Marry Your Sister?" In H. Ellison, ed., *Dangerous Visions.* New York: Signet.

Tavris, C. (1993). "Beware the Incest-Survivor Machine." *New York Times Book Review,* January 3, 1993, pp. 1, 16–17.

Varley, J. (1974). *The Persistence of Vision.* New York: Dell.

Weinberg, S. K. (1955). *Incest Behavior.* New York: Citadel Press.

Weitzel, W. D.; Powell, J. P.; and Penick, E. C. (1978). "Clinical Management of Father-Daughter Incest: A Critical Reexamination." *American Journal of Diseases of Children* 132: 127–30.

Westermarck, E. (1889). *The History of Human Marriage.* New York: Allerton Press.

Williams G. J., and Money, J. (1980). *Traumatic Abuse and Neglect of Children at Home.* Baltimore: John Hopkins University Press.

Yates, A. (1982). "Children Eroticized by Incest." *American Journal of Psychiatry* 139: 482–85.

4

Rape and Sadomasochistic Paraphilias*

Peter M. Sheridan and Steven Hucker

INTRODUCTION

Within recent years the forensic definition of rape has undergone major modification so that it includes not only violent sexual assault of a stranger by an intruder but also date, acquaintance and spousal rape. This chapter presents various types of rape, the diverse forms this phenomenon may take, and current views on violent and aggressive versus sexual motivation in rape. A brief review of male rape is also provided, as this is an area where only limited research has been conducted to date. Paraphilic rape and sadistic rape are discussed within the context of these new definitions of rape.

In a latter part of the chapter sadomasochistic paraphilia is considered. The term sadism was introduced by Richard von Krafft-Ebing (1886, 1965), borrowing the moniker of the Marquis de Sade, whose novels are replete with descriptions of cruelty, torture and murder designed to stimulate his fictional characters. Krafft-Ebing viewed sadism as the association of sexual arousal with cruelty ranging from verbal humiliation to serial murder. A. von Schrenk-Notzing (1895, 1956) used the term *algolagnia* (literally "pain craving") to emphasize the necessity of inflicting pain; he referred to both active algolagnia, which corresponds to sadism, and passive algolagnia, or masochism. Albert Eulenberg (1911) broadened this concept of sadism to include infliction of mental pain in the form of humiliation and degradation. Other authors have stressed the importance of feelings of domination, power and control

*The authors gratefully acknowledge the assistance of Rosemary L. Scaglione in the preparation of this chapter.

over the victim (Brittain 1970; Hazelwood, Dietz, and Warren 1992; Karpman 1954; Weinberg 1987).

The term *masochism* was also introduced by Krafft-Ebing (1886, 1965) and can be traced to Leopold von Sacher-Masoch, whose novels portray males dominated by women who humiliate and physically abuse them. Masochism is essentially the mirror image of sadism. The masochist is sexually aroused by the idea of being completely and unconditionally subject to the will of another person as if this person were the master, and of being humiliated and abused, rather than inflicting this treatment on someone else. Sadistic and masochistic fantasies often coexist in the same person (Arndt et al. 1985; Spengler 1977). Both sadism and masochism may be associated with other paraphilias (Abel et al. 1988), especially transvestitism and fetishism (Gosselin & Wilson 1980).

TYPES OF RAPE

In clinical usage, the term rape is typically employed to describe the sexual assault of nonconsenting adult females by adult males. This includes not only forced vaginal intercourse but also fellatio, cunnilingus, and anal intercourse. Researchers typically do not distinguish among these acts in their classification of rapist subtypes (e.g., Knight & Prentky 1990; Knight et al. 1985; Prentky et al. 1985; Quinsey 1984; Rosenberg et al. 1988), although there are those (e.g., Groth 1979) who attempt to distinguish rapists on the basis of the inferred motives in their assaults. Exceptions to this general rule are those men deemed to be rape-prone (i.e., those for whom an erotic preference exists for raping as opposed to intercourse with a consenting partner).

To date, two types of rape-proneness have been identified: *sadistic rape,* in which the act of raping appears to be only a byproduct of the sexual gratification achieved by causing fear, pain, injury or even death to one's victim (Brittain 1970; Langevin et al. 1985); and *preferential rape,* in which a man has persistent urges and fantasies to rape, usually of female strangers, despite access to willing sexual partners (Freund et al. 1986; Freund et al. 1972; Freund & Steiner 1980). These will be considered in further detail below.

The occurrence of vaginal penetration is not necessary in this definition of rape. Rapists may use instruments such as bottles for penetration. Degradation and humiliation of the victim may be accomplished by nonverbal actions (spitting, ejaculating or urinating on her) and verbal abuse of both a sexual and nonsexual nature (Darke 1990; Holmstrom & Burgess 1980). Victim compliance may be gained through verbal and/or physical coercion, physical restraint and assault, or threats of physical harm or even death, often with a weapon such as a knife or gun. Amir (1971) reported that 60 percent of rapes involved beating in varying degrees of brutality. In some cases, a victim may be taken advantage of in a state of alcohol or drug intoxication or unconsciousness.

Forcible, or forensic, rape historically has a narrower definition in law than that employed by most social science researchers. The basic legal definition of rape in the United States, until relatively recently, was the act of perpetration involving sexual intercourse with a female other than one's wife, against her will and consent, whether her will is overcome by force, by drugs or intoxicants, or because she is incapable of exercising rational judgment in giving her consent. In many states, the crime of rape required penile-vaginal penetration although full erection and ejaculation were not necessary. Forced acts of oral and anal sex, although frequent occurrences in rape, were legally considered a separate class of sexual offense (Sadoff 1978). With the introduction of the Michigan Criminal Sexual Code, the criteria of sexually assaultive acts were broadened, protection under law was extended to separated spouses as well as males, and use of a victim's sexual history in court was restricted. By the mid-1970s, forty-nine other states had revised or were revising their rape statutes to reflect similar changes (McConaghy 1993).

The emphasis that the traditional legal definition of rape places on penile-vaginal penetration has tended to obscure the context in which this act takes place, namely, a violent assault with, more often than not, multiple forced sexual activities (Muehlenhard et al. 1992). As Sheffield (1987) notes, the exclusive focus on this sexual component often meant that evidence demonstrating that the victim was not willing, that she resisted, must be forthcoming. Rape is one of the few crimes in which the victim is required to prove nonconsent. Victims of sexual assaults who avoid being raped, according to this narrow definition, and who do not suffer serious physical injuries, may be thought of as having tacitly given consent or permission to their assailants by their lack of resistance (Sheffield 1987; Stanko 1985; Stermac et al. 1990).

The legal definition of rape was originally drawn to exclude the possibility of marital sexual assault because of the presumption that a wife's sexual services were part of the contract of marriage and to protect the husband's "sexual property" (Russell 1982). A number of celebrated media cases in North America challenged this particular legal definition and in many states marital rape is now considered a criminal offense. *Marital rape* occurs when a woman is forced to have sex, or to engage in sexual acts to which she objects, by her husband. This may occur in battering relationships, in which sexual violence is yet another aspect of abuse, or in relationships where the frequency or quality of sexual activities is in conflict. Additionally marital rape may occur in relationships in which husbands are involved in atypical sexual obsessions, often involving the consumption of pornography, and in which wives are pressured or physically coerced to participate in recreating the husband's fantasies (Finkelhor & Yllo 1985; Yllo & Finkelhor 1985). These patterns of sexual assault in marriage are not typical of rapists seen in forensic settings, and thus this form of rape will not be discussed in detail here. According to the new definitions, however, prevalence estimates from two studies have found that marital rape is the most common form of sexual assault; between 10 percent and 14 percent of married women reported rape by their husbands involving the use or threat of force to obtain sexual activities, not exclusively vaginal intercourse (Russell 1982; Yllo & Finkelhor 1985). Similarly, the new definition has led to some estimates of marital rape which suggest that 24 percent to 26 percent of women were raped by their husbands or male lovers (Kilpatrick et al. 1988; Sorenson et al. 1987).

Statutory rape typically refers to sexual intercourse between an individual who is below the legal age of consent and an older offender, where the parties are not married. There is some form of statutory rape law in every state, although few states employ this terminology. Most states have a number of laws relating to statutory rape, which depend on the type of sexual activity involved, the ages of the victim and offender, and their relationship to each other.

Nearly all states now have gender-neutral statutory rape laws; a handful (Alabama, the District of Columbia, Georgia, and Idaho) prohibit only statutory rape of females. Many statutes require a specific age difference between the offender and victim; such an age difference affects the characterization of the offense in most states (e.g., Sexual Assault in the 3rd Degree versus Sexual Assault in the 2nd Degree where the victim and offender are close in age). Age differences specified in the statutes vary considerably from state to state; some require only that the offender be older than the victim (e.g., Mississippi), while others range from a two-year (e.g., Alabama) to a ten-year (e.g., California) age difference. In 32 states, the age of the offender makes no difference when the victim is below a certain age, ranging from ten years of age in South Dakota to sixteen years in the District of Columbia and Missouri. Age of consent to sexual intercourse obviously varies from state to state, and in some states there may be no minimum age of consent if the victim and offender are close in age (National Victim Center 1992).

The age of consent (or age of majority) is an arbitrary dividing line between competency and incompetency to make decisions. The concept of a set age of consent implies that, by a certain age, any individual has acquired the knowledge and experience to make decisions in his or her best interests. Under certain circumstances, consent may be given by individuals prior to the age of majority (Gaylin 1982). Finkelhor (1979) has suggested that, rather than focusing on moral and legal arguments, it is better to examine whether informed consent has been given. In order for the requirement of informed consent to be satisfied, the individual whose consent is sought must have what Finkelhor characterizes, but does not define, as the capacity to understand what is proposed, the ability to assess the advantages and disadvantages of his or her actions, and the ability to refuse consent. In addition, the decision-making process must be free from coercion and pressure.

The legal age of consent is intended to differentiate adults, who can provide informed consent, from children, who are believed to be unable to provide such consent. Children, it is claimed, cannot adequately give consent to sexual acts because they are unable to understand what they are consenting to; hence they cannot appreciate the possible consequences of that consent given their limited understanding of accepted sexual standards of their community. A further barrier to children giving informed consent to sexual activity with adults is the inherent power differential between children and adults which may lead to coercion playing a role in the child's decision (Abel et al. 1984).

Unfortunately, it is difficult from a legal standpoint to determine a standard acceptable age of consent given that this does not necessarily follow uniformly from sexual maturation. Other difficult issues in statutory rape cases include the defendant's mistaken belief that his partner was above the age of consent, and the willing, even initiating, participation of some partners. The issue of informed consent also arises in some cases where, because of mental deficiency, an individual is incapable of providing such consent. In some states (e.g., Wisconsin), statutes specifically prohibit sexual intercourse with a mentally ill person if that person is unable to understand the consequences of his or her conduct and the accused is aware of this condition. A number of sensational media cases, including those of Amy Fisher and "Sarah," a woman diagnosed with multiple personality disorder (Grogan & Tamarkin 1990) have brought the issue of consent in rape cases to the public's attention.

A number of authors distinguish between blitz and confidence rape (Bowie et al. 1990; Burgess & Holmstrom 1980). *Blitz rape,* typically referred to as stranger rape, is a sudden, surprise attack by an unknown assailant. Such rapes typically occur in settings deemed secure by victims, such as their own homes, or in secluded outdoor areas where victims are taken by surprise. Stranger or blitz rapes are more likely to involve threats to a victim's life, involve the use or threat of a weapon significantly more often than in confidence rapes, and result in greater violence and trauma to the victim (Bowie et al. 1990; Bownes et al. 1991; Ellis et al. 1981; Katz & Mazur 1979).

Confidence rape is characterized by interaction between the rapist and the victim for some duration prior to the sexual assault and is more commonly known as date rape, or acquaintance sexual assault. In this form of rape, the assailant is known to the victim; he may be a casual acquaintance or a romantic partner. Compared to blitz rape, date or confidence rape more often involves the consumption of alcohol or drugs by either the perpetrator or the victim, more often occurs in the rapist's car or home, and more often is a prolonged incident. Unlike stranger or blitz rape, verbal coercion plays a prominent role in gaining victim compliance in date rape, and the use of weapons and signific t physical trauma is uncommon; over half of all victims of date rape report sustaining no physical injury (Bownes et al. 1991). Conciliatory behaviors (apologizing, asking for another date, assisting the victim home) and aggressive behaviors (threatening victim, warning her not to report rape) on the part of assailants may occur with equal frequency (43 percent and 48 percent, respectively) following acquaintance assaults, whereas these behaviors are very rare (7 percent and 3 percent respectively) in stranger assaults (Bownes et al. 1991). Koss (1985) found that 13 percent of female university students reported experiencing coercive oral, anal or vaginal intercourse with someone they knew, but only half identified this as rape. The terms blitz and confidence rape convey a more comprehensive description of the sexual assault than stranger and date rape, which focus narrowly on the relationship between victim and perpetrator.

RAPE OF MALES

In the foregoing discussion of definitions and descriptions of the diverse forms rape may take, victims are assumed to be female and perpetrators male. Indeed, in some states rape is defined as a crime against women and requires forced penile-vaginal penetration. The problem of male rape has been largely ignored by researchers, or has been considered an anomaly of institutional life where the sex object of choice is unavailable (Cotton & Groth 1982; Nacci & Kane 1983; Sagarin 1976; Weiss & Friar 1974; Wooden & Parker 1982). The prevalence of sexual assault of noninstitutionalized adult males has been estimated to be between 5 percent and 10 percent (Forman 1982; Kaufman et al. 1980) but the figures do not carry statistical certainty. Little attention has been paid to males who experience sexual violence as adults in the community.

To date there are few clinical and research papers that deal with male rape (Anderson 1982; Calderwood 1987; Duncan 1990; Forman 1982; Goyer & Eddleman 1984; Groth 1979; Groth & Burgess 1980; Hillman et al. 1990; Kaufman et al. 1980; Mezey & King 1989; Myers 1989). The popular conception of male rape is that of homosexual rapists overpowering heterosexual men and boys. This notion is not only false but may even represent an inversion of reality. The majority of assailants in some reports of male rape (e.g., Groth 1979; Groth & Burgess 1980; Hillman et al. 1990) are perceived to be heterosexual, while victims usually consider themselves to be homosexual or bisexual. Groth (1979; Groth & Burgess 1980) found that assailants in cases of male rape were more likely to be strangers to the victim than in cases of female sexual assault. Groth (1979) belongs to the school of thought that considers such rapists to be similar to rapists of women; their rapes, he believes, are the sexual expression of aggression and hostility. As such, sexual gratification is of secondary, or nonexistent, importance. Groth understands male rape to serve a variety of motives, including the expression of mastery and control through conquest; the desire for revenge and retaliation, provoked by anger toward the victim; the erotic gratification of sadism and degradation of the victim; the punishment of another as a means of warding off anxiety resulting from unresolved conflict over one's sexual orientation; or the need for status and affiliation, as in gang rape. A number of these motives are clearly operative in antigay violence, or "gay bashing"; as many as 10 percent of men who are victims of antigay violence report experiencing sexual assault by heterosexual male perpetrators (Berrill 1990).

Recent investigations of sexual assault of adult males (Duncan 1990; Hillman et al. 1990; Mezey & King 1989), including our own (Stermac et al. 1993), and studies of sexual coercion in the relationships of adult males (McConaghy & Zamir, cited in McConaghy 1993), have challenged this model of the heterosexual male perpetrator and homosexual victim of stranger rape. Such research suggests that the majority of sexual assaults occur within the context of homosexual relationships, in a manner analogous to heterosexual date rape. Few cases of male rape conform to the stereotype of blitz rape described above; most assaults occur in the victim's or perpetrator's home, involve use of alcohol or drugs by both parties, and tend to involve verbal coercion, intimidation, threats, and restraint more often than physical violence. Few victims are attacked by complete strangers; often the assailant is the victim's partner or former partner, an acquaintance, or someone the victim met in a gay bar or known gay cruising area, such as a public park. The assault behaviors reported by victims consist primarily of receptive oral and anal intercourse or attempted intercourse (Hillman et al. 1990; Mezey & King 1989; Stermac et al. 1993). Of particular note in one study is that over a third (35 percent) of victims were physically or cognitively disabled, and 21 percent indicated that they were assaulted when unconscious (intoxicated, drugged or sleeping) (Stermac et al. 1993).

It may be that these patterns of male rape represent two distinct groups of perpetrators: heterosexual males who rape other males as a means of punishing and degrading them, possibly an extension of other forms of violence targeted specifically toward subordinate males (e.g., in prison); and gay or bisexual males who coerce partners or acquaintances into sexual activity by use of threats or intimidation, as in date rape. In the opinion of the authors, the former pattern does occur, but is more rare than the latter. The emergence in the research literature of the date rape pattern may reflect the growing awareness of clinicians and researchers to this form of sexual violence as well as the willingness of victims to acknowledge their sexual orientation.

Furthermore, research with offenders, as opposed to victims, would appear to be particularly biased in terms of reporting of sexual orientation; sex offenders are known to deny their sexual preferences, and those who assault males may be loath to admit that they are homosexual or bisexual (see, for example, Groth 1979).

Sexual assault of adult males by females is not unknown, although true sexual aggression, characterized by physical restraint and fear for safety, is rare (Sarrel & Masters 1982). It appears that men are also subjected to sexually exploitative pressure, most often psychological, such as not wanting to appear homosexual, unmasculine, inexperienced, or shy (Muehlenhard & Cook 1988; Struckman-Johnson 1988). Where female perpetrators have been identified, however, it is most often in the context of a sexual assault involving another male (Stermac et al. 1993; see also Hillman et al. 1990). For example, victims have reported that they were engaged in consenting activity with a male partner, who was then joined by a female against the victim's wishes and forced sexual activity ensued (Stermac et al. 1993).

Effects of sexual assaults on men appear similar to those of women (Anderson 1982; Calderwood 1987; Groth 1979; Groth & Burgess 1980; Kaufman et al. 1980; Mezey & King 1989), although special needs populations have been identified. The heterosexual victim of male assault may have fundamental beliefs about his sexuality and masculinity challenged. Dysfunction in affectional and sexual relationships following assault by male or female assailants is not uncommon (Masters 1986). The gay male victim of acquaintance sexual assault may experience fearful or aversive feelings associated with normal sexual behavior and may blame himself—as female victims of date rape do—for not resisting vehemently enough, or being somehow complicitous in the rape (Garnets et al. 1990). Victims of antigay violence in which sexual assault is a part have special treatment needs which must be addressed, including internalized homophobia, stigmatization and marginalization (Stermac & Sheridan 1993).

RAPE AS A PARAPHILIA

A problematic area for mental health professionals of all disciplines is whether rape constitutes a true paraphilia. The concern raised by the discussion of this issue appears to arise out of the fear that the extensive work done by women's groups to raise public consciousness regarding the severe impact sexual assault has on victims will be reversed. The popular perception is that individuals may escape punishment for their actions by using the psychiatric diagnosis of paraphilic rape (paraphilic coercive disorder). Abel and Rouleau (1990) point out that as the ability of the victim to resist sexual assault decreases (such as in pedophilia) or the degree of force used in the perpetration of the crime increases (as in rape), society is less accepting of a psychiatric justification for such crimes and is more in favor of punishment through the criminal justice system. In practice, however, psychiatric treatment in response to a paraphilic diagnosis does not preclude incarceration for the illegal act. Indeed, court mandated psychiatric or psychological treatment may well prolong, rather than reduce, time served.

Additional controversy over this issue tends to be generated by some contemporary feminist scholars and some social science researchers who argue that rape is primarily a crime of power and aggression, and represents only one dramatic instance of patriarchal society's general hostility toward women (Brownmiller 1975; Burt 1980; Clarke & Lewis 1977; Russell 1975; Stanko 1985). Such theorists tend, as a whole, to dismiss any arguments about the sexual nature of rape. Careful review of the relevant literature, however, reveals that sexual and aggressive impulses are fused in sexual assault and neither variable alone can account for all aspects of the phenomenon. Recent developments in the taxonomy of sexual offenders, including rapists, recognize the diverse routes which end in sexual assault (e.g., Knight & Prentky 1990). Furthermore, these two perspectives on motivation in rape are not incompatible; elucidation of the mechanisms whereby power and aggression become eroticized is critical in understanding the etiology of sexual violence.

Support for the classification of rape among the other paraphilias comes from a number of sources. Clinical interviews with rapists reveal that in many cases recurrent, repetitive, compulsive urges or fantasies to commit rape are present. These tend to have a cyclical nature: the individual experiences urges of increasing intensity which he attempts to control, the urges become too strong, control breaks down, the urges are acted upon, and a temporary reduction of urges follows. This cyclical pattern is similar to the clinical picture present in traditionally recognized paraphilias (American Psychiatric Association [APA] 1987).

Additional support for the conception of rape as a paraphilia comes from the developmental history of the disorder and its association with other common paraphilias. Similar to the early onset of deviant arousal in other paraphilias, 50 percent of individuals who rape experience the onset of this type of arousal by the age of twenty-one (Abel & Rouleau 1990). In one study, rapists had a high likelihood of past or present history of other paraphilia in addition to rape, most commonly nonincestuous (44 percent) and incestuous (24 percent) female pedophilia, exhibitionism (28 percent), voyeurism (18 percent), frotteurism (11 percent) and sadism (10 percent) (Abel et al. 1988).

Recognition of the co-occurrence of multiple paraphilia in rapists is not new (c.f., Gebhard et al. 1965; Yalom 1960), yet systematic study of this has occurred only relatively recently. Freund (1990; Freund & Blanchard 1986;

Freund et al. 1983, 1984), who proposes that a number of the paraphilias, including preferential rape, represent disorders of normal courtship with a common underlying cause, has also demonstrated the high co-morbidity of other sexually anomalous activities with rape-proneness. The lower overall percentages for rapists in Freund's studies compared with Abel's (voyeurism, 9 percent; exhibitionism, 19 percent; toucheurism/frotteurism, 13 percent; sadism, 16 percent; Freund 1990) may reflect the small number of rape cases in his sample showing the preferential rape pattern. That there may be a shared etiology among expressions of courtship disorder lends support to the belief that at least some forms of rape may best be classified among the other paraphilias, although the mechanism itself, while intriguing, is not understood.

Further support for a paraphilic model of rape comes from psychophysiological research. Abel et al. (1977) suggest that, in a manner analogous to pedophilia, rapists are paraphilic in the sense that they demonstrate anomalous erotic preference for nonconsensual aggressive sexual interactions. Abel and his colleagues conducted the first major investigation of erotic preference in rapists using penile plethysmography. These authors found that, relative to nonrapists, rapists did demonstrate greater arousal to descriptions of forced sex, although they did not show an erotic preference for rape. Rapists were equally aroused to consenting and nonconsenting sexual descriptions, while nonrapists were considerably less aroused by the nonconsenting than consenting descriptions (Abel et al. 1977). These results have been supported by a number of other authors (Barbaree et al. 1979; Quinsey & Chaplin 1984; Quinsey et al. 1981). Rapists in these early studies failed to discriminate between consensual and forced sex.

A number of subsequent researchers have provided support for the sexual preference hypothesis in rapists. Quinsey et al. (1984), for example, reported that rapists demonstrated stronger arousal to rape descriptions than did nonoffenders, and stronger arousal to rape than to consensual descriptions. Similar results have been reported by Earls and Proulx (1987). Numerous researchers have, however, reported equivocal results: equivalent arousal to rape and nonrape descriptions, at least in some nonoffender subjects, has been reported (Abel et al. 1978; Baxter et al. 1986), as has lower arousal of rapists to depictions of rape than to consenting sexual depictions (Baxter et al. 1984; Baxter et al. 1986; Murphy et al. 1984).

These mixed results suggest not only that rapists are a heterogeneous group with regard to sexual preference, but that great variability is also present in nonoffender males. Indeed, apparently deviant erotic preferences are shown by "normal" heterosexual males under a variety of circumstances, including alcohol consumption (e.g., Barbaree et al. 1983), permissive instructions (e.g., Quinsey et al. 1981), angering subjects prior to testing (Yates et al. 1984), conditions of victim blame (e.g., Sundberg et al. 1991), descriptions which portray victims as becoming sexually aroused during rape (Malamuth et al. 1980), and pre-exposure to aggressive pornography (Marshall et al. 1991).

Two methodological difficulties must be noted in the interpretation of these findings. First, differentiation of rapist from nonrapist males is sometimes achieved with difficulty, and the diverse methods employed by the above authors may contribute to the conflicting results. Careful stimulus construction (e.g., Barbaree et al. 1979) is often crucial in obtaining differential responding by rapist and nonrapist subjects. Second, although phallometric measures of sexual arousal are less susceptible to voluntary distortion than is self-report, subjects are able to inhibit or enhance sexual arousal (Quinsey & Bergersen 1976; Wydra et al. 1983).

Taken as a whole, the literature on the anomalous erotic behavior of rapists suggests that arousal to sexually aggressive stimuli, under laboratory conditions, is not an essential or exclusive characteristic of rapists. These results should not be surprising, given that rape is a complex, multidetermined behavior. As with the sexual assault of children, where not all perpetrators demonstrate a pedophilic erotic preference, we should not expect all rapists to demonstrate an erotic preference for sexual aggression. However, some relationship between arousal to sexual violence and the commission of rape does exist in some offenders. One recent study (Barbaree et al. 1993) found that rapists subtyped as sexual or nonsexual according to Knight and Prentky's (1990) taxonomy differed in their sexual arousal patterns. Rapists classified independently of phallometric data as sexually motivated subsequently demonstrated greater arousal to nonconsensual sexual depictions than did their nonsexual counterparts.

Barbaree and his colleagues (Barbaree & Marshall 1991; Barbaree et al. 1993) suggest that there are at least two separate cognitive-behavioral processes which lead to rape: a paraphilic process operating in sexual subtypes and a nonparaphilic, impulsive-hostile process operating in nonsexual subtypes. The sexual preference hypothesis may best account for the arousal which occurs in rape in the paraphilic group, while in the nonparaphilic group a stimulus-disinhibition model (Barbaree 1990; Barbaree et al. 1979) may be operative. This model describes the process by which men's arousal to rape fails to be inhibited by the victim's nonconsent and the violence of the assault. Disinhibition may be precipitated by a number of conditions, including alcohol intoxication, anger, and victim blame.

Rapists are clearly not a homogeneous group. The diversity of characteristics seen in such men defies a single explanation. Recent approaches to understanding rape (Barbaree & Marshall 1991; Malamuth 1988; Marshall & Barbaree 1990) recognize the value of the sexual preference hypothesis in at least a subgroup of rapists. Degree of deviant arousal appears to be associated with the frequency and degree of violence in sexual assault (Abel et al. 1977, 1978), suggesting that deviant arousal characterizes the most violent and habitual rapists. In some such men, a strong preference for sexually aggressive stimuli has been noted.

PREFERENTIAL AND SADISTIC RAPE

Individuals who show a preferential rape pattern (Freund et al. 1983, 1984), also referred to as paraphilic coercive disorder (Abel 1989; APA 1987) or biastophilia (Money 1990), are sexually aroused by fantasies and urges of forcing themselves on their victims. In contrast to the sadist, who is stimulated by the use of gratuitous force, the preferential rapist is thought not to use greater force than necessary to gain victim compliance (Abel 1989). The sadistic rapist is also distinguished in phallometric assessment by a higher level of arousal to descriptions of physical, but nonsexual, assault on female victims (Abel 1989). A simple dichotomy between sadistic and nonsadistic rape has not been supported by the work of Knight and Prentky (1990), however. It is likely that a range of force is utilized by rapists and that degree of force is a continuous rather than a categorical variable (McConaghy 1993).

Most researchers (Abel et al. 1988; Freund et al. 1983, 1984; Groth 1979) have reported that only 5 percent to 10 percent of rapists fulfill *DSM-III-R* (APA 1987) criteria for sexual sadism, although a number of authors have reported prevalence estimates as high as 45 percent (Fedora et al. 1992; Hucker et al. 1988). Such disparate estimates may reflect the fact that cases studied are derived from very different populations, namely, mental health patients versus correctional inmates, although it is also likely that different researchers have held varying conceptualizations of sexual sadism.

Freund (1993) has suggested that the term dangerous or predatory sadism be restricted to mean the erotic drive to cause bodily harm or physical suffering to another organism, whereas the broader concept, involving the desire to humiliate and dominate a partner, be referred to as erotic hyperdominance. When one reviews the definition of sexual sadism in the *DSM-III-R* (APA 1987) it is clear that Freund's categories are subsumed under the one term. The *DSM-III-R* suggests that some rapists are sexually aroused by forcing their victims to engage in intercourse but that their arousal is neither increased nor inhibited by the victim's suffering. Rapists do respond with greater arousal to nonsexual violence than do nonrapists (Barbaree et al. 1979; Quinsey et al. 1984), and violent rapists tend to respond more strongly to depictions of nonsexual violence than do comparatively less violent rapists (Quinsey & Chaplin 1982). The absolute magnitude of these responses is quite small, however. Furthermore, rapists do not respond with significant arousal to nonsexual violence perpetrated by men against men. The relative arousal to descriptions of nonsexual violence between men and women appears to occur because of the implied sexual element in the act, rather than as a pure response to aggression (Quinsey et al. 1984).

Further complicating discussion of the conceptualization of sexual sadism is the finding that many "normal," nonoffender males acknowledge sexual fantasy arousal to the idea of raping and hurting a woman. Of men who indicate a likelihood they could rape, 16 percent to 20 percent indicate that they experience greater arousal to descriptions of sadomasochistic scenes (Malamuth et al. 1980) and to descriptions in which the victim experiences pain (Malamuth & Check 1983) than those who do not admit to this proclivity. Similarly, most young men appear to be more aroused by pictures of women bound and in distress than by women who are smiling and cooperative (Heilbrun & Leif 1988), and about half report a willingness to engage in bondage and a third in whipping and spanking (Malamuth 1989). Among the general male population, 30 percent report fantasies of tying up and raping a woman and 10 to 20 percent report fantasies of torturing or beating a woman (Crepault & Couture 1980). Women have corresponding fantasies of being sexually abducted and seduced.

In one college student study respondents estimated that approximately 45 percent of men would commit what they thought to be a rape if certain that they would not be caught, and that 32 percent of women would enjoy being raped if no one were to know (Malamuth et al. 1980). When asked about their own potential, 51 percent of these men report some likelihood that they would commit a rape if assured they would not be caught, while only 2 percent of women report believing they would enjoy being raped. On average, about 35 percent of college-age males admit that they might commit a rape under certain circumstances (Malamuth 1981), although in some samples as many as 60 percent of males admit to such desires (Briere & Malamuth 1983). What appears to be sexually arousing to such males is the fantasy of engaging in aggressive, but not brutal, sexual activity with a complete stranger, overcoming her initial resistance, and stimulating her to the point that she eventually enjoys the experience. These elements are also present in the fantasies of some sadists, though victim enjoyment of aggression and rape are less salient than the perpetrator's pleasure or gratification. Self-reported likelihood of raping is correlated with acceptance of rape myths, fantasies about forced sex, and sexual arousal to rape depictions (Malamuth 1981).

Although these academic studies may be of questionable real-life validity, one study showed that at least one-quarter of males acknowledged using coercion to achieve sexual relations with an unwilling partner (Koss et al. 1987) and another study showed that 10 percent to 15 percent of women reported initially being coerced into, and then enjoying, sexual activity (Mc-

Conaghy 1993). It would appear that some degree of coercion in sexual relationships can lead to arousal and enjoyment in both men and women, and plays a part in traditional heterosexual courting behavior. Common though aggressive themes may be in fantasy or courtship, however, such studies do not provide information on the frequency with which truly sadistic fantasies are acted upon, or, more importantly, on whether they relate to a preferred method of sexual arousal.

SADOMASOCHISTIC PARAPHILIAS

There is little available data on the prevalence of sadistic and masochistic preferences in the general population. Hunt (1974) reported that approximately 5 percent of men and 2 percent of women claimed to derive sexual pleasure from inflicting pain, and 3 percent of men and 5 percent of women from receiving it. Women tend not to report early sadistic fantasies and typically do not discover domination on their own, but are drawn into it by men wanting to be dominated; they then discover that they find the role exciting (Scott 1983). Most of our knowledge of sadistic and masochistic behaviors is derived from clinical histories of individual patients or from small series of cases that have been published (e.g., Dietz et al. 1990).

A distinction is often drawn between major and minor sadism. Major sadism, corresponding to Freund's (1993) concept of dangerous or predatory sadism, is reserved for such savage acts as erotic stabbing, lust murder, and perhaps sexual activities with human cadavers (Hirschfeld 1956). Minor sadism includes sadistic fantasies that are not acted upon as well as actual humiliation of a consenting partner by means of bondage, mild flagellation, or submission to degrading acts.

Those who participate in giving and receiving acts of minor sadism in a consenting relationship often refer to the activity as bondage and discipline, dominance and submission, or sadomasochism (Gosselin 1987; Weinberg et al. 1984). In these activities the dominant partner places the submissive one in a position of helplessness and then administers some form of discipline. Administration of pain, humiliation or bondage is effected through whipping, piercing or fisting (insertion of a fist into the anus or vagina). Use of such roles as master-slave and governess-pupil ensures a tone of humiliation as does cross-dressing the submissive, treating him or her like an animal, and sometimes urinating or defecating on his or her body. The submissive may be further humiliated by being forced to wear a diaper or to lick the dominant's boots. Verbal degradation usually accompanies these activities.

Flagellation or flogging, almost exclusively applied to the buttocks, and bondage, including the use of gags and blindfolds to render the submissive helpless and immobile, are common sadomasochistic elements. The breasts of a female submissive may be bound tightly and clothespins or clamps may be attached to the nipples of either sex or to the penis in the case of the male submissive. In "water sports" the submissive partner is urinated upon or forced to drink the dominant's urine. Enemas may be administered to deprive the submissive of control of his or her bodily functions or the submissive may be forced to retain the enema for an uncomfortably long period. Sadomasochistic partnerships are a specialized subculture in the homosexual community and in large cities networks exist for those who have this interest.

Major, dangerous or predatory sadism includes piqueurism, in which the assailant stabs a female victim, usually in the breast or buttocks, and then escapes (de River 1958; Eulenberg 1911). Vampirism, a rare anomaly, involves sexual arousal from drawing and sometimes drinking blood by cutting or biting. In some cases, the individual will draw blood from him- or herself for this purpose (McCully 1964; Prins 1985; Vanden Bergh & Kelly 1964). Closely related to vampirism are the phenomena of necrophilia, the erotic attraction to corpses, and lust murder, both of which represent extreme manifestations of sexual sadism.

As with sadism, some data are available on the frequency of masochistic practices in the general population. Hunt (1974) reported that 10 percent of unmarried females and 6.3 percent of unmarried males claimed to derive sexual pleasure from receiving pain. Crepault and Couture (1980) found that, among mostly married subjects, 11.7 percent of men fantasized about being humiliated and 5.3 percent imagined being beaten up by a woman. Once again, however, these data do not provide a clear picture of the prevalence of an actual sexual preference for masochistic interactions. Interestingly, only 15 percent of Spengler's (1977) members of a sadomasochistic club needed such interactions to reach climax.

Living masochists may present to physicians for removal of rings, bottles and other objects from body orifices or from the penis. Some masochists use electricity to stimulate themselves sexually (Hucker 1985). Serious damage caused by masochistic activity seems to be rare, however (Hucker 1985). One extreme variant of masochism, or perhaps a separate but related entity, autoerotic asphyxia, may present as a fatality.

REFERENCES

Abel, G. G. (1989). "Paraphilias." In H. I. Kaplan and B. J. Sadock, eds., *Comprehensive Textbook of Psychiatry*. 5th ed. Vol. 1: 1069–85. Baltimore, Md.: Williams & Wilkins.

Abel, G. G.; Barlow, D. H.; Blanchard, E. B.; and Guild, D. (1977). "The Components of Rapist's Sexual Arousal." *Archives of General Psychiatry* 34: 895–903.

Abel, G. G.; Becker, J. V.; and Cunningham-Rathner, J. (1984). "Complications, Consent, and Cognitions in Sex Between Children and Adults." *International Journal of Law and Psychiatry* 7: 89–103.

Abel, G. G.; Becker, J. V.; Cunningham-Rathner, J.; Mittelman, M. S.; and Rouleau, J.-L. (1988). "Multiple Paraphilic Diagnoses among Sex Offenders." *Bulletin of the American Academy of Psychiatry and the Law* 16: 153–68.

Abel, G. G.; Blanchard, E. B.; Becker, J. V.; and Djenderedjian, A. (1978). "Differentiating Sexual Aggressives with Penile Measures." *Criminal Justice and Behavior* 5: 315–32.

Abel, G. G., and Rouleau, J.-L. (1990). "The Nature and Extent of Sexual Assault." In W. L. Marshall, D. R. Laws, and H. E. Barbaree, eds., *Handbook of Sexual Assault: Issues, Theories and Treatment of the Offender,* pp. 9–21. New York: Plenum Press.

American Psychiatric Association. (1987). *Diagnostic and Statistical Manual of Mental Disorders.* 3rd ed., rev. Washington, D.C.: Author.

Amir, M. (1971). *Patterns of Forcible Rape.* Chicago: University of Chicago Press.

Anderson, C. L. (1982). "Males as Sexual Assault Victims: Multiple Levels of Trauma." *Journal of Homosexuality* 7: 145–62.

Arndt, W.; Foehl, J.; and Good, F. (1985). "Specific Sexual Fantasy Themes: A Multidimensional Study." *Journal of Personality and Social Psychology* 48: 472–80.

Barbaree, H. E. (1990). "Stimulus Control of Sexual Arousal: Its Role in Sexual Assault." In W. L. Marshall, D. R. Laws, and H. E. Barbaree, eds., *Handbook of Sexual Assault: Issues, Theories and Treatment of the Offender,* pp. 115–42. New York: Plenum Press.

Barbaree, H. E., and Marshall, W. L. (1991). "The Role of Male Sexual Arousal in Rape: Six Models." *Journal of Consulting and Clinical Psychology* 59: 621–30.

Barbaree, H. E.; Marshall, W. L.; and Lanthier, R. D. (1979). "Deviant Sexual Arousal in Rapists." *Behavior Research and Therapy* 17: 215–22.

Barbaree, H. E.; Marshall, W. L.; Yates, E. P.; and Lightfoot, L. O. (1983). "Alcohol Intoxication and Deviant Sexual Arousal in Male Social Drinkers." *Behavior Research and Therapy* 21: 365–73.

Barbaree, H. E., Seto, M. C., Serin, R. C., Amos, N. L., and Preston, D. L. (1993). "Comparisons between Sexual and Nonsexual Rapist Subtypes: Sexual Arousal to Rape, Offense Precursors and Offense Characteristics." *Criminal Justice & Behavior* 21: 86–104.

Baxter, D. J.; Barbaree, H. E.; and Marshall, W. L. (1986). "Sexual Responses to Consenting and Forced Sex in a Large Sample of Rapists and Nonrapists." *Behavior Research and Therapy* 24: 513–20.

Baxter, D. J.; Marshall, W. L.; Barbaree, H. E.; Davidson, P. R.; and Malcolm, B. P. (1984). "Deviant Sexual Behavior: Differentiating Sex Offenders by Criminal and Personal History, Psychometric Measures, and Sexual Response." *Criminal Justice and Behavior* 11: 477–501.

Berrill, K. T. (1990). "Anti-Gay Violence and Victimization in the United States: An Overview." *Journal of Interpersonal Violence* 5: 274–94.

Bowie, S. I.; Silverman, D. C.; Kalick, S. M.; and Edbril, S. D. (1990). "Blitz Rape and Confidence Rape: Implications for Clinical Intervention." *American Journal of Psychotherapy* 44: 180–88.

Bownes, I. T.; O'Gorman, E. C.; and Sayers, A. (1991). "Rape—A Comparison of Stranger and Acquaintance Assaults." *Medicine, Science and the Law* 31: 102–109.

Briere, J., and Malamuth, N. M. (1983). "Self-Reported Likelihood of Sexually Aggressive Behavior: Attitudinal versus Sexual Explanations." *Journal of Research in Personality* 17: 315–23.

Brittain, R. (1970). "The Sadistic Murderer." *Medicine, Science and the Law* 10: 198–207.

Brownmiller, S. (1975). *Against Our Will: Men, Women and Rape.* New York: Simon & Schuster.

Burgess, A. W., and Holmstrom, L. L. (1980). "Rape Typology and the Coping Behavior of Rape Victims." In S. L. McCombie, ed., *Rape Crisis Intervention Handbook,* pp. 27–42. New York: Plenum Press.

Burt, M. R. (1980). "Cultural Myths and Supports for Rape." *Journal of Personality and Social Psychology* 38: 217–30.

Calderwood, D. (1987). "The Male Rape Victim." *Medical Aspects of Human Sexuality* 21: 53–55.

Clark, L., and Lewis, D. J. (1977). *Rape: The Price of Coercive Sexuality.* Toronto, Canada: Canadian Women's Educational Press.

Cotton, D. J., and Groth, A. N. (1982). "Inmate Rape: Prevention and Intervention." *Journal of Prison and Jail Health* 2: 47–57.

Crepault, E., and Couture, M. (1980). "Men's Erotic Fantasies." *Archives of Sexual Behavior* 9: 565–81.

Darke, J. L. (1990). "Sexual Aggression: Achieving Power through Humiliation." In W. L. Marshall, D. R. Laws, and H. E. Barbaree, eds., *Handbook of Sexual Assault: Issues, Theories and Treatment of the Offender,* pp. 55–72. New York: Plenum Press.

De River, P. (1958). *Crime and the Criminal Psychopath.* Springfield, Ill.: Charles C Thomas.

Dietz, P. E.; Hazelwood, R. R.; and Warren, J. (1990). "The Sexually Sadistic Criminal and His Offenses." *Bulletin of the American Academy of Psychiatry and the Law* 18: 163–78.

Duncan, D. F. (1990). "Prevalence of Sexual Assault Victimization among Heterosexual and Gay/Lesbian University Students." *Psychological Reports* 66: 65–66.

Earls, C. M., and Proulx, J. (1987). "The Differentiation of Francophone Rapists and Nonrapists Using Penile Circumferential Measures." *Criminal Justice and Behavior* 13: 419–29.

Ellis, E. M.; Atkeson, B. M.; and Calhoun, K. S. (1981). "An Assessment of Long-Term Reaction to Rape." *Journal of Abnormal Psychology* 90: 263–66.

Eulenberg, A. von. (1911). *Sadism and Masochism.* New York: Bell.

Fedora, O.; Reddon, J. R.; Morrison, J. W.; Fedora, S. K.; Pascoe, H.; and Yeudall, L. T. (1992). "Sadism and Other Paraphilias in Normal Controls and Aggressive and Nonaggressive Sex Offenders." *Archives of Sexual Behavior* 21: 1–15.

Finkelhor, D. (1979). "What's Wrong with Sex between Adults and Children?" *American Journal of Orthopsychiatry* 49: 692–97.

Finkelhor, D., and Yllo, K. (1985). *License to Rape: Sexual Abuse of Wives.* New York: Holt, Rinehart and Winston.

Forman, B. D. (1982). "Reported Male Rape." *Victimology* 7: 235–36.

Freund, K. (1990). "Courtship Disorder." In W. L. Marshall, D. R. Laws, and H. E. Barbaree, eds., *Handbook of Sexual Assault: Issues, Theories and Treatment of the Offender,* pp. 195–207. New York: Plenum Press.

——— (1993). "Courtship Disorder within the Framework of the Other Paraphilias." Unpublished manuscript.

Freund, K., and Blanchard, R. (1986). "The Concept of Courtship Disorder." *Journal of Sex and Marital Therapy* 12: 79–92.

Freund, K.; Scher, H.; and Hucker, S. (1983). "The Courtship Disorders." *Archives of Sexual Behavior* 12: 369–79.

——— (1984). "The Courtship Disorders: A Further Investigation." *Archives of Sexual Behavior* 13: 133–39.

Freund, K.; Scher, H.; Racansky, I. G.; Campbell, K.; and Heasman, G. (1986). "Males Disposed to Commit Rape." *Archives of Sexual Behavior* 15: 23–35.

Freund, K.; Seeley, H. R.; Marshall, W. E.; and Glinfort, E. K. (1972). "Sexual Offenders Needing Special Assessment and/or Therapy." *Canadian Journal of Criminology* 14: 345–65.

Freund, K., and Steiner, B. W. (1980). "Disorders of Sexual Behavior." In S. E. Greben, R. Pos, V. M. Rakoff, A. Bonkalo, F. H. Lowy, and G. Voineskos, eds., *A Method of Psychiatry,* pp. 211–20. Philadelphia: Lea and Febiger.

Garnets, L.; Herek, G. M.; and Levy, B. (1990). "Violence and Victimization of Lesbians and Gay Men: Mental Health Consequences." *Journal of Interpersonal Violence* 5: 366–83.

Gaylin, W. (1982). "The Competency of Children: No Longer All or None." *Hastings Center Report* 12: 333–38.

Gebhard, P. H.; Gagnon, J. H.; Pomeroy, W. H.; and Christenson, C. V. (1965). *Sex Offenders.* New York: Harper and Row.

Gosselin, C. C. (1987). "The Sadomasochistic Contract." In G. D. Wilson, ed., *Variant Sexuality: Research and Theory,* pp. 229–57. Baltimore, Md.: Johns Hopkins University Press.

Gosselin, C. C., and Wilson, G. D. (1980). *Sexual Variations.* London: Faber and Faber.

Goyer, P. F., and Eddleman, H. C. (1984). "Same-Sex Rape of Nonincarcerated Men." *American Journal of Psychiatry* 141: 576–79.

Grogan, D., and Tamarkin, C. (1990, Nov. 26). "The Six Faces of Sarah Bear Witness to a Sexual Assault." *People:* 107–109.

Groth, A. N. (1979). *Men Who Rape: The Psychology of the Offender.* New York: Plenum Press.

Groth, A. N., and Burgess, A. W. (1980). "Male Rape: Offenders and Victims." *American Journal of Psychiatry* 137: 806–810.

Hazelwood, R. R.; Dietz, P. E.; and Warren, J. (1992). "The Criminal Sexual Sadist." *FBI Law Enforcement Bulletin* 61: 12–20.

Heilbrun, A., and Leif, D. (1988). "Autoerotic Value of Female Distress in Sexually Explicit Photographs." *Journal of Sex Research* 24: 47–57.

Herman, J. L. (1981). *Father-Daughter Incest.* Cambridge, Mass.: Harvard University Press.

——— (1990). "Sex Offenders: A Feminist Perspective." In W. L. Marshall, D. R. Laws, and H. E. Barbaree, eds., *Handbook of Sexual Assault: Issues, Theories and Treatment of the Offender,* pp. 177–93. New York: Plenum Press.

Hillman, R. J.; O'Mara, N.; Taylor-Robinson, D.; and Harris, J. R. W. (1990). "Medical and Social Aspects of Sexual Assault of Males: A Survey of 100 Victims." *British Journal of General Practice* 40: 502–504.

Hirschfeld, M. (1956). *Sexual Anomalies.* New York: Emerson.

Holmstrom, L. L., and Burgess, A. W. (1980). "Sexual Behavior of Assailants during Reported Rapes." *Archives of Sexual Behavior* 9: 427–40.

Hucker, S. J. (1985). "Self-harmful Sexual Behavior." *Psychiatric Clinics of North America* 8: 323–27.

Hucker, S. J.; Langevin, R.; Wortzman, G.; Dickey, R.; Bain, J.; Handy, L.; Chambers, J.; and Wright, P. (1988). "Cerebral Damage and Dysfunction in Sexually Aggressive Men." *Annals of Sex Research* 1: 33–47.

Hunt, M. (1974). *Sexual Behavior in the 1970s.* New York: Playboy Press.

Karpman, B. (1954). *The Sexual Offender and His Offenses: Etiology, Pathology, Psychodynamics and Treatment.* New York: Julian Press.

Katz, S., and Mazur, M. A. (1979). *Understanding the Rape Victim: A Synthesis of Research Findings.* New York: Wiley.

Kaufman, A.; DiVasto, P.; Jackson, R.; Voorhees, D.; and Christy, J. (1980). "Male Rape Victims: Noninstitutionalized Assault." *American Journal of Psychiatry* 137: 221–23.

Kilpatrick, D. G.; Best, C. L.; Saunders, B. E.; and Veronen, L. J. (1988). "Rape in Marriage and in Dating Relationships: How Bad Is It for Mental Health?" *Annals of the New York Academy of Sciences* 528: 335–44.

Knight, R. A., and Prentky, R. A. (1990). "Classifying Sexual Offenders: The Development and Corroboration of Taxonomic Models." In W. L. Marshall, D. R. Laws, and H. E. Barbaree, eds., *Handbook of Sexual Assault: Issues, Theories and Treatment of the Offender,* pp. 23–52. New York: Plenum Press.

Knight, R. A.; Rosenberg, R.; and Schneider, B. (1985). "Classification of Sexual Offenders: Perspectives, Methods and Validation." In A. Burgess, ed., *Rape and Sexual Assault: A Research Handbook,* pp. 222–93. New York: Garland.

Koss, M. P. (1985). "The Hidden Rape Victim: Personality, Attitudinal, and Situational Characteristics." *Psychology of Women Quarterly* 9: 193–212.

Koss, M. P.; Gidycz, C.; and Wisniewski, N. (1987). "The Scope of Rape: Incidence and Prevalence of Sexual Aggression in a National Sample of Higher Education Students." *Journal of Consulting and Clinical Psychology* 55: 162–70.

Krafft-Ebing, R. von. (1965). *Psychopathia Sexualis.* New York: Stein and Day. (Originally published 1886).

Langevin, R. (1990). "Sexual Anomalies and the Brain." In W. L. Marshall, D. R. Laws, and H. E. Barbaree, eds., *Handbook of Sexual Assault: Issues, Theories and Treatment of the Offender,* pp. 103–113. New York: Plenum Press.

Langevin, R.; Bain, J.; Ben-Aron, M.; Coulthard, R.; Day, D.; Handy, L.; Heasman, G.; Hucker, S. J.; Purins, J. E.; Roper, V.; Russon, A.; Webster, C. D.; and Wortzman, G. (1985). "Sexual Aggression: Constructing a Predictive Equation." In R. Langevin, ed., *Erotic Preference, Gender Identity, and Aggression in Men,* pp. 39–76. Hillsdale, N.J.: Lawrence Erlbaum.

Malamuth, N. M. (1981). "Rape Proclivity among Males." *Journal of Social Issues* 37: 138–57.

——— (1988). "A Multidimensional Approach to Sexual Aggression: Combining Measures of Past Behavior and Present Likelihood." In R. A. Prentky and V. L. Quinsey, eds., *Human Sexual Aggression: Current Perspectives,* pp. 123–32. New York: New York Academy of Sciences.

Malamuth, N. M., and Check, J. V. P. (1983). "Sexual Arousal to Rape Depictions: Individual Differences." *Journal of Abnormal Psychology* 92: 55–67.

Malamuth, N. M.; Haber, S.; and Feshbach, S. (1980). "Testing Hypotheses Regarding Rape: Exposure to Sexual Violence, Sex Differences and the Normality of Rapists." *Journal of Research in Personality* 14: 121–37.

Malamuth, N. M.; Heim, M.; and Feshbach, S. (1980). "Sexual Responsiveness of College Students to Rape Depictions: Inhibitory and Disinhibitory Effects." *Journal of Personality and Social Psychology* 38: 399–408.

Marshall, W. L., and Barbaree, H. E. (1984). "A Behavioral View of Rape." *International Journal of Law and Psychiatry* 7: 51–77.

——— (1990). "An Integrated Theory of the Etiology of Sexual Offending." In W. L. Marshall, D. R. Laws, and H. E. Barbaree, eds., *Handbook of Sexual Assault: Issues, Theories and Treatment of the Offender,* pp. 257–75. New York: Plenum Press.

Marshall, W. L.; Seidman, B. T.; and Barbaree, H. E. (1991). "The Effects of Prior Exposure to Erotic and Nonerotic Stimuli on the Rape Index." *Annals of Sex Research* 4: 209–220.

Masters, W. H. (1986). "Sexual Dysfunction as an Aftermath of Sexual Assault of Men by Women." *Journal of Sex and Marital Therapy* 12: 35–45.

McConaghy, N. (1993). *Sexual Behavior: Problems and Management.* New York: Plenum Press.

McCully, R. S. (1964). "Vampirism: Historical Perspective and Underlying Process in Relation to a Case of Auto-Vampirism." *Journal of Nervous and Mental Disease* 139: 440–51.

Mezey, G., and King, M. (1989). "The Effects of Sexual Assault on Men: A Survey of 22 Victims." *Psychological Medicine* 19: 205–209.

Money, J. (1990). "Forensic Sexology: Paraphilic Serial Rape (Biastophilia) and Lust Murder (Erotophonophilia)." *American Journal of Psychotherapy* 44: 26–36.

Muehlenhard, C. L., and Cook, S. W. (1988). "Men's Self-Reports of Unwanted Sexual Activity." *Journal of Sex Research* 24: 58–72.

Muehlenhard, C. L.; Powch, I. G.; Phelps, J. L.; and Giusti, L. M. (1992). "Definitions of Rape: Scientific and Political Implications." *Journal of Social Issues* 48: 23–44.

Murphy, W. D.; Krisak, J.; Stalgaitis, S.; and Anderson, K. (1984). "The Use of Penile Tumescence Measures with Incarcerated Rapists: Further Validity Issues." *Archives of Sexual Behavior* 13: 545–54.

Myers, M. F. (1989). "Men Sexually Assaulted as Adults and Sexually Abused as Boys." *Archives of Sexual Behavior* 18: 203–215.

Nacci, P. L., and Kane, T. R. (1983). "The Incidence of Sex and Sexual Aggression in Federal Prisons." *Federal Probation* 47: 31–36.

National Victim Center. (1992). *Statutory Rape.* Arlington, Va.: Author.

Prentky, R. A.; Cohen, M. L.; and Seghorn, T. K. (1985). "Development of a Rational Taxonomy for the Classification of Sex Offenders: Rapists." *Bulletin of the American Academy of Psychiatry and the Law* 13: 39–70.

Prins, H. (1985). "Vampirism: A Clinical Condition." *British Journal of Psychiatry* 146: 666–68.

Quinsey, V. L. (1984). "Sexual Aggression: Studies of Offenders against Women." In D. Weisstub, ed., *Law and Mental Health: International Perspectives,* vol. 1: 84–121. New York: Pergamon Press.

Quinsey, V. L., and Bergersen, S. G. (1976). "Instructional Control of Penile Circumference in Assessments of Sexual Preference." *Behavior Therapy* 7: 489–93.

Quinsey, V. L., and Chaplin, T. C. (1982). "Penile Responses to Nonsexual Violence among Rapists." *Criminal Justice and Behavior* 9: 372–81.

——— (1984). "Stimulus Control of Rapists' and Non-Sex Offenders' Sexual Arousal." *Behavioral Assessment* 6: 169–76.

Quinsey, V. L.; Chaplin, T. C.; and Upfold, D. (1984). "Sexual Arousal to Nonsexual Violence and Sadomasochistic Themes among Rapists and Non-Sex Offenders." *Journal of Consulting and Clinical Psychology* 52: 651–57.

Quinsey, V. L.; Chaplin, T. C.; and Varney, G. (1981). "A Comparison of Rapists' and Non-Sex Offenders' Sexual Preferences for Mutually Consenting Sex, Rape, and Physical Abuse of Women." *Behavioral Assessment* 3: 127–35.

Rosenberg, R.; Knight, R. A.; Prentky, R. A.; and Lee, A. (1988). "Validating the Components of a Taxonomic System for Rapists: A Path Analytic Approach." *Bulletin of the American Academy of Psychiatry and the Law* 16: 169–85.

Russell, D. E. H. (1975). *The Politics of Rape: The Victim's Perspective.* New York: Stein and Day.

——— (1982). *Rape in Marriage.* New York: Macmillan.

Sadoff, R. L. (1978). "The Psychiatrist and the Rapist: Legal Issues." In R. T. Rada, ed., *Clinical Aspects of the Rapist,* pp. 215–25. New York: Grune and Stratton.

Sagarin, E. (1976). "Prison Homosexuality and Its Effect on Post-Prison Sexual Behavior." *Psychiatry* 39: 245–57.

Sarrel, P., and Masters, W. (1982). "Sexual Molestation of Men by Women." *Archives of Sexual Behavior* 11: 117–33.

Schrenk-Notzing, A. von. (1956). *The Use of Hypnosis in Psychopathia Sexualis.* New York: Julian Press. (Originally published 1895.)

Scott, G. G. (1983). *Dominant Women, Submissive Men.* New York: Praeger.

Sheffield, C. J. (1987). "Sexual Terrorism: The Social Control of Women." In B. B. Hess and M. M. Ferree, eds., *Analyzing Gender: A Handbook of Social Science Research,* pp. 171–89. Beverly Hills: Sage.

Sorenson, S. B.; Stein, J. A.; Siegel, J. M.; Golding, J. M.; and Burnam, M. A. (1987). "The Prevalence of Adult Sexual Assault." *American Journal of Epidemiology* 126: 1154–64.

Spengler, A. (1977). "Manifest Sadomasochism of Males: Results of an Empirical Study." *Archives of Sexual Behavior* 6: 441–56.

Stanko, E. A. (1985). *Intimate Intrusions: Women's Experience of Male Violence.* New York: Routledge and Kegan Paul.

Stermac, L. E.; Segal, Z. V.; and Gillis, R. (1990). "Social and Cultural Factors in Sexual Assault." In W. L. Marshall, D. R. Laws, and H. E. Barbaree, eds., *Handbook of Sexual Assault: Issues, Theories and Treatment of the Offender,* pp. 143–59. New York: Plenum Press.

Stermac, L. E., and Sheridan, P. M. (1993). "Anti-Gay/Lesbian Violence: Treatment Issues." *Canadian Journal of Human Sexuality* 2: 33–38.

Stermac, L. E.; Sheridan, P. M.; Davidson, A.; and Dunn, S. (1993). "Sexual Assault of Adult Males." Manuscript submitted for publication.

Struckman-Johnson, C. (1988). "Forced Sex on Dates: It Happens to Men, Too." *Journal of Sex Research* 24: 234–41.

Sundberg, S. L.; Barbaree, H. E.; and Marshall, W. L. (1991). "Victim Blame and the Disinhibition of Sexual Arousal to Rape Vignettes." *Violence and Victims* 6: 103–120.

Vanden Bergh, R. L., and Kelly, J. F. (1964). "Vampirism: A Review with New Observations." *Archives of General Psychiatry* 11: 543–47.

Weinberg, M. S.; Williams, C. J.; and Moser, C. (1984). "The Social Constituents of Sadomasochism." *Social Problems* 31: 379–89.

Weinberg, T. S. (1987). "Sadomasochism in the United States: A Review of Recent Sociological Literature." *Journal of Sex Research* 23: 50–69.

Weiss, C., and Friar, D. (1974). *Terror in the Prisons.* New York: Bobbs-Merrill.

Wooden, W. S., and Parker, J. (1982). *Men behind Bars: Sexual Exploitation in Prison.* New York: DaCapo.

Wydra, A.; Marshall, W. L.; Earls, C. M.; and Barbaree, H. E. (1983). "Identification of Cues and Control of Sexual Arousal by Rapists." *Behavior Research and Therapy* 21: 469–76.

Yalom, I. D. (1960). "Aggression and Forbiddenness in Voyeurism." *Archives of General Psychiatry* 3: 305–319.

Yates, E. P.; Barbaree, H. E.; and Marshall, W. L. (1984). "Anger and Deviant Sexual Arousal." *Behavior Therapy* 15: 287–94.

Yllo, K., and Finkelhor, D. (1985). "Marital Rape." In A. Burgess, ed., *Rape and Sexual Assault: A Research Handbook,* pp. 146–58. New York: Garland.

5

Genital Exhibitionism and Voyeurism: Theories and Treatment*

Ron Langevin

The Diagnostic and Statistical Manual of Mental Disorders, third edition, revised (*DSM-III-R*), provides a seemingly straightforward definition of genital exhibitionism: "Recurring intense sexual urges and sexually arousing fantasies of at least 6 months duration involving the exposure of one's genitals to a stranger." However, there are many facets of exhibitionism that make it a surprisingly complex sexual anomaly. Consider the following examples:

1. A 30-year-old woman is walking with her 9-year-old daughter through the park late in the afternoon. No one else is around. Suddenly a man approaches from a distance and, a few feet in front of the woman and her daughter, he drops his pants to expose his genitals. The woman and her daughter giggle and walk on quickly.

2. A 25-year-old woman on her way to work is waiting in a bus shelter at 6 A.M. She is alone when a man in his mid-twenties crosses the street and stands in the doorway, blocking the exit from the bus shelter. He opens his pants and masturbates in front of the frightened woman, making obscene remarks to her while he masturbates. The woman is shaking as she looks to see if the bus is coming.

Both incidents may satisfy the *DSM-III-R* definition of Genital Exhibitionism, but there are many questions that arise which indicate the multi-

*The author wishes to thank Dennis Marentette and Robin J. Watson for their comments to an earlier draft of this paper.

faceted nature of exhibitionism. For example, in the first case, is the flasher exposing to the woman, to her daughter, or to both of them? Is he a pedophile as well as an exhibitionist? Is it significant that he has no erection while he exposed and he did not masturbate, whereas the exhibitionist in the second example did? Did the first male hope that the woman or her daughter would receive enjoyment or pleasure from the exposing? Did the second male hope that the woman would be frightened? Did he deliberately corner her so that she could not get away? Could one of these exhibitionists more readily progress to a rape, or other dangerous sexual assault, than the other? The answers to these questions have important implications for understanding the etiology and treatment of genital exhibitionism. Exhibitionism may co-occur with a number of other sexual anomalies. In particular, the victim of indecent exposure is frequently a juvenile female, so pedophilia is a possible diagnosis.

The available literature on the topic of exhibitionism has been reviewed by Blair and Lanyon (1981), Cox and Daitzman (1980) and Langevin (1983). It is maintained in the professional literature that exhibitionism is one of the most common sexual offenses committed in North America. However, the exact frequency with which exhibitionism occurs with juvenile or with adult victims, or appears in conjunction with other unusual sexual behavior, remains, for the most part, unknown. Cox (1988) has reviewed the criminological data, and Cox and Daitzman (1980) have reviewed the legal information available on the subject. They note that exhibitionists account for almost one third of paraphilic men involved in the legal system in the USA, the United Kingdom, and Canada. Cox's own interesting studies on college women in the USA and Hong Kong indicate that the frequency of reported indecent exposure is far greater than the numbers of men convicted. Cox, Tsang, and Lee (1982) compared the responses of 128 female undergraduates enrolled in introductory psychology in Hong Kong with those of 450 American female college students from nine universities, randomly selected from across the USA. Although 35 percent of the Hong Kong students and 33 percent of the American students had been victims of indecent exposure on at least one occasion, none of the Hong Kong students and only 15 percent of the American students reported the occurrence to the police. A further study by Cox (1988) on 846 college women showed similar results and indicated that, for the most part, incidents of indecent exposure are not reported to the police (see also Zverina et al. 1987). Cox et al.'s study also shattered the myth that indecent exposure is rare outside of the Western world. It may be less frequently reported, but it appears to occur with a frequency similar to that in the USA and Canada.

An important issue in genital exhibitionism (and seen in example two above) is the potential for violence. Little systematic information is available on this topic, in spite of the commonly held belief that exhibitionism is a frequent companion of rape and indecent sexual assaults. MacDonald (1973) and Lang et al. (1987) both found that between one-fifth and one-third of men who were undergoing assessment and/or treatment for genital exhibitionism had a prior sexual assault conviction. Although the majority were not sexually aggressive and fit the prevailing stereotype of the exhibitionist as a "relatively harmless, hands-off sex offender," clearly significant numbers can be dangerous and do either progress to, or concurrently engage in sexual assaults.

Romero and Meyer-Williams (1985) conducted a ten-year followup of 231 adult males convicted of sex offenses and placed on probation in Philadelphia between October 1966 and November 1969. Their sample included 48 exhibitionists who were examined ten years after release for number of arrests for both sexual and nonsexual offenses. The recidivism rate for the total sample was low, at 11.3 percent committing a further sex offense, and thus was consistent with earlier reports on the subject (see Mohr, Turner and Jerry 1963). However, whereas the recidivism rate was 6.2 percent for pedophiles and 10.4 percent for sexual assaulters, exhibitionists had the highest rate at 20.5 percent. Among the exhibitionists seen at followup, 10.6 percent were involved in a violent nonsex crime and of the individuals rearrested, exhibitionists accounted for the highest percentage related to a sex offense (41 percent). Although one may argue about the peculiarity of the sample in Romero and Meyer-Williams' study, or about different base rates of exhibition versus other sexually anomalous activity which can influence likelihood of detection, the results do indicate that some exhibitionists can be aggressive both in sexual and nonsexual contexts (see also Berah and Myers 1983; Lamontagne et al. 1984; Stermac and Hall 1989).

The chronology of the development of exhibitionistic behaviors and more aggressive sexual offenses may be difficult to discern. Fehrenbach et al. (1986) noted that the criminal history of sex offenders can begin early. Characteristically, adolescence is a time for the emergence of anomalous sexual behavior; however, juveniles frequently escape court proceedings. In their sample, 11 percent of the 305 adolescent sex offenders, whose average age was 14.8 years, had engaged in indecent exposure, with victims equally divided between child peers and adults. Particularly noteworthy was that 64.7 percent of those adolescents currently being assessed for indecent exposure had committed a previous sexual offense. These results indicate that exhibitionists may be a greater concern than historically has been the case. The results also suggest that there may be distinct aggressive and nonaggressive subtypes of exhibitionists.

Exhibitionism remains predominantly a male act, although a number of authors have questioned its existence in women. A few female case studies have been presented but financial gain (e.g., nude display for pornographic magazines) (cf. Rhoads and Blekelheide 1985) and mental illness (cf. Langevin 1983) remain paramount motives in female genital exhibitionism, although some cases may reflect true genital exhibitionism (cf. Grob 1985). However, the case presentations are usually atypical. Some authors have raised the issue that exhibitionism may be legal for females (e.g., the stripper), and illegal for males, which may account for the low incidents of female exhibitionists who face criminal charges (see also Cassell & Gomez 1987; Schneider 1982). In the past decade, more male strippers have appeared in clubs, so the logic of this claim may no longer be valid.

The current psychological literature continues to document poorly the nature of genital exhibitionism. In particular, the victim's age and sex are rarely mentioned, although characteristically the victims are female. One is unsure whether there is a concurrent pedophilic interest, or whether some other sexual anomaly is more prominent. Rarely are other sexual response anomalies (i.e., voyeurism, rape, transvestitism, etc.) mentioned. A complete sex history is almost never reported, so our understanding of genital exhibitionism has not advanced much in the decade since the literature was reviewed by the present author (Langevin 1983).[1] Moreover, a number of confounding factors may have played a significant role in the behavior of genital exhibitionists as well as other sexually anomalous men but these are rarely noted. Substance abuse, for example, while a most prominent factor, is almost never discussed.

Langevin and Lang (1990) examined a group of 461 male sex offenders. Over half of them scored in the alcoholic range on the Michigan Alcoholic Screening Test (MAST) (Selzer 1971) and although the group of exhibitionists was small (N = 16), it did not differ remarkably from other sex offenders on the abuse of both alcohol and street drugs, with approximately half of them being alcoholics. Myers and Berah (1983) found that 25 percent of the forty-five exhibitionists in their study were consumers of alcohol but only 4 percent were intoxicated at the time of their offense, in contrast to 49 percent of the sixty-five pedophiles examined. Other important factors that play a role in unusual sexual behavior also have not been documented (e.g., mental illness, poor socialization, history of violence, neuropsychological impairment, or endocrine factors) (Langevin 1992). Findings in the last decade suggest that the etiology of exhibitionism, as well as other sexual anomalies, is more complex than it was considered to be twenty years ago.

Voyeurism remains more of an enigma than exhibitionism, even though the two behaviors are often associated (cf. Langevin 1983). The literature on voyeurism is scant and professionals have remained, for the most part, silent about the etiology and treatment of voyeurism. The literature on voyeurism was reviewed by Langevin (1983, 1985), Smith (1976), and Yalom (1960): as the reviewers noted, empirical studies of voyeurism are rare. In part, this may be so because peeping is difficult to detect and may readily be labeled as another crime (e.g., "causing a disturbance", "trespassing" or "mischief"), and may not come to the attention of clinicians and researchers. However, even when voyeurism is noted in clinical samples, it is difficult to isolate. Langevin et al. (1985), for example, did not find one exclusive voyeur in a sample of 422 sexually anomalous men tested in a forensic clinic over a six-year period. Moreover, based on sexual behavior alone, a criterion of ten instances of "peeping" was required to distinguish the "voyeurs" from healthy community controls, although only one instance of orgasmic peeping was needed to discriminate between the groups. Freund and Watson's (1990) results were similar. Of 1,572 heterosexual paraphilic men studied, only 125 peeped (8 percent) and of these, 10.1 percent were exclusive voyeurs—0.8 percent of the total sample. It seems that, using *DSM-III-R* criteria to search for recurring intense desires to peep, one rarely encounters pure voyeurism. Like exhibitionism, voyeurism is multifaceted and, even more than exhibitionism, may be a common behavior that is part of other sexual anomalies or a precursor of them.

Many of the questions raised about exhibitionism can be repeated here: does the voyeur go on to commit more violent and dangerous sexual offenses? Who are the victims of voyeurism? Are there subtypes of voyeurs? It is also possible that voyeurism is such a broad clinical concept that it is useless diagnostically (see Langevin 1983).

The incidence of voyeurism in the community at large is difficult to ascertain. Unlike what happens in exhibitionism, the victims of voyeurism are often unaware of what has transpired because the offender does not want to be seen or to have any physical contact with them.

Voyeurism has been linked to violence by Yalom (1960), who suggests it is associated with murder, arson, and burglary. He described voyeurism as "sadistic" since the intention of the voyeur is to injure or humiliate the victim. However, Yalom presented no systematic empirical data to support his thesis.

Many of the criticisms of the literature on exhibitionism apply to voyeurism as well, only empirical studies of the latter are much rarer. In the following sections, theories of genital exhibitionism and voyeurism will be outlined with supporting data, followed by a review of current treatment studies.

THE THEORIES

A number of theories have attempted to explain genital exhibitionism and voyeurism. It should be kept in mind that when empirical evidence is presented for these theories, it is frequently based on inaccurate assessments (e.g., exhibitionism and pedophilia are mixed; exhibitionism may or may not occur with voyeurism; and it may even be labeled as sadistic or even homosexual, although females are usually the primary victims of indecent exposure). Both exhibitionism and voyeurism may be common pathways for the expression of a variety of sexually anomalous preferences. Therefore, conclusions must be considered with caution until more systematic research is available.

Psychoanalytic Theory

Exhibitionism and voyeurism, like many sexual anomalies, are explained by psychoanalytic theory in terms of castration anxiety, unconscious homosexuality, and feelings of inferiority. Scoptophilia was a term used by Freud to explain the common association of voyeurism and exhibitionism. The primary satisfaction for these two behaviors comes through the act of looking rather than through tactile behavior. Other psychoanalytic hypotheses have been reviewed and will not be repeated here (see Langevin 1983) because no additional systematic empirical evidence has been accumulated in the past decade to test the hypotheses. In general, psychoanalytic theory is short on empirical data, so validation of theoretical claims is often quite poor compared to other theories. One of the difficulties with the analytical literature is that the concept of scoptophilia, which includes exhibitionism and voyeurism, often transcends the sexual realm. Therefore, the intense desire to look or derive satisfaction from looking may be labeled exhibitionism or voyeurism, when, in fact, the individuals described are not evidently deriving erotic gratification in the usual sense of the term (cf., for example, Mahoney 1989).

Only a few case studies have been reported in the past decade which support the psychoanalytic theory that (1) the exhibitionist is protecting himself against castration anxiety by having a woman watch him expose; (2) the fear of the female assures him that he has a penis; and (3) it is a triumphant act in which the exhibitionist says, "I will show you what I hope you could show me." Buzov (1988) examined cases of genital exhibitionism through their manifest dream content and found support for the theory. In a more detailed case presentation, Fuerstein (1984) also found support for the theory. It is noteworthy that Stoller (1975) has defined perversion as "an erotic form of hatred" which has found acceptability in some psychoanalytic circles.

In reviewing the literature in 1983, the present author found that the available evidence indicating exhibitionists have some feelings of inferiority about their bodies or are overly concerned about castration had only equivocal support. When asked twenty-four questions about their bodies, exhibitionists, in comparison with other individuals with heterosexual anomalies and non-patient controls, differed only on six items. Exhibitionists, more than controls, wished that they were more athletic and had a more athletic build, had a larger penis, and were better looking. They more often felt that there was something wrong with their penis and that their fathers were concerned that they take care of it and keep it clean. However, the exhibitionists did not differ from other sexually anomalous men, only from the controls. In general, the concerns about body image and cleanliness were not specific to exhibitionists.

Similarly, psychoanalytic claims that exhibitionists differ from controls in their relationships with their mothers, were not supported by empirical data. In fact, the exhibitionists did not differ from controls in any remarkable ways in terms of their mother relationships, although they did see their fathers as stricter than did controls. The contention that exhibitionism is a form of latent homosexuality has not been supported by sexual behavior or phallometric studies. Characteristically, exhibitionists have a heterosexual history and react most to adult females in phallometric testing (cf. Langevin, et al. 1979).

Voyeurism has been described as sadistic by Yalom (1960), who maintains the voyeur wants to injure and humiliate his victim. Both Yalom (1960) and Karpman (1957) stressed that voyeurism is sexually gratifying because it is undetected and forbidden. Consequently, voyeurs are not interested in strip shows. Karpman also hypothesized that voyeurs have an unusual lack of curiosity. Langevin, Paitich and Russon (1985) in two empirical studies of forty-five and thirty-one voyeurs did not find support for either hypothesis. To this writer's knowledge, there have been no other empirical studies of voyeurism conducted in the past decade.

Personality Theory

A variety of sex offenders are believed to be anxious and unassertive or aggressive when facing conventional heterosexual relationships (Langevin 1985). These personality characteristics, then, are the driving force in their sexually anomalous behavior. The genesis of their personality problems and unusual sexual behavior may lie in disturbed family relations.

Some research has suggested that the family background of exhibitionists is disturbed, but the patterns of disturbance may vary and it is not clear that the families differ between sex offender groups and criminals in general. Marshall et al. (1991), for example, noted that their samples of exhibitionists reported their childhood experiences with their parents to be more unpleasant than normal controls reported.

Dwyer (1988) has examined a variety of sex offenders with a number of instruments. In her study of fifty-six exhibitionist/voyeurs, offenders had a poor or nonexistent relationship with their father and they were often ignored by him throughout early development. She argued that exhibitionist/voyeurs also had overprotective mothers and/or later sought out overprotective wives.

Myers and Berah (1983) compared forty-five exhibitionists and sixty-five pedophiles who were referred for psychiatric assessment. In contrast to Dwyer's results, 71 percent of the exhibitionists reported a positive relationship with their fathers compared to 43 percent of pedophiles. Eighty-seven percent of the exhibitionists, compared to 68 percent of pedophiles, also reported a positive relationship with their mothers. Only 9 percent of the exhibitionists did not have a positive relationship with either parent.

Two studies using the Clarke Parent Child Relations (PCR) Questionnaire (Paitich & Langevin 1976) have examined exhibitionists and voyeurs. The questionnaire consists of fourteen scales that examine, retrospectively, aggression among mother, father and child; and parents' strictness, overindulgence, affection, competence and the respondent's identification with parents. Paitich and Langevin found that forty-two exhibitionists did not differ from forty community controls in mother relationships; however, they did rate their fathers as more strict. Langevin et al. (1985) found the PCR of forty-five voyeurs to be more disturbed than those of fifty-two nonvoyeur sexually anomalous men and fifty-two community controls. Voyeurs' parents were more aggressive to each other and to their children. Parental affection was low and mother's strictness was high. Identification with parents was lowest in the voyeur group.

Some theorists have argued that child sexual abusers were themselves sexually abused as children and, in effect, are repeating a compulsive pattern of behavior. Hanson and Slater (1988) have reviewed the literature on this topic for sex offenders with the conclusion that child sexual abuse is more commonly reported by a sex offender population than by community controls. However, criminals in general also report the abuse more often with 27 percent claiming the experience as a child. The difference between sex offenders and criminals in general is not statistically significant.

Langevin et al. (1989) examined 418 sex offenders and community controls. Within that group were sixteen exhibitionists. The exhibitionists did not differ significantly from the other groups in terms of the frequencies of childhood sexual contacts with adults. In Dwyer's (1988) survey of over 200 exhibitionists/voyeurs, 56 percent reported sexual and/or physical abuse experiences as children. She noted that in the early stages of treatment many offenders may not recall these experiences, but do so in the course of therapy.

Overall, the support for the theory of childhood sexual abuse as an etiological factor in sexual anomalies, including exhibitionism and voyeurism, is weak. However, those sex offenders who have experienced either sexual or physical abuse in childhood do have special problems in therapy; they may show a wider range of symptoms and a greater level of emotional disturbance upon presentation at a mental health clinic (cf. Langevin et al. 1989).

A number of theorists have postulated that exhibitionists and voyeurs are shy, unassertive, or else aggressive. Available empirical studies do not support these claims in general (Blair & Lanyon 1981; Langevin et al. 1979, 1983; Langevin et al. 1985). Whereas exhibitionists had normal personalities, the results for voyeurs were mixed. Voyeurs showed more overall clinical pathology than either community controls or nonvoyeur paraphilic men in one study, but not in a second study (Langevin et al. 1985). As predicted, voyeurs showed more overall hostility than the other groups in both studies.

Psychoanalytic theory predicts that exhibitionists are more narcissistic than average. They have an inordinate interest in their own bodies and believe they are conferring a service on their victims. Narcissism is a complex concept and measures are poor at present (Raskin & Terry 1988; Raskin & Novack 1989; Svrakic 1987; Anechiarico 1990; Buss & Chiodo 1991), so it is difficult to test the hypothesis empirically. However, Langevin et al. (1979) showed four exhibitionists pictures of themselves in the nude, among other pictures, and found that penile volume changes did not differ between sexually neutral materials and the pictures of the exhibitionists' own bodies, thus failing to support the narcissism theory.

On the other hand, Langevin (1983) reported that the exhibitionist hopes the female victim will enjoy seeing his penis and be impressed by its size more often than he desires to have intercourse with her. Moreover, this narcissistic desire relates more to frequency of masturbation while exposing than to the total frequency of exposing. Evidently, more research is needed on the question (see also Lang et al. 1987).

As an adjunct issue on this topic, theorists have debated the role of marriage in the exhibitionist's rehabilitation. Some argue that intercourse is aversive while others see it as a "prophylaxis against exposing" (cf. Langevin 1983). Empirical information on this issue is scant. Langevin et al. (1979), in the only study on the topic, found no differences between exhibitionists and controls on the frequency of divorce or separation, or on marital adjustment.

The results of personality theory have been disappointing for exhibitionism (cf. Levin & Stava 1987). More work is needed to explore the personality of voyeurs.

Courtship Disorders Theory

Using an ethological model, Freund et al. (1983) have developed a courtship disorder theory that links exhibitionism and voyeurism with toucheurism, frottage, rape, and obscene telephone calling. Courtship is divided into four stages: searching for a partner, pretactile interaction, tactile interaction, and genital union. Exhibitionism, voyeurism and associated sexual anomalies are intensified distortions or exaggerations of the courtship stages. Voyeurism represents the searching stage in which all sexual energy is invested and the remaining courtship stages appear only in a vestigial way, or not at all, before climax is reached. Exhibitionism and obscene phone calls are a distortion of the pretactile stage; toucheurism and frottage the tactile stage; and rape, the genital union stage.

Freund et al. (1983) noted from the literature the frequency with which the so-called courtship disorders are co-reported (see, for example, Dalby 1988). In their own study, they examined 139 men for the co-occurrence of courtship disordered behaviors and claimed support for the theory. Of the eighty-six cases referred for exhibitionism, 26 percent also showed voyeurism, 24 percent toucheurism and frottage, 1 percent rape and 13 percent obscene calls. Noteworthy, 55 percent of the cases only showed/reported the presenting sexual anomaly, and 48 percent of the exhibitionists only exhibited. As noted above, pure voyeurism was rare.

Results of a further study (Freund & Blanchard 1986) of 950 sexual offenders also supported the courtship disorder hypothesis, but the link of exhibitionism with voyeurism was stronger with 73.5 percent of voyeurs also exhibiting and 27.9 percent of exhibitionists also peeping. Again, approximately one half of the exhibitionists exposed only. The most recent study of this group (Freund & Watson 1990) on 1,572 paraphilic men was similar. One has to wonder if the pure exhibitionist group is different in significant ways. Freund and Blanchard compared men who were charged with sexual offenses on minors versus offenses on adults. Of the former, 32.8 percent were also exhibitionists compared to 47.5 percent of the latter (see also Freund 1988; Freund & Blanchard 1986; Freund et al. 1986).

Freund and his associates have also carried out a number of phallometric studies to test the courtship disorder hypothesis. In their 1983 study, Freund, et al. compared the phallometric responses of fifteen exhibitionists and eighteen controls to audio descriptions of exposing, toucheurism, conventional tactile interaction, intercourse, and sexually neutral stimuli. The exhibitionists responded significantly more to the exhibiting and toucheurism stimuli while controls responded more to conventional touching and intercourse in support of the courtship theory. In a further study, Freund et al. (1984) compared the responses of sixteen exhibitionists and sixteen controls to the 4 stages of courtship and found no group differences (see also Freund et al. 1986, for a study of mixed exhibitionists, voyeurs and toucheurs).

Although Freund's own work has provided some support for the courtship disorder theory, Marshall et al. (1991) suggested that Freund's results and their own results do not support his theory. Moreover, Marshall et al. argued that penile plethysmography is not valuable in differentiating exhibitionists and nonexhibitionists. They also denied the primacy of sexual motivation in exhibiting behavior. In their own study, they compared forty-four convicted exhibitionists with twenty community controls. All subjects were male and the two groups did not differ significantly in age or social class. The men were presented three audiotapes describing mutually consenting sexual activities culminating in intercourse, and three other stimuli describing an adult male exposing to unwilling adult females. The exhibitionists and controls differed significantly in their responses both to consenting intercourse and exhibiting. As expected, the nonoffenders responded significantly more to consenting intercourse than the exhibitionists but significantly less to exposing stimuli. However, because the exhibitionist group responded more to consenting intercourse than to exhibiting, Marshall et al. argued that only some exhibitionists have deviant arousal and the degree of this deviance was not profound in any of their subjects.

Other studies have also shown that it is difficult to discriminate sex offenders, including exhibitionists, from nonoffenders based on response preference as measured by phallometric testing (cf. Langevin 1983). One might be tempted to conclude from Marshall et al.'s article that phallometric testing is useless. However, the discrimination of body shape (such as age and gender preferences), based on phallometric testing, is highly reliable as shown by the work of Freund and Watson (1991) and Frenzel and Lang (1989). Determination of erotic response preferences such as exhibitionism, voyeurism, sadism, and rape, as well as other response preferences has been difficult (cf. Langevin 1985). It would seem premature to conclude that exhibitionists are not primarily sexually motivated. Many factors play a role in the erotic potency of a stimulus (e.g., whether slides or movies are shown) (Freund et al. 1974). Other factors may also potentially play a role in erotic valence but have not been explored in systematic phallometric research (e.g., the use of color versus black and white film, the state of undress of the stimulus subjects, the use of male versus female voices in the descriptions, and the duration of the stimulus, among others). Marshall et al.'s study does point to the difficulty of validating the courtship disorder hypothesis via phallometric evaluation of sexual response preferences.

The courtship disorder hypothesis faces other incongruities which are difficult to incorporate. For example, Kolarsky and Madlafousek (1983) found in a phallometric study that exhibitionists tended to respond more to nonerotic cues from females than to their erotic behavior (see also Fedora et al. 1986). Whether it was specific features of the female stimulus or possible voyeurism that may have attracted the individuals to this situation is unknown. It is also difficult for the courtship theory to incorporate the findings of Lang et al. (1987) that 41 percent of thirty-four persistent exhibitionists had a history of cross-dressing but not gender dysphoria; a feature also reported in rapists (cf. Langevin et al. 1985). Freund and Watson (1990) studied 1,572 paraphilic men and found similar results. Interestingly, in their sample only 6.6 percent of 258 exhibitionists and 8.8 percent of 125 voyeurs engaged in "nongender dysphoric cross-dressing," whereas 39.5 percent of the forty-three men labeled "nondysphoric transvestites" engaged in exhibitionism and 25.6 percent engaged in voyeurism. Their results suggest that both exhibitionism and voyeurism are multifaceted sexual anomalies. Their results also showed that the courtship disorders clustered more than they did with other sexual anomalies. In total, 39.9 percent of exhibitionists engaged in voyeurism whereas 82.4 percent of voyeurs exposed. Freund's theory, more than any other in this area, has generated empirical data, and remains promising.

Neuroendocrine Theories

Literature dating back to the 1960s and earlier presented case studies and some systematic research indicating that brain abnormalities, especially in the temporal lobes, are sometimes associated with unusual sexual behavior (cf. Purins & Langevin 1985 for review). The first systematic study in this area was carried out by Kolarsky et al. (1967), in which patients in a neurology clinic were referred to a sexology clinic for investigations of unusual sexual behaviors. The results showed that unusual sexual behavior was much more common in temporal lobe epilepsy than in epilepsy associated with other brain locations.

The sexual behavior reported in association with brain abnormalities has varied and includes both exhibitionism and voyeurism, although fetishism has been noted most. A few case reports have indicated exhibitionism as a primary feature associated with the brain abnormality (cf. Purins & Langevin 1985). One difficulty in evaluating these studies is that they are frequently reported by neurologically oriented researchers or clinicians rather than sexologists. The definition of sexual terms and description of sexual behavior tends to be imprecise. Reported sexual behavior may be atypical of sexually anomalous men in general. For example, an individual who is "indecently exposing" himself may or may not be behaving in a sexual way. It could be the inappropriate behavior of someone who is having a nonconvulsive or partial seizure or the behavior of someone who is disoriented. The sexual motivation for the behavior may not even be described in the case. Even if it is, it may remain difficult to evaluate the sexual motivation of the patient. For example, the author saw a 55-year-old male referred for "indecent exposure." He would drop his trousers on a busy street, frequently losing his personal effects, including his wallet, which the police used to identify him. He was arrested for indecent exposure after a woman filed a complaint to the police. It was not clear from the evidence provided to me whether he masturbated or not, nor whether any obscene remarks were made to the woman. This married "exhibitionist" with a conventional sexual history could not reveal the details of his indecent exposure, of which he had no memory. Progressive brain deterioration due to a disease process was uncovered and the neurologist gave him less than two years to live.

Pandita-Gunawardena (1990) reported a case of a 80-year-old man who suffered a head injury at the age of six when he was kicked in the head by a horse. When he was arrested by the local police, he had been "indecently exposing" himself to a neighbor. Prior to his arrest he seemed disturbed and anxious. The patient had invited the neighbor to examine some household effects. He then adopted a baby posture, inviting her to "change his nappy" and to feed him, after which he masturbated. He also visited her the next day and exposed himself on her doorstep. Although there was masturbation and some sexual motivation involved, it was certainly not typical exhibiting behavior. This patient also showed a considerable amount of aggressive behavior throughout the course of his life subsequent to the head injury. Neurological findings did not show temporal lobe involvement.

De Fazio and Cunningham (1987) reported a case of exhibitionism associated with spinal cord injuries. Complete sensory motor deficits were noted below the injury. The client was unable to obtain physiological feedback, maintain an erection or ejaculate, but he persisted in exhibiting. No prior history of sexual anomaly was reported.

Very rarely is voyeurism noted in association with brain pathology (see Kolarsky et al. 1967 and Taylor 1969), possibly because of the even greater than usual difficulty of defining voyeurism in such cases. The author saw a 34-year-old married man suffering from temporal lobe epilepsy. Between seizures, he felt an overwhelming compulsion to peep on his sister-in-law while she undressed. Ironically, he was married to her identical twin. He was not sexual during his seizures, as far as one could tell.

Ellison (1982) has divided the expected alterations in sexual behaviors in temporal lobe epilepsy into the ictal [seizure], post-ictal, and inter-ictal stages. Ellison indicated that ictal sexual behaviors reported are: erotic thoughts, sexual arousal, copulatory movements, masturbation, undressing, and orgasms. Post-ictally, one sees sexual arousal and exhibitionism. In the inter-ictal stage one sees hyposexuality, impotence, fetishism, transvestitism, sadomasochism, pedophilia, voyeurism, exhibitionism, homosexuality, and transsexualism (see also Blumer & Walker 1975). Ellison's own study of four cases supports the theory that the temporal lobes are central to the presence of unusual sexual behavior. He also noted that in a number of studies, lobectomy improved seizure control in 82 percent of the cases, improved sexual behavior in 21 percent, worsened sexual behavior in 11 percent, and had no effect on sexual behavior in 68 percent of the cases. With such results, one has to wonder whether the sexual manifestations are coincidental to the epilepsy rather than focal to it (see also Taylor 1969).

Pitman (1983), Comings and Comings (1982), and Kerbeshian et al. (1985) have reported case studies of unusual sexual behavior associated with Gilles de la Tourette Syndrome. The Tourette Syndrome is characterized by multiform and changing vocal and motor tics, as well as a large range of accompanying behavioral symptoms (Kerbeshian et al. 1985). Comings and Comings' (1982) case of a 32-year-old male with Tourette Syndrome showed severe symptoms of exhibitionism. This was treated with low doses of Haloperidol, an antipsychotic drug, which eliminated all exhibitionistic urges. Other family members with Tourette Syndrome showed mild exhibitionism as well, suggesting a possible genetic component to the sexual anomaly.

Pitman (1983) associated the abnormalities in Tourette Syndrome that may lead to exhibitionism with Austro-German ethology, as Freund et al. (1983) have done in their courtship disorder theory. Pitman noted that there are innate motor patterns, innate releasing mechanisms and central motor generators involved in the basic universal building blocks of human behavior. Pitman argued that exhibitionism may be understood in ethological terms as a sequence of appetitive and consummatory behaviors. In the appetitive phase, drive builds while the performer seeks out the appropriate releasing stimulus situations, in this case, the presence of an adult female observer. The drive is reduced during the consummatory acts, which include being viewed. Comings and Comings have argued that exhibitionists may show a hypersensitivity of dopamine receptors, which bind the neurotransmitter substance, dopamine, to brain cells that are involved in their disease. Pitman notes that this may be a problem in patients with Tourette Syndrome as well.

Case studies always present a difficulty in that one never knows whether they represent the population at large. For example, do all exhibitionists show some neurological impairment, structural or otherwise? From the neurologist's perspective, would all Tourette Syndrome cases show genital exhibitionism as a feature and, if so, is this "exhibitionism" typical of the behavior seen in sex offender exhibitionists? In the last decade a number of systematic studies have been conducted to examine the brains of exhibitionists, rather than neurology patients, to determine if there are abnormalities, particularly in the temporal lobes; the hypothesized brain center for the initiation and maintenance of sexual arousal.

Flor-Henry and his associates (Flor-Henry et al. 1988) proposed a brain dysfunction theory of sexual anomalies. They argued that a number of electrical brain processes are operative during sexual arousal. They stated that ideational processes in the left frontal-temporal lobes identify sexual stimuli and send a message to the right temporal lobe wherein further brain processes lead to sexual arousal. This chain of events can be impaired in a number of ways in sex offenders. First, there may be some disruption in the left temporal-frontal area associated with verbal processing and ideation related to sexual arousal. Secondly, there may be problems of interhemispheric transfer of information to the right temporal regions associated with sexual arousal. Finally, there may be anomalies in the right hemisphere, affecting arousal itself.

Flor-Henry and his associates have examined these hypotheses in exhibitionists and found support for their theory. Groups of exhibitionists and controls were successfully discriminated based on EEG results generated during administration of verbal processing tasks (Flor-Henry et al. 1988), various neurocognitive tests (Flor-Henry 1987), and neurocognitive and neurolinguistic tests (Langevin et al. 1989). O'Carroll (1989), however, failed to replicate these results, although the number of cases in this study was quite small.

Little neurological investigation of exhibitionists has been carried out. Those studies with larger samples suggest some disturbance in the temporal area. Reports on voyeurs consist only of a few case studies, noted earlier.

Very few studies have examined endocrine function or sex hormone values in exhibitionists. Langevin et al. (1979) examined sixteen exhibitionists for baseline testosterone levels and found no significant difference from sixteen controls. More recently, Lang et al. (1989) examined sixteen exhibitionists and fifteen controls on a number of hormones; cortisol, prolactin, DHEA-S, estradiol, LH (Luteinizing Hormone), FSH (Follicle Stimulating Hormone), androstenedione, and testosterone (total and free) as well as on SHBG. They also found no significant differences between groups. Bradford and McLean (1984) examined a group of fifty sex offenders, including seven exhibitionists. They reported no overall group differences in plasma testosterone levels. However, the exhibitionist subjects were not separated from other offenders for analysis. No hormonal data are available on groups of voyeurs, to our knowledge. There are also no reports on endocrine challenge tests (e.g., HCG [Human Chorionic Gonadotropin] or GnRH [Gonadotropin Releasing Hormone] tests on exhibitionists or voyeurs). The challenge tests may show dynamic differences in the endocrine system of exhibitionists and voyeurs that would not be evident in static samples of peripheral blood.

TREATMENT METHODS

Group Therapy

As with other sexually anomalous behavior, exhibitionism and voyeurism have been treated primarily by one variant or another of aversion therapy, in which the undesired sexual behavior is repeatedly followed by an unpleasant stimulus (e.g., an unpleasant smell or an electric shock). However, group therapy has been discussed most for exhibitionists (for reviews, see Langevin 1983; Lester 1982). In the 1960s and 1970s, for some unknown reason, exhibitionism was the sexual anomaly that epitomized the issues of compliance in treatment (cf. Langevin 1983). The debate concerned whether it was worthwhile to treat exhibitionists if they had been coerced into therapy. The value of group therapy versus individual therapy was also debated. In the past decade, the role of compliance in treatment has come to the forefront of treatment issues for sex offenders in general. Langevin et al. (1988) examined eighty-seven varied sex offenders. Approximately one-half of the sample saw no need for treatment and did not think there was anything wrong with their unusual sexual behavior. Hucker et al. (1988) found similar results in a study of one hundred pedophiles. Simkins et al. (1990) found that the men who are most open about their sexual behavior and engage in the least denial, make the most progress in sex offender therapy. It appears that the therapy issues for the 1990s will center on enhancing treatment compliance through various motivational strategies.

Perhaps because of economic restraints and increased crowding, group therapy has also become a method of choice, especially in correctional systems. However, to this writer's knowledge, no systematic report of group therapy for exhibitionists per se has appeared in the last decade. The classic work of Hackett (1971) remains the most thoughtful evaluation of therapy issues for exhibitionists to date. Hackett, by a trial and error process, arrived at a group therapy process for exhibitionists in which the discharge of anger was a critical factor to the success of treatment. He successfully treated thirty-four of thirty-seven cases, with followup ranging from six months to fourteen years after release.

Maletzky examined one hundred patients, comprised of thirty-eight homosexual pedophiles and sixty-two exhibitionists. The groups were subdivided into self-referred and court-referred. There were fifteen self-referred and twenty-three court-referred pedophiles, while thirty exhibitionists were self-referred and thirty-two were court-referred. Maletzky was careful to exclude individuals who were pressured into seeking therapy by friends and relatives. There were few significant differences between any of the groups in terms of demographic characteristics, treatment response, and outcome. All groups responded significantly to treatment and there were no significant group differences on variables measured which included penile plethysmographic responses to deviant and conventional stimulus materials, attendance in therapy, or followup using police records. Persons were treated weekly for twenty-four weeks and then followed with booster sessions every three months for three years. Of a total of 2,400 sessions, only forty-three were missed by the clients. There were no statistically significant differences in the four sub-groups, although 67 percent of missed appointments were by self-referred patients. When legal records were examined, only eleven legal charges involving eight patients were filed over a 36-month period. Again there were no significant subgroup differences. Thus, it would appear that it makes little difference whether the individual is self-referred or court-referred. Perhaps results would be different for group therapy than for covert sensitization (see below).

The issue raised about forced or voluntary treatment remains unresolved to this date, although Maletzky (1980) found it made little difference. It is generally believed, at present, that without some kind of legal coercion, sex offenders in general, including exhibitionists, will not seek treatment on their own.

Aversion Therapy—Covert Sensitization

Covert sensitization has been most frequently reported as the effective aversion therapy of choice for exhibitionists and voyeurs. In this method, both the undesired sexual behavior and the unpleasant stimulus that follows are imagined by the client. In some cases unpleasant odors (smelling salts or valeric acid) are used to supplement the imagined aversive stimulus (see Maletzky 1991). The majority of studies are case reports (Alford et al. 1980; Carney & Hong 1982; Fensterheim 1974; Lamontagne & Lesage 1986; Polk 1983; Rangaswamy 1987), with the notable exception of Maletzky's (1980) work. The case reports provide additional support for the effectiveness of the covert sensitization method. However, these studies are a continuation of earlier research in the 1960s and 1970s in which a comprehensive sexual history of the individuals treated and other important factors, such as substance abuse, socialization, personality, mental illness, or criminal history, are not reported. Followup of treatment continues to be relatively short, as was the case in earlier studies.

Aversion methods may have short-term effects on behavior, but long term effectiveness remains unknown. Exhibitionism is especially problematic in this regard because some individuals can go for long periods of time without exposing. For some, it appears to be seasonally driven (cf. Langevin et al. 1979). It is exceptional in these studies for any penile plethysmographic evaluation to be made. Once again, Maletzky's (1980) and Alford et al.'s (1980) studies are exceptions. As noted earlier, the phallometric evaluation of an exhibitionist's and voyeur's erotic preferences is difficult, but one can evaluate the arousal level to an individual's own deviant fantasies before, during, and after a course of treatment. As the individual gains more control over his responses, the level of erection should decrease. This provides an objective indicator of the effectiveness of treatment. However, one must have a co-operative and motivated individual in treatment.

Maletzky (1977) addressed the issue of the permanence of assisted covert sensitization, in which the fantasies of unwanted sexual behavior was paired with an aversive odor (usually valeric acid). Maletzky examined eighteen homosexual and twelve exhibitionistic patients to compare those who required booster sessions and those who did not. Of the twelve exhibitionists, four showed increases in anomalous sexual behavior within twelve months of treatment termination; that is, approximately one-third of the men showed recurrence of symptoms. The booster sessions appeared to be an important addition to treatment. Although Maletzky found no differences in those requiring booster sessions and those who did not, in terms of duration or frequency of problems, marital status, age, etc., those who did not require the booster were able, by themselves and through therapy, to rearrange their environments so that strong provocation to expose did not frequently occur. Maletzky concluded that the frequency of required booster sessions remains unknown at this time.

The most noteworthy study of exhibitionists treated by covert sensitization was carried out by Maletzky (1980), as noted above. He not only showed that covert sensitization is effective in reducing the frequency of exhibiting behavior, but he examined, in the only study known to this writer, self-referred versus court-referred cases in treatment, discussed earlier.

Covert sensitization procedures are not unlike those used in hypnotherapy. In fact, Polk (1983) assisted covert sensitization of an exhibitionist with hypnosis. Epstein and Deyoub (1983) used hypnosis by itself and one can see many similarities in the procedures (see also Langevin 1983 for review of this topic). Epstein and Deyoub noted that exhibitionists appear to dissociate during exposure; therefore, the use of hypnosis may be particularly valuable since dissociation is a classic situation wherein hypnosis is used. Their case of a 38-year-old exhibitionist who had been active for fourteen years was treated in eight sessions, (a significantly shorter period than used for covert sensitization), and there were no known exposures at two-year followup.

Positive Behavioral Methods

Some therapists have attempted to use positive behavioral procedures alone, or in conjunction with aversion procedures. In two of these studies, carried out on mentally challenged (retarded) individuals, the therapist reinforced the exhibitionists at the times they were not exposing with a hug and attention, but did not reinforce or pay attention when they exposed (Hurley & Sovner 1983; Lutzker 1974). The operant approach to behavioral change is not a new one, but when applied to the mentally retarded, a range of other problems arise that involve communication with the individual and determining whether the behavior in question is really deviant or merely inappropriate (cf. Griffiths et al. 1989; Hurley & Sovner 1983). Just evaluating the nature of the sexual preference can be a time-consuming and unreliable task requiring specialized training in the area of learning disabilities and mental retardation. Nevertheless, these two studies indicate that a positive approach can be effective with retarded individuals.

Multitreatment Approaches

Historically, behavior therapists have dealt with a range of problems present in sexually anomalous men. Exhibitionists and voyeurs are no exception. Thus, aversive conditioning might be used to reduce deviant sexual impulses, while social skills training or assertiveness training would be used to enhance heterosexual skills. For example, Marshall et al. (1991) in two studies compared the effectiveness of modifying deviant sexual behavior versus changing cognitions, enhancing relationships in interpersonal skills, and relapse prevention. In the first study, Marshall et al. compared twenty-three treated with twenty-one untreated exhibitionists. They were followed between 64 and 161 months. The men were treated with four procedures, electrical aversion, orgasmic reconditioning, masturbatory satiation, and ammonia aversion; in other words, classic behavior therapy aversion methods to reduce deviant sexual arousal. Fifty-seven percent of the untreated men versus 39 percent of the treated men re-offended, based on official police records. Although the results indicate some advantage of treatment versus no treatment, the results were not statistically significant. In the second study, seventeen exhibitionists were treated with the focus on cognitive procedures. The treated groups in both studies carried smelling salts, but, in the second study, they were told that this was to develop control over their thoughts rather than to punish deviant sexual feelings. Covert sensitization was used with this group as well as relapse prevention training that, however, was not uniform across all cases. The treatment focused on unassertiveness, a need to be perfect, and inability to achieve a sense of intimacy in adult relations. Assertiveness training, stress management, cognitive restructuring, and training in relationship skills were the main treatment elements to deal with the problems. This group was followed up for a much shorter time, forty-eight months, but only 24 percent had recidivated. In many ways, Marshall et al.'s study indicated that the use of more positive techniques and a focus on self-control resulted in enhanced treatment outcomes, compared to the more passive, aversive behavioral methods.

Johnson and Edinger (1981) also presented the multimethod treatment of a 36-year-old schizophrenic referred for exhibitionism. They successfully employed self-monitoring, relaxation training, desensitization, guided imagery, and "substitution" methods. The exhibitionistic fantasies and behavior disappeared altogether and did not recur during a five-month followup period.

Although a holistic approach to treatment is appealing from the perspective of dealing with a variety of problems that an individual faces, such an approach has provided great difficulty for evaluation studies. One cannot know whether one aspect of therapy is more effective than another or if some combination and interaction of treatments has produced the desired result. As the number of treatment procedures increases, the number of interactions between the therapies grow, so that the task of knowing which component is effective becomes extremely difficult to determine. One has to ask how cost effective such multimethod therapies are, and whether some simpler procedure might not do the job just as well.

Antiandrogens and Other Drugs

Historically, cyproterone acetate (Androcur) and medroxyprogesterone acetate (Provera and Depo-Provera) have been used in the treatment of sex offenders. Both drugs have some demonstrated value in reducing circulating levels of testosterone in the blood stream, decreasing sexual fantasies and actual sexual behavior. Scattered studies continue to support the value of these drugs (cf. Cooper 1988; Hucker et al. 1988). Case reports once again leave many unanswered questions compared to control studies, although they do provide support for the use of the medication (Ross et al. 1987; Kenyon 1989). Hucker et al's. study of one hundred consecutive cases of pedophilia is illustrative here. Of their initial sample, fifty-seven did not acknowledge a problem with their sexual behavior. Of the forty-three who agreed to take part in the assessment/drug treatment program, only twenty would accept Provera for a three-month term. Of these twenty, only twelve completed the treatment and one faked taking his pills in this double blind study. Thus, from one hundred referrals, Hucker et al. ended up with 11 percent compliance in taking the medication, even for a three-month period. This kind of information is not available in case reports wherein the representativeness of the cases remains unknown.[2]

Although Androcur and Provera have been used since the mid-1960s as sex drive-reducing medications, some newer drugs became available in the 1980s. Bianchi (1990) used fluoxetine (Prozac) in the treatment of a case of exhibitionism. The author noted that the client had been unsuccessfully treated with Provera previously. The patient's sexual fantasies and desires to act out decreased over a three-to-four-week period on fluoxetine. Perilstein et al. (1991) also examined fluoxetine treatment of three cases, one of which was of exhibitionism. The fluoxetine significantly decreased the exhibitionist's fantasies that included violence. Perilstein et al. noted, however, that one of the side effects of fluoxetine is retarded ejaculation.

It is interesting that fluoxetine has been effective in the treatment of obsessive compulsive disorders. Some authors have equated the "compulsive quality" of paraphilias to the obsessive compulsive disorders in which there is a buildup of tension and subsequent relief through the obsessive behavior. However, using this logic, one would have to consider all sexual behavior as compulsive. The major differences between obsessive compulsive disorder and sexual behavior, including paraphilias, is that the obsessive compulsion occurs with high frequency and is motivated by anxiety. Sexual behavior, on the other hand, is motivated by pleasure. There is disputable evidence that paraphilics in general have a very high level of sexual outlet and that their frequency of sexual release is any different from an age-matched sexually conventional group. However, a few paraphilic individuals do present with very high frequencies of sexual release and they appear to be obsessive in their acts.

It is noteworthy that Konopacki and Oei (1988) treated two cases, one of exhibitionism and one of voyeurism, using a behavioral approach and considered both problems as analog compulsive disorders. They used an ABAB single-case experimental design to examine their hypothesis. In the case of the exhibitionist, the procedure was designed to remove and undermine the development of sexual arousal by increasing accessibility to the controlling stimuli and by increasing the duration of exhibitionistic responses. This was made possible by the client's membership in a "nudist camp" which he attended once weekly. Over a three-year period, there were no convictions from his exhibiting behavior and his wife reported less inappropriate nudity around their home. Konopacki and Oei's method has its analogy in masturbatory satiation, as described by Marshall and Lippens (1977).

Rousseau and his associates (1990) have examined two other drugs in combination: an LHRH (Luteinizing Hormone Releasing Hormone) agonist and the antiandrogen, flutamide. Although LHRH would influence the release of androgens via the hypothalamic-pituitary axis, it does not affect the adrenal androgens. Rousseau et al. used a combination of LHRH and flutamide (Eulexin) in the treatment of an exhibitionist who had exposed over 2,000 times. The study was illustrative, showing the effect of the combined drugs on sexual fantasies and outlet. At the termination of treatment, the deviant fantasies and exhibitionism returned. The combination of drugs would appear to be useful, although a systematic study of the long-term side effects of these drugs is needed.

The primary problem in the use of antiandrogenic drugs is their poor acceptability by patients. They appear to be effective for a number of individuals who are willing to take them. However, if these drugs are to be used further in the treatment of exhibitionists and voyeurs, strategies for motivating the offenders to accept them need to be developed.

An unusual case of exhibitionism is reported by Evans (1970). This individual started to exhibit himself at age thirty. A medical examination revealed that there was a history of diabetes in his family and that the patient himself was hypoglycemic. When his hypoglycemia was treated, the exhibitionistic behavior stopped. Diabetes can be a significant factor in the occurrence of unusual behavior, sexual and otherwise, and a routine full medical evaluation can be valuable.

Other Approaches

Relapse prevention has become a prominent treatment goal, especially for convicted sex offenders. Preventively the thoughts, feelings and stressors leading up to acting out sexually are explored and alternative coping strategies are developed to deal with the "relapse cycle" (cf. Bays & Freeman-Longo 1989). Although the method appears valuable, treatment of exhibitionists and voyeurs has not been examined specifically.

Victim empathy methods have also been explored in the past decade but work with exhibitionists has not been reported.

The question has been raised, particularly in the last decade, whether sex offenders need treatment or are "just bad" and need to be punished (cf. Kosky 1989). Undoubtedly, sex offenders can harm their victims, but it has been argued that treatment can help to reduce future victimization of others. Early prevention programs to help individuals deal with their own difficult history and/or sexual problems may be more effective than leaving their future behavior to chance.

Kilmann et al. (1982) reviewed the effects of treating paraphilias in general and exhibitionism in particular. This included as well a separate review of exhibitionism. They critiqued the professional literature and noted that most of the studies available are single case reports. Further, the studies failed to control for social desirability factors, especially in the case of sex offenders, and relied excessively on verbal self-reports in the evaluation of treatment outcome. Although the studies generally report positive results, there may be a selection bias in publication of successful treatments.

CONCLUSIONS

Snaith (1983) has described genital exhibitionism as a disorder without a satisfactory explanation. This remains true today. Snaith noted that the behavioral act does not signify a homogeneous population. The same can be said for voyeurism. Nor does there appear to be a single unifying factor, be it personality, attitude toward women, erotic gratification in the act, or presence of other deviant behavior. The clinician assessing the exhibitionist or voyeur must examine a wide range of sexual behaviors to evaluate erotic preference and dangerousness.

The literature on treatments has not progressed beyond what was known ten years ago. Drug therapies and aversive conditioning have had some reported effectiveness. However, these treatment methods are limited by their unacceptability to sex offenders (cf. Langevin 1988). Maletzky (1980) reported a 67 percent refusal rate for electrical aversion and 63 percent for aversive behavioral rehearsal. Offenders prefer individual counseling to deal with their life issues. At many times, their goals and the therapy goals of the correctional system are not the same (cf. Langevin et al. 1988).

A number of studies have used covert sensitization successfully and, based on the literature, one might believe that it was the treatment of choice. The more current therapies such as relapse prevention and behavioral management techniques are almost unmentioned in the literature on exhibitionism and voyeurism of the past decade. There is only a minimal literature on denial and minimization in exhibitionists, problems that are common to sex offenders in general. Presumably work such as that of Simkin et al. (1990), evaluating openness versus rationalization as factors in effective treatment, could be generalized to exhibitionists as well.

It would seem that the satisfactory direction for exploring the etiology of exhibitionism and voyeurism would be, first, to provide thoroughly documented sexual histories, as examined in the Clarke Sex History Questionnaire (Langevin 1991), and to note confounding factors such as substance abuse, among others, that may have an important bearing on acceptability of treatment or treatment success. Second, neuroendocrine factors in exhibitionism should be explored thoroughly in a variety of samples. The hormonal challenge tests (Bain et al. 1988) would be a valuable addition to our knowledge of exhibitionism. Neuropsychological and imaging studies would also be valuable. Third, a differentiation of subgroups of exhibitionists is needed. Are there personality and/or other differences between those who are violent/aggressive or have sadistic intent and those who want a positive response from their victims? Are there important differences between the orgasmic and nonorgasmic subgroups of exhibitionists? How do cross-dressing exhibitionists differ from those who do not engage in such behavior? Is one subgroup of exhibitionists more likely to show courtship-disordered behavior and/or be more violent and dangerous? These results would have an important bearing on assessment and treatment effectiveness as well. It would be valuable to have more systematic studies, even if the sample sizes were small, than to continue case reports. Hopefully exhibitionism and voyeurism will not remain a neglected area of research in the next decade.

NOTES

1. A noteworthy exception remains Gebbard et al. (1965).

2. Editor's Note: An additional consideration is that to ensure compliance the hormone should be administered as a long-acting injectable or subcutaneous implant. Orally administered, the hormone is rendered ineffectual by the digestive secretions of the gut.

REFERENCES

Alford, G. S.; Webster, J. S.; and Sanders, S. H. (1980). "Covert Aversion of Two Interrelated Deviant Sexual Practices: Obscene Phone Calling and Exhibitionism. A Single Case Analysis." *Behavior Therapy* 11: 15–25.

Anechiarico, B. (1990). "Understanding and Treating Sex Offenders from a Self-Psychological Perspective: The Missing Piece." *Clinical Social Work Journal* 18: 281–92.

Bain, J.; Langevin, R.; Hucker, S.; Dickey, R.; Wright, P.; and Schonberg, C. (1988). "Sex Hormones in Pedophiles." *Annals of Sex Research* 1: 443–54.

Bays, L., and Freeman-Longo, R. (1989). *Why Did I Do It Again? Understanding My Cycle of Problem Behaviors.* Orwell, Vt.: The Safer Society Program and Press.

Berah, E. F., and Myers, R. G. (1983). "The Offense Records of a Sample of Convicted Exhibitionists." *Bulletin of the American Academy of Psychiatry and Law* 11: 365–69.

Bianchi, M. D. (1990). "Fluoxetine Treatment of Exhibitionism." *American Journal of Psychiatry* 147: 1089–90.

Blair, C. D., and Lanyon, R. I. (1981). "Exhibitionism: Etiology and Treatment." *Psychological Bulletin* 89: 439–63.

Blumer, D., and Walker, A. E. (1975). "The Neural Basis of Sexual Behavior." In F. Benson and D. Blumer, eds., *Psychiatric Aspects of Neurologic Disease.* New York: Gune and Stratton.

Bradford, J. W., and McLean, D. (1984). "Sexual Offenders, Violence and Testosterone: A Clinical Study." *Canadian Journal of Psychiatry* 29: 335–43.

Buss, D. M., and Chiodo, L. M. (1991). "Narcissistic Acts in Everyday Life." *Journal of Personality* 59: 179–215.

Buzov, I. (1988). "Exhibitionism: The Essential Psychic Conflict in Manifest Dream Content." *The American Journal of Psychoanalysis* 48: 180–83.

Carney, R. N., and Hong, B. A. (1982). "Effects of Covert Sensitization on Facial EMG: A Pilot Study." *Perceptual and Motor Skills* 55: 655–58.

Cassell, D., and Gomez, J. (1987). "Indecent Exposure—A Report of a Female." *British Journal of Psychiatry* 151: 867.

Comings, D. E., and Comings, D. G. (1982). "A Case of Familial Exhibitionism in Tourette's Syndrome Successfully Treated with Haloperidol." *American Journal of Psychiatry* 139: 913–15.

Cooper, A. J. (1988). "Medroxyprogesterone Acetate as a Treatment for Sexual Acting Out in Organic Brain Syndrome." *American Journal of Psychiatry* 145: 1179–80.

Cox, D. J. (1988). "Incidence and Nature of Male Genital Exposure Behavior as Reported by College Women." *Journal of Sex Research* 24: 227–34.

Cox, D. J., and Daitzman, R. J. (1980). *Exhibitionism: Description, Assessment and Treatment.* New York: Garland Press.

Cox, D. J.; Tsang, K.; and Lee, A. (1982). "A Cross-Cultural Comparison of the Incidence and Nature of Male Exhibitionism among Female College Students." *Victimology: An International Journal* 7: 231–34.

Dalby, J. T. (1988). "Is Telephone Scatologia a Variant of Exhibitionism?" *International Journal of Offender Therapy and Comparative Criminology* 32: 45–49.

De Fazio, A., and Cunningham, K. A. (1987). "A Paraphilia in a Spinal-Cord-Injured Patient: A Case Report." *Sexuality and Disability* 8: 247–54.

Dwyer, M. (1988). "Exhibitionism/Voyeurism." *Journal of Social Work and Human Sexuality* 7: 102–112.

Ellison, J. M. (1982). "Alterations of Sexual Behavior in Temporal-Lobe Epilepsy." *Psychosomatics* 23: 499–509.

Epstein, S. J., and Deyoub, P. L. (1983). "Hypnotherapeutic Control of Exhibitionism: A Brief Communication." *The International Journal of Clinical and Experimental Hypnosis* 31: 63–66.

Evans, D. R. (1970). "Exhibitionism." In C. G. Costello, eds., *Symptoms of Psychopathology: A Handbook.* New York: J. Wiley.

Fedora, O.; Reddon, J. R.; and Yeudall, L. T. (1986). "Stimuli Eliciting Sexual Arousal in Genital Exhibitionists: A Possible Clinical Application." *Archives of Sexual Behavior* 15: 417–427.

Fehrenbach P. A.; Smith, W.; Monastersky, C.; and Deisher, R. W. (1986). "Adolescent Sexual Offenders: Offender and Offense Characteristics." *American Journal of Orthopsychiatry* 56: 225–33.

Fensterheim, H. (1974). "Behavior Therapy of the Sexual Variations." *Journal of Sex and Marital Therapy* 1: 16–28.

Flor-Henry, P. (1987). "Cerebral Aspects of Sexual Deviation." In G. D. Wilson, ed., *Variant Sexuality: Research and Theory.* Bechenham, Kent, England: Croom Helm Ltd.

Flor-Henry, P.; Lang, R.; Koles, Z. J.; and Frenzel, R. R. (1988). "Quantitative EEG Investigations of Genital Exhibitionists." *Annals of Sex Research* 1: 49–62.

Frenzel, R. R., and Lang, R. A. (1989). "Identifying Sexual Preferences in Intrafamilial and Extrafamilial Child Sexual Abusers." *Annals of Sex Research* 2: 255–75.

Freund, K. (1988). "Courtship Disorder: Is This Hypothesis Valid?" *Annals of the New York Academy of Sciences* 58: 172–82.

Freund, K., and Blanchard, R. (1986). "The Concept of Courtship Disorder." *Journal of Sex and Marital Therapy* 12: 79–92.

Freund, K.; Langevin, R.; and Barlow, D. (1974). "Comparison of Two Penile Measures of Erotic Arousal." *Behavior Research and Therapy* 12: 355–59.

Freund, K.; Scher, H.; and Hucker, S. (1983). "The Courtship Disorder." *Archives of Sexual Behavior* 12: 369–79.

——— (1984). "The Courtship Disorder: A Further Investigation." *Archives of Sexual Behavior* 13: 133–39.

Freund, K.; Scher, H.; Racansky, I. G.; Campbell, K.; and Heasman, G. (1986). "Males Disposed to Commit Rape." *Archives of Sexual Behavior* 15: 23–35.

Freund, K., and Watson, R. (1990). "Mapping the Boundaries of Courtship Disorder." *Journal of Sex Research* 27: 589–606.

Fuerstein, L. A. (1984). "A Case of Exhibitionism: Self-Hatred Beneath a Mask." *Psychoanalytic Approaches to Sexual Problems, Current Issues in Psychoanalytic Practice* 1: 69–81.

Gebbard, P.; Gagnon, J.; Pomeroy, W.; and Christenson, C. (1965). *Sex Offenders.* New York: Harper and Row Co.

Griffiths, D.; Quinsey, V. L.; and Hingsburger, D. (1989). *Changing Inappropriate Sexual Behavior: A Community Based Approach for Persons with Developmental Disabilities.* Baltimore: P. H. Brookes Pub.

Grob, C. S. (1985). "Female Exhibitionism." *Journal of Nervous and Mental Disease* 173: 253–56.

Hackett, T. P. (1971). "The Cycle Therapy of Exhibitionist in a Court Clinic Setting." *Seminars in Psychiatry* 3: 297–306.

Hanson, R. K., and Slater, S. (1988). "Sexual Victimization in the History of Sexual Abusers: A Review." *Annals of Sex Research* 1: 485–99.

Hucker, S.; Langevin, R.; and Bain, J. (1988). "A Double Blind Trial of Provera for Pedophiles." *Annals of Sex Research* 1: 227–42.

Hurley, A. D., and Sovner, R. (1983). "Treatment of Sexual Deviation in Mentally Retarded Persons." *Psychiatric Aspects of Mental Retardation Newsletter 2,* no. 4: 13–16.

Johnson, S., and Edinger, J. (1981). "A Case Study: Treating the Multiple Problem Exhibitionist Fantasies in a Restrictive Setting." *Corrective and Social Psychiatry and the Journal of Behavior Therapy* 27: 100–104.

Karpman, B. (1957). *The Sexual Offender and His Offenses.* New York: Julian Press.

Kenyon, E. D. M. (1989). "The Management of Exhibitionism in the Elderly: A Case Study." *Sexual and Marital Therapy* 4: 93–100.

Kerbeshian, J.; Burd, L.; Fisher, W.; Martsolf, J. T.; and Wikenhaiser, M. (1985). "Gilles de la Tourette Disease and Multiply Disabled Children." *Rehabilitation Literature* 46: 255–58.

Kilmann, P. R.; Sabalis, R. F.; Gearing, M. L., II; Bukstel, L. H.; and Scovern, A. W. (1982). "The Treatment of Sexual Paraphilias: A Review of the Outcome Research." *Journal of Sex Research* 18: 193–252.

Kolarsky, A.; Freund, K.; Machek, J.; and Polak, O. (1967). "Male Sexual Deviation: Association with Early Temporal Lobe Damage." *Archives of General Psychiatry* 17: 735–43.

Kolarsky, A., and Madlafousek, J. (1983). "The Inverse Role of Preparatory Erotic Stimulation in Exhibitionists: Phallometric Studies." *Archives of Sexual Behavior* 12: 123–48.

Konopacki, W. P., and Oei, T. P. S. (1988). "Interruption in the Maintenance of Compulsive Sexual Disorder: Two Case Studies." *Archives of Sexual Behavior* 17: 411–19.

Kosky, R. J. (1989). "Should Sex Offenders Be Treated?" *Australian and New Zealand Journal of Psychiatry* 23: 176–80.

Lamontagne, Y., and Lesage, A. (1986). "Private Exposure and Covert Sensitization in the Treatment of Exhibitionism." *Journal of Behavior Therapy and Experimental Psychiatry* 17: 197–201.

Lamontagne, Y.; Boyer, R.; Lamontagne, C.; and Giroux, J. (1984). "Viols à deux et viols en bandes à Montréal." *Revue Canadienne de Psychiatrie* 29: 564–69.

Lang, R. A.; Langevin, R.; Bain, J.; Frenzel, R. R.; and Wright, P. (1989). "Sex Hormone Profiles in Genital Exhibitionists." *Annals of Sex Research* 2: 67–76.

Lang, R. A.; Langevin, R.; Checkley, K. L.; and Pugh, G. (1987). "Genital Exhibitionism: Courtship Disorder or Narcissism?" *Canadian Journal of Behavior Science* 19: 216–32.

Langevin, R. (1983). *Sexual Strands: Understanding and Treating Sexual Anomalies in Men.* Hillsdale, N.J.: Lawrence Erlbaum Associates.

——— (1985). "An Overview of the Paraphilias." In M. H. Ben-Aron, S. J. Hucker, and C. D. Webster, eds., *Clinical Criminology: The Assessment and Treatment of Criminal Behavior.* Toronto: M & M Graphics.

——— (1991). *Clarke Sex History Questionnaire for Males: Manual.* Etobicoke, Canada: Juniper Press.

Langevin, R.; Bain, J.; Ben-Aron, M. H.; Coulthard, R.; Day, D.; Handy, L.; Heasman, G.; Hucker, J. J.; Purins, J. E.; Roper, V.; Russon, A. E.; Webster, C. D.; Wortzman, G. (1985). "Sexual Aggression: Constructing a Predictive Equation; A Controlled Pilot Study." In R. Langevin, ed., *Erotic Preference, Gender Identity, and Aggression in Men: New Research Studies,* pp. 39–76. Hillsdale, N.J.: Lawrence Erlbaum Associates.

Langevin, R., and Lang, R. A. (1990). "Substance Abuse among Sex Offenders." *Annals of Sex Research* 3: 397–424.

Langevin, R.; Lang, R. A.; Wortzman, G.; Frenzel, R. R.; and Wright, P. (1989). "An Examination of Brain Damage and Dysfunction in Genital Exhibitionists." *Annals of Sex Research* 2: 77–88.

Langevin, R.; Paitich, D.; Hucker, S.; Newman, S.; Ramsay, G.; Pope, S.; Geller, G.; and Anderson, C. (1979). "The Effects of Assertiveness Training, Provera, and Sex of Therapist in the Treatment of Genital Exhibitionism." *Journal of Behavior Therapy and Experimental Psychiatry* 10: 275–82.

Langevin, R.; Paitich, D.; Ramsay, G.; Anderson, C.; Kamrad, J.; Pope, S.; Geller, G.; and Newman, S. (1979). "Experimental Studies in the Etiology of Genital Exhibitionism." *Archives of Sexual Behavior* 8: 307–331.

Langevin, R.; Paitich, D.; and Russon, A. E. (1985). "Voyeurism: Does It Predict Sexual Aggression or Violence in General?" In R. Langevin, ed., *Erotic Preference, Gender Identity, and Aggression in Men: New Research Studies,* pp. 77–98. Hillsdale, N.J.: Lawrence Erlbaum Associates.

Langevin, R.; Wright, P.; and Handy, L. (1988). "What Treatment Do Sex Offenders Want?" *Annals of Sex Research* 1: 363–86.

——— (1989). "Characteristics of Sex Offenders Who Were Sexually Victimized as Children." *Annals of Sex Research* 2: 227–54.

Lester, D. (1982). "The Treatment of Exhibitionists." *Corrective and Social Psychiatry and the Journal of Behavior Technology* 28: 94–98.

Levin, S. M., and Stava, L. (1987). "Personality Characteristics of Sex Offenders: A Review." *Archives of Sexual Behavior* 16: 57–79.

Lutzker, J. R. (1974). "Social Reinforcement Control of Exhibitionism in a Profoundly Retarded Adult." *Mental Retardation* 12: 46–47.

MacDonald, J. M. (1973). *Indecent Exposure.* Springfield, Ill., Charles C Thomas Co.

Mahoney, P. J. (1989). "Aspects of Nonperverse Scoptophilia within an Analysis." *Journal of the American Psychoanalytic Association* 37: 365–99.

Maletzky, B. M. (1977). " 'Booster' Sessions in Aversion Therapy: The Permanency of Treatment." *Behavior Therapy* 8: 460–63.

——— (1980). "Self-Referred versus Court-Referred Sexually Deviant Patients: Success with Assisted Covert Sensitization." *Behavior Therapy* 11: 306–314.

——— (1991). "Treating the Sexual Offender." Newbury Park, Calif.: Sage Publications.

Marshall, W. L.; Eccles, A.; and Barbaree, H. E. (1991). "The Treatment of Exhibitionists: A Focus on Sexual Deviance versus Cognitive and Relationship Features." *Behavior Research Therapy* 29: 129–35.

Marshall, W. L., and Lippens, K. (1977). "The Clinical Value of Boredom: A Procedure for Reducing Inappropriate Sexual Interests." *Journal of Nervous and Mental Disease* 165: 283–87.

Marshall, W. L.; Payne, K.; Barbaree, H. E.; and Eccles, A. (1991). "Exhibitionists: Sexual Preferences for Exposing." *Behavior Research and Therapy* 29: 37–40.

Mohr, J.; Turner, R. E.; and Jerry, M. (1964). *Pedophilia and Exhibitionism.* Toronto: University of Toronto Press.

Myers, R. G., and Berah, E. F. (1983). "Some Features of Australian Exhibitionists Compared with Pedophiles." *Archives of Sexual Behavior* 12: 541–47.

O'Carroll, R. (1989). A Neuropsychological Study of Sexual Deviation. *Sexual and Marital Therapy* 4: 59–63.

Paitich, D., and Langevin, R. (1976). "The Clarke Parent-Child Relations Questionnaire: A Clinically Useful Test for Adults." *Journal of Consulting and Clinical Psychology* 44: 428–36.

Pandita-Gunawardena, R. (1990). "Paraphilic Infantilism: A Rare Case of Fetishistic Behavior." *British Journal of Psychiatry* 157: 767–70.

Perilstein, R. D.; Lipper, S.; and Friedman, L. J. (1991). "Three Cases of Paraphilias Responsive to Fluoxetine Treatments." *Journal of Clinical Psychiatry* 52: 169–70.

Pitman, R. K. (1983). "Tourette's Syndrome and Ethology." *American Journal of Psychiatry* 140: 652.

Polk, W. M. (1983). "Treatment of Exhibitionism in a 38-Year-Old Male by Hypnotically Assisted Covert Sensitization." *The International Journal of Clinical and Experimental Hypnosis* 31: 132–38.

Purins, J. E., and Langevin, R. (1985). "Brain Correlates of Penile Erection." In R. Langevin, ed., *Erotic Preference, Gender Identity, and Aggression in Men: New Research Studies.* Hillsdale, N.J.: L. Erlbaum Associates.

Rangaswamy, K. (1987). "Treatment of Voyeurism by Behavior Therapy." *Child Psychiatry Quarterly* 20: 73–76.

Raskin, R., and Novacek, J. (1989). "An MMPI Description of the Narcissistic Personality." *Journal of Personality Assessment* 53: 66–80.

Raskin, R., and Terry, H. (1988). "A Principal-Components Analysis of the Narcissistic Personality Inventory and Further Evidence of Its Construct Validity." *Journal of Personality and Social Psychology* 54: 890–902.

Rhoads, J. M., and Boekelheide, P. D. (1985, Winter). "Female Genital Exhibitionism." *Psychiatric Forum:* 1–6.

Romero, J. J., and Meyer-Williams, L. (1985). "Recidivism among Convicted Sex Offenders: A 10-Year Follow-Up Study." *Federal Probation* 49: 58–64.

Romero, J. J., and Williams, L. M. (1983). "Group Psychotherapy and Intensive Probation Supervision with Sex Offenders." *Federal Probation* 47: 36–42.

Ross, L. A.; Bland, W. P.; Ruskin, P.; and Bacher, N. (1987). "Antiandrogen Treatment of Aberrant Sexual Activity." *American Journal of Psychiatry* 144: 1511.

Rousseau, L.; Couture, M.; Dupont, A.; Labrie, F.; and Couture, N. (1990). "Effect of Combined Androgen Blockade with a LHRH Agonist and Flutamide in One Severe Case of Male Exhibitionism." *Canadian Journal of Psychiatry* 35: 338–41.

Schneider, R. D. (1982). "Exhibitionism: An Exclusively Male Deviation?" *International Journal of Offender Therapy and Comparative Criminology* 26: 173–76.

Selzer, M. (1971). "The Michigan Alcoholism Screening Test: The Quest for a New Diagnostic Instrument." *American Journal of Psychiatry* 127: 1653–58.

Simkins, L.; Ward, W.; Bowman, S.; Rinck, C. M.; and de Souza, E. (1990). "Predicting Treatment Outcome for Child Sexual Abusers." *Annals of Sex Research* 3: 21–58.

Smith, S. R. (1976). "Voyeurism: A Review of the Literature." *Archives of Sexual Behavior* 5: 585–608.

Snaith, P. (1983). "Exhibitionism: A Clinical Conundrum." *British Journal of Psychiatry* 143: 231–35.

Stermac, L., and Hall, K. (1989). "Escalation in Sexual Offending: Fact or Fiction?" *Annals of Sex Research* 2: 153–62.

Stoller, R. (1975). *Perversion: The Erotic Form of Hatred.* New York: Pantheon Books.

Svrakic, D. M. (1987). "Clinical Approach to the Grandiose Self." *American Journal of Psychoanalysis* 47: 167–81.

Taylor, D. C. (1969). "Sexual Behavior and Temporal-Lobe Epilepsy." *Archives of Neurology* 21: 510–16.

Yalom, I. (1960). "Aggression and Forbiddenness in Voyeurism." *Archives of General Psychiatry* 3: 305–319.

Zverina, J.; Lachman, M.; Pondelickova, J.; and Vanek, J. (1987). "The Occurrence of Atypical Sexual Experience among Various Female Patient Groups." *Archives of Sexual Behavior* 16: 321–26.

6

The Medicolegal Investigation of Autoerotic Asphyxial Deaths

Lauren R. Boglioli and Mark L. Taff

INTRODUCTION

Autoerotic asphyxial (AEA) deaths or sexual asphyxias are perhaps the most fascinating accidental deaths encountered by medical examiners and coroners. Because of the rarity of their occurrence, many health care professionals and death scene investigators are unfamiliar with such cases and misdiagnose them as suicidal or homicidal hangings.

AEA results from the excessive application of an asphyxial mechanism used for the purpose of increasing sexual excitement (Hazelwood et al. 1983). It has been estimated that 250–1,000 autoerotic asphyxial deaths occur in the United States each year (Brody 1984; Hazelwood et al. 1979). Due to the lack of familiarity with this sexual act by both professionals and lay persons, the actual number of AEA deaths each year is unknown.

BRIEF HISTORY

Sexual hanging has been reported since 1791 in the Marquis de Sâde's *Justine,* with Roland's hanging being assisted by Thérèse (Hazelwood et al. 1983). This account suggests that sexual pleasure accompanies hanging and choking. That same year, a prostitute was tried for murdering Francis Kotzwarra in Prague for assisting him in hanging himself for sexual pleasure. During the time of judicial execution by hanging, many people were aware that hanged men developed an erection. Even Herman Melville's *Billy Budd* questions the origin of priapism in hanging (Resnik 1983). Such erections were, in fact, spinal reflexes. In the late nineteenth and early twentieth centuries, many references were made to young boys who accidentally hanged themselves. Anthropologists have noted that certain Eskimo and other cultural groups are known to choke each other during sexual activity (Lowery & Wetli 1982). In 1927, a case of a 24-year-old man who hanged himself using a woman's high-heeled shoe and an elaborate arrangement of weights and ligatures was reported in the psychiatric literature (Auden 1927). An Austrian encyclopedia of sexuality published from 1928–1931 devoted chapters to strangulation and "penis strangulation" as autoerotic practices. In 1935, Bloch described the practice of choking women during intercourse, and in 1936, Ellis described the "impulse to strangle the object of sexual desire." In 1940, Gonzales, Vance and Helpern introduced sexual asphyxia to the forensic community for the first time by adding a single sentence about the subject in his textbook on forensic medicine. In 1953, Stearns published a review of 97 suicides occurring among young people in Massachusetts during 1941–1950. He found twenty-five to be probable suicides in young persons without obvious motivation, suggesting accidental death or sex hanging (Stearns 1953).

Although this ritual has apparently been practiced for centuries, many people are still unaware of its occurrence. Due to the paucity of literature on this subject, nearly all of which appear in the forensic medical/psychiatric literature, this sexual phenomenon is greatly underreported.

THE AEA SYNDROME

The AEA syndrome has been previously described by Resnik (1972) as the "eroticized repetitive hanging" syndrome and includes the following components: an adolescent male or young adult male; ropes, belts, or other binding material so arranged that compression of the neck may be produced and controlled voluntarily; evidence of masturbation (e.g., semen); partial or complete nudity; a solitary victim; evidence that the deceased had consistently tried to hide any visible marks on his person; no apparent wish to die; the presence of erotic pictures or literature; binding of the body and/or the extremities and/or genitals with ropes, chains or leather; and the presence of female attire.

Autoerotic fatalities are deaths occurring as a result of or in association with autoerotic activity (masturbation). An "autoerotic death" is one that results from self-strangulatory asphyxia as part of a paraphilic masturbatory ritual. Paraphilia is a medical term used to classify unusual or bizarre sexuoerotic behavior or imagery which is fixated and necessary for sexual gratification

(Berlin & Coyle 1981; Meyer 1980; Money 1981, 1984, 1985, 1986, 1988; Money & Lamacz 1989). Paraphilic erotic fantasies and their practices are popularly known as "kinky" or bizarre. The popular term for asphyxiophilia is "scarfing." The law refers to paraphilias as "sexual perversions."

Asphyxiophilia is a paraphilia in which sexuoerotic arousal and attainment of orgasm depend on self-strangulation and asphyxiation up to, but not including, loss of consciousness (Money 1986). Each self-asphyxiating, near-death episode represents a symbolic killing-off of an alter ego (an alternate version of the self as in the dual personality syndrome) in whom exists the corrupting embodiment of lust (Money et al. 1991).

The neurophysiologic mechanism by which sexual arousal is heightened is based on constriction of the neck. This results in interruption of the arterial blood supply to the brain and hence, decreased oxygenation, as well as increased carbon dioxide retention. Both conditions result in altered physiologic states, producing feelings of giddiness, lightheadedness, and exhilaration which heighten the sexual response (Resnik 1983). Similar conditions were observed in deep sea divers who reported giddiness and "highs" due to increased carbon dioxide retention. While transient hypoxia (i.e., decreased oxygen level) heightens sexual arousal, bilateral pressure on the carotid sinuses results in immediate unconsciousness and possibly death.

The four basic methods of inducing asphyxia include (a) neck compression (b) oxygen exclusion (c) airway obstruction, and (d) chest compression. Neck compression is usually accomplished by hanging or strangulation, which causes asphyxia by compression of the neck with a ligature. Hanging differs from strangulation in that hanging requires the weight of the body to pull on a ligature attached to a suspension point, whereas strangulation requires a force other than the weight, or partial weight, of the body to pull on the ligature (Resnik 1983). Compression of the neck causes death by interrupting arterial and venous blood flow and/or compression of carotid baroreceptors,* which result in a fall in heart rate and blood pressure leading to unconsciousness. Approximately 5 kilograms of rope tension is sufficient to cause carotid artery occlusion and rapid loss of consciousness (Polson 1985). Those who practice autoerotic asphyxia attempt to apply slow pressure to the neck. They relax their body weight progressively by manipulating the tension on the neck with ropes tied to the upper and lower extremities. Split-second failure to release the noose or gag at the onset of the orgasm results in death. The autoerotic ritual may be repeated for years before the critical moment is miscalculated and death ensues.

Oxygen exclusion is caused by suffocation or with exclusion of oxygen

*Sensory receptors in the blood vessels which are stimulated by changes in pressure within the vessel.

with gas or chemical replacement. Suffocation results from the exhaustion of a limited supply of oxygen, generally when the head is enclosed in an airtight space, for example, a plastic bag. In such cases, death occurs more slowly, usually requiring two to five minutes from the time the oxygen supply has been exhausted (Polson 1965). The use of chemicals, gases, or anesthetic agents reduces the available oxygen supply and cause unconsciousness in a similar manner. Reports indicate that nitrous oxide or "laughing gas" heightens fantasy formation and giddiness. Freon, isobutane, and amyl and isobutyl nitrite inhalation have also been used to enhance the hypoxic effect during masturbation.

Airway obstruction or choking is rare in autoerotic deaths. Fatal asphyxia develops in three phases: hypoxia and slight cyanosis (turning blue), accumulation of carbon dioxide, and quickening and deepening of respirations; vascular congestion associated with petechiae formation,* labored breathing, and convulsions; and infrequent respirations, complete loss of consciousness, dilated pupils, and death, sometimes associated with terminal vomiting (Simpson & Knight 1985; Taff & Boglioli 1989). Death usually occurs in two to five minutes by inability of the victim to inspire oxygen and expire carbon dioxide. Many factors contribute to the length of time that it takes for mechanical interference with respiration to cause death, including the degree of obstruction and force applied by the assailant or ligature, the age and sex of the victim, struggling, and the effect of drugs and/or alcohol.

Chest compression or traumatic asphyxia is also rare in autoerotic cases. Extrinsic restriction of the chest wall and muscles controlling respiration may produce a slow death in these cases.

A PROFILE OF THE VICTIM

Typically, the victim is an adolescent or young adult male. AEA is seen in all races, in all parts of the world, and at all socioeconomic levels. In 132 autoerotic fatalities reported by Hazelwood et al., the majority of the victims were white males with a mean age of 26.5 years (1983). AEA behavior typically begins during adolescence. Most deaths occur in this age group because the practitioners lack experience. As some participants mature and elicit the assistance of partners in their fantasy, death is often prevented by the other individual. Cases of lethal sexual asphyxia among females are extremely rare and there has been debate over the accuracy of the few cases reported in the literature (Danto 1980; Hazelwood et al. 1983). Seventy percent of the victims were single and 27 percent were married. In a series of 157 autoerotic fatalities only 6.3 percent of the victims had clear evidence of homosexual

*A pinpoint, round, purplish red spot caused by a hemorrhage.

orientation (Hazelwood et al. 1983). Based on the low prevalence of recognized homosexuality among decedents, the authors concluded that autoerotic asphyxia is not disproportionately associated with homosexuality.

DEATH SCENE

It is recommended that investigators at the death scene be aware of the complex and bizarre findings of accidental autoerotic death. One of the findings that death by ligature or hanging was accidental is the position of the body, the presence of protective measures such as padding about the neck, and evidence of an attempt not to leave any telltale marks on the body. Another finding is evidence of sexual activity, usually in the form of masturbation or so-called perversion (transvestism, masochism, or other paraphilic fixation). In addition, there is no evidence of suicidal ideation or intent, whereas, by contrast, evidence of prior episodes of self-strangulation may be retrievable (Boglioli et al. 1991).

Hangings commonly occur in secluded locations, such as the decedent's own room, closet, basement, attic, or motel room in order to conceal the victim's sexual fantasies (Boglioli et al. 1991; Hazelwood et al. 1991). The majority of the victims will have used some type of ligature to suspend themselves by the neck from some point within their reach. Some individuals engage in bondage activities and utilize materials or devices to restrain or humiliate themselves, physically or mentally, for erotic arousal. The presence of hooks and bondage materials, such as ropes, straps, parachute rigging, handcuffs, chains, hoods, leather, rubber, gags, blindfolds, scarves, silk undergarments, pantyhose, wire, and belts, chains, and other elaborate devices for hanging and bondage will be present at the scene. These ligatures are arranged so that compression of the neck may be produced and controlled voluntarily. Knotting and wrapping may be quite complex. These devices might show extensive wear from previous use.

Electricity is also occasionally used for sexual stimulation in a paraphilic ritual of autoerotic bondage (Money et al. 1991). Accidental deaths resulting from electrocution have been reported in the literature during such activities. Electric shock can occur depending on the site of application to the body, skin moisture, and characteristics of the current itself (Hazelwood et al. 1983). Death by electrocution can result from either a cardiac dysrhythmia or asphyxia due to paralysis of respiratory muscles and/or the respiratory center of the brain. The death scene will reveal the presence of electrical devices, wires, cords, and clamps in contact with the subject's genitals, breasts, or anorectum. Small burns from electrocution may be found on the body and hands of the deceased. The electrical devices should be retained and analyzed by a qualified electrician to rule out the possibility of faulty equipment and product liability.

The death scene will often contain extensive women's apparel. In the study by Hazelwood et al., 20.5 percent of male decedents were cross-dressed at the time of death. The women's apparel worn at the time of death, in order of decreasing frequency, included brassieres, panties, stockings, slips, blouses, skirts, pantyhose, women's shoes, garter belts, girdles, sweaters, women's wigs, makeup, and nightgowns. In many cases, the women's clothing belonged to the victim's wife, daughter, or girlfriend. In the male, the wearing of female clothing may symbolize what is self-perceived as the corrupting embodiment of homosexual lust as a concomitant of a partial transposition of gender identity toward transsexuality (Money et al. 1991).

Pornographic literature, videotapes, and VCR equipment are often recovered at the scenes of accidental sexual asphyxias. Sadomasochistic literature portraying individuals engaged in bondage activities may also be present at the scene. It is believed that many, although not all, participants learn about AEA by word of mouth, sex manuals, medical books, pornographic literature, and detective magazines, as well as through the news media (newspapers and/or television) (Brody 1986; Dietz 1989; Dietz & Evans 1982; Dietz et al. 1986; Donnerstein & Malamuth 1983; Goldstein & Kant 1973; Hazelwood et al. 1981; O'Brian 1987; O'Halloran & Lovell 1988; Wade 1984). Alternatively, the idea of AEA is self-generated.

Drugs and/or alcoholic beverages may be present at the scene. Walsh et al. (1977) reviewed twenty-one post-mortem drug screens performed in cases of autoerotic fatalities selected from the Armed Forces Institute of Pathology and found only two significant blood-alcohol concentrations and one toxic level of barbiturates. These drugs should be collected at the scene and saved for comparison with the post-mortem toxicological analysis performed on the body fluids and tissues of the decedent.

Evidence of klismaphilia, in which enemas are the primary source of sexual gratification, may also be present at the scene (Boglioli et al. 1991). This is a rare finding at most AEA fatalities.

AUTOPSY

A complete autopsy should be conducted on the body. Photographs of the decedent, as received, with clothing and scene paraphernalia should be taken. The clothing, beauty aids (e.g., wigs, false eyelashes and fingernails), jewelry, and paraphernalia should be carefully itemized and incorporated into the written autopsy report. Ligatures, rope burns, masochistic activity (such as burns, puncture wounds, and erotic jewelry), and tattoos should also be documented. Trace evidence (e.g., seminal stains, foreign objects, hairs, fibers, lubricants, makeup) should be collected for possible future analysis by the crime laboratory. All of the above evidence should be properly labeled and retained.

A complete external and internal examination should be performed. Careful attention should be paid to the skin for the presence of electrical burns, masochistic-related injuries, and sexually transmissible diseases. Oral, anorectal, and penile swabs and smears should be saved for serological and cytological analysis. The entire digestive tract should be examined for the presence of foreign objects, as well as a ruptured viscus with hemorrhage and/or peritonitis. Specimens of such body fluids and tissues as blood, bile, urine, vitreous humor, brain, liver, lungs, and kidneys, as well as stomach contents, should be collected for a post-mortem drug screen. Alcohol and recreational drugs are occasionally found in body specimens at autopsy. The results of the post-mortem toxicological analysis should be compared with the medicational/recreational drugs recovered at the death scene. A sample of blood should also be collected to test for AIDS (human immunodeficiency virus [HIV] antibody titre [level]). and/or other potentially lethal infections.

PSYCHOLOGICAL AUTOPSY

In order to make the diagnosis of an autoerotic fatality, a psychological autopsy with a behavioral analysis and reconstruction must be conducted in conjunction with the death (Hazelwood et al. 1981, 1982).

The psychological autopsy is a retrospective behavioral analysis consisting of interviews with relatives and significant others in order to obtain information regarding the personality of the deceased, as well as the circumstances surrounding death (Boglioli et al. 1988; Hazelwood et al. 1982; Huffine 1971; Tabachnick et al. 1966). A psychological autopsy is often used to clarify the manner of death in equivocal cases, such as AEA. It is recommended that a reconstruction of the decedent's behavioral pathology be conducted after the autopsy, through individual interviews of relatives and friends, so that a profile can be established. It is important that suicide be ruled out to satisfy both the medical examiner and the family of the deceased.

Usually, there is no apparent indication of suicidal intent and the AEA fatality is a shock for friends and family. The psychological autopsy will help to clarify the state of mind of the decedent shortly before his death. The victim is commonly described as being in good spirits and goal-oriented shortly before death. The victims are also described as being in good physical condition, mentally and physically active, as well as being intelligent and independent. In summary, the psychological autopsy aids the medical examiner investigating the case and often acts as a catharsis for the family.

DEATH CERTIFICATION

Medical examiners are obliged to sign death certificates and render opinions as to the cause and manner of death. The immediate cause of death in these cases should be listed as either sexual asphyxia or autoerotic asphyxia. The use of drugs and/or alcohol can be included as associated conditions contributing to death. The information on the death certificate is public knowledge and thus it is not necessary to describe the details of the circumstances on the document. The medical examiner classifies deaths into five categories: natural, accident, suicide, homicide, or undetermined. The manner of AEA deaths should be classified as accidental because of the circumstances surrounding the deaths and the lack of other factors consistent with either a suicide or a homicide. Therefore, the next of kin are entitled to receive accidental insurance death benefits.

COUNSELING

The bizarre nature of AEA deaths leaves a void in the surviving next of kin that requires medical examiners and other health care professionals to assist the bereaved during the acute grief period (Dusick 1985; Hirsch 1984; Valdes-Dapena 1983). In addition to comforting the next of kin with condolences, it is important for the medical examiner to explain the syndrome of AEA. This requires speaking directly with family members in a private, professional setting. The syndrome must be explained in a clear way that is understandable to lay persons. If necessary, the subject matter should be repeated in two or three different ways because a bereaved individual may be inattentive and distracted. The subject of paraphilias and sexual perversions must be explained in a mature fashion.

It is recommended that the medical examiner not pass judgment about the normalcy or abnormalcy of the victim's behavior. The subject matter can be presented in such a way that the family understands AEA to be a potentially dangerous behavior involving a single person. The issue of conscious pain and suffering should not be raised by the medical examiner unless the family specifically asks. In the event a question about survival time is asked, the counselor should answer truthfully within a reasonable degree of medical certainty. Asphyxial deaths are rapid deaths, usually occurring within a few minutes.

The medical examiner should be prepared to provide the family with literature about AEA, as well as the names of support groups. It should be emphasized that other families have also experienced the shock of AEA deaths. The counselor should explain to the family that the reaction to an AEA death is to be expected. It is not necessary to provide details of the death scene and recovered paraphernalia. It is best to inform the family that the criteria used by medical examiners to diagnose an AEA death were met by the scene findings and autopsy results.

If the family totally rejects the diagnosis of the medical examiner because of denial, another medical examiner should be recommended to the family for an independent review of the case. Therefore, it is imperative that the death scene and autopsy be properly documented with color photographs. The autopsy report should be clearly written and made available to the family and insurance companies in a timely fashion. The medical examiner should avail himself in the event additional questions are raised by the family. The family should never be abandoned during their period of crisis, nor should they feel guilty about the activities of their dearly departed. One should not hesitate to discuss AEA with families. They are likely to be relieved to hear the death was an accident and not a suicide.

PUBLIC HEALTH ROLE OF THE MEDICAL EXAMINER IN AEA DEATHS

The medical examiner holds an unusual position in the medical community in that he has the most experience amongst physicians with AEA deaths. The medical examiner should be prepared to educate his colleagues, as well as the news media, regarding the dangers inherent in AEA activities. The medical examiner should present this sensitive subject to members of the press and the public in the same manner he would discuss the subject with the decedent's next of kin. The best policy is always to be truthful. The most important function of the medical examiner in AEA deaths is to convince others of the dangers inherent in this sexual activity and to prevent them from engaging in such. If the medical examiner can dissuade one other person from experimenting with AEA, he will have succeeded in his role as a practitioner of preventive medicine.

REFERENCES

Auden, G. A. (1927). "An Unusual Form of Suicide." *Journal of Mental Science* 73: 428–30.

Berlin, F. S., and Coyle, G. S. (1981). "Sexual Deviation Syndromes." *Johns Hopkins Medical Journal* 149: 119–25.

Bloch, I. (1935). *Anthropological and Ethnological Studies in the Strangest Sex Acts in Modes of Love of All Races Illustrated.* New York: Falstaff Press.

Boglioli, L. R.; Taff, M. L.; Green, A. S.; Lukash, L. I.; and Lane, R. (1988). "A

Bizarre Case of Vehicular Suicide." *American Journal of Forensic Medicine and Pathology* 9: 169–78.

Boglioli, L. R.; Taff, M. L.; Stephens, P. J.; and Money, J. (1991). "A Case of Autoerotic Asphyxia Associated with Multiplex Paraphilia." *American Journal of Forensic Medicine and Pathology* 12: 64–73.

Brody, J. E. (1984, March 27). " 'Autoerotic Death' of Youths Causes Widening Concern." *The New York Times,* pp. 17, 20.

——— (1986, August 27). "Personal Health—Researchers Say That Sexual Fantasy Is Almost Universal." *The New York Times,* p. C8.

Danto, B. L. (1980). "A Case of Female Autoerotic Death." *American Journal of Forensic Medicine and Pathology* 1: 117–21.

Dietz, P. E. (1989). "Television-Inspired Autoerotic Asphyxiation" (Letter). *Journal of Forensic Science* 34: 528–29.

Dietz, P. E., and Evans, B. (1982). "Pornographic Imagery and Prevalence of Paraphilia." *American Journal of Psychiatry* 139: 1493–95.

Dietz, P. E.; Harry, B.; and Hazelwood, R. R. (1986). "Detective Magazines: Pornography for the Sexual Sadist?" *Journal of Forensic Science* 31: 197–211.

Donnerstein, E., and Malamuth, N. (1983). "Pornography: Its Consequences on the Observer." In L. B. Schlesinger and E. Revitch, eds., *Sexual Dynamics of Anti-Social Behavior,* pp. 41–50. Springfield, Ill.: Charles C Thomas.

Dusick, C. (1985, May 20). "Parents of Sons Hanged During Autoerotic Activity Speak Out." *Sexuality Today* 8: 1.

Ellis, H. (1936). *Studies in the Psychology of Sex.* 4 vols. New York: Random House.

Goldstein, M. J., and Kant, H. S. (1973). *Pornography and Sexual Deviance.* Berkeley, Calif.: University of California Press.

Gonzales, T. A., Vance, M., and Helpern, M. (1940). *Legal Medicine and Toxicology.* New York: D. Appleton-Century.

Hazelwood, R.; Burgess, A.; and Groth, A. (1981). "Death during Dangerous Autoerotic Practice." *Social Science Medicine* 15: 129–33.

Hazelwood, R.; Dietz, P.; and Burgess, A. (1981). "The Investigation of Autoerotic Fatalities." *Journal of Political Science and Administration* 9: 404–411.

——— (1982). "Sexual Fatalities: Behavioral Reconstruction in Equivocal Cases." *Journal of Forensic Sciences* 27: 763–73.

——— (1983). *Autoerotic Fatalities.* Lexington, Mass.: D. C. Heath (Lexington Books).

Hirsch, C. S. (1984). "Talking to the Family after an Autopsy." *Archives of Pathological Laboratory Medicine* 108: 513–14.

Huffine, C. L. (1971). "Equivocal Single-Auto Traffic Fatalities." *Life-Threatening Behavior* 1: 83–95.

Lowery, S. A., and Wetli, C. V. (1982). "Sexual Asphyxia: A Neglected Area of Study." *Deviant Behavior: An Interdisciplinary Journal* 4: 19–39.

Meyer, J. K. (1980). "Paraphilias." In H. I. Kaplan, A. M. Freedman and B. J. Sadock, eds., *Comprehensive Textbook of Psychiatry,* III, vol. 2. Baltimore, Md.: Williams and Wilkins.

Money, J. (1981). "Paraphilias: Phyletic Origins of Erotosexual Dysfunction." *International Journal of Mental Health* 10: 75–109.

Money, J. (1984). "Paraphilias: Phenomenology and Classification." *American Journal of Psychotherapy* 38: 164–79.

——— (1985). *The Destroying Angel: Sex, Fitness and Food in the Legacy of Degeneracy Theory, Graham Crackers, Kellogg's Corn Flakes and American Health History.* Buffalo, N.Y.: Prometheus Books.

——— (1986). *Lovemaps.* New York: Irvington.

——— (1988). *Gay, Straight and In-Between.* New York: Oxford University Press.

Money, J., and Lamacz, M. (1989). *Vandalized Lovemaps.* Buffalo, N.Y.: Prometheus Books.

Money, J.; Wainright, G.; and Hingsburger, D. (1991). *The Breathless Orgasm.* Buffalo, N.Y.: Prometheus Books.

O'Brian, B. (1987). "Auto-Erotic Asphyxiation: Magazine Cleared in Death." *National Law Journal* 9: 8.

O'Halloran, R. L., and Lovell, F. W. (1988). "Autoerotic Asphyxial Death Following Television Broadcast." *Journal of Forensic Science* 33: 1491–92.

Polson, C. J. (1965). *The Essentials of Forensic Medicine.* 2d ed. Oxford, England: Pergamon Press.

——— (1985). "Hanging." In C. J. Polson, D. J. Gee and B. Knight, eds., *The Essentials of Forensic Medicine.* 4th ed., pp. 357–88. Oxford, England: Pergamon Press.

Resnik, H. L. P. (1972). "Eroticized Repetitive Hangings: A Form of Self-Destructive Behavior." *American Journal of Psychotherapy* 26: 4–21.

——— (1983). "Eroticized Repetitive Hangings." In L. B. Schlesinger and E. Revitch, eds., *Sexual Dynamics of Anti-Social Behavior,* pp. 228–45. Springfield, Ill.: Charles C Thomas, Pub.

Rosenblum, S., and Faber, M. M. (1979). "The Adolescent Sexual Asphyxia Syndrome." *Journal of the American Academy of Child Psychiatry* 18: 546–58.

Simpson, K., and Knight, B. (1985). *Forensic Medicine.* 9th ed., pp. 87–106. Baltimore, Md.: Edward Arnold.

Stearns, A. (1953). "Cases of Probable Suicide in Young Persons without Obvious Motivation." *Journal of the Maine Medical Association* 44: 16–26.

Tabachnick, N.; Litman, R. E.; Osman, M.; Jones, W. L.; Cohn, J.; Kaspar, A.; and Moffat, J. (1966). "Comparative Psychiatric Study of Accidental and Suicidal Death." *Archives of General Psychiatry* 14: 60–68.

Taff, M. L., and Boglioli, L. R. (1989). "Strangulation: A Conceptual Approach for Courtroom Presentation." *American Journal of Forensic Medicine and Pathology* 10: 216–20.

Valdes-Dapena, M. A. (1983). "The Post-Autopsy Conference with Parents." In M. Valdes-Dapena and D. S. Huff, eds., *Perinatal Autopsy Manual,* pp. 95–98. Washington, D.C.: Armed Forces Institute of Pathology.

Wade, C. (1984). "Autoerotic Asphyxiation—The Choking Climax." *High Society* 9: 85.

Walsh, F. M.; Stahl III, C. J.; Unger, H. T.; Lilienstern, O. C.; and Stephens III, R. G. (1977). "Autoerotic Asphyxial Deaths: A Medicolegal Analysis of Forty-Three Cases." In C. H. Wecht, ed., *Legal Medicine Annual 1977,* pp. 155–82. New York: Appleton-Century-Crofts.

7

Prostitution

Nancy Lee

INTRODUCTION

Perkins and Bennett (1985: 4) define prostitution as a "business transaction where both parties understand it is a business transaction and see it as a short term contract." In *Ladies of the Night,* Susan Hall quotes one prostitute who puts it quite succinctly:

> Prostitution may not be legal but it is quite legitimate. Business would crumble without it—if businessmen didn't use prostitutes as a means of manipulating, entertaining, increasing sales, and pacifying clients. We consummate deals. We're like a barter system. Our backs are the bridges which link business deals. (1973: 204).

Those "business transactions" are the subject of this chapter, from the social structure of prostitution to the different forms by which it is manifested, constrained, and defined by ever-changing sociopolitical climates and sexual mores. Prostitution and its legal status will also be explored.

PROSTITUTION'S SOCIAL HIERARCHY

A social hierarchy exists in prostitution, with the highest status position given to the call girl and the lowest status given to the "five dollar ho" or the street hooker who is unable to command the going rate for her services. Massage parlors, escort service workers, brothel workers, club dancers, hostesses and road workers fall in between.

Call girls rarely tell of being forced into prostitution; instead, they come of their own volition seeking excitement, glamour, and money. The call girl is the least likely to suffer physical harm or to be arrested, often having a lawyer on retainer. She is also the least likely to become addicted to drugs or to contract a venereal disease. When she does become addicted to drugs, she usually does so after entering the profession, whereas the street prostitute is more likely to be addicted prior to entering prostitution. The call girl is more likely than the street prostitute to seek regular medical care and she is more knowledgeable about detecting signs of disease in her clients.

A call girl who works out of hotels or an escort service is usually better educated and comes from a higher social background than the street worker. Her clients are usually professional persons, business executives or visiting foreigners. Because she often fulfills exotic fantasies for her customers, a service for which she may command $300 to $500 an hour, she rarely sees more than one customer a night, working in the client's hotel room, where she is less likely to be disturbed or arrested (Reynolds & Thomas 1986: 13). The call girl is probably the most businesslike of the various types of prostitutes in her dealings with the client.

"Johns," or customers, usually assume the call girl or escort to be a higher class, more professional sex provider, but many street hookers have also become more sophisticated in their approach to soliciting customers, using pagers and newspaper advertising to contact new and regular customers. This type of call girl is more likely to go to the john's place of business, offering a shorter sexual package, more typical of the type of service she offers on the street, since she realizes that she is more well known to the police, less sophisticated, and out of place in higher class hotels. Local customers or repeat out-of-towners learn which services provide which type of girl and often pass this information along to their cohorts.

Traditional escort services are run by a manager who quotes a specific fee, takes information from the prospective client for verification, and sets a time and place for the date. Once the escort arrives, she will call the manager to confirm her arrival. She will then double check the information the john gave the manager over the phone, checking out driver's license, credit cards, personal questions—anything that will confirm that the john is a legitimate customer and not a police officer. As one undercover officer put it, "it's harder than cashing a check."

If the woman has any suspicions regarding the legitimacy of the john, she will call the manager, state her suspicions and leave. Undercover officers report that soon after the girl has left the room, they may receive a call from the manager asking if the girl left before collecting the required fee. The manager may offer to send a second girl over but rarely does so. Escort service and massage parlor personnel are more vulnerable to arrest than call girls simply because they advertise in the phone book or newspaper, whereas the call girl operation relies more on word of mouth and the customer's desire for anonymity.

Since most states require some type of licensing and training in order to open a massage parlor, men often see them as a type of legal brothel or sex parlor. Parlors fear losing their license and managers are careful to instruct their girls in how to approach customers so they are not seen as soliciting. Because the massage parlor customers often must take responsibility for verbally arranging for extra services, the man who doesn't understand his role in the process often gets exactly what he pays for—a massage.

The number of massage parlors and escort services is growing all across the country, indicating a social need of some type which is not being met by conventional methods. Clients are most likely to be persons with enough money to meet the cost of the service. The client may be a businessman who needs to relieve the stress of everyday business, the college student who wants sexual relief without the stress of having to date or socialize, the elderly man who visits three times a week for conversation and occasional sexual release, or the woman who finds herself without a loving partner because her husband travels or has died.

The female client is a fairly recent phenomenon. She often calls the parlor or service not knowing what to expect. She may be confused when she learns that most services have only females working for them and may therefore simply request a massage or a visit. She does not consider herself bisexual or homosexual. Therefore, she may be reluctant to address her need for sexual pleasure. Once the massage has begun, she realizes that this is strictly a business arrangement and relaxes to the point where she is able to relate to the masseuse as a friend, often asking her to spend the night or accompany her on outings. Because of the increase in the number of women seeking escorts, many services traditionally using females are beginning to add male escorts and masseurs to their staff.

Prostitutes who work as club dancers see themselves as better off than the street prostitute, working inside with a regular schedule, and making their arrangements within the safer environment of the club under the protection of the manager or bouncer. While some go-go dancers or strippers are adamant in their refusal to make sex a part of their jobs, many dancers use their dancing as an advertisement for sexual services.

A more recent phenomenon is the male dancer who performs in clubs or private parties. Like his female counterpart, he is often approached for sexual favors. Many say they are accepting these offers and do not see this as prostitution, but as an extended business arrangement.

THE STREET PROSTITUTE

Street prostitutes are the most visible of all categories of prostitutes. The street prostitute is the one most likely to have entered prostitution because of economic need and few legitimate means of meeting that need. She is most likely to be black, to be addicted to drugs, to have severe medical problems, and to suffer physical abuse during her work. She is also the most likely to be prosecuted and jailed for her activities. She is also the most able to use psychology and to understand human needs. While the call girl, escort, masseuse or dancer has the help of a manager, bouncer, or club owner to weed out the unsavory or abusive trick, the street "ho" has only her intuition. She quickly learns to assess her chances with a john or she doesn't survive on the street.

As in the past, certain areas of the city are considered red light districts, and while there may be harassment from the authorities and residents, the street "ho" can usually work there with some degree of ease. The number of hookers working a certain area or stroll depends on the number of tricks frequenting that area. Where there are more hookers than johns, hookers may become more aggressive in their approach and in their dress. Whereas the public pictures the hooker as the over- (or under-) dressed woman in the short tight skirt or shorts, fishnet stockings, heavy makeup and wild jewelry, the person who fits this description is more likely to be your neighbor's teenage daughter. Instead, most hookers try to dress in a way that helps them blend in with the general population and learn to attract a trick in other ways. Those women who do dress in the stereotypical fashion are working with a pimp, see themselves as a romantic character, or are competing in a buyer's market.

The street hooker follows a pattern for soliciting which is the same almost anywhere you go. While in some areas, prostitutes are highly visible and aggressive in their approach, even soliciting men in front of their wives, most hookers are not so visible; thus it is not unusual for people in an area to admit they have never seen a hooker. The solicitation pattern is one where the woman always stands in the same area during her working hours. She may walk around in order to appear less conspicuous but seldom leaves her general stroll area. Since she depends on her regular customers for the majority of her money and for extra money or help when she needs it, she must remain close to the area where they expect to find her (Freund et al. 1989). Regular customers will search a general area for one or two specific hookers and may leave without having sex if those women are not available. Others, while they may prefer certain women, will choose another woman if their first choice is not around (Freund et al. 1991). In a red light district, car customers will often cruise an area for some time, driving past the same spot several times before stopping. This helps the john assess the availability of certain hookers and the safety factor. Availability is established by direct eye contact, a nod of the head or by stepping closer to the curb. When a woman does not feel safe, is not working for some reason or simply does not want to date a particular john, she will avoid eye contact and walk away. Occasionally a john will get out of his car to pursue an unwilling prostitute or to talk, but this is not common practice since it is not safe.

The one-time john may be a businessman passing through town, a student on a dare, or a man who feels insecure about dating again following a divorce or death of a spouse. The hooker may discourage the younger john from returning as he is more likely to cause trouble or physically harm her. It is the younger client who is more likely to perceive societal expectations of access to a woman's body as a man's right and to become violent when a women has the audacity to demand payment for this right. As Perkins and Bennett (1985) point out, when this happens, the hooker is unlikely to report the violence, feeling that society may well agree with this perceived right and offer her little protection or support.

On the other hand, she encourages the older man to return, offering support, consoling him, listening to him and making him feel cared about. In return, these men are often the ones who help the hooker when she is in financial trouble, or needs money for bail, presents for her children, or medical care.

While the street hooker meets the sexual, psychological and social needs of her clients, her own needs are seldom met. The study of resident street prostitutes in the New Jersey town of Camden showed a small percentage of women with no permanent residence, relying instead on their tricks to provide a place to bathe and rest (Freund et al. 1989). Since they had no mailing address, they were ineligible for social service benefits, and so had no access to medical or dental treatment. Because of their multiple sex partners, prostitutes tend to have a higher rate of cervical and uterine cancer and sexually transmitted diseases. They are also more likely to suffer from malnutrition and tuberculosis, and to miscarry.

While the prostitutes in the Camden study denied using the penal system for access to medical care, observation indicated otherwise. When a woman was ill, she appeared to be less likely to avoid police or bounty hunters, making herself more visible and subject to arrest. However, at the time of the study, overcrowding in the jail led officials to release women with medical problems back onto the street, removing their one access to the system. This was especially tragic for those women who used incarceration for a drug treatment program, since few inpatient drug treatment programs are available to indigent women, especially those with children.

Women who are unable to earn enough to support their addictions have three alternatives: arrest; to become a bag bride (the woman of a dealer or person who can meet her drug needs in return for sex); or to move into a shooting gallery or crack house where she will be given a share of a buyer's drug in return for sex. Shooting galleries and crack houses are generally located in abandoned houses where one room has been set up to accommodate the user. A pallet provides the place for sex in full view of the dealer and other addicts. It is not uncommon for very young children to accompany their mothers to these houses and to observe sex being traded for drugs, thus conditioning them for the future. It is also not unusual for children to witness death from overdoses or violence in these houses, which may thus further rationalize self-destructive behavior in the future.

Simple hygiene is difficult for the street prostitute, even when she has a place to live. Since most street encounters take place in a john's car and since survival depends on the woman being able to have sex with as many johns as possible in a day, she rarely leaves her stroll long enough to go somewhere to shower and clean up. She may try to convince a john to rent a room by offering him a special cut rate, or special acts, so that she can shower and perhaps rest before the next date. Failure to secure a room forces her to use public restrooms in restaurants, hospitals or public buildings for bathing. Many prostitutes are sensitive to the public's impression of them as "dirty, smelly hos."

While the call girl may report no sexually transmitted diseases (STDs) during her career, the street prostitute is subject to many different types of diseases. The Centers for Disease Control (CDC) reported a sharp rise in 1992 of syphilis among women. Syphilis is often a correlate of AIDS, and some reports estimate that 50 to 70 percent of street prostitutes are HIV positive depending on the area in which they work. Street prostitutes are also more inclined to suffer from pelvic inflammatory disease, genital warts, herpes and gonorrhea. Unlike the managed hooker who is usually given instruction in recognizing signs of venereal diseases, the street hooker learns on the street and her discussions of disease and treatment are often filled with folklore and misinformation.

The social service system fails to protect the sex worker, often giving only lip service to educational programs designed to reach the street. Programs whose funding requires them to provide information on AIDS and other STDs may do nothing more than hand out a pamphlet or require their clients to watch a short film with no followup discussion. In addition, most education is directed toward men with blame directed toward women, the prostitute being seen and studied as the person responsible for the spread of STDs. While it is known logically that any receiver of body fluids is at increased risk for infection with the HIV virus, gay and female prostitutes are singled out for their role in the spread of AIDS.

Another system failure occurs insofar as health care agencies responsible for monitoring and treating STDs do not always maintain confidentiality. Clinic workers sometimes pass on messages to hookers or their johns regarding test results, especially if they are STD positive. In some places, names of people positive for STDs are posted prominently in public places.

Even among street prostitutes there is a hierarchy. Where pimp/hooker relationships are the norm in an area, the independent hooker is lower in the social hierarchy. Where the independent hooker is the norm, the pimp managed hooker is not necessarily lower on the social scale but outside the norm. For both groups, the queen, or gay prostitute, is lower than the twenty dollar ho, or woman who charges the going rate for sexual favors, even when the queen or gay charges the same rate. Lowest on the social scale is the "five-dollar ho," designating the hooker who will have sex for a lesser amount of money than the going rate. This is usually the woman who is so heavily addicted that it is difficult for her to earn enough money to support her habit, since she is less attractive to johns either because of personal habits, age, or attitude.

Angel was a 62-year-old participant in the Camden study and an example of a "five-dollar ho." Being a long-time drug user, Angel's physical appearance was less than appealing and her approach was more begging than soliciting. Some of her old customers would give her money but refuse to have sex with her. These donations failed to meet Angel's drug and personal needs, and she was forced to perform oral sex, or "blow jobs," for cigarettes or food when she could find a willing john.

Male prostitutes may be gigolos who date women, homosexual males who date men, male hustlers who date men or women, or drag queens who pass as females and predominantly date men. Male prostitutes observe the same pattern of solicitation as do female prostitutes, using visual signs, body language and dress codes to make themselves known. In a gay area, gay male prostitutes are subject to the same hierarchical structure as female prostitutes; but where they compete with females, they are subject to more harassment and abuse than are females.

Queens are most likely to engage in oral or anal sex in confined places such as cars, allowing them to maintain their disguise as women. Some queens who wish to appear as females often take female hormones, shave their bodies and dress provocatively, sometimes being so successful as to confuse arresting police who bring them to a female unit officer. Some jails isolate queens upon arrest, saying that their presence is a source of potential trouble in the male unit. They are treated differently than jailed female prostitutes, often being ridiculed by prison personnel and straight male prisoners. At the same time queens are often given more freedom to engage in sexual activity with each other and with certain prison staff.

PIMPS AND MADAMS

Most of the straight world believes that behind every prostitute is a controller/manager—a pimp or madam. The pimp is usually pictured as a flamboyant figure who leads girls into drug addiction and then forces them into prostitution. Living off their earnings, the pimp beats the girls into producing even more money to support his insatiable desire for proof of his success. The madam, on the other hand, is often pictured as having a heart of gold, caring for her girls like a mother or a big sister. While there is some historical basis for these stereotypes, the real world of the procurer is something not quite so clear.

Most prostitutes do have someone monitoring their moves and that someone is usually male. He may be her pimp, her "man" or something in between. Eleanor Miller (1986) defines a pimp as the man a woman works for and her "man" as someone she works with. The pimp manages a stable of women. By contrast, the "man" has one woman or else his "bottom woman" and another woman whom they have taken in. His control over them is limited. This is especially true on the street, where the man may be dependent on the woman to earn enough to support his drug habit as well as hers. The pimp flaunts his position, dressing in a flashy manner to stand out in the crowd; the "man," on the other hand, dresses to blend in, in order to give the impression of being in a straight relationship. Pimps are more likely to operate in an area where women come in from other areas: the woman who works in her home town area is more likely to have a "man."

Black men in our society are less likely to be upwardly mobile than either black women or white men. Therefore, many black males from lower socioeconomic groups see their future in professional sports or professional street life. They see prostitution as a profession and the pimp as a professional manager. The successful pimp is seen as a real player, a man of power who puts other people to work for him while he remains a man of leisure. While the use of force to control his female employees is seen as a legitimate form of management and elicits respect from his fellow hustlers, today's pimp is more likely to use psychological coercion rather than brute force. Nevertheless, control is the name of the game and, when he feels a woman deserves it, the pimp is capable of using as much force as necessary to bring her back into line and keep the respect of his other women. The pimp believes that women not only need to be, but want to be, controlled. The pimp becomes a patriarchal power, laying down rules and controlling his "family" (Hall 1972).

Many of the women who have pimps are from good families where they were spoiled children, never making any decisions on their own, being completely taken care of and controlled by the men in their lives. This is especially true of child prostitutes. It is easy for them to allow the pimp to take over this role, controlling their lives, giving them orders and punishing them when they are "bad." As an expression of rebellion, a young white girl may be drawn to the black pimp whom she sees as being mysterious, different—a free and easy soul who, unlike the white men she knows, doesn't care what other people think.

The pimp sees white women as being more controllable than black women, since most white women are socialized to take care of men. Black women will test him to see who can get the better of him, to prove they are street-wise. White women compete for him, rather than with him, cooking or doing domestic jobs that show how much the pimp needs them, or buying him gifts with the allowance he gives them from their earnings (Hall 1972).

The pimp prefers white women for other reasons as well. Black women can earn as much as white women but have less opportunity because the police harass them more often. Statistically, black hookers are more likely to use drugs. The last thing a pimp wants is a whore who is addicted: an addicted hooker is untrustworthy, spending her earnings on her own habit, and is more difficult to control. While he may do drugs himself, he has little interest in a woman who does them. While some pimps have only white women in their stable, other pimps have no problem with black women. However, the more common stable of women is a racially mixed one, since the smart pimp knows that variety is the spice of life and that some men are turned on by having sex with someone who is racially different.

No matter who his girls are, the pimp discourages them from mixing with other women. Part of the psychology he uses is to convince them that because they are with him they are better off than other women, and that they have a man who will take care of them, protect them and make all their decisions for them. The women are made to feel that while they are with him, they will have a place to stay, food to eat, and clothes to wear. They see other hookers scrounging for food and working all night on the street rather than sleeping when business is slow, and their greatest fear is being out there alone and on their own.

Most hookers, knowing that they will not always be able to make money on the street, have fantasies of retirement. The pimp encourages them in their fantasies and assures them that their money is being kept safe for them until they need it. In the beginning they may believe him; but as they gain wisdom, they know it is their money that is being used to create the aura of success with which the pimp surrounds himself (Hall 1974). Although there are variations, the true pimp displays the earnings of his wives flamboyantly. He dresses in custom-made clothes, wears excessive amounts of gold and drives a distinctive car, adding expensive options—not the least of which is a car phone and a CB (Citizen's Band) radio.

In addition to food, medical care and bail money, it is not unusual for a pimp to reward his wives with gifts or vacations when they have made a big score or when the stress of the street has become too much for them. One or all the "wives" may benefit. The successful pimp is cognizant of the stress of working the street. When a woman produces for him on a regular basis, he will see that she gets needed relief so that she in turn will see him as her savior and return to the street even more willing to earn money for him.

The pimp is rarely sexual with a girl from his established stable, basing their relationship on money rather than sex and reducing the potential for jealousy. The girls are rarely jealous of each other since, as one woman put it, "I can't possibly make enough money on my own to support his needs" (Hall 1973). Supporting their man is as important to the hookers as it is to the woman who knows that her ability to make her husband look good to his boss and co-workers is helping him gain status in the corporate world. It is this type of thinking that allows the women to accept a new woman into the group.

"Copping" or bringing a new woman into the group is more difficult when the community fails to show proper respect for the pimp, since part of the copping process is to convince the newcomer that being with him will bring her respect as well. Therefore, the pimp is more likely to look for women in places where he is known as a big player. He searches for a woman who associates with people on the fringes of "the life" and sets out to seduce her into his stable. His other women know to back off during this dating period as the pimp will be spending most of his time with his new woman.

The seduction process is much the same as any man uses in the bar scene. He may buy the woman a drink, dance with her, tell her how special she is and offer to take her to another party or club where she can see how respected he is and how she will be treated as his woman. (It should also be noted here that he may offer her pot or cocaine: most street people and addicts do not consider these to be drugs since they are supposedly not addictive.) The pimp does not immediately talk to the woman about working for him; instead, he treats her like a lover.

Once the newcomer moves in with him, as far as she is concerned, theirs is a straight relationship. She knows that the pimp has other women working for him but sees her relationship with him as being different. While they will not necessarily have sex, the pimp will lavish all his attention on her for a period of time, learning her fears and dreams, and making himself ever more important to her. Eventually, he will suggest to her that his other women love him more since they support him and give him gifts. By this time, the woman's need for the pimp's attention and fear of losing him will work in his favor, so he can "turn her out" to work on the street or in a club or parlor.

On the street, the woman usually works with at least one other wife-in-law for protection since a pimp's wives rarely associate with independent hookers. They maintain contact with the pimp by phone, advising him of police harassment, potential danger, or fear for one of their partners. The adult female is expected to solicit enough customers on her own to cover the pimp's "operating costs." The pimp is only visible when he collects her earnings or bails her out of jail.

The major difference in the pimp's management of adult and child prostitutes lies in the role he plays as procurer. With the child, the pimp must play a more active role, often having a picture portfolio which he uses to actively solicit customers. When the risk becomes too great he may negotiate to place the children in brothels on a rotating basis (Campagna 1988). Placing children in truck stops is also lucrative for the pimp as a child may turn as many as twenty to thirty tricks a night there. However, truck stops require the pimp to remain on site in his car, where he sets up dates by phone and CB radio, thus increasing his risk of arrest.

Even though pimps are reviled in the straight world as men who live off women, in fact, the "sweet" or "good" pimp provides protection for his women, ensures that they have a place to live and food to eat, sees that they get medical care, insists they stay drug-free and practice safe sex, and rewards them with small gifts or trips when they are stressed out.

Whereas pimps flaunt their status on the street, the madam or manager maintains a lower profile. Managers run call girl operations, massage parlors, escort services or brothels; most allow their workers to keep a larger portion of their earnings than a pimp does. A manager of a modeling agency, escort service or massage service may collect a designated fee for service and allow the worker to keep anything she contracts for above that set fee, or the worker may be paid a set wage based on the number of clients she sees in a night.

Most important, however, is the interest the madam or manager takes in her workers. While not all managers treat their workers alike, managers pick their workers carefully. The women who work in parlors may be upper middle class women who find themselves in need of extra money, divorcees, students who need extra money for school, or wives earning money for a new car or the down payment on a house. Because of their position in the community, they are likely to pay attention to the training on how to spot the police, examine for venereal diseases, avoid problems with clients and require regular health exams. Many women start out by adamantly refusing to do anything but a full body massage, which is a massage with a hand release (allowing the man to ejaculate while they massage his genitals).

Some parlors charge a minimum fee for a half hour or full hour total body massage. Once in the room, the client may negotiate for additional activities for which the girl receives a tip. For example, a nude massage with a hand release requires a fifty-dollar tip; a light bondage episode for a half hour may require a hundred-fifty-dollar tip. In some parlors, the girl receives no part of the house fee and the house may or may not receive a percentage of her tip. Other parlors charge a flat fee for a half hour or an hour, with no hidden charges. In this case, the girl will receive a paycheck based on the number of hours she worked or the number of clients she saw during the week. This is also typical of brothels.

Upper-class parlors and escort services are often owned by silent partners who are respected business people in the community. Owners may also act as managers, remaining on the premises during business hours. It is here that you are most likely to see the madam/manager with a heart of gold. In conversations with managers, you may hear them refer to their employees as though they were beloved children or, at the very least, protégées. They encourage the women to set goals and limit the amount of time they will work to reach that goal. They advise them as to investments or brokers, and are concerned about them when they are arrested or found out by their husbands or boyfriends.

TRICKS AND JOHNS

Tricks, also known as johns, are as varied as the reasons for which they date prostitutes. In the Camden study of street prostitutes, Lee (1989) interviewed over one hundred johns and met them again later in social, political and business settings. Some clients she saw in marriage counseling were later found to be regular customers of the prostitutes she had interviewed. Husbands of couples she saw socially were also regulars. Men who were interviewed during the study ranged from politicians, doctors, judges, and social workers to businessmen, factory workers, retirees, and street hustlers. The oldest person interviewed was eighty-two and had someone bring him into town twice a month. The youngest interviewee was a fourteen-year-old street hustler.

In the Camden study, about 50 percent of the men interviewed were married, and the remainder were single, widowed or divorced (Freund et al. 1991). Their reasons for dating hookers were varied: women are there to be used; they don't have time to woo a woman into bed; regular dates are too expensive; they are uncomfortable in social situations; there is the element of danger; they are trying to outsmart the hustler; and nice women don't do what they like. Some johns are always looking for variety, choosing different women each time, going to new areas whenever possible, and always seeking new sexual adventures. A surprising number, however, are committed to one or two particular women, seeking them out, waiting until they return from the previous date—waiting their turn or leaving rather than going with someone they don't know.

While it is easy to understand the sexual adventurer, it is more difficult to understand the long-term client. Prostitutes survive because they are good at what they do, and what they do is to fulfill a man's needs and fantasies. But prostitutes are often puzzled by a man's attraction and devotion to a fellow prostitute whom they find offensive even by street standards. In observing some of these unlikely liaisons, I found such women were expert in assessing a man's emotional needs and meeting those needs consistently.

One woman who was totally disliked by others on the street had several long-term relationships, one of which had lasted eighteen years. One trick had given her a house to live in, another paid her utility bills and still another was always good for a loan; but when she was with a man, she made him feel that he was the only one in her life. She teased, smiled, listened and made him feel important. Like most long-term johns, these men were financially secure and socially inept, e.g., excessively shy and unassertive with women.

Occasionally, there is a true caretaker who takes a woman in, helps her to get medical or dental care, outfits her, and allows her to stay for as long as she wishes with no strings attached. Sex is usually a part of the package, but is not demanded by the caretaker. The caretaker often believes that some day he may save the hooker from the street and make a decent woman of her. Sometimes the hooker will engage in this fantasy with him, but other times she will tell him that she is only there for a short period.

Similar to the long-term john is the man who dates one woman at a time, attempting to establish a quasi-normal relationship with her. This can be a man who sees himself either as a savior of women or as one who would not attract a straight (i.e., "respectable") woman. It is not uncommon for him to work within the system as a corrections officer, prison guard or social worker. This type of john does not see himself as a regular date but as a boyfriend or lover. He may even marry the woman, but usually the relationship does not last long enough for that.

In return for sex, the john may give the woman a place to stay. He may support her drug habit to keep her away from her old friends. He may introduce her selectively to his own friends, so as to simulate a normal relationship. However, once the relationship ends, the john may act in the same way as the pimp or "man" who keeps the woman's clothes and personal articles, and perhaps beats her up before turning her out on the street with no money. This type of relationship is not to be compared with the man/mistress relationship, since there is no true affection between the two, but a love/hate relationship which meets the control issues of both parties.

Johns, even educated ones, are naive regarding the safety and health issues involved in dating a hooker, especially a street worker. Men tend to be unrealistic in their assessment of their ability to control all aspects of a male-female relationship. They do not see themselves in any real danger from a woman. They seldom take into account that a woman may have an accomplice or that she may have a sexually transmitted disease. Men in the Camden study often voiced a belief in their ability to look at a prostitute and tell if she used drugs, was HIV positive, or even if she was dangerous. They also believe that by confining their sexual activities to hand release or oral sex they are completely safe from disease. They are almost totally unaware that diseases such as herpes can be transmitted orally (Freund et al. 1991).

THE PROSTITUTION OF CHILDREN

There are two important differences to be considered when the street prostitute is a child. While most adult street prostitutes are black, the majority of child prostitutes are white (Weisberg 1985: 87) and while most child prostitutes come from a lower socioeconomic or working class background, there has been an increase in children, many of them teenage runaways, from middle-class professional families since the 1960s.

Male youths rarely hook up with a pimp or manager. Instead, a youth becomes either a part of a hustler group, a full-time independent prostitute, or he finds a benefactor who will keep him. For the hustler, selling his body is just one more hustle—a con he is pulling on a willing adult. He rarely calls what he is doing prostitution, nor does he consider himself as one engaging in homosexual activity (although he calls the tricks queers or fags). He sees himself as a heterosexual male who is working a job—no more, no less. This rationalization is agreed to and reinforced within the peer group.

Not all hustlers are males, nor do they all live on the street. In fact, they may be attending school and participating in activities which cover up their sexual behavior. For example, one group of upper-middle-class male hustlers were football players on a high school team, and one member of the group was class president. Approximately twenty boys from this group had regular sexual contact with a local business owner who paid them fifty dollars to perform oral sex on them and a hundred dollars to perform anal sex on him. None of the boys interviewed considered this to be prostitution or homosexual activity; instead, they saw it as taking advantage of a man who was crazy enough to pay you to "get your rocks off." For them, it was an easy way to get money for the prom, new clothes, and drugs. They also stated that none of their parents ever questioned where their money came from.

A young male prostitute, or chicken, is most successful if he is feminine-looking, not muscular, and is sexually skilled. This child usually finds it easy to get a benefactor, at least until he begins to mature or age. The younger the child, the less importance he places on money, sometimes performing oral sex for as little as five dollars. The younger child rarely has any sense of money and, if there are no immediate needs, may have sex with an adult for no money, settling instead for a gift or a movie (Campagna 1988).

Sometimes the very young child, ten to fourteen, may be part of a sex ring. In Camden, N.J., a "chicken ring" of youths nine to twelve years old was recruited and managed by schoolmates fourteen to sixteen years old. The lure was money. In this case, a boy was brought to a pickup site by the procurer, picked up by the john and taken out of the area. Later the boy was brought back to the original pickup site and returned home by the procurer.

Homosexual adolescent prostitutes often see prostitution as a way to make money as well as to socialize with other gay males. While street prostitution is dangerous for all children, it is even more dangerous for the gay youth. Not only must he fear violence from the tricks, or "chicken hawks" as they are known on the street, but he must constantly be on the alert for those who would harass or hurt him because of his homosexuality. Violence is more likely to occur if he engages in solicitation in the rougher leather bar sections of town than if he does his stroll in a "lace" area where he is more likely to encounter middle-aged business men who are married or have not publicly come out as homosexuals.

Should the young prostitute work as a drag queen, the stress and danger are even greater, since he must work to ensure that most tricks do not discover that he is a male. Oral sex is least likely to lead to detection and anal sex is possible if the youth acts as recipient and is in a setting where he is not required to undress completely. "Michelle" performed as a go-go dancer at the age of fifteen at a lawyer's convention in Atlantic City. He and a female dancer were both asked to stay and provide sex for the participants. Although each of them serviced approximately thirty men apiece, none of the men knew that one of the hookers they had hired was a male nor how old he was. Even police are often surprised to find they have arrested a male instead of a female.

A few young males will service female clients, but this usually occurs at hotels where women feel safer and can make the contact through the bell captain or a call service.

As stated earlier, female juvenile prostitutes operate much the same way as do adult females. The major difference is that the girl may join a hustler group for protection rather than work with a pimp, and spend any money earned more quickly. When she does work with a pimp, she may be forced to work in a brothel or at truck stops, constantly being moved from place to place to protect the pimp. Given the option, the teenage girl prefers the street. It offers her more freedom, time to hang out with her friends, and opportunity to flirt in much the same way as her former schoolmates do at the mall.

No matter how much money the young prostitute makes, she is never able to save anything. What her pimp does not take, she gives to her friends, buying a place for them to sleep, copping drugs or taking a day trip to the beach. She is remarkably uninformed about her body and has little information on how to avoid pregnancy, believing, for instance, that urinating immediately after sex prohibits pregnancy or that douching with Coca-Cola acts as a spermicide.

While many young people on the street are runaways, there is another group of children whose parents know that they are soliciting. This group enters prostitution when their parents are approached by someone who proposes to buy or lease the child for a short period of time. The child may be solicited for pornographic sessions or for work in a brothel. Parents accepting such an offer are usually in financial need or are totally self-absorbed. Alternatively, a pimp may deliberately pick a woman with a young daughter, threatening to withdraw from the relationship if she refuses to allow him to pimp her daughter.

Sandi, one of the Camden street prostitutes, had her two children on the street with her. Because of this it was difficult for her to find a place to stay. In her case, a female offered to take her in and to look after the children should Sandi be arrested. In fact, when Sandi was arrested, the woman took Sandi's twelve-year-old daughter, Trina, into local bars and pimped her to the customers. Trina never told her mother what was going on because she loved the attention, the makeup and the sexy clothes. However, one must assume that her mother was aware of the situation, since it was common knowledge on the street and continued even after Sandi was released.

LEGALIZATION

Prostitution is seen as a victimless crime, and is usually treated as a misdemeanor rather than a felony. As courts become overburdened and as sexually transmitted diseases increase, the question of legalization arises. Prostitutes' rights organizations push for decriminalization, which would make prostitution legal, at least in cases involving consensual sex between two adults, with few regulatory or monitoring systems. Professional managers of prostitutes, however, are willing to have legalization despite its bureaucratic limitations because they see benefits for the profession as a whole.

Professional managers from Philadelphia, discussing a crackdown on "legitimate" massage parlors and escort services, argued that their girls were required to stay drug-free, use condoms and maintain high standards of behavior in return for a regular salary, a lawyer on retainer, and fairly secure working conditions. The only real threat came from the police and not the customer. The managers were willing to tolerate municipal intervention and licensing regulations, having no problem with the health requirements for both establishment and worker. They were aware that in poorly run parlors and escort services, the prostitutes may be on drugs, and not practicing sanitary or safe sex.

Many sociologists agree with these managers' assessment that they are providing a vital service to society by allowing clients to act out their fantasies in a regulated environment that relieves clients of the need to act them out publicly. Thus, a teacher has sex with a 23-year-old "child of six"; a doctor acts out his fantasies about his "patients"; a business person relieves the pressure of constantly having to make decisions by being "dominated" a few hours a week; or, an elderly person who needs to be held and made to feel important goes once or twice a month in order to keep on living. With the services of the paid prostitute, a patron may be able to control an impulse to assault someone sexually, and not lose control on the job. The fact that over one hundred bondage and dominance parlors operate in the Camden-Philadelphia area alone indicates that a major social need exists. Scientifically, it is difficult to predict behavior, but not difficult to investigate the crime rate where sex is open and prostitution is legal.

Should prostitution become legalized, this would not necessarily eliminate underground operations dealing in child prostitution or life-threatening activities. In fact, some professionals fear that without a simultaneous effort to meet the needs of the addicted hooker, there could possibly be a dramatic rise in robbery and assault if addicts have fewer options for earning money to support their habits.

CONCLUSION

Prostitution may be the oldest profession but it still remains the least understood. Historically, prostitutes have been revered and reviled, encouraged and punished, reflecting the social values of the times. These mixed attitudes continue to coexist in modern society, reflecting our own confusion about sex in general and women in particular. Prostitution exists as a subculture with its own stratification system, values, socialization process and economic system.

The prostitute coexists with other members within that subsystem as well as with members of the larger society, represented by social service workers, correctional personnel, johns and family members. Failure to understand this subculture can result in a service provider becoming enmeshed in the system and rendered ineffectual.

REFERENCES

Campagna, D., and Poffenberger, D. (1988). *The Sexual Trafficking of Children.* Dover, Mass.: Auburn House.

Diana, L. (1985). *The Prostitute and Her Client.* Springfield, Ill.: Charles C Thomas, Pub.

French, D. (1988). *Working.* New York: E. P. Dutton.

Freund, M.; Lee, N.; and Leonard, T. (1991). "Sexual behavior of Clients with Street Prostitutes in Camden, N.J." *Journal of Sex Research* 28: 579–91.

——— (1989). "Sex Behavior of Resident Street Prostitutes in Camden, N.J." *Journal of Sex Research* 26, no. 4: 460–78.

Goldstein, P. J. (1979). *Prostitution and Drugs.* Lexington, Mass.: Lexington Books.

Hall, S. (1972). *Gentleman of Leisure.* New York: New American Press.

——— (1973). *Ladies of the Night.* New York: Trident Press.

Miller, E. (1986). *Street Women.* Philadelphia: Temple University Press.

Perkins, R., and Bennett, G. (1985). *Being a Prostitute.* Sydney, Australia: George Allen and Unwin Press.

Reynolds, H. (1986). *The Economics of Prostitution.* Springfield, Ill.: Charles C Thomas, Pub.

8

Transsexualism, Sex Reassignment, and the Law*

Louis J. G. Gooren and Frans A. van der Reijt

PSYCHOMEDICAL ASPECTS OF TRANSSEXUALISM

Description of the Syndrome

Transsexualism, the condition of crossing over to live full-time in the role of the other sex, once considered to be a moral or social deviance and outside the realm of medicine, is now classified as a medical disorder. The criteria for its diagnosis are specified in the psychiatric diagnostic classification system of the *Diagnostic and Statistical Manual of Mental Disorders* (*DSM-III-R*) of the American Psychiatric Association (1987). Guidelines for its diagnosis and more particularly for its treatment have been detailed in the standards of care of the Harry Benjamin International Gender Dysphoria Association (Walker et al. 1985).

The term "transexualism" was coined by Cauldwell (spelled by him with one s) in 1949. It was, however, the pioneering work of Harry Benjamin (1966), laid down in his book *The Transsexual Phenomenon* that set the stage for worldwide programs of hormonal and surgical sex reassignment of transsexuals.

The largest scholarly contribution to the field has been made by John Money, director of the Psychohormonal unit of Johns Hopkins Hospital in

*The help of John Money and of Keith Courtney in editing, and of W. Harmsen-Louman and of Jos Megens in the technical preparation of this work is thankfully acknowledged.

Baltimore, Md. In 1955 Money proposed the term "gender role" and subsequently "gender identity/role" (Money 1955). Gender identity is the sameness, unity and persistence of one's individuality as male, female or ambivalent, and is introspective. Gender role is everything that a person says and does to indicate to others and him- or herself the degree that he or she is male or female or ambivalent, and is extrospective. Gender identity and role constitute an inseparable unity. In search of factors that shape one's own perception as being male or female, Money needed a new term: gender identity/role.

The terms "sex" and "sexual identity" as understood in English refer to the *bodily* characteristics of being male or female. These preclude the concept of *sex* as a unified entity. It is now well documented that sexual differentiation, becoming a man or a woman, is a multi-step process. At each stage the differentiating organism is at a bifurcation of male or female development; in other words, at each stage of this process the developing organism must make a decision to develop further along male or female lines.

Each step has its own critical period; there is a window of time in which each specific part of sexual differentiation can take place. Before or past this critical period, the organism is not yet or no longer sensitive to the differentiating stimulus. In other words: there is no back tracking in case of differentiation errors. Money's aim was precisely to identify independently each variable, at every stage of sexual differentiation, as a possible shaping factor in a subject's place in society as boy or girl, man or woman. He needed a term to investigate the degree of adherence to traditional social coding and stereotyping of activities and interests by which people, particularly those who have suffered a mishap in one or more of the stages of sexual differentiation, identified themselves as male or female.

In the vast majority of human beings there is a continuum between the characteristics of their bodily sex and their gender identity/role. Not so in the so-called (pseudo) hermaphrodites, in whom there are contradictions between the components of the sexual differentiation process, namely the chromosomes, gonads and internal/external genitalia. Classic examples are the androgen-insensitivity syndrome and the congenital virilizing adrenal hyperplasia syndrome (Money 1994a, b). In gender dysphoria, of which transsexualism is the extreme degree, there is sexually a contradiction between body and mind.

The phenomenon of transsexualism shows that in human beings the sexological reality of gender identity/role can conflict with that of the chromosomal/gonadal/hormonal/genital sex. Extensive endocrinal investigations have never succeeded in producing convincing evidence for attributing the transsexual condition to prenatal/perinatal or subsequent hormonal abnormalities. It is not presently known through which biological mechanisms the concept and perception of oneself as man, woman or ambivalent is brought about and fixed in adulthood. It is clear, however, that transsexuals cannot be persuaded by the evidence of their anatomical reality to modify their gender identity/role. Dependent on their degree of gender dysphoria they see sexual reassignment of their bodies as the means of easing their dilemma. Transsexualism strikes the layman and the scientist with disbelief.

John Money's major study has been to follow up individuals in whom one or more of the stages of sexual differentiation has been atypical in relation to the others. One of his conclusions has been that the sex of assignment and rearing in cases of (pseudo)hermaphroditism is more accurate than any other variable as a prognosticator of the gender identity/role established by these subjects later in life. The other variables are the nature of the chromosomal sex, gonadal sex, sex hormone levels and genital anatomy. With this information the discrepancy between body and gender identity/role in transsexuals becomes more comprehensible. Money's conclusions have often been misinterpreted to assert that the future gender identity/role of a child with a defective sexual differentiation is determined solely and exclusively by "nonbiological" factors, specifically, the sex of assignment and rearing. In fact his work demonstrates only the predominance of such "nonbiological" factors in relation to the other (likewise significant) factors.

Apart from accomplishing a theoretical framework of gender identity and its disorders, Money's work has been pivotal in devising the clinical approach to sex reassignment. To cite Money:

> No diagnostic test that can be carried out within a hospital clinic or physician's office substitutes for the two-year, real-life test prior to the final and irreversible step of surgical sex-reassignment. This is a difficult test. It requires that the patient become socially, vocationally, economically, and emotionally rehabilitated in the sex of reassignment prior to surgical change of the genital anatomy. During the two-year test, hormonal reassignment is permitted, for its effects can be reversed, even in the most difficult instance of surgically reversing vocal cord masculinization in the female-to-male transsexual.
>
> The two year, real-life test allows both the patient and the physician to monitor from waking to sleeping, week by week and month by month, the experience in the new sex status as he/she habituates his/her responses to other people. Without this test of how other people react, and how he/she reacts to other people, the patient knows only his/her private convictions and fantasies of being a member of the opposite sex.
>
> Convictions and fantasies can be notoriously unreliable. They may include a covert and magical proposition in which the reassignment operation is equated with being born again, fully accommodated, as a member of the new sex, to the gender-dimorphic expectancies and responses of other people. Such accommodation does, however, require time. It should be accomplished prior to the irreversible step of surgery. Sex-reassignment surgery should occupy a place in a person's life that corresponds rehabilitatively to hys-

terectomy in the life of a woman, or prostatectomy in the life of a man. (Money & Ambinder 1978)

The state of the art of medical treatment of transsexuals has been summarized by Money as follows:

> Transsexualism is not a reversible condition, judging by today's therapeutic techniques. Nor is it a progressively deteriorative condition, but it does represent a chronic disability, requiring a patient's life to be rehabilitated. Sex reassignment—social, hormonal, surgical, and legal—is an ameliorative and rehabilitative treatment for transsexualism. It is not a cure. There cannot be a clearly formulated cure for this condition in the absence of a clearly formulated etiology so far not discovered. (Money 1971)

Several studies have evaluated the results of rehabilitative sex reassignment of transsexuals. In spite of the methodological difficulties inherent in the assessment of success, the overall impression is that hormonal and surgical reassignment relieves gender dysphoria and is an important factor in emotional, social, sexual and physical well-being over time (Kuiper et al. 1988; Mate-Kole et al. 1990). Among the factors that contribute to the outcome is the social and legal position in society of reassigned transsexuals.

The Etiology of Transsexualism

Science has not yet advanced to being able to formulate a causal explanation of gender identity and its transposition in transsexualism. Sex steroids or, more precisely, testicular hormones play a decisive role prenatally in the sexual differentiation of the genitalia both in the animal kingdom and in the human species. Since the pioneering work of Steinach in the early twentieth century, evidence has accumulated from animal experimentation that not only the genitalia but also the brain undergo a sexual differentiation. From this animal experimentation it is now firmly established that sex steroids act not only on the prenatal but also on the postnatal central nervous system to permanently alter its function and the behavior it mediates. This action has been termed an organizational effect and it is exerted at a rather circumscribed period of prenatal or early postnatal life.

It is of note that in some species the last step in sexual differentiation, that of the brain, has not been completed at birth.

The inherent tendency of the brain is to develop feminine coital patterns but exposure to androgens (normally occurring in males) induces defeminization (reduction of the capacity to display feminine coital behavior) and masculinization (enhancement of the ability to display masculine coital patterns).

These well-documented mechanisms operative in animal sexology have been extrapolated, sometimes dogmatically, to the development of gender identity/role and sexual orientation in the human. In principle it is doubtful, however, that an animal model of gender identity can be found. By virtue of its definition, assessment of gender identity requires insight into the subjective judgment of one's gender status for which no animal experimental model is available.

The only reliable sources of information on hormonal or other biological influences on human gender identity formation are clinical syndromes in which the hormonal environment of the fetus has been atypical for its sex. Followup studies of such patients have provided evidence for possible effects of prenatal sex steroids on brain lateralization, sexual orientation, and gender role stereotypes. However, a straightforward hormonal (or other biological) effect on gender identity viewed as self-identification as male or female or ambivalent, has been difficult to ascertain up the present time (Gooren 1990).

Sex Differences in Brain Morphology

Over the last few years research on sex differences in the brain has yielded some interesting results. Total brain weight is sexually dimorphic (Swaab et al. 1992) but only the hypothalamus, a small part of the brain area is thought to be the prime substrate of sex differences, in view of its regulatory function in reproductive processes. It has been difficult to establish reliably sex differences in brain morphology, and only as recently as in 1985 was the sex dimorphic nucleus in the preoptic area of the hypothalamus described. The volume and cell number of this nucleus is twice as large in adult men as in adult women (Swaab & Fliers 1985). Another sex difference was reported in 1990 in another very small part of the brain, the "darkly staining posteromedial component of the bed nucleus of the stria terminalis," again larger in volume in men than in women (Allen & Gorski 1990).

So far the brains of only three male-to-female transsexuals have been investigated. In two of them the sex dimorphic nucleus was smaller and in one larger than in control men. A nearby nucleus, also very small, the suprachiasmatic nucleus (which is reportedly larger in homosexual than in heterosexual men) was large in the first two and small in the third one (Swaab et al. 1992). These preliminary results suggest that transsexualism may have a demonstrable brain substrate, but it is clear that much more research is needed before the evidence is conclusive.

Research on development of the sex dimorphic nucleus has provided thought-provocative results with regard to transsexualism. The sex dimorphic nucleus becomes distinguishable in the human fetal brain in mid-pregnancy. At birth the cell number and volume are only around 18 to 20 percent of the values found between two and four years of age postnatally. In the second half of pregnancy and in the first two years of postnatal life there is no significant male/female difference. During the first postnatal years the cell numbers of the sex dimorphic nucleus rapidly increase in both boys and girls up to the age of two to four years. Only at this stage does the sex dimorphic nucleus differentiate according to sex due to a decrease in volume and cell number in females, whereas in males both parameters remain constant (Swaab et al. 1992).

This observation is pertinent to the understanding of transsexualism. It appears from the above that the human brain also undergoes male/female differentiation. This process takes place between the ages of two to four years postnatally. Its determinants have not been established. At that stage there are no significant differences in levels of sex steroids between the sexes.

Transsexualism may turn out to be a form of pseudohermaphroditism involving and limited to the brain. Pseudohermaphroditism is defined as a condition in which the gonads are of one sex but one or more contradictions exist in the other morphologic criteria of sex.

On the basis of the above preliminary findings in the brains of transsexuals, it is no longer hypothetical to suppose that in transsexualism sexual differentiation has followed the course of differentiation prognosticated by the chromosomal pattern up to the development of the external genitalia and that the next step, that of the sexual differentiation of the brain, has followed a cross-sex development.

Sexual differentiation is a developmental process that takes place in distinct steps, each characterized by a bipotentiality to develop along either male or female lines. Clinical syndromes such as the androgen-insensitivity syndrome in males and the congenital adrenal virilizing hyperplasia syndrome in females are paradigms of sexual differentiation that may cross over from a male to a female path of development (or vice versa).

Implications for Transsexualism

Most legal systems abide by the principle of assigning a newborn to the sex that the external genitalia indicate. Generally the law allows that an apparent misjudgment of the nature of the external genitalia can be rectified. In the case of transsexuals it is maintained that no error has been made in assessing sex immediately after birth since in transsexuals the external genitalia are unambiguously male or female. Neuroscience now provides evidence that the sexual differentiation is a stepwise process which has not been completed at birth. Sexual differentiation of the brain does not take place earlier than between the ages of two to four years postnatally. It must be admitted that assignment of the newborn to a sex by the criterion of the appearance of the external genitalia is an expedient practice. Only as few as an estimated 1:12,000 males and 1:30,000 females will experience a contradiction between his/her gender identity/role and the actual genital morphology (Bakker et al. 1993).

Statistically, the external genitalia are excellent, reliable prognosticators of most babies' future gender identity/role. Nonetheless, on the basis of recent neuroanatomical evidence the law must make provisions for those rare individuals in whom the formation of gender identity has not followed the course prognosticated by the external genitalia.

TRANSSEXUALISM AND THE LAW

Law is the body of knowledge which contrives to bring a balanced order within a society. In this context, the discussion frequently arises whether the law, in an attempt to achieve order, finds its norms and values from within its own constructs, or whether they are derived from other domains of human existence or culture. By posing this question to the subject of gender dysphoria one is confronted with the struggle to make sense of rather abstract phenomena. Those who struggle with the legal issues concerning transsexualism find that they move quickly from abstractions to arguments that concern themselves with the basic tenets of the legal system.

Legal Order

The basic question is whether the law is an implementation of the norms and values encountered in the domain of human existence or whether it is a formulation of the norms and values found within its own system, with a ranking or priority deduced from within the system itself.

Obviously, the facts of life that require regulation by the law are found outside of the legal system. However, the precise etiologies of these influences remain a matter of debate. Some religious groups argue that the Mosaic laws as formulated in the Ten Commandments are absolute, unchallengeable norms, with the legal system being derived from these norms. Consequently, the task of the law is to convert these commandments into prescriptions that can be implemented and enforced. In this scenario the law is a subservient science.

One can argue against the acceptance of absolute external imperatives or axioms which transcend and govern the law. No precept, value, or norm can be defended as being absolute or sacrosanct. Turning back to the example of the Ten Commandments, one is confronted with the axiom, "Thou shalt not kill." However, society permits certain groups to carry weapons with the calculated risk and expectation that, under certain conditions, these weapons will be used to kill. These conditions include warfare, law enforcement, and capital punishment.

Rapid progress in the biomedical sciences has further contributed to the relativization of the aforementioned commandments. In an attempt to create order in society, one looks to the law to dictate choices and decisions with regard to controversial issues, such as abortion and euthanasia. A task of the law is to implement principles of justice adapted to the facts of life while not giving way to opportunism or special interest groups.

In attempting to order society, law has evolved into its own unique theoretical paradigm. However, one should not lose sight of the fact that the law is a reflection and interpretation of society, influenced by combinations of products such as science, religion, and prevailing societal values and norms. It is through this dynamic reinterpretation and interaction of society that the law strives to maintain a balanced and measured order in society.

Legal Principles and Transsexualism

With regard to transsexualism, this balanced notion of the law accepts prevailing norms and values and for the most part ignores contributions made by the sciences and medicine. In this instance traditional norms and values would appear to be accepted as absolute, inviolable organizing principles imposed on the legal system. Instead of a closed system that models the life of the individual human being on the preconceived values and norms of a society, a plea is made for a primacy of order that continually struggles to explain and justify its conduct when confronted with the complexity, multiformity, and diversity of human lives by drawing from the full range of society's products.

At stake are the attitudes and dispositions from which legislators and judges perform their duties. How does the legislator arrive at the choices of what he deems necessary to regulate and carry out these regulations? The importance of these basic attitudes with regard to legal implications of transsexualism will become evident from the following five transcripts awaiting legislative and court rulings.

(1) From Mr. van Dis, Proceedings of the Second Chamber of the States General of the Netherlands, September 4, 1984, p. 5797:

> It is an inalienable part of our confession that man is created whole and perfect. The Gallic and Belgian creeds state: "and God said, 'Man is made in Our own image, in Our own likeness." In Genesis it states: "And God created man in His own likeness, in the image of God He created him, man and woman created He them."

Comment: These citations from Scripture imply that legislation offering the transsexual a procedure to change his or her sex is improper and condemnable.

The dichotomy of the sexes is God's immutable creation to which men, women, and their legislatures are completely subordinate.

(2) From the second statement issued by the Supreme Court of the Netherlands, January 3, 1975:

> . . . that the legislator, in pronouncing the sex of the child, has taken no other facts into consideration other than the external sex characteristics of the newborn; that in drawing up the certificate of birth of the child the sex of the child could and will be registered not other than faithful to the above considerations; that apparently the Supreme Court takes this position but subsequently expresses the view that the registration of the birth certificate on the criterion of the external sex characteristics must be considered an error if, in the opinion of experts in this area, the adult, according to other constitutional characteristics not discernible at the moment of birth, but stemming from the mental development of the child starting prior to birth, already at the time of birth must have been, at least in part, a member of the opposite sex.
>
> This position finds no legal ground in the law as it offers no point of departure for the determination of the sex to be registered on the birth certificate. The proposal has been made that the assignment at birth be made in accordance with the externally perceived genitalia. However, should this designation be disputed at a later time by an expert in the field, a judge has the right to change a person's designation, retroactive to the time of birth. In the opinion of the Supreme Court this practice would damage the legal security which the registers of civil registration intend to provide, particularly with regard to the legal evidential value of the birth certificate in relation to a person. Only the legislator has the legal power to enact a modification of the certificate of civil registration. This modification is not retroactive.

Comment: In this instance the Supreme Court attempts to recognize the primacy of the law as a principle of order. However, the Supreme Court would appear either to be oblivious of or to doubt recent scientific evidence regarding transsexuals.

(3) From the Civil Courts of Mechelen, Belgium, June 17, 1975:

> Determination of the sex should come not only from the assertion of the external sex characteristics, but that other characteristics be considered, including psychological, hormonal and genetic influences. Currently, the law refers only to the externally apparent characteristics of the sex. With the present state of legislation an artificial medical intervention cannot be grounds to legally change a person's sex.

Comment: The judge appears to express no doubts regarding scientific evidence. He states, more clearly than the Supreme Court of the Netherlands, that the existing laws provide no solution for transsexuals regarding change in sex status. By phrasing sex reassignment as an "artificial medical intervention" he finds an excuse for the present legislation not to offer a solution to the sex status of transsexuals.

(4) From the Court of Antwerp, Belgium, October 27, 1987:

> In consideration of the fact that the determination of the sex at birth was certain and correct; that the sex has later changed as a consequence of the disorder of transsexualism, which is outside the domain of the free will of the person involved; that the status of transsexualism has as a consequence the existence of a discrepancy between the legal sex and the perceived sex status of that person in the same vein as an ambiguous sexual differentiation at the time of birth; that the proper legal remedy for this problem cannot be the same; that the amendment of the birth certificate cannot be permitted in view of the fact that the present sexual status was not in existence at the time of birth; that an alteration of the "ex tunc" (on the basis of the facts at the time of birth) in such cases would be unacceptable; in view of the fact that the applicant has been married and a child has been born of the marriage; that the fatherhood of the child is certain; that, in the given circumstances, a legal claim to change one's sexual status is the only way out of the problem; in consideration that the claim to change of legal sex has not been regulated by the present laws; that such a claim is not prohibited by any legal rule; that the immutability of sex cannot be postulated if it is assumed that such action constitutes a violation of Article 8 of the European Charter of Human Rights each time a subject is forced to maintain a legal sexual status that no longer corresponds with his or her factual sexual status; in consideration that it is not only in the interest of the applicant but also in the interest of societal order in view of the social role that the applicant fulfills and constitutes a justification of the request for legal alteration of the sexual status; that the applicant functions as a female and is recognized from this point in time on as a member of the female sex "ex nunc" (on the basis of the present situation) must be granted which can be enacted by a legal claim of a change of sex.

Comment: In this case the judge makes creative use of the existing law. In making use of the "factual situation" to bring order to society he finds a legal solution for what previously seemed to be an insurmountable dilemma between the factual situation and the legal situation.

(5) From the dissenting opinion of Judge Martens in the case of Miss Cossey for the European Council of Human Rights in Strasbourg, France, September 1990:

> Sexual identity is not only a fundamental aspect of everyone's personality but, through the ubiquity of the sexual dichotomy, also an important societal fact. For postoperative transsexuals sexual identity has, understandably, a very special and sensitive importance because they acquired theirs deliberately, at high cost in mental and bodily suffering. To be condemned to live, as far as that identity is concerned, in opposition to and thus "outlawed" by their country's legal system must therefore cause permanent and acute personal distress to post-operative transsexuals. . . .

Comment: This opinion exposes a true assessment of the factual situation of the post-operative transsexual. As well, it also exposes the legal system which outlaws the factual situation of the transsexual.

These five citations serve to shed light on the philosophical and abstract natures of the thema. They display, in decreasing order, an observance of the absolute, external norm for the orderly regulation of society.

The first quotation of the parliamentarian van Dis demonstrates a refusal to change any law that would subsequently conflict with an external religious prescript. The Supreme Court of the Netherlands declares a "non possumus" (we are not able to do so) in abidance with the law, while at the same time being somewhat diffident regarding the scientific evidence of transsexualism. The Court of Mechelen, being more aware of the reality of transsexualism, states that there is no legal room for enacting a change of legal sex. The Court of Antwerp finds a solution on the basis of a broader application of the legal rights of persons. Finally, Judge Martens, who views sexual dichotomy not as a God-given norm of creation, declares it to be subject to the sexual identity that an individual citizen experiences and socially expresses. He arrives at the conclusion that the national state cannot neglect to provide a legal regulation.

It is evident that the last two judges do not subscribe to the ideas and concepts of law expressed by the first religious fundamentalist parliamentarian. They apply relativism to the law as a regulating principle. This relativism was so well apparent in the rulings of the Supreme Court of the Netherlands and the Court of Mechelen. If one rejects an absolute external norm as an imperative for the legislator, it follows that the law also will constitute a less absolute norm. The law will be viewed as a product of the present time, with ideas, insights and developments requiring adaptation and alteration in view of new facts of life. This results in a creative use and interpretation of the law as seen in the court ruling of Antwerp and several United States courts.

In conclusion, the less dogmatic, less fundamentalist approach a judge has to the law, the more adaptive and accommodating the law will be for a subject like transsexualism.

In Europe there are two legal traditions, Continental and Anglo-Saxon. The Continental tradition emphasizes statutory regulation and must find a solution for transsexuals in a change of the law. The other prevailing tradition, Anglo-Saxon, provides more room for the judge to interpret the law, thus providing a greater emphasis on case law. Concordance between the two systems is problematical for European unity on transsexuals' rights.

Judge Martens and other judges who supported his dissenting opinion in the *Cossey* case are motivated by developments in society with regard to transsexualism. A "supranational" European court has been instituted to protect fundamental human rights and to view social developments as the determining criterion for questions concerning whether certain laws must be observed and protected. This court no longer considers religion or "pseudoscience" as a determining criterion. This ideology supports the view that the law, to a high degree, formulates its own legal orders and priorities.

The best legal solution for the problem of transsexualism is to accept that human beings have a fundamental right to self-realization and that "pseudonorms" and irrational inhibitions should not interfere with these decisions. With this approach most legal systems will be able to produce a solution for transsexuals that does justice to them in the same way that justice is provided to citizens in whom this condition does not occur. This can be achieved either by an adjustment of the existing laws or by a creative interpretation of the prevailing juridical system. This approach to the issue of transsexualism would also result in the application of relativistic thinking to other "sacred cows" in the legislation that affects other groups in society. There are many articles in the law in the areas of marriage and lineage that are redundant and discriminatory. For example, there is no fundamental legal argument that rationalizes treating a homosexual relationship differently than a heterosexual relationship, or a transsexual relationship differently than a nontranssexual one.

A similar argument can be used with regard to adoption and paternal lineage. Biological parentage can now be established with an almost 100 percent certainty, yet the law currently accepts an oral statement regarding lineage. Legal and biological parentage are not required to coincide to be legally acceptable.

The Problems of the Various Legal Systems

Limiting legal regulations to issues that are absolutely necessary to secure the equality of citizens may provide solutions for legal systems with seemingly immutable arguments to maintain certain legal inequalities.

The administration of the law in the United Kingdom is not favorable to the case of transsexuals. In an attempt to be pragmatic it states that the birth certificate constitutes an historical document, mentioning solely historical facts. As the reasoning goes, historical facts are immutable, no matter how badly this may suit the case of the transsexual.

It is beyond the scope of this paper to fully examine the precise differences between the English and the European Continental concepts with regard to the function of the birth certificate in the registration of a citizen's civil identity. The major distinction is that in the Continental legal system the birth certificate functions as the basic document for civil registration, being instrumental to conscription, registration of voters or matrimonial competence. However, a strictly systematic civil registration is nonexistent in most Anglo-Saxon countries.

Recognition of this fundamental difference in the significance and legal power of the birth certificate between countries such as France and the United Kingdom has given rise to differing opinions in the European Court for Human Rights in Strasbourg, France, with regard to complaints of citizens that their states refused to change their legal sex status or refused to change the pertaining law to enable such a change. Indeed, the difference in legal systems of the two countries has been the deciding factor in the different judgments of the Court for the same question. It is morally questionable whether such recognition of the two legal systems must lead to a granting of rights to transsexuals in one country, France, and the denial of such rights in another country, the United Kingdom. In any case it does not do justice to the case of transsexualism as a fact of life. This fact of life is the following: "the applicant has already submitted that the disclosure of his birth certificate and his sexual identity before surgery, and the embarrassment that such a disclosure causes, is only part of his complaint under Article 8 of the European Charter of Human Rights. At the heart of the complaint is the very issue of the non-recognition of the identity itself" (note 15 of the dissenting opinion of Judge Martens in the *Cossey* case). Phrased differently, the English law may pretend that it considers a birth certificate as a purely historical document, whose content has to be respected, but it is an unacceptable fact for the transsexual that it contains a description of a sexual identity which is not experienced by the person involved. It is further of note, as outlined in the introduction, that the sex of the birth certificate is determined by the nature of the external genitalia, which is only one of five criteria of biological sex in the human. To claim that the sex at the time of birth can satisfactorily be determined solely on the criterion of the external genitalia is obsolete and blind to developments and insights in the biological sciences with regard to sexual differentiation.

A Possible Solution

Most people feel that in daily life there are two sexes and that they are biologically different. The question forces itself whether, from the viewpoint of social order, it is necessary that the law recognize the difference. In other words, is there a legal necessity to register newborns as either male or female on their birth certificate? It goes without saying that in certain areas of life the sex of the citizen is relevant, but one can seriously question the exigency that, at the level of the birth certificate, the sex of the newborn is to be mentioned.

If one takes this position, it implies that one believes that legislation or civil registration are not ends in themselves but solely serve to bring order to the domains of society where it is needed for proper functioning. On the basis of this premise there is no necessity to register the sex of the newborn in the birth certificate. No mention of the sex in the birth certificate would provide a solution for the problem transsexuals encounter in their relations with the state.

The position of the legislator of the United Kingdom that a birth certificate is a historical, unchangeable, inexorable document may be convincing at first sight, if one postulates the unchangeableness of an official document on the grounds that an alteration would mean a falsification of historical facts. There are a number of data that are irrefutable and incontestable. These include the place and time of birth and the woman from whom the child is born. If the woman is married, then the assumption is made that her husband is the father of the child unless this is contested. Finally, the sex of the child is mentioned. It is of note that it is not the external sex characteristics that are mentioned but the assigned sex. The latter is an act of faith and, in the vast majority, an appropriately expedient practice. The sexual differentiation of the brain has still to occur and one has to wait to see what gender identity the child will develop. This information on gender identity development hinges on self-reflection and is of a different order than the objective data mentioned in the certificate. In other words, it is arguable whether a birth certificate can be viewed as an historical document that contains incontestable facts. It would call for evidence stronger than that on which the document is based if it is contended that the birth certificate is a historical document of which no mutation can be tolerated. With regard to the United Kingdom, it would be recommendable not to mention the sex in the birth certificate. Assignment to one sex or the other at birth is a fallible practice and it does not serve any purpose in present-day society.

Legally speaking, no true arguments can be found as to why sex should be mentioned in the birth certificate. The registration of sex is pertinent only when such a document lies at the basis of other legal documents, e.g., conscription or a marriage license, as is the case in most of the countries of continental Europe. Notably, several of those countries have made provisions for transsexuals to change their legal sex status. Given this, it would appear that the absence of the mention of the sex on the birth certificate does not produce insurmountable difficulties with regard to social order.

The nonmention of sex on the birth certificate does not mean that there are no domains of life where sex is a relevant item. These domains may for their own purpose define sex (e.g., hospital wards, military barracks, or sports). However, there is no true necessity that sex for those domains be derived from the birth certificate. In other words, the birth certificate can remain a workable document without mention of sex.

Inventory of the Present State of Legal Sex of Transsexuals

The Council of Europe met on this subject on April 14–16, 1993, in Amsterdam and the outcome of this conference will be influential in the member states. Several European countries, Sweden (1975), Germany (1980), Italy (1982), the Netherlands (1985), and Turkey (1988), have made provisions for the change of sex. Switzerland has a long history of law of precedent dating back to a case in 1931. Austria, Norway and Denmark have found administrative solutions to the problem. (For review see: Will 1992). A similar situation prevails in Spain (Cantero 1991). The European Court ordered France (decision of March 25, 1992) to show due respect for the privacy of its subjects, implying that the legal sexual status of a subject must be in concordance with his or her social sex role. On the basis of this ruling it can be expected that France, Belgium and Luxembourg will find solutions to this issue. Portugal and Greece have laws of precedent enabling a legal sex change. It is not known whether it has indeed occurred. In Poland a similar solution has been found, but most lawyers would favor a change of law instead of having to rely on the law of precedent.

With regard to the United Kingdom and Ireland, it is questionable whether the European Court will any longer accept their position that the birth certificate is a historical, unchangeable document. In the opinion of the Court, a dominant social common consent with regard to human rights has to be respected by the member states and overrules the discretionary competence of single member states. In the rest of the world, Australia (Otlowski 1990) and Quebec, Canada (Rivet 1987), have made provisions. The situation in the United States of America is not fully clear since this issue has no federal competence. Individual states have found solutions sometimes on the basis of antidiscrimination laws. It can be expected that some states will follow the reasoning of the United Kingdom. Of the Far East little factual information is available, but it seems that solutions are created. South Africa has a liberal stand on the problem. Central and South America, for the most part, do not. India has long given a traditional societal status, part caste and part religious, to its sex-changing *hijras.*

In conclusion, legal systems defined sex in a period of history when insight into the sexual differentiation process was limited. According to the time-honored criterion that the external sex characteristics should be in conformity with the self-experienced gender identity, medical technique has been applied to adapt the bodily sex to the self-experienced gender identity. Problems as to the legal sex status of the individual in such cases have arisen (Bailey-Harris 1989; Hurley 1984; Richardson 1983). Several law systems have found solutions for this problem (Bradley 1991). Others adhere to the definition of sex by the criterion of the external genitalia. The latter position can no longer be defended in view of modern insights into the sexual differentiation which is not complete at the time of birth but is an ongoing process as far as the sexual differentiation of the brain is concerned.

REFERENCES

Allen, L. S. and Gorski, R. A. (1990). "Sex Differences in the Bed Nucleus of the Stria Terminalis of the Human Brain." *Journal of Comparative Neurology* 302: 697–706.

American Psychiatric Association (1987). *Diagnostic and Statistical Manual and Mental Disorders,* 3d ed., rev. Washington D.C.: American Psychiatric Association.

Bailey-Harris, R. (1989). "Sex Change in the Criminal Law and Beyond." *Criminal Law Journal* 13: 353ff.

Bakker, A.; Van Kesteren, P. J. M.; Gooren, L. J. G.; and Bezemer, P. D. (1993). "The Prevalence of Transsexualism in the Netherlands." *Acta Psychiatrica Scandinavica* 87: 237–38.

Benjamin, H. (1966). *The Transsexual Phenomenon.* New York: Julian Press.

Bradley, D. (1991). "Transsexualism and Legal Policy." *Gender Dysphoria* 1: 25–40.

Cantero, G. G. (1991). "Spain: Sex Change and the Courts." *Journal of Family Law* 29: 425–29.

Cauldwell, D. O. (1949). "Psychopathia Transexualis." *Sexology* 16: 274–80.

Gooren, L. J. G. (1990). "The Endocrinology of Transsexualism. A Review and a Commentary." *Psychoneuroendocrinology* 15: 3–14.

Hurley, R. (1984). "Constitutional Implications of Sex-Change Operations: Mind over Matter?" *Journal of Legal Medicine* 5: 633–64.

Kuiper, A. J., and Cohen-Kettenis, P. (1988). "Sex Reassignment Surgery: A Study of 141 Dutch Transsexuals." *Archives of Sexual Behavior* 17: 439–57.

Mate-Kole, C.; Freschi; M. and Robin, A. (1990). "A Controlled Study of Psychological and Social Change after Surgical Gender Reassignment in Selected Male Transsexuals." *British Journal of Psychiatry* 157: 261–64.

Money, J. (1955). "Hermaphroditism, Gender and Precocity in Hyperadrenocorticism: Psychologic Findings." *Bulletin of Johns Hopkins Hospital* 96: 253–64.

——— (1971). "Transsexualism and the Philosophy of Healing." *Journal of the American Psychosomatic and Dental Medicine* 18: 25–26.

——— (1994a). "Hormones, Hormonal Anomalies, and Psychologic Healthcare." In M S. Kappy, R. M. Blizzard, and C. J. Migeon, eds. *Wilkins: The Diagnosis and Treatment of Endocrine Disorders in Childhood and Adolescence.* 4th ed. Springfield, Ill.: Charles C Thomas, Pub.

——— (1994b). *Sex Errors of the Body and Related Syndromes: A Guide to Counseling Children, Adolescents, and Their Families.* 2d ed. Baltimore, Md.: Paul H. Brookes.

Money, J., and Ambinder, R. (1978). "Two-Year, Real-Life Diagnostic Test: Rehabilitation versus Cure." In J. P. Brady and H. K. H. Brodie, eds., *Controversy in Psychiatry.* Philadelphia: Saunders.

Otlowski, M. (1990). "The Legal Status of Sexually Reassigned Transsexual: R. v. Harris and McGuinness and Beyond." *The Australian Law Journal* 64: 67–74.

Pfäfflin, F., and Junge, A. (1992). "Nachuntersuchungen nach Geschlechtsumwandlung. Eine kommentierte Literaturübersicht 1961–1991. (Followup Studies on Sex-Reassignment. A Literature Survey and a Commentary 1961–1991)." In F. F. Pfäfflin and A. Junge, eds., *Geschlechtsumwandlung.* Stuttgart: Schattauer.

Richardson, L. (1983). "The Challenge of Transsexuality: Legal Responses to an Assertion of Rights." *Northern Illinois University Law Review* 4, no. 1: 119–52.

Rivet, M. (1987). "La verité et le status de la personne en droit québécois." *Revue Générale de Droit* 18: 843–68.

Swaab, D. F., and Fliers, E. (1985). "A Sexually Dimorphic Nucleus in the Human Brain." *Science* 228: 1112–14.

Swaab, D. F.; Gooren, L. J. G.; and Hofman, M. A. (1992). "The Human Hypothalamus in Relation to Gender and Sexual Orientation." *Progress in Brain Research* 93: 141–48.

Walker, P. A.; Berger, J. C.; Green, R.; Laub, D. R.; Reynolds, C. L.; and Wollman, L. (1985). "Standards of Care: The Hormonal and Surgical Sex Reassignment of Gender Dysphoria Persons." *Archives of Sexual Behavior* 14: 79–90.

Will, M. R. (1992). "Ein Leiden reit Recht." Zur Namens-und Geslechtsänderung bei transsexuellen Menschen in Europa. ("Suffering from the Law." On the Change of Name and Sex of Transsexuals in Europe). In F. F. Pfäfflin and A. Junge, eds., *Geschlechtsumwandlung,* pp 113–47. Stuttgart: Schattauer.

9

Sexual Harassment in the Workplace and in Psychotherapeutic Relationships*

Herman Musaph

SEXUAL HARASSMENT IN THE WORKPLACE

Definition

The American Psychological Association has defined sexual harassment (SH) as deliberate or repeated comments, gestures, or physical contacts of a sexual nature that are unwanted by the recipient. This definition, however, gives no insight into the spectrum of SH.

Variations in Sexual Harassment

The many forms of SH can be divided into two categories (Divasto et al. 1984): invasive (fondling, attempted rape, and rape) and noninvasive (offensive disrespect, obscene telephone calls, exposure, and peeping). Noninvasive SH

---

*Editor's Note: It is with regret that we note the passing of Herman Musaph in November 1992, before his manuscript could be completed. We have chosen to publish this last work of Dr. Musaph posthumously, in honor of a career dedicated to sexology and human welfare. Typically, writing in a nonnative language generates questions about intent and language usage. Unfortunately, prior to his death, the editing process by which Dr. Musaph would have clarified these issues had not been completed. Consequently the reader is left with some possible ambiguities. Nevertheless, the chapter provides needed insight, partly professional, partly cultural, on a topic about which there remains a paucity of rational debate.

is usually committed by strangers while invasive SH is usually engaged in by friends, acquaintances, or relatives. SH can also be divided into physical and nonphysical in form.

This chapter will only describe SH in the workplace and in therapeutic relationships. In her book, *Sex and the Workplace,* Barbara Gutek (1985) reported the survey results obtained from 872 women and 405 men aged eighteen and older and employed outside of the home for twenty hours a week or more. The survey asked participants to identify whether certain forms of conduct constituted sexual harassment. The results are presented in Table 1 below.

Table 1
What Is Sexual Harassment?

	Males	*Females*
Complimentary comments	21.9%	33.5%
Insulting comments	70.3%	85.5%
Complimentary looks, gestures	18.9%	28.9%
Insulting looks, gestures	61.6%	80.3%
Non-sexual touching	6.6%	7.3%
Sexual touching	58.6%	84.3%
Expected socializing	91.1%	95.8%
Expected sexual activity	94.5%	98.0%

Source: B. A Gutek (1985). *Sex and the Workplace.* San Francisco: Jossey-Bass.

It is obvious that one can speak of SH only when the recipient of the act experiences it as such. It is easy to imagine that a perpetrator could be unpleasantly surprised to hear of an accusation based on differential attributions of the same behavior. Furthermore, it is possible that both partners accept the behavior, but that others in the surroundings, either in the workplace or at home, experience this behavior as SH and therefore demand legal action. Table 1 shows a large difference in the evaluation of behavior with respect to SH by males and females. More must be known about the situation and the victim's attitude toward eroticism and sexual behavior before an objective judgment can be reached. To some, including this author, the criteria can be nothing but subjective, with the result that judgments are situationally and dispositionally determined (Storms 1973).

Pryor (1988) recognized consistency, distinctiveness, and consensus as aspects of SH. The perpetrator could make sexual overtures toward a target consistently over time; he/she could also make similar overtures to different targets (low distinctiveness) or to targets toward whom other perpetrators did not behave similarly (low consensus). Such behavior is viewed by Pryor as SH.

Powell (1986) found in her research on 249 undergraduate students (57 percent male, 94 percent single, 97 percent business majors) that women perceived SH more often than men did. Subjects high on a scale of femininity perceived SH more readily than those rated low in femininity. The lone significant univariate test for the interaction found that masculinity had a negative association with behavior considered SH by men versus a positive association by women. The difference was, however, only 8 percent.

Incidence

There have been various research studies conducted on the occurrence of SH in different settings. Gutek's research (1985) has shown that one really cannot speak of typical groups of people where the risk factor for SH is higher or lower. SH in the workplace is a commonly occurring phenomenon that hardly differs in incidence based on the sociological stratification. The opinion that SH has to do with a shortcoming in one's innate refinement and thus occurs more in the lower classes is a very persistent prejudice.

Another extensive study was conducted on the federal workforce in the United States (Powell 1986). These researchers found that 42 percent of all female employees and 15 percent of all male employees reported having been harassed in the previous twenty-four months.

Stereotypes

In the Western Hemisphere, certain stereotypes play an important role in the preconceptions of SH. Most of these stereotypes are used by men to place the blame for SH on the female victim. A few examples follow:

1. Any woman who shows her legs by wearing short skirts or who is dressed in a sexually provocative manner is asking for sexual contact or intercourse.

2. Any woman who walks alone on the streets at night is asking for sexual contact or is a woman of easy virtue.

3. Any woman who, after a date, asks her partner to join her for a cup of coffee in her room, is asking for sexual contact.

4. Any woman who greets male visitors while wearing night apparel is also asking for sexual contact.

Another stereotype is that SH is practiced only by males and that only women are victims. Gutek's research (1985), including only American data, states that 37.3 percent of males and 53.1 percent of females reported experiencing at least one social-sexual behavior they considered SH during their working life.

One of the most common responses of women to SH is simply "doing nothing" (Murnen et al. 1989). This response may be interpreted as indicating consent or approval of the action, thus promoting its continuation. The most common argument used by men to pardon their SH behavior is that they were seduced by the woman's "hungry looks," body exhibition, or voice. Following this way of thinking, the man would thus please the woman by approaching her in a sexual manner. Her "no," in such circumstances, always means "yes." If this were true, the term "unwanted" in the definition of SH would have no meaning, with the consequence being that the woman would be treated as a sex object without volition. This manner of thinking belongs to a patriarchal culture where the balance of power lies in favor of the male, and is diametrically opposed to the concept of body ownership (Krivacska 1990).

Transcultural Problems

SH is also seen in societies transculturally. The uninvited active sexual approach by a man will have a different meaning in a patriarchally structured society than in a matriarchal one or in a Western society where there is greater equality between the sexes. One clear example derives from the anthropological research conducted in rural Turkey by de Jong (1991). He found families that live within a patrilineage where authority and power lie with the man. Marriages were endogamously arranged and virilocation frequently occurred; i.e., the newlyweds resided in the village where the groom lived before the marriage. Such behavior is also true of the Arabian Moroccans and the Berbers of the Atlas Range in North Africa. For these people, the male is the person of authority; he determines the sexual behavior within the community.

An example of matrifocal behavior is found among the city Creole of Suriname. The mother is the head of the family and also the person of authority. She usually has many children from different men with whom she has successive sexual relationships. There exists, therefore, a matrifocal concubinage. Her sexual behavior and that of her children is mainly determined by women—mother and grandmother. It must be clear, therefore, that men and women from a matrilineal culture will react differently to SH in the workplace than will men and women from a patrilineal cultural background.

When judging the SH committed in the workplace by men or women immigrants to Europe from other cultural backgrounds, one should keep in mind the degree of adaptation and assimilation the perpetrator has achieved within the European cultural pattern in which the SH has occurred.

Antisexual Attitude as a Side Effect of Feminism: Pleasure Contaminated by Sexism

The sexual revolution in America in the 1960s has contributed greatly to the emancipation of women both within and beyond American society. As in every emancipation movement, unintended adverse side effects have arisen, among them the devaluation of sexual feelings.

Feminism has rightly denounced the power situation favoring men. However, some feminists have denounced all erotic and sexual expressions by men, equating them with male abuse of power. One example of this attitude states, "Each sexual arousal outside the marriage lowers the woman to a lust object." Pleasure is contaminated by sexism (Kate 1990; Money 1980; Money 1991). This attitude has not caught on as strongly in Western European society as in America.

A clear example of such antisexualism in the USA is the Senate Confirmation Hearings involving Anita Hill and Clarence Thomas (Sept./Oct. 1991) in which Thomas was accused of SH that had presumably taken place in the workplace ten years before. This hearing was crucial for the nomination of Thomas as a Supreme Court Judge. The incensed aversion of millions of women to a man who may have committed SH a decade earlier cannot be explained simply by the possibility that Anita Hill was telling the truth. There apparently exists in many men and women an attitude toward sexuality in general, independent of the SH judged in these hearings, that is an example of an emotional balance gone awry. Naturally SH should be condemned, but the hate expressed during these hearings against any form of erotic or sexual contact in general was alarming.

Motivation

According to feminist views, SH can be linked to the exercise of power. An SH relationship is usually seen as the result of a power struggle in which the male is in a position superior to the female, and the male's wish to humiliate the female plays a large role (Leigh 1989). Besides the exercise of power, there are other factors, for example, risk and excitment that differ from person to person, not only qualitatively but quantitatively (Leigh 1989; Marshall 1989). SH can combat a threatening or chronic dullness in the workplace. As so often occurs in certain situations, when conversation lags and boredom threatens, one can always start erotic or sexual games. It is obvious that a sado-masochistic cat-and-mouse game can arise in such situations (Halberstadt-Freud 1991).

It is clear that erotic seduction can take on many meanings for the unconscious, not only to combat boredom but also to express nonsexual emotions. The masking of strong aggressive feelings and fears frequently occurs in both men and women. It is understandable that dentists and surgeons are usually the ones who experience sexual seduction by young and not-so-young women in the consultation room: the fear of pain and anger over enforced helplessness can be warded off by flirtation. Aggression against the oppressor and the fear of pain and surrender can be seen as the driving forces in such behavior. Kernberg (1991) expresses it clearly: "Sexual excitement includes an element of surrender and acceptance of the state of enslavement to the other, while also being the master of the other's fate."

In this context one must consider the Stockholm Syndrome (Strentz 1980). In 1973 the Sveriges Kreditbank in Stockholm was held up by a 32-year-old thief, burglar, and prison escapee named Jan-Erik Olson. He held four young bank employees hostage for 131 hours with a submachine gun, thus permanently affecting their lives. During the ordeal one of the female employees fell in love with Olson. At the end of the captivity, she broke with her former boyfriend and married the terrorist. It is not difficult to imagine that the fear felt during this terrifying period was sexualized and that it led to feelings of infatuation.

An entirely different set of motives for SH is the wish for intimacy (Marshall 1989). Young people who are single and feel a great need for eroticism and sexuality may be especially vulnerable to the temptation that colleagues in the workplace provide. If SH should occur in such a situation, it is possible for a more or less permanent sexual relationship to grow from the SH that is first rigorously repulsed and condemned.

Gender Differences in Motivation

It is obvious that sexual relationships can arise from very different motives. This is, of course, true for heterosexual as well as homosexual relationships. There are also gender differences in the motivation for sex. One traditional example is the heterosexual relationship in which the woman, in general, is ostensibly more motivated by the expression of romantic emotions in having sex, while the man is more concerned with the expression of lusty emotions (Leigh 1989). The fear of pregnancy is, of course, stronger in women. In the early 1980s, the fear of HIV infection and AIDS was stronger in homosexuals (Juhaz 1990), whereas now there is hardly any difference between homosexuals and heterosexuals, men and women regarding HIV.

Leigh (1989) was correct when he stated that gender differences in the motivations for sex persist in all kinds of relationships. This is also true for SH. The common occurrence of SH in societies where the male still dominates the situation in the workplace and outside makes one wonder whether in certain situations SH belongs to the traditional sex role stereotype. SH would be one manner in which to accentuate and continue the traditional power situation. Combating SH is thus also a problem of emancipation.

THERAPIST-PATIENT SEXUAL INVOLVEMENT

Incidence in the USA and Europe

Nanette Gartrell and Judith Herman (Gartrell et al. 1986; Gartrell et al. 1987) together with a number of colleagues from the psychiatric departments of the Harvard Medical School, the Beth Israel Hospital (Boston), and the New York Medical College, reported that in their study of psychiatrists (n = 1423), 26 percent of those who received a questionnaire returned it completed. The survey showed eighty-four offenders of the injunction: "Psychiatrists are expected to refrain from having any sexual contact with their patients, even if the patient asks for it." Of these eighty-four offenders, 70 percent of respondents were male and 30 percent were female. Twelve respondents thought that sexual contact between therapist and patient should not be condemned. Of the offenders, 81 percent declared that they had fallen in love with the patient and that sexual contact was begun after termination of the sessions. Twenty of the responding psychiatrists (1.6 percent) had had sexual contact with their own therapist or analyst. This usually occurred when the junior psychiatrist in training was female. A total of 41 percent of the offending senior psychiatrists consulted a colleague to help them out of the situation. Of these, 50 percent turned out to be one-time offenders. The researchers concluded that psychiatrists responsible for training are poorly counseled in how to cope with their countertransference to those they train.

Gafnit Aghassy (1984) of the Psychology Institute of the University of Amsterdam, Holland, surveyed Dutch psychotherapists (n = 823) and reported data on 193 respondents (23 percent). Of these, 37 percent were members of a professional society. The distribution of sexual contact with a client or patient was 31 percent in psychoanalytical-dynamically oriented therapy, 12.5 percent in Rodgerian therapy, 10.5 percent in behavioral therapy, 7 percent in Gestalt therapy, 5.5 percent in eclectic therapy, and 33 percent other or unspecified. Of the therapists who had had sexual contact with a client/patient, 39 percent were psychiatrists, 34.5 percent psychologists, 11 percent social workers, and 15.5 percent other or unspecified. From the data, Aghassy concluded that when the offender is a man, he is, on average, ten years older than the client, and when a woman, she is usually single.

Apfel and Simon (1985) reported from Boston that 5–10 percent of male therapists were involved in sexual contact with patients. Of these offenders, 5–7 percent had had sexual intercourse.

The Canadians Carr and Robinson (1990) reviewed the existing literature and reported that 7.1–10.9 percent of male therapists and 1.9–3.5 percent of female therapists had admitted to engaging in intimate contact with patients.

A change in attitude occurred in psychotherapeutic circles during the 1960s and 1970s. There was a psychotherapeutic proliferation of, for example, nude group therapy and various degrees of sexual permissiveness in group and individual therapies, especially on the West Coast of America. This phenomenon definitely influenced the psychotherapeutic methods used in the entire Western world. It coincided with the rise of anti-psychiatric and anti-authoritarian doctrine, the antibiotic control of veneral diseases, the breakthrough in the use of oral contraception, the emphasis on the unlinking of sexuality and reproduction, and the accentuation of the woman's right to sexual fulfillment. One of the consequences of this emancipatory current was the breakdown of the taboos on speaking and writing about extramarital sexual relationships, such as those between psychotherapists and their patients/clients.

These irregular forms of psychotherapy resulted in the gradual acceptability of having sexual feelings and of expressing sexual behavior which was not a priori condemned. For some, this may have been regarded as a blessing. One example was the acceptance of the sexuality of mentally and physically handicapped people and a desire to help them with their sexual behavior (Heslinga 1977). Another example is the practice of allowing prisoners to receive their partners in their cells. By contrast, however, in the routine psychotherapeutic situation, sexual contact is considered harmful even for the patient/client who, either verbally or nonverbally, requests contact.

Psychodynamic Perspectives: Implications for the Patient

There have been studies carried out, especially in the USA, on the harmful results for the patient of patient-therapist contact (Carr & Robinson 1990; Heslinga 1977). While studying these harmful results, I noticed that a number of patients who have asked for my help after having sexual contact with a previous therapist, had suffered abuse or incestuous experiences. The sex that occurred in the previous therapy is then a repetition of the earlier incestuous relationship, together with its unsolved conflicts. In explorative psychotherapy, the return of the repressed behavior is a tool in the hands of the therapist to clear up the unsolved conflicts. Every good therapist has positive feelings for each patient/ client, and not only those originating from the countertransference. The patient can feel this and will try to discover the limits of its possibilities. The patient, consciously or unconsciously, tries to seduce the therapist so that he/she can relive the as yet unsolved conflict situation. However, psychotherapy should be carried out in abstinence. Otherwise the feelings of guilt, shame, anger, and impotence that belong to a prior infantile or childhood experience will be intensified, not diminished.

In psychotherapy sessions, the patient finds him/herself in a state of dependency and of unilaterally relinquishing personal privacy. This state is strengthened by a sexual relationship with the therapist. The dignity of both patient and therapist can become damaged to no small degree.

Experience shows that sex between therapist and patient makes termination of psychotherapy difficult, if not impossible. The dependence combined with ambivalence, with its infantile roots, is endorsed and strengthened rather than decreased. Termination of the psychotherapeutic relationship because of the commencement of a sexual relationship usually brings the patient into a crisis paired with overwhelming feelings of guilt, shame, fear, anger, and impotence, together with a disturbance in his/her self-concept (Sonne et al. 1985). This crisis can then no longer be worked out and can lead to cognitive dysfunction and suicidal risk (Pope 1986).

A study on the harmful consequences for the patient of sexual relationships with the therapist was undertaken by the Rutgersstichting (marriage guidance clinics) and the Ministerie van Welzijn, Volksgezondheid en Cultuur (Ministry of Welfare, Health and Cultural Affairs) in the Netherlands (Rutgers Foundation 1991). It found that one of the serious results of sex with a therapist was the loss of the patient's trust in therapists in general. The victim becomes too inhibited to see another therapist, despite existing psychological problems, so that PTSD (post-traumatic stress disorder) keeps growing.

Implications for the therapist

All bona fide therapists know that they morally transgress the ethical code of their profession when engaging in sexual relationships with patients. Many rationalizations can be forwarded to excuse such relationships and certain alternative theories promoted to support such rationalizations. Furthermore, undisclosed circumstances in the personal life of the therapist, not only current circumstances but previous ones as well, may collusively reinforce the therapist's dependency on the patient, which in turn appeals to the unacceptable infantile conflicts in the therapist. Thus, dependency of the therapist on the patient may originate. This dependency can be felt intuitively by the patient. Because of this, a concerted unconscious action between the two can evolve that forms the basis for the sexual relationship. It goes without saying that this concerted action does not have to lead to a sexual relationship. It is possible for a psychotherapist, on the basis of unacceptable unconscious infantile conflicts in the aggressive sphere, to block psychotherapeutic progress. In such a case, the situation does not become a sexual one. Nonetheless, the therapist-patient relationship is impaired and may need to be terminated.

The power differential in the therapist-patient relationship resembles the traditional imbalance of power in the parent-child and in the male-female relationship (Carr & Robinson 1990). This culturally determined differential is used in sexual abuse, whereby the normal development of a child to adulthood, and the neurotic to normal development of the adult client, is blocked. The inequality of power is in itself not sufficient to explain sexual abuse. On the contrary, in the psychotherapeutic process, this very inequality can be a starting point for emotional growth whereby the patient, through acceptance, working alliance, and dignity, learns how to obtain more insight into his/her own problems and to control his/her conflicts better (Bouhoutsos 1985).

The therapist's chronic fear of discovery of an illicit sexual relationship with a patient can interfere with the psychotherapeutic and medical treatment of other patients. Also, the perception that there is something fundamentally wrong with his/her own emotional development can seriously damage normal psychosocial functions. The inner struggle against existing misconduct can also cause other indiscretions. It is a known psychological mechanism that by provoking a more serious conflict, one can fight and overshadow the uneasiness felt in an existing conflict. In certain cases, the fear and guilt feelings of therapists are strengthened by patients who threaten to make the relationship public or to kill themselves. A colleague of my own acquaintance committed suicide after having had a pedophilic relationship with a patient.

False Accusations

Individual psychotherapy takes place on a one-to-one basis. Because the patient must give up personal privacy, all sorts of fantasies are freed that can be used in the psychotherapeutic process. These fantasies are usually infantile in nature (Kirkendall & McBride 1990) whereby unaccepted Oedipal conflicts can play a role. Seduction situations directed at the therapist can then arise, derived from the period of the seduction situation of the Oedipal phase. If the patient's sense of reality is seriously disturbed and his/her personality structure distorted to such an extent that one can speak of a borderline personality (Gutheil 1989) or a pseudologia fantastica, then there is a great chance that the therapist will be falsely accused of sexual abuse. It seems obvious that in this situation, agitation of the patient's feelings of revenge of infantile origin can play a role.

It is not easy to diagnose false accusation. Sometimes the reliability of the patient's statement is debatable when, along with the accusation, there are other things claimed that cannot possibly be true. Pseudological complainers often betray themselves by adding a number of other people to their charge. Other false accusers give conflicting testimony that can be proven false. There is, however, a group of psychologically impaired people of high intelligence who can make life very difficult for the falsely accused therapist. These accusers usually lay the onus of proof on the defendant, who can be put in an extremely awkward position.

People underestimate the enormous amount of grief, fear, anger, and impotence that the therapist feels when falsely accused, even though he/she knows theoretically that these feelings originate in the unconscious of the accuser and threaten to become real only because of a *lex artis*. The patient unconsciously knows how to evoke such feelings in the therapist as a defense against the threatening revival of his/her own conflicts.

In certain cases the judge will require the accuser to undergo a psychiatric examination with a therapist other than the accused. This is sometimes seen as a threat to the accuser's own reliability. This threat, which has been felt for years by a psychopathic personality, can be disputed with the reaction: "How dare you question my charge! I will not undergo a new psychiatric examination. That would confirm the possibility that I am wrong."

Therapists can sometimes feel the threat of a false accusation during a session. Using good psychotherapeutic techniques they can express and thoroughly discuss this feeling with their patients or clients. If therapists find that because of the personality structure of some patients, such discussions are not sufficient, they will terminate therapy.

Sexual Involvement after Dismissal from Therapy

From the data of Gartrell et al. (1986, 1987), it seems that 81 percent of the offenders had fallen in love with a patient and, after termination of the treatment, had started sexual contact. One can then speak of a bad start, because all sorts of psychological mechanisms that belong to the therapeutic process have contributed to the infatuation. If the relationship proves lasting, then it shows that the partners can handle the mechanisms without showing too many neurotic symptoms. The psychological growth process can then open new perspectives. Overcoming a bad start together, handling the guilt feelings together, can strengthen and intensify a relationship. There are many marriages that have turned out well after a bad start.

SANCTIONED THERAPIST-PATIENT INVOLVEMENT

The Surrogate Women of Masters and Johnson

Masters and Johnson (1966) developed a method to help male patients with sexual dysfunctions by allowing them to practice therapeutic exercises in bed with women especially trained for that purpose. The training, for which only selected women were accepted, was designed very seriously. The surrogate women received daily instructions from Masters and Johnson on the manner in which they must execute the caressing exercises, after the patients had been seen by the sexologists. The way in which this sex therapy was carried out is thoroughly described by Herbert d'H. Lee (1971). The report of forty-one men who were treated by thirteen surrogate women over a period of thirteen years, cites a success rate of more than 80 percent. Most of the women treated one male patient at a time, and had no other patient for approximately one year. During the treatment periods, the surrogates had no long-term partners. They were coached in how to achieve insight into the causes of the men's sexual dysfunctions, especially with regard to their fear of performance. The women reported back daily to Masters and Johnson.

Seen from the psychodynamic viewpoint, one could say that Masters and Johnson looked over the shoulders of the patient during the exercises with the surrogate. With such a setup a strong feeling of acceptance of having sexual intercourse can be produced combined with a lessening of the guilt feelings, which by itself can work therapeutically. These psychological bonuses are independent of the exercises. They allow a possible touching taboo to be lessened or even removed. At the same time a strong positive influence on the patient's ego can occur when he is accepted not only by a woman but by two famous psychotherapists.

This treatment method found little following in the 1980s. The reason is undoubtedly linked to the political situation in America and Europe during that era. The official sexual morals propagated by church, political, and governmental authorities were clearly shifting toward antisexuality, quite apart from the emergence of the HIV/AIDs epidemic. It is possible that the therapy with surrogate women has taken place more often without publicity. In Europe, so far as I know, this form of sexual therapy is not conducted. However, the method of Masters and Johnson without the surrogate women is commonly used by sex therapists.

Helping Handicapped People Have Sex

In their Dutch rehabilitation center, Heslinga (1977) and Verkuyl (1977) have pioneered methods of helping physically handicapped patients satisfy their sexual needs. These patients are frequently unable to masturbate let alone have sexual intercourse with their partners. Caressing exercises can often be achieved, but sometimes even kissing another physically handicapped person is impossible without the help of a healthy outsider.

Most of the patients in the Dutch center were young people who had had an automobile accident but whose libido was completely intact. If the patients were married, their partners were instructed in the sexual treatments. There were, however, other young patients without regular partners who remained for months or years in the center, did their physiotherapy exercises and had their treatments, and remained deprived of sex. Naturally, there were infatuations involving the nursing staff who, however, were usually already married and had a normal sex life at home.

The problem was solved by instructing women, on a volunteer basis, in how to help the patients realize their sexual needs in a manner they asked for themselves. This meant that a certain female nurse or social worker helped a male patient into a female patient's bed and vice versa. The paralyzed appendages were arranged in such a way that bodily, sexual, and genital contact was possible. Instruments were also used. Sometimes the women themselves volunteered as partner in the sexual game. For such events to take place, long-term, comprehensive training discussions are needed, as is an atmosphere in which the inclinations of the patients can be respected and realized. It is obvious that the board of such an institution must be knowledgeable of such methods, as well as able to create such an atmosphere and organize the trainings.

In such surroundings, a possible SH by the invalid is not taken on face value, but is placed in the context of the total living pattern. We know of no such case in all the years during which this helping sex has occurred that has led to police or judicial action.

COPING WITH UNWANTED SEXUAL HARASSMENT

General Prevention

Prevention of SH must be directed at social education in which the misuse of power in interpersonal relationships is no longer accepted. It is clear that this social education must also include sex education (Musaph 1990). However, a change in mentality is not something that occurs overnight. Much time is needed, as well as a host of other preventive measures. For example, the government must start an active prevention and counseling policy, and the early signs or threats of SH must be discussed. Silence about SH must be broken down. This has already begun with the numerous publications on the subject in the professional literature. However, media communication resources should also be used to this end. The facts must be imparted, not sensationally but in a plain and simple manner. In this way, the fear that exists in many people about sexual violence and sex in general can be minimized.

For example, a film was made recently in Holland, on the initiative of the government, to inform teenagers around sixteen years of age about SH. A girl meets a male friend in an outdoor cafe. The girl then asks the boy to come and see her room. The boy considers this invitation as permission for sexual contact. When he tries to have sexual contact, the girl is frightened and refuses him categorically. The boy leaves and later calls the girl to apologize for his actions. The film ends as it began: the two are sitting in an outdoor cafe enjoying a cup of coffee. Feminists have protested against this film, stating that it confirms the power situation of the male sex: the boy thinks that the sexual approach must come from him. The government meant the film to show that the resistance of women and girls against sexual abuse should increase one's pride and self-respect.

Prevention of SH in the Workplace

In the workplace, employees may demand that employment contracts include the statement, "Sexual Harassment is forbidden and may give cause for judicial measures." Women and girls will then feel that they will be protected after reporting SH. Furthermore, women may be reassured that it is acceptable to report SH without hestitation. In practice, many victims are paralyzed by repeated offenses. Protesting becomes more difficult with time, because it can then be said that the victim wanted the SH, or otherwise would have done something about it earlier. Increasing the possibilities of resistance for women and girls against sexual violence must be organized as quickly as possible.

Depending on the seriousness of the psychological disturbance caused by SH, social workers, clinical psychologists, or psychiatrists can care for the victims. In some settings group discussions among personnel, guided by a social worker or a personnel manager, can work therapeutically for prevention as well as for the care of the victim. These group discussions can also have a preventive effect on potential abusers. If the cohesion of the group is good, then it is possible that the abuser will not be reported to the police or judicial authorities and the problem will be solved internally.

Nevertheless, it must also be mentioned that not all erotic expressions uttered in the workplace are SH. A pleasurable working atmosphere with job satisfaction does not exclude erotic utterances brought with humor, insofar as workers intuitively feel that each person has and knows his/her own limit.

PREVENTING THERAPIST-PATIENT SEXUAL INVOLVEMENT

It is necessary that each caretaker, social worker, doctor, or psychologist is comprehensively informed during his/her education about the dangers of sexual involvement, especially when unconscious motives threaten to surface. This educational program on therapist-patient sexual involvement must apply to all forms of psychotherapy and all practitioners.

However, sex education alone is not sufficient. There are caretakers with an excellent education who belong in the category of sex offenders. The character structure and the unaccepted infantile conflicts of some caretakers are also responsible for sex offending. Therefore, in most cases it is pointless immediately to involve the judicial system. Neither prison sentences nor fines have ever cured anyone of his/her neurotic symptoms.

How to Handle Therapist-Patient Involvement

Sexual abuse is subject to discipline by not only professional organizations but also by the law. A prison sentence, in my view, is needed only when society must be protected from pathological behavior. The judge can determine in his sentence whether the abuser must undergo psychotherapy and may then, if the abuser agrees, put the offender on probation. A harsher sentence will not be more effective. It is better to hire a mediator or therapist at an early stage. Then the therapist does not have the added difficulty of a therapy being forced on the offender.

Many psychiatrists all over the world favor mandatory reporting (Gartrell et al. 1988). It is unknown how many psychiatrists or other therapists are treating patients with a prior history of sexual contact while in treatment. Many doctors plead professional confidentiality. They do not know whether their patient wishes to report the incident to a judge or ethical committee. Even if the patient wishes that such action be taken by the new therapist, it is still not certain that he/she will take it. Reporting means that the therapist will be making public the occurrence of sexual abuse within the profession he loves and perhaps by a colleague he knows well. Since in real life there are numerous factors that can limit the new therapist's behavior, it is difficult for me to state general guidelines. If one feels that the behavior of the previous therapist forms a danger for future patients, then action is necessary. This action will usually entail making contact with the colleague. The advice to this colleague is pretty obvious: "Look for a senior therapist and let him/her trace the origin of the lapse." The abuser is then treated as a patient and privacy (Stone 1983) is maintained. This seems to me the most elegant solution, which, unfortunately, is not always possible.

Reporting the offender's background to an ethical commission of the professional organization or to a judge can be sparked by various motives. Honest indignation does not have to ruin a colleague. The senior therapist will have to thoroughly inspect the motives of his/her actions, which should not include gloating over another's failure or personal revenge. The most important motive for mandatory reporting is knowledge of recidivism after the offender has been advised to undergo therapy.

It seems unjust to me to make sexual harassment a criminal act. Coleman (1988) is correct when he states: "Criminal liability seems extremely unlikely and inappropriate. Civil liability appears to be the best solution in especially egregious cases." Following this train of thought, mandatory reporting in less egregious cases is definitely not the first action one should think of. However, most American therapists favor such a measure (Gartrell et al. 1987).

It is only natural that a respectful demeanor be used toward a patient who was sexually offended in a previous therapy (Burgess 1981). In the new situation, the therapist must search for unconscious motives that may be of significance. In this way, feelings of shame and guilt (Musaph 1982) can be discussed.

In Minneapolis there is a nonprofit agency, the Walk-In Counseling Center, that has taken an active role in evaluating exploitive therapists to determine their rehabilitation potential (Musaph 1990). I do not think it reasonable to require all psychiatrists to report sexual misconduct by any psychiatric colleague to the ethics committee of their professional organization. The best manner seems to me to make use of well-educated confidential psychotherapists who have specialized in this issue. At the beginning of psychotherapy sessions, the therapist should inform the patient/client of the existence of such a confidential mediator and mention that this person can be contacted if and when a threatening or an actual sexual contact occurs. Each caretaker who feels that the contact with the patient/client is threatening to go awry can also contact such a confidential mediator, who then has the task of placing both the patient and the therapist under the care and supervision of an appointed expert.

REFERENCES

Aghassy, R. (1984). "Sexual Contact between Clients and Psychotherapists." Dissertation Psychol. Lab. University of Amsterdam, Holland.

Apfel, J. R., and Simon, B. (1985). "Patient-Therapist Sexual Contact. Psychodynamic Perspectives on the Causes and Results." *Psychotherapy and Psychosomatics* 43: 57.

Bouhoutsos, J. C. (1985). "Therapist-Client Sexual Involvement: A Challenge for Mental Health Professionals and Educators." *American Journal of Orthopsychiatry* 55: 177.

Burgess, A. W. (1981). "Physician Sexual Misconduct and Patient's Responses." *American Journal of Psychiatry* 138: 1335.

Cart, M., and Robinson, G. E. (1990). "Fatal Attraction. The Ethical and Clinical Dilemma of Patient-Therapist Sex." *Canadian Journal of Psychiatry* 35: 122.

Coleman, P. H. (1988). "Sex between Psychiatrist and Former Patient: A Proposal for a 'No Harm, No Fool' Rule." *Oklahama Iowa Review* 41: 1.

Divasto, P. V.; Kaufman, A.; and Rosner. L. (1984). "The Prevalence of Sexually Stressful Events among Females in the General Population." *Archives of Sexual Behavior.*

Gartrell, N.; Herman, J.; Olarte, S.; Feldstein, M.; and Localio, R. (1986). "Psychiatrist-Patient Sexual Contact: Results of a National Survey." *American Journal of Psychiatry* 143: 1126.

——— (1987). "Reporting Practices of Psychiatrists Who Knew of Sexual Misconduct by Colleagues." *American Journal of Orthopsychiatry* 57: 287.

Gartrell, N.; Herman, J.; Olarte S.; Feldstein, M.; and Localio, R. (1988). "Management and Rehabilitation of Sexually Exploitive Therapists." *Hospital and Community Psychiatry* 39: 1077.

Gutek, B. A. (1985). *Sex and the Workplace.* San Francisco: Jossey-Bass.

Gutheil, T. H. G. (1989). "Borderline Personality Disorder, Boundary Violations, and Patient-Therapist Sex: Medicolegal Pitfalls." *American Journal of Psychiatry* 146: 597.

Halberstadt-Freud, H. (1991). *Freud, Proust, Perversion and Love.* Amsterdam: Swats and Zeitlinger.

Heslinga, K. (1977). "Psychosexual Problems of the Motor-Disabled." In J. Money and H. Musaph, eds., *Handbook of Sexology.* Amsterdam: Elsevier.

Jehu, D. (1989). "Sexual Dysfunction among Clients Who Were Sexually Abused in Childhood." *Behavioral Psychotherapy* 17: 53.

Jong, J. T. V. M. de (1991). "Strange Fantasies? System Therapy with Moroccans, Turkish and Surinamese Migrants." (In Dutch with a summary in English.) *Maandbl. Geest. Volksgez.* 9: 924.

Juhasz, A. (1990). "The Contained Threat: Women in Mainstream AIDS Documentary." *Journal of Sex Research* 27: 25.

Kate, E. (1990). "Essay Fatal Attraction, or the Postmodern Prometheus." *Journal of Sex Research* 27: 111.

Kernberg, O. (1991). "Sadomasochism in the Perversions." *Journal of American Psychoanalytic Association* 39: 741.

Kirkendall, L. A., and McBride, L. G. (1990). "Preadolescent and Adolescent Imagery and Sexual Fantasies: Beliefs and Experiences." In M. E. Perry, ed., *Handbook of Sexology* 7: 263. Amsterdam: Elsevier.

Krivacska, J. J. (1990). "Child Sexual Abuse and Its Prevention." In M. E. Perry, ed., *Handbook of Sexology* 7: 395. Amsterdam: Elsevier.

Lee, d'H. H. (1971). *Surrogate Wife.* New York: Dell Publishers.

Leigh, B. C. (1989). "Reasons for Having and Avoiding Sex: Gender, Sexual Orientation, and Relationship to Sexual Behavior." *Journal of Sex Research* 26: 199.

Marshall, W. L. (1989). "Intimacy, Loneliness and Sexual Offender." *Behavior Research and Therapy* 17: 491.

Masters, W. H., and Johnson, V. E. (1966). *Human Sexual Response.* Boston: Little, Brown, and Co.

Money, J. (1980). *Love and Lovesickness. The Science of Sex, Gender Differences, and Pairbonding.* Baltimore, Md.: Johns Hopkins University Press.

——— (1991). "Semen-Conservation Theory, Semen Investment Theory, Antisexualism, and the Return of Freud's Seduction Theory." *Journal of Psychology and Human Sexuality* 4, no. 4: 31–55.

——— (1994). *Sex Errors of the Body and Related Syndromes: A Guide to Counseling Children, Adolescents, and Their Families.* 2nd ed. Baltimore: Paul H. Brookes.

Murnen, S. K.; Perot, A.; and Byrne, D. (1989). "Coping with Unwanted Sexual Activity: Normative Responses, Situational Determinants, and Individual Difference." *Journal of Sex Research* 26: 85.

Musaph, H. (1982). "The Role of the Liaison Psychiatrist in Sex Difficulties in Patient-Doctor Relationship." In Z. Hoch and H. Lief, eds., *Sexology International Congress Series,* p. 329. Amsterdam: Excerpta Medica.

——— (1990). "First Sexual Intercourse." In M. E. Perry, ed., *Handbook of Sexology* 7: 287. Amsterdam: Elsevier.

Pope, K. S. (1986). "Research and Laws Regarding Therapist-Patient Sexual Involvement: Implications for Therapists." *American Journal of Psychotherapy* 40: 564.

Pryor, J. B., and Day, J. D. (1988). "Interpretation of Sexual Harassment: An Attributional Analysis." *Sex Roles* 18: 405.

Rowell, G. N. (1986). "Effects of Sex Role Identity and Sex on Definitions of Sexual Harassment." *Sex Roles* 14: 9.

Rutgers Foundation and Ministry of Culture. (1991). *Documentary and Library Ministry of Culture.* The Hague, The Netherland. (In Dutch.)

Sonne, J.; Meyer, C. B.; Bory, D.; and Marshall, V. (1985). "Client's Reaction to Sexual Intimacy in Therapy." *American Journal of Orthopsychiatry* 55: 183.

Stone, A. A. (1983). "Sexual Misconduct by Psychiatrists: The Ethical and Clinical Dilemma of Confidentiality. A Commentary." *American Journal of Psychiatry* 140: 195.

Storms, M. D. (1973). "Videotape and the Attribution Process: Reversing Actor's and Observers's Point of View." *Journal of Personality and Social Psychology* 27: 165.

Strentz, T. H. (1980). "The Stockholm Syndrome: Law Enforcement Policy and Ego Defenses of the Hostage." *Annals of the New York Academy of Science* 11: 137

Verkuyl, A. (1977). "Some Neuromotor Syndromes and Their Sexual Consequences." In J. Money and H. Musaph, eds., *Handbook of Sexology,* p. 945. Amsterdam: Elsevier.

Part Two

Identification and Case Management of Sex Offenses

Introduction

Whereas the previous section examined the nature and etiology of paraphlic behavior and the social framework within which some of it becomes labeled as illegal, this section examines current strategies for assessment and intervention. Illustrating how pervasive the degeneracy model of sex offending has become, despite the overall focus of this volume away from such a model, many of the authors remain stuck with terminology that is more evocative of judgmental emotionality than of impartial rationality in the consideration of offending behavior, its etiology, and its consequences. This is particularly evident in the terminology used by Hollida Wakefield and Ralph Underwager in their chapter on assessment and identification of child sexual abuse and in Charlene Steen's contribution on the case management of sexual abuse victims.

There remains much work to be done regarding official policy in response to accusations of abuse which may be accurate or confabulated, or a mixture of both. Steen, for example, provides a framework for case management of the child abuse victim, but does not fully resolve the issue of how to handle the child in initial stages of the investigative or therapeutic processes without assuming the authenticity of victimhood while it is still in question. Even more troublesome is the response of mental health professionals to accusations of abuse which they strongly believe to be false, and to situations in which a parent or other significant person in the child's life holds a view different from the child's as to the reality of the alleged abuse. No matter what, one seems to be stuck with terminology that labels the child a victim prior to any determination of whether abuse actually occurred. Unfortunately, given the current response protocols used by both the child protection and legal systems, this victimological nomenclature may paradoxically reflect the true reality of the child who becomes a victim of alleged abuse in the absence of actual abuse.

Part of the dilemma here is mentioned tangentially by nearly all the authors in this section, and relates to the newly enhanced forensic role of healthcare workers as adjuncts in the legal prosecutory process. Mental health professionals have allowed themselves to become aligned with law enforcement agencies. The goals of the helping professions are incompatible with those of law enforcement, and are inevitably compromised when healthcare professionals become disguised co-conspirators in the pursuit of criminal convictions. Psychologists, social workers, counselors, therapists, and physicians should avoid the role of validating accusations of abuse, noting the similarity to the role ostensible science played in validating the religious dogma of the seventeenth through nineteenth centuries. Their proper business is to document the psychosocial history of the individual brought to them, so as to understand the dynamics and possible dysfunction of the family relative to the accusations of abuse.

Wakefield and Underwager discuss how subscribing to the validator role can contaminate the investigative process. In their chapters, Lee Coleman and Jeffrey Victor describe two of the latest phenomena to demonstrate the perversion of science in support of fundamentalist dogma on the role of evil in sexuality. Coleman discusses recovered memories of alleged sexual assault in childhood which have remained dormant and out of awareness for years until emerging in adulthood. Victor places the current hysteria of "Satanic sexual abuse" of children in a broader sociological perspective, which attempts to explain the factors permitting the birth, expansion, and maintenance of beliefs in Satanism in a modern society.

Margretta Dwyer and Eli Coleman explore assessment, case management, and treatment approaches to alleged sex offenders. Gregory Lehne provides a comprehensive review of outcome studies. These two chapters together challenge the postulation of evil intent and voluntary choice as progenitors of sex offending behavior.

10

The Alleged Child Victim and Real Victims of Sexual Misuse

Hollida Wakefield and Ralph Underwager

INTRODUCTION

Neither the science of psychology nor the exercise of law is perfectly accurate. The lawyer and the psychologist each agree that improved accuracy is the goal for each. Everyone involved in the justice system—judges, attorneys, accusers, victims, defendants, law enforcement, and society as a whole—benefits from increasing the accuracy of the decision-making process. As Saks and Kidd (1980–81) observe:

> Through legal decision making we seek to avoid the classic errors of convicting an innocent defendant or acquitting a guilty one, or finding liability when there is none or failing to find liability when it is present. Whatever justice may be, surely it is not error. (p. 123)

The science of psychology has been asked to provide information to aid in the decision-making process when there are allegations of child sexual abuse. Psychologists have responded to this request, but often in the absence of accurate and reliable information.

Ravetz (1971) notes that when a field of inquiry is immature and the relationship to the events it purports to describe is tenuous, it may mask this true state of imprecision by producing aphorisms. An aphorism is a deeply felt personal doctrine presented in a superficially comprehensible fashion, which often is in error. This is what took place in the development of the system to handle allegations of child sexual abuse in the last fifteen years. Aphorisms such as "Child sexual abuse is a raging epidemic," "Society actively chooses to ignore sexual abuse," "Children don't lie about sexual abuse," "Children can't talk about things they have not experienced," "Children are no more suggestible than adults," and "Children must be believed at all costs," have been advanced as truisms and given the patina of scientific authority. On this basis, politicians, law enforcement, and social welfare authorities have constructed, in the absence of facts, a system of laws, policies, regulations, bureaucratic structures, techniques, and procedures now entrenched in our justice system and established as the way our society responds to child abuse.

Any decision-making structure built on error is liable to produce error at an indeterminate, unrecognized, but significant level that causes harm (Gambrill 1990). Evaluation of the extent of error and thus the potential for harm may best be done by the application of Bayes Theorem (Fischoff & Beyth-Marom 1983).

The Bayes approach rests on the principle that the degrees of belief in an ideally rational person conform to the mathematical principles of probability theory (Horwich 1982). This concept should be acceptable to a scientifically trained person or to anyone who respects science. A number of scientists have applied Bayesian inference to child sexual abuse in the interest of assessing the level of error and type of error produced by the system. *Every Bayesian analysis of the decisions made by the child abuse system that we have found concludes that the most probable and most frequent type of error is false positive, that is, identifying an individual as abused or an abuser when it is not true* (e.g., Altemeier et al. 1984; Caldwell et al. 1988; Gambrill 1990; Horner 1992; Horner & Guyer 1991a, 1991b; Kotelchuck 1982; Milner et al. 1984; Paradise 1989; Realmuto et al. 1990; Starr 1979; Wakefield & Underwager 1988; Zeitlin 1987). This is true even when a 95 percent accuracy level for the decision making is assumed, as in Gambrill (1990). Starr (1979) assumes a procedure that is 83 percent accurate in correctly identifying abusive situations. Still he reports a ratio of twenty false positives to one true positive. Horner (1992) finds the ratio of false positive to false negative classificatory errors ranging across studies from 3:1 to an astonishing 2000:1. More realistic and probable lower estimates of the accuracy of the decision-making process but higher base rates produce unconscionable and unacceptable levels of false positives, ranging to a ratio of nine false positives to one true positive.

Much has been made of the harm to children if there is a false negative decision, that is, a failure to identify a child as abused when it is true. This conclusion ignores the damage done to innocent people who represent the false positives generated by the system. Also, the severity of damage may be greater when a nonabused child is treated as if abused than when an abused child is not correctly identified. The justice system must begin to consider this possible reality and to ask how the accuracy of decision making may be improved.

There is now enough credible scientific knowledge that we can improve the accuracy of the decision-making process. We do not need to continue making the kinds of error that have been made up to the present. There are no good reasons for being opposed to efforts to increase accuracy, only bad ones.

THE AFTERMATH OF ERROR

If adults make a mistake and treat nonabused children as if they have been abused, this is not innocuous or benign. Smith (1991), a psychotherapist, describes a letter brought to him on her fourth visit by Stephanie, a 17-year-old psychotherapy client:

> I am so miserable, Dr. Smith, I need your help now. As you know, I have told you how my mother and I just don't like each other. We fight and argue all the time. But I have never told you why. When I was little, six I think, I dearly loved my dad. I think he and I were very close and did many things together. I knew my mom and dad didn't get along but somehow things were all right between me and my parents.
>
> Then one day, my mother told me my father was very sick and needed to go to a doctor to get well. She told me I would have to say that my dad had hurt me by touching me [in] places that were nasty. She said if I would say this Dad would have treatment and get better and be a nicer dad to me and bring me more presents.
>
> My mother rehearsed with me what I was to say and then took me to a doctor in another city and practiced with me again what I was to say and I said what she told me to say.
>
> Later my mom said that Dad had to go to a hospital to get the help he needed, but when I was twelve I found out he was in prison because he had molested me.
>
> Once I got to go see Dad in prison. He told me he had written me many times, but Dr. Smith, I never received any of those letters. I think Mom burned them. Later Mom told me that Dad was living in another state.
>
> Just last night my mom and I got in a big fight and she told me Dad had committed suicide. I feel so bad. I'm to blame because I lied for my mom. I hate her and I hate myself. I can't stand myself! I can't wait to leave home when I get older.
>
> Please help me Dr. Smith. (p. 203)

The next night Stephanie died from an overdose of her mother's sleeping medication.

William H. Yanco, a policeman, committed suicide after a complaint was made that he had kissed a 10-year-old boy on the lips. Yanco, who had specialized in working with disturbed children for fourteen years, was judged to have died in the line of duty. Yanco wrote in a letter to his two sons, "No matter what I say, people will always be suspicious. I can't stand the way people are going to think of me" (Associated Press 1992). Douglas Tarrant killed himself after being accused of sexual abuse which he claimed was false in a videotape he left behind for his family. The 15-year-old girl who had accused him had retracted her story two days before Tarrant killed himself, but he had not been told of the recantation (Landry 1988).

A Canadian mother who had been falsely accused of sexual abuse by her former husband got her three children returned to her by judicial order (*Stuart-Mills* v. *Cher* 1990). They had been subjected to interrogation techniques known to the husband who was a member of the Mossad, the Israeli intelligence agency. The children hated their mother so violently they cut up her clothes, tried to burn down the house, attacked her, cursed, swore, skipped school, and refused to cooperate in any way. Now, two years after the event, the mother believes she and her children have repaired the breach but it will never be the same (Stuart-Mills 1992, personal communication).

The assessment of an accusation is seldom a neutral event for anyone. Mantell (1988) notes that the process of evaluating an accusation may result in more damage to the interests of the child and to the child's primary relationships than the original act in question. Tyler and Brassard (1984) report that a sexual abuse investigation can be devastating to families and children, especially to the alleged victim, who may be placed in a shelter or foster care. Diorio (1992) reports that parents whose children had been removed invariably perceived the actions of the protection system as oppressive, unfair, insensitive, harsh, cruel, and tyrannical. Baurmann (1983) found that secondary victimization was common in his sample of 8,058 sexual abuse victims in lower Saxony; he reported that for at least one-fifth of his sample, the main cause of the damage was judged by the victims to be the behavior of relatives, friends, or the police rather than actual abuse.

Even if an allegation is eventually judged to be false, the family, including the alleged child victim, will have been severely traumatized by the allegation. Schultz (1989) surveying one hundred families falsely charged with sexual abuse, found that almost all reported major disruption and trauma. Davis and Reppucci (1992) surveyed eighty-five men who had claimed to have been falsely charged with abusing their children or stepchildren. Almost all, regardless of whether they had been found guilty of abuse or not, reported a variety of negative effects in diverse areas of their lives. Robson (1991) comments on the aftermath for the Scott County, Minnesota, families, in which twenty-five adults were accused of abusing their own and other children. The charges were dropped after the only one to go to trial ended in an acquittal and the children eventually were returned home. However, the families all experienced severe dysfunction and distress, and "perhaps permanent emotional damage to the accused and the accusers alike" (p. 50). Weinbach (1987) remarks: "Acquittal of charges cannot undo the damage. Even unsupported charges tend to leave lingering doubt among friends, family, and associates" (p. 532).

A study of thirty families where erroneous charges of sexual abuse were made was recently carried out in England by Westminster College, Oxford. The study examined the process of investigation, outcomes, and the effects on children, parents, and extended families. All suffered post-traumatic shock. The report also suggests that the type of counseling required by these families is unique and the closest model is that of victims of violence. They are disabled because an external force has assaulted them and torn their lives apart (Prosser and Lewis 1992).

Children are often placed in foster care as a result of a sexual abuse allegation. Foster care is seldom positive; Besharov (1985b) reviews its effects and concludes it is an emotionally jarring experience which confuses younger children and unsettles older ones. The trauma for a child who has been sexually abused is likely to be increased if the child is removed from home (Gomes-Schwartz et al. 1990).

A court-appointed panel of thirteen experts reviewed the entire Illinois child welfare system and their handling of the 23,000 children in their custody. The report establishes that the agency charged with preventing child abuse and neglect is itself abusing and neglecting thousands of children (Final Consolidated Report of Rule 706 Panel of Experts 1990). Silberberg and Silberberg (1982) observe that parents who abuse children are accused of child abuse while officials who abuse children say they are rehabilitating the child.

Jones (1991) describes nine possible components of iatrogenic (doctor-induced) harm by the system when children have actually been abused. They are (1) overzealous professional intervention, (2) repeated interviewing, (3) repeated physical examinations, (4) decline in living standards, (5) defensive decision making, (6) attendance at court, (7) withholding treatment, (8) over-treatment, and (9) foster care. Jones also reports a number of studies demonstrating that there is a higher frequency of abuse in foster care families than in matched-comparison natural families (families of birth).

If an abused child is traumatized by the consequences of a sexual abuse disclosure, investigation, and justice system involvement, the effects can be even worse for a child who has, in fact, not been abused. Not only may the child be placed in foster care or be separated from a parent, but the child is often put in sexual abuse therapy where the false allegation is encouraged and reinforced. The child may be forced to be fixated on feelings of having been abused and to talk about the abuse and the abuser for months or even years.

Campbell (1992b) reports on a 7-year-old girl who was in therapy for two years. As part of the therapy, the child was required to keep diaries of her thoughts and feelings for nine months. There were 246 entries in the diaries, mostly descriptions of dreams. The girl's mother was portrayed negatively in 121 entries and her stepfather in 120 entries. There was a steady progression of hatred and hostility toward both. When the trial was held, the girl testified to abuse by the mother and stepfather, recounting the content of her dreams as if they were reality. The environment of a divorce/custody conflict and the development of the allegations strongly suggested that this was a false allegation and the jury acquitted both the mother and stepfather. This kind of therapy experience can be an assault on the child's developing ability to differentiate reality from fantasy.

This is the kind of harm that can be done to children and families. If it is the case, as Horner and Guyer (1991a, 1991b) suggest, that for every false negative there are over twenty false positives, the sheer amount of human misery and anguish caused by the system that aims at protecting children demands an immediate improvement in accuracy of decision making.

HOW MANY ALLEGATIONS ARE FALSE?

The reports of suspected child abuse have greatly increased in the past twenty years, particularly for reports of child sexual abuse. This increase results from the broadening of the reporting laws along with the public and professional attention given to child abuse. But as Davis and Reppucci (1992) observe, the reforms that have increased reporting and made prosecution easier have also made it easier wrongfully to accuse and to prosecute innocent people.

Child sexual abuse allegations present great difficulties to the justice system. Often the child is the only witness and there is no corroborating evidence of the abuse. Several highly publicized day care cases in the last several years have highlighted the problem of sorting out the truth. The McMartin preschool case ended in acquittals, hung juries, and dismissals because the jury concluded that the suggestive interviews of the children by the prosecution clouded the actual facts of the case. But parallel trials, namely the Little Rascals case in Edenton, North Carolina, and the Kelly Michaels case in New Jersey ended in convictions.

Child sexual abuse allegations arising during a divorce and custody dispute are especially difficult because of the young age of the children involved, the possible motivations of adults, and the need to balance the rights, interests, and welfare of the child and the accused parent. In all cases, particularly if the child has been interviewed repeatedly, there is a question of the extent to which the account has been contaminated by the adults' influence (Doris 1991; Underwager & Wakefield 1990).

While many professionals believe that most allegations are true, there has been a continuing dispute about the proportion that are false, with some professionals claiming they are extremely rare (e.g., Berliner 1988; Faller 1984 & 1990; Jones & McGraw 1987; Summit 1983) and others maintaining that the frequency of false allegations has become a serious problem (e.g., Coleman & Clancy 1990; Raskin & Yuille 1989; Wexler 1990; Wakefield & Underwager 1988). Victims of Child Abuse Laws (VOCAL) cites the percentage of unsubstantiated allegations to support their claim that most allegations are false, since 65 percent of all reports of suspected child abuse turn out to be unfounded (Besharov 1985a, 1986). Others respond by saying that "unsubstantiated" does not mean the abuse did not occur.

Much of the disagreement over the proportion of false allegations comes from differences in how a false allegation is defined. Substantiation by child protection agencies, the opinion of a mental health professional or police investigator, or the justice system outcome have been used by various researchers and writers.

The terms *substantiated* and *unsubstantiated* cause confusion. Corwin et al. (1987), Paradise et al. (1988), and Quinn (1988) note that *unsubstantiated* does not mean the allegation is *false*. The allegation may have been true but the investigating authorities did not get enough information to substantiate it. At the same time, an ostensibly *substantiated* allegation may not be *true*. A study conducted for the U.S. National Center of Child Abuse and Neglect found that in about half of the cases of families under the supervision of child protection, the parents had never actually maltreated their children (Besharov 1985a). In addition, the legal meaning of *substantiated, founded,* and *indicated* can differ from state to state.

Some writers use the term *false allegation* to include all cases that cannot be substantiated (Thoennes & Pearson 1988b; Sink 1988b), while others use it only when there is a deliberate falsification and exclude misunderstandings made in good faith. In order to estimate the proportion of false allegations, the definition must be specified since if the definition excludes cases that are not deliberately fabricated, there will be a much smaller proportion of them. For example, Jones and McGraw (1987) reported that only 8 percent of the cases they studied were false. But examination of their data indicates that only 53 percent were founded, even including cases that were later recanted. Of the remaining 47 percent, there was insufficient information in 24 percent, 17 percent were unsubstantiated, and 6 percent were judged to be deliberately fictitious. The 8 percent comes from dropping cases with insufficient information and recalculating the percentages. This also inflated the percentage that was defined as founded, with the result that Jones and McGraw stated that 70 percent of the reports were "reliable."

The estimate of the proportion of sexual abuse cases that are false will differ according to the definitions used as well as to the experience and opinion of the person making the estimate. If true abuse is defined as all substantiated cases and false allegations are limited to deliberate fabrications, there will be a small proportion of false allegations. There will be more if false allegations refer to unsubstantiated cases. If false allegations are defined in terms of the judicial system outcome, there will be still more since not all substantiated allegations result in an abuse finding in court.

In this chapter, we differentiate between *false* and *fabricated* allegations. A false allegation occurs when abuse is judged not to occur, while a fabricated allegation is limited to a purposefully and deliberately false allegation.

DIVORCE AND CUSTODY DISPUTES

Many professionals believe that the largest percentage of false allegations are in divorce and custody disputes, but there is disagreement over exactly how often this happens. Thoennes and her colleagues (Thoennes & Pearson 1988a, 1988b; Thoennes & Tjaden 1990) attempted to get information on the incidence and validity of sexual abuse allegations through telephone interviews and mail surveys from court administrators, judges, custody mediators, and child protection workers throughout the United States. They report that the initial survey and interviews revealed a general consensus that sexual abuse allegations in custody disputes occur in "a small but growing" number of cases (Thoennes & Pearson 1988a). They estimate that accusations of sexual abuse are found in approximately 2 percent of contested custody cases (the range across court sites was 1 percent to 8 percent). They observe that there are approximately one million divorces annually, and of these, about 55 percent, or 550,000 involve minor children. About 15 percent of these (82,500) result in court involvement due to custody and/or visitation disputes. Their estimate of 2 percent sexual abuse accusations in 82,500 custody disputes translates into 1,650 cases of sexual abuse accusations annually within the environment of a divorce/custody dispute.

Others, however, suggest a higher frequency. Esplin (1990) estimates that sexual abuse allegations occur in 15 percent of contested custody situations in Arizona. Many professionals believe that various factors in the divorce and visitation situation increase the possibility of false sexual abuse allegations (Benedek & Schetky 1985a, 1985b; Blush & Ross 1987, 1990; Cooke & Cooke 1991; Ekman 1989; Elterman & Ehrenberg 1991; Fisk 1989; Gardner

1992; Green & Schetky 1988; Guyer & Ash 1986; Hindmarch 1990; Horner & Guyer 1991a, 1991b; Kaser-Boyd 1988; Levy 1989; Raskin & Yuille 1989; Ross & Blush 1990; Sheridan 1990; Spiegel 1986; Wakefield & Underwager 1991). There is disagreement over how many of these accusations are false, although most estimates range between 20 percent and 80 percent.

Others, however, believe that most allegations arising in divorce and custody disputes are true. Faller (1990) suggests three possible reasons for an abuse disclosure surfacing during a divorce in addition to a false allegation: (1) the nonoffending parent finds out about the sexual abuse and decides to divorce the offending parent; (2) there is long-standing sexual abuse that is revealed only in the context of divorce; or (3) there is sexual abuse that has been precipitated by the marital dissolution.

Several authors (Berliner 1988; Corwin, et al. 1987; Faller 1990; MacFarlane 1986; Sink 1988b) suggest reasons why valid allegations of sexual abuse may not surface until the time of a divorce. A sexually abused child may be afraid to disclose while the family is still together. A child who has been threatened with the breakup of the family may tell once this has already happened. It is more difficult for the abusing parent to persuade the child to keep the secret once he or she is not living with the child. A child may become genuinely terrified at the prospect of spending time alone with the abuser and therefore tell in order to avoid a visit. Increased distrust between parents results in willingness to suspect sexual abuse. Some writers believe, without substantiating evidence, that the divorce itself is a risk factor for actual abuse and that the father may begin sexually abusing his child because of the stress and emotional devastation of the divorce (Corwin, et al. 1987; Goodwin et al. 1989; MacFarlane 1986).

EVALUATING SEXUAL ABUSE CASES

Memory, Suggestibility, and Interviews of Children

Understanding the nature of memory is necessary in evaluating child sexual abuse. The fact that memory is reconstruction and not recall is supported both in laboratory studies and in surveys (Bradburn et al. 1987; Dawes 1988; Goodman & Hahn 1987; Loftus & Ketcham 1991; Loftus et al. 1989). Although people introspectively believe that their memories are a process of uncovering what actually happened, as though a videotape had been made in the brain and is being replayed, in reality our memories are also reconstructed in accordance with our current beliefs and feelings. Loftus and Ketcham (1991) describe the reconstruction process and how people can come to believe firmly in events that never happened:

> Truth and reality, when seen through the filter of our memories, are not objective facts but subjective, interpretative realities. We interpret the past, correcting ourselves, adding bits and pieces, deleting uncomplimentary or disturbing recollections, sweeping, dusting, tidying things up. Thus our representation of the past takes on a living, shifting reality; it is not fixed and immutable, not a place way back there that is preserved in stone, but a living thing that changes shape, expands, shrinks, and expands again, an amoeba-like creature with powers to make us laugh, and cry, and clench our fists. Enormous powers—powers even to make us believe in something that never happened. (p. 20)

Children are often subjected to repeated interviews, sexual abuse therapy, and interactions with adults who believe that the abuse is real. The adults may ask a series of leading questions in which they provide information to the child about what supposedly happened. They may even tell the child that they already know about the abuse. Through this process of adult social influence, the adults may create stories about abuse that can become incorporated into the child's memory.

Understanding this process of adult social influence is necessary in assessing a child's statements about abuse. Although repeated and/or suggestive interviews do not mean that a child has not been abused, they can make it very difficult to sort out what, if anything, has happened. The influence of multiple interviews over time by persons who have a prior belief about what they think happened and who ask suggestive questions is discussed by several researchers in a recent American Psychological Association study edited by John Doris (1991).

A number of writers have examined the factors of memory development, cognitive and moral development of children, and suggestibility of children to adult social influence (e.g. Ceci & Bruck 1993; Doris 1991; Garbarino & Stott 1989; Lassiter, Stone, & Weigold 1987; Lepore 1991; Lindsay 1990; Loftus & Ketcham 1991; Wakefield & Underwager 1988; Underwager & Wakefield 1990). There is no doubt that children can be led to make statements about and sometimes believe in events that have not happened. This does not mean that children lie, but rather that they are influenced by the adult's agenda and beliefs (Wakefield & Underwager 1988).

Research on Memory and Suggestibility of Child Witnesses

After the turn of the century there were many studies done on children's memory and suggestibility. Many professionals concluded from this that children were not reliable witnesses, and demanded that children's testimony be excluded from the court record. The overall picture from the early studies is of a potentially accurate witness, who can recount events and answer non-leading questions fairly accurately, but whose report can easily be contaminated by suggestion (Goodman 1984).

Later studies compared the memory and suggestibility of children to that of adults. Loftus (1979) and Loftus and Davies (1984) summarize the results of studies that demonstrate how adults' memories are influenced by suggestion. The question that has been investigated in studies of children's memory and suggestibility is how suggestible they are as compared with adults.

Until recently, there was some disagreement concerning whether children are more susceptible than adults to distortions of memory caused by leading questions. The older studies concluded that children were more suggestible. Later studies found that both adults and children are influenced by leading questions but were inconsistent as to whether children were more suggestible. However, recent studies that have used younger children and attempted to employ a more natural or "ecologically valid" context have found young children to be more suggestible than adults and younger children to be more suggestible than older children (Doris 1991; Underwager & Wakefield 1990). Some recent studies have provided dramatic demonstrations of the degree to which young children can be influenced by an interviewer (Ceci & DeSimone 1992; Clarke-Stewart et al. 1989; Haugaard & Alhusen 1992; Thompson et al. 1991).

One of the most consistent research findings is that, although young children can provide accurate information, they recall less than do adults (Lepore 1991). But the less information the child gives in free recall, the sooner the interviewer will turn to using leading questions, which can influence the child and distort the story. Children may have a different perception of the interview than do the adults and therefore try to tell the interviewer what they believe the interviewer wants them to say (Ceci et al. 1987; Cole & Loftus 1987). They may answer questions they do not understand and about which they have no information (Hughes & Grieve 1983).

Although the newer research comes closer to duplicating the situation of a child witness in an actual case of alleged sexual abuse, the situation faced by a child witness in a real case cannot be reproduced in a laboratory study. With a few exceptions, the suggestions asked in the typical suggestibility experiment are much weaker than are found in an actual interview. Children are presented the misleading information once and may be given two or three misleading questions. But in the real world, interviews with young children often include many leading and suggestive questions and use significant pressure and coercion for the child to affirm abuse (DeLipsey & James 1988; Slicner & Hanson 1989; Underwager & Wakefield 1990; Warren et al. 1992).

In laboratory studies, children are generally tested immediately or after several days. But in sexual abuse cases in which children are required to testify as witnesses, they are often interviewed many times by a variety of people over a long period of time. Poole and White (1992) found young children were consistent if repeated but appropriately open-ended questioning was used immediately or one week after the event. However, when the children were questioned again two years later, repeated questioning increased inaccuracy. The authors noted that the children often seemed simply to make up responses. They conclude that, although children can be prompted to discuss a remote event, this procedure is not without risks. It cannot be assumed that results from studies using short retention intervals can be generalized to actual cases which often have long delays.

When the child eventually testifies, the memory will consist of a combination of recall and reconstruction influenced by all of the interviews, conversations, and therapy sessions that have occurred during the delay. The longer the delay, the greater the possibility of social influence and the more the memory may consist of reconstruction rather than recall. In addition, as Raskin and Yuille (1989) note, providing testimony in a sexual abuse case may have profound effects on the child's life. Whereas in the laboratory studies, the child's statements have no serious consequences, in real life, what the child says about sexual abuse may lead to the breakup of the home, inability to see a parent, or placement in a foster home.

Ceci and Burke (1993) determined that there are three conclusions which can be said to be generally accepted in the scientific community. First, there are significant age differences in suggestibility, with younger children more vulnerable to suggestion than older children and adults. Second, extreme positions, such as "Children never lie" versus "Children cannot distinguish reality and fantasy," are not supported. Young children do in fact make false claims about central events, particularly events that could be construed as sexually abusive. Third, children are capable of recalling much that is forensically relevant. However, it is of utmost importance to examine carefully and critically the conditions at the time of initial disclosure and the process since then to which the child has been subjected.

Unsupported Interview Techniques

Although so-called anatomically correct dolls are the most frequently used interview technique, investigators of sexual abuse also use a variety of other techniques with children (Kendall-Tackett 1992). These include the use of books, puppets, drawings, projective cards, play dough, games, and play therapy. None of these are reliable or valid techniques in assessing possible sexual abuse. Their use is likely to contaminate and influence the statements children may make. The suggestive nature of these techniques is increased when the interviewer encourages the child "to pretend."

Anatomical Dolls

Anatomically detailed dolls that are genitally differentiated are used by professionals from a variety of disciplines (Boat & Everson 1988; Conte et al. 1991; Kendall-Tackett & Watson 1992). The dolls, however, have proven to be extremely controversial and there is disagreement in the professional community as to whether they should be used (e.g., Yates & Terr 1988).

White and her colleagues (White, Strom, and Santilli 1986; White, Strom, and Halpin 1986) developed a structured protocol for the use of the dolls, but this has not been validated or accepted in clinical practice. Realmuto et al. (1990) used this protocol and found that their raters were unable to correctly classify the children as abused or nonabused. Only a few researchers, however, attempt to use any kind of protocol.

The American Psychological Association (APA Council of Representatives 1991) issued a statement concluding that there are no normative data for the dolls and their use, and that there are no uniform standards for conducting interviews with the dolls. But despite this, they are often used. Unfortunately, the persons actually using the dolls are often untrained, unsophisticated, and vary widely in their interpretation of children's behavior with the dolls (Boat & Everson 1988). Skinner et al. (1992) observe that dolls users are likely to develop personal norms based on their own experience and caution practitioners against equating their own experience with scientific evidence.

Modeling the dolls can be a learning experience for a child. Interviewers modeling the dolls suggest that they be undressed (or undress them for the child) and label them for the child. They ask the child to show with the dolls what the accused perpetrator did and may even place the dolls in sexually explicit positions for the child. This is, in effect, a teaching experience for the child. Several studies suggest that some nonabused children engage the dolls in sexual play (Dawson & Geddie 1991; Dawson et al. 1992; Everson & Boat 1990; McIver et al. 1989).

The rationale given for using the dolls is that it enables young children who have difficulty verbalizing their abuse to demonstrate it. But there are no data supporting the belief that a child who is unable to talk about what happened can then accurately demonstrate the event using a doll. In fact, one study found decreased accuracy when young children were asked to show on a doll where they were touched compared to being asked to show on their own bodies (DeLoache 1991).

Another rationalization offered is that the dolls enable an interviewer to go through a body parts naming procedure and learn the child's idiosyncratic terms for the genitals. This is often done early in the interview. When the questioning about body parts ends with the identification of the genitalia, as it often does, the child has likely been taught that the purpose of the interview is to talk about sexuality. There is no evidence to support the efficacy of this procedure. An interviewer does not need dolls to talk to children about sexuality or to learn the child's vocabulary. Props are not used to talk to children about anger, violence, play, kindness, or any other behavior about which they may have a unique, individualized vocabulary.

In summary, there is no evidence that doll interviews are a reliable method for obtaining accurate information about sexual abuse. The studies that claim to show differences between the responses of sexually abused and nonabused children have major methodological shortcomings which limit any conclusions that can be drawn from them (Ceci & Bruck 1993; Underwager & Wakefield 1990, Wakefield & Underwager 1989a; Wolfner et al. 1993). In a recent review of the empirical research, Skinner, et al. (1992) conclude that distinct patterns of play of abused versus nonabused children have not been identified and that the lack of norms calls into question the forensic use of the dolls. Wolfner et al. (1993) assert that there is no scientific evidence to justify clinical or forensic diagnosis of sexual abuse on the basis of doll play. Levy (1989) argues that any statement by a child that is the product of a doll-aided evaluation should be inadmissible as evidence.

Drawings

Children's drawings, such as the House-Tree-Person (HTP) and Kinetic Family Drawings, as well as free drawings, are often used in assessing possible sexual abuse. The assumption is that the drawings of children with emotional problems will differ from the drawings of normal children (DiLeo 1973; Koppitz 1968; Myers 1978; Yates et al. 1985). Qualitative features of the drawings may be seen as signs that the child has been sexually abused. These may include features such as the colors used, the size and detail of body parts such as hands, and the shape of the figures.

However, drawings lack validity and reliability as projective assessment devices. In a review of the Draw-A-Person test in the *Seventh Mental Measurements Yearbook,* Harris (Buros 1972) notes that there is very little evidence for the use of "signs" as valid indicators of personality characteristics. With children's drawings there is so much variability from drawing to drawing that particular features of any one drawing are too unreliable to say anything about them. The *Tenth Mental Measurements Yearbook* (Buros 1989), in reviews by Cundick and Weinberg (pp. 422–25), continues the consistent finding since the first edition (1938) that interpretations of drawings (as are often done in forensic evaluations) are not supported by data. Both reviewers note that there are no normative data establishing reliability and validity of the Kinetic Drawing System.

There are serious difficulties in the few research studies that report differences between the drawings of abused and nonabused children (Wakefield & Underwager 1988, 1989a). There is no good research establishing that the drawings can be used diagnostically to substantiate sexual abuse.

The only valid use of drawings lies in establishing rapport and encouraging the child to talk. For example, Burgess and Hartman (1993) describe a technique for using drawings as an associative tool in assessing and accessing stored memory. However, if drawings are used this way, the interviewer must avoid selective reinforcement and cueing of responses.

Another type of drawing often used is an outline of the back and the front of a boy or a girl. The child is shown the outline and instructed to put an X where he or she was touched. There is no research on this technique. The way it is often used may well give the child the message: "You were touched, now show me where."

Books and Projective Cards

Children's books about sexual abuse are often used in assessment sessions with children who are thought to have been sexually abused. A typical book is *Red Flag Green Flag People* (Rape and Crisis Abuse Center, 1985). In this book, the child is led through a series of pages that present good touch and bad touch. After several pages, a child is asked to color portions of a figure that may have been touched. When the child colors a genital area, this is regarded as evidence that the child has been abused. However, neither this book nor any others have been validated for diagnosing child sexual abuse. They may teach the child about what is expected to be said in the interview.

Two special techniques have been developed for assessing suspected Satanic ritual abuse. The *Projective Story Telling Cards* (Northwest Psychological Publishers 1990) and *Don't Make Me Go Back, Mommy: A Child's Book about Satanic Ritual Abuse* (Sanford 1990) contain explicit pictures illustrating Satanic rituals and are used to encourage the child to describe the abuse. These unvalidated techniques are likely to frighten a child as well as teach about what is supposed to occur in Satanic ritual abuse.

Play Therapy Observations

A child's behavior in play therapy may be used to substantiate abuse. Such therapy is sometimes called *disclosure-based* and the sessions focus on reenactments and talking about the alleged abuse. Although there is little evidence that play therapy is an effective therapeutic procedure for victims of child sexual abuse (Campbell 1992a; Underwager & Wakefield 1990; Wakefield

& Underwager 1988), children are frequently given disclosure-based play therapy for sexual abuse before there has been any legal determination that sexual abuse has occurred. Jones (1991) says that the use of the term "disclosure work" itself suggests the interrogator has a preconceived bias and is not able to consider the alternative, namely, that there is nothing to disclose.

A child who does not produce abuse statements or behaviors symbolically interpreted as suggesting abuse may be seen as being "in denial" and the questioning continues relentlessly. The play is often combined with questions and the behavior of the child in the play sessions is used to form conclusions about abuse. But there is no support for the supposition that behaviors in play therapy can be used as signs to establish the truth of past events. Campbell (1992b) notes that play therapy can influence children to accept the beliefs of the therapist and can be a contributing factor to false allegations.

Children's play has been shown to be aggressive, to use pretend monsters, and to express in behavior what may appear to be concepts of anxiety, fear, and sexuality (Archer et al. 1988; Best 1983; Bretherton 1982; Bretherton & Beeghly 1982; Fein 1981; Gundersen et al. 1981) but which instead may be normal, nonpathological behavior (Trad 1990). Of male and female children ages three to six, 75 percent tell stories that are violent and aggressive (Ames 1966). Fantasies of children express fear of monsters and mishaps (Pitcher & Prelinger 1966). Boys and girls show different patterns of play behavior; boys' aggressive behavior may be expressions of friendliness (Condry & Ross 1985; Maccoby 1990).

Many of the persons using play therapy and interpreting the play behavior appear to be uninformed about the research literature and the actual nature of children's play activities. Their personal and idiosyncratic values are then the basis for erroneous and unrealistic overinterpretations and misinterpretations. An example is a 5-year-old boy who played with the figures of popular mythical TV heroes and depicted aggressive behaviors. A sexual abuse "validator" interpreted these behaviors to mean that the child had been sexually abused.

Effective Interviews

Even very young children can provide accurate and useful information if the adults know how to interview them effectively. As mentioned above, the free recall of children is accurate. If the child is interviewed carefully and leading questions and suggestions avoided, the child can provide forensically useful information. Jones and Krugman (1986) describe a case of a 3-year-old girl, who had been abducted, sexually abused, and left to die in a mountain outhouse. When found and later interviewed by the police she was able to describe what had happened and to pick out the perpetrator from a lineup. The perpetrator ultimately confessed, confirming the accuracy of the child's description. Therefore, the task of the interviewer is to tap into a child's accurate free recall by encouraging the child to tell in his or her own words what has happened. Garbarino and Stott (1989) conclude that the problem is not that children cannot give reliable information, but rather that adults do not know how to get it from them.

Several professionals have suggested guidelines for conducting an unbiased evaluation and noncontaminating interview (e.g., Daly 1991, 1992a, 1992b; Quinn et al. 1989; Raskin & Yuille 1989; Slicner & Hanson 1989; Underwager & Wakefield 1991b; Wakefield & Underwager 1988; White 1990). The interviewer must enter the interview with an open mind about what may or may not have happened. There should be a conscious decision and continued conscious determination to delay decision making.

Unfortunately, mental health professionals often reach a quick diagnosis, within thirty to sixty seconds, and on the basis of idiosyncratic and unvalidated pathognomic signs (Gauron & Dickinson 1969). When this happens, the likelihood of error is increased, for once a choice is made, evidence may be fabricated to support the decision and contrary information ignored (Arkes & Harkness 1980). To prevent this, all possible alternatives should be considered until there are sufficient data to rule out those that are inapplicable. This might be done by using a form or writing out the alternatives to be considered. This approach has been shown to be effective in eliminating clinicians' bias (Arkes 1991).

Steller (1990) and Daly (1992b) also recommend formulating all possible alternative hypotheses about what led to the accusations of abuse. These hypotheses are successively explored and ruled out during the interview. Throughout, the interviewer should ask open-ended questions and encourage the child to provide a free narrative. Details should be encouraged by responses such as "and then what happened." Pressure and coercion, leading questions and selective reinforcement of responses, and unvalidated techniques must be avoided.

The interviewer should be fully informed about the serious consequences that may result if there is an error. For example, the reality of foster care should be known so that there is not the automatic assumption that the state can be a better and effective parent. This is a possible way to increase the response costs to decrease strategy-based errors (Arkes 1991). In-service training programs should include material that clarifies the potential for harm by the system.

King and Yuille (1987) stress that the child be told that the interviewer is only interested in what the child remembers, and that admissions of memory failure and memory gaps are expected. The child should be instructed (in an appropriate fashion), "I don't want you to say something that didn't happen, but if something did happen, I want you to tell me about it." Repeated questions should be avoided since this tells the child that the previous answers were not acceptable. Discussions of "good touch" and "bad touch" should not be used since these are confusing and potentially contaminating.

There is beginning research on a European procedure for interviewing children suspected of being abused and for analyzing the resulting interview. Criterion Based Content Analysis/Statement Validity Analysis (CBCA/SVA) assumes that an account based on memory of an actual event will differ in content and quality from accounts that are based on fabricated, learned, or suggested memory. The procedure requires a relatively complete statement obtained as soon as possible after the child has disclosed an incident; the interview must also be designed to obtain as much free narrative as possible. Leading questions and suggestions must be avoided. The interview is tape-recorded and transcribed for later analysis (Khnken & Steller 1988; Raskin & Esplin 1991; Rogers 1990; Undeutsch 1989).

Preliminary research on CBCA/SVA is promising. Raskin and Esplin (1991) found that the techniques discriminated between twenty interview statements of children independently determined to have been abused and twenty statements in cases determined to be false. Horowitz et al. (1992) found high reliability for the criteria used in CBCA/SVA as a whole, although there was variability for individual criteria.

A professional may be asked to assess a case after the child has been interviewed by others. In such cases, the progress of the case and the procedures followed by the previous evaluators must be carefully examined in order to assess possible contamination (Wakefield & Underwager 1988; White & Quinn 1988). What happens to a child during the process of investigation and the interim between beginning an investigation and reaching trial or dispositional hearing is crucial for making the best possible and most accurate decisions (Ceci & Burke 1993). Children are often interviewed repeatedly by a variety of trained and untrained adults, and may be put into disclosure-based sexual abuse therapy. When children have been subjected to leading and coercive interviews, their recollections may become so contaminated that it is extremely difficult to determine what happened. Therefore, it is essential to analyze all contacts with the child in which abuse was discussed.

All interviews of the child should be videotaped, or at least audiotaped, since a tape is the only means whereby the procedures and information obtained during the interview can be accurately documented (DeLipsey & James 1988; Herbert et al. 1987; Raskin & Yuille 1989; Underwager & Wakefield 1990, Wakefield & Underwager 1988, 1989a). In practice, this is often not done. Many prosecutors do not want the defense to have access to a tape so that they can criticize the interviewer's techniques during the trial (Stern 1992). This is hardly a legitimate argument if the goal is accuracy and avoidance of harm to children by the system.

Behavioral Indications

Lists of behaviors thought to be caused by sexual abuse have been widely publicized (e.g., Cohen 1985; Council on Scientific Affairs 1985; Sgroi 1982). These behaviors are quite inclusive; nearly every problem behavior exhibited by children has been offered by someone as a sign of possible sexual abuse. As a result, when these behaviors are observed, an adult may become suspicious and begin questioning the child. Particularly when the questioning adult is untrained and believes abuse is likely, the questioning may result in answers that are interpreted as indicating abuse.

However, all of the behaviors mentioned on the lists are found in nonabused children. They appear in many different situations, including conflict between parents; divorce; economic stress; wartime separations; father absence; natural disaster; and physical, emotional, but nonsexual abuse (Emery 1982; Hughes & Barad 1983; Jaffe et al. 1986; Porter & O'Leary 1980; Wallerstein & Kelly 1980; Wolman 1983). Although children who are distressed for whatever reason may show behavior changes, there are no behaviors exclusive to victims of sexual abuse. A recent review of the literature concluded that with the exception of sexualized behavior, the majority of symptoms shown in sexually abused children characterize child clinical samples in general (Beitchman et al. 1991).

Even sexualized behavior cannot be used as proof of abuse. What children normally do sexually is more involved than most people believe (Best 1983; Gundersen et al. 1981; Langfeldt 1981; Martinson 1981; Okami 1992). Friedrich et al. (1991) asked mothers of 880 nonabused 2- to 12-year-old children to complete questionnaires concerning sexual behavior. Although behaviors imitative of adult sexual behaviors were rare, the children exhibited a wide variety of sexual behaviors at relatively high frequencies. Mannarino et al. (1991) report no differences in sexual behavior between abused girls and a clinical control group, although both scored higher than did the normal controls. Haugaard and Tilly (1988) found that approximately 28 percent of male and female undergraduates reported having engaged in sexual play with another child when they were children.

On the other hand, since many sexually abused children do not suffer significant trauma (Browne & Finkelhor 1986; Gomes-Schwartz, et al. 1990; Wakefield & Underwager 1988) an abused child may not exhibit any behavioral signs. It is thus a mistake to use the absence of behavioral signs as support for an allegation being false.

Therefore, using behavioral indicators to assess sexual abuse may result in a mistake in either direction. Besharov (1990) observes that behavioral indicators by themselves are not a sufficient basis for a report, Levine and Battistoni (1991) state that none of these indicators, in any combination, are valid without a direct statement by the child about sexual involvement or sexual knowledge.

This entire procedure of attempting to infer *a posteriori* to an alleged prior event and claim that a present observation establishes the facticity of the alleged earlier event is the logical error of affirming the consequence. It will result in increased error and will produce harm (Gambrill 1990). In the absence of credible data supporting a strong causal relationship, this procedure should not be used.

Physical Evidence

Although medical examinations are common when there is an allegation of sexual abuse, the results are frequently ambiguous. Much abuse involves exhibitionism, fondling, and masturbation of the perpetrator rather than anal, oral or vaginal penetration, and therefore there will be no physical or medical evidence. However, police, social workers, juries, prosecutors, defense attorneys, and therapists have come to rely on physicians to find evidence that will either rule out or substantiate the abuse (Coleman 1989; Paradise 1989). It may be that too much credence is given to medical evidence when there are no conclusive data for almost all of the physical observations that are made.

Nevertheless, a physical examination is important, particularly when the allegations are of behaviors likely to result in physical sequelae. There have been attempts made to classify the physical findings in terms of how specific they are to sexual abuse (Bays & Chadwick 1993). For example, the presence of semen or sperm would be classified as a definitive finding of sexual abuse; marked enlargement of the hymenal opening, recent lacerations of the hymen, or laboratory confirmation of a venereal disease would be a specific finding, and various abnormalities of the genitals would be a nonspecific finding.

The examination should take place as soon as possible since genital injuries heal rapidly and physical signs will be difficult to detect if the examination is not performed immediately after the alleged event (Bays & Chadwick 1993; McCann et al. 1992). Paul (1990) describes the expected physical signs when there is abuse but cautions physicians concerning the risks of an incorrect interpretation. Sometimes the absence of an expected finding can be important, such as an intact hymen when full vaginal penetration is alleged, or the failure of the child to describe severe pain during penetration or when defecation is attempted after allegations of anal rape.

Unfortunately, there is generally little consideration given as to whether the physician's conclusions are speculation or legitimate scientific evidence. A 1983 paper by Cantwell is still frequently cited in support of the belief that a vaginal opening size above four millimeters indicates abuse, although there has never been empirical support for this claim. Other normal findings, or vague and ambiguous findings, such as genital redness, are seen as "consistent with" sexual abuse. Physicians often rely on the history given by the person who brings the child in for the examination and conclude, "sexual abuse based on history." Such statements are taken seriously by others and repeated as evidence that the physical examination has substantiated the allegation. An analysis by Paradise (1989) suggests that 65 percent false positives occur when assessing penile penetration and 73 percent false positives with assessment of digital penetration. This raises serious questions about the validity and reliability of medical examinations.

Until recently, a major difficulty in evaluating physical findings was the absence of baseline data—that is, information about the appearance of the genitals in normal, nonabused children. This situation has now changed. Adams (1992) observes that there are now enough data on normal and presumably nonabused children to classify many findings as either normal or nonspecific.

McCann and his colleagues conducted research on 267 prepubertal children, screened to rule out sexual abuse (McCann et al. 1989, 1990; McCann et al. 1990). They found a high incidence of nonspecific findings such as erythema (redness of the skin), tags, fissures, scars, adhesions, notches, thickening, and anal relaxation in their sample of nonabused children; therefore, they urge physicians to exercise caution in giving an opinion about the significance of such findings. They also found a large range of vertical and horizontal hymenal orifice diameters and report that this varied not only by age group, but according to the technique and position used to measure it. Emans et al. (1987) also found a large range of hymenal openings in their subjects and report that the genital findings of sexually abused girls were similar to nonabused girls who had other genital complains such as vaginitis, vulvitis, bleeding, or dysuria (difficulty in urinating). Bays and Chadwick (1993) note that there are a variety of dermatologic, congenital, traumatic, and infectious conditions that may mimic findings caused by sexual abuse.

Coleman (1989), after analyzing 158 medical examinations in cases of alleged sexual abuse, reports that nearly all the findings attributed to abuse were found by McCann in substantial numbers of the normal children he had examined. Coleman, however, does not differentiate between children who were later determined to be abused or nonabused. In 216 cases we have analyzed arising in the context of divorce, similar vague and nonspecific findings were commonly interpreted as supporting the allegation. This was also true in the majority of the cases we classified as false allegations and where abuse was not found by the justice system.

Sexually transmitted diseases support a suspicion of sexual abuse since sexual contact is the most common means of transmission. Sexual transmission of diseases outside of the perinatal period is rare (Bays & Chadwick 1993). However, since there can be alternative explanations for the transmission of sexual diseases, a finding of a venereal disease does not conclusively establish sexual abuse (Wakefield & Underwager 1988). In addition, the testing performed may be inaccurate or inappropriate. For example, a chlamydia screening test meant for an adult may be highly inaccurate with a child, and produce false positives because the test reacts positively to certain bacteria normally found in the intestinal tract of children (Fay 1991).

The only specific and unambiguous physical findings demonstrating sexual contact are pregnancy or sperm in the vagina or anus. Krugman (1989) concludes: "The medical diagnosis of sexual abuse usually cannot be made on the basis of physical findings alone. With the exception of acquired gonorrhea or syphilis, or the presence of forensic evidence of sperm or semen, there are no pathognomic signs for sexual abuse" (pp. 165–66).

SUGGESTED CRITERIA FOR DIFFERENTIATING BETWEEN REAL AND FALSE ALLEGATIONS

The Origin and Timing of the Original Disclosure

The allegations are less likely to be correct when the parent, rather than the child, initiates the disclosure (Yates & Musty 1988; Yates 1988). The disclosure may have come about only after the parent becomes suspicious after observing one of the behavioral indicators and begins questioning the child (Wakefield & Underwager 1988; Rogers 1990). Although adolescents sometimes initiate false allegations for a variety of reasons, young children almost never initiate false allegations without influence from an adult. Klajner-Diamond et al. (1987) note that false allegations are most likely the result of adult indoctrination rather than childhood fantasy. A spontaneous disclosure made by a young child without evident adult influence is more likely to be true.

The timing and circumstances of the allegation are also important, especially in the divorce and custody context. Although both true and false accusations of sexual abuse can occur at at any point (Blush & Ross 1987; Underwager & Wakefield 1988; Wakefield & Underwager 1991), there is a difference between an accusation that appears in a continuing marriage and an accusation that first appears during a custody or visitation battle. If the allegation appears in the midst of a custody or visitation dispute, it is more likely to be false. But if it can be determined that the divorce occurs as a result of the abuse disclosures, the abuse is more likely to be true. Sirles and Lofberg (1990) studied 128 families in which sexual abuse occurred: approximately half of these families ended in separation and/or divorce.

The Age of the Child

Allegations that turn out to be false appear to involve very young children. Schaefer and Guyer (1988) report that the children in their false cases were most often under five years old. Everstine and Everstine (1989) note that a younger child whose parents are divorcing may be more vulnerable to the manipulations of an angry and vengeful parent. Our analysis of 216 cases of sexual abuse allegations arising in a divorce context, which involved 325 children, found that the median age was 8.6 when the allegations were probably true, and 4.6 when the allegations were probably false.

The Nature of the Allegations

Schaefer and Guyer (1988) observe that in cases involving false allegations in the divorce and custody context, the allegations were often extremely vague. Often the allegation involved no specific behavior but only a vague observation that something was happening. Also, normal parenting behaviors such as bathing, toileting, and tickling may be mistakenly labeled as sexual abuse (Cooke & Cooke 1991). Rosenfeld and his colleagues (Rosenfeld et al. 1986; Rosenfeld et al. 1987) stress getting normative information on nakedness, genital touching and bathing practices before deciding whether any of these behaviors supports a suspicion of sexual abuse, since they found that many behaviors that could trigger suspicion of abuse occurred often in normal families.

When there is no corroborating evidence, and the behaviors alleged are highly improbable, it is unlikely that the allegations are true (Wakefield & Underwager 1988, 1991, 1992b). There is information about the behavior of known sexual abusers (e.g., Erickson et al. 1988; Tollison & Adams 1979). Fondling is common and aggression and physical violence are rare. Bribery is more common than threat. Vaginal and anal penetration are rare in very young children because it is so painful. Girls are more likely than boys to be victims.

Allegations of ritual abuse should be treated with great suspicion. Although such allegations are often directed at multi-perpetrator, multi-victim day care situations, they are occasionally seen in divorce and custody battles. Both parents are also occasionally accused of ritual abuse with their own children. However, despite hundreds of investigations by the FBI and police, there is no independent evidence supporting the existence of organized cults of outwardly normal people who engage in ritual abuse, animal and human sacrifice, murder, and cannibalism of children (Bromley 1991; Hicks 1991; Jenkins & Maier-Katkin 1991; Lanning 1991, 1992; Mulhern 1991; Noll 1989; Nathan 1991; Putnam 1991; Russell 1991; Underwager & Wakefield 1991a; Victor 1991a, 1991b; Wakefield & Underwager 1992a; see also Victor in this volume).

Therefore, when the allegations are of very low frequency behaviors such as rape, physical violence, vaginal or anal penetration of a very young child, use of feces and urine, and/or ritual abuse with several people involved, the allegations are unlikely to be true.

Characteristics of the Accused

Deviant and bizarre allegations are even less likely to be true if the accused has been evaluated and found to be psychologically normal. Although child sexual abusers form a heterogeneous group, they tend to have behavioral and psychological difficulties. Studies on the Minnesota Multiphasic Personality Disorders (MMPIs) of sex offenders may show elevations on scales reflecting poor impulse control and judgment, antisocial behavior, a history of "acting out," lack of self-esteem, feelings of inadequacy, a schizoid social adjustment, much time spent in fantasies, and/or thought disorders and confusion.

However, since some sex offenders produce MMPIs within normal limits—Erickson et al. (1987) found this in 19 percent of their convicted sex offenders sample—a "normal" personality profile on the MMPI or other assessment technique does not rule out the possibility that the individual is a sexual abuser. But knowledge of the accused person's personality characteristics becomes more useful as the alleged abusive behaviors become more bizarre and deviant. It is not likely that a psychologically normal individual would engage in sadistic and violent sexual behaviors.

Characteristics of the Child's Statement

There is general agreement concerning the characteristics of a child's statement in cases of actual abuse compared to false allegations, although little research has been done thus far on this important variable. Contextual details are seen by most professionals as important. DeYoung (1986) notes that affective details, specific action, and contextual details are found in valid accounts and that in a false allegation, the child will be unlikely to give such details. Jones and Seig (1988) observe that when the allegation is false, the child will give an inconsistent, sparse, or unrealistic account. Sink (1988a) believes that in real abuse the child will spontaneously provide contextual descriptive information and that the child's affect will be appropriate to the report. Jones and McGraw (1987) state that a child's account of actual abuse will have, relative to age, a sufficient amount of uniqueness and idiosyncracy of detail, appropriate emotion, and reports of secrecy, coercion, or threats.

Faller (1988) analyzed 103 cases in which the perpetrator had confessed to some level of the abuse. She examined the child's statements for contextual details, the description or demonstration of the sexual victimization, and the child's emotional state. She reports that a description of the sexual behavior of the sort said to be found in a true allegation as well as an emotional reaction to the sexual abuse was found in over four-fifths of the statements. Contextual details were found in over three-fourths. Over two-thirds of the allegations contained all of these characteristics. Faller therefore concluded that this study supports the clinical assumptions concerning these criteria.

These characteristics are similar to several of the criteria looked for in the CBCA/SVA procedure described earlier (Horowitz, et al. 1992; Köhnken & Steller 1988; Raskin & Esplin 1991; Rogers 1990; Undeutsch 1989). Therefore, the quantity, quality and contextual embedding of details and appropriate affect and emotion are useful criteria when evaluating the child's statement. However, the statement must be obtained as soon as possible from a child who has made a spontaneous disclosure. It must also be based upon the child's narrative account and not on yes or no answers to the interviewer's leading questions.

In divorce and custody cases, strong hatred expressed toward the accused parent based upon trivial and vague reasons may result from learning from the accusing parent rather than from actual abuse (Gardner 1992). Ross and Blush (1990) report that in a false allegation, the child may describe "horrible" and traumatic events while not appearing to be traumatized. Also, a young child who is very eager to talk about the abuse may have learned that adults reward such talk (Wakefield & Underwager 1988).

Telltale Signals of the Parties Involved

Personality disorders and other psychiatric problems have been reported in parents who make false allegations (Ross & Blush 1990; Green & Schetky 1988; Jones & McGraw 1987; Rogers 1990; Klajner-Diamond, et al. 1987; Wakefield & Underwager 1990). Faller (1990) notes that a childhood history of abuse in the mother may result in distortions of events or hypervigilance. However, as Bresee et al. (1986) point out, a troubled woman with vengeful motives may nevertheless have discovered genuine evidence of sexual abuse.

Several writers have described differences in the behavior of an accusing parent when there is real abuse compared to cases of false allegations (e.g., Bresee et al. 1986; Cooke & Cooke 1991; Faller 1990; Gardner 1992; Jones & Seig 1988; Wakefield & Underwager 1991). The natural response of a reporting parent is to hope that the child was not sexually abused and to be relieved when the evaluator believes abuse is unlikely. The parent will consider other explanations for the behaviors that aroused her suspicions and she may initially report not believing the abuse, or thinking that the child was mistaken. If the evaluator concludes that abuse was likely, she will probably be upset, distressed, and embarrassed.

But in a false allegation, the accusing parent may remain firmly convinced the abuse is real. She is likely to feel vindicated if her suspicions are validated by the interview or medical examination, and may even tell everyone what happened and what a terrible person her former spouse was. If the evaluator says that abuse is unlikely, this parent may seek out another professional to confirm her suspicions. She may even involve the child in multiple examinations and interviews despite the effect of this on the child (Bresee et al. 1986; Cooke & Cooke 1991; Rand 1989, 1990; Schaefer & Guyer 1988). Such an experience can be iatrogenically negative for the child (Jones 1991).

Although observations of the behavior and motivations on the part of the person reporting the abuse may be helpful in the divorce and custody situation, teachers, day care workers, and therapists may also be primed to find sexual abuse. They may have attended sexual abuse workshops, learned the behavioral indicators, been told to be alert to any sign of sexual abuse, and believe that sexual abuse is rampant. They may therefore observe an ambiguous behavior, conclude that the child has likely been abused, and begin questioning the child in a way that results in the child giving answers that are interpreted as supporting their suspicions.

The professionals who have interviewed the child may be biased. Klajner-Diamond et al. (1987) note that one factor suggesting a false accusation is a professional committed prematurely to the truth of the allegation. Blush and Ross (1990) observe that false cases are characterized by a loss of control early on when professionals decide that abuse is real before doing a careful investigation. This is seldom deliberate, although there may be an occasional professional who will collude with parents to develop false accusations (Wakefield & Underwager 1989b).

ANTISEXUALITY

A final observation about the current sexual abuse system is that it represents a violent and virulent antisexualism, the likes of which the world has not known since the days of Tertullian, the second-century Christian apologist who maintained that the only proper way to be a Christian was to emasculate oneself. In a recent interview, Judith Herman, a Harvard psychiatrist and early feminist who has specialized in sexual abuse, said about molesters, "They are just evil. They do it because they want to and it gives them satisfaction" (Hawkins 1991: 50). This stance is also demonstrated in the effort to link child sexual abuse with Satanic, ritualistic abuse allegations.

Money (1991) sees the antisexualism of the child sexual abuse system as a new specialty of victimology and maintains there is a strong element of man-bashing that is part of a more generalized hostile reaction to the sexual revolution of the 1960s. He also sees victimology as equating sex with wrongdoing (Money 1982). Mosher (1991) traces the development of the view of children presented in the history of American child-saving: "The *rebellious child* became the *deprived child* who became the *sick child* who has now become the *victimized child*" (p. 15). This aspect of antisexualism is accepted without criticism within professional societies and accorded respectability in the professional community (Money 1992).

At the same time, professional societies support the politically correct hangovers of the sexual revolution with their stances toward abortion, gay rights, and feminist rhetoric. The earliest child abuse prevention programs were proliferated by feminists. Sexual abuse prevention programs that have proliferated throughout the country are based on empowerment theory. The orientation of empowerment theory is political ideology, which has antisexualism at its core (Krivacska 1991).

Antisexualism may be discerned in the language game of sexual abuse with its own peculiar, idiosyncratic usage of terms such as "hurt," "touch," "feel funny," "body parts," "yucky," and "uncomfortable." The system does not permit direct language about sexuality but uses circumlocutions such as "parts covered by a bathing suit." This can only communicate to children that sex is viewed negatively and cannot be talked about freely and openly. If a young child who has little knowledge of adult sexual behavior is questioned repeatedly about deviant sexuality, that child has been taught a negative view of sexuality. The focus on genitals teaches a genitalized and partial view of sex that will hinder the development of concepts of intimacy and sexuality (Krivacska 1990; Nelson 1978).

A distressing trend is the tendency to label childhood sexual play as sexual abuse (Okami 1992). This criminalization of what used to be understood as relatively normal sexual play and curiosity reflects the antisexualism of the sexual abuse system. An example is Cantwell's (1988) discussion of what she terms "very young perpetrators." She does not adequately define normal sexual behavior and includes in her examples a 7-year-old who was "playing sexually with a 5-year-old neighbor" (p. 580).

Haugaard (1990) emphasizes that there is no justification for labeling mutually enjoyable sex play as sexually abusive or for labeling one or both of the children as an abuser. But this is happening. Thompson (1992) describes a situation where consensual fondling of a 14-year-old girl's breasts by her 16-year-old boyfriend resulted in the boy being convicted of sexual abuse.

Very young children may be sentenced to therapy programs or to various forms of detention. In Phoenix boys as young as seven were sentenced to a treatment program for young offenders using a penile plethysmograph and avoidance conditioning. They were shown specific sexual stimuli, including heterosexual, homosexual, and pedophilic acts; if the plethysmograph registered penile engorgement they are subjected to a noxious stimulus (Young 1992).

Insurance companies may pay large sums of money rather than go to trial when there are allegations of sexual play between children. We consulted in one case where an allegation of sexual play between a 4-year-old boy and a 3-year-old girl in a day care setting resulted in the parents of the girl collecting from the insurers. In another case, a man who had befriended a single mother was accused of sexual abuse when he kissed her 10-year-old boy good night and patted him on the buttocks. The man was sentenced to two years in prison. The prosecutor in the closing argument told the judge that no man should ever be able to do anything that makes a child uncomfortable and excuse it by claiming he was being affectionate.

CONCLUSIONS

The real victims of sexual abuse of children include all of us, because the system we have set up to eliminate abuse of children may be doing more damage than good. Children may be harmed by the intervention. Families, including extended family members, may be destroyed. Grandparents may never see their grandchildren again. Occupations that involve work with children become suspect: Teachers, preachers, boy scout leaders, big brothers, athletic coaches, day care workers, counselors, mental health professionals, and others are watched suspiciously by a society that asks why they choose to work with children. Lonely people learn quickly to avoid all friendly actions toward children (Weinbach 1987). Men learn that in spite of twenty years of rhetoric telling them they can have feelings and be gentle, if they are affectionate with children they can go to prison.

Raymond Buckey (Buckey et al. 1990), who surely has the credentials to claim being damaged by the system, spoke of how everyone was a victim in the McMartin preschool case:

> These families and the children are victims just like us. We were all victims. We were sucked into the system and we were pawns just like the families were. We would not attack those children and those families on the stand because we realize what they went through also and we can sympathize with them but at the same time we had to show that what they said wasn't true. . . . But no, we don't attack those people. (p. 224)

Unfortunately, many professionals who have worked hard and long to raise public awareness of child sexual abuse react defensively to legitimate questions about unjustified costs and false victims (Weinbach 1987). Those professionals who believe they have been ill treated by the system have great difficulty letting go of their emotional investment in establishing their innocence. Colleagues are sharply and deeply polarized. Charges and countercharges fly back and forth at personal, associational, institutional, and societal levels.

It must be possible for all who are concerned with reducing the abuse of children to agree cognitively that increasing the accuracy of the process is both desirable and attainable. There is more credible and reliable information now than a few years ago. It is possible now to assert, as Ceci and Burke (1993) do, that there is a general consensus in the scientific community about some basic facts. Potentially this information can be used to develop a more accurate and reliable way to make decisions about child sexual abuse which will result in greater protection of abused children and less harm to innocent persons.

REFERENCES

Adams, J. A. (1992). "Significance of Medical Findings in Suspected Sexual Abuse: Moving toward Consensus." *Journal of Child Sexual Abuse* 1, no. 3: 91–99.

Altemeier, W.; O'Connor, S.; Vietze, P.; Sandler, H.; and Sherrod, K. (1984). "Prediction of Child Abuse: A Prospective Study of Feasibility." *Child Abuse and Neglect* 8: 393–400.

Ames, L. B. (1966). "Children's Stories." *Genetic Psychology Monographs* 73: 337–96.

APA Council of Representatives (1991, February 8). *Statement on the Use of Anatomically Detailed Dolls in Forensic Evaluations.* Washington, D.C.: American Psychological Association.

Archer, J.; Pearson, N. A.; and Westeman, K. E. (1988). "Aggressive Behavior of Children Aged 6–11: Gender Differences and Their Magnitude." *British Journal of Social Psychology* 27: 371–84.

Arkes, H. R. (1991). "Costs and Benefits of Judgment Errors: Implications for Debiasing." *Psychological Bulletin* 110: 486–98.

Arkes, H. R., and Harkness, A. R. (1980). "Effects of Making a Diagnosis on Subsequent Recognition of Symptoms." *Journal of Experimental Psychology: Human Learning and Memory* 6: 568–75.

Associated Press (1992, June 27). "Policeman Kills Self after Accusation He Kissed Boy He Was Counseling." *Star Tribune,* Minneapolis, Minn., p. 7A.

Baurmann, M. (1983). *Sexualität, Gewalt und psychische Folgen.* Eine Langsschnittuntersuchung bei opfern sexueller Gewalt und sexuellen Normverletzungen anhand von angezeigten Sexualkontakten. Wiesbaden.

Bays, J., and Chadwick, D. (1993). "Medical Diagnosis of the Sexually Abused Child." *Child Abuse and Neglect* 17: 91–110.

Beitchman, J. H.; Zucker, K. J., Hood, J. E.; daCosta, G. A.; and Akman, D. (1991). "A Review of the Short-Term Effects of Child Sexual Abuse." *Child Abuse and Neglect* 15: 537–56.

Benedek, E. P., and Schetky, D. H. (1985a). "Allegations of Sexual Abuse in Child Custody and Visitation Disputes." In E. Benedek and D. Schetky, eds., *Emerging Issues in Child Psychiatry and the Law,* pp. 145–56. New York: Brunner/Mazel.

——— (1985b). "Custody and Visitation: Problems and Perspectives." *Psychiatric Clinics of North America* 8: 857–73.

Berliner, L. (1988). "Deciding Whether a Child Has Been Sexually Abused." In E. B. Nicholson and J. Bulkley, eds., *Sexual Abuse Allegations in Custody and Visitation Cases,* pp. 48–69. Washington, D.C.: The American Bar Association.

Besharov, D. J. (1985a, Spring). "Right versus Rights: The Dilemma of Child Protection." *Public Welfare,* pp. 19–27.

——— (1985b). *The Vulnerable Social Worker.* Silver Spring, Md.: The National Association of Social workers.

——— (1986). "Unfounded Allegations—A New Child Abuse Problem." *The Public Interest* 83: 18–33.

——— (1990, Spring). "Gaining Control Over Child Abuse Reports." *Public Welfare,* pp. 34–41.

Best, R. (1983). "Fun and Games in the Primary Grades." In *We've All Got Scars: What Boys and Girls Learn in Elementary School,* pp. 109–125. Bloomington, Ind.: Indiana University Press.

Blush, G. L., and Ross, K. L. (1987). "Sexual Allegations in Divorce: The SAID Syndrome." *Conciliation Courts Review* 25, no. 1.

——— (1990). "Investigation and Case Management Issues and Strategies." *Issues in Child Abuse Accusations* 2: 152–60.

Boat, B. W., and Everson, M. D. (1988). "Use of Anatomical Dolls among Professionals in Sexual Abuse Evaluations." *Child Abuse and Neglect* 12: 171–79.

Bradburn, N. M.; Rips, L. J.; and Shevell, S. K. (1987). "Answering Autobiographical Questions: The Impact of Memory and Inference on Surveys." *Science* 236, no. 10: 157–61.

Bresee, P.; Stearns, G. B.; Bess, B. H.; and Packer, L. S. (1986). "Allegations of Child Sexual Abuse in Child Custody Disputes: A Therapeutic Assessment Model." *American Journal of Orthopsychiatry* 56: 560–69.

Bretherton, I. (1984). "Representing the Social World in Symbolic Play: Reality and Fantasy." In I. Bretherton, ed., *The Development of Social Understanding,* pp. 3–41. New York: Academic Press.

Bretherton, E., and Beeghly, M. (1982). "Talking about Internal States: The Acquisition of an Explicit Theory of Mind." *Developmental Psychology* 18: 906–921.

Bromley, D. G. (1991). "Satanism: The New Cult Scare." In J. T. Richardson, J. Best, and D. G. Bromley, eds., *The Satanism Scare,* pp. 49–72. New York: Aldine De Gruyter.

Browne, A., and Finkelhor, D. (1986). "Initial and Long-Term Effects: A Review of the Research." In D. Finkelhor, *A Sourcebook on Child Sexual Abuse,* pp. 143–79. Beverly Hills, Calif.: Sage Publications, Inc.

Buckey, P.; Buckey, R.; Buckey, P. A. (1990). "After the McMartin Trials: Some Reflections from the Buckeys." *Issues In Child Abuse Accusations* 2: 220–25.

Burgess, A. W., and Hartman, C. R. (1993). "Children's Drawings." *Child Abuse and Neglect* 17, no. 1: 161–68.

Buros, O. K., ed., (1972). *The Seventh Mental Measurements Yearbook,* pp. 401–405). Highland Park, N.J.: Gryphon Press.

——— (1989). *The Tenth Mental Measurements Yearbook,* pp. 422–25). Highland Park, N.J.: Gryphon Press.

Caldwell, R. A.; Bogat, G. A.; and Davidson, W. S. (1988). "The Assessment of Child Abuse Potential and Prevention of Child Abuse and Neglect: A Policy Analysis." *American Journal of Community Psychology* 16, no. 5: 609–624.

Campbell, T. W. (1992a). "Promoting Play Therapy: Marketing Dream or Empirical Nightmare." *Issues in Child Abuse Accusations* 4: 111–17.

——— (1992b). "False Allegations of Sexual Abuse and the Persuasiveness of Play Therapy." *Issues in Child Abuse Accusations* 4: 118–24.

Cantwell, H. B. (1983). "Vaginal Inspection As It Relates to Child Sexual Abuse in Girls Under Thirteen." *Child Abuse and Neglect* 7: 171–76.

——— (1988). "Child Sexual Abuse: Very Young Perpetrators." *Child Abuse and Neglect* 12: 579–84.

Ceci, S. J., and Bruck, M. (1993). "The Suggestibility of the Child Witness: A Historical Review and Synthesis." *Psychological Bulletin.*

Ceci, S. J., and DeSimone, M. (1992, March 14). "Group Distortion Effects in Preschooler's Reports." Paper presented at the American Psychology-Law Society Biennial Meeting, San Diego, Calif.

Ceci, S. J.,;Ross, D. F.; and Toglia, M. P. (1987). "Age Differences in Suggestibility: Narrowing the Uncertainties." In S. J. Ceci, M. P. Toglia, and D. F. Ross, eds., *Children's Eyewitness Memory,* pp. 178–208. New York: Springer-Verlag.

Clarke-Stewart, A.; Thompson, W.; and Lepore, S. (1989, April). "Manipulating Children's Interpretations through Interrogation." Paper presented at the biennial meeting of The Society for Research in Child Development, Kansas City, Mo.

Cohen, A. (1985). "The Unreliability of Expert Testimony on the Typical Characteristics of Sexual Abuse Victims." *Georgetown Law Journal* 74: 429–56.

Cole, C. B., and Loftus, E. F. (1987). "The Memory of Children." In S. J. Ceci, M. P. Toglia, and D. F. Ross, eds., *Children's Eyewitness Memory,* pp. 178–208. New York: Springer-Verlag.

Coleman, L. (1989). "Medical Examination for Sexual Abuse: Have We Been Misled?" *Issues in Child Abuse Accusations* 1, no. 3: 1–9.

Coleman, L., and Clancy, P. E. (1990). "False Allegations of Sexual Abuse: Why Is It Happening? What Can We Do?" *Criminal Justice* 5, no. 3: 14–47.

Condry, J. C., and Ross, D. F. (1985). "Sex and Aggression: The Influence of Gender Label on the Perception of Aggression in Children." *Child Development* 56: 225–33.

Conte, J. R.; Sorenson, E.; Fogarty, L.; and Rosa, J. D. (1991). "Evaluating Children's Reports of Sexual Abuse: Results from a Survey of Professionals." *American Journal of Orthopsychiatry* 61: 428–37.

Cooke, G., and Cooke, M. (1991). "Dealing with Sexual Abuse Allegations in the Context of Custody Evaluations." *American Journal of Forensic Psychology* 9, no. 3: 55–67.

Corwin, D.; Berliner, L.; Goodman, G. S.; Goodwin, J.; and White, S. (1987). "Child Sexual Abuse and Custody Disputes: No Easy Answers." *Journal of Interpersonal Violence* 2: 91–105.

Council on Scientific Affairs (1985). "AMA Diagnostic and Treatment Guidelines concerning Child Abuse and Neglect." *Journal of the American Medical Association* 254: 796–800.

Daly, L. W. (1991). "The Essentials of Child Abuse Investigation and Child Interviews." *Issues in Child Abuse Accusations* 3: 90–98.

——— (1992a). "Who Evaluates Child Interviews and Interviewers?" *Issues in Child Abuse Accusations* 4: 1–16.

——— (1992b). "Child Sexual Abuse Allegations: Investigative Approaches to Identifying 'Alternative Hypotheses.' " *Issues in Child Abuse Accusations* 4: 125–31.

Davis, S. M., and Reppucci, N. D. (1992, March 12–15). "Accusations of Child Sexual Abuse: A Study of Process and Consequences." Paper presented at the Biennial meeting of the American Psychology-Law Society, San Diego, Calif.

Dawes, R. M. (1988). *Rational Choice in an Uncertain World.* San Diego: Harcourt Brace Jovanovich.

Dawson, B., and Geddie, L. (1991, August). "Low Income, Minority Preschoolers' Behavior with Sexually Anatomically Detailed Dolls." Paper presented at the American Psychological Association in San Francisco, Calif.

Dawson, B.; Vaughan, A. R.; and Wagner, W. G. (1992). "Normal Responses to Sexually Anatomically Detailed Dolls." *Journal of Family Violence* 7, no. 2: 135–52.

DeLipsey, J. M., and James, S. K. (1988). "Videotaping the Sexually Abused Child: The Texas Experience, 1983–1987." In S. M. Sgroi, ed., *Vulnerable Populations: Evaluation and Treatment of Sexually Abused Children and Adult Survivors,* 1: 229–64. Lexington, Mass.: Lexington Books.

DeLoache, J. (1991, August 18). Discussant at invited address by Gail Goodman at the 99th Annual Convention of the American Psychological Association, San Francisco.

DiLeo, J. H. (1973). *Children's Drawings as Diagnostic Aids.* New York: Bruner/Mazel.

Diorio, W. D. (1992). "Parental Perceptions of the Authority of Public Child Welfare Caseworkers." Families in Society: *The Journal of Contemporary Human Services,* April, pp. 222–35.

de Young, M. (1986). "A Conceptual Model for Judging the Truthfulness of a Young Child's Allegation of Sexual Abuse." *American Journal of Orthopsychiatry* 56: 550–59.

Doris, J. (1991). *Suggestibility of Children's Recollections.* Washington D.C.: American Psychological Association.

Ekman, M. (1989). "Kid's Testimony in Court: The Sexual Abuse Crisis." In P. Ekman, *Why Kids Lie,* pp. 152–80. New York: Charles Scribner's Sons.

Elterman, M. F., and Ehrenberg, M. F. (1991). "Sexual Abuse Allegations in Child Custody Disputes." *International Journal of Law and Psychiatry* 14: 269–86.

Emans, S.; Woods, E.; Flagg, N.; and Freeman, A. (1987). "Genital Findings in Sexually Abused, Symptomatic and Asymptomatic Girls." *Pediatrics* 79: 778–85.

Emery, R. E. (1982). "Interparental Conflict and the Children of Discord and Divorce." *Psychological Bulletin* 92: 310–30.

Erickson, W. D.; Luxenberg, M. G.; Walbek, N. H.; and Seeley, R. K. (1987). "Frequency of MMPI Two-Point Code Types among Sex Offenders." *Journal of Consulting and Clinical Psychology* 55, no. 4: 566–70.

Erickson, W. D.; Walbek, N. H.; and Seely, R. K. (1988). "Behavioral Patterns of Child Molesters." *Archives of Sexual Behavior* 17: 77–86.

Esplin, P. (1990, March 23–25). Workshop on Statement Validity Analysis/Criterion Based Content Analysis, Salt Lake City, Utah.

Everson, M. D., and Boat, B. W. (1989). "Sexualized Doll Play among Young Children: Implications for the Use of Anatomical Dolls in Sexual Abuse Evaluations." *Journal of the American Academy of Child and Adolescent Psychiatry* 29: 736–42.

Everstine, D. S., and Everstine, L. (1989). *Sexual Trauma in Children and Adolescents: Dynamics and Treatment.* New York: Brunner/Mazel.

Faller, K. (1984). "Is the Child Victim of Sexual Abuse Telling the Truth?" *Child Abuse and Neglect* 8: 473–81.

——— (1988). "Criteria for Judging Credibility of Children's Statements about Their Sexual Abuse. *Child Welfare* 67: 389–401.

——— (1990). *Understanding Child Sexual Maltreatment.* Newbury Park, Calif.: Sage Publications.

Fay, R. (1991). "A Critical Analysis of a Medical Report in a Case of Suspected Child Sexual Abuse." *Issues in Child Abuse Accusations* 3: 199–202.

Fein, G. G. (1981). "Pretend Play in Childhood: An Integrative Review." *Child Development* 52: 1095–1118.

Final Consolidated Report of Rule 706 Panel of Experts (1990). *Court Appointed Expert's Report on* B. H. et al., *v.* Gordon Johnson. Director of Illinois Department of Children and Family Services.

Fischhoff, B., and Beyth-Marom, R. (1983). "Hypothesis Evaluation from a Bayesian Perspective." *Psychological Review* 90, no. 3: 239–60.

Fisk, M. C. (1989, July 17). "Abuse: The New Weapon." *The National Law Journal,* pp. 1, 20–25.

Friedrich, W. N.; Grambsch, P.; Broughton, D.; Kuiper, J.; and Beilke, R. N. (1991). "Normative Sexual Behavior in Children." *Pediatrics* 88: 456–64.

Gambrill, E. (1990). *Critical Thinking in Clinical Practice.* San Francisco: Jossey-Bass.

Garbarino, J., and Stott, F. M. (1989). *What Children Can Tell Us.* San Francisco: Jossey-Bass.

Gardner, R. A. (1992). *The Parent Alienation Syndrome.* Cresskill, N.J.: Creative Therapeutics.

Gauron, E. F., and Dickinson, J. K. (1969). "The Influence of Seeing the Patient First on Diagnostic Decision Making in Psychiatry." *American Journal of Psychiatry* 126: 85–91.

Gomes-Schwartz, B.; Horowitz, J. M.; and Cardarelli, A. P. (1990). *Child Sexual Abuse: The Initial Effects.* Newbury Park, Calif.: Sage.

Goodman G. S. (1984). "Children's Testimony in Historical Perspective." *Journal of Social Issues* 40, no. 2: 9–31.

Goodman, G. S., and Hahn, A. (1987). "Evaluating Eyewitness Testimony." In I. B. Weiner and A. K. Hess, eds., *Handbook of Forensic Psychology*, pp. 258–92. New York: John Wiley and Sons.

Goodwin, J. M.; Sahd, D.; and Rada, R. T. (1989). "False Accusations and False Denials of Incest: Clinical Myths and Clinical Realities." In J. M. Goodwin, *Sexual Abuse: Incest Victims and Their Families*, pp. 19–36. Chicago: Year Book Medical Publishers, Inc.

Green, A. H., and Schetky, D. H. (1988). "True and False Allegations of Child Sexual Abuse." In D. H. Schetky and A. H. Green, *Child Sexual Abuse*, pp. 104–124. New York: Brunner/Mazel.

Gundersen, B. H.; Melas, P. S.; and Skar, J. E. (1981). "Sexual Behavior in Preschool Children: Teachers' Observations." In L. L. Constantine and F. M. Martinson, eds., *Children and Sex: New Findings, New Perspectives*, pp. 45–51. Boston: Little, Brown and Company.

Guyer, M., and Ash, P. (1986, October 17). "Child Abuse Allegations in the Context of Adversarial Divorce." Paper presented at the Annual Meeting of the American Academy of Psychiatry and the Law. Los Angeles, Calif.

Haugaard, J. (1990). Letter to the Editor. *Child Abuse and Neglect* 14: 294–95.

Haugaard, J., and Alhusen, V. (1992, March 13). "Children's Definitions of Lies." Paper presented at the American Psychology-Law Society Biennial Meeting, San Diego, Calif.

Haugaard, J. J., and Tilly, C. (1988). "Characteristics Predicting Children's Responses to Sexual Encounters with Other Children." *Child Abuse and Neglect* 12: 209–218.

Hawkins, J. (1991). "Rowers on the River Styx." *Harvard Magazine* 93, no. 4: 43–52.

Herbert, C.; Grams, G.; and Goranson, S. (1987). *The Use of Anatomically Detailed Dolls in an Investigative Interview: A Preliminary Study of "Non-Abused" Children.* Vancouver, British Columbia: Department of Family Practice, University of British Columbia.

Hicks, R. D. (1991). *In Pursuit of Satan.* Buffalo, N.Y.: Prometheus Books.

Hindmarch, B. (1990). "Allegations of Child Sexual Abuse in the Context of Custody/Access Disputes." *Alberta Psychology* 19, no. 1: 18–19.

Horner, T. M. (1992). "Expertise in Regard to Determinations of Child Sexual Abuse." Unpublished manuscript.

Horner, T. M., and Guyer, M. J. (1991a). "Prediction, Prevention, and Clinical Expertise in Child Custody Cases in Which Allegations of Child Sexual Abuse Have Been Made: I. Predictable Rates of Diagnostic Error in Relation to Various Clinical Decision-Making Strategies." *Family Law Quarterly* 25: 217–52.

——— (1991b). "Prediction, Prevention, and Clinical Expertise in Child Custody Cases in Which Allegations of Child Sexual Abuse Have Been Made: II. Prevalence Rates of Child Sexual Abuse and the Precision of 'Tests' Constructed to Diagnose It." *Family Law Quarterly* 25: 381–409.

Horowitz, S. W.; Lamb, M. E.; Esplin, P. W.; Boychuk, T. D.; Krispin, O.; and Reiter-Lavery, L. (1992, June 21). "Reliability of Criteria-Based Content Analysis of Child Witness Statements." Paper presented at the annual meeting of the American Psychological Society, San Diego.

Horwich, P. (1982). *Probability and Evidence.* Cambridge, Mass.: Cambridge University Press.

Hughes, H. M., and Barad, S. J. (1983). "Psychological Functioning of Children in a Battered Woman's Shelter: A Preliminary Investigation." *American Journal of Orthopsychiatry* 53: 525–31.

Hughes, M., and Grieve, R. (1983). "On Asking Children Bizarre Questions." In M. Donaldson, R. Grieve, and C. Pratt, eds., *Early Childhood Development and Education: Readings in Psychology,* pp. 105–114. New York: The Guilford Press.

Jaffe, P.; Wolfe, D.; Wilson, S.; and Zak, L. (1986). "Similarities in Behavioral and Social Maladjustment among Child Victims and Witnesses to Family Violence." *American Journal of Orthopsychiatry* 56: 142–46.

Jenkins, P., and Maier-Katkin, D. (1991). "Occult Survivors: The Making of a Myth." In J. T. Richardson, J. Best, and D. G. Bromley, eds. *The Satanism Scare,* pp. 127–44. New York: Aldine De Gruyter.

Jones, D. P. H. (1991). "Professional and Clinical Challenges to Protection of Children." *Child Abuse and Neglect* 15, Supp. 1: 57–66.

Jones, D. P. H., and Krugman, R. D. (1986). "Can a Three-Year-Old Child Bear Witness to Her Sexual Assault and Attempted Murder?" *Child Abuse and Neglect* 10: 253–58.

Jones, D. P. H., and McGraw, J. M. (1987). "Reliable and Fictitious Accounts of Sexual Abuse to Children." *Journal of Interpersonal Violence* 2: 27–45.

Jones, D. P. H., and Seig, A. (1988). "Child Sexual Abuse Allegations in Custody or Visitation Cases: A Report of 20 Cases." In E. B. Nicholson, ed., *Sexual Abuse Allegations in Custody and Visitation Cases,* pp. 22-36. Washington, D.C.: American Bar Association.

Kaser-Boyd, N. (1988). "Fictitious Allegations of Sexual Abuse in Marital Dissolutions." *Family Law News* 11, no. 4: 45, 50–52.

Kendall-Tackett, K. A. (1992). "Beyond Anatomical Dolls: Professionals' Use of Other Play Therapy Techniques." *Child Abuse and Neglect* 16: 139–42.

Kendall-Tackett, K. A., and Watson, M. W. (1992) "Use of Anatomical Dolls by Boston-Area Professionals." *Child Abuse and Neglect* 16: 423–28.

King, M. A., and Yuille, J. C. (1987). "Suggestibility and the Child Witness." In S. J. Ceci, M. P. Toglia, and D. F. Ross, eds., *Children's Eyewitness Memory,* pp. 24–35. New York: Springer-Verlag.

Klajner-Diamond, H.; Wehrspann, W.; and Steinhauer, P. (1987). "Assessing the Credibility of Young Children's Allegations of Sexual Abuse: Clinical Issues." *Canadian Journal of Psychiatry* 32: 610–14.

Köhnken, G., and Steller, M. (1988). "The Evaluation of the Credibility of Child Witness Statements in the German Procedural System." In G. Davies and J. Drinkwater, eds., *Issues in Criminological and Legal Psychology,* pp. 37–45. Leiceister: British Psychological Society.

Koppitz, E. M. (1968). *Psychological Evaluation of Children's Human Figure Drawings.* New York: Grune and Stratton.

Kotelchuck, M. (1982). "Child Abuse and Neglect: Prediction and Misclassification." In R. H. Starr, Jr., ed., *Child Abuse Prediction: Policy Implications.* Cambridge, Mass.: Ballinger.

Krivacska, J. J. (1990). *Designing Child Sexual Abuse Prevention Programs.* Springfield, Ill.: C. C. Thomas.

——— (1991, June 9). "Child Sexual Abuse Prevention Programs: The Prevention of Childhood Sexuality?" Paper presented at the annual meeting of the Midwestern Regional Society for the Scientific Study of Sex, Kansas City, Mo.

Krugman, R. D. (1989). "The More We Learn, the Less We Know 'With Reasonable Medical Certainty'?" *Child Abuse and Neglect* 13: 165–66.

Landry, S. (July 18, 1988). "Girl Recanted Story before Official's Suicide." *Tampa Bay State,* p. 1B.

Langfeldt, T. (1981). "Childhood Masturbation: Individual and Social Organization." In L. L. Constantine and F. M. Martinson, eds., *Children and Sex: New Findings, New Perspectives,* pp. 63–72. Boston: Little, Brown and Company.

Lanning, K. V. (1991). "Ritual Abuse: A Law Enforcement View or Perspective." *Child Abuse and Neglect* 15: 171–73.

——— (1992). *Investigator's Guide to Allegations of "Ritual" Child Abuse.* Quantico, Va.: National Center for the Analysis of Violent Crime.

Lassiter, G. D.; Stone, J. I.; and Weigold, M. F. (1987). "Effect of Leading Questions on the Self-Monitoring—Memory Correlation." *Personality and Social Psychology Bulletin* 13: 537–45.

Lepore, S. J. (1991). "Child Witness: Cognitive and Social Factors Related to Memory and Testimony." *Issues In Child Abuse Accusations* 3: 65–89.

Levine, M., and Battistoni, L. (1991). "The Corroboration Requirement in Child Sex Abuse Cases." *Behavioral Sciences and the Law* 9: 3–20.

Levy, R. J. (1989). "Using 'Scientific' Testimony to Prove Child Sexual Abuse." *Family Law Quarterly* 23: 383–409.

Lindsay, D. S. (1990). "Misleading Suggestions Can Impair Eyewitnesses' Ability to Remember Event Details." *Journal of Experimental Psychology: Learning, Memory, and Cognition* 16: 1077–83.

Loftus, E. F. (1979). *Eyewitness Testimony.* Cambridge, Mass.: Harvard University Press.

Loftus, E. F., and Davies, G. M. (1984). "Distortions in the Memory of Children." *Journal of Social Issues* 40, no. 2: 51–67.

Loftus, E., and Ketcham, K. (1991). *Witness for the Defense.* New York: St. Martin's Press.

Loftus, E. F.; Korf, N. L., and Schooler, J. W. (1989). "Misguided Memories: Sincere Distortions of Reality." In J. C. Yuille, ed., *Credibility Assessment,* pp. 155–74. Dordrecht, The Netherlands: Kluwer Academic Publishers.

McCann, J.; Voris, J.; and Simon, M. (1992). "Genital Injuries Resulting from Sexual Abuse: A Longitudinal Study." *Pediatrics* 89: 307–310.

McCann, J.; Voris, J.; Simon, M.; and Wells, R. (1989). "Perianal Findings in Prepubertal Children Selected for Nonabuse: A Descriptive Study." *Child Abuse and Neglect* 13: 179–93.

McCann et al. (1990). "Comparison of Genital Examination Techniques in Prepubertal Girls." *Pediatrics* 85: 182–87.

——— (1990). "Genital Findings in Prepubertal Girls Selected for Nonabuse: A Descriptive Study." *Pediatrics* 86: 428–39.

Maccoby, E. E. (1990). "Gender and Relationships. A Developmental Account." *American Psychologist* 45: 513–20.

MacFarlane, K. (1986). "Child Sexual Abuse Allegations in Divorce Proceedings." In K. MacFarlane and J. Waterman, eds., *Sexual Abuse of Young Children*, pp. 121–50. New York: The Guilford Press.

McIver, W.; Wakefield, H.; and Underwager, R. (1989). "Behavior of Abused and Nonabused Children in Interviews with Anatomically Correct Dolls." *Issues in Child Abuse Accusations* 1, no. 1: 39–48.

Mannarino, A. P.; Cohen, J. A.; Smith, J. A.; and Moore-Motily, S. (1991). "Six- and Twelve-Month Followup of Sexually Abused Girls." *Journal of Interpersonal Violence* 6: 494–511.

Mantell, D. M. (1988). "Clarifying Erroneous Child Sexual Abuse Allegations." *American Journal of Orthopsychiatry* 58: 618–21.

Martinson, F. M. (1981). "Eroticism in Infancy and Childhood." In L. L. Constantine and F. M. Martinson, eds., *Children and Sex: New Findings, New Perspectives*, pp. 23–35. Boston: Little, Brown and Company.

Milner, J. S.; Gold, R. G.; Ayoub, C.; and Jacewitz, M. M. (1984). "Predictive Validity of the Child Abuse Potential Inventory." *Journal of Consulting and Clini·al Psychology* 52, no. 5: 879–84.

Money, J. (1982). "Sexosophy and Sexology, Philosophy and Science: Two Halves, One Whole." In Z. Hoch and H. I. Lief, eds., *Sexology, Sexual Biology, Behavior and Therapy*. Selected papers of the 5th World Congress of Sexology, Jerusalem, Israel, June 21–26, 1981. Amsterdam: Excerta Medica.

——— (1991a). "Semen-Conservation Theory vs. Semen-Investment Theory, Antisexualism, and the Return of Freud's Seduction Theory." *Journal of Psychology and Human Sexuality* 4, no. 4: 31–55.

——— (1991b, June). "Epidemic Antisexualism: From Onanism to Satanism." In W. Bezemer, P. Cohen-Kettenis, K. Slab, and N. van Son-Schoones, eds., *Sex Matters: Proceedings of the Tenth World Congress of Sexology*. Amsterdam: Elsevier.

Mosher, D. L. (1991). "Ideological Presuppositions: Rhetoric in Sexual Science, Sexual Politics, and Sexual Morality." *Journal of Psychology and Human Sexuality* 4, no. 4: 7–29.

Mulhern, S. (1991). "Satanism and Psychotherapy: A Rumor in Search of an Inquisition." In J. T. Richardson, J. Best, and D. G. Bromley, eds., *The Satanism Scare*, pp. 145–74. New York: Aldine De Gruyter.

Myers, D. V. (1978). "Toward an Objective Evaluation Procedure of the Kinetic Family Drawing (KFD): An Interpretive Manual." *Journal of Personality Assessment* 42: 358–65.

Nathan, D. (1991). "Satanism and Child Molestation: Constructing the Ritual Abuse Scare." In J. T. Richardson, J. Best, and D. G. Bromley, eds., *The Satanism Scare*, pp. 75–94. New York: Aldine De Gruyter.

Nelson, J. B. (1978). *Embodiment.* Minneapolis, Minn.: Augsburg Publishing House.

Noll, R. (1989). "Satanism, UFO Abductions, Historians and Clinicians: Those Who Do Not Remember the Past. . . ." *Dissociation* 2, no. 1: 251–54.

Northwest Psychological Publishers, Inc. *Projective Storytelling Cards.* P.O. Box 494958, Redding, Calif.

Okami, P. (1992). "Child Perpetrators of Sexual Abuse: The Emergence of a Problematic Deviant Category." *Journal of Sex Research* 29, no. 1: 109–130.

Paradise, J. E. (1989). "Predictive Accuracy and the Diagnosis of Sexual Abuse: A Big Issue About a Little Tissue." *Child Abuse and Neglect* 13: 169–76.

Paradise, J. E.; Rostain, A. L.; and Nathanson, M. (1988). "Substantiation of Sexual Abuse Charges When Parents Dispute Custody or Visitation." *Pediatrics* 81: 835–39.

Paul, D. M. (1990). "The Pitfalls Which May Be Encountered during an Examination for Signs of Sexual Abuse." *Medical Science and the Law* 30, no. 1: 3–11.

Pitcher, E. G., and Prelinger, E. (1966). *Children Tell Stories: An Analysis of Fantasy.* New York: International University Press.

Poole, D. A., and White, L. T. (1992, April 30). "It Happened Two Years Ago: Question Repetition and the Eyewitness Testimony of Children and Adults." Paper presented at the meetings of the Midwestern Psychological Association, Chicago, Ill.

Porter, B., and O'Leary, D. (1980). "Marital Discord and Childhood Behavior Problems." *Journal of Abnormal Psychology* 8: 287–95.

Putnam, F. W. (1991). "The Satanic Ritual Abuse Controversy." *Child Abuse and Neglect* 15: 175–79.

Quinn, K. M. (1988). "Credibility of Children's Allegations of Sexual Abuse." *Behavioral Sciences and the Law* 6: 181–99.

Quinn, K. M.; White, S.; and Santilli, G. (1989). "Influences of an Interviewer's Behaviors in Child Sexual Abuse Investigations." *The Bulletin of the American Academy of Psychiatry and the Law* 17: 45–52.

Rand, D. C. (1989). "Munchausen Syndrome by Proxy as a Possible Factor When Abuse Is Falsely Alleged." *Issues in Child Abuse Accusations* 1, no. 3: 32–34.

——— (1990). "Munchausen Syndrome by Proxy: Integration of Classic and Contemporary Types." *Issues in Child Abuse Accusations* 2: 83–89.

Rape and Crisis Abuse Center (1985). *Red Flag Green Flag People.* Fargo, N.D.: Red Flag Green Flag Resources.

Raskin, D. C., and Esplin, P. W. (1991). "Assessment of Children's Statements of Sexual Abuse." In J. Doris, ed., *The Suggestibility of Children's Recollections,* pp. 153–64. Washington, D.C.: American Psychological Association.

Raskin, D. C., and Yuille, J. C. (1989). "Problems in Evaluating Interviews of Children in Sexual Abuse Cases." In S. J. Ceci, D. F. Ross, and M. P. Toglia, eds., *Children Take the Stand: Adult Perceptions of Children's Testimony,* pp. 184–207. New York: Springer-Verlag.

Ravetz, J. R. (1971). *Scientific Knowledge and Its Social Problems.* Oxford University Press.

Realmuto, G.; Jensen, J.; and Wescoe, S. (1990). "Specificity and Sensitivity of Sexually Anatomically Correct Dolls in Substantiating Abuse: A Pilot Study." *Journal of the American Academy of Child Adolescent Psychiatry* 29, no. 5: 743–46.

Robson, B. (1991, March). "The Scars of Scott County." *Mpls/St Paul* (Minneapolis./St. Paul, Minn.), pp. 48–53, 123, 125–31.

Rogers, M. L. (1990). "Coping with Alleged False Sexual Molestation: Examination and Statement Analysis Procedures." *Issues in Child Abuse Accusations* 2: 57–68.

Rosenfeld, A.; Bailey, R.; Siegel, B.; and Bailey, G. (1986). "Determining Incestuous Contact between Parent and Child: Frequency of Children Touching Parents' Genitals in a Nonclinical Population." *Journal of the American Academy of Child Psychiatry* 25, no. 4: 481–84.

Rosenfeld, A.; Siegel, B.; and Bailey, R. (1987). "Familial Bathing Patterns: Implications for Cases of Alleged Molestation and for Pediatric Practice." *Pediatrics* 79, no. 2: 224–29.

Ross, K., and Blush, G. (1990). "Sexual Abuse Discriminators in the Divorced or Divorcing Family." *Issues in Child Abuse Accusations* 2, no. 1: 1–6.

Russell, J. (1991). "The Historical Satan." In J. T. Richardson, J. Best, and D. G. Bromley, eds., *The Satanism Scare,* pp. 41–48. New York: Aldine De Gruyter.

Saks, M. J., and Kidd, R. F. (1980–81). "Human Information Processing and Adjudication: Trial by Heuristics." *Law and Society Review* 15, no. 1: 123–59.

Sanford, D. (1990). *Don't Make Me Go Back, Mommy: A Child's Book about Satanic Ritual Abuse.* Portland, Or.: Multnomah Press.

Schaefer, M., and Guyer, M. (1988, August). "Allegations of Sexual Abuse in Custody and Visitation Disputes: A Legal and Clinical Challenge." Paper presented at the 96th Annual Convention of the American Psychological Association, Atlanta, Ga.

Schultz, L. (1989). "One Hundred Cases of Unfounded Child Sexual Abuse: A Survey and Recommendations." *Issues in Child Abuse Accusations* 1, no. 1: 29–38.

Sgroi, S. M. (1982). *Handbook of Clinical Intervention in Child Sexual Abuse.* Lexington, Mass.: Lexington Books.

Sheridan, R. (1990). "The False Child Molestation Outbreak of the 1980s: An Explanation of the Cases Arising in the Divorce Context." *Issues in Child Abuse Accusations* 2: 146–51.

Silberberg, N. E., and Silberberg, M. C. (1982). "Abusing Poor Children by Trying to Protect Them." In R. Hanson, ed., *Institutional Abuse of Children and Youth,* pp. 133–38. Binghamton, N.Y.: Haworth.

Sink, F. (1988a). "A Hierarchal Model for Evaluation of Child Sexual Abuse." *American Journal of Orthopsychiatry* 58: 129–35.

——— (1988b). "Studies of True and False Allegations: A Critical Review." In E. B. Nicholson, ed., *Sexual Abuse Allegations in Custody and Visitation Cases,* pp. 37–47. Washington, D.C.: American Bar Association.

Sirles, E. A., and Lofberg, C. E. (1990). "Factors Associated with Divorce in Intrafamily Child Sexual Abuse Cases." *Child Abuse and Neglect* 14: 165–70.

Skinner, L. J.; Berry, K. K.; and Giles, M. K. (1992, June 21). "Anatomically Detailed Dolls: The Lack of Normative Play Patterns for Validation Interviews." Paper presented at the annual meeting of the American Psychological Society, San Diego, Calif.

Slicner, N. A., and Hanson, S. R. (1989). "Guidelines for Videotape Interviews in

Child Sexual Abuse Cases." *American Journal of Forensic Psychology* 7, no. 1: 61–74.

Smith, J. (1991). "Aftermath of a False Allegation." *Issues in Child Abuse Accusations* 3: 203.

Spiegel, L. D. (1986). *A Question of Innocence: A True Story of False Accusation.* Morris Plains, N.J.: The Unicorn Publishing House.

Starr, R. H. (1979). "Child Abuse." *American Psychologist* 34, no. 10: 872–78.

Steller, M. (1990, March 23-25). Workshop on Statement Validity Analysis/Criterion Based Content Analysis, Salt Lake City, Utah.

Stern, P. (1992). "Videotaping Child Interviews: A Detriment to an Accurate Determination of Guilt." *Journal of Interpersonal Violence* 7: 277–88.

Stuart-Mills, P., v. *Cher, A. J.* (1990). Child custody. No. 500–12–184613-895. Montreal district court.

Summit, R. (1983). "The Child Sexual Abuse Accommodation Syndrome." *Child Abuse and Neglect* 7: 177–93.

Thoennes, N., and Pearson, J. (1988a). "A Difficult Dilemma: Responding to Sexual Abuse Allegations in Custody and Visitation Disputes." In D. J. Besharov, ed., *Protecting Children from Abuse and Neglect,* p. 91–112. Springfield, Ill.: Charles C Thomas, Pub.

——— (1988b). "Summary of Findings from the Sexual Abuse Allegations Project." In E. B. Nicholson, ed., *Sexual Abuse Allegations in Custody and Visitation Cases,* pp. 1–36. Washington, D.C.: American Bar Association.

Thoennes, N., and Tjaden, P. G. (1990). "The Extent, Nature, and Validity of Sexual Abuse Allegations in Custody/Visitation Disputes." *Child Abuse and Neglect* 14: 151–63.

Thompson, J. E. (1992). "Defense of Child Molestation Charges." *Issues in Child Abuse Accusations* 4: 132–40.

Thompson, W. C.; Clarke-Stewart, A.; Meyer, J.; Pathak, M. K.; and Lepore, S. (1991). "Children's Susceptibility to Suggestive Interrogation." Paper presented at annual meeting of the American Psychological Association, San Francisco, Calif.

Tollison, C. D., and Adams, H. E. (1979). *Sexual Disorders: Treatment, Theory, and Research.* New York: Gardner Press.

Trad, P. V. (1990). *Conversation with Preschool Children: Uncovering Developmental Patterns.* New York: Norton and Company.

Tyler, A. H., and Brassard, M. R. (1984). "Abuse in the Investigation and Treatment of Intrafamilial Child Sexual Abuse." *Child Abuse and Neglect* 8: 47–53.

Underwager, R., and Wakefield, H. (1990). *The Real World of Child Interrogations.* Springfield, Ill.: Charles C Thomas, Pub.

——— (1991a). "*Cur alii, prae aliis?* (Why Some and Not Others?)." *Issues in Child Abuse Accusations* 3: 78–193.

——— (1991b, May 2). "More Effective Child Interviewing Procedures in Sexual Abuse Allegations." Workshop presented at the Seventh Annual Symposium in Forensic Psychology, Newport Beach, Calif.

Undeutsch, U. (1989). "The Development of Statement Reality Analysis." In J. Yuille, ed., *Credibility Assessment,* pp. 101–119. Boston: Kluwer Academic Publishers.

Victor, J. (1990). "Satanic Cult Rumors as Contemporary Legend." *Western Folklore* 49, no. 1: 51–81.

——— (1991a). "The Dynamics of Rumor-Panics about Satanic cults." In J. T. Richardson, J. Best, and D. G. Bromley, eds., *The Satanism Scare,* pp. 221–36. New York: Aldine De Gruyter.

——— (1991b). "The Satanic Cult Scare and Allegations of Ritual Child Abuse." *Issues in Child Abuse Accusations* 3: 135–43.

Wakefield, H., and Underwager, R. (1988). *Accusations of Child Sexual Abuse.* Springfield, Ill.: Charles C Thomas, Pub.

——— (1989a). "Evaluating the Child Witness in Sexual Abuse Cases: Interview or Inquisition?" *American Journal of Forensic Psychology* 7, no. 3: 43–69.

——— (1989b). "Manipulating the Child Abuse System." *Issues in Child Abuse Accusations* 1, no. 2: 58–67.

——— (1990). "Personality Characteristics of Parents Making False Accusations of Sexual Abuse in Custody Disputes." *Issues in Child Abuse Accusations* 2: 121–36.

——— (1991). "Sexual Abuse Allegations in Divorce and Custody Disputes." *Behavioral Sciences and the Law* 9: 451–68.

——— (1992a). "Assessing Credibility of Children's Testimony in Ritual Sexual Abuse Allegations." *Issues in Child Accusations* 4: 32–44.

——— (1992b). "Recovered Memories of Alleged Child Sexual Abuse: Lawsuits against Parents." *Behavioral Sciences and the Law* 10, no. 4: 483–507.

Wallerstein, J. S., and Kelly, J. B. (1980). *Surviving the Breakup: How Children and Parents Cope with Divorce.* New York: Basic Books.

Warren, A.; Boyd, C.; and Walker, A. G. (1992, March 13). "Interviewing Child Witnesses: Beyond Leading Questions." Paper presented at the American Psychology-Law Society Biennial Meeting, San Diego, Calif.

Weinbach, R. W. (1987). "Public Awareness of Sexual Abuse: Costs and Victims." *Journal of the National Association of Social Workers* 32: 532–33.

Wexler, R. (1990). *Wounded Innocents: The Real Victims of the War against Child Abuse.* Buffalo, N.Y.: Prometheus Books.

White, S. (1990). "The Investigatory Interview with Suspected Victims of Child Sexual Abuse." In A. LaGreca, ed., *Through the Eyes of Children,* pp. 368–84. Boston: Allyn & Bacon.

White, S.; Strom, G. A.; and Santilli, G. (1986, February). "Clinical Protocol for Interviewing Preschoolers with Sexually Anatomically Correct Dolls." Unpublished manuscript.

White, S.; Strom, G.; Santilli, G.; and Halpin, B. (1986). "Interviewing Young Sexual Abuse Victims with Anatomically Correct Dolls." *Child Abuse and Neglect* 10: 519–29.

White, S., and Quinn, K. M. (1988). "Investigatory Independence in Child Sexual Abuse Evaluation: Conceptual Considerations." *The Bulletin of the American Academy of Psychiatry and the Law* 16: 269–78.

Wolfner, G.; Faust, D.; and Dawes, R. (1993). "The Use of Anatomically Detailed Dolls in Sexual Abuse Evaluations: The State of the Science." *Applied and Preventive Psychology* 2: 1–11.

Wolman, B., ed. (1983). *Handbook of Developmental Psychology.* Englewood Cliffs. N.J.: Prentice Hall.

Yates, A. (1988). "Sex Abuse Study Challenges 'Sine qua non.' " *Convention Insights.* 140th Annual Meeting of the American Psychiatric Association, Chicago, Ill., p. 3.

Yates, A.; Beutler, L.; and Crago, M. (1985). "Drawings by Child Victims of Incest." *Child Abuse and Neglect* 9: 183–89.

Yates, A., and Musty, T. (1988). "Preschool Children's Erroneous Allegations of Sexual Molestation." *American Journal of Psychiatry* 145: 989–92.

Yates, A., and Terr, L. C. (1988). "Debate Forum: Anatomically Correct Dolls: Should They Be Used as a Basis for Expert Testimony?" *Journal of the American Academy of Child and Adolescent Psychiatry* 27, no. 2: 254–57.

Young, A. (1992, June 14). "Sex-Case Treatment Is Called Child Abuse." *The Arizona Republic,* p. 1.

Zeitlin, H. (1987, October 10). "Investigation of the Sexually Abused Child." *The Lancet,* pp. 842–45.

11

Case Management of Sexual Abuse Victims: Child, Adolescent, and Adult

Charlene Steen

Sexual abuse victims usually suffer emotional damage from their abuse (Bagley & Ramsey 1986; Briere 1987; Conte & Berliner 1987; Friedrich 1986; Gomes-Schwartz et al. 1985). Unfortunately, they and their families often suffer further victimization by the criminal and civil justice and child welfare systems. Personalized case management can be an effective way to ameliorate these problems. Because many different systems come into play and each case may interface with a different constellation of entities, case management of sexual abuse victims is a complex and varying concept. Age of the victim, type of crime, type or lack of legal action, relationship of the parties involved, and arena of management are all aspects of case management which determine its structure.

Case management has become a kind of buzzword for mental health and social welfare agencies in the 1990s (Netting 1992); yet definitions vary from coordination of community agencies and services to a form of therapeutic intervention and/or provision of a support system. It includes assessment, service planning, agency and treatment coordination, provision of resources, and followup services. Moore (1990) summed it up most succinctly when he stated ". . . case management is just old-fashioned social work wearing new clothes." As this chapter will demonstrate, different forms of case management will be required for each aspect of the legal and treatment intervention processes.

Identifying the client and the case manager is the first step in the case management process, but client and case manager can differ in different cases. Ideally, in cases of child sexual abuse, the suspected child victim is the client and the case manager is a designated agent of the statutory child protection agency. If the focus is on the child and the child's needs, the roles of the other parties can be relegated to a lower rung of the hierarchical ladder, and the maximum protection of the child from further traumatization can be effected. While the needs of the other parties, such as parents (whether secondary victims, perpetrators, or the innocent accused), are to be considered, the child's needs are foremost, since the child has the least power and access to resources.

In some child victim cases, however, there is no child protection agency involved. In cases of child sexual abuse by a stranger, out-of-home friend, relative or babysitter, and in some cases of sexual abuse by a divorced non-custodial parent, the child protection agency either never gets involved, because it is merely a criminal or civil law matter; or else it drops jurisdiction rapidly, because the child is deemed safe in his or her home situation. Similarly, child protection agency personnel do not maintain involvement with cases, particularly of preschool-aged children, where the charges of abuse cannot be adequately substantiated.

While the child is ideally still the client in these cases, there may be different case managers in different settings. In most states, there are victim-witness agencies to help the victim through the court and victim-witness funding mazes. The victim-witness agency's advocate for the child may serve as the case manager through the court processes and recommend treatment modalities. In some cases, crisis intervention and longer term therapeutic treatment may even be afforded through these agencies. More commonly, however, case management by the advocate does not extend to the treatment realm and the therapist working with the child must also fulfill the role of case manager in non-courtroom arenas.

Sometimes there is a conflict between persons serving in the role of case manager in different agencies. For example, a court or probation officer may see him/herself as case manager and prohibit or permit the alleged perpetrator to have contact with the child, whether or not the child is ready for such contact. Similar problems may arise when the victim acts out in a delinquent manner and is under the guidance of a probation officer who makes determinations based on the new offense rather than the victimization issues. Sometimes court jurisdiction over an incestuous family may be dropped by the court before the family is ready to reunify.

In the case of adults, no protective agency is usually available to provide case management. While adults are much more capable than children of getting what they need, adult victims are often in a state of crisis, know little about and fear the court system, and lack knowledge of needed therapeutic interventions and victim-witness resources. Victim-witness advocates, rape crisis center staff, outside therapists, or probation officers must often fill the case manager role. All too often there is no decision made as to case management with an adult, and planning for successful recovery from victimization is left to chance. It is therefore critical that a case manager be designated.

An effective approach to coordinating case management procedures is to get representatives of all of the involved entities, agencies and individuals working with sexual abuse cases to sit down together and draw up a written protocol for all types of sexual abuse cases (Lurigio et al. 1990). This protocol should designate the case managers for children, adults and elders in various situations. It should establish the procedures for investigation, child and elder protection, medical examination, treatment planning and referral, and court assistance.

The person who is designated as the case manager should act in a supervisory role, working cooperatively with the other concerned agencies and individuals to assess the needs of the victim, developing a flexible but comprehensive individualized plan (following, of course, overall protocol guidelines) for legal system participation, treatment, development of support systems and financial compensation. The other involved professionals should be seen as submanagers, case managing within their particular realms, under the coordination of the supervising case manager and following the agreed-upon written procedures. Periodic meetings, written reports and telephonic communication between all of the professionals involved in a particular case to assess progress, modify the plan, and coordinate activities are critical.

Active rather than reactive management is recommended (Sgroi 1982). Reactive management leaves the case manager vulnerable to conflicting and competing demands of court officials, child protective services (CPS) workers, parents, attorneys, and others. The end result of reactive management is often disorganization of parts or manipulation by the more active protagonists, with the victim's interests often not adequately served.

Active management, on the other hand, takes a proactive stance, legitimately exercising authority for the betterment of the client. An active management style is like a chess game, where the object is clearly stated, elements analyzed, plan of action formulated, and necessary moves made by the requisite player. In addition, periodic review and modification of actions as needed assure accomplishment of goals.

Because the interventions will have profound effects on the victim and other principals in the sexual abuse recovery drama, it is essential that the case manager and submanagers be well trained not only in their individual disciplines, but in sexual abuse dynamics and mechanics, civil and criminal law, and community resources. Training in each of these areas should be coordinated and provided to all professionals involved in sex offense cases. Additionally, by using professionals from the community and legal jurisdictions (including lawyers, judges, prosecutors, therapists, and CPS specialists) case managers not only acquire knowledge and status but also establish communication networks (Giarretto 1982).

REPORTING AND EMERGENCY PLACEMENT CONSIDERATIONS

The essential precursor to the institution of legal action is the report of sexual abuse. Since, in most cases, the perpetrator is not apprehended while committing the criminal act and does not voluntarily come forward, reporting becomes a critical element. While adult victims often report their own sexual abuse to law enforcement agencies, most children are not capable of doing so. They usually tell teachers, counselors, therapists, friends, family members, or doctors. Because of this lack of capacity and the public obligation to prevent further abuse, almost all states have laws requiring professionals to report suspected child sexual abuse. Usually it is a misdemeanor not to report, and civil liability may also attach. Good faith reporters, on the other hand, are usually protected from civil liability.

Some states also have laws requiring reporting of elder sexual abuse, since old people also are often incapable of reporting abuse themselves. The sexual abuse of most competent adults does not have to be reported, because adults are deemed capable of making their own reports if they so desire.

It is important that all professionals working with children and the elderly know the reporting laws in their particular jurisdiction. These laws usually state who must report, what must be reported, and to whom reports must be made. Often this is a painful process, as in cases where a child does not want the adult to report child sexual abuse or an adult caretaker does not want to report his/her child's sexual abuse, because the abuse was in the past or the person is afraid of the consequences. Despite the betrayal of trust that may ensue, the professional must by law make required reports in a timely manner. Particularly with adults, adolescents, or older children who may feel that making a report contrary to their wishes is one more extirpation of their power, it is strongly recommended that the professional state the legal necessity to report in advance of the revelation. In this way victims understand the consequences and feel less violated.

While prior notification of the duty to report may suppress some disclosures, not telling victims leads them into a sense of false trust. When report of a supposedly confidential revelation is then made, victims are likely to perceive it as a devastating deceit. Trust has already been breached by the offender. When the system deliberately betrays victims, all safe havens are eliminated. Usually, even if victims withhold after notification, if there is a continuation of abuse, they will eventually reveal the information. An additional method of preserving adults', adolescents', or older children's power after an accidental revelation is made is to allow them to make the oral report to authorities themselves in the professional's presence.

Some therapists and sexual abuse prevention teachers may become overzealous in their desire to investigate and establish child sexual abuse, particularly when they believe a child has been molested and the child is silent. They may interrogate and lead the child, or provide suggestive play or drawing activities, sometimes to such an extent that the alleged victim's statements become contaminated, truth is lost, and future testimony is so tainted that it should or must be barred. Additionally, repetitive questioning may cause the child eventually to shut down. It is important that everyone working with a suspected sexual abuse victim recognize and abide by their appropriate role.

To avoid problems of unreliability, false accusation, and inadmissibility, there should be a section in the jurisdiction's formal sexual abuse protocol designating the person or agency who will do the questioning and determining how each further step of the investigatory process will be managed. This protocol should be distributed and discussed with educators, therapists, and all other mandatory reporters to lessen the likelihood of unprofessional and/or misguided behavior.

Sexual abuse investigators should be experts, completely competent and certified. They should be on a staff of the child protection and/or law enforcement agency, but not invariably so. They should be extensively trained for this task and should follow accepted questioning and play informational techniques, understand the legal requirements regarding leading questions, utilize standardized methods to check veracity, and carefully assess the effects of external influences. Investigators should be as neutral as possible in their gathering of evidence.

Concurrent collection of any physical evidence should be made, and a medical examination should be performed if needed. Accompaniment by a family member and/or well-trained sexual assault victim services representative who will be able to maintain contact with the child through all future proceedings can help minimize the secondary trauma and should be part of the protocol.

If the case is one of suspected intrafamilial child molestation, the investigator often must make critical decisions regarding safe placement of the suspected victim after the initial investigation. Is it necessary to separate the child from the alleged offender? Can the alleged offender be removed? Can the nonoffending parent(s) keep the child safe? Will the nonoffending family members emotionally abuse the child for telling? If the child must be removed, is there a trustworthy relative, or must an emergency foster home or shelter be found? Should the other children in the family also be removed? There is often no happy solution. It is usually best to err on the side of safety of the child (and other children), with the alleged perpetrator being the one to move, so as to minimize feelings of wrongdoing on the part of the suspected child victim. Only decisions necessary to ensure the immediate safety of the child should be made by the investigator. Subsequently the overall case manager assumes responsibility for making short- and long-term arrangements with input from an interdisciplinary team.

For the adult sexual assault victim (younger than sixty-five in jurisdictions with elder reporting laws), confidentiality is a more significant issue. The sexual assault or victim-witness services agency should be contacted to provide assistance to the victim and the victim's family only with the victim's permission. Likewise, unless the victim gives express permission, in most jurisdictions therapists may not notify law enforcement or anyone else, unless there is reason to believe a minor (or older person) is in present danger. If the victim is a minor or older person (as appropriate), a report of abuse made without the victim's consent should be limited to only the legally required information. Similarly, any report made with permission of an adult may not exceed the scope of the consent.

The case of Mary, an 18-year-old who lived at home in California with her parents, illustrates some of the problems inherent in required reporting. Mary told her therapist that her father had been molesting her for a number of years, and that she was upset because he was now molesting her 14-year-old sister. Mary was terrified of her father and did not want the molestation reported; in fact, she said she would deny everything if a report was made. In California, the law requires that the molestation of a minor be reported if there is reasonable suspicion that the abuse has occurred. The therapist believed there was a reasonable suspicion that Mary's younger sister had been molested, and made a report as required to Child Protective Services. Mary's molestation would remain confidential unless Mary either chose to report it herself or gave permission to her therapist to report it for her.

This story does not have a happy ending. Mary dropped out of therapy, feeling that she had been betrayed. To authorities she denied having said that her younger sister had been molested. The younger sister acknowledged the molestation when questioned by authorities, but was not believed by her mother. The father denied all molesting behavior. The younger sister was removed from the home for her safety. The father was tried in criminal court but found not guilty of the molestation of the younger sister, despite her very specific testimony. A civil action, requiring a lower standard of proof than the criminal court action ("preponderance of the evidence" instead of the "beyond a reasonable doubt" standard) found the parents unfit and took away the younger sister until such time as the parents completed a family sexual abuse treatment program. Since they refused, the younger child could not return home. Mary continued to live in the family, since she was legally an adult. It is not known whether her father continued to molest her. The younger sister was kept safe in foster placement and participated in therapy with others similarly abused where she could talk out her powerlessness, hurt, and frustration.

Such outcomes, unfortunately, are not uncommon. However, an effective case manager and a nonjudgmental treatment provider might have made a difference. In a very similar case, where the case manager was seen as a helper and advocate for the whole family as well as for the victim, the family was encouraged to participate in a sexual abuse therapy program. The mother gradually came to believe the child, the father gradually admitted some of his actions, a multi-faceted treatment program was completed, and eventually the family was reunified.

When the marital relationship remains intact, healthy family reunification is a positive goal. Separation of either the perpetrator or the victim from the family is usually painful for all family members. Although most victims do not want to be further abused, they miss and need their families, even their perpetrating family member. Overzealous case managers often forget this need in their desire to protect the child absolutely. The system should be responsive to the victim's and other family members' desires for contact. Protective guidelines to assure safety in contact are more helpful to the victim and family as a whole than the all too frequent absolute isolation of either victim or offender from each other or the rest of the family.

Thus, although the safety of the victim should be a principal concern, a helping nonjudgmental case management model can sometimes lessen the degree of damage to the family system in incest cases.

LEGAL SYSTEM CONSIDERATIONS

There are many different types of legal action likely to be encountered by the sexual abuse victim—criminal, dependency or wardship, family law, and various types of civil actions. Often victims have no understanding of the various procedures, are terrified at the thought of having to go to court and having to confront their perpetrator, and have no idea what will be expected of them. Most of their families are equally uninformed and fearful. Sometimes multiple legal actions are being simultaneously pursued in the courts, each with its own set of rules and demands on victims, with the potential of further confusing the parties involved. Particularly confusing may be the dismissal of criminal actions, while civil actions are sustained due to the different standards of proof. In addition, victims may not know what the ramifications of the different actions can be. It is important that the case manager or other designated contact person clarify for victims and their family what the court procedures will be, and what the victims can expect.

Often there are conflicting interests. In incest cases in particular, there may be subtle or even overt pressures by family members on the victim to retract in order to keep the family together and prevent notoriety, incarceration of the perpetrator, and/or economic loss. Where there is a divorce case, the opposite may occur. Pressure may be brought to coerce unfounded accusations or to elaborate on sexual abuse. This pressure may be due to malice or paranoia on the part of the accusing parent who does not trust the other parent. In still other cases, victims may feel pressured not by anyone else, but by their own knowledge that they may lose a family member or cause hurt to someone else.

There is no easy method of preventing pressure from conflicting interests. Supportive intervention and education may be quite effective. Usually, in intrafamilial child abuse cases, it is necessary to prevent contact between the perpetrator and victim during the pendency of the case, so as to prevent pressure from being placed on the victim to recant. In addition, where there is likely to be pressure one way or another from family members, it is often beneficial to give the family members written directives of what may and may not be talked about, with the sexual crime being strictly taboo. In extreme cases, it may be necessary to remove a child victim from the influences of family members via foster care for the duration of the court processes.

The case of Julia, a 7-year-old who was repeatedly molested by her father, illustrates the problem. After family reunification subsequent to the first molestation charges, Julia told her therapy group that her father was coming into her room and molesting her again. Child Protective Services was then notified, but when Julia was questioned by authorities she denied the molestation, saying that she had just dreamed it. Julia returned to therapy and reiterated the dream story. Many months later, when the molestation became too disturbing, she broke down in group and acknowledged what was happening. Julia said her mother told her that if she ever reported being molested again, her father would not only go to prison forever, but Julia would be removed and never see any of the family again. Julia did not want be removed from her home, but it was necessary. She did testify to what her father had done to her, and he was convicted and sent to prison. Julia's mother, through therapy, became stronger and able to appropriately protect her children, and eventually Julia was returned to her mother.

A suspected child victim may also have to be removed from an angry or paranoid custodial parent who keeps encouraging a child to invent or embellish a sexual abuse scenario. Openness and impartiality of the case manager are critical to making removal decisions.

Another pretrial issue is preparation of the victim so as to avoid contamination of subsequent testimony. It is important that the victim know the court procedures and what to expect. Usually a victim-witness services advocate, often attached to the prosecutor's office, will be available for this preparation.

It is helpful, especially for child victims, to go into the courtroom in advance of any hearing and be shown where each participant will sit. Many courts now allow an advocate or parent to hold the hand of a child victim for comfort and support while testifying. If that will be the case, assurance that the support person will be present in that capacity can alleviate some of the fear victims may have. It should be clarified, however, that no matter what the victim says, whether the victim testifies against the alleged perpetrator or retracts prior statements, that the support will still be there. There is concern on the part of defense attorneys that such support on the witness stand could make the alleged victim look much more vulnerable and honest and influence a jury unfairly. This is a very real concern, and should also be given consideration.

There are many ways court preparation can taint evidence, resulting in either inaccurate convictions or dismissals. For example, it is important, if a suspected child victim is in group therapy where the children playact the court process, that the situations used bear no resemblance to the specific victims' cases, so that evidence is not contaminated by confusing truth with play. In such cases, the children should be encouraged to playact nonsexual crimes such as theft or murder and include both true and false accusations to prevent peer pressure from influencing testimony. In addition, the difference between playacting and reality should be reiterated to the children. Therapists should also remain as neutral as possible at this stage, neither encouraging nor discouraging disclosures.

A key rule in court preparation is to inform suspected child victims what the procedure will be, while assiduously avoiding telling the child what to say. As noted above, it is important not to have the young child keep reiterating what happened, because there is a tendency for some children to shut down and stop talking, or for others to begin to develop fictional elaborations in an effort to please.

The emotional well-being of the suspected victim is a concern with respect to court participation. Ideally, each offender should take responsibility for his/her offense, and the victim then would not have to be subjected to the court processes. While many of the cases do not go to full trial, some do, and others require the victims to go through various pre- or post-trial processes, such as a preliminary hearing and/or sentencing. Some victims are not emotionally capable of this. Others want to have their day in court and are upset if a case plea bargains or settles and they cannot appear.

According to the United States Constitution, defendants in a criminal action have a right to confront and cross-examine their accuser. An exception to the Confrontation Clause was admitted under the doctrine of "spontaneous utterances" in the U.S. Supreme Court cases of *Ohio* v. *Roberts* (1980), where the declarant was unavailable—the lack of availability being the critical element allowing the exception. Some states codified the exception, incorporating it into their codes of evidence. However, in *White* v. *Illinois* (1992), a U.S. Supreme Court case decided January 15, 1992, the Court went a step further, allowing introduction of a child molestation victim's "spontaneous declaration" without any demonstration that the victim was unavailable. Basically, this opens the door to admission of a child's spontaneous statements about being molested without the victim's having to testify and disallows confrontation and cross-examination of the accuser by the perpetrator. For example, parents or teachers could testify to what a child told them about being sexually abused without the alleged victim having to appear and answer any questions.

Victim advocates have worked for this nonconfrontation for a long time, based on the tendency of the courtroom process and defense counsel confrontation to further traumatize sexual assault victims, especially children. In addition, child victims are often afraid to tell what happened to them when the seemingly powerful perpetrator is there watching them, particularly when that perpetrator is a father figure who previously has had total power over them. However, this creates the very real problem of discrediting any unfounded or spurious accusation if the accuser is not present.

Various solutions have been proposed and tried, including televised confrontation rather than in-person confrontation. One of the most creative solutions, which occurred at a parole violation hearing at a California State Prison, was to have the child victim stand behind a one-way glass mirror, where the deciders of fact and the alleged perpetrator could see and question the victim, while the victim did not have to see the alleged perpetrator or the courtroom.

When it would be injurious to the victim's emotional well-being to go through the court processes and to testify, it is particularly important that the victim's therapist immediately notify the prosecutor, so that the prosecution does not go forward. It is possible, in most cases, for actions to be dismissed without prejudice and be refiled if and when the victim is capable of testifying. In some cases, where a victim is not currently capable of testifying, plea bargains are instituted.

In most jurisdictions, psychologists, psychiatrists or other therapeutic experts are appointed by the courts, child protective agency, or attorneys to evaluate the alleged perpetrator, suspected victim, accusatory parent and/or family situation. These evaluators usually are not and should not be the treating therapists, because the treating therapists' views will be biased based on experiences with their clients. Independent evaluating psychologists who can perform objective and unbiased tests as well as structured interviews are recommended to assess the parties and testify in court.

Conflicts arise when treating therapists are called to testify. Sometimes this testimony is necessary because the treating therapist has information not available to anyone else. For example, if a child says that his father anally penetrated him weekly for six years, and he is now retracting and denying any more than a one time fondling, the treating therapist may be called by the prosecutor. In such a case, the therapist should notify the patient in advance of the necessity of this testimony. Testimony by the treating therapist may result in the therapist being unable to further treat the involved party after the court appearance due to destruction of the therapeutic rapport and breach of trust. Whether or not the therapist is the treater of the victim or the perpetrator or of another family member, this schism may occur due to the revelation of the therapist's opinions in a nontherapeutic manner, which may not be positive for the patient to hear. Bifurcation of the roles of evaluating and treating therapist is the best way to preserve the therapeutic relationship.

Another conflict occurs when the treating therapist takes the stand and tends to advocate for the patient rather than give an unbiased view of the facts, due to the relationship that has developed between therapist and patient. If the therapist must testify, it is important to recognize this problem and minimize it to the best of the therapist's ability. This can also occur when any party with a continuing relationship with a witness testifies regarding that witness.

An exception may also occur where, after an initial evaluation, a therapist is assigned by the court to work with parent or parents and child with the express purpose of assessing and improving the interactions between them and report back to the court. This treating therapist should also be an independent professional, not the therapist of one or the other parent.

Such circumstances notwithstanding, on issues of emotional condition, amenability to treatment and risk of harm to self or others, the independent psychologist who is solely an evaluator, not a treater, is highly preferable, because there are fewer potential problems.

If the treating therapist is called to testify, it is critical that he/she know the rules of privilege with respect to therapist testimony. Each state has its own set of rules. The patient (and/or patient's parents) holds the privilege, which may result in prevention of the therapist from testifying. However, there are exceptions to the privilege, which may require the therapist to testify when subpoenaed, particularly in child (and elder) abuse cases and where the patient's state of mind is at issue. Careful review of the scope of the exceptions can protect both therapist and client.

In child sexual abuse cases, the case manager within the child welfare department should have the most complete data possible on the child and family for purposes of court testimony regarding safety of visitation and reunification of a molesting family. Team conferences with the various parties involved in the case should be instituted as soon as possible after jurisdiction is obtained over the family so that input from all therapists, visitation supervisors, and probation officers are incorporated. Ideally, this case manager should follow the case from beginning to end. Unfortunately, there are usually different workers at different stages of the court processes, or case managers may change due to personnel transfers. This problem is further complicated by incomplete record keeping.

Welfare workers supervising visitation between some parents and children in placement may also be called to testify, with possibly tainted results. The workers may develop bonds with the estranged parents, feeling sorry for them, or, conversely, become overly protective of the child. Some have little knowledge of, or training in, assessing the mental condition and behavior of the parent(s), and may miss some of the pathology of the interactions. Others can give perceptive and informed opinions. Adequate and ongoing training of welfare workers is the best solution to this problem.

While criminal (and criminal juvenile) court actions essentially determine whether an alleged perpetrator is legally guilty of the sexual crime beyond a reasonable doubt, other court actions also make determinations as to whether some type of sexual activity may have taken place by using a lower standard of proof, usually that of the "preponderance of the evidence." This determination may be part of an action filed by child welfare to determine the fitness of the parents to retain custody of the victim and siblings. It may be a part of family law divorce and visitation actions brought by one parent against another to determine who should have custody of children and to what extent child victims need visitation protection from an allegedly guilty parent. The issue may also arise in tort actions, which are civil procedures to recover money damages for sexual abuse brought by the injured party, who must prove that the sexual abuse occurred in order to recover.

While a plea or determination of guilt (not "no contest" or "nolo contendere") in criminal court is binding on all of the other types of actions, findings that the alleged perpetrator committed the offense in the other types of actions are not binding on the criminal action. This is because of the higher standard of proof required in the criminal action. Thus, the issue of guilt must be retried in a criminal action even though it may have been proven that the alleged perpetrator committed the crime for purposes of being an unfit parent, or for purposes of monetary recompense, or even at a probation or parole violation hearing. Conversely, even though alleged perpetrators may not have been found guilty in a criminal action, they can be determined to have been guilty for purposes of these other actions.

In addition, all of these different types of actions can be brought with respect to the same case. The prosecutor may file criminal charges; the child welfare department through their legal agent may file unfit parent charges; the victim or victim's parent(s) may file tort charges; one parent may file in family court for custody and/or visitation limitations due to the offense;

and if the alleged perpetrator was already on probation or parole, violation charges based on the same offense might be filed concurrently. The victim, perpetrator and other witnesses may thus be required to be in court to testify in all these cases.

Different jurisdictions determine which action should be heard at what time. Sometimes the procedures occur concurrently; in other cases they follow one another. Because of the possible confusion arising out of all the potential court actions, it is important that the jurisdiction's sexual abuse protocol set up an orderly procedure.

One other potential area of chaos occurs when sexual abuse of one or more victims may have occurred in more than one jurisdiction. In such cases, since criminal actions must be held in the jurisdiction in which the crime occurred, more than one prosecution can be instituted at a time. Usually the jurisdiction where the alleged perpetrator is located will prosecute first.

With these various actions possible, plus the propensity of the court to postpone hearings to other dates, both victim and witnesses can potentially undergo great strain due to the time demands. This can affect testimony, victim recovery, and therapeutic relationships. Utilization of a case manager during the court proceedings to communicate with attorneys, court and parties to coordinate scheduling can ease the pressure and strain of such proceedings.

Another trial-related issue has to do with court orders issued, particularly in the child sexual abuse arena. It is important for the case manager to communicate with the attorneys in the various actions to assure that orders for therapy and contact are made with respect to the alleged perpetrator, suspected victim, and family members, and that they are consistent if there are multiple court actions addressing the same issues. (Even if the accusations are spurious, therapy may be needed to mend relationships.)

POST-TRIAL AND NO TRIAL CONCERNS

Many issues arise after the trial. A conviction, an acquittal, recognition and nonrecognition of the fact of the sexual abuse or denial of damages—all impact on the emotions of the victim, whether a child or adult, as does the court proceeding itself. Numerous variables come into play which affect the mental status of the victim. It is important for the case manager and therapist, in particular, to be aware of the potential and present reactions of victims.

For victims of incest in particular, conviction may be a double-edged sword. They usually lose no matter what the outcome. While conviction may reaffirm the truth for them, helping them regain power and esteem, it also results in further alienation from the offending parent, and possible economic disaster for the family. Victims may also be the target of anger from other family members who see the victim's accusations rather than the perpetrator's acts as being responsible for their losses. On the other hand, where either the prosecutor refuses to prosecute due to inadequate proof of the crime or the court fails to uphold the accusations of victims, the results may include further feelings of powerlessness, disbelief and discredit, and even possible punishment by the perpetrator and other family members.

Often overlooked is what happens after the trial when the alleged perpetrator is found innocent, especially in incest cases. This may occur either with or without a conviction or other court determination of guilt. It is important to recognize that there is no known way to determine absolutely whether or not an alleged perpetrator has committed an offense. Mistakes are made, even by case managers, evaluating psychologists, clinicians, criminal justice system personnel and jurors. If the court has found that sexual abuse was committed in a family, protection of the child and therapeutic treatment has to be instituted based on the assumption that the court finding is true. On the other hand, if the court finds that no sexual abuse occurred, usually formal case management is dropped. The sexual abuse protocol should offer a format for assistance in these situations.

If the child firmly believes such abuse occurred, even if it probably did not, the terminating case manager should encourage the child to remain in therapeutic treatment and encourage the alleged perpetrator to work with the child's therapist. Care should be taken not to confuse the child further. A change of the child's therapist may be needed if the therapist overzealously implanted unfounded molestation beliefs in the child's head. Similarly, if the false allegations were the result of the paranoia or malevolence of a divorced parent spouse, therapy between the two parents and between the child and accused parent should be ordered (if possible, or at least encouraged) to try to increase communication and trust.

Even if the court process concludes optimally with truth prevailing and a victim of sexual abuse having adequate support, there is often a letdown after a trial concludes. Victims must put their lives back together, reorganizing priorities and values, while often dealing with symptoms of post-traumatic stress disorder. There may also be fears of retaliation, whether founded or not, by the family or friends of a perpetrator or by the perpetrator himself when released from incarceration.

The case manager should continue to assist the victims after the court procedures have concluded. Ascertaining and providing adequate resources are the principal functions at this point. Government funding and psychotherapy are two of the major resources. If not already in process, an application for victim of crime compensation should be made. Victim of crime compensation is funding administered by the state to help crime victims. In most jurisdictions, it will cover the costs of medical and mental health treatment and financial losses caused by the crime, such as loss of wages. Participation by victims, perpetrators and families in sexual abuse specific group therapy as well as individual therapy should be encouraged and/or instituted if not previously begun.

Sometimes threats may have been made against a victim, for example, by the brothers of the man found guilty of raping the victim. Helping the victim obtain adequate police protection may be a necessary service of the case manager, who may be a member of a rape crisis center staff in the case of an adult. If the victim is too traumatized to return to his/her former employment, vocational rehabilitation agencies should be contacted when the victim is ready to be retrained. It is easy to see the necessity of therapist input with respect to readiness of an adult victim to go back to work or move on with vocational training. Sometimes, too, the victim was attacked on the job, and the case manager must tackle the often very difficult task of assisting the victim through the Worker's Compensation system.

In the case of the child incest victim, the case manager must determine if there is physical or emotional danger to the victim from an angry, dysfunctional family. The case manager may have to arrange for in-home services to help the family relate appropriately or bring the case back to court for further action and possible removal of the victim from the home. Some families also violate court no-contact orders, and it may be necessary to return to court as a consequence. A plan for contact between the victim and family, and victim and perpetrator will have to be made. If either the child victim and/or perpetrator are removed from the home, decisions about when the child and/or perpetrator may be returned will have to be made.

If the child victim is placed in foster care, there is the additional element of the foster parents to be considered in making decisions about treatment, contact, and permanency planning. It is important to ensure that the foster family in which a sexually abused child is placed has had training in sexual abuse victim dynamics, in order that the child not be further traumatized. Foster parents may have very judgmental attitudes toward the parents of a sexual abuse victim, resulting in sabotage of family reunification plans, or may disbelieve the victim and stigmatize him/her by their attitudes. Child and adolescent victims may also act out inappropriately in sexual and other ways, which could cause problems in the foster home. Mediation and encouragement of participation of one or both foster parents in the child's therapy program are thus an important part of case management.

It is critical that the various agencies and treatment providers involved continue to interface after the principal court actions have been resolved. This is where multiple treatment provider and agency interaction problems occur. Particularly in the sexually abusive family cases, there may be a multitude of different people with different clients and interests involved, such as therapists for each of the family members, group therapists, probation officers and welfare workers with various functions. The court may have made orders which need modification. Whose voice wins out?

This is where it is particularly crucial to have a designated case manager coordinating a team approach, with periodic meetings of all of the players to discuss and work through the necessary decisions. This is also where a proactive stance is particularly valuable. A comprehensive plan, albeit a flexible one, should be made for all of the prospective changes and interactions. Input of each of the team members should be acknowledged in a way where all can feel that they are working together for the victim's welfare. Inclusion of the victim's family and/or victim, if old enough, in the planning process can also result in increased cooperation.

Input on progress and noteworthy occurrences are major themes of the periodic case management team meetings. Depending on the input, modifications can be made to increase the relevance and effectiveness of the plan. Different steps in the plan will have to be coordinated with the different treatment providers. For example, in the molesting family that wants to reunify, the recommended progression regarding therapy often takes the following format: The victim, perpetrator, spouse and nonvictim children participate in separate therapy groups with other victims, perpetrators, spouses and siblings, and also in individual therapy. Family therapy focused on rebonding the victim with the nonoffending parent and the siblings comes next. Meanwhile, perpetrators and their spouses should also be working in therapy to develop a better, more appropriate and communicative relationship. When victims are deemed ready by their therapists, and the therapists for the perpetrators find them ready as well, victim and offender therapy and whole family therapy are finally instituted.

The most common situation is that of the incestuous family wanting reunification when the perpetrator has been removed from the home for the safety of the victim, and the victim and siblings have remained with the nonoffending spouse. Visitation and return home by the perpetrator must be orchestrated with the needs of the child victim foremost. Usually, this is effected in a gradual progression, beginning with short supervised visits when the victim's therapist determines the victim to be ready. These initial visits may occur within the therapy setting or outside with a trained supervisor. Longer visits and visits supervised by family members or friends who can be trusted, and eventually by the nonoffending spouse, follow. It is only when the child feels ready and the perpetrator has completed a significant period of therapy that nonsupervised visits should be allowed. Eventually the perpetrator spends a night or two at home, and then may move home. At each step of the way, the parties involved should process with the therapist the interactions between family members in therapy.

Often child abuse cases occur around a divorce, where the nonoffending parent wants the abusive parent neither to return nor, oftentimes, to see the children again. It is important for the case management team to remain as neutral as possible, not pushing husband and wife apart or together, since resumption of the parents' relationship or total disengagement are personal decisions the parents should make for themselves. However, resumption of a relationship between the children, victim and siblings, and the perpetrator is an area where case management must intervene for the children's benefit. The children's emotional needs for their offending parent as well as their protection from further sexual assault are delicate issues requiring sensitive handling.

Where a divorced or separated parent is highly antagonistic to the offending parent, it is especially important that all parties work through their feelings and interactions in psychotherapy. If possible, joint therapy between antagonistic spouses should also take place, to decrease the friction and create some type of working relationship where the probability of a future healthy relationship between victim and offending parent can be increased.

It is also important that a format for safe visitation by the perpetrating parent be drawn up and presented in any divorce or separation action, so that the court does not, due to ignorance of the composite knowledge and plan of the treatment team, order visitation contrary to the best interests of the child. Likewise, periodic case evaluations by the case manager, which include the input of individual therapists, can be very helpful to judges making some of the necessary and difficult decisions regarding custody, modifications of custody and visitation, and reunification. In many jurisdictions, where the child is made a dependent of the court, semiannual reports are mandated. In family court actions, such as divorce or custody suits, the courts often send the parties to Conciliation Court counselors who report back to the judge with custody and visitation recommendations. It is particularly important that these counselors receive reports from the designated case managers regarding the plan for and progress of the parties in treatment.

What happens when there has been no trial? Sometimes the perpetrator has not been apprehended, there is insufficient evidence, or the victim is afraid or emotionally incapable of testifying. No court jurisdiction attaches, so there usually is no formal case management. This happens more frequently with adult sexual assault victims. The sexual abuse protocol should address the needs of this population and develop an assistance and referral procedure. Centers of the rape crisis type can afford valuable help with emergency and crisis intervention, therapy or referral to qualified therapists, assistance in completing victim of crime compensation applications, and general support. Where there is no rape crisis-type operation, these services need to be provided by other agencies and individuals, such as mental health agencies or professionals and victim assistance programs.

SUMMARY AND CONCLUSIONS

Case management is a means of reducing the impact of primary and secondary traumatic experiences on sexual abuse victims. For effective case management to take place, the most important tool is a written protocol developed by all the persons in the locale who will have contact with the victim. It should not only delineate procedural steps to take with different types of sexual abuse victims, but also identify a treatment team and case manager. The case manager and treatment team should proactively develop a plan of assistance for victims, particularly children, which is geared to the victim's needs. Communication between courts, agencies and individuals interfacing with the victim should be facilitated as a part of this plan.

For such intervention to be efficacious, it is important that the case management team be well educated and trained in victimology, legal procedures, child and adolescent development and sexual abuse dynamics; work cooperatively for the benefit of the victim, meeting at periodic intervals; and be conversant with all relevant community resources. Everything depends, of course, on who has the resources to cover the costs.

REFERENCES

Bagley, C., and Ramsey, R. (1986). "Sexual Abuse in Childhood: Psychosocial Outcomes and Implications for Social Work Practice." *Journal of Social Work and Human Sexuality* 4: 33–47.

Briere, J. (1987). "Post Sexual Abuse Trauma: Data and Implications for Clinical Practice." *Journal of Interpersonal Violence* 2.

Conte, J., and Berliner, L. (1987). "The Impact of Child Sexual Abuse: Empirical Findings." In L. Walker, ed., *Handbook on Sexual Abuse of Children: Assessment and Treatment Issues.* New York: Springer.

Friedrich, W. (1986). "Behavior Problems in Sexually Abused Young Children." *Journal of Pediatric Psychology* 11: 47–57.

Giarretto, H. (1982) *Integrated Treatment of Child Sexual Abuse.* Palo Alto, Calif.: Science and Behavior Books, Inc.

Gomes-Schwartz, B.; Horowitz, J.; and Sauzier, M. (1985). "Severity of Emotional Distress among Sexually Abused Preschool, School-age and Adolescent Children. *Hospital and Community Psychiatry* 35: 505–508.

Lurigio, A. J.; Skogan, W. G.; and Davis, R. C., eds. (1990). *Victims of Crime: Problems, Policies and Program.* Newbury Park, Calif.: Sage Publications.

Moore, S. T. (1990). "A Social Work Practice Model of Case Management: The Case Management Grid." *Social Work* 35: 385–480.

Netting, F. E. (1992). "Case Management: Service or Symptom?" *Social Work* 37, no. 2: 160–64.

Ohio v. *Roberts,* 448 U.S. 56, 66 (1980).

Sgroi, S. M. (1982). *Handbook of Clinical Intervention in Child Sexual Abuse.* Lexington, Mass.: Lexington Books.

White v. *Illinois,* 112 S. Ct. 736 (1992).

12

The Manufacture of Sexual Abuse "Memories": Psychiatry's Latest Fad

Lee Coleman

INTRODUCTION

The reality of false allegations of child sexual abuse is now widely recognized. Less often understood is the central role of psychiatry in creating this problem, through its influence on the training of law enforcement and child protection workers (Coleman 1986; Coleman & Clancy 1990; Coleman 1990).

My own experience in studying hundreds of cases of alleged child sexual abuse, involving over one thousand children, as well as the findings of numerous mental health professionals (see, for example, Wakefield & Underwager 1988) and official investigations (Humphrey 1985; San Diego County Grand Jury 1992), indicate that the heart of the problem is the way children are being interviewed by police, child protection investigators and therapists. We now know that if an interviewer assumes abuse has occurred, and is intent on corroborating what is already assumed, the child will often adopt the same point of view, "figure out" the details (with help from the interviewer), and describe with real sincerity events that never took place. The child comes to believe in what is said, not understanding that the story has been learned rather than remembered.

Emerging now, however, is yet another chapter in this tragic story. Adults, almost always women, are being victimized in the same way by overzealous and crusading professionals who have decided to specialize in a new kind of therapy. This therapy is aimed at treating patients for sexual abuse trauma, even though the patient gives no history of such abuse. The lack of such history is considered by the therapists to be itself a symptom of the disorder created by the assumed abuse. The patient has, in other words, "repressed," or "blocked," or "dissociated" the trauma, and is "in denial."

This therapy starts with a few symptoms from a list so ubiquitous that no person would fail to have some of them. The patient is then taught, either in individual or in group sessions (or both), that such symptoms are indicative of child sexual abuse, and asked for memories of such experiences. If the patient produces no memories, he or (usually) she is told that it is common to block such experiences from conscious awareness, and that progress in therapy requires the uncovering of such hidden "memories."

These themes run consistently through the cases in which I have had the opportunity to study the complete documentation and interview major participants. They are strikingly similar to patterns communicated not only by others who have questioned these new trends (see, for example, Wakefield & Underwager 1992; Wakefield & Underwager, undated manuscript) but also by the counselors and therapists describing their own work.

EMERGING PATTERNS IN "BLOCKED MEMORY" ALLEGATIONS

Large-scale, reliable data have yet to be gathered on this newly emerging phenomenon, but some data are available.

Recently, a grass-roots support group of parents accused by their adult sons or daughters of sexual abuse, calling itself the "False Memory Syndrome Foundation," has attempted to quantify certain aspects of this phenomenon. Responding to requests for information via newspaper articles and other media venues, over 600 families have made themselves known,* and 115 of them have completed and returned surveys (False Memory Foundation 1992). While hardly more than a small beginning, the data are the first available and seem instructive. They also tend to match a number of patterns from my own experience as well as patterns described by therapists claiming to be helping adults discover previously "blocked" memories of sexual abuse.

First, neither the accusing son nor daughter, nor the family, appears generally to have a history of major psychosis or overwhelming family breakdown. Family income is typically upper-middle-class, with divorce lower than the national average, and higher education prominent.

Ninety percent of accusing persons were daughters. Only one third of

*A more recent statistic, as reported by Victor, chapter 13 of this volume, places the number of families at 4,000 as of spring 1993.

these daughters had received psychotherapy as children. *In almost all cases, the "recovered memories" emerged in therapy.* The therapists were female about 75 percent of the time, and about evenly distributed among social workers, psychologists and other types of counselors. The book *The Courage to Heal* (Bass & Davis 1988) and similar works were prominent in the therapy, as was the use of survivor groups, dreams as evidence of assumedly real events, and a variety of techniques such as age regression, hypnosis, meditation, trance writing, and psychodrama.

In nearly half of the survey responses, accusations included repeated violence or anal/vaginal rape. Eighteen percent included what has been termed satanic ritual abuse, in which orgies of murder, mayhem, and sadistic sexual torture allegedly took place. In 86 percent of the cases, siblings did not corroborate any of the allegations, and three-fourths did not believe anything happened.

In a recent report from therapists engaging in this new type of therapy (Shaffer & Cozolino 1992), similar data emerge. Limiting themselves to cases in which the patient eventually described "sacrificial murder of animals, infants, children, and/or adults," in which "corpses were often subjected to sexual violations and cannibalistic feasting," and in which the patients claimed they were "suspended on hooks . . . arms and legs twisted, being given electric shocks, having hair and body parts burned, and confined in coffins that often contained insects, spiders, and snakes," Shaffer and Cozolino report that in all cases these claims emerged only in therapy in which "uncovering of memories was reported as the primary focus of the therapy." These patients had come because of:

> addictions, fears, and phobias. . . . [M]any subjects progressed from memories of sexual abuse by acquaintances, to memories of sexual abuse by family members, and finally, to memories of ritualistic victimizations that included sexual abuse by multiple perpetrators of both sexes . . . participation in twelve-step programs as well as support groups such as Incest Survivors Anonymous, Victims Anonymous, and Adults Molested as Children was reported by the majority as necessary adjuncts to psychotherapy. *This served to provide virtual substitute families* for many victims who had cut ties with their biological families as a result of either their disclosures of earlier abuse being met with denial and/or discovering that the families were cult involved. (italics added)

It seems, then, that both the believers and the nonbelievers are gathering similar data. My own experience has been the same, the most important factors being that the accusers were young white women, well educated, who had entered therapy for problems involving depression, anxiety, and frequently drug, alcohol, or eating disorders; they had come across therapists who urged upon them the idea that their symptoms were the ones to be expected from a history of sexual abuse. Those ultimately "discovering" previously "hidden memories," in other words, are those patients who gradually accept a point of view that is promoted in individual and group sessions.

This pattern, reported by both critics and believers alike, would seem to indicate that suggestibility and group influence may be an important focus for scholarly attention. The most important parallel between my own experience and the beginning data from other sources is that the allegations, even the most fantastic (see below), are the result not of psychotic breakdown, but of the gradual adoption of ideas through the susceptibility to psychological contagion which we all possess to a greater or lesser degree.

The emergence of these patterns is perhaps best illustrated by a case example.

MEETING MS. JONES

A 36-year-old woman I'll call Ms. Jones sought treatment for alcoholism. Her background included two failed marriages, sexual promiscuity (her words) before marriage and several extramarital affairs, and bulimorexia (an eating disorder that alternates between food binges and fasting). Several prior courses of psychotherapy had never included any mention of incest.

Admitted as an inpatient to an alcohol treatment center, Ms. Jones was asked about any sexual abuse in her past. She mentioned a boy who forced himself on her as a teenager, and also recounted that on weekends her father would come into bed with her and her sister. She herself described no improper contact with her father, but a 'sexual recovery program counselor' nonetheless wrote:

> she was able to identify a limited amount of incestuous behavior . . . Dad would climb into bed with her or her sister on Sunday mornings. She was very uncomfortable about that.

With nothing more to show, it was concluded that Ms. Jones had "multiple incest issues with her family of origin." She was put into "Sexual Concerns Group" and upon discharge referred for outpatient therapy.

Her new outpatient therapist inquired about these "incest issues." Ms. Jones repeated the same recollections as before, but the therapist noted in her records that Ms. Jones was "probably blocking others." Within a month, Ms. Smith would fulfill her therapist's expectations, and produce "memories of incest."

Because Ms. Jones was keeping a diary, required in the type of therapy she had fallen into, it is possible to study how these "memories" emerged. In her first entry after discharge from inpatient treatment, she wrote:

> Something happened during my childhood that gave an incredibly powerful message of shame about my body and sexuality. My gut level is that I was incested and beaten by my mother for it.

In another entry, describing her inpatient treatment, she wrote, "They [hospital staff] kept asking me—'Why are you protecting your father?' "

Ms. Jones now acceded to her therapist's recommendation to join a group to work on these issues, while also continuing her individual therapy. In both, she was encouraged to do "anger work." As her journal noted, "they kept asking me—'why are you protecting your father?' I thought and thought. I didn't think I was, but I really felt and saw nothing."

That night, she wrote, "Have come to realize . . . I'm running from a feeling or memory . . . why the sex, why the food, am I protecting my father?"

Within days, Ms. Jones finally accomplished what her therapist and her group therapy peers had urged upon her: she had her first "memories" of incest. Yet she also wrote in her journal, "This is a game I'm playing with myself. It didn't really happen. I'm imagining this. It's just because they told me something happened that I think this happened. I'm misremembering things. I'm making this up."

As her journals began to be more and more taken up with these mental pictures, Ms. Jones abandoned all doubt and gave herself completely to the process. In the ensuing months, her claims grew to include:

- repeated intercourse, sodomy and oral sex with her father
- repeated beatings by her father and mother
- repeated rape by her mother
- repeated insertion of foreign objects into her vagina and anus
- surgery in which her mother cut her vagina and inserted foreign objects, thereby stretching her vagina for later intercourse with her father
- multiple murders of children and adults, perpetrated by members of the "cult" which fronted as a normal church
- three pregnancies, all resulting in live births, prior to age twelve, with each baby murdered in "cult" rituals
- sterilization at age twelve
- electroshock treatment to her at home
- gradual recognition of her 112 personalities
- torture by electric shock via wires inserted into her vagina and rectum
- multiple rapes by other members of the "cult."

Absorbing the messages from her therapist and group therapy peers, who (as her journals and my subsequent interview with her indicated) had by now become her only friends, Ms. Jones was able to "understand" how she lost her awareness of these events. She had "blocked" the memories; she was a "multiple personality."

Along with these new "memories" came other ideas. She filed a lawsuit against her parents, and planned to write a book. Her therapist's notes, which I was also able to study, made it clear that she accepted Ms. Jones' claims as reality. So much so, in fact, that when Ms. Jones said several times she thought that she had exhausted her storehouse of memories, her therapist urged her to keep digging for more.

But whatever fantastic allegation might have been considered a sign of progress, Ms. Jones was nonetheless continuing her alcohol abuse and was also in trouble at work. She was then admitted to another inpatient program, this time one solely devoted to treatment of sexual abuse.

Every allegation was accepted at face value by the new treatment team. Not once were the parents contacted to ask for their statements. No attempt was made to corroborate anything. Despite Ms. Jones' claim that she had, by age eleven, delivered her third child in a hospital in a nearby city, no attempt was made to obtain medical records.

By the time of discharge, Ms. Jones was now a bona fide *DSM-III-R** 300.4, multiple personality disorder, and 309.89, post traumatic stress disorder. Her discharge summary offers a hint of what must have been happening in her treatment: "The patient attended an Anger to Power lecture, two Anger experiential groups, and the Anger and Letters to Perpetrators Workshops."

Months later, Ms. Jones decided to sue her parents for what she claimed they had done to her. Asked by defense attorneys to consult in this lawsuit, I had an opportunity to interview her. As with similar cases I have studied, it was clear that Ms. Jones was not "lying." She believed with utmost sincerity, it seemed to me, that all her claims were accurate. I expect that she will continue to believe these allegations for the rest of her life.

When, however, the Court ordered Ms. Jones to be physically examined to see if there was evidence of the multiple childbirths and mutilations she claimed, she dropped her lawsuit.

STUDYING THE THERAPISTS

The above example should make it clear that an understanding of the recent emergence of the "blocked memory" phenomenon will require more a study

**Diagnostic and Statistical Manual of Mental Disorders,* 3rd ed., rev. (1987)

of the thinking and practices of certain mental health professionals than, as some would argue, a new understanding of memory, repression, and the dynamics of trauma. Let us begin such an inquiry with a brief look at an example of the ideas being presented to patients by therapists of the persuasion encountered by Ms. Jones.

E. Sue Blume, in *Secret Survivors: Uncovering Incest and Its Aftereffects in Women* (1991), recommends her "Incest Survivors' Aftereffects Checklist, reproduced in Table 1.

For those inclined to assume that only a tiny fringe of therapists could fail to see the meaninglessness of such a shopping list, my own experience would indicate that Ms. Blume is correct when she writes:

> The Incest Survivors' Aftereffects Checklist has spread from its . . . origins to international distribution among incest survivors, professionals, conference attendees, participants in self-help and recovery groups for sexual and substance abuse, and adult children of alcoholics.

Here are a few of Blume's ideas, offered as representative of this new therapeutic approach emerging among "specialists" in child sexual abuse. (Blume, Preface & Introduction 1991):

> Incest is easily the greatest single underlying reason why women seek therapy or other treatment. . . .
>
> Many, if not most, incest survivors *do not know* that the abuse has even occurred! . . .
>
> Through the Incest Survivors' Aftereffects Checklist, numerous incest survivors have finally been able to piece together the disjointed fragments of their lives: Difficult though it is to face that one is an incest survivor, this is the first step in ending confusion and finding a direction for healing. . . .
>
> After introducing the broadened definition of incest upon which my work is based . . . I discuss the tactics commonly used . . . to protect against awareness of a reality that cannot be faced: amnesia, blocking, splitting (depersonalization, shutdown, and others). . . .
>
> Among women who had not been aware of childhood sexual abuse but who recognized characteristics in themselves on the checklist, a surprising number began to uncover previously repressed incest. . . .
>
> Whether or not actual memories are uncovered, the checklist then presents a structure for identifying and addressing the consequences of incest. (italics added).

Table 1
Incest Survivors' Aftereffects Checklist
(Blume 1991)

- Nightmares, night terrors
- Swallowing or gagging sensitivity
- Alienation from the body
- Failure to heed body signals
- Failure to take care of one's body
- Poor body image
- Avoidance of sexual attention
- Gastrointestinal problems
- Gynecological disorders
- Headaches
- Arthritis or joint pains
- Wearing a lot of clothing
- Baggy clothes
- Unwillingness to remove clothing
- Excessive bathroom privacy
- Eating disorders
- Drug or alcohol abuse
- Total drug or alcohol abstinence
- Other addictions
- Compulsive disorders
- Self-destructiveness
- Skin carving, self-abuse
- Phobias
- Need to be invisible
- Need to be perfect or perfectly bad
- Suicidal thoughts or behaviors
- Depression
- Anger issues
- Splitting (depersonalization)
- Creating fantasy world
- Creating fantasy relationships
- Creating fantasy identities
- "Sensory flashes" of unknown meaning
- Ambivalent relationships
- Avoidance of mirrors
- Desire to change one's name
- Limited tolerance for happiness
- Aversion to making noise
- Verbal hypervigilance
- Stealing
- Starting fires
- Going into shock
- Shut down in crisis
- Psychic numbing
- Pain with a memory or emotion
- Numbness with memory or emotion
- Rigid control of thought process
- Multiple personality
- Humorlessness or extreme solemnity
- Childhood hiding or cowering in corners
- Nervous about being watched or surprised
- Feeling watched
- Startle response
- Inability to trust
- Total trust, trusting indiscriminately
- High risk taking, inability to take risks
- Boundary issues
- Control, power, territoriality issues
- Fear of losing control
- Obsessive-compulsive behaviors
- Guilt, shame
- Low self-esteem
- High appreciation of favors by others
- Pattern of being a victim
- No sense of own power
- No sense of right to set limits and say no
- Relationships with much older persons
- Feeling demand to "produce and be loved"
- Abandonment issues
- Blocking out some period of early years
- Feeling of carrying an awful secret
- Feeling crazy, different, unreal
- Denial
- Repression of memories
- Sexual issues, aversion to being touched
- Confusion of sexuality and emotionality
- Sexual acting-out
- Compulsively seductive
- Compulsively asexual
- Must be the sexual aggressor
- Cannot be the sexual aggressor
- Promiscuity
- Prostitution, becoming a stripper or porn actress

Mulhern (1991a, 1991b, 1992) has studied the question of why and how in recent years a growing number of patients claiming to have "discovered" memories of abuse have gone on to make allegations involving extreme acts of group violence and mayhem, including mutilation of animals, infanticide, sexual orgies, and other acts sometimes called satanic ritual abuse (SRA). Her findings, I believe, tell us much about the underlying causes of the entire "blocked memory" phenomenon, and not only those cases which eventuate in ritual abuse claims.

Mulhern concludes that it is the intense networking among professionals, during "professionally accredited courses" aimed at "offering training in the identification and treatment of victims of [satanic] ritual abuse," which accounts for the emergence of, and similarity between, accounts coming from patients in recent years. She has, after studying these training workshops, found a pattern which is similar to my own findings. First, she writes:

> Listeners are admonished, threatened and exhorted to believe. Belief is presented as vital. . . . SRA seminars assert that the vast majority of SRA victims enter therapy amnesic for the extraordinary abuses which they have suffered. Clinicians are warned that unless these memories are recovered, any hope for significant recovery will be compromised. The recovery of SRA memories, whether they be those of adults or children, is said to depend on the efficient use of specialized therapeutic techniques. . . . (Mulhern 1992)

G. K. Ganaway has also discussed the emergence of this phenomenon, and his unsparing criticism of therapists who uncritically adopt this stance is worthy of careful consideration. He writes:

> As empirical evidence accumulates . . . that an apparent international, highly organized conspiratorial system of criminal satanic cults may not, in fact, exist outside the collective minds of those who believe in it, the *true* cult may prove to be comprised of a network of individuals who intentionally or unintentionally are more interested in proving the hypothesis than in discovering what is really there. Due to the emotionally charged nature of the subject . . . it is not difficult to see how otherwise level-headed and rational authorities and leaders in their fields of psychiatry, psychology, social work, law enforcement, and pastoral care could themselves be drawn into a cult-like group through consensual validation with the evolving generic SRA stories of alleged cult survivors providing the dogmatic glue that keeps the group cohesive. Many of these individuals unfortunately appear to have literally staked their reputations on the validity of the "survivor" accounts. . . . (Ganaway 1991)

Despite the strong emphasis by commentators like Mulhern and Ganaway on therapeutically induced claims of "ritual abuse," neither my own experience nor that of others who have reviewed a number of these cases (Wakefield & Underwager 1992) would indicate that escalation to murder and mayhem is a necessary element in therapeutically induced "memories" of sexual abuse. The literature on human suggestibility is too well documented to require separate comment here. (In this context, see Ceci & Bruck, Loftus 1992). Even a casual study of recently publicized allegations of "recovered memories" of incest soon reveals that something other than true memory is the explanation. When, for example, TV comedienne Roseanne Arnold alleges that she can remember, *at age six months,* sexual abuse by her father, it is obvious that such statements are not the product of memory.

INCEST SURVIVORS ANONYMOUS

As important as is the study of training seminars for professionals, complete understanding of the emergence of the "blocked memory" phenomenon requires a look at another piece of the puzzle. Self-help groups of the kind briefly mentioned by Ms. Jones in her journals are now operating throughout the United States and other countries. A brief look at their activities will be instructive.

Modeled on the twelve steps program of Alcoholics Anonymous, Incest Survivors Anonymous (ISA) is the most influential of the recently emerging "survivor" groups, and is similar in philosophy and practice to others that I have been able to study. ISA was started in 1980 by Erin M., who has described the process by which she "discovered" her incest (Incest Survivors Anonymous 1988).

> The first forty-eight years I lived my family's lies of which I was innocent, having no conscious memory of the family secret. I had only remembered what they had programmed me to remember. . . . The second section of my life began the day I had my first incest memory breakthrough at the age of forty-eight in 1975 and began the tedious, painful road to recovery from a childhood of incest, and then in 1982 the memories of ritual abuse broke through the blocking. . . . For a while I had been seeing funny little black flicks in front of my eyes. . . . Today I know it was my system on overload and memories pushing up to breakthrough. . . .

The moment of "breakthrough," we learn, came in a dentist's chair:

> The male dentist in the white coat, standing over me, smiling, light shining off glasses, the light shining down on me, the shining cold instrument to hold my mouth open, the needle full of drugs in my gums triggered cell memory, feelings and pictures. It was in my breakthroughs that I remembered our family dentist had molested me and was in the rituals.
>
> . . . The restless sleep, anxiety attacks, early morning sweats and shakes, and panic attacks were getting more and more frightening. . . . I had worked my AA and Alanon programs hard and prayed for help. . . . I had worked so long and so hard for recovery from alcoholism, I was not going to give up now. One night as I was falling asleep I heard the floor squeak and my eyes popped open and what I saw triggered me into a terrifying state. What I saw with my eyes I also saw deep in my gut. It was like a shutter on a camera opening and closing fast. It was black deep inside and a door opened, a yellow shaft of light silhouetted a dark figure of a man, wearing a white shirt, standing in the doorway with his arms out in front of him.

As it turned out, the man was her husband, getting ready for bed.

> He had done nothing wrong to trigger such a reaction. . . . Several months later I felt ready. I went for help . . . having no conscious memory of the family abuse. . . . It didn't help any that I had been given electric shock to the left side of my brain during the rituals to block my memory so I could be used over and over. This was revealed to me later.

Now ISA's future founder had taken the critical step, making the connection which I have found in every case of "blocked memories" of incest: *She started therapy in which the therapist taught her to believe in the reality of whatever mental images she could conjure up.*

> He [the therapist] taught me to look within and tell what I saw. As I did, feelings and pictures of terrible intensity broke loose and roared to the surface. . . . The blocking was so intense that until the moment of breakthrough I had no conscious memory of what I was now beginning to remember in a living smell-a-vision, color-vision, tel-a-vision, taste-a-vision, hear-a-vision. . . . It was like watching a horror movie or television or slide show that I couldn't turn off. . . .
>
> When the memories would surface and the wrenching would churn my gut, I would sit in my rocking chair and rock, crying, streams of tears washing my face, talking to Jesus whose picture hung on my living room wall, hugging my cat "Bigfoot," my AA Big Book and my Bible. . . . Over a period of time . . . horrific memories were coming up—initiators too numerous to mention: father, mother, older sister, aunts, uncles, cousins, family dentist, family doctor, grammar school principal, business acquaintance, minister, the list went on and on. . . .

> Five years after my first breakthrough, knowing all along that God was getting me ready for something, the stark reality hit me that God wanted me to start a worldwide twelve steps program for incest survivors. . . . This was God's vision. . . . This is how, when, where and why ISA was founded July 15, 1980, with our first meeting of eight women survivors who met in my living room . . . we now have 110 groups that we know about across the country. . . .

By the time of this writing, the number of such groups must surely be many times larger than this. In each one, vulnerable persons coming not only with a need for help but the likely desire to place their trust in both therapist and peer, are being taught,

> When you are able, and not before, your mind will slowly remind you of the experience in the mind's own language, MEMORY. Often in dreams, and/or during your awake hours. These memories may appear to be hallucinations, fantasies or unreal but they are not. . . . When you translate these memories you will go through a breakthrough to recovery. (Incest Survivors Anonymous 1988)

This, then, was the milieu into which Ms. Jones was thrust and to which thousands of vulnerable women have been exposed in the last decade. Is it any wonder that a growing number of them are coming up with claims remarkably similar to those of Ms. Jones, and Erin M. before her? Not only are such groups proliferating across the nation; they have become intimately associated with the new wave of psychotherapists who specialize in such "blocked memories." Their members attend the same seminars, read the same materials, and refer patients to one another just as Mulhern and Ganaway have described. Thus, patients caught up in this network are often subjected to the profound influence, simultaneously, of both individual therapist and group therapy peers.

It is also inevitable that a certain percentage of persons who hear or read the same ideas in written materials or from the broadcast media will embrace this new movement. With the ever-widening dissemination of materials, both written and broadcast, repeating these ideas, it becomes increasingly possible for persons with no direct contact in the therapy milieu to absorb the same misguided notions. Some of them will then seek out those very therapists and groups promoting these ideas and methods.

As it turns out, precisely such a source has been around for quite a while, but only recently has receieved the attention it doesn't deserve.

THE POWER OF THE WRITTEN WORD

To illustrate how even nonpatients may, simply by reading certain books or articles on this subject, become exposed to these ideas, let us consider an early and potent source of inspiration for the wave of "remembering." The year 1980 saw the publication of *Michelle Remembers,* co-authored by psychiatrist Lawrence Pazder and his patient Michelle Smith (Smith & Pazder).

We learn that Michelle's sessions were lasting hours at a time, as Pazder encouraged her to keep trying to bring out something she said was hidden.

"It's sort of like going back to a haunted house," he told her. "You can't go back all alone—because it scared you before, too much, and all you'd have would be the same person you had before—yourself. If you're going back to a haunted house, you've got to have someone you trust to go with you, someone you know it's safe with. . . . Just try to let yourself go."

Before long, Michelle was ready to do that.

> As Dr. Pazder watched, her hands flew up in front of her face, the fingers splayed wide and stiff. Her eyes squeezed almost painfully closed. Her mouth opened round, stretching her white lips thin. She drew a deep, deep breath. And then the terror broke. She screamed. It was a cry so violent that it drove her down into the couch. Dr. Pazder sat quietly as Michelle screamed, his hand on her head. After twenty-five minutes, the screaming began to ebb.

We learn (as well) that the screams were not those of Michelle Smith, twenty-seven years old, but a five-year-old, the first of Michelle's "multiple personalities." She was being tortured by "Malachi," as her parents and many others watched.

"I never even knew about any of this before today," Michelle told Pazder, even adding that she was worried she was making it up. Pazder had no such doubts, however. He told Michelle, "You were obviously almost re-experiencing some terrible memory, about a time when you were a little girl. . . . You did well." The session had lasted four and a half hours.

In subsequent meetings, Michelle described satanic rituals, complete with silver goblets, candles, and black robes. A woman in a black cape dipped a stick into a vile mixture from a goblet, and inserted it into her nose, her mouth, her ears, as the rest of the coven watched.

Did Dr. Pazder have any doubts about any of this? Evidently not. "Privately, Dr. Pazder was convinced that the group—whoever they were—had been using very sophisticated techniques of ego destruction."

Michelle was now seeing Pazder every day, "often as much as six hours a day." The "therapeutic relationship" was as robust as the rapidly escalating stories. When Michelle spoke of her desire for a "link to the present," before entering her next memory, Pazder was ready to accommodate. ". . . [T]hey shifted so that he could sit on the sofa with her head against his shoulder. This seemed to give her the closeness and security she needed."

In the ensuing months, escalating claims of ritual orgies, murders, tortures, and trips to graveyards emerged. We also read:

> Their working postures had evolved too. They seldom used the sofa . . . it was not stable enough for the shaking and trembling that Michelle went through as she relived. They had moved to the mat. Sometimes Dr. Pazder would sit on the floor beside it. At other times would lie back, a pillow under his head. It was the only way to work, considering that the sessions often went on for five or six hours . . . she needed contact. Dr. Pazder did not look upon her as an attractive twenty-eight-year-old woman. . . . Sometimes she would have her head on his shoulder. But he was careful about the way he touched her. . . . (Smith & Pazder 1980: 100)

Eventually, Dr. Pazder divorced his wife, and he and Michelle were married.

Dressed in a more scholarly veneer are the increasing number of books by therapists and counselors (some self-taught), which are having a growing impact on large segments of the population. Most influential is the best-selling book *The Courage to Heal* (Bass and Davis 1988). Bass (who describes herself as "not academically educated as a psychologist. I have acquired counseling skills primarily through practice"), and Davis (who "remembered" her sexual abuse while in counseling with Bass) are cited by a large percentage of women when asked about sources that helped them "unblock" their memory, and is considered "must" reading for professionals interested in this new and exciting field.

These authors have cast a wide net indeed. Children "forced to listen to sexual talk," "subjected to unnecessary medical treatments," ". . . kissed or held in a way that made you uncomfortable," "bathed in a way that felt intrusive," and "objectified and ridiculed about your body" are all victims of sexual abuse. They add, moreover, that "If you are unable to remember any specific instances like the ones mentioned, but still have a feeling that something abusive happened to you, it probably did" (p. 21).

Even those with "no conscious memory" of being abused need not be left out. Pazder and Smith write:

> You may think you don't have memories, but often as you begin to talk about what you do remember, there emerges a constellation of feelings, reactions, and recollections that add up to substantial information. . . . Often the knowledge that you were abused starts with a tiny feeling, an intuition. It's important to trust that inner voice and work from there. Assume your

> feelings are valid. . . . If you think you were abused and your life shows the symptoms, then you were.

Given the growing impact of such writings, not only on lay persons but on the mental health community as well, it is time to take a closer look at the alleged basis for this newly discovered phenomenon—"blocked memories" of major trauma. Is there any evidence, beyond anecdotal material, to support the claim that major trauma is being legitimately retrieved? Are we dealing with "memory" or suggestibility?

EXAMINING THE EVIDENCE FOR "REPRESSED MEMORY" OF SEXUAL ABUSE

The core of the "evidence" for the reality of repressed memories of sexual abuse is the claims of alleged victims. While such claims, because they are anecdotal, have no inherent reliability, some persons nevertheless argue that several factors make these claims reliable (Gleason 1985; Gould & Cozolino 1992; Shaffer & Cozolino 1992; Young et al. 1991). They point out the similarity in the claims of the many thousands of women who have remembered their abuse only in adult life. Since these women have never met each other, it is argued, their stories could not be the product of rumor, contagion, or suggestibility.

But as a number of commentators have pointed out (including Victor, chapter 13 in this volume), this is a rather simplistic understanding of the dynamics of how ideas spread among people. As Putnam (1991) has stated:

> Studies of the sociometric patterns of rumor contagion have demonstrated that rumors, urban-legends, and other folk tales can be rapidly disseminated throughout our society and are shared in common by large numbers of people who have never directly met each other. The child abuse community is particularly susceptible to such a rumor process as there are multiple, interconnected communication/education networks shared by therapists and patients alike. In addition, there is massive media dissemination of material . . . through dramatic autobiographical accounts, sensational talk shows, and news reports of alleged cases, not to mention the numerous movies and television programs. . . . Contagion and contamination are very real and powerful processes. . . . (p. 177)

Similarly flawed are statistics which claim to document the relative frequencies of cases of sexual abuse repressed until adulthood, and those cases where the adult merely failed to tell of abuse during childhood. An article by Briere and Conte (1993) may be taken as typical of such statistics. They claim that 59.6 percent of 279 subjects were "amnesic for their abuse," and go on to describe variables which allegedly influence whether abuse will be remembered or repressed.

As it turns out, however, these figures resulted from self-reported questionnaires of persons enmeshed in the very web of influences described in this discussion. "Subjects were recruited," Briere and Conte (1993) write, "by their therapists, who were part of an informal sexual abuse treatment referral network connected with Childhelp, U.S.A." "Amnesia was assessed," they continue, "by the question 'During the period of time before the first forced sexual experience happened and your eighteenth birthday was there ever a time when you could not remember the forced sexual experience?' "

A simple checkmark was all it took to create the "evidence" reported with such confidence by Briere and Conte. Nowhere do they even mention the evidence that the "informal sexual abuse treatment referral network" is intimately connected with the recent emergence of so many false claims of abuse. With no way to know how many of these patients were in fact victims of sexual abuse, and how many were influenced to create events that never took place, the "findings" of Briere and Conte, like those of so many similar reports, prove nothing.

The methodological problems go deeper yet. Briere and Conte go on to encourage therapists to engage in the same methods which the "sexual abuse recovery" groups have disseminated so widely.

> . . . [T]he clinician who has some reason to believe that his or her client was molested as a child (e.g., in terms of her current clinical presentation) may be well advised to continue to entertain that hypothesis during treatment, *even in the absence of client abuse memories*. . . . Such amnesia may partially or totally remit as therapy continues, especially if the structure and pace of treatment communicates safety and encourages exploration, and the therapist remains open to the possibility that sexual abuse occurred. (italics added)

Efforts to support the reality of "repressed memories" of sexual abuse sometimes turn to theoretical, psychodynamic explanations. A growing number of authors, usually already steeped in controversial diagnoses (such as multiple personality disorder, dissociative disorders, psychogenic amnesia, and post-traumatic stress disorder), are claiming that an upsurge of new knowledge has recently established that major psychic trauma is the leading cause of these disorders (Loewenstein 1991). Massive denial and dissociation, they claim, can lead to a total block of memory for the events of the trauma. This so called "state-dependent amnesia" may be lifted by appropriate therapy, or by a retraumatization, which may bring back memories of the original trauma.

When one looks for evidence to support such notions, a noteworthy circularity is immediately evident. Either the "evidence" for the original trauma consists merely of statements of patients who have been in therapies that increasingly engage in what has been termed "memory chasing," (Agosta & Loring 1988) or the "amnesia" is itself considered proof that there must have been trauma as a cause.

EXAMINGING THE EVIDENCE AGAINST "REPRESSED MEMORY" OF SEXUAL ABUSE

It is, of course, impossible to *disprove* most allegations. That is why a groundless accusation is not one that *could not have happened,* but one for which there is no credible evidence. Several factors related to the "repressed memory movement," however, add up to solid evidence that such claims are completely unreliable.

First, a significant percentage of cases of alleged "recovered memory" contain allegations involving what has been termed "ritual abuse." These claims include:

> the alleged existence of a vast international, multigenerational, conspiracy practicing religious worship of Satan through sex and death rituals involving torture, incest, perverted sex, animal and human sacrifice, cannibalism, and necrophilia. In addition to suffering rape, bizarre tortures and being forced to participate in victimizing others, alleged victims of satanic ritual abuse are often reported to have been "brainwashed" with the aid of hypnosis and drugs and implanted with suggestions to kill themselves or commit other acts on command. (Putnam 1991)

I have seen such claims in many of the cases I have personally studied. They inevitably were later stages of a buildup of allegations which began in therapy encouraging "recovery of memories." The fact that both the believers (Cozolino 1989; Gould & Cozolino 1992; Shaffer & Cozolino 1992) and those claiming to be falsely accused (False Memory Foundation 1992) agree that many of these cases involve allegations of satanic ritual abuse (SRA) means that data on the reality or unreality of SRA will tell us a great deal about the wider phenomenon of alleged "unblocking" of sexual abuse memories.

Of the hundreds (perhaps thousands by now) of allegations of SRA, *not a single* case has been substantiated by investigative agencies. This makes a mockery of the unwavering faith of those who persist in claiming that such cases are real. Kenneth Lanning, an FBI Special Agent, has focused for more than a decade on "all aspects of the sexual victimization of children" (Lanning 1989). He writes:

> When I first began to hear stories of what sounded like satanic or occult activity in connection with allegations of sexual victmization of children, I tended to believe them. . . . But the number of alleged cases began to grow and grow. We now have hundreds of victims alleging that thousands of offenders are abusing and even murdering tens of thousands of people as part of organized satanic cults, and there is little or no corroborative evidence. The very reason many "experts" cite for believing these allegations (i.e., many victims, who never met each other, reporting the same events), is the primary reason I began to question. . . . (Lanning 1992)

And as Putnam (1991) has commented:

> there is a complete absence of independent evidence corroborating the existence of such cults or their alleged activities such as human sacrifice, cannibalism, and sex and death orgies. Despite hundreds of investigations in the United States by local police departments and the Federal Bureau of Investigation, there has never been a single documented case of satanic murder, human sacrifice, or cannibalism. (p. 175)

Why does this tell us something about the alleged process of "recovering memories" of sexual abuse? Because if so many of these cases ultimately lead to allegations of ritual abuse which is clearly not happening, then we may safely conclude that the *process leading to the claims is fatally flawed.*

Finally, if accounts of alleged survivors are the major "evidence" being cited to support the reliability of "recovered abuse memories," perhaps I will be forgiven for offering a different kind of survivor account. This one is from a woman subjected to the very therapeutic manipulations I have discussed, who for a while adopted the belief that she had, with the help of her therapist and group therapy peers, retrieved memories of childhood sexual abuse. Eventually, she had a different opinion:

> . . . I'd had some sexual abuse by an uncle, . . . it was not anything that I ever forgot. . . . Once I got into therapy, . . . it began to be things like, I feel uncomfortable hugging my father so there must be something to that. My father must have sexually abused me. . . . The fact that I didn't like my mother washing my hair when I was eight or nine . . . that was an indicator that my mother had done more than that in the bathtub . . . different little things like this were indications that something more than I was willing to say or knew about was going on and the fact that I wouldn't reveal the specifics was only a sign of my denial. . . . So by the time you get through, you've got every school teacher, pastor, every neighbor, anybody . . . I began to believe that possibly my parents had been involved . . . and even began to have almost visualizations . . . based on what he'd told me that I'd suffered this traumatic sexual abuse . . . that the MMPIs [Minnesota Multiphasic

> Personality Inventories] and different tests showed all this, I began to believe . . . my brothers and sisters came in and . . . they got to hear from my therapist how bad my parents are and how unless I have the support of my brothers and sisters, I'm liable to kill myself. . . . Someone has taken everything you thought you knew about your family, the people you love, and twisted it and told you that everything you knew was wrong. These people that you loved, the values . . . are all garbage, they're really a bunch of satanic cult people who kill and eat babies and flesh . . . It put me in a very serious medical place. . . . I'd never tried to kill myself till I started therapy. (Price 1992)

This woman also described the role of the "survivor group" foisted upon her by her therapist:

> The therapists have told me that I need to make this group of sick, dependent women my new family . . . I love those women, . . . but we were not a group that needed to be dependent . . . now you really are depressed so you don't go to work as much, you don't communicate with people on the outside because what are you going to tell them. All you talk about is flashbacks, . . . incest and cutting and eating. . . . You go to therapy, you work enough to pay for therapy and you just call each other with flashbacks and that's how my life went for a while.

A QUESTION OF TIMING

Further evidence that "recovered memories" of sexual abuse are not memories at all, involves the matter of timing. Only in the last few years have such claims been made. Does this mean that a new and dramatic discovery has been made, one that drastically alters our common sense notions about memory? Or is the sudden emergence of such claims merely a fad?

The psychodynamic concept of repression, postulated by Freud, is unprovable (because there is usually no way to verify retrospective information gained from patients in therapy) but nonetheless widely respected by therapists (Holmes 1990). The impossibility of *proving* that repression is real doesn't mean that feelings and impulses may not disappear from awareness, as psychodynamic theory teaches, but it does mean that statements do not automatically become reliable indicators of past events, simply because they are uttered by a patient engaged in some kind of "uncovering" therapy.

Generally, the timing of the phenomenon of "repressed memory for sexual abuse," coming as it does on the heels of the explosion of sexual abuse allegations during the last decade, and the related emergence of false allegations by children in some cases, has been ignored by apologists for the "recovered memory" phenomenon. In a recent case on which I consulted, however, a therapist specializing in techniques aimed at encouraging emergence of sexual abuse memories offered her explanation as to why such claims are only now emerging:

> It is precisely because the emotional intensity of sexual abuse in childhood is greater than what most children can integrate that these experiences are quickly lost to memory. The ensuing forgetting and denial are the mind's way of protecting the individual from total disruption of their cognitive functioning. This was particularly true of survivors of sexual abuse whose experiences occurred more than ten years ago. The reason for this is that there was not the social awareness nor the professional expertise for dealing with these problems at that time. Children instinctively know when the adults around them are going to be able to help them. When they find themselves in situations where they may . . . be disbelieved . . . this forgetting and denial comes into play even more strongly. . . . (Personal communication)

In this same case, many other children had allegedly been abused. None of them (now adults) corroborated any of the claims. This was no surprise to this therapist:

> . . . It is highly likely that most or all of the [now grown] children . . . will be unable to remember these experiences. This does not mean they did not occur any more than Ellen's (not her real name) former amnesia means that these events had not happened to her. One of these [youngsters] may be precipitated to remember and recapture the experiences through a process similar to what occurred for Ellen. (personal communication)

If the mental apparatus of human beings was such that repeated, traumatic events could be completely blocked from awareness (some even claim *while it is happening*), surely this phenomenon would have been noted prior to the last few years. Instead, the emergence of such claims corresponds precisely with the emergence of a crusade aimed at ferreting out child sexual abuse.

The work of those who have spent their careers studying memory, in more dispassionate settings than the child abuse community, offers no support for such an idea, and much to contradict it (Ceci & Toglia 1987; Ceci & Bruck 1993; Loftus 1992). There is a general consensus among students of memory that recall of past events is easily influenced by subsequent events and feelings. It is also generally agreed that the final, composite image, while in fact being a mixture of actual events and subsequent influences, may nonetheless be perceived as nothing but the original event. The person believes he or she remembers things exactly as they happened.

What is also clear is that this process is capable of creating mental images which are honestly felt to represent past experiences but which in fact are not memories of actual events. Jean Piaget's famous example, in which he believed for years that he remembered an attempted kidnapping, only later to find that his nanny had contrived the story to cover an indiscretion on her part, illustrates the point.

More recently, the "blocked memory" fad has caused some researchers to demonstrate, once again, that the creation of false memory is not particularly difficult. E. Loftus, for example, reports that when "Jim," by prior arrangement, falsely told his younger brother "Chris," age fourteen, that at age five Chris was lost in a shopping mall, just two days later Chris said he remembered the incident. He described it in great detail, and when later informed that it was an experiment, that it never happened, Chris maintained that it indeed had happened. His memory told him so (Loftus 1992).

Another instructive example involved a man accused of sexual abuse. After intensive interrogation, the suspect eventually not only agreed to the charges against him, but claimed to be part of a satanic cult. The prosecution called in a "cult expert," sociologist Richard Ofshe, hoping he would uncover even more. Ofshe, however, sensed something was wrong, so he fabricated a story of abuse of two children whom he knew could never have had contact with the suspect. Just like "Chris," the suspect initially said he could not remember anything, but gradually, with encouragement, began to have some mental picture of the allegation. Eventually, he described his abuse of these children in detail, and wrote out a three-page confession (Loftus 1992).

CONCLUSION

The vulnerability of all human beings, of all ages, to persuasion, suggestion, and group influence, and the ease with which all human beings may sincerely confuse genuine memory with mental images coming from other sources, is so well known historically, so well documented in the scientific literature, and so much a part of all of our lives, that there is no excuse for mental health professionals to ignore the obvious role of such factors in the recent emergence of the "blocked memory" phenomenon.

The behavior of one segment of the mental health community is leading to a shameful chapter in the history of efforts to apply the art of psychotherapy in a reasonable and professional attempt to aid troubled persons. The longer this trend continues, with insurance plans paying these practitioners who sustain it, the more difficult it will be to expose the deception for what it is.

REFERENCES

Agosta, C., and Loring, M. (1988). "Understanding and Treating the Adult Retrospective Victim of Child Sexual Abuse." Vol. 1 of S. Sgroi, ed., *Vulnerable Populations.* Lexington, Mass.: Lexington Books.

Bass, E., and Davis, L. (1988). *The Courage to Heal.* New York: Harper and Row.

Blume, E. S. (1991). *Secret Survivors: Uncovering Incest and Its Aftereffects in Women.* New York: Ballantine Books.

Briere, J. and Conte, J. (1993). "Self-Reported Amnesia for Abuse in Adults Molested as Children." *Journal of Traumatic Stress* 6: 21–31.

Ceci, S., and Toglia, M. (1987). "Suggestibility of Children's Memory: Psycholegal Implications." *Journal of Experimental Psychology* 116, no. 1: 38–49.

Ceci, S., and Bruck, M. (1993). "The Suggestibility of the Child Witness: A Historical Overview and Synthesis." *Psychological Bulletin* 113: 403–39.

Coleman, L. (1986). "False Allegations of Child Sexual Abuse: Have the Experts Been Caught with Their Pants Down?" *Forum,* January/February, pp. 12–21.

——— (1990b). "False Accusations of Sexual Abuse: Psychiatry's Latest Reign of Error." *Journal of Mind and Behavior* 11, nos. 3 & 4: 545–56.

Coleman, L., and Clancy, P. (1990, Fall). "False Allegations of Child Sexual Abuse: Why Is It Happening? What Can We Do?" *Criminal Justice,* p. 14.

Cozolino, L. (1989). "The Ritual Abuse of Children: Implications for Clinical Practice and Research." *The Journal of Sex Research* 26, no. 1: 131–138.

False Memory Foundation (1992). *Newsletter of the False Memory Foundation,* published June 12, 1992. (Available from FMF, 3508 Market St., Suite 128, Philadelphia, Pa. 19104.)

Ganaway, G. K. (1991, August 19). "Alternate Hypotheses Regarding Satanic Ritual Abuse Memories." Paper presented at the 99th Anual Convention of the American Psychological Association, San Francisco, Calif.

Gleason, W. (1985, May 21). "Satanic Related Child Abuse Investigations in Kern County-Lamont Area." (Available from Los Angeles County Sheriff's Department, 2600 The Strand, Manhattan Beach, Calif. 90266.)

Gould, C., and Cozolino, G. (1992, Fall). "Ritual Abuse, Multiplicity, and Mind-Control." *Journal of Psychology and Theology* 20, no. 3: 194–96.

Humphrey, H. H., III (1985, February). *Report on the Scott County Investigations.* Minneapolis, Minn: Minnesota Attorney General.

Holmes, D. S. (1990). "The Evidence for Repression: An Examination of Sixty Years of Research." In I. L. Singer, ed., *Repression and Dissociation: Implications for Personality Theory, Psychopathology and Health,* pp. 85–102. Chicago: University of Chicago Press.

Incest Survivors Anonymous (1988, March). *I.S.A Talks to Friends, Professionals, and Survivors!* (Available from ISA World Service Office, P.O. Box 5613, Long Beach, Calif. 90805-0613.)

Lanning, K. (1989, October). *Satanic, Occult, Ritualistic Crime: A Law Enforcement Perspective.* Quantico, Va.: FBI Academy, National Center for the Analysis of Violent Crime.

——— (1992, January). *Investigator's Guide to Allegations of "Ritual" Child Abuse.* Quantico, Va.: FBI Academy, National Center for the Analysis of Violent Crime.

Loewenstein, R. (1991). "Psychogenic Amnesia: A Comprehensive Review." In A. Tasman and M. Goldfinger, eds., *Annual Review of Psychiatry* 10: 189–222. Washington, D.C.: American Psychiatric Association Press. (See generally Part Two of this volume.)

Loftus, E. (1992, August). "The Reality of Repressed Memories." Paper presented at the Centennial meeting of the American Psychological Association, Washington, D.C.

Mulhern, S. (1991a). Letter to the Editor. *Child Abuse and Neglect* 15: 609–610.

——— (1991b). "Satanism and Psychotherapy: A Rumor in Search of an Inquisition." In J. T. Richardson, J. Best, and D. G. Bromley, eds., *The Satanism Scare,* pp. 145–72. New York: Aldine de Gruyter.

——— (1992). "Ritual Abuse: Defining a Syndrome versus Defending a Belief," *Journal of Psychology and Theology* 20: 230–32.

Price, L. (1992, April 20). Untitled presentation at the Midwest Regional False Memory Syndrome Foundation Meeting, Benton Harbor, Mich.

Putnam, F. (1991). "The Satanic Ritual Abuse Controversy." *Child Abuse and Neglect* 15: 175–79.

Report of the Ritual Abuse Task Force (1989, September 15). *Ritual Abuse.* Los Angeles: Los Angeles County Commission for Women. (Available from author, 500 West Temple St., Los Angeles, Calif. 90012.)

San Diego County Grand Jury (1992, June 29). *Child Sexual Abuse, Assault, and Molest Issues: Report No. 8.* (Available from San Diego County Grand Jury, 1420 Kettner Blvd, Suite 310, San Diego, Calif. 92101–2432.)

Shaffer, R., and Cozolino, L. (1992). "Adults Who Report Childhood Ritualistic Abuse." *Journal of Psychology and Theology* 20, no. 3: 188–93.

Smith, M., and Pazder, L. (1980). *Michelle Remembers.* New York: Congdon and Lattes.

Wakefield, H., and Underwager, R. (1988). *Accusations of Child Sexual Abuse.* Springfield, Ill.: Charles C Thomas, Pub.

——— (1992). "Recovered Memories of Alleged Sexual Abuse: Lawsuits against Parents." *Behavioral Sciences and the Law* 10: 483–507.

——— (undated). "Magic, Mischief, and Memories: Remembering Repressed Abuse." Unpublished draft; see generally *Issues in Child Abuse Accusations* 3 (Summer 1991).

Young, W. C.; Sachs, R. G.; Braun, B. G.; and Watkins, R. (1991). "Patients Reporting Ritual Abuse in Childhood: A Clinical Syndrome of 37 Cases." *Child Abuse and Neglect* 15: 181–89.

13

Allegations of Satanism and Ritual Sex Abuse

Jeffrey S. Victor

THE AMBIGUOUS MEANING OF RITUAL ABUSE

Rumors of satanic cult ritual abuse of children initially arose from the "survivor" stories of multiple personality patients, beginning with the publication of *Michelle Remembers* in 1980 (Smith & Pazder 1980). They spread rapidly after ostensible satanic ritual abuse was alleged by children in the McMartin Preschool case in 1983. By the end of the 1980s, the concept of ritual abuse had become taken for granted among many police, journalists, therapists and social workers. The prefix "satanic cult" was quickly dropped, however, from the term "ritual abuse," in order to make it more acceptable to secular audiences, such as trial juries, who might reject satanic conspiracy theories as being too bizarre to be credible.

In most cases, the satanic cult accusations circulate only in local rumors. Many prosecutors in these cases worry that some jurors might be unable to believe children's more fantastic claims about bizarre rituals, torture, orgies and infant sacrifices. Instead, satanic cult activity is merely implied through the use of the euphemistic term "ritual child abuse" during police investigations and legal proceedings (Richardson 1991). The term "ritual abuse" has now become a trendy buzzword for people who believe in the existence of secret satanic cults.

The concept of "ritual abuse" is now at the center of a heated controversy in law enforcement and in the mental health professions (Kohn 1992). Before adequate behavioral science research can be done and before any reliable police investigation can be conducted, the concept of "ritual abuse" needs to be clearly defined. Unfortunately, the term is ambiguous. It is unclear exactly what behavior needs to be found in scientific research or in police investigations in order for the term "ritual abuse" to be applied. There are many meanings given to the term "ritual abuse" and these meanings are usually burdened with unspoken connotations of Satanism.

A California state criminal justice report on "occult crime," for example, defines ritualistic abuse as: "repeated physical, sexual, psychological and/or spiritual abuse which utilizes rituals" (Office Criminal Justice Planning 1989: 33). Certainly, when we start talking about "spiritual abuse", we are on very shaky ground if we need to specify acts which might be clearly illegal as well as scientifically verifiable based on careful research.

A more elaborate definition appears in some recent articles in professional journals. For example, Susan Kelley, a psychiatric nurse, defines ritual abuse as follows:

> Ritualistic abuse refers to the systematic and repetitive sexual, physical, and psychological abuse of children by adults engaged in cult worship. The purpose of ritualistic abuse is to induce a religious or mystical experience for adult participants. Perpetrators of ritualistic abuse involve children in group religious practices and ceremonies that often include the ingestion of human excrement, semen, or blood; witnessing the mutilation of animals; threats with supernatural or magical powers; ingestion of drugs; and use of songs or chants. The child victims are threatened with supernatural powers and physical harm to prevent disclosure of the ritualistic activities. For example, children may be threatened that the devil or demons will harm them. (Kelley 1990: 25)

Claims about ritual sex abuse are being made by some very prominent therapists, who see it as being a manifestation of an international network of criminals motivated by devil worship. These claims are very similar to those being made across America in popular magazine articles, on television talk shows, at police and social work conferences, and in local neighborhood gossip.

The Office of Criminal Justice Planning of the State of California published a special report in 1989 titled "Occult Crime: A Law Enforcement Primer," which presents claims made by several prominent professionals about satanic cult ritual child abuse.

> Dr. Bennett Braun has personally worked with over 70 adults with Multiple Personality Disorder (MPD) and has conducted two recent studies on data collected from 40 states. He estimates that of the approximate 200,000 Americans who suffer from MPD, up to one-fourth, 50,000, could be victims of Satanic Ritual Abuse. . . .
>
> Psychiatrist Roland Summit, whose subspecialty is child sexual abuse, calls ritual abuse of children "the most serious threat to children and to

> society that we must face in our lifetime." Dr. Summit's experiences point to "no less than 1,000 children who stated their involvement in ritualistic systems." . . .
>
> Dr. Lawrence Pazder, psychiatrist, describes the motives and pervasiveness of ritualized abusers who are "normal-looking and carry on normal lives. They are members of every stratum of society which they have carefully infiltrated. Any position of societal power or influence should be seen as a target for infiltration. The perpetrators have masses of money available. Many have impeccable credentials—doctors, ministers, professionals of every kind." (Office of Criminal Justice Planning 1989: 39)

In sharp contrast, Kenneth Lanning, special agent for the FBI's Behavioral Science Unit, pointed out the inherent ambiguities in attempts to construct a new category of harm done to children, which focuses upon ritualistic activity. Lanning suggests that police investigation and scientific research needs to focus upon concrete acts of physical, sexual, or emotional harm, rather than shift the focus to the social context of those acts (e.g., rituals).

> The author [Lanning] has been unable to precisely define ritualistic abuse and prefers not to use the term. It is confusing, misleading and counter-productive. . . .
>
> When a victim describes and investigation corroborates what sounds like ritualistic activity, several possibilities must be considered. The ritualistic activity may be part of the excessive religiosity of a mentally ill, psychotic offender. It may be a misunderstood part of sexual ritualism. The ritualistic activity may be incidental to any real abuse. The offender may be involved in ritualistic activity with a child and also may be abusing a child, but one may have little or nothing to do with the other. (Lanning 1989a: 69–70)

THE HISTORY OF RITUAL ABUSE ALLEGATIONS

The first known satanic cult "survivor" testimonial was published in 1980 in the book *Michelle Remembers* (Smith & Pazder 1980). It was written by a Canadian psychiatrist, Dr. Lawrence Pazder, from a case study of one of his patients, Michelle Smith, whom he diagnosed as suffering from multiple personality disorder, and is discussed in detail in Lee Coleman's chapter in this volume (see chapter 12).

In treating Michelle, Pazder used some rather unconventional therapy. In one session, for example, Pazder arranged to have Michelle baptized a Catholic by a priest. Curiously, Pazder who is himself a Catholic, later divorced his wife and married Michelle, who had divorced her spouse.

There is no external evidence to corroborate Michelle's bizarre tale.

Michelle's claims of encountering supernatural beings should provoke skepticism. A reporter who investigated Michelle's story found that Michelle's two sisters, who were not mentioned in her book, deny her story, as does her father (Grescoe 1980).

Dr. Pazder had been a physician in West Africa, where he became very much interested in the study of black magic rituals in ceremonies he observed. He gathered an extensive collection of photographs of these ceremonies, according to his own admission. Pazder's interest in African black magic could have influenced his preconceptions about Michelle's story while his photographs could have become cues for ideas incorporated into her imaginings.

Michelle's survivor story attracted a large audience. Even before *Michelle Remembers* was published, her story was featured in *People* magazine, which reported that the authors had received an unusually high $100,000 advance for the hardback edition and an additional $242,000 for a paperback version (McMurran 1980). Another article quickly appeared in *The National Enquirer,* spreading the story to an even wider audience (Lyons 1988). Michelle and Dr. Pazder have since appeared frequently on television and radio, as well as at conferences, speaking as experts on satanic cult ritual abuse. The point is that Michelle's satanic cult "survivor" story was widely disseminated and quite likely became a model imitated by later self-proclaimed MPD satanic cult "survivors."

Some researchers suspect that the early satanic cult "survivor" stories of adult MPD patients influenced the development of allegations of ritual sex abuse voiced by children. What is known with certainty, however, is that the book *Michelle Remembers* was used by police and prosecutors in the early 1980s, in preparing several cases against people accused of sexually molesting children in day care centers (Charlier & Downing 1988). It is also known that Michelle Smith and several other "survivors" met with parents and children involved in the famous McMartin case after it was reported in the press (Nathan 1991). The initial prosecutor in the McMartin case, Glenn E. Stevens, believes that Michelle Smith and child protection counselors influenced the children's testimony against the accused (Carlson 1989).

Rumors that Satanists were sexually molesting children in day care centers first surfaced in the McMartin Preschool case, which began in 1983 in Manhattan Beach, California. It went on to become the longest and most expensive trial in American history, with an ultimate cost over seven years of 15 million dollars (Reinhold, Jan. 24, 1990; Reinhold, Feb. 1, 1990). The initial allegations linked sexual child abuse in the day care center to rituals of a "devil worship" cult. These allegations led to the arrest of 62-year-old Peggy McMartin Buckey, her son, Raymond Buckey, and five other child care workers. They were accused of victimizing 360 children in weird and bizarre sexual and nonsexual acts, carried out over a period of five years.

This case was particularly important because it gave rise to the organization of volunteer groups of parents and child protection advocates, such as Believe the Children, which were committed to alerting the general public to the hidden dangers of a newly identified kind of child abuse and molestation which they labeled "ritual abuse." Unfortunately, the process of the McMartin trial did nothing to clarify the facts of the case. In January 1990, there were only two remaining defendants. Peggy Buckey was found innocent. Later that year, the few remaining charges against Raymond Buckey were dropped by the prosecution (Mydans 1990).

Soon after the McMartin case attracted national attention, a host of other, similar accusations of ritual sexual abuse sprang up not only in this country but abroad. In some cases, accusations of satanic cult activity were made public during trials. In Kern County, California, during 1984 and 1985, a local panic over rumors of a satanic cult resulted in the investigations of 77 people whom local police believed to have been involved in a criminal satanic cult. In several panic-driven trials, dozens of people were convicted and sent to the state prison (Snedeker 1988). In one such case, seven people were convicted and imprisoned for sexually molesting children as part of a satanic cult. The only direct evidence against them came from the testimony of children, who claimed that they had been injected with drugs, forced to drink urine and to engage in bizarre sexual acts with adults as well as with other children, while the activities were filmed. The children also accused the defendants of murdering at least twenty babies, using their blood in rituals and engaging in cannibalism. Some of the children later recanted their stories (Mathews 1989). Then, in 1990, the convictions were overturned after being appealed.

As these cases continued, passions ran high and almost anyone who cautioned against presuming the guilt of those accused, became a "suspect" in the eyes of the outraged parents in one community. In a case in Jordan, Minnesota, in 1983–84, for example, a policeman who vouched for the character of an accused person was soon charged with the same crimes (Charlier & Downing 1988). In another case in Chicago, two women who publicly expressed support for an accused person, shortly thereafter found their names on a list of child molesters being circulated by a concerned parents group (Charlier & Downing 1988). Trials involving accusations of satanic cult ritual abuse have continued to occur across the United States in the 1990s.

INVESTIGATIONS OF RITUAL SEX ABUSE ALLEGATIONS

As yet, there are no comprehensive, scientific studies of the extent, content and outcomes of allegations of ritual child sex abuse which go to court. Most of the available information has been collected by journalists. There are also a few relevant behavioral science reports.

A journalist who has investigated many cases of alleged ritual abuse, Debbie Nathan, offered her conclusions about these allegations in an award-winning article titled "The Ritual Sex Abuse Hoax." It stands as the best summary of investigations of ritual abuse allegations.

> Investigations usually began because of vague medical symptoms or after an upper-middle-class child did something inappropriately sexual. Then, even though most sexual abuse occurs within the family, investigators immediately directed their inquiries outside the home. Sometimes they suspected community sex rings, but most often they focused upon elite child care centers. The first allegation sometimes seemed plausible. But in remarkable departures from traditional forensics, police, social workers, doctors and therapists badgered children to name more victims and perpetrators, ignoring answers that contradicted a ritual abuse scenario. As a result, many men were charged; but women were too, and this was especially shocking, since women have not been thought of as child molesters, much less sex torturers.
>
> From 1984 to 1989, some 100 people nationwide were charged with ritual sex abuse; of those, 90 or so were tried and convicted, with no evidence but testimony from children, parents, "experts" expounding on how the children acted traumatized and doctors talking about tiny white lines on anuses or bumps on hymens—"signs of abuse" that later research would show appear on nonabused children. (Nathan June 12, 1990: 38)

As Nathan indicates, the moral crusade against ritual abuse has resulted in a zealous rush to judgment in which the lives of innocent people have been ruined. In many prominent cases, such as those in Kern County, California, and Jordan, Minnesota, people who were convicted of ritual sex abuse have had their convictions overturned upon appeal. There is mounting evidence from investigations done by journalists into specific cases that many innocent people have been accused, put on trial, and even convicted of ritual abuse.[1]

In 1988, reporters Tom Charlier and Shirley Downing of the Memphis, Tennessee, *Commercial Appeal* published a careful study of thirty-six cases of accusations of ritual sexual abuse of children. In these cases, only about one-fourth of those people arrested were eventually convicted, and most of the convictions had little to do with any kind of "ritual" sexual abuse. Charlier and Downing concluded:

> Allegations of Satanism—of rites involving mutilation, infant sacrifice and devil worship—have since emerged in more than 100 child sex abuse cases across the country. . . . In four years, though, investigators have found no evidence to support fears that cults are preying on the nation's children.

> The *Commercial Appeal* studied ritual sexual abuse allegations in 36 cases and found instead that many of the stories labeled "satanic" or "ritual" have the hallmarks of urban legends. (Charlier & Downing Jan. 18, 1988)

Charlier and Downing identified some possible channels through which this urban (or contemporary) legend was transmitted. They noted that satanic cult sexual child abuse stories have been disseminated, since the McMartin case in 1983, by Satan hunters across the country and through seminars, workshops and conferences about ritual child abuse and satanic cult crime. These conferences attract parents, social workers, therapists, police and prosecutors. The central importance of these seminars and conferences is that they function as organizing agencies for communication networks carrying the satanic cult legend (Hicks 1991).

It is likely that the continuing satanic cult scare has produced an increasing number of allegations of "ritual abuse." The American Bar Association's Center on Children and the Law is conducting a survey of local prosecutors, to obtain an estimate of the national incidence of different types of cases of child abuse. Preliminary data indicate that about one-third of local prosecutors have handled cases involving "ritualistic or satanic abuse" (Goretsky, personal communication, April 19, 1991). If these preliminary findings are representative of the eventual survey conclusion, that would mean that courts across the country are now dealing with a great number of accusations of ritual abuse.

Many local psychotherapists are now confirming or "validating" the satanic cult allegations of patients they diagnose as having MPD. Some therapists have made a thriving enterprise out of identifying clients whom they regard as having MPD and being childhood victims of "ritual" abuse by satanic cults. A recent national survey of clinical psychologists who reported treating cases of alleged ritual abuse (as alleged by children or MPD patients) was conducted by psychologists at the State University of New York at Buffalo. The survey found that sixteen clinical psychologists reported having treated over a hundred cases each. In sharp contrast, among the other clinical psychologists surveyed, 1,908 reported treating no such cases, and 785 therapists reported treating only one or two cases (Bottoms et al. 1991). The survey also found that clinical psychologists in practice in a small number of predominantly rural states (Iowa, Montana, Mississippi, Utah, and Tennessee) reported proportionately higher numbers of ritual abuse cases. These data suggest that clusters of relatively few therapists account for a disproportionately large number of allegations of satanic cult ritual abuse.

ALLEGATIONS OF RITUAL SEX ABUSE AGAINST WOMEN

An estimate of the extent of ritual abuse allegations can be found in research studies that attempt to determine the national incidence of child sexual abuse. The best known and most commonly cited study of this kind was that done by sociologist David Finkelhor and published in a book titled *Nursery Crimes* (Finkelhor et al. 1988). The study focuses upon allegations of sexual abuse in day care centers across the country, from 1983 to 1985. It collected information on 270 cases. The information about these cases was obtained primarily from child protection agencies, which regarded the cases as being "substantiated," meaning that these agencies considered the allegations to be "true." This, of course, did not mean that any legal charges were necessarily filed in court. Actually, fewer than a third of the cases were prosecuted, and less than a tenth resulted in guilty pleas or convictions. The famous McMartin case, for example, which resulted in bizarre allegations against seven original defendants, but no convictions, was one of the cases included. Unfortunately, the Finkelhor study is often distorted and cited as evidence of actual ritual sexual abuse in child care centers, rather than simply as a study of sexual and ritual abuse allegations.

The Finkelhor study identified thirty-six cases of alleged ritual abuse in day care centers. These constituted 13 percent of the total cases of sexual abuse. Curiously, women were accused sexual abusers in all these ritual abuse cases. In some of the cases, women alone, without male associates, were the accused perpetrators. The high proportion of women appearing in these cases throws doubt on the validity of ritual abuse allegations.

Research on sexual behavior has found that it is rare to find cases of women, especially those not under the coercive influence of male accomplices, who sexually molest very young children (Faller 1987). It is rare for women to sexually molest children either outside or within the family, or to sexually exploit a combination of boys and girls.

THE INTERACTION PROCESS THAT CREATES RITUAL ABUSE ALLEGATIONS

In order to understand the process that gives rise to allegations of ritual sex abuse, one needs to focus attention on the interactive social process that gives rise to the children's stories. In other words, one must examine interaction between the behavior of the child protection workers, who may be believers in ritual abuse, and the children whom they are questioning. Only then can one determine if the stories may have been fabricated in a process of joint storytelling. Arguments about whether or not children's stories of ritual sex abuse are factual accounts, fabrications, or outright lies, and questions about the presumed motives of the children for honesty or dishonesty are likely to be emotionally charged distractions from the pursuit of observable and verifiable evidence.

Insight into the dynamics of the interactive creation of allegations of ritual sex abuse can be found in careful studies of the origins of false allegations of sexual child abuse. The interaction process whereby children's false stories of sexual abuse are socially created is described in detail by psychiatrist Lee Coleman and attorney Patrick Clancy, both of whom have had considerable experience dealing with cases of child sexual molestation. Their findings were published in a benchmark article titled "False Allegations of Child Sexual Abuse" (Coleman & Clancy 1990). In their article they state:

> In our experience, which adds up to hundreds of allegations and about fifteen hundred hours of audio- or videotaped interviews with children being investigated for possible molestation, children quite regularly make allegations that can be factually proven not to be true. When this happens, it is rare for the child to be the true initiator of the false statements. In most cases, the child's false statements are the product of an interviewing style that leads the child gradually to construct a mental picture of abuse. This picture becomes the child's "memory." The result can be disastrous, not only for the Justice process, but also for the child's emotional well-being. . . .
>
> It is common practice for police or child protection investigators to refer a child for therapy at the very outset of an investigation. The stated purpose is either to help the child disclose information about abuse or to help the child with the trauma secondary to abuse. If the child is a true molestation victim, both of these purposes may be fulfilled with no harm done to the truth-seeking process. But, if the child has not been abused, such therapy can have a profoundly contaminating impact. Week after week, the child is questioned about abuse and encouraged to "tell the secret." In our experience, children may "learn" in such sessions that they are in danger and may develop major fears and anxieties. They may learn to believe they were abused and gradually construct the details. They may come to believe in these inventions with all the sincerity that real events would call forth. (Coleman & Clancy 1990: 18)

Coleman and Clancy point out that child protection workers are not expected to be impartial investigators searching for evidence of wrongdoing. Instead, they are advocates for children and commonly act on the presumption that children have been victimized in some way when allegations have been made by parents, or neighbors, or even sometimes by anonymous telephone callers.

Once in the child protection system, children are caught in a catch-22 situation. If the child denies being involved in sexual acts, that is taken as evidence that the child is "repressing" his or her memories of terrifying abuse, which the child protection worker is morally responsible to "bring out," gradually and carefully. If the child expresses anxiety, the anxiety is regarded as evidence of repressed memories of sexual molestation, rather than anxiety due to being repeatedly interrogated by unfamiliar child protection workers and police (Coleman & Clancy 1990).

This catch-22 situation is partly a result of widespread acceptance among child protection workers of the faulty concept of "the child sexual abuse accommodation syndrome," first proposed by psychiatrist Roland Summit in 1983. (Summit more recently has become a prominent proponent of satanic cult ritual abuse conspiracy beliefs.) The concept is not grounded in careful and controlled data collection; it derives instead from Summit's clinical observations of clients involved in cases of incest. The crucial construct for present concerns is the idea that child victims of incest (and by extension, any kind of sexual abuse) can be expected to deny any evidence of sexual molestation and to recant their stories of such experience after they voice them. This circular reasoning, when applied by child protection workers, results in taking children's denials of sexual abuse and later recantations of abuse as evidence of sexual abuse. In practice, this means that allegations of sexual abuse from almost any source, including community gossip and rumors, are assumed to be true and must be disproven.

Coleman and Clancy's examination of videotapes of the interaction between therapist and children being interviewed found that overzealous child advocates often use leading questions, cueing of desired responses, praise for desired answers and manipulated fantasy play to gradually implant ideas about sexual abuse in the communication process between the child and therapist (Coleman & Clancy 1990). Studies by Underwager and Wakefield of videotaped interactions came to same conclusion (Wakefield & Underwager 1988, 1990).

Social psychologists call this interaction process "priming" (Herr 1986; James 1986). Research on priming indicates that it is most likely to happen when an authority figures questions a person who is anxious and highly suggestible. The process is not necessarily conscious and deliberate. Priming can easily occur if a child protection worker, as an authority figure, inadvertently shapes the discourse with a child around his or her preconceptions about ritual sex abuse.

When overzealous therapists "prime" the discourse between themselves and children, they may gradually implant reconstituted memories of events, which become shaped by the verbal discourse. These pseudomemories may then become reinforced by later conversations outside of the interview situation, such as those between the child and his or her parents, other children and police. If these other people frequently reaffirm the pseudomemories of ritual abuse, they can easily become subjectively "real" events in the memory of the child. In this way, it is possible for children to "remember" events that never occurred. Research on childhood memories suggests that childhood memories may largely be a product of language learning, constructed from the discourse between a child and adults who tell the child what happened to him or her in the past (Lindesmith et al. 1991).

Contrary to popular belief, eyewitness accounts are not invariably accurate. People's minds do not work like photographic cameras. Memories represent a reconstruction of events, the storage and retrieval of which can be distorted: by severe anxiety; by preconceptions to see what one expects to see; by the power of suggestion from others, particularly from authority figures; and by contamination of memories filled in since the original event (Loftus 1979, 1980).

Priming by poorly trained therapists is not the only source of distortion in children's testimony about events. Several additional explanations for children's bizarre stories of ritual sexual molestation are suggested by the FBI's Kenneth Lanning, who has studied many cases of alleged ritual abuse since they emerged in 1983 (Lanning 1989b). In some cases, the traumatic fears of children in response to actual sexual abuse in their homes may produce elaborate fantasies about events in day care. In other cases of actual sexual abuse, child molesters may deliberately use threats of magic spells, witches and demons in order to intimidate the children; but not as part of any commitment to a satanic ideology. Child molesters may be familiar, as are most people today, with the satanic cult legend, and appropriate it for their own exploitive use.

Sometimes children's stories of satanic cult ritual abuse are outright lies fabricated by the children, with the assistance of adults with a score to settle. Evidence comes from some cases in which children have recanted their stories. In one such case in 1989, four brothers, who had appeared on an "Geraldo" TV show to testify about satanic ritual abuse, recanted accusations that they had made against their mother and her boyfriend (Bamberger 1989). The boys' allegations included accusations of killing babies and drinking their blood. It appeared that the boys' divorced father had coached the boys to tell the same fabricated stories. In another case in England in 1991, two sisters admitted under cross-examination in court that they had lied about being sexually abused in devil-worshiping rituals (MacKinnon 1991; Linton 1991). Five people, including the girls' parents, had been arrested on the basis of the accusations by the older sister, age ten. The girl admitted in court to making up the stories, which included, once again, the killing of babies and being forced to eat their flesh. The girl said that she had fabricated the stories to please her grandmother, with whom the girls had been sent to live after their parents had separated. Cases such as these, where children recant stories of satanic cult torture, are given much less attention in newspaper reports than are the initial atrocity stories of ritual abuse. Furthermore, in a classic catch-22 scenario, the recantation may itself be used as confirmation of the ritual scenario.

THE COLLECTIVE BEHAVIOR PROCESS IN RITUAL ABUSE ALLEGATIONS

There is simply no corroborating evidence for the existence of an organized network of satanic cults that sexually molest children in order to "brainwash" them into a devil-worshiping ideology. Instead, allegations about satanic cults and ritual abuse arise from a complex process of collective behavior. One effect is that children in different parts of the country report very similar content in stories of satanic ritual abuse.

What are the social dynamics of the collective behavior which leads to allegations of ritual abuse made by children? Historical concepts drawn from psychiatry of "mass hysteria," "emotional contagion" and "collective delusions" have long since proven insufficient to explain the collective behavior involved in rumors, contemporary legends and social movements. Instead, one needs to examine also the roles of ideological preconceptions, communication networks, organizational activities and the mass media in the dissemination of claims, rumors and allegations about satanic cult crime. Processes of collective behavior are not necessarily activities consciously and deliberately planned and coordinated by coherent groups seeking specific goals or motivated by particular ends.

THE ROLE OF IDEOLOGY: FRAMING THE PROBLEM

A key question for a sociologist is: How do people attribute shared meaning to an unclear, ambiguous social situation (such as the allegations of children and MPD patients of bizarre torture by organized groups), and communicate that meaning so that the ideas coalesce into the joint activity of a social movement?

When moral crusaders strive to arouse public awareness about a newly recognized social "evil," they must be able to offer explanations of the causes of that "evil" and propose credible ways of getting rid of it. They must cut through the inevitable complexity and ambiguity by framing the problem in a way that can be widely comprehended. Framing the problem sets the "evil" within a much broader scope of moral concerns. It provides the basic interpretive assumptions through which the "evil" can be redefined and linked to other social "evils" in society.

Meanings are attributed to ambiguous situations, events or activities that enable them to be labeled "satanist," through perceptual frames for understanding "evil" in society. These frames are drawn from people's personal belief system, including sociopolitical-religious ideologies. The different personal frames are connected by the demonology of the satanic cult legend, which offers a broader explanation for the ambiguous circumstances (Stevens 1991).

A frame functions like a cultural model or paradigm, which organizes people's shared preconceptions. Once a new definition of deviant behavior is given a frame for interpretation, people who have little or no direct contact with that behavior can "make sense" of the claim about it. Most importantly, framing the problem in a convincing way can recruit volunteers to spend some of their time, energy and money in the joint effort of a social movement (Snow 1986). A way of framing a problem provides the context for personal motivation to people who are moved to do something about the problem. A shared frame for a problem also enables people from different occupations and holding different belief systems to work together with a shared definition of the situation.

The Christian Religious Frame

The initial frame for the problem of satanic cult "ritual" abuse was drawn from fundamentalist Christian religious ideology. Fundamentalist moral crusaders, especially clergymen, view Satanists as being actual agents of the devil, who are trying to spread immorality of all kinds, in order to destroy the moral order of American society and hasten Satan's takeover of the world. The logic is that if good people are working for God, then evil people must be working for Satan. Satanic cult crime is seen simply as being one manifestation of the conspiratorial work of Satan and his earthly followers. In the fundamentalist framing of the problem, "ritual" abuse is simply one more example of the growing moral corruption (especially sexual perversion) in American society by "evil" people, who reject God and true Christianity. The assertion that organized "devil worshipers" are infiltrating the nation's child care centers in search of children to torture and corrupt, can be taken on faith alone, without any necessary verification.

This frame can be found in religious books about Satanism and in the public speeches of Christian moral crusaders, including not only clergymen, but also many police officers and public prosecutors who are Satan hunters. Variations of it have also been voiced by a new breed of Christian psychotherapists, counselors and child protection workers.

Christian psychotherapy and counseling became one of the most rapidly growing movements in the helping professions during the 1980s (Goleman 1991; Stafford 1993). This therapy approach uses Christian (evangelical Protestant) religious ideology as a frame for understanding and treating people's psychological problems.

A Dallas city magazine describes the background of Christian counseling in an article about a young woman who "remembered" having been a victim of satanic cult "ritual abuse" by her parents only after being treated by a Christian therapist. The therapist had a history of identifying a great number of cases of ritual sex abuse among his clients.

> For years, "Christian counseling" meant going to confession, or asking the pastor for help with marital problems. But in the late seventies and early eighties, psychologists such as James Dobson, Larry Crabb, and Paul Meier and psychiatrist Minirth began to attract the enthusiasm of the evangelical community with their integration of scriptural teachings and current methods of psychological treatment. The new approach involves Christians who are trained in psychiatry and psychology, disciplines often considered antithetical to Christianity. While the methods used by Christian psychologists are as varied as those of secular therapists, there's an emphasis on gaining insight into undesirable behavior through psychological methods, then dealing with the behavior "biblically." (Whitley 1991: 46)

Therapists who use a traditionalist Christian ideology in their therapy practice may be particularly receptive to believe in the satanic cult legend and to find indications of satanic "ritual abuse" in their most deeply disturbed patients.

There are several small businesses which specialize in supplying local law enforcement officials with materials about satanic cult crime, including ritual sex abuse. Many are ideologically fundamentalist. Many of the materials used at police training seminars about ritualistic crime, or distributed by police at community meetings, derive from these sources. Therefore, they convey a religiously traditionalist way of framing the problem of satanic influences in American society.

A questionnaire study of police Satan hunters found a correlation between religious activity and interest in Satanism. Those police who attended church most frequently were also those most likely to believe that satanic cult crime was common and should be a serious police concern (Crouch & Damphousse 1991). This finding suggests that religious ideology may be central for many police Satan hunters in motivating their concern for the pursuit of criminal Satanists. Less traditionally religious police probably give other types of crime greater priority in their expenditure of time and effort, even if they accept satanic crime as being a real entity.

It should not be concluded that there is a uniformity of belief among all Christian fundamentalists in the imminent danger of a huge, secret conspiracy of Satanists. A few Christian religious writers, among them those working for *Cornerstone* magazine, have provided important investigative reports refuting false and exaggerated claims about satanic cults and ritual abuse (Passantino et al. 1990).

The Social Conservative Frame

The initial frame for interpreting crimes attributed to satanic cults was modified by activists using a compatible conservative sociopolitical perspective. In this frame, so-called "ritualistic" crime is seen as a response to the hedonistic pursuit of pleasure and power. Satanism is regarded as an extension of the climate of moral permissiveness which had its source in the moral anarchy of the 1960s, and which continues to be encouraged by "permissive liberals" today. It is viewed as being one more manifestation of the moral decline and corruption of American society. This frame is most commonly found in articles and public speeches by police Satan hunters.

The Child Advocate Frame

Many child protection workers and therapists frame the problem of "ritual" abuse in terms of an analogy with the way female victims of male sexual aggression, in cases of rape, incest and sexual harassment, have been callously discredited when they have come forward. The child advocate framing of the problem perceives any skepticism about "ritual" abuse as being simply one more attempt to discredit testimony about sexual aggression against women and children. (The contradictory fact that many of the people accused of the "ritual" sexual abuse of children are women is ignored.) A recent book about the psychological effects of incest illustrates this implicit analogy:

> Ritual abuse—also called cult abuse and satanic abuse—is a phenomenon whose pervasiveness is only now becoming clear to those who deal with child sexual abuse. The chilling stories told by unrelated victims around the country are virtually identical. The truths of this abuse are so shocking to society that the victimizers are protected by our own disbelief. . . . Their flashbacks and memories may represent an unwanted truth, but a truth nonetheless. Believe them. (Blume 1990: 60)

This appeal demonstrates the child advocate frame for dealing with the ambiguity of "ritual" abuse allegations. It's simple: believe the children. The basic assumption is that a wall of silence and skepticism, similar to that alleged in cases of incest, protects the satanist perpetrators of vicious child torture. It can be found in many publications about "ritual abuse" by therapists and child protection workers. In this frame, an interest in elaborate stories about Satanism is quite secondary, and flows from a concern to protect children from one of the many threats to children in contemporary society.

This frame may appear, at least superficially, to be an expression of some kind of feminist ideology. However, it is not. It only uses some of the rhetoric of feminism which touches upon perceived threats to children. It differs from a feminist ideology in the sense that it is not drawn from any broad structural critique of society, but instead focuses upon the need to protect children from vaguely defined "evil" forces in society.

THE ORGANIZATIONAL BASIS OF THE MORAL CRUSADE

The Role of Communication Networks

The moral crusade against ritual abuse is likely to persist for a long time to come. One reason for its persistence is that the moral crusade has developed an effective communication network able to disseminate elaborate assumptions about "ritual" abuse, even in the absence of scientific and law enforcement evidence to verify those claims.

Conferences, seminars and training workshops on "ritual" abuse for police and child protection workers function as organizing agencies, enabling moral crusaders from different occupations to make contact with one another and to share their differing concerns and expertise. These meetings also enable moral crusaders to recruit more and more professionals, including social workers, psychiatrists, psychologists, physicians and police, in the moral crusade. These professionals then become "experts" on ritual abuse and disseminate claims about it to the local level, where they alert people in public speeches and small town newspaper articles to the so-called signs of "ritual" abuse. As a result, more and more "signs" are detected and allegations made.

Child Protection Organizations

There is a wide variety of child protection organizations which are part of the moral crusade against Satanism. Most of them have a much broader agenda of concerns about perceived threats to children beyond Satanism. Most have assimilated claims about satanic cult crimes into their agendas only after these claims have already been widely disseminated.

Some child protection groups focus their efforts on educating the general public about dangerous satanic influences on children from the entertainment media and children's fantasy games. These groups include: Parents Music Resource Center, the National Coalition Against Television Violence, and Bothered about Dungeons and Dragons (BADD).

Other child protection organizations focus their efforts on fighting satanic "ritual" abuse as part of a broader agenda of concerns about child abuse. They include Believe the Children, a volunteer organization composed largely of parents, which was first established by scores of the parents whose children made allegations of satanic ritual against the Buckeys and other child care workers at the McMartin Preschool in Manhattan Beach, California. It now has affiliates in Chicago and Lincoln, Nebraska. Its advisory board is diverse and consists of several prominent therapists (including Dr. Roland Summit), clergymen and police Satan hunters. The activities of Believe the Children are directed mainly at educating the public about "ritual abuse," by providing information to journalists, sending speakers to community meetings, holding seminars about child abuse, and publishing a newsletter.

National and local professional associations concerned with child abuse sponsor conferences, sometimes offering special training workshops about ritual abuse for social workers and other interested professionals. These workshops are organized for the official purpose of simply sharing technical expertise. Nevertheless, they provide a vehicle for moral crusaders against satanic "ritual" child abuse to manufacture more "experts." Since the work of dealing with child sexual abuse has itself taken on the character of a moral crusade, these workshops and conferences are forums where heated scientific debate and critical analysis are neither expected nor desired. There are a great many of these local gatherings across the country.

Some child abuse conferences feature psychotherapists who work with multiple personality disorder (MPD) patients who claim to have been ritually abused by satanic cults as children. Many of these therapists suggest that MPD "survivors" and children purported to be victims of "ritual" abuse in child care centers are both victims of the same secret satanic conspirators (Mulhern 1991). Some of the training workshops on "ritual" abuse are co-sponsored by feminist groups concerned with sexual aggression. For example, one two-day conference in Minneapolis in September 1990 (Underwager & Wakefield 1991) was sponsored by the Minnesota Awareness of Ritualistic Abuse Network and the Sexual Violence Center of Hennepin County.

Numerous business enterprises produce materials that have the effect of promoting the social construction of ritual abuse as a distinct form of social deviance. For example, several companies make training films about ritual abuse for therapists and law enforcement officials. At least one company now sells sets of drawings of supposed satanic cult ritual abuse scenes, which are designed for use by therapists in interviewing children suspected of having been victims of "ritual" abuse (Northwest Psychological Publishers 1990). Another company publishes a children's book about "ritual" abuse for the same purpose (Sanford 1990).

Even some government agencies have entered the moral crusade against Satanism via concerns about child abuse. The Los Angeles County Commission for Women, for example, established a Ritual Abuse Task Force which published a widely circulated report about Satanism and ritual abuse

(Ritual Abuse Task Force 1990). The report is as ideologically distorted as other publications by fervent moral crusaders.

In sharp contrast, other child protection agencies have published reports about ritual abuse which are carefully put together and which recognize the ambiguity and lack of consensus covering the whole issue of Satanism and ritual abuse. One example is a report published by The National Resource Center on Child Sexual Abuse titled, "Ritual Child Abuse: Understanding the Controversies" (Lloyd 1990). A similarly well-reasoned report for therapists and the general public was published by the National Center for Missing and Exploited Children. The report, titled *Child Sex Rings,* was written by FBI special agent Kenneth Lanning (Lanning 1989b).

Mental Health Organizations

The main organization disseminating claims about Satanism and "ritual abuse" to mental health professionals is the International Society for the Study of Multiple Personality and Dissociation. The organization has about 11,000 members, including psychiatrists, clinical psychologists, social workers and nurses. It also has nonprofessionals as members who are interested in MPD. Some of the nonprofessionals are MPD satanic cult "survivors."

The national and regional conferences of the society regularly include lectures and professional training seminars for therapists about satanic cult "ritual abuse" of MPD patients. Lecturers on the topic have included prominent moral crusaders against Satanism, such as Pat Pulling (the organizer of BADD), and detective Robert "Jerry" Simandl. One of the missions of the society is to educate the public about MPD, which now includes claims about ritual abuse. The conferences offer training seminars on satanic cult "ritual abuse," at which elaborate claims are presented without scientifically verifiable evidence (Mulhern 1991).

Papers about the ritual abuse of MPD patients from these conferences find their way into the hands of police Satan hunters and are used to give scientific credibility to various claims about satanic cult crimes. Some of the most prominent psychiatrists specializing in the study of MPD are "believers" in the satanic cult conspiracy explanation of "ritual" abuse.

There is also an increasing number of psychiatric clinics and hospital programs around the country specializing in providing psychotherapy to patients who claim to be victims of satanic cult ritual abuse. The costs for a course of treatment may range from fifteen to twenty thousand dollars. In some states, these costs are passed on to the taxpayer through Medicaid programs. Otherwise, the costs are paid by health insurance companies and ultimately result in increased costs for medical insurance.

THE ROLE OF THE MASS MEDIA

Another reason for the persistence of allegations of "ritual" abuse is that they provide sensational "atrocity stories" for the mass media. Small town newspapers are particularly likely to simply report the stories of bizarre "satanic" activities, without much skepticism or critical analysis.

The McMartin Preschool case offers an excellent example of the social dynamics of media sensationalism. As described earlier, the case involved a proliferation of allegations by hundreds of children who claimed to have been subjected to a bizarre series of sexual rituals and torture over the course of many years.

The Los Angeles Times published a detailed analysis of the media's coverage of the case, including its own reporting (Shaw Jan. 19; Jan. 20; Jan. 22, 1990). Its conclusions apply equally well to similar cases which arise continually in other locations but do not receive national attention.

> More than most big stories, McMartin at times exposed basic flaws in the way contemporary news organizations function. Pack journalism. Laziness. Superficiality. Cozy relationships with prosecutors. A competitive zeal that sends reporters off in a frantic search to be the first with the latest shocking allegation, responsible journalism be damned. A tradition that often discourages reporters from raising key questions if they aren't first brought up by the principals in a story.
>
> In the early months of the case in particular, reporters and editors often abandoned two of their most cherished and widely trumpeted traditions—fairness and skepticism. As most reporters now sheepishly admit—and as the record clearly shows—the media frequently plunged into hysteria, sensationalism and what one editor calls "a lynch mob syndrome." (Shaw Jan. 19, 1990: A20)

Media sensationalism helps to spread rumors about satanic cult crimes from one location to another. Research on rumors has found that people tend to recall the most sensational aspects of news reports and forget later published denials (Kapferer 1990). In this way, the sensational reports provide a plausible scenario for similar rumors to pop up, sometimes years later, in distant locations. After the initial sensational reporting about the McMartin case, for example, eight other preschools in the area were identified as being centers of satanic cult activity; and shortly thereafter, over one hundred preschools across the country became targets of similar allegations and police investigations (Foster 1990).

UNDERLYING SOCIAL STRUCTURAL CAUSES OF THE SATANIC CULT SCARE

In the past, threats of subversion have swept over Western societies in response to shared sources of stress when social conditions created sudden and widespread insecurity. The most common source of shared social stress has been a rapid decline in the economic conditions of people in a society. Other conditions, however, may also account for people's perception of a threat to their security in a society. The "Red Scare" of the 1950s, for example, arose during a period of increasing economic prosperity. But it occurred at the beginning of the cold war and in response to the sudden realization that the Soviets had atom bombs that could destroy American cities.

In his book on the satanic cult scare, J. S. Victor presents evidence that the major current source of shared social stress is the rapid decline of occupational opportunities in the United States (Victor 1993). In addition, several other social stresses have contributed to a widespread perception that American society is beset by some kind of ambiguous threat to people's security. One is the disintegration of stable family relationships. Another is the widening gap, growing for three decades, between the publicly preached ideals and actual practices of powerful, wealthy and prestigious people; people who provide the social models for others to emulate. These social conditions have led to the widespread belief that American society is in a moral decline.

These conditions are particularly disturbing for young, economically stressed, blue-collar parents, who must worry about fragile family bonds and the difficulties of providing a moral foundation for their children. As a result, the satanic cult scare has symbolically focused upon perceived threats to children and teenagers.

In conditions of shared social stress with complex, unclear and ambiguous causes, people want a quick, easy explanation for their plight. The easiest explanation is to find scapegoats. In Western societies, the scapegoating process has traditionally been guided by the blueprint provided in a demonology which attributes the causes of "evil" to a small, conspiratorial group seeking to undermine the moral order of society. The satanic cult legend is a product of that Western demonology. In the past, that demonology has targeted heretics, Jews, witches, Freemasons, and even Catholics in some societies, as scapegoats.

PRACTICAL APPLICATIONS

Allegations of satanic cult ritual sexual abuse of children in child care centers need to be carefully investigated, avoiding undue emotional overreaction. These allegations can easily lead to false arrests and ruined community reputations, as they have in many past cases. The allegations may also distort and confuse the painful realities of actual sexual abuse, perhaps experienced in a child's home.

Such allegations are most likely to be interactive products of children's fear-filled imaginings, combined with priming by overzealous interviewers who believe in the existence of criminal satanic cult conspirators. Police investigators need to be cautiously aware that allegations of satanic ritual abuse heard from children be the result of such priming.

Most importantly, police and child protection workers need to be aware that there is no evidence whatsoever for the existence of groups of so-called Satanists who sexually abuse children, whereas there exist plenty of rumors about satanic cults circulating in communities today (Victor 1993). These rumors may influence the preconceptions of some therapists and some local police. Children my also overhear them when the rumors are subjects of adult gossip and television news.

There is abundant research information about the sexual molestation of children by adults. Police and child protection workers need to be guided by that body of research, rather than by rumors or by speculative claims presented by moral crusaders at conferences, seminars and training workshops about satanic cult crime, ritual abuse, or multiple personality disorder.

Responsible authorities need to avoid imparting legitimacy to moral crusaders, who are constructing a fictional form of deviance. Agencies that provide educational credit for attendance at seminars conducted by these "experts" in satanic cult crime should be required to reconsider their rationale for doing so. These may be mental health seminars about teenage Satanism or "ritual abuse," or MPD satanic cult "survivors." They may be police conferences on so-called occult or ritualistic crime. People in this country are free to hear the freely expressed beliefs of any speaker. However, that does not mean that professional agencies must lend credibility to fearmongering, or that taxpayers' money should be used to support the attendance of government employees (police, social workers) at these conferences.

The stories of satanic cult torture told by people suffering from MPD are manifestations of their deep psychological disorder. The fact that many therapists, including some who are eminent psychiatrists, believe the stories, is another example of therapists being seduced and deceived by the fantasies of their disturbed patients. The circumstances are very similar to those of cases in which credulous psychotherapists believe their patients' accounts of being abducted by UFOs or having returned from a near-death experience.

The MPD "survivor" stories are manifestations of an interaction process in which both patients and therapists are collusive storytellers. The contemporary legend of satanic cults as learned from many popular culture sources is retold by the MPD patient and then affirmed by the authority of the therapist in search of a breakthrough discovery. Police need to keep in mind that therapists are not trained in criminal investigation and that many of them are not even adequately trained in careful scientific methods of research. (Moreover, many people who call themselves "therapists" or "counselors" are paraprofessionals, who are not extensively trained in psychology, sociology and anthropology.)

The proliferating number of sexual child abuse "survivors," whose purported "repressed memories" were brought out by believing therapists, has resulted in the victimization of thousands of emotionally troubled adult women and their aging parents (Ofshe 1993). Many of these psychotherapy patients also claim to be "survivors" of satanic cult ritual sex abuse. This psychotherapy hoax has destroyed the relationships between patients and their elderly parents whom they accuse of having sexually molested and tortured them in secret satanic cult rituals. A national organization of parents, called the False Memory Syndrome Foundation, was formed in 1992 to fight this hoax.[2] By the spring of 1993, the organization had gathered information from about 4,000 families affected by accusations originating from purported "repressed memories" of sexual child abuse, about 20 percent of which include accusations of satanic ritual abuse. Some of this "repressed memory therapy" may be unethical, if it is a form of disguised religious proselytism that preys upon the psychological problems of people as a means of converting them to a particular ideology (see chapter 12 of this volume).

Responsible authorities need to investigate whether this bogus psychotherapy is being used deliberately by some psychiatric clinics and hospital programs to profit from the suffering of psychologically disturbed clients, the costs of which are passed on to taxpayers and medical insurance companies.

NOTES

1. Studies done by investigative journalists of cases involving false allegations of ritual child sex abuse include: Alexander 1991; Bamberger 1989; Bernhardt 1990; Buser 1991; Mathews 1989; Nathan 1987, 1988, 1990; Passantino, et al. 1991; Rabinowitz 1990; Snedeker 1988; Watters 1991; Williams 1988; Whitley 1991; Wright 1993a, 1993b.

2. The address of the False Memory Syndrome Foundation is: 3401 Market Street, Suite 130, Philadelphia, Pa. 19104

REFERENCES

Alexander, D. (1991, Sept./Oct.). "Still Giving the Devil More Than His Due." *The Humanist* 42: 22–33.

Bamberger, M. (1989, Oct. 21). "Sons Tell a D.A. That They Lied." *Philadelphia Inquirer.*

Bernhart, K. (1990). *Guilty Until Proven Innocent.* Hannibal, Mo.: Hannibal Books.

Blume, S. (1990). *Secret Survivors: Uncovering Incest and Its Aftereffects in Women.* New York: John Wiley and Sons.

Bottoms, B. L.; Shaver, P. R.; and Goodman, G. G. (1991, Aug. 19). "Profile of Ritualistic and Religion-Related Abuse Allegations Reported to Clinical Psychologists in the United States." Paper presented to the annual meeting of the American Psychological Association, San Francisco, Calif.

Buser, L. (1991, Feb. 21). "Court Voids Child Abuse Conviction of Ballard." *Commercial Appeal* (Memphis, Tenn.).

Carlson, S.; and Larue, G.; with O'Sullivan, G.; Masche, A.; and Frew, D. (1989). *Satanism in America.* El Cerrito, Calif.: Gain Press.

Charlier, T., and Downing, S. (1988, Jan. 17). "Facts, Fantasies Caught in Tangled Web." *Commercial Appeal* (Memphis, Tenn.). (This and the following three articles were included in a six-part series titled "Justice Abused: The 1980's Withhunt.")

——— (1988, Jan. 17). "Allegations of Odd Rites Compelled Closer Look." *Commercial Appeal* (Memphis, Tenn.).

——— (1988, Jan. 18). "Allegations Rife, Evidence Slight." *Commercial Appeal* (Memphis, Tenn.).

——— (1988, Jan. 18). "Links to Abuse of Children Hard to Prove." *Commercial Appeal* (Memphis, Tenn.).

Coleman, L., and Clancy, P. E. (1990, Fall). "False Allegations of Child Sexual Abuse." *Criminal Justice,* pp. 14–20, 43–47.

Cruoch, B., and Damphousse, K. (1991). "Law Enforcement and the Satanic Crime Connection: A Survey of 'Cult Cops.' " In J. Richardson, J. Best, and D. Bromley, eds., *The Satanism Scare,* pp. 191–217. New York: Aldine de Gruyter.

Faller, K. C. (1987). "Women Who Sexually Abuse Children." *Violence and Victims* 2, no. 4: 263–76.

Finkelhor, D.; Williams, L. M.; and Burns, N. (1988). *Nursery Crimes: Sexual Abuse in Day Care.* Newbury Park, Calif.: Sage Publications.

Foster, S. E. (1990, Summer). "The Satanic Preschool: A Contemporary Legend." *California Folklore Society Newsletter,* p. 9.

Goleman, D. (1991, Sept. 10). "Therapists See Religion As Aid, Not Illusion." *New York Times,* CI and C8.

Goretsky, S. R. (1991, April 19). Personal communication. Washington, D.C.: Center on Children and the Law, American Bar Association.

Grescoe, P. (1980, Oct. 27). "Things That Go Bump in Victoria." *Maclean's* (Canada), p. 30–31.

Herr, P. M. (1986). "Consequences of Priming: Judgment and Behavior." *Journal of Personality and Social Psychology* 51, no. 6: 1106–1115.

Hicks, R. (1991). *In Pursuit of Satan.* Buffalo, N.Y.: Prometheus Books.

James, K. (1986). "Priming and Social Catergorizational Factors: Impact on Awareness of Emergency Situations." *Personality and Social Psychology Bulletin* 12: 462–67.

Kapferer, J. N. (1990). *Rumors: Uses, Interpretations and Images.* New Brunswick, N.J.: Transaction Publishers.

Kelley, S. J. (1990). "Parental Stress Response to Sexual Abuse and Ritualistic Abuse of Children in Day-Care Centers." *Nursing Research* 39, no. 1: 25–29.

Kohn, A. (1992, June). "A Comparative Analysis of the Views of Law Enforcement Agencies and the Mental Health Community on Ritual Child Abuse." Master of Philosophy dissertation. University of Cambridge (U.K.), Institute of Criminology.

Lanning, K. V. (1989a). "Satanic, Occult, Ritualistic Crime: A Law Enforcement Perspective." *The Police Chief,* pp. 69–70.

——— (1989b). *Child Sex Rings: A Behavioral Analysis.* Arlington, Va.: National Center for Missing and Exploited Children.

Lindesmith, A. R.; Strauss, A. L.; and Denzin, N. K. (1991). *Social Psychology.* 7th ed. Englewood Cliffs, N.J.: Prentice-Hall.

Linton, M. (1991, Nov. 20). "Satan Case Collapses After Girl's Evidence." *The Guardian* (London, U.K.).

Loftus, E. F. (1979). *Eyewitness Testimony.* Cambridge, Mass.: Harvard University Press.

——— (1980, Oct.). "The Eyewitness on Trial." *Trial,* pp. 31–36.

Lloyd, D. W. (1990, Aug. 10). *Ritual Child Abuse: Understanding the Controversies.* Wheaton, Md.: The National Center on Child Sexual Abuse.

Lyons, A. (1988). *Satan Wants You.* New York: Warner Books.

MacKinnon, I. (1991, Nov. 19). "Sister in 'Ritual Sex' Trial Lied Over Names." *The Independent* (London, U.K.).

McMurran, K. (1980, Jan. 1). "A Canadian Woman's Bizarre Childhood Memories of Satan Shocks Shrinks and Priests." *People,* pp. 14, 28–30.

Mathews, J. (1989, May 31). "In California, a Question of Abuse." *Washington Post,* p. DI.

Mulher, S. (1991). "Satanism and Psychotherapy: A Rumor in Search of an Inquisition." In J. Richardson, J. Best, and D. Bromley, eds., *The Satanism Scare,* pp. 145–72. New York: Aldine de Gruyter.

Mydans, S. (1990, July 28). "Seven Years Later, McMartin Case Ends in a Mistrial." *New York Times,* p. A1.

Nathan, D. (1987, Sept. 29). "The Making of a Modern Witch Trial." *The Village Voice,* pp. 19–32.

——— (1988, Aug. 2). "Victimizer or Victim? Was Kelly Michaels Unjustly Convicted?" *The Village Voice,* pp. 31–39.

——— (1990, June 12). "The Ritual Sex Abuse Hoax." *The Village Voice,* pp. 36–45. (Reprinted in Nathan, D. [1991]. *Women and Other Aliens.* El Paso, Tex.: Cinco Punts Press.)

——— (1991). "Satanism and Child Molestation: Constructing the Ritual Abuse Scare." In J. Richardson, J. Best, and D. Bromley, eds., *The Satanism Scare,* pp. 75–94. New York: Aldine de Gruyter.

Northwest Psychological Publishers. (1990). *Projective Story Telling Cards.* Redding, Calif.: Author.

Office of Criminal Justice Planning, State of California. (1989–1990). *Occult Crime: A Law Enforcement Primer*. Sacramento, Calif.: Author.

Ofshe, R., and Watters, E. (1993, March/April). "Making Monsters." *Society*, pp. 4–16.

Passantino, G.; Passantino, B.; and Trott, J. (1990). "Satan's Sideshow: The True Lauren Stratford Story." *Cornerstone* 18, no. 90: 24–28.

Rabinowitz, D. (1990, May). "From the Mouths of Babes to a Jail Cell." *Harper's*, pp. 52–63.

Reinhold, R. (1990, Jan. 24). "McMartin Case: Swept Away by Panic about Molestation." *New York Times*, p. A1.

——— (1990, Feb. 1). "Longest Trial Over, Child Abuse Suspect Faces a Retrial." *New York Times*, p. AI.

Richardson, J. T. (1991). "Satanism in the Courts: From Murder to Heavy Metal." In J. Richardson, J. Best, and D. Bromley, eds., *The Satanism Scare*, pp. 205–220. New York: Aldine de Gruyter.

Ritual Abuse Task Force. (1989, Sept. 15). *Report*. Los Angeles: Los Angeles County Commission for Women.

Sanford, D. (1990). *Don't Make Me Go Back, Mommy*. Portland, Or.: Multnomah Press.

Shaw, D. (1990, Jan. 19). "Where Was Skepticism in Media?" *Los Angeles Times*, pp. A1, A20–21.

——— (1990, Jan. 20). "Reporter's Early Exclusiveness Triggered a Media Frenzy." *Los Angeles Times*.

——— (1990, Jan. 22). "Times McMartin Coverage Was Biased, Critics Charge." *Los Angeles Times*.

Smith, K., and Pazder, L. (1980). *Michelle Remembers*. New York: Congdon and Latte. (Paperback edition New York: Pocket Books, 1981).

Snedeker, M. (1988). "The Rise and Fall of the Devil in Kern County, California." *California Prisoner*, part 1, April, pp. 4–6; part 2, June.

Stafford, T. (1993, May 17). "The Therapeutic Revolution." *Christianity Today*, pp. 24–32.

Stevens, P., Jr. (1991). "The Demonology of Satanism: An Anthropological View." In J. Richardson, J. Best, and D. Bromley, eds., *The Satanism Scare*, pp. 21–40. New York: Aldine de Gruyter.

Summit, R. C. (1983). "The Child Sexual Abuse Accommodation Syndrome." *Child Abuse and Neglect* 7: 177–93.

Underwager, R., and Wakefield, H. (1990). *The Real World of Child Interrogations*. Springfield, Ill.: Charles C Thomas, Pub.

——— (1991). "*Cur alii, prae aliis*? (Why Some, and Not Others?)." *Issues in Child Abuse Accusations* 3, no. 3: 178–93.

Victor, J. S. (1993). *Satanic Panic: The Creation of a Contemporary Legend*. Peru, Ill.: Open Court Publishing Co.

Wakefield, H., and Underwager, R. (1988). *Accusations of Child Sexual Abuse*. Springfield, Ill.: Charles C Thomas, Pub.

Watters, E. (1991, July/Aug.). "The Devil in Mr. Ingram." *Mother Jones,* pp. 30–33, 65–68.

Whitley, G. (1991, Oct.). "The Seduction of Gloria Grady." *D Magazine* (Dallas), pp. 45–49, 66–71.

Williams, M. A. (1988). "Witch Hunt." *Chicago Lawyer* 11, no. 10: 1, 7–9, 24–27.

Wright, L. ((1993a, May 17). "Remembering Satan–Part I." *The New Yorker,* pp. 60–81.

——— (1993b, May 24). "Remembering Satan–Part II." *The New Yorker,* p. 54–76.

14

Assessment of the Adult Alleged Offender*

S. Margretta Dwyer and Eli Coleman

INTRODUCTION

The predominant view around the world is that sex offenders should be punished, the effect of which would be to deter them from committing further offenses. Punishment has included incarceration, physical punishment, castration and, in some cases, death. Recognizing sex offenses as a symptom of an underlying disorder in need of treatment is a relatively new concept, but one that has found increasing favor in contemporary Western cultures. Thus, evaluating sex offenders for possible disorders is part of a new and emerging field within forensic sexology.

While there is more support for understanding and treating the sex offender, the clinician is still called upon to prove that a disorder exists and that society would be better off attempting prevention as well as rehabilitation through medical and psychological treatment rather than through punishment alone. The clinician is still under intense pressure to gather substantive and abundant data to support a recommendation of treatment for rehabilitation.

Fortunately, there is emerging scientific knowledge which clinicians can utilize in going about their task. However, this task is still difficult. Current knowledge of the underlying disorders and of assessment techniques and treatment methodologies is in an early stage of development. Since this field is an emerging one, most psychotherapists or psychiatrists have not been adequately trained to conduct assessments. The clinician must have specialized training and expertise in the growing body of knowledge of assessing and treating sex offenders.

*Special thanks are due to Melva Dunn for her work on the manuscript.

Even with this knowledge, determining whether sex offenders pose serious threats to others, are not dangerous, or have a treatable condition, is a challenge to the clinician. Opinions are exactly that—opinions. And yet, these opinions carry great weight in decisions regarding sentencing of a sex offender. The burden upon the clinician is great—including legal risk to the clinician (Melella et al. 1987).

In order to assist the professional who is called upon to evaluate an alleged or convicted sex offender, this chapter reviews the current assessment methodology of nonviolent sex offenders, violent offenders, and those falsely accused. Some of the limitations of assessment are also addressed.

In assessing alleged or convicted offenders, information must be gathered from many sources, including the offenders themselves, their families, court and police reports, victim statements, and probation officers' investigative reports. Even after initial evaluation, there is a process evaluation that occurs through the course of treatment. As much data as possible is collected to diagnose and determine treatability. Because the acquired material will often be contradictory, excellent differential diagnostic skills are required on the part of the clinician.

DETERMINING THE DIAGNOSIS

Determining the diagnosis is one of the clinician's most important tasks. Most sex offenders suffer from a paraphilic disorder, a type of psychosexual disorder. Not all paraphilias are illegal. It is important to differentiate a sex offense, which is a *legal* concept, from a paraphilia, which is a *psychiatric* concept.

According to John Money, a paraphilia is diagnosed when an individual is compulsively responsive to, or dependent upon, an unusual and unacceptable stimulus in the imagery of fantasy for optimal initiation and maintenance of erotosexual arousal, and for the facilitation or attainment of orgasm (Money 1986). Paraphilic imagery may be replayed in fantasy during solitary masturbation or intercourse with a partner. According to the *Diagnostic and Statistical Manual,* 3rd ed. (rev.) (*DSM-III-R*) of the American Psychiatric Association (American Psychiatric Association 1987), paraphilias are a type of impulse control disorder. Some argue that the paraphilias may be a variant of an obsessive-compulsive disorder (Coleman 1991).

According to the *DSM-III-R,* a paraphilia must occur over a period of at least six months, involve recurrent, intense sexual urges and sexually arousing fantasies of a socially unacceptable behavior, and be disparate from love or intimacy. The person must also have acted on these urges, or be markedly distressed by them. The authors of *DSM-III-R* consider paraphilias as Axis I disorders. Often, someone with a paraphilia also suffers from an additional

Axis I psychiatric disorder, such as an anxiety or depressive disorder or a variety of Axis II personality disorders. It is important to recognize comorbid psychiatric diagnoses in order to complete a comprehensive assessment of either nonviolent sex offenders, violent offenders, or those falsely accused.

ASSESSMENT OF NONVIOLENT SEX OFFENDERS

The nonviolent offender is one who has not used a weapon during the crime and has not injured the victim's body in any manner. A nonviolent offender has usually touched, fondled, or befriended the victim and/or spent considerable time manipulating the potential victim to cooperate, or has committed a "hands off" offense such as exposing, voyeurism, or obscene phone calls. He/she has no history of violent behavior (Langevin et al. 1983).

As with all offenders, assessment of the nonviolent offender must include personal interviews. These interviews must take place over a period of time in order to develop a complete picture of the individual. Completing all interviews in one or two days is not recommended, as offenders may be in a state which precludes them giving accurate or honest information. A one-hour and one-time-only interview is useless. Interviews over a period of time are needed to develop a trusting therapeutic relationship. Time in between interviews also elicits more and more accurate information. Weekly one-hour interviews conducted over one or two months can best yield the necessary information.

Structure of the Interview

A series of six to eight interviews will yield substantial information for assessment. The first interview should be nonthreatening, as the alleged or convicted offender is likely to be extremely defensive. It is important for the clinician to explain the purpose of the assessment and describe the limits of confidentiality. Federal and state guidelines in the United States, for example, mandate the reporting to authorities of cases of sexual abuse of children or vulnerable (incapacitated) adults. Clinicians must be honest and direct if they are to expect the same from alleged or convicted offenders.

Few details of the offense should be taken in the first interview, as most of the truth will not be gathered until a positive bond has formed between the clinician and the offender. It is to be expected that offenders have reason to be distrustful and suspicious of anyone who might have a say over the outcome of their sentence. In addition, sex offenders normally feel extreme guilt and are cautious in divulging information (Wilson et al. 1986). Adding to the difficulty of the assessment process is the fact that offenders may have a deficient range of social skills (Becket et al. 1978; Boozer 1975; Dwyer & Amberson 1985; Dwyer & Amberson 1989; Dwyer & Myers 1990; Laws & Serber 1975; Pacht 1975). With high guilt operating and low social skills the norm, the offender is sometimes mislabeled as "lying" or "in denial."

Present relationship status; sexual functioning or dysfunction; fantasy life; medical condition, including current medications, use of alcohol or other drugs; psychological functioning; employment; education and career; previous evaluation(s) or treatment(s)—all these topics are good for the first interview. It is also important to elicit information regarding the current legal situation, including the nature of the allegations, whether sentencing has taken place and, if so, conditions of sentencing or probation.

The second interview should serve to gather family of origin information and relationship history. Depending on the complexity of the family of origin and the number of previous relationships and/or marriages, this may take more than one session.

By the third or fourth interview, offenders should be ready to divulge details of their offending behavior(s), including how such behavior was concealed up until they were caught and charged with the sex offense. Clinicians should also elicit a more detailed description of offenders' fantasy life and erotosexual orientation. An attempt should be made to identify their primary arousal pattern as well as the boundaries of the *lovemap* (Money 1986).[1]

Patients should also be asked how they masturbate and should be asked for complete details about their fantasies during masturbation. Fantasies during masturbation often reveal erotosexual orientation. Many offenders must use their paraphilic fantasies as a means of achieving an orgasm.

Fifth and sixth interviews should elicit a year-by-year sex history. During this verbalization, offenders begin to remember incidents in their sexual development. It is best to proceed chronologically, starting at about age four, and to try to elicit, in detail, offenders' earliest recollection regarding their sexual development. Particular importance should be paid to critical events that may have played a role in offenders' sexual development, including: childhood sex play; punishment for sex play; sex education; age of and response to puberty; content of sex dreams during childhood, pubescence and adolescence; adolescent sexual and intimate experience; same- and opposite-sex experience; and any traumatic events, including child abuse.

If offenders are in a long-term relationship, interviews are needed with their partners to help corroborate the information obtained from offenders as well as to better understand their relationship patterns and their sexual and intimacy functioning. Good evaluative practice calls for looking at multiple sources of information and data, and searching for a convergence of the data, while engaging in a process of ruling out competing hypotheses. For example, partners can be very helpful in corroborating or challenging the reported alcohol or drug use by offenders. Many substance abuse and other disorders are diagnosed with the assistance of information provided by partners.

Not all partners are cooperative or forthright. Some are invested in "protecting" the offender and/or their observations are sometimes distorted by their own psychopathology.

Because most therapies for sex offenders utilize a systemic approach, partners must be evaluated for their ability and willingness to engage in the process of treatment for offenders. In most treatment programs available today, partners must be amenable to treatment or sex offenders will not be accepted into treatment. In many cases, partners are given individual treatment as well as regarded as part of the family system. Several sessions involving partners are necessary to complete this aspect of the evaluation. A separate and more complete evaluation of partners may be needed for their individual treatment plan to be developed.

Besides arriving at a complete differential diagnosis, the clinician must assess the type of treatment that will be required and the likelihood of successful treatment.

During this extensive assessment one of three types of sex offenders can be identified:

1) offenders with psychopathic personalities or those who are psychotic and are not amenable to current treatments;

2) offenders who have little or no impulse control but can be successfully treated in inpatient facilities; and

3) offenders who have sufficient control or can be controlled through treatment on an outpatient basis.

In the final assessment session, the clinician should review the assessment data and interpret the results to the offender. In situations where the assessment will be sent to legal authorities, the clinician must have a written and signed authorization from the client to release the information. Further, in building a trusting relationship, it is helpful for the clinician to review the assessment with the offender before it is sent to the authorities.

Psychometric Testing

No one test can really describe a person, but testing may give a global overview of the offender. By utilizing a battery of psychometric instruments, the clinician can derive an overview of an offender's psychological functioning and assist in the overall assessment process. Testing should be conducted in a controlled and supervised environment such as a private room in a clinic.

There are a number of instruments which the clinician might find helpful.

In terms of general psychological functioning, the Minnesota Multiphasic Personality Inventory (MMPI) has been used extensively in evaluations. It cannot, by itself, identify an offender. Several profiles of offenders have been identified—including one that is completely within normative limits. The MMPI is helpful in identifying mental disorders and personality characteristics. Among pedophiles or incest patients, it has also been shown to be helpful in subclassifying the offender with variable predictions for treatment success or difficulty (Kalichman & Dwyer 1992; Kalichman, Henderson, et al. 1992; Kalichman, Russell, et al. unpublished). Most of the literature indicates that an MMPI 4,8 profile is fairly typical for an offender, and does not necessarily indicate psychopathology for sex offenders (Erickson et al. 1987). By contrast, most psychiatric patients with the 48/84 code tend to be diagnosed as schizophrenic (paranoid type) or antisocial, schizoid, or suffering from paranoid personality disorder. Sex offenders' MMPI patterns change during treatment.

Further, most of the literature indicates that the MMPI cannot be used to distinguish an "offender" from a "nonoffender." Many evaluators try to read more into the MMPI than is appropriate. Nonetheless, it is a helpful tool. Other suggested tests alongside the MMPI are: an additional personality test (of choice); a depression and an anxiety scale (of choice); the Tennessee Self-Concept Scale (Fitts 1964); the Derogatis Sexual Functioning Inventory (Derogatis 1978); the Multiphasic Sex Inventory (Nichols & Molinder 1984); the Bem Sex Role Inventory (Bem 1978); and the Dissociative Experiences Scale (Bernstein & Putnam 1985). Many of these tests will give the clinician a cross-validation between scales and clinical impression. For example, the MMPI can indicate depression, and a scale such as the Beck Depression (Beck et al. 1961) will help validate a clinical impression. Cross-validating an assessment is important for evaluations that will be used in legal proceedings where clinical impressions alone may be subject to scrutiny and criticism regarding reliability. By the same token, the outcome of a psychometric test should be interpreted only in light of the clinical picture and cross-validated by other psychometric instruments.

Questionnaires and Inventories

Patients will not always be able to narrate unusual sexual practices. Often, they will be able to indicate their occurrence when answering a questionnaire. Conversely, some patients will not put anything down on paper but will be willing to discuss these matters with the clinician directly. Both interview and questionnaire methods are needed to complete an assessment.

Even with a thorough assessment, it is likely that the clinician will not get a clear picture of all the sexual behaviors in which the individual has engaged. Disclosing this highly personal information involves a high degree of trust. In many cases, clinicians will gather more and more of this information as treatment proceeds. Patients themselves may unconsciously block some of this information. The behaviors are "remembered" in the course of therapy. For example, it is certainly not uncommon for offenders to report having had sexual relations with one or two minors and then in the course of therapy to remember other pedophilic occasions.

Neurological Assessment

Many nonviolent sex offenders have neurological abnormalities or damage. Sensory deprivation during the formative periods of brain development results in functional and microstructural abnormalities of the developing brain (Prescott 1975). The emotional-social engaging parts of the brain are reflected in a person's emotional-social behaviors, which of course are connected with sexuality (Prescott 1975). The limbic system (having to do with the circumferential portion of the brain) and the temporal and frontal lobe are involved in sexual behaviors; damage to these areas or congenital abnormalities within them can lead to sexually aberrant behavior, including sex offenses. It is important to look for subtle evidence of neurological disorders such as learning disabilities, difficulties in concentration or memory, psychomotor deficiencies, and/or sensory deficits.

Psychometric testing can detect sources of brain dysfunction and can pinpoint areas of cognitive dysfunction which could interfere in any psychotherapeutic intervention. An electroencephalogram (EEG) (including a nasopharyngeal EEG), and brain imaging tests, namely, computer axial tomography (CAT Scan) or magnetic-resonance-imaging (MRI), may determine gross or subtle abnormalities, especially in the limbic system, and the temporal and frontal lobes. The clinician would want to rule out Tourette's Syndrome, temporal lobe epilepsy, focal supratentorial lesions or epileptiform abnormalities, brain malformations, and post-encephalopathic brain damage. In the future, one may use a positron-emission tomography (PET Scan) which can identify abnormalities in brain activity. This has been a useful tool in research documenting obsessive-compulsive and other psychiatric disorders. If neurological deficits are suspected, then a psychiatrist should determine if a full-scale neurological battery is needed. Such a neurological battery may include CAT and other scans (Langevin 1987, 1991).

Even with minimal neurological impairment, the patient may benefit from medication. Medications such as the serotonergic fluoxetine and the anxiolytic buspirone have been found to affect the temporal lobe and frontal lobe areas of the brain, areas associated with sexual activity. Some medications tend to lessen obsession with deviant sexual arousal (Coleman & Cesnik 1991; Kafka 1991).

Physical Examination

Many patients appearing for assessment have not had a physical examination for many years. A thorough physical should be conducted as part of the assessment. This includes a complete review of systems and appropriate laboratory tests. The physician must determine the existence of general health problems, not only to determine if there may be organic problems that might help explain the offending behavior, but also to determine whether the individual can endure the stress of treatment or the use of certain medications.

Before patients enter intensive therapy for sex offenders they should be screened for heart problems, high blood pressure, and other problems that could interfere with healthy living or therapy. Hormonal assays should be conducted to rule out overt hormonal abnormalities, disorders, or tumors. In males, testosterone and LH (luteinizing hormone) levels should be measured. Testosterone and LH blood samples should be drawn and used also to measure sugar levels and cholesterol. The evaluator should bear in mind that laboratories differ in their ranges of what constitutes normality. Typically, the normal range for testosterone is between 300–1200 ng/dl. When there are abnormalities in testosterone, it is always important to check the pituitary hormones (the gonadotropins, FSH [follicle-stimulating hormone] and LH, which in men stimulate the testicles to produce testosterone). It is also important to rule out hyperpituitarism, for example, by measuring prolactin. Hyperpituitarism is sometimes due to a tumor, either adenoma or carcinoma. Such tumors occur more often in males than in females.[2]

Treatment should be given for any nonsexual conditions diagnosed prior to, or concomitant with, sex offender treatment.

Plethysmography or Phallometric Testing

Plethysmography or phallometric testing are methods for measuring physical arousal in response to standardized erotic stimuli. Most plethysmography equipment measures only changes in penile circumference through changes in a strain gauge that is placed around the penis. Phallometric testing involves measurement of volumetric changes in total penis size. Both these methods are valuable in assessing male offenders. These tests distinguish sexual arousal from stimuli differentiated by age, gender and depiction of violence. Results are not usually admissible in court. If they are, they must be interpreted carefully: arousal to a person of a certain age does not imply action; attraction may exist only in the offender's fantasy life.

It should be noted that in using phallometric or plethysmographic testing, incest perpetrators can have "normal" profiles that do not indicate eroto-sexual attraction to children. However, some incest perpetrators are pedophilic as well (Langevin 1983; Langevin et al. 1985).

Suppression and faking are frequently a problem with this test. A variety of ways exist to detect this and evaluators may develop some of their own. The patient can be asked to "suppress" and then "not to suppress" his response in order to obtain a reading on suppression or faking. If the penile gauge moves up too rapidly at any one time, this could indicate the patient is pulling on the gauge to make himself "look appropriately normal" at certain times. If the Galvanic Skin Response (GSR) is used, this, too, can be a clue indicating suppression readings. When the GSR responds in an abnormal pattern for a particular patient after a pattern has been established, this could also indicate suppression. The patient can be asked at the end of the evaluation about faking; frequently he will acknowledge it. It is also important to make sure no round objects are close by the patient during the test, so that he can place the penile gauge on the object instead of himself. If evaluators have access to this type of testing procedure, they should be acquainted with the literature on faking procedures.

Clearly, not all clinicians will have access to a psychophysiological lab. While plethysmography is much more available than phallometric testing, and is less complicated and expensive, plethysmography equipment is not available in most countries and in many rural areas, small towns and clinics in the United States. If this type of testing is not available, the clinician must rely on self-report and clinical skills to make an accurate diagnosis.

Polygraph

A "lie detector" or polygraph can sometimes elicit the truth from a patient who is denying involvement in or responsibility for an offense. This assessment tool is only as good as the operator, and can be valid only when the proper questions are asked and phrased correctly. Even when right questions are *phrased* wrongly, the patient may pass this test. It is helpful when a number of physiological measures are recorded, such as galvanic skin response, pulse, heart beat, respiration, and voice stress. Results on multiple measures help corroborate the interpretation of the test. There is much debate about the accuracy of the polygraph, which is why it is rarely, if ever, admissible in court. However, like any assessment tool, it can be useful if used correctly and interpreted cautiously.

ASSESSMENT OF VIOLENT SEX OFFENDERS

A violent sex offender is one who has used a weapon, used force in committing the crime, or has mutilated or killed his/her victim. The entire evaluation process described for nonviolent sex offenders is also essential for evaluating violent sex offenders. In addition, several issues complicate the assessment of violent sex offenders.

There is enormous societal pressure to punish rather than to rehabilitate violent sex offenders. Consequently, the pressure on the clinician to substantiate the diagnosis and prognosis is greater in these cases than in cases of nonviolent offenders.

Most violent sex offenders are punished rather than offered treatment. If treatment is offered, it is usually limited to inpatient treatment, unless it can be determined that they have sufficient self-control to get help on an outpatient basis.

In the assessment process of violent sex offenders, a developmental history is particularly important. Sexual aggression in adulthood, especially in rapists, is related to distinct aspects of developmental history. The quality of early interpersonal attachments and the experience of sexual abuse as a child both play a significant role in sexual aggression in adulthood (Cerce et al. 1984). Relationships in the family and with significant others during formative years is critical (Buikhuisen et al. 1985; Ensminger et al. 1983; Loeber & Dishion 1983; Magnusson et al. 1983; Prentky et al. 1989).

Frequent changes in caretakers, repeated losses, and lack of stable role models predict greater violence (i.e., rape in sexual encounters) (Prentky et al. in press). Others have noted that disrupted attachments seem related to criminal/violent outcome (Burgess et al. 1986; Mawson 1980).

Motive for the offender's use of a weapon needs to be determined. A person may have "loosely" or "carelessly" used a weapon in the crime; this in and of itself does not make him a "violent sex offender." He may have thought one is supposed to carry a weapon and may have been more frightened of it than anything.

Little is understood about the nature of amnesic or "fugue-like" states, where the facts of a crime are not remembered. Still less is known about how to determine whether a report of amnesia is genuine (Schacter 1986). Claims of amnesia occur frequently after the commission of a violent crime. Sometimes the ego is not strong enough to face what has really transpired. Lengthy therapy may be required.

If it is determined that the violent offender can possibly benefit from treatment, then most likely inpatient treatment is recommended.

FALSE ACCUSATION CASES

Men can be and have been falsely accused of sexual offenses. If a false accusation is suspected, an evaluation must include many persons and will take much longer to accomplish. All the above techniques and tools need to be used in the assessment process along with some additional assessments.

Once all the above interviews and testing have been completed on the alleged abuser, a full-scale workup must also be completed on the accuser. Using the same testing battery that was used on the alleged perpetrator is recommended, as well as a voice stress and polygraph for the accused and the accuser. The plethysmograph may be unnecessary for the accuser, unless for some reason the evaluator needs to assess his arousal patterns also.

Stepfathers, biological fathers, and uncles, as well as male friends of the mother (or the accuser), should be interviewed extensively if they have been in frequent close contact with the alleged victims. All of this is time-consuming and expensive to the parties involved. If the alleged victim is a child, then an assessment by a child psychologist/psychiatrist must be completed.

If the alleged victim(s)' stories are too contaminated from previous interviews, then caution should be used in proceeding with the interviews.

Even with the best interviewing and sophisticated testing, one can never say with absolute certainty that the accused did or did not commit the offense. Unless an admission is obtained, only an opinion can be rendered. There are, however, some fictitious admissions, irrespective of this being self-incriminating. Clear conclusions and recommendations should be given to the parties involved based on the evaluation. These recommendations may have to be conditional, and the parties told to use them with caution, especially if they are based for the most part on opinion. Evaluators are encouraged to be creative in their recommendations. Creative planning can sometimes improve the family relationships or at least make for more peaceful living conditions for the victim and all involved.

SUMMARY

Evaluating the sex offender for possible disorders is part of a new and emerging field within forensic sexology. The clinician must have specialized training and expertise in the growing body of knowledge of assessing and treating sex offenders. These are skills which most health care professionals do not have.

The assessment must be thorough and comprehensive. The diagnosis must determine the type of psychological/psychiatric/organic disorder as well as shed light on the prognosis of treatability. Some offenders have psychopathic personalities or are psychotic and therefore not amenable to current treatments. Many offenders can be treated in inpatient or outpatient facilities, depending upon their impulse control and their risk of reoffending during treatment.

Evaluations of violent offenders and those who may have been falsely accused are particularly difficult. For the violent offender, establishing the motive for the offender's use of a weapon is critical. Sociopathy and psychopathy are difficult to diagnose. A developmental history is especially important in evaluating these individuals.

In today's social climate, a number of men have been falsely accused of committing sexual offenses. The evaluation of the person who denies committing an alleged offense is a challenging one. In addition to evaluating the accused, it is critical to evaluate the accuser and the alleged victim(s). Even then, the truth may never be known—especially in cases where an admission of the offense is not forthcoming. Some admissions are false, however.

It is a greater challenge to support rehabilitation for sex offenders rather than to acquiesce to the calls for punishment. This task is made more difficult because our science is new and emerging. Therefore, evaluations can only be "informed" opinions. Hopefully, they are as objective as our science permits. It is also to be hoped that forensic sexologists will continue to be challenged to refine our evaluation methodologies so that they can be more accurate in the future.

At this point suggested Standards of Care regarding sex offenders (Coleman & Dwyer 1990) can be helpful reading, as can the references attached to this chapter.

NOTES

1. An individual's erotosexual arousal and behavior patterns are "stored" in the brain as a template, toponymic representation, or lovemap. John Money sees the striking parallel of erotosexual development to language development in children. Like language, a lovemap, once developed, is extremely difficult to change.

2. This is true except for Cushing Syndrome which is not, however, associated with paraphilia.

REFERENCES

Beck, A. T.; Ward, G. H.; Mendelson, M.; Mock, J.; and Erbaugh, J. (1961). "An Inventory for Measuring Depression." *Archives of General Psychiatry* 4: 561–71.

Becker, J. V.; Abel, G. G.; Blanchard, E. B.; Murphy, W. D.; and Coleman, E. (1978). "Evaluating Social Skills of Sexual Aggressives." *Criminal Justice and Behavior* 5: 357–68.

Bem, S. (1978). *Bem Inventory*. Palo Alto, Calif.: Consulting Psychologist Press.

Bernstein, E., and Putnam, F. W. (1985). *Dissociative Experiences Scale*. Beloit, Wis.: Beloit College.

Boozer, G. (1975). "Offender Treatment: Programming." Paper presented at Sixth Alabama Symposium on Justice and the Behavioral Sciences, University of Alabama, Tuscaloosa.

Buikhuisen, W.; van der Plas-Korenhoff, C.; and Bontekoe, E. H. M. (1985). "Parental Home Deviance." *International Journal of Offender Therapy and Comparative Criminology* 29: 201-210.

Burgess, A. W.; Hartman, C. R.; Ressler, R. K.; Douglas, J. E.; and McCormack, A. (1986). "Sexual Homicide: A Motivational Model." *Journal of Interpersonal Violence* 1: 251–72.

Cerce, D.; Day, S. R.; Prentky R. A.; and Knight, R. A. (1984). "The Correlative Relationship between Family Instability in Childhood and Sexually Aggressive Behavior in Adulthood." Paper presented at the Second National Conference for Family Violence Researchers, University of New Hampshire, Durham.

Coleman, E. (1991). "Compulsive Sexual Behavior: New Concepts and Treatments." *Journal of Psychology and Human Sexuality* 4, no. 2: 37–52.

Coleman, E., and Cesnik, J. (1991, September). "Use of Serotonergic Medications in the Treatment of Nonparaphilic and Paraphilic Compulsive Sexual Behavior." Paper presented at the Second Annual International Conference on the Treatment of Sex Offenders, Minneapolis, Minn.

Coleman, E., and Dwyer, S. M. (1990). "Proposed Standards of Care for the Treatment of Adult Sex Offenders." *Journal of Offender Rehabilitation* 16, nos. 1/2: 93–106.

Derogatis, L. R. (1978). *Derogatis Sexual Functioning Inventory.* Baltimore, Md.: Derogatis Publishers.

Dwyer, S. M., and Amberson, J. I. (1985). "Sex Offender Treatment Program: A Follow-Up Study." *American Journal of Social Psychiatry* 4: 56–60.

——— (1989). "Behavioral Patterns and Personality Characteristics of 56 Sex Offenders: A Preliminary Study." *Journal of Psychology and Human Sexuality* 2, no. 1: 105–117.

Dwyer, S. M., and Myers, S. (1990). "Sex Offender Treatment: A Six-Month to Ten-Year Follow-Up Study." *Annals of Sex Research* 3: 305–318.

Ensminger, M. E.; Kellam, S. G.; and Rubin, B. R. (1983). "School and Family Origins of Delinquency: Comparisons by Sex." In K. van Dusen and S. Mednick, eds., *Prospective Studies of Crime and Delinquency,* pp. 73–97. Boston: Kluwer-Nijhoff Pub.

Erickson, W. D.; Luxenberg, M. G.; Walbek, N. H.; and Seely, R. K. (1987). "Frequency of MMPI Two-Point Code Types among Sex Offenders." *Journal of Consulting and Clinical Psychology* 55: 566–70.

Fitts, W. (1964). *Tennessee Self-Concept Scale.* Los Angeles: Western Psychological Services.

Kafka, M. (1991, September). "Fluoxetine in the Treatment of Paraphilias and Nonparaphilic Sexual Addictions in Males." Paper presented at the Second Annual International Conference on the Treatment of Sex Offenders, Minneapolis, Minn.

Kalichman, S., and Dwyer, S. M. (1992). "Psychological and Sexual Functioning among Outpatient Sexual Offenders against Children: An MMPI Cluster Analytic Study."

Journal of Psychopathology and Behavioral Assessment 14, no. 3: 259–76.

Kalichman, S.; Henderson, M.; Shealy, L.; and Dwyer S. M. (1992). "The Assessment of Sex Offenders: Psychometric Properties of the Multiphasic Sex Inventory." *Criminal Justice and Behavior* 19, no. 4: 384–96.

Kalichman, S.; Russell, R.; Hoffman, L.; Henderson, M.; and Dwyer, S. M. *Aberrant Sexual Behavior and the Golden-Meehl "Schizotypy" Indicators: A Dimensional Analysis.* Submitted for publication.

Langevin, R. (1983). *Sexual Strands: Understanding and Treating Sexual Anomalies in Men.* Hillsdale, N.J.: Lawrence Erlbaum.

——— (1987). "An Overview of the Paraphilias." In M. H. Ben-Aaron, S. J. Hucker, and C. D. Webster, eds., *Clinical Criminology,* pp. 179–90. New York: Plenum Press.

——— (1991, November). "Biological Factors Contributing to Sex Offenses." Paper presented at the Tenth Annual Conference of the Association for the Treatment of Sexual Abusers, Ft. Worth, Tex.

Langevin, R.; Handy, L.; Russon, A. E.; and Day, D. (1985). "Are Incestuous Fathers Pedophilic, Aggressive and Alcoholic?" In R. Langevin, ed., *Erotic Preference, Gender Identity, and Aggression in Men.* Hillsdale, N.J.: Lawrence Erlbaum.

Langevin, R.; Paitich, D.; and Russon, A. (1983). "Are Rapists Sexually Anomalous, Aggressive or Both?" In R. Langevin, ed., *Erotic Preference, Gender Identity, and Aggression.* Hillsdale, N.J.: Lawrence Erlbaum.

Laws, D. R., and Serber, M. (1975). "Measurement and Evaluation of Assertive Training with Sexual Offenders." In R. E. Hosfort and C. S. Moss, eds., *The Crumbling Walls: Treatment and Counseling Prisoners.* Champaign, Ill.: University of Illinois Press.

Loeber, R., and Dishion, T. (1983). "Early Predictors of Male Delinquency: A Review." *Psychological Bulletin* 94, no. 1: 68–99.

Magnusson, D.; Stattin, J.; and Duner, A. (1983). "Aggression and Criminality in a Longitudinal Perspective." In K. T. Van Dusen and S. A. Mednick, eds., *Prospective Studies of Crime and Delinquency,* pp. 277–301. Boston: Kluwer-Nijhoff Publishing.

Mawson, A. R. (1980). "Aggression, Attachment Behavior, and Crimes of Violence." In T. Hirschi and M. Gottfredson, eds., *Understanding Crime,* pp. 103–116. Beverly Hills, Calif.: Sage Publications.

Melella, J.; Travin, S.; and Cullen, K. (1987, Spring). "The Psychotherapist's Third-Party Liability for Sexual Assaults Committed by His Patient." *Journal of Psychiatry and Law:* 83–116.

Money, J. (1986). *Lovemaps: Clinical Concepts of Sexual/Erotic Health and Pathology, Paraphilia, and Gender Transposition in Childhood, Adolescence, and Maturity.* New York: Irvington Pub. (Buffalo, N.Y.: Prometheus Books, 1993, Paperback).

Nichols, H. R., and Molinder, I. (1984). *Multiphasic Sex Inventory.* Tacoma, Wash.: Nichols and Molinder.

Pacht, A. (1975). "The Rapist in Treatment: Professional Myths and Psychological Realities." Paper presented at Sixth Alabama Symposium on Justice and the Behavioral Sciences, University of Alabama, Tuscaloosa.

Prentky, R. A.; Knight, R. A.; Sims-Knight, J. E.; Straus, H.; Rokous, F.; and Cerce, D. "The Developmental Antecedents of Sexual Aggression." *Development and Psychopathology* 1: 153–69.

Prescott, J. W. (1975). "Body Pleasure and the Origins of Violence." *The Futurist* 9: 64–74.

Schacter, D. L. (1986). "Amnesia and Crime: How Much Do We Really Know?" *America Psychologist* 41: 286–93.

Wilson, K. M.; Abel, G. G.; Rouleau, J. L.; and Coyne, B. J. (1986). Untitled paper obtained from Dr. Abel, Georgia State University and Behavioral Medicine Institute (unpublished).

15

Case Management and Prognosis of the Sex Offender

Gregory K. Lehne

INTRODUCTION

Various approaches have been taken to the case management of sex offenders. Criminal justice approaches primarily involve incarceration and/or supervision on parole or probation. Different approaches to rehabilitation have also been incorporated into criminal justice management of sex offenders. Psychological treatment methods may use combinations of individual and group therapy, educational programs, and cognitive and behavioral techniques. Relapse prevention, based upon treatments of addictions, is the latest approach being tried for the case management of sex offenders. Medical pharmacological approaches utilize medications to reduce sexual arousal and performance. Surgical castration has a similar effect but, being irreversible, is much disputed.

Do different approaches to the case management of sex offenders have different effects on recidivism, the likelihood that a sex offender will engage in a sexual (or other criminal) offense in the future? Does recidivism vary in relationship to the type of offense, or characteristics of the offender? Is there an interaction between offender characteristics and case management approaches which influences recidivism? The data to answer these questions remain largely unascertained (see Furby et al. 1989; Abel et al. 1993 for reviews of recent literature; and chapters 4 and 5 of this volume).

As these questions suggest, there are three classes of variables to be considered in evaluating case management and prognosis for sex offenders: type of sex offense, characteristics of the offender, and case management approaches, all in various combinations of interaction. The general outcome measure of concern is whether the sex offender subsequently engages in criminal sexual behavior (or any criminal behavior).

TYPES OF SEX OFFENSES

A sex offender is, by definition, an individual who has been criminally convicted as a result of engaging in sexual behavior in a situation which is proscribed by law. The specific types of sexual behavior that may be illegal vary according to the jurisdiction, historical period, and relationship with the victim. The criminal justice system classifies sex offenders according to the nature of their offense(s) and victim(s). The term "sex offender" is, therefore, strictly a legal term which does not describe any characteristics of an individual other than adjudication for a sex offense.

Recently, the *Crime Classification Manual* (*CCM*), a standardized system for classifying violent crimes, was developed through the support of the FBI's National Center for the Analysis of Violent Crime (Douglas et al. 1992). This classification system is gradually being introduced in the United States and other countries in the world to aid in compiling and comparing crime data and developing criminal personality profiles. This process was inspired by psychiatric classification, as exemplified in the *Diagnostic and Statistical Manual of Mental Disorders,* 3rd ed. (rev.) (*DSM-III-R*), published by the American Psychiatric Association (1987). The *CCM* was developed on the basis of the concept that different types of crimes are committed by criminals who manifest different personality characteristics. As this system is further developed and applied in forensic sexological research, it should be possible to develop more homogenous groupings of sex offenses and sex offenders. This is one indicator of the developing convergence of criminal justice and biomedical concepts of criminal sexual behavior (see Honey & Lehne 1983).

The *CCM* differentiates numerous types of *sexual homicide, rape* (criminal enterprise; entitlement; power-reassurance; exploitation; anger; sadism; abduction), *sexual assault* (nuisance offenses; domestic violence), *pornography, sex rings,* and *group sexual assault.* A subcategory of classification is whether the victim is a *child, adolescent,* or *adult.* Empirical data about offender characteristics have been used in compiling these categories of offense. However, the classification is based upon analysis of the characteristics of the offense and victim, rather than on an evaluation (with cooperation) of the offender.

In forensic practice and research, sex offenders are typically categorized as a unitary group differentiated from nonsex offenders. In some instances, sex offenders may be differentiated according to their type of offense. Part of the difficulty in interpreting and generalizing from the research literature on sex offenders is the lack of standardization in characterizing or defining the sample of sex offenders under study. Different studies rarely have indisputably comparable groups. Men convicted of "rape" or sexual assault, for example, may have engaged in very different types of sexual activities depending upon the laws in the jurisdiction at the time they were convicted. Sex with a 15-year-old girl, for example, might be included in the category of rape, or listed as a sexual offense against a minor, or be classified as incest or child abuse, or not be counted as a sexual offense at all, depending upon the legal jurisdiction, charging practice, and the age of the offender.

In the criminal justice system, sex offenders are sentenced or their cases managed according to the severity of their offense (in terms of its effect upon the victim), and in the interest of protecting the public from future offenses (although this implies a prognosis which may not be ascertainable with any scientific validity). General demographic criteria are commonly used in criminal justice policy as a factor in determining sentencing recommendations for case management. These criteria are not specific to sex offenses. They include age at time of first offense, number and seriousness of prior offenses, present age, employment, and marital status. Social class, racial and geographical differences, and the history of recidivism may also be related to the likelihood of being arrested, and to case management, and may affect how an individual is treated by the criminal justice system. Characteristics of the victim and offense (such as injury or use of a weapon) may also be part of the criteria used by the criminal justice system in developing case management recommendations for sex offenders.

CLASSIFICATION ACCORDING TO PSYCHOLOGICAL CRITERIA

Classification systems for sex offenders have been developed which are not based solely upon the criminal offense, but take into account some characteristics or hypothesized motivations of the offender. For example, men who rape have been classified according to the criteria of sexual motivation, anger, power, or opportunity (e.g., Groth & Birnbaum 1979). Sexual motivation might be differentiated as *fixated,* which means reflecting a primary sexual focus, or as *regressed,* which means being in association with contributory stressors. Some of these criteria have been incorporated into the *CCM.*

Presently, there is no consensus among mental health professionals regarding the defining criteria for the classification of sex offenders. However, there is some correspondence between a diagnosis of certain types of psychiatric disorder and certain crime classifications. For example, what the *CCM* describes as preferential offenses generally corresponds to what mental health professionals would consider behavioral evidence for the presence of a paraphilia.

Thus *CCM* preferential types of "Nuisance Offenses" include behaviors subsumed under *DSM-III-R* diagnostic categories of exhibitionism, voyeurism, and acts of fetishism. Likewise, *CCM*'s "Subordinate Rape, Child" is generally limited to acts committed by individuals who would be diagnosed as pedophiles. *CCM*'s "Power-Reassurance Rape" would include paraphilic rapists, while "Criminal Enterprise Rape" would include antisocial personality-disordered men, with men committing "Secondary Felony Rape" probably also being diagnosed as suffering from a sexual disorder.

Psychiatric diagnosis based upon the *DSM-III-R* may be used in developing case management recommendations in certain criminal justice decisions. Some sex offenders do have officially recognized psychiatric disorders, although many offenders do not. Because of this limitation, psychiatry may not be able to make recommendations for case management or prognosis for sex offenders who do not meet diagnostic criteria for psychiatric disorders. In all cases, psychiatric diagnosis must be based upon the evaluation of the offender. Psychiatric diagnosis cannot be inferred simply from an analysis of the offense, criminal charges, or convictions.

Some sex offenses are committed by men who suffer from sexual fixations, obsessions, or compulsions, which constitute psychiatric disorders. Men whose primary sexual interests are in prepubescent children may be diagnosed as suffering from the disorder of *pedophilia,* either heterosexual, homosexual or bisexual. Note that the medical definition of children is more limited than the legal definition, in that the medical definition does not include adolescence while the legal one does—up to age 18 depending on the jurisdiction. Men who compulsively expose their penis to female strangers, with no fantasies or behavior involving sexual contact with the victim, may be diagnosed as suffering from the disorder of *exhibitionism.*

There are sexological disorders and conditions that have been identified but are not presently listed in *DSM-III-R.* For example, Money (1986) and Money and Lamacz (1989) have described many more paraphilias than are listed in *DSM-III-R.* Other paraphilias are subject to controversy and excluded from *DSM-III-R* for political reasons, such as *paraphilic rapism* or *raptophilia.* This is a relatively rare disorder in which the individual is driven by sexual fixation, obsession, or compulsion to rape nonconsenting women, usually strangers, in serial succession. Money has broadened the concept of paraphilia significantly with his sexological conceptualization of lovemaps and vandalized lovemaps (Money and Lamacz 1989). Some paraphilic sexual offenses are an acting out of a developmentally vandalized and paraphilic lovemap, although the individual may not suffer from an officially recognized psychiatric disorder.

Various nonsexual psychiatric and personality disorders may be present in an individual who has committed a sex offense. For example, antisocial personality disorder may be diagnosed in men with a history of multiple illegal behaviors, including sex offenses. Alcoholism or substance abuse disorder may also occur in individuals who commit sex offenses. These disorders may influence the likelihood of committing an offense, and thus influence recidivism. The presence of these additional disorders requires different approaches to case management, such as combined psychotherapy and pharmacotherapy for a personality disorder or a substance addiction.

The research literature on personality characteristics of sex offenders fails to document any consistent relationship between sex offending and disordered personality characteristics or other psychopathology as measured by psychological tests (see Levin & Stava 1987 for a review of the literature). Thus, when psychological or psychiatric criteria are used with reference to case management for sex offenders, these criteria must be assessed or diagnosed for each individual offender, rather than inferred from the conviction for any specific sex offense.

It is important to note that there is no direct correspondence between legal definitions of sex offenses and psychiatric diagnoses. Sometimes the forensic psychiatric literature refers to the men who have been convicted of sexual behavior with juveniles as child molesters (not a psychiatric label) or pedophiles (a *DSM-III-R* psychiatric diagnosis). Yet it is possible that many of these men would not fulfill the psychiatric criteria for a diagnosis of pedophilia, in the sense of a preferred or exclusive sexual fixation and preoccupation with prepubescent children.

Forensic sexology continues to develop new conceptualizations of sexological conditions related to sex offenses that may not be defined as psychiatric disorders. Forensic sexology is not inherently a division of psychiatry. Many aspects of sexology relate to other branches of medicine or other professional disciplines. Some terms such as "power rapist" or "gang rape" or "date rape" are not psychiatric or medical concepts, and not scientifically sexological, but political and moral concepts. Sexological approaches to case management are being developed which are different from psychiatric management approaches. Sexology has its own specialized body of knowledge and evaluative and treatment techniques, such as Sexual Attitude Restructuring workshops or use of the penile plethysmograph.

CRIMINAL JUSTICE APPROACHES TO CASE MANAGEMENT

Criminal justice deals with the offender by utilizing deterrence, supervision on probation, incarceration and parole. In some jurisdictions, incarceration may occur in a special facility with programs for the rehabilitation of sex offenders. Several jurisdictions (Canada, for example, and the states of California, Florida, Massachusetts, and Washington in the U.S.) are notable for having established treatment programs for incarcerated sex offenders, and conducting followup programs on the effectiveness of correctional intervention.

Criminal justice approaches are concerned with recidivism. Thus, the basic unit of efficacy is whether the offender is arrested or convicted for a new offense committed after the adjudication of the prior offense. Recidivism may be based upon committing another sex offense, or committing any other type of criminal act which leads to arrest or conviction. The base-time period for recidivism does not include time awaiting sentencing or incarceration, but does include time while on parole or probation, and the period following. Sex offender recidivism research studies are reviewed by Furby et al. (1989).

Two to five years represents a minimum period for measuring recidivism. However, even this period of followup may be inadequate. For example, in Soothill & Gibbens' (1978) English study of adjudicated but untreated sex offenders, about 17 percent of the offenders had been rearrested for any criminal offense within their first two years in the community, increasing to about 25 percent by five years, and rising to nearly 50 percent having been rearrested for any offense by the twenty-fourth year of followup. General criminal recidivism occurred in more than 40 percent of convicted felons within three years of their release on supervised probation, according to recent U.S. Justice Department studies. However, in the majority of cases, the new offense was different from that of the prior conviction; for example percent only 3 percent of the rapists were charged with another rape within three years of release.

Several research studies have compared recidivism for treated and untreated sex offenders in states with treatment programs for mentally disordered sex offenders in the criminal justice system. Contrary to expectations, the untreated sex offenders often had recidivism rates as low or lower than the treated offenders. These studies were conducted with types of treatment programs no longer in general use, and differences in the offender groups and followup time make comparisons to present treatment programs and offender samples difficult (see Furby et al. 1989).

In one California study, "nonamenable" and consequently untreated sex offenders had a 12 percent recidivism rate compared to 21 percent for sex offenders released as cured (Dix 1976). Similar results were found in a different sample of child molesters, where after at least three years following release from prison, 11 percent of the untreated offenders had committed new sex offenses, compared to a 19 percent recidivism rate for the offenders released from the sex offender treatment program (Frisbie 1969). However, the untreated offenders had higher nonsexual recidivism (46 percent) compared to the treated offenders (31 percent).

Furby et al. (1989) compared recidivism in Florida criminal justice programs that provided incarceration with and without treatment. Sex offenders considered nonamenable to treatment had an 11 percent recidivism rate for sex offenses compared to 14 percent for offenders who had completed treatment, within a mean of thirty months of followup. However, the nontreated sex offenders had a higher recidivism rate for all offenses, 35 percent compared to 19 percent for the treated sex offenders. In another Florida study, there was no difference in recidivism (about 5 percent in the first year) for sex offenses between offenders treated in state hospitals and those held without treatment in correctional facilities.

A similar pattern of results was found for sex offenders on probation, who were randomly assigned to probation only or probation plus specialized group therapy. After a ten-year followup, the offenders on probation without treatment had a lower recidivism rate for sex offenses (7.2 percent) as compared to those offenders who received group therapy while on probation (13.6 percent) (J. J. Peters Institute 1980).

In summary, past programs that provided treatment through the criminal justice system have not demonstrated a reduction in ascertained sex offense recidivism (Furby et al. 1989). However, sex offenders treated through criminal justice programs may have lower rates of nonsexual recidivism than do untreated sex offenders. If earlier treatment programs did have an effect on recidivism, it was not specific for sex offenses. The inference may be drawn from these studies that more specific attention needs to be paid to the characteristics of the offenders as matched to the types of treatment that are offered.

Psychological Approaches to Sex Offender Treatment

From a psychological perspective, sex offenders do not constitute a unitary group, but rather are a collection of diverse individuals who have committed different, though possibly related, types of sexual offenses. The case management and prognosis for sex offenders is based upon an assessment of the characteristics of the offender, rather than the legal category of offense. Treatment is then specifically matched to the characteristics of the offenders. Treatment may be based upon psychiatric diagnostic categories, or it may be individualized as in types of cognitive-behavioral or relapse prevention treatment models.

One primary distinction for psychological case management of sex offenders is whether or not the sex offense is perpetrated by an individual suffering from a psychiatric disorder, namely paraphilia. The diagnosis of a psychiatric disorder must be based upon an evaluation of the offender; it cannot be based only upon the nature of the sex offense.

Psychological treatment models use the concept of relapse, instead of recidivism, when evaluating the effectiveness of treatment. A relapse is a recurrence of any of the primary symptoms associated with the diagnosed disorder or problem. Relapses vary in degree, and may not be expressed in the florid form of sex offense behavior resulting in legal charges. Thus a recurrence of certain types of sexual dreams, fantasies, masturbation, or thinking about behavior or situations related to a sex offense might be considered a relapse (depending upon treatment goals or approach), even if there is no overt sexual behavior involving a victim. Most paraphilic relapses would not correspond to criminal recidivism. Criminal recidivism involving a nonsex offense would not necessarily be considered a relapse or an indication that treatment was not effective.

Unfortunately, there are not yet effective techniques to consistently define and measure the frequency of relapses in sex offender populations. While self-report is generally used as a measurement of relapse in other areas of medicine and human behavior, it is not considered accurate in the evaluation of sex offenders. A lack of confidentiality in treatment and legal requirements for reporting suspected offenses have had a chilling effect on patients' self-reporting of relapses in most settings.

In psychological treatment, a certain frequency of relapse is tolerated, even expected, without indicating that treatment is ineffective. Relapses may provide information which is used to change the course or intensity of treatment. The potential seriousness or consequences of a relapse influence decisions about whether an individual can be treated in the community or in some more secure setting, such as a psychiatric hospital or criminal justice facility. Assessment of risk to self or others is an ongoing part of psychological treatment. Many psychiatric disorders are controlled or ameliorated, not cured.

There is an extensive literature on the treatment, case management and prognosis for a variety of psychiatric disorders as listed in the *DSM-III-R*. When these disorders are diagnosed in individuals who commit sex offenses, and are causally associated with the sex offense, then the treatment and prognosis would be highly similar to any other individual suffering from a similar disorder (see Berlin et al. in press). A sex offense, for example, may be committed by a person during a manic episode of a bipolar disorder, or during a psychotic episode in an individual suffering from schizophrenia. If the sex offense is a direct product of these psychiatric states, then the relevant literature on the management of manic episodes or psychotic episodes in individuals similarly diagnosed will provide the necessary information on management and prognosis. In these types of conditions medication may be necessary to maintain stable and nonoffending behavior. As long as there are no problems with medications, including compliance in taking them, behavior is usually well controlled.

Of particular concern is the case management of individuals who suffer from sexual disorders (mainly the paraphilias). Individuals with these disorders usually have obsessional thoughts and compulsive urges to engage in sexual behaviors of a highly specific type, such as involvement with children (pedophilia), or exposure of the genitals (exhibitionism), or rape (usually serial rape, as in paraphilic rapism). Since these disorders are chronic, there is a great likelihood that without treatment paraphilic individuals will repeat their offenses, or, with ineffective treatment, suffer a relapse.

The recent research literature on treatment of paraphilia has been reviewed by Abel et al. (1992). Other literature reviews include Kilmann et al. (1982) for earlier and small sample studies, Scharsch et al. (1990) for individual therapy, and chapters in Marshall et al. (1990) and Laws (1989).

In general, the psychological treatment literature is biased toward the publication of successful treatment outcomes, with most studies having inadequate controls or followup time. Treatment approaches have been changing, with practitioners being optimistic about the more recently developed methodologies. Psychoanalytic and psychodynamic approaches to individual therapy as a primary mode of treatment are considered to be ineffective. Attempts to "cure" individuals of sexual disorders by uncovering the origin of the disorder and to focus treatment on early life experiences have given way to approaches based upon alleviating symptoms or managing chronic sexual disorders.

Most current psychological treatment programs utilize group therapy as their primary method, with individual treatment or pharmacological treatment as an adjunct for specific cases. Treatment approaches are usually cognitive-behavioral. Treatment programs may use behavioral techniques to modify patterns of inappropriate sexual behavior, teach relevant social skills, identify and alter the cognitive distortions of the patients, and develop individualized plans for relapse prevention. While these approaches can be provided in individual treatment, group treatment when available tends to be more cost-effective. Some programs are time-limited, others vary in length of treatment according to presence of symptoms, and still other programs maintain patients in long-term therapeutic followup.

Some treatment programs have been developed specifically for groups of offenders with similar disorders or behavior patterns, such as exhibitionists, pedophiles, incest offenders or rapists. Treatment of sex offenses within families usually involves specific protocols that work on couple and family relationships, including rebuilding a new relationship with the incest victim, if appropriate. Otherwise, couple or family therapy is not a central component of most sex offender treatment programs, although it probably should be.

Abel et al. (1992) provide a good descriptive and evaluative overview of psychological therapies. Behavior therapies may assist individuals in reconditioning their pattern of arousal and acting out to include negative consequences (imagining bad things happening) or negative associations. Masturbatory reconditioning is incorporated into some programs, to help the individual masturbate only to nonoffending sexual imagery (see review by

Laws & Marshall 1991). Many sex offenders have deficits in social skills, assertiveness, or sex education and healthy sexual functioning (Abel et al. 1984). Educational and prosocial behavior development activities may be incorporated into treatment, based upon individual needs assessment. Distorted thinking about sex offenses and victims is common among sex offenders. Corrective therapeutic experiences could include cognitive restructuring, confronting and challenging distortions, role play reversals, and activities developing awareness of victims' perspectives (Murphy 1990).

In evaluating treatment effectiveness, there are difficulties because different types of offenders may have different relapse or recidivism rates without treatment. For example, incest offenders tend to have low recidivism rates (4–10 percent), while exhibitionists often have high recidivism rates (41–71 percent). Recidivism rates for pedophiles (10–40 percent) and rapists (7–35 percent) vary greatly between studies (see Marshall & Barbaree 1990). In the research literature, almost never is an untreated control group used, and followup time is inadequate, so there is no benchmark for evaluating treatment effectiveness compared to nontreatment. The literature tends to report outcomes for programs that are deemed successful. But programs also change over time, so that results from previous studies cannot be generalized to new or developing treatment protocols. The results of programs in general also cannot be easily generalized to specific cases. The present state of knowledge is that the effectiveness of treatment cannot be predicted for any individual sex offender. There is a growing body of knowledge on the different therapeutic components which might be incorporated into a treatment program, and the effectiveness or lack of effectiveness of some of those components (see Abel et al. 1992).

Representative recent outcome studies of cognitive-behavioral programs deemed successful are reviewed by Abel et al. (1992). Studies usually report recidivism outcomes, rather than relapse frequencies and characteristics. Despite the use of the concept of relapse in psychology, there is virtually no research literature dealing with relapse frequencies among sex offenders.

Some programs were conducted while the offenders were incarcerated, and these programs tend to use a similar treatment model for all types of sex offenders. Gordon (1989) followed a mixed group of Canadian sex offenders for two to seven years after their release from a cognitive-behavioral program, and reported only a 10 percent recidivism rate. Relapse prevention techniques were incorporated into a California State Hospital program, and the recidivism rate was 8 percent in the first year following release for a mixed group of sex offenders (Marques et al. 1989). Pithers et al. (1989) reported different recidivism rates according to offender category, within their prison-based relapse prevention program. They reported only 3 percent recidivism for pedophiles, but 20 percent recidivism for rapists, with six years of followup.

Community-based programs for sex offenders show different recidivism rates within the same types of programs, according to offense groups. With periods of followup variable, but longer than one year, Maletzky (1987) found different recidivism rates according to offense types: molesters of girls (5 percent), molesters of boys (14 percent), rapists (26 percent), and exhibitionists (7 percent—one of the lowest rates in the literature). This program was cognitive-behavioral and also used medication in some cases. Exhibitionists had the highest recidivism rate (48 percent) in Marshall and Barbaree's (1990) report on their cognitive-behavioral program in Canada. They reported much lower recidivism for men who molested their own children (8 percent), girls outside the family (18 percent), or boys (13 percent), with followup time ranging from one to ten years.

Relapse prevention is the newest approach to psychological treatment for sex offenders (Abel et al. 1992; Laws 1989; Marshall et al. 1990). Essentially the specifics of relapse prevention are highly individualized for each offender according to his pattern of acting out sexual behavior, identifying the progression he goes through which leads to acting out of inappropriate sexual behavior, and then developing individualized techniques for monitoring and modifying that progression. Relapse prevention is not based upon psychiatric diagnostic categories or offense types, but operates on the basis of a model that assumes a general human tendency to repeat prior patterns of sexually motivated behavior.

Relapse prevention should be differentiated from treatment approaches based upon the concept of sexual addiction and the use of community-based twelve-step self-help groups (Carnes 1989; 1990). Research is not available which validates the conceptualization of human sexuality as an addiction, or the effectiveness of this approach for controlling sexual behavior. While individuals may find this approach useful, as they do for alcoholism and drug dependency, it has not achieved verified effectiveness sufficient to recommend it for forensic applications. The criminal justice system's experience with Alcoholics Anonymous programs cannot be generalized at this time to requiring participation in Sexaholics Anonymous or other such types of group as part of sentencing for sexual behavior offenses.

Medical and Pharmacological Treatments

Medical and pharmacological treatments for sex offenders utilize either medication or, much less frequently, surgical castration to alter the balance of sex-regulating hormones in the body. A lowered sex drive then facilitates individual control over sexual behavior. Despite evidence of the effectiveness of these methods of treatment, they are not often utilized in the criminal justice system. Ethical and political considerations have made courts leery of requiring them as part of case management.

Pharmacological treatments for sex offenders are typically combined with psychological treatments. The pharmacological intervention lowers the sex drive, making it easier for the offender to control his sexual behavior while he continues to take the medication. This increases public safety when offenders are treated in the community. In some cases offenders may be on pharmacological treatment for long periods of time. Although medication does not cure or resolve the sexual problem permanantly, it may ameliorate the problem's manifestations..

The effectiveness of pharmacological treatment, and problems with side effects, must be specifically determined for each patient and each medication. There are two types of hormonal treatment, one with steroidal antiandrogens, and the other with neuropeptides that suppress hypothalmic-pituitary regulation of androgen secretion from the testicles. Neuropeptide treatment for sex offenders is new and relatively untried. One antiandrogenic steroid is cyproterone acetate (Androcur), available only in Europe. The other, medroxyprogesterone, MPA (Depo-Provera) is used in the United States.

Medroxyprogesterone acetate is a synthetic progestenic hormone which operates, in part, by calming sexual regulatory centers in the hypothalmus of the brain (Lehne 1988; Money 1970; 1987; Michael & Zumpe 1993). It is also an antiandrogen which, like cyproterone acetate, acts by lowering the circulating testosterone level and its cellular uptake to that of prepuberty (Bradford 1985, 1990). In general, antiandrogenic treatments appear to be quite effective in virtually eliminating relapses while patients are receiving the medication. But when patients are not receiving adequate doses of medication, or when medication is discontinued, recidivism rates increase. Thus, medication can be useful for facilitating living in the community, but its effectiveness has been established only during the period of active treatment. Longer-term recidivism rates, after the patient is off medication, appear more related to other aspects of the treatment programs.

The treatment programs of the Sexual Disorders Clinic, formerly at the Johns Hopkins Hospital, combined the use of medroxyprogesterone acetate (Depo-Provera) with group therapy for 40 percent of its patients (see Berlin et al. 1991). Treatment effectiveness was influenced by long-term compliance with the treatment program. Relapses and recidivism were tracked both while patients were in the outpatient treatment program, and also following discharge under conditions of compliance or noncompliance. Recidivism differed for three groups, pedophiles (7.4 percent), exhibitionists (23.4 percent), and a diagnostically mixed group of sexual aggressives (4.6 percent), with the mean period at risk for recidivism being about five years. Recidivism rates for treatment-compliant groups of patients were about half the rates for the whole group. Data on patients receiving medication were not analyzed separately, since the use of medication was based upon diagnosis and was an integral part of the treatment program.

In some case reports, different types of psychotropic medications, such as anti-anxiety, antidepressant, or antipsychotic medications, have been used in the treatment of individual sex offenders. These cases are distinct from those in which primary nonsex-offending psychiatric diagnoses alone justified the use of those medications. The published case reports are biased toward reportedly successful outcomes. However, not enough data are available yet on the effectiveness of these types of treatment with medication to support their more widespread use in forensic settings.

Castration has been used in Europe, although rarely, mainly in Germany and Scandinavia, to reduce recidivism in sex offenders. Although there are criticisms of this research literature (see Heim & Hursch 1979), the general findings are of low recidivism rates of 3–5 percent even with long followup periods (see Sturup 1960; Ortmann 1980; Wille & Beier 1989). Noncastrated comparison groups had recidivism rates as high as 50 percent. Castrates seemed to be relatively satisfied with their lives, and better socially adjusted than the noncastrates. For political and ethical reasons, castration is rarely recommended forensically in North America. Individuals who are castrated typically have not been required to participate in any other type of case management for their sexual behavior.

CONCLUSION

Forensic sexology is developing into a specialty in which it may be possible in the future to specify recommendations for case management for specific subgroups of sex offenders. Clearly, reliance on incarceration alone does not keep sex offenders from recidivating while they are in the community.

Recidivism rates vary according to the type of offense and offender. Due to difficulties in classifying sex offenses and sex offenders, recidivism data are inaccurate or difficult to interpret. However, it does appear that incest perpetrators have generally lower recidivism rates, while recidivism varies for other types of child sexual offenses. There are great variations in recidivism for men convicted of rape. Exhibitionists in general appear to have higher recidivism rates.

Treatment programs vary in their effectiveness, with many past programs not demonstrating a significant reduction in sex offense recidivism compared to untreated offenders. However, it is not yet possible to generalize from research findings to make specific predictions for any specific offender or any particular approach to case management. Generalized psychotherapy approaches, such as psychoanalytic or psychodynamically oriented individual psychotherapy, are not considered effective.

Standardized classification and reporting of sexual offenses, such as that based upon the system developed for the *CCM,* should facilitate the collection of more consistent and interpretable criminal data in the future, although such a taxonomy may be more reflective of a criminologic perspective than a biomedical one. Treatment and research programs should describe and analyze their populations in ways that permit comparisons and generalizations. Followup periods of at least two years, and preferably five years, are necessary to assess the effectiveness of different case management approaches. Use of the concept of relapse, rather than recidivism, requires the development of new approaches to evaluation and data collection. Problems related to the possible unreliability of self-report data, and the limitations related to the lack of confidentiality in some treatment settings, will need to be resolved.

While many sex offenders do not have psychiatric disorders, the more sexually compulsive offenders probably do suffer from paraphilias. Psychiatric disorders, including the paraphilias, need specialized treatment, including medication in some cases, for maximum treatment effectiveness. The field of sexology is broader than sexual psychiatry, and will need to incorporate the concept of psychiatric disorders as well as other conceptual categories for working with sex offenders. New treatment approaches that are not based strictly upon psychiatric diagnostic categories, such as relapse prevention, offer promise for the future.

REFERENCES

Abel, G. G.; Becker, J. V.; Cunningham-Rathner, J.; Rouleau, J. L.; Kaplan, M.; and Reich, J. (1984). *The Treatment of Child Molesters.* Atlanta, Ga.: Behavioral Medicine Institute of Atlanta.

Abel, G. G.; Osborn, C.; Anthony, D.; and Gardos, P. (1992). "Current Treatments of Paraphiliacs." *Annual Review of Sex Research* 3: 255–90.

American Psychiatric Association. (1987) *Diagnostic and Statistical Manual of Mental Disorders.* 3rd ed., rev. Washington, D.C.: Author.

Berlin, F. S.; Hunt, W. P.; Malin, H. M.; Dyer, A.; Lehne, G.; and Dean, S. (1991). "A Five-Year Plus Follow-Up Survey of Criminal Recidivism within a Treated Cohort of 406 Pedophiles, 111 Exhibitionists and 109 Sexual Aggressives: Issues and Outcome." *American Journal of Forensic Psychiatry* 12: 5–28.

Berlin, F. S.; Malin, H. M.; and Lehne, G. (in press). "The Eroticized Violent Crime: Special Treatment Issues." In L. J. Hertzberg, ed., *Violent Behavior,* vol. 2. Costa Mesa, Calif.: AMA Pub.

Bradford, J. M. W. (1990). "The Antiandrogen and Hormonal Treatment of Sex Offenders." In W. L. Marshall, D. R. Laws, and H. E. Barabee, eds., *Handbook of Sexual Assault,* pp. 297–310. New York: Plenum.

———. (1985). "Organic Treatments for the Male Sex Offender." *Behavioral Sciences and the Law* 3, no. 4: 355–75.

Carnes, P. (1989). *Contrary to Love: Helping the Sexual Addict.* Minneapolis, Minn.: CompCare.

——— (1990). "Sexual Addiction: Progress, Criticism, Challenges." *American Journal of Preventive Psychiatry and Neurology* 2, no. 3: 1–8.

Dix, G. E. (1976). "Determining the Continued Dangerousness of Psychologically Abnormal Sex Offenders." *Journal of Psychiatry and the Law* 3: 327–44.

Douglas, J. E.; Burgess, A. W.; Burgess, A. G.; and Ressler, R. K. (1992). *Crime Classification Manual.* New York: Lexington.

Frisbie, L. V. (1969). *Another Look at Sex Offenders in California. Mental Health Research Monograph,* No. 12. Sacramento: State of California, Department of Mental Hygiene.

Furby, L.; Weinrott, H. R.; and Blackshaw, L. (1989). "Sex Offender Recidivism: A Review." *Psychological Bulletin* 105: 3–30.

Gordon, A. (1989). "Research on Sex Offenders: Regional Psychiatric Centre (Prairies)." *Forum on Correctional Research* 1: 2021.

Groth, A. N., and Birnbaum, H. J. (1979). *Men Who Rape: The Psychology of the Offender.* New York: Plenum.

Heim, N., and Hursch, C. J. (1979). "Castration for Sex Offenders: Treatment or Punishment? A Review and Critique of Recent European Literature." *Archives of Sexual Behavior* 8: 281–304.

J. J. Peters Institute. (1980). *A Ten-Year Follow-Up of Sex Offender Recidivism.* Philadelphia: Author.

Kilmann, P. R.; Sabalis, R. F.; Gearing, M. L., II; Bukstel, L. H.; and Scovern, A. W. (1982). "The Treatment of Sexual Paraphilias: A Review of the Outcome Research." *The Journal of Sex Research* 18: 193–252.

Laws, D. R., ed. (1989). *Relapse Prevention with Sex Offenders.* New York: Guilford.

Laws, D. R., and Marshall, W. L. (1991). "Masturbatory Reconditioning with Sexual Deviates: An Evaluative Review." *Advances in Behavior Research and Therapy* 13: 13–25.

Lehne, G. (1988). "Treatment of Sex Offenders with Medroxyprogesterone Acetate." In *Pharmacology and Endocrinology of Sexual Function,* pp. 516–25. Vol. 6 of J. M. A. Sitsen, ed., *Handbook of Sexology.* Amsterdam: Elsevier.

Levin, S. M., and Stava, L. (1987). "Personality Characteristics of Sex Offenders: A Review." *Archives of Sexual Behavior* 16: 57–79.

Marques, J. D.; Day, D. M.; Nelson, C.; and Miner, M. H. (1989). *The Sex Offender Treatment and Evaluation Project, Third Report to the Legislative in Response to PC 1365.* Sacramento, Calif.: California State Department of Mental Health.

Marshall, W. L., and Barabee, H. E. (1990). "Outcome of Comprehensive Cognitive-Behavioral Treatment Programs." In W. L. Marshall, D. R. Laws, and H. E. Barabee, eds., *Handbook of Sexual Assault,* pp. 363–85. New York: Plenum.

Marshall, W. L.; Laws, D. R.; and Barbaree, H. E., eds. (1990). *Handbook of Sexual Assault: Issues, Theories, and Treatment of the Offender.* New York: Plenum.

Michael, R. P., and Zumpe, D. (1993). "Medroxyprogesterone Acetate Decreases the Sexual Activity of Male Cynomolgus Monkeys (*Macaca fascicularis*): An Action on the Brain?" *Physiology and Behavior* 53: 783–88.

Money, J. (1970). "Use of an Androgen-Depleting Hormone in the Treatment of Male Sex Offenders." *Journal of Sex Research* 6: 165–72.

—— (1986). *Lovemaps: Clinical Concepts of Sexual/Erotic Health and Pathology, Paraphilia and Gender Transpositions in Childhood, Adolescence and Maturity.* New York: Irvington.

—— (1987). "Treatment Guidelines: Antiandrogen and Counseling of Paraphilic Sex Offenders." *Journal of Sex and Marital Therapy* 13: 219–23.

Money, J., and Lamacz, M. (1989). *Vandalized Lovemaps: Paraphilic Outcome of Seven Cases in Pediatric Sexology.* Buffalo, N.Y.: Prometheus Books.

Money, J., and Lehne, G. K. (1983). "Biomedical and Criminal-Justice Concepts of Paraphilia: Developing Convergence." *Medicine and Law* 2: 257–61.

Murphy, W. D. (1990). "Assessment and Modification of Cognitive Distortions in Sex Offenders." In W. L. Marshall, D. R. Laws, and H. E. Barabee, eds., *Handbook of Sexual Assault*, pp. 331–42. New York: Plenum.

Ortmann, J. (1980). "The Treatment of Sexual Offenders, Castration and Antihormonal Therapy." *International Journal of Law and Psychiatry* 3: 443–51.

Pithers, W. D.; Martin, G. R.; and Cumming, G. F. (1989). "Vermont Treatment Program for Sexual Aggressors." In D. R. Laws, ed., *Relapse Prevention with Sex Offenders*, pp. 292–310. New York: Guilford.

Scharsch, E.; Galedary, G.; Haag, A.; Hauch, M.; and Lohse, H. (1990). *Sex Offenders.* New York: Springer-Verlag.

Soothill, K. L., and Gibbens, T. C. N. (1978). "Recidivism of Sexual Offenders." *British Journal of Criminology* 18: 267–76.

Sturup, G. (1960). "Sex Offenses: The Scandinavian Experience." In M. Shimm, ed., *Law and Contemporary Problems*, pp. 361–75. Durham, N.C.: Duke University Press.

Wille, R., and Beier, K. M. (1989). "Castration in Germany." *Annals of Sex Research* 2: 103–133.

Part Three

Public Policy, Sexology, and the Law

Introduction

The main premise of this section is that sexology has much to contribute to the debate about the appropriate role of government, the law, and public policy in legislating and regulating the private sexual behavior of its citizenry. Donald Mosher sets the stage for this debate with his analysis of the foundations of a moral law which is based on reason rather than dogmatic moralizing founded on intolerance of diversity. By advocating the existence of a moral imperative for the individual exercise of sexual rights, Mosher reframes the debate as one which challenges government to restrict its role to one justified by preventing actual harm to individuals, and by establishing a right to sexual expression within a moral code of conduct with expressly stated values. The dividing line between individual and social rights is not static but historically mutable—it is different now than before the advent of HIV/AIDS, for example.

James Krivacska elaborates on these principles by providing an argument for rethinking the role of sexuality in our lives from childhood onward. He discusses the assumptions, or lay theories, which currently guide social policy and decision making on both a governmental and an individual level. He then offers an alternative set of assumptions logically derived from rational theories from which societal policy may be constructed so as to promote normophilic development throughout childhood and into adulthood. The expressed intent of sex-positive child rearing practices and social policies is to prevent the formation and expression of paraphilias that plague contemporary society and impair the mental health of its citizenry.

Ferrel M. Christensen jumps head-on into the debate over pornography and its relationship to societal problems such as rape and sexual violence. He challenges research purporting to show a positive relationship by critiquing its methodology and conclusions, as well as by summarizing the overwhelming evidence to the contrary. He strengthens his argument with a reasoned attack on society's perception of sex, and therefore on its depiction of sex as pathological, degrading, and demeaning, especially of women.

Philip Meredith draws upon past and current perceptions of sexuality in Western society to shed light on the debate over sexuality education, contraception, and abortion policy, demonstrating how the trends of the last fifty years have impact on social policy, legislation, and regulation in these areas, particularly in Great Britain.

Detailing the psychological sequelae of HIV infection and subsequent manifestation of AIDS, Herman Sno reframes the nature of this disease as a threat to our humanity; in this way, he helps to force the debate on the response to AIDS away from a position of moral posturing and moral condemnation. His research into the psychological costs of AIDS serves as another justification for legal and public policy initiatives that will promote AIDS prevention and secure the human rights of those infected.

This section includes also two general discussions of the status of sexology and the role of government with respect to the sexual lives of its citizenry in two societies that have remained, for nearly half a century, closed to the scrutiny of the international scientific community. Fang-fu Ruan provides an overview of sex policy in Communist China and some recent moves toward liberalization in that politically still very closed society. A. A. Tkachenko similarly gives a glimpse into the wasteland of sexological research characteristic of the former Soviet Union, as well as into the new-found anticipation and excitement born in the wake of the dissolution of the former Communist state.

Ralph Underwager and Hollida Wakefield, and Paul Okami close the debate over the role of sexology in forensic endeavors. Underwager reviews a 1993 Supreme Court decision incorporating the principles of Sir Karl Popper's philosophy of science—specifically, falsifiability as the essential element of a scientific theory—into legal standards of admissibility of expert testimony. He analyzes the potential impact of this decision on the role of the expert in legal proceedings, and draws some surprising conclusions. Okami exposes the tendency for professionals, including sexologists, to become manipulated and used by the political system they hope to influence, and decries the devaluation of empirical science in favor of social advocacy as the driving force of contemporary social science.

In his epilogue, Jerome Miller reminds sexologists of their responsibility as scientists and cautions them against an unholy alliance with the legal establishment. For Miller, the adversarial principle of the law is incompatible with the prevention principle of biomedical science. Such alliances serve neither system, and have failed to impact on the incidence of paraphilias in the general population. Moreover, such alliances compromise the therapeutic relationship and are evidence of an abandonment of the ethical traditions of the helping professions.

16

Public Policy and Sex Offenses: Social Tolerance versus Criminalization

Donald L. Mosher

There is a moving and welcome humility in the conception that society should not be asked to give its reason for refusing to tolerate what in its heart it feels is intolerable. (A journalist's response to Sir Patrick Devlin's Maccabaean lecture on "The Enforcement of Morals.")

I am afraid we are less humble than we used to be. We once burnt old women because, without giving our reasons, we felt in our hearts that witchcraft was intolerable. (A second journalist's rejoinder, both quoted by H. L. A. Hart 1959/1988: 51)

INFORMING PUBLIC POLICY

Public policy entails governmental action designed to achieve its purposes. These purposes can vary from liberal to conservative, from promoting human welfare to maintaining law and social order. Policy making requires the review of information, including scientific information, to determine appropriate action. A public policy often allocates governmental resources as one means of achieving its ends. It puts its money where its values are.

Without question, public policy making is a complex social and political process. Nonetheless, public policy is best informed at the conceptual intersection of moral and political philosophy with science. Both conceptual clarity and factual discovery are necessary to inform public policy; it is, however, currently formed by pragmatists, who are neither philosophers nor scientists but rather concerned with the practical use of law and the practical role of government in promoting its purposes.

An old argument concerns the proper role of government in regulating sexual conduct. Some "sex offenses" make up a portion of the so-called offenses against morality. Much of the argument centers on whether sexual acts historically characterized as "immoral" and "offensive," such as fornication, adultery, sodomy, and homosexuality, should be criminalized and penalized by the law or tolerated by society when they do not harm others.

If public policy is concerned with a practical wisdom for solving the social problem of sexual moral offenses, then reasoned argument from empirical evidence has its place within the context of publicly announced value stances. At their best, the input of sexologists will be theory-driven; empirically persuasive; and embedded in historical, social, cultural, and ethical contexts. But ultimately, practical wisdom is based upon the rationality, impartiality, and morality of the polity and its policy makers. Experts can inform the public without manipulating it whenever such experts acknowledge their values as well as their facts, while seeking to educate, even to persuade, by reasoned argument.

As a citizen, the sexologist can best influence other citizens by arguing within the context of an educative discourse that can be both understood and questioned by fellow citizens. Lacking the coercive power of government, sexology's task is persuasion, using reasoned argument and empirical data.

Adopting a liberal and humanistic stance, the argument presented in this chapter favors true tolerance instead of the criminalization of so-called sex offenses. According to the philosopher J. Budziszewski (1992), true tolerance is a virtue, a complex disposition of character that aids in the art of knowing when and how to tolerate, including the developed ability to distinguish good moral rules from bad, and to make judgments when there are no rules or apparently contradictory rules about what can be tolerated. True tolerance requires distinguishing morality from mores, conformity from good character, and traditional moral values from a critical morality. While recognizing that practical wisdom and many other virtues are to be cultivated by society, the tolerant person also recognizes that a wide variety of sexual choices, lifestyles, and cultures can be consistent with a critical morality.

FRAMING THE ARGUMENT

The epigraphs from the two journalists frame the issue of the enforcement of morals through the criminalization of nonharmful sex offenses. On the one hand, the conservative moralist believes that the affects of moral indignation, repugnance, and disgust justify intolerance and criminalization of certain sexual acts. On the other hand, the liberal fears any irrational cruelty that is justified as necessary for the enforcement of sexual morals.

While believing that moral considerations do indeed justify the criminal law, the liberal also believes that not all traditional moral considerations can be used to justify the criminal law. Public policy must be founded upon moral principles, but not all moralistic and paternalistic principles are worthy of the name "moral." To found public policy about so-called sexual moral offenses on moralistic and paternalistic grounds is to justify a cruel infringement by government upon personal freedom. It is to immorally justify intolerance through criminalization of sexual choices and lifestyles.

THE DEBATE ON MORALITY AND THE LAW

Harms to Persons or the Enforcement of Morals?

If certain sexual conduct is considered immoral by religious or traditional moral standards, is that sufficient warrant to justify making that conduct punishable by the law?

In *On Liberty,* John Stuart Mill (1859/1986) argued:

> The only purpose for which power can rightfully be exercised over any member of a civilized community against his will is to prevent harm to others. (p. 16)

Mill contrasted this liberty-limiting principle of *harm to others* with government coercion and public disapproval that is justified either paternally—as being for one's own good—or morally—as preserving one's own morality. Mill said:

> He cannot rightfully be compelled to do or forbear because it will be better for him to do so, because it will make him happier, because in the opinions of others, to do so would be wise or even right. (ibid.)

In assuming a liberal position, Mill placed a high value on the primacy of freedom of expression and the defense of personal autonomy. For Mill, it was not enough for the ordinary person to feel offended at the mere thought of someone else engaging in sexual acts that were conventionally regarded as immoral; instead, the offended person must demonstrate that the sexual acts have interfered with the real interests of persons. Otherwise, as David Richards (1986) indicated:

> . . . conventional morality mandates legal and social prohibitions that narrow the range of permissible actions to those simply of the most unquestioned popular prejudices based on crass stereotypes, elementary failures of moral and human imagination, and group ignorance and bigotry. (p. 238)

Mill's harm principle restricted the scope of the criminal law to acts that may be properly made criminal *only if they inflict concrete harms on assignable persons.* It excludes as improper either criminalizing an act *solely* on the ground of preventing harm to the actor or because the mere thought of it gives offense to others.

With Mill and moral offenses in the law in mind, James Fitzjames Stephen (1873, 1967) rejoined:

> There are acts of wickedness so gross and outrageous that . . . [protection of others apart], they must be prevented at any cost to the offender and punished if they occur with exemplary severity. (p. 163)

Severe punishment is warranted, so the argument goes, because its threat deters immoral conduct and erases past evils. In the skeptical words of Joel Feinberg (1988):

> Thus, punishment, it is said, contributes to the intrinsic value of the universe in two ways: by canceling out past sins and preventing future ones. (p. 59)

From the liberal perspective, without a *victim* who has been unjustly harmed, "setting things straight" has no plausible intuitive meaning.

In England, the argument continued in the twentieth century following the submission of the 1957 Wolfenden Report on Homosexual Offenses and Prostitution. The Wolfenden Report proposed that homosexuality no longer be considered a legal offense because of the importance of freedom of choice and action in matters of private morality.

In rejoinder to Wolfenden, Sir Patrick Devlin gave his 1959 Maccabaean lecture on "the enforcement of morals." Devlin (1965/1988) argued that there was indeed a *public* morality, because society was composed of a web of moral ideas whose common bondage held the social order together. He claimed that society, moreover, had a right to make judgments on morals because a recognized morality was as necessary to society as a recognized government. Society can rightly protect itself from the *public* danger of sexual immorality that exploits human weakness, said Devlin, just as it can justly protect itself from treason or political subversion. Not everything is to be tolerated, according to Devlin, when the majority feels "a real feeling of reprobation" at the practice (or at the thought of the practice). Devlin argued, "No society can do without intolerance, indignation, and disgust; they are the forces behind the moral law . . ." (p. 27).

One hundred years after Mill, H. L. A. Hart (1959/1988) championed Mill's Harm Principle in response to Devlin. Hart saw Devlin as advocating *legal moralism,* a belief that enforcing sexual morality was part of the business of law. First, Hart distinguished "positive [conventional] morality," the morality actually accepted and shared by a given social group, from "critical morality," the moral principles used in criticizing existing social institutions, including positive morality. Second, Hart argued that the call for the enforcement of positive morality required justification because of two *prima facie* objectionable outcomes: (1) actual punishment would deprive individuals of liberty, and (2) the coercive threat of legal punishment would restrict the *prima facie* value of free choice—to experiment with living—and would create a special form of suffering for those whose sexual desires were so frustrated. Finally, for Hart, the distinction between positive and critical morality made clear that the argument is about *which* morality to enforce—one based upon legal moralism or one based upon the harm principle.

For Hart, the flaw in Devlin's approach is the faulty comparison between the suppression of sexual immorality and the suppression of treason or subversive activity, because the former is "private" and the latter is "public." Hart states:

> But it is grotesque, even where moral feeling against homosexuality is up to concert pitch, to think of homosexual behavior of two adults in private as in any way like treason or sedition either in intention or effect. (p. 51)

Morality and Liberty-Limiting Principles

In four volumes on the moral limits of the criminal law, Joel Feinberg addressed the question, "What sorts of conduct may the state rightly make criminal?" Feinberg defended the liberal position that the harm and offense principles, duly clarified and qualified, exhaust the class of good reasons for criminal prohibitions.

The Harm Principle

According to Feinberg (1984), the extreme liberal position accepts only the Harm Principle:

> It is always a good reason in support of penal legislation that it would probably be effective in preventing (eliminating, reducing) harms to persons other than the actor (the one prohibited from acting) *and* there is probably no other means that is equally effective at no greater costs to other values. (p. 26)

Feinberg writes, "Where coercive law stops, there liberty begins" (p. 7). By this, he means to distinguish both *duties* that are required and punishable by law and *crimes* that are prohibited and punishable by law from a zone that is free of legal coercion, where the citizen has a moral claim to be *at liberty to do or to forbear doing.*

In clarifying the harm principle as a morally legitimate liberty-limiting (or coercion-legitimating) principle, Feinberg indicated that an *act of harming* is the object of criminal law. A "harm" was defined as a "setback of interests." The Harm Principle is concerned with harms that are simultaneously *wrongful setbacks*: either setbacks of interests that are wrongs or wrongs that are setbacks to interests.

"Interests" were defined as the *welfare interests* (e.g., the continuance of life, health, and normal functioning of the body and mind, minimal income, a tolerable environment) which are the minimal and necessary generalized means to all focal aims, because when one's welfare is set back, so too are the ultimate ends or interests of any citizen, whatever they might be.

Not everything that we dislike or wish to avoid is harmful in this sense. Harm as a setback of interests must be distinguished from tolerable *hurts or offenses* that are temporary and passing. The harm principle requires some concept of normalcy, so that the actor is not prevented from normal activities that might create more than temporary and tolerable hurt or offense in an individual with an abnormal susceptibility. According to Feinberg:

> It is the person of normal vulnerability whose interests are to be protected by coercive power; the person, who figuratively speaking, can be blown over by a sneeze cannot demand that other people's vigorous but normally harmless activities be suspended by government power. (1984: 50)

To *set back* an interest is to reverse its progress, creating a worse condition. To set back an interest includes: to *impede* an interest, slowing or delaying its advancement; to *thwart* (or block or frustrate) an interest, stopping its progress without reversing it; to *defeat* an interest, irrevocably and conclusively putting it to utter rout; and, to *doom* an interest, foreordaining its defeat from the beginning.

Thus, Feinberg argues that A harms B when: A acts in a manner that is defective or faulty in respect to the risks it creates for B, with intention to produce the consequences that follow, or similarly adverse ones, or with negligence and recklessness in respect to those consequences, and A's acting in the moment is neither excusable nor justifiable, and A's action is the cause of the setback to B's interest, which is also a violation of B's rights (Feinberg 1984: 105–106).

A right is a valid claim. To wrong someone is to act in such a way as to violate his or her rights. Many rights are double claims against an individual as *moral rights* and against the state as *legal rights* to force performance to insure protection by threats against unwarranted interference from others. But, according to Feinberg:

> When legally enforceable claims are arbitrary and supported for no [morally valid] reasons (for example, a slaveowner's right to beat and starve his slave), they are *legal rights merely*. (1984: 110, original italics).

From the perspective of a critical morality, the moral limits of the criminal law do not encompass the right to limit sexual freedom by coercive laws whenever sexual conduct does not create harm (or offense, duly clarified and qualified). Such laws, against fornication and sodomy for example, are *merely* legal, while being immoral and coercive transgressions by government into the moral rights of citizens. As Feinberg puts it:

> Given the inherent costs of criminalization, when a particular legal prohibition oversteps the limits of moral legitimacy, it is itself a serious moral crime. (1984: 4)

The Offense Principle

Feinberg's (1985) Offense Principle states:

> It is always a good reason in support of a proposed criminal prohibition that it is probably necessary to prevent serious offense (as opposed to injury or harm) to persons other than the actor and that it is probably a necessary means to that end. (p. 1)

Feinberg is using "offense" in a general sense to refer to the whole miscellany of universally disliked mental states (disgust, shame, hurt, shock to moral sensibilities, and the like), and in a normative sense to refer to those states only when caused by the wrongful (right-violating) conduct of others. Feinberg warns of the great caution required in responding to claims of offense. He writes, "Offensive behavior as such is no kind of menace, but at its worst only severely irritating nuisance" (p. 5).

Following the model of "nuisance" laws, Feinberg proposed that legislators apply a balancing test to proposed legislation that would limit offensive conduct: weigh the seriousness of offense caused to unwilling witnesses against the reasonableness of the offender's conduct.

According to Feinberg:

> The seriousness of the offensiveness would be determined by (1) the intensity and durability of the repugnance produced, and the extent to which repugnance could be anticipated to be the general reaction of strangers to conduct displayed or represented (conduct offensive only to persons with an abnormal susceptibility to offense would not count as *very* offensive); (2) the ease with which unwilling witnesses can avoid the offensive displays; and (3) whether or not the witnesses have willingly assumed the risk of being offended either through curiosity or the anticipation of pleasure. (1985: 26, original italics)

Feinberg continues:

> These factors would be weighed as a group against the reasonableness of the offending party's conduct as determined by (1) its personal importance to the actors themselves and its social value generally, remembering always the enormous social utility of unhampered expression (in those cases where expression is involved); (2) the availability of alternative times and places where the conduct in question would cause less offense; (3) the extent, if any, to which the offense is caused by spiteful motives. (p. 26)

Liberal principles cannot support a criminal prohibition against private (unwitnessed) and harmless conduct on the ground that some "morally sensitive" person needs protection from "a real feeling of reprobation" at the bare knowledge that some "immoral" sexual conduct might be taking place somewhere behind drawn blinds. Since he witnessed no homosexual conduct, Devlin had no grievance. "The offense-causing action," said Feinberg (1988), "must be more than wrong; it must be a *wrong* to the offended party, in short, a violation of *his* rights" (p. xiv, original italics). Punishing private and harmless sexual behavior to prevent bare-knowledge offense cannot be justified by liberal liberty-limiting principles.

The Principle of Legal Paternalism

Legal paternalism is excluded from the liberal position as a legitimate reason for criminalization. According to Feinberg (1986), this principle states:

> It is always a good and relevant (though not necessarily decisive) reason in support of a prohibition that it will prevent harm (physical, psychological, or economic) to the actor himself. (p. 4)

Feinberg distinguished "hard paternalism" from "soft paternalism," which he does not regard as paternalism at all. Hard paternalism is said, arguably, to justify state interference with self-regarding dangerous behavior even when it is wholly voluntary. Soft paternalism warrants state interference only when behavior dangerous to the self is substantially nonvoluntary or only temporarily to determine whether such a choice is voluntary.

Feinberg believes that a convincing conception of personal autonomy serves as a moral trump card over claims of hard legal paternalism. He views autonomy—the capacity for self-government—as the *sovereign authority* to govern one's self, which is absolute within the self's moral boundaries.

Whereas legal paternalism subordinates a person's *right* of self-determination to the person's own *good,* Feinberg argues that it is a violation of personal sovereignty whenever an autonomous person's liberty is interfered with in the name of his own good. Moreover, Gerald Dworkin regards paternalism as the denial of autonomy by substituting the state's judgment for that of the person. According to Dworkin (1988):

> Autonomy is a second-order capacity to reflect critically upon one's first order preferences and desires, and the ability either to identify with these or to change them in light of higher-order preferences and values. (p. 108)

Thus the exercise of autonomy defines the self and takes responsibility for one's actions, giving meaning and coherence to one's life.

The Principle of Legal Moralism

As an alternative to the liberal view, Feinberg (1988) first stated the Principle of Legal Moralism broadly:

> It can be morally legitimate for the state, by means of the criminal law, to prohibit certain types of action that cause neither harm nor offense to anyone, on the grounds that such actions constitute or cause evils of other kinds. (p. 3)

A more narrow and strict second definition focused only on the use of legal moralism to enforce morality:

> It can be morally legitimate . . . to prohibit conduct on the ground that it is inherently immoral, even though it causes neither harm nor offense to the actor or to others. (p. 4)

The broader definition of legal moralism is often said to be necessary to preserve a traditional way of life. Moral conservatism, what Hart called the "conservative thesis," holds that it can be morally legitimate to preserve a society's traditional way of life from radical or essential change through the use of coercive law.

As society changes, the conservative laments that it is unfair that he has come to feel an alien in his own land and a stranger in his own family. The "moral majority" seeks to defend its lifestyle from the lifestyles of the "immoral minority" as an unfair encroachment upon their traditions. Yet, according to Feinberg:

> If we assume, as seems natural, that human nature comes in different sizes and shapes, so to speak, that there are deep and morally significant differences among normal people in respect to basic temperament and emotional needs, then to insist that only some of these types of character, even if they are the most common ones, are entitled to satisfaction, would seem to be unfair to others, a form of discrimination as arbitrary as racial prejudice. (1988: 54)

Moreover, moral conservatives claim that "moral offenses" harm them by producing an indirect harm to their interests in living in a certain homogeneous, conventionally moral community. But any individual's interest in how he lives his own life is more important than any conservative's interest in how another person lives his life; it is the same difference in the interests of the owner of a purse and its thief that Mill pointed out: the desire of the owner to keep it and of the thief to take it are incommensurate.

Therefore, autonomy necessarily trumps both the thief's interest in theft and the conservative's *external* interest in others' self-regarding behavior. A democratic community must honor the personal autonomy of anyone or risk losing the personal autonomy of everyone. Justice Brandeis's "right to be let alone" requires the toleration of differences in religious views and in sexual lifestyles.

Still, the moral conservative argues that it is necessary to protect traditional family values. Feinberg dryly notes:

> When inanimate objects like rocks or bicycles, or abstractions like institutions, are said to be harmed, this is often an indirect way of referring to the [supposed] harm suffered by those who have an interest in the maintenance of these objects. (1988: 72)

Protecting so-called traditional family values is a gloss that protects the males' patriarchal interests in dominating family life (Mosher 1989).

Just as there is a difference between a species of animals changing by evolving over time and that same species becoming extinct at once by the shooting of all its members, there is a difference, Feinberg argues, between the natural social change of the family and its extinction: continuous growth is evolution, not an abrupt extinction. Dominant marriages can become egalitarian marriages; patriarchal families can become democratic families; new family forms can evolve without the institution of the family becoming extinct.

Hart (1967) distinguishes the "moral minimum" from the "moral residuum." The *moral minimum* refers to "those restraints and prohibitions that are essential to the existence of any society of human beings whatever (p. 9), including rules against violence, homicide, mendacity, and fraud—each derivable from the Harm Principle and legitimately subject to legal coercion. Nonuniversal moral rules that are found within any particular society's code but that do not prevent individual harms can be designated the *moral residuum.* To preserve a particular community's way of life is not a legitimate plea to preserve the moral minimum, but instead is an intolerant plea to preserve a particular way of life by maintaining an unchanging moral residuum that is essential only to that society which a conservative favors. Protecting the moral residuum—by preserving the family, by avoiding the pollution of the moral environment, and by preventing the corruption of youth from free-floating evils—strikes most liberals as morally perverse. "Where there are no individuals who can voice personal grievances over an unforced change," wrote Feinberg, "then tears shed in advance over the 'destruction of a way of life' are more sentimental than moral or humane" (1988: 80). Unlike the moral conservative who is concerned with protecting a way of life, the strict legal moralist elevates conventional morality to an ultimate morality in which "morals offenses," even when private and harmless, are such odious evils that they should be forbidden solely on the grounds of their evil nature. Feinberg stated that the full theory of strict legal moralism holds three tenets: (1) true moral evil, even when free-floating (independent of anyone's interests), should be prohibited by law; (2) some serious moral evils *are* free-floating, leaving no individual with a specific grievance; and (3) even when moral wrongdoers harm no one, their misdeeds should be punished as an end in itself.

In contrast, according to Feinberg, the liberal holds, "All of the justifying aims of the criminal law consist of moral considerations," but the liberal does not believe that, "All moral considerations are part of the justifying aims of the criminal law" (1988: 153).

For the liberal, to be criminal, an act must be simultaneously harmful and wrongful. Immorality as such is not sufficient for criminalization when no individual has a grievance, when no one has been wronged by such actions. Thus, for the liberal, the only legitimate reason for criminalization is a thoroughly moral one: the protection of moral rights; but, this cannot include so-called sexual and moral offenses that do not violate the moral rights of other parties. Feinberg wrote:

> He may be [considered] morally blameworthy for his beliefs and desires, his infractions of taboo, his tastes, his harmless exploitations, and other free-

> floating evils, but *these* moral judgments are not the business of the criminal law. (1988: 154, original italics)

Is punishment of evil an end in itself? After considering the Puritans' desire to ban harmless immoralities, Bertrand Russell (1935) concluded:

> The laws in question [morals offenses] can, therefore, only be justified by a theory of vindictive punishment, which holds that certain sins, though they may not injure anyone except the sinner, are so heinous as to make it our duty to inflict pain upon the delinquent. (p. 122)

Stephen (1873/1967) is often viewed as just such a moral retributionist. When Feinberg examines Stephen's position, however, he unearths a paradox: if a crime has no victim, who is there to want revenge? He concluded that Stephen is not a retributionist at all, simply an advocate of hatred as the automatic response of right-thinking people, given their disgust or repugnance at "unnatural sex." According to Feinberg:

> Stephen teaches the liberal to identify one of the moral presuppositions of his own liberal position, that *it is not appropriate to hate people except (at most) for their disposition to harm and wrong others.* (1988: 165, original italics)

In conclusion, the moral residuum of conventional sexual morality and the conservative preservation of the traditional family are offered as justifications for laws against fornication, sodomy, adultery, divorce, homosexuality, pornography, prostitution, contraception, and abortion. Yet, from a liberal perspective, neither legal moralism nor legal paternalism can legitimate government coercion. Although a critical morality is a legitimate basis for the legislation of laws and for punishment to enforce the law, such a system of criminal justice must found its laws upon the principles of harm and offense. Although for the law to be justified by morality is a legitimate aim of the law, morality is not justified merely because it is culturally conventional or historically traditional. Neither majority opinions nor historical precedents within a particular society provide a justified account for a critical morality.

THE JUSTIFICATION OF MORAL RULES

How are moral rules justified? Although the analyses of Mills, Hart, and Feinberg offer useful guides to the legislature, specifying when it is morally legitimate to use law's coercive force to prevent harm (and some forms of offense) to others, they do not specify moral rules useful to the individual in making moral judgments about his or her conduct. The liberal program has been predominantly concerned with preserving negative liberty and with reducing the government's coercive role to the minimum necessary to maintain peace and social order. Yet, this does not mean that a liberal position must entail an ethical emotivism, subjectivism, nihilism, skepticism, or relativism. It is fair to say that everyone follows moral rules; the question is which moral rules are to be followed.

Sexual conduct is governed by the same moral rules as human conduct in general, although the intimacy of sexual conduct may evoke moral ideals as well.

Justified Moral Rules

The moral philosopher's task is to explain and justify the rules of morality. For example, Bernard Gert (1988) offered a justification for the moral rules. Gert analyzed the major concepts of *rationality, impartiality,* and *morality.* Then he advanced an account of a moral system—guidelines for making moral judgments—and a justification for it.

Morality

For Gert:

> *Morality is a public system applying to all rational persons governing behavior which affects others and which has the minimization of evil as its end, and which includes what are commonly known as moral rules as its core.* (1988: 6, original italics)

By a *public system,* Gert means a system that is understood and could be accepted by all rational persons who are subject to it. All impartial rational persons can understand and accept the moral rules as a guide to their conduct and the conduct of others.

Rationality

Action is central in making judgments of rationality or irrationality. Gert regards irrational acts as those that are always to be avoided; calling an act "irrational" is to advocate that it not be done. On the other hand, to call an act "rational" is not to advocate that it be done, since there may be more than one rational alternative.

Rationality requires the optimum satisfaction of desires—the harmonizing of desires that are neither rationally required nor prohibited. As Gert defines it:

> *A desire is irrational if and only if one knows (or should know) that acting on that desire will result in one failing to satisfy some desire or set of desires which in a cool moment one has decided is significantly more important.* (1988: 27, original italics)

Moreover, a desire is irrational if it is always irrational to act on it simply in order to satisfy it (that is, without the person having a *reason* for acting on it). Desires to die, to be disabled, to suffer pain and negative affect, to suffer loss of freedom, and to suffer loss of pleasure are irrational unless there is a reason for so acting. Gert writes, "*Reasons for acting are conscious beliefs that can make rational what would otherwise be an irrational action*" (1988: 34, original italics).

For Gert:

> A reason is a conscious belief, not obviously inconsistent with what one knows, that one's actions will, directly or indirectly, help someone, oneself or someone else, avoid an evil or gain a good. (1988: 283)

Since rationality is not equated with self-interest, a person might rationally give his or her life to save others. Although one can rationally benefit others, one is not *required by rationality* to benefit others, to lay down one's life for the other.

Good and Evil

Gert recognizes that "evil plays a much more important role in morality than good does" (p. 47). He defines evil as the object of irrational desires. This definition includes a list of evils: death, pain, disability, loss of freedom, and loss of pleasure. Gert's concept of evil is both objective and precise. "No rational person," writes Gert, "chooses an evil for himself unless he has a reason, but some rational person may choose to inflict evils on others, even without a reason" (p. 49).

Gert continues by defining "a good as that which no rational person will avoid without a reason" (p. 50). A *personal good* would never be avoided by a rational person. A *social good* increases personal goods or decreases personal evils. What is crucial for Gert is that death, pain, disability, loss of freedom, and loss of pleasure are personal evils and that life, positive affect, ability, freedom, and pleasure are personal goods.

Impartiality

Gert offers the following definition of impartiality:

> A is impartial in respect R with regard to group G if and only if A's actions in respect R are not influenced at all by which member(s) of G benefit or are harmed by these actions. (1988: 80, original italics)

For Gert, morality requires impartiality of all rational persons with respect to obeying or violating a moral rule. But impartiality is not required with respect to following the moral ideals. It would be impossible to satisfy this requirement since impartial rational persons who may rank the goods and evils differently need not always agree on the answer they would give to every moral question.

Moral impartiality must include rationality, whereas rationality does not necessarily include impartiality. "Moral impartiality," wrote Gert, "requires that one never violate a moral rule unless one can advocate that such a violation be publicly allowed, which requires that it be understood and could be accepted by all rational persons" (p. 95). Impartiality extends the scope of morality beyond friends, family, and society to a minimal group of all presently existing rational persons and persons who were once rational.

Moral Rules

Gert seeks the logically necessary and sufficient conditions for a rule to be defined as a moral rule, including both the formal properties and the content of moral rules. Gert's formal properties of moral rules are: (1) moral rules are universal, applying to all persons who can understand (rational persons) and follow them (have the requisite voluntary abilities); (2) moral rules are general, known by all rational persons without having to achieve special knowledge; (3) moral rules concern actual actions, real possibilities of evil action or inaction in all societies at all times; (4) moral rules are unchanging and unchangeable, discovered rather than invented; (5) moral rules are not dependent upon the will or decision of any person or groups of persons; (6) moral rules have exceptions, not being absolute prohibitions even though they are universal and general ones; and (7) moral rules are prohibitions intended to avoid causing evil, rather than to prevent evil or to promote good.

The *moral attitude* toward the moral rules is an attitude that requires impartial obedience. Gert stipulates:

> Justifying a moral system requires providing a public system that incorporates the moral rules and that applies to all rational persons and then showing

> that all impartial persons would advocate adopting that system as the public system that all rational persons should use as a guide for their conduct and a basis for their judgments. (1988: 97)

For Gert, showing that impartial rationality requires the moral attitude toward the rule means that he has justified the moral rule.

Gert introduces five basic justified moral rules: (1) *Don't kill*—prohibits causing permanent loss of consciousness, whether or not the organism dies; (2) *Don't cause pain*—prohibits causing physical pain and mental suffering; (3) *Don't disable*—prohibits causing the loss of ability; (4) *Don't deprive of freedom*—prohibits causing the loss of opportunity; and (5) *Don't deprive of pleasure*—prohibits causing loss of future as well as present pleasure.

Gert argues that all rational persons would adopt an egocentric attitude toward these five rules in order to protect themselves and those they care for from evil consequences. What is more, an *impartial rational person* would adopt this moral attitude:

> Everyone is to obey the rule with regard to everyone except when an impartial rational person can advocate that the violation of the rule be publicly allowed. Anyone who violates the rule when no impartial person can advocate that such a violation be publicly allowed may be punished. (p. 119)

Gert introduces five more "discovered and unchanging" moral rules: (6) *Don't deceive;* (7) *Keep your promise;* (8) *Don't cheat;* (9) *Obey the law;* and (10) *Do your duty.* Each of these rules is viewed as independent.

All these moral rules apply to sexuality but none of them is specific to sexuality. Gert argues that those who hold a "traditional" and those with a "new" sexual morality are, in fact, not having a *moral dispute,* because whatever side one takes on sexuality, it should not affect one's attitudes toward the ten moral rules. The confusion enters, Gert believes, when both parties think that there is an independent rule governing sexual behavior that shares all of the features of the other basic moral rules. For example, rape is immoral. It is immoral not because it is concerned with sexual matters, but because it necessarily involves a violation of the moral rules against the infliction of pain and the deprivation of freedom. At the same time, deprivation of the pleasure of sex is itself immoral unless such deprivation avoids a greater evil. Thus, Gert states:

> Unless nonmarital sexual relations between consenting adults causes harm to someone, no impartial rational person could favor a public rule prohibiting such activity. (1988: 135)

Moral Ideals

Morality also includes moral ideals that advocate both preventing evils such as death, pain, disability, and losses of freedom and pleasure as well as promoting life, positive affect, freedom, and pleasure.

Moral rules can be obeyed impartially by all rational persons continuously throughout a day and a lifetime; they only require not causing death, pain, disability, and so on. But the moral ideals cannot be always followed impartially toward all rational persons, since these ideals define an unending and expansive duty beyond a human being's grasp. Although "Eschew evil; do good" is a pithy summary of morality, the most Gert believes that can be required is, "Always be just; be kind when you can."

The goal of morality is to minimize the amount of evil suffered by persons; not causing evil takes precedence over preventing evil, which takes precedence over promoting good. Punishment is justified for a violation of moral rules, which causes harm to others, but not for failing to live up to moral ideals. Neither the government nor the family can coerce any rational person to follow moral ideals. Promoting moral ideals is a matter of socialization, education, and persuasion.

The Moral System

Gert's moral theory implies a moral system for making judgments about whether moral violations are publicly acceptable. He distinguishes eight morally relevant features (for example, what moral rules are being violated; what evils are being avoided, prevented, or caused; and the like). In considering such questions, the kind of evil or good, its seriousness, its duration, its probability, the number of people affected, and the distribution of effects must be considered. The *morally decisive question* is: "What effect would this kind of moral violation of the rules have if publicly allowed?" (p. 285) The answer may be clear. When it is not, it may be that the facts are disputed or that the evils and goods are ranked differently by impartial rational persons. Gert believes most disputes about morality concern the interpretation of facts.

SOCIAL TOLERANCE VERSUS CRIMINALIZATION

Such disputes, about both the facts and the nature of the good, litter the terrain of public policy. Still, it remains easier to secure agreement on the evils than on the good.

The exercise of tolerance preserves civil tranquility by giving all parties a wide and fair scope in which to lead their lives as they see fit. Tolerance embraces the freedom to be let alone. Oppression of individuals is minimized when the state refrains from condemning any individual's private moral choices that do not harm others. Of course, by nature of their being private they cannot offend others.

Locke's Liberal Solution of Tolerance

For two hundred years after the Reformation, religious strife and wars disrupted civil peace.

Seeing diversity as a threat only when a government was repressive, John Locke (1955, 1975) proposed the liberal solution of "toleration." William Galston (1991: 261) summarizes Locke's thesis in three propositions: (1) because religious truth cannot be known with certainty, efforts to impose it through coercion lack rational warrant; (2) even if religious truth could be established, inward faith cannot be imposed through external coercion; (3) and even if coercion could succeed, it would be wrong to employ it. For Locke, tolerance required reliance on persuasive speech rather than on coercion.

Locke's liberalism was born in fear: of evil, of cruelty, of bloody conflict, and of arbitrary and tyrannical authority, both magisterial and religious. This liberal view was a secular one, antipathetic to all cruelty, particularly religious cruelty. Putting cruelty first disregarded the idea of sin as understood by revealed religion. Moreover, according to Judith Shklar (1984):

> By putting it [cruelty] unconditionally first, with nothing above us to excuse or to forgive acts of cruelty, one closes off any appeal to any order other than that of actuality. (p. 9)

Diversity and Liberal Neutrality

Diversity in religions, values, and ways of life is a basic social fact in pluralistic American society. Liberalism endorses a wide neutrality over ways of life because of the values placed upon individual autonomy and political freedom. But liberalism does not endorse an immoral neutrality that says, "Anything goes." The state can legitimately legislate laws against harming others and, very carefully, against the nuisance of serious offense against others when it outweighs the reasonableness of the prohibited conduct. The person can choose a way of life, making personal choices so long as these choices are consistent with a moral attitude that seeks to avoid causing evils to others.

The diversity of people and societies suggests that human good must contain many varieties of good, with each life tailored to each person's purposes and capacities within this pluralism of rational possibilities. "When combined with the empirical diversity of human purposes," writes Galston (1991), "the liberal account of purposiveness leads directly to a vindication of tolerance, interpreted as the settled disposition of each individual to minimize interference with the strivings of others" (p. 228).

The stance of liberal neutrality is a procedural constraint against state coercion that follows whenever a particular conception of positive (conventional or traditional) morality is adopted at the expense of critical morality.

According to Charles Larmore's (1987) interpretation of *neutrality of procedure,* state policies should be justified "without appealing to the presumed intrinsic superiority of any particular conception of the good life" (p. 43). Just as the rules of evidence constrain trial advocacy, and the rules of science constrain knowledge claims, neutrality of procedure constrains the reasons that can be invoked to justify public policy.

Procedural neutrality is linked to several key liberal concepts: (1) *liberal equality,* as an expression of equal respect due to all persons; (2) *minority rights,* as limiting what a majority can rightly do with its power; (3) *privacy,* as a protected sphere of personal autonomy; and (4) *freedom of conscience,* as permitting a justified opposition to liberty-limiting coercion by policies that are based upon the majority's conventional conception of the good. A commitment to civil peace, to the resolution of disputes by rational argument—persuasion rather than coercion—mutes conflict generated by a narrow specification of the sole good life in favor of life itself. The rational resolution of disputes recognizes that citizens' lives embody a plurality of plans and diverse ways of living.

The rational defense of negative liberty is an easier task than securing an embracing and convergent definition of positive liberty. The essence of liberty remains the prevention of tyranny and the provision of personal and political freedom. Liberal neutrality favors the principle of equal respect for persons, valuing personal autonomy and the capacity for justice (Rawls 1971).

Rational Life Plans and Rational Liberty

From his theory of justice, Rawls (1971) introduced a natural duty of *mutual respect,* "the duty to show a person the respect which is due him as a moral being, that is, as a being with a sense of justice and a conception of the good" (p. 337). Mutual respect is manifested by a willingness to see a situation from the other's point of view, from their perspective of the good, and by a willingness to give reasons for our actions whenever the interests of others are materially effected. For Rawls,

> . . . our good is determined by the plan of life that we would adopt with full deliberative rationality if the future were adequately foreseen and adequately realized in the imagination. [p. 421] . . . A rational plan—con-

> strained as always by the right—allows a person to flourish, so far as circumstances permit, and to exercise his realized abilities as much as he can. (p. 429)

R. M. Smith (1985) has championed the role of Locke's *rational liberty* in American constitutional law. Rational liberty—the preservation and enhancement of human capacities for understanding and reflective self-direction—was the core of Locke's political and moral vision. For Locke, liberty is a power, involving a capacity for rational self-determination as the distinctive feature of human nature. Social cooperation and tolerance are required to develop the human capacity for rational liberty. For Smith, Mill's praise of "mental expansion and elevation," Dewey's advocacy of the "method of intelligence," and Rawls's rational life plans for the moral person, taken together, indicate that the ideal of the deliberative, self-directing, morally autonomous person is deeply ingrained in liberalism.

Smith writes:

> The rational liberty view contains a standard for the process of moral decision making, the requirement of rational deliberation on our alternative goals and their consequences, as well as a substantive standard, the insistence that we must strive not to endanger anyone's capacities for such self-deliberation. (p. 210)

Smith holds that the liberal society can insist that it is wrong to destroy or injure the capacities for rational self-direction. He argues that:

> it [rational liberty] commissions us to act so that we do not harm the capacities for rational understanding and self-control of ourselves or others, which is the minimum basis for self-respect, and to strive to realize those capacities insofar as we are able, which is the ground for greater moral self-esteem. (p. 217)

Choices of sexual activities, life plans, and lifestyles are morally justified if and only if moral agents, as impartial rational persons, publicly accept the moral rules: moral sexual acts do not kill, cause pain, disable, deprive of freedom, deprive of pleasure, break promises, deceive, or cheat. A moral sexuality respects others' capacity for rational liberty, for making choices consistent with their need for autonomy and their plan of life. Legislating against justifiable sexual lifestyles as "morals offenses" prevents the individual from performing his or her moral duty to obey the law. Thus, morally justified exceptions exist for laws that are merely legal, such as those on fornication, sodomy, and homosexuality.

Disrespect for law occurs when laws are not morally justified; morally unjustified laws are immoral in their consequences. Exceptions to anachronistic and unenforced laws against sexual moral offenses can be advocated on grounds that an impartial rational person can advocate that they be publicly allowed. Oral and anal sexual acts between consenting adults do not necessarily violate moral rules. We publicly allow this conduct in half of the states of the nation, whereas it is proscribed in the remaining states. The arbitrarily illegal conduct in question causes no evil effects; such laws are both commonly breached and rarely enforced. Moreover, their violation in states still having these laws creates no noticeable differences in consequences for the polity than does their legitimate expressions in morally enlightened states where obeying the law does not require abjuring from such sexual acts. To obey such blindly unjust laws would undermine autonomy, freedom of conscience, the capacity for rational liberty, and many rational plans of life.

Harms of Criminalization

The criminalization of sexual activities and sexual lifestyles that do not cause harm to an identifiable other interferes with individual autonomy, the rational life plan of many persons, and the rational liberty of all. Laws against heterosexual and homosexual fornication and sodomy are particularly objectionable because they insult the dignity of moral persons, reducing their self-respect and self-esteem. The failure to enforce these laws clarifies that their purpose is symbolic—to express intolerant moral disapproval, backed up by the threat of legal consequences. The intolerant moralist feels indignant, disgusted, and repulsed owing to the knowledge that such sexual acts are occurring somewhere and involving someone because they view such sexual acts as evil-in-themselves. Not only do these laws interfere with the rightful autonomy of persons to make sexual choices, but they are used to justify the unfair restriction of the civil liberties of individuals who are presumed to violate such laws.

David Richards has examined toleration and the American Constitution. For Richards, criminalization of oral and anal sex coercively abridges the rights of many heterosexual men and women, certain disabled people, and homosexual men and women. According to Richards (1986):

> The best contemporary evidence about the nature and role of sexuality in the life of the person makes clear the rightful dignity, grounded in the traditional American commitment to an abstract right of privacy, of the right of persons to engage in forms of sexual expression central to the integrity of their intimate relations and personal lives. (p. 270)

Richards argues that criminal prohibitions bear a substantial burden of justification. Of course, such justification requires distinguishing between reflective ethical argument and noncritical, conventional sexual morality. For Richards, ethics treats other persons as one would want oneself to be treated with respect for one's basic demands for those liberties central to a free and self-governing person and moral agent. Such equal respect for persons—which ensures the basic liberties to form different religious, philosophical, and political allegiances—requires that the scope of the criminal law must itself express such respect for persons.

Justifying a general prohibition on oral and anal sex, whether heterosexual or homosexual, cannot rest on appeals to traditional moral condemnation of such acts. "The appeal to 'morality and decency,' without more [i.e., alone]," Richards argues, "falsely begs the central issue in dispute, supposing precisely the kind of homogeneity in moral values that the general history of Western ethics and the specific history of constitutional privacy belie" (p. 275).

Sexual freedom is a liberty central to a free and self-governing moral agent. Thus the criminal law should include equal respect for all persons with morally justified sexual lifestyles.

Richards warns of the harms done by these laws on the lives of exclusively homosexual men and women: (1) such laws deny practicing homosexuals their just moral independence in building personal relationships with confidence and security; (2) criminal penalties reinforce employment risks and social prejudice, which fragment emotions, physical expression, and self-image, corrupting the integrity essential to a free and morally responsible person; (3) the deepest damage is the spiritual violence on the human heart—on the imagination of, desire for, and achievement of a love that organizes and expresses the essentially human moral powers. False social stereotypes that are supported by law make it difficult for gay men and lesbians to esteem their own emotional propensities, their natural expression, or their love objects. Thus any law forbidding exclusive homosexuals the option to express sexual love in the only ways they may find natural deprives them not only of love but of the moral independence required to live a life of personal and moral value. Richards concludes, "The right to constitutional privacy is the precise remedy for this wrong" (p. 280).

Therefore, these pitiful laws against "moral offenses" are themselves immoral, causing unjust harms to persons. Such unjust juridical contempt creates needless evil: causing pain, depriving both freedom and opportunity, depriving sexual pleasure, disabling voluntary abilities, and even rationalizing the assault and murder of gay men and lesbians.

For Gert (1988), tolerance is not a moral ideal; instead, it is required by the moral rules. Tolerance consists of not doing certain things. To be intolerant is to violate the first five moral rules because of some morally indifferent characteristic like sexual orientation. But a tolerant person will not kill, cause pain to, disable, deprive of freedom or pleasure, any person because of racial, ethnic, religious, or sexual diversity. Gert concluded that, "An intolerant person is necessarily an immoral person, for he violates a moral rule unjustifiably" (p. 169).

UNDERSTANDING THE RATIONAL PUBLIC

Benjamin Page and Robert Shapiro (1992) have summarized fifty years of trends in America's policy preferences based upon a comprehensive integration of hundreds of opinion surveys conducted between 1935 and 1990. When they have changed, opinions about social issues have done so in understandable and sensible ways, reacting to changes in circumstances or information. Page and Shapiro found that opinion change was not at all common, but, nonetheless, some social opinions revealed a number of exceptionally large changes. According to Page and Shapiro:

> While one should not forget the continued conservatism of Americans on questions involving law and order (e.g., drugs and capital punishment), school prayer, pornography, the flag, and other matters, the great story about social issues in the mid-twentieth century United States remains the gradual, sweeping liberalization that occurred over several decades: the strong trends toward increased support for civil rights, civil liberties, women's rights, and the legal tolerance of diversity [gay rights]. (p. 115)

They indicate that the public's policy preferences are often more tolerant than their personal social attitudes. For example, despite extremely widespread public distaste for the idea of homosexuality in the 1970s and 1980s (over 80 percent agreeing that "homosexuality is always/almost always wrong"), far fewer people wanted homosexuality to be *illegal.* A temporary rise in opinions that homosexuality should not be legal followed the outbreak of AIDS in the 1980s. According to Page and Shapiro:

> By 1989, the idea that homosexual relations between consenting adults should be legal rebounded sharply (by 19 percent), from 38 percent to 57 percent, according to Gallup. (Kagay 1989: 13) (p. 99)

They conclude, "while tolerating homosexuality, most Americans did not want to encourage it" (p. 100).

The major thesis of Page and Shapiro is, that given accurate information, the public is rational, justifying a majoritarian democracy in which the public has the capacity to govern. Still, this faith in a rational public depends upon the quality of information that is made available to it. Collective deliberation works well when citizen's preferences are *well informed,* reflecting exposure to empirical evidence, justified morality, and reasoned debate.

Bias is often introduced in the process of getting items included on the agenda for public discussion. Without inclusion on the public agenda, the public cannot become well informed. How the issue is framed by opinion leaders often predetermines the response to it. Public debates of experts inform and educate the citizenry.

Government response to what the public wants is out of harmony roughly one-third of the time (Monroe 1979; Page & Shapiro 1983). When salience of and attention to issues are low, such a discrepancy is more likely. Elites can control what is on the agenda as a public problem, and what is seen as a solution.

Joel Best (1989, 1990) analyzed the tactics by which claims-makers seek to place their interests on the public agenda. To succeed, they must persuade the public the problem is important; moreover, ultimately they want *ownership* of the problem: to control the way in which the problem is to be seen, defined, or construed. First, claims-makers *typify* the problem—giving it an image that characterizes the problem in a preferred way. Second, the problem is defined in the broadest and most inclusive way possible in order to expand its significance—making it a pressing problem. Third, "experts" cite large numbers of instances of the problem—creating awareness of its danger. Fourth, "experts" claim the problem is growing in incidence and prevalence—increasing the threat and danger. Fifth, the problem is blamed upon social change or immorality—portraying a threat to "the American way" of life. Sixth, with the immensity and danger of the problem having been established, the typification is further expanded into new territory by recognizing the similarity of the "new" problem to the "old" one—staking an expanding claim. Seventh, a call for action is issued that, given the *typification* of the problem, requires response from any moral and right-thinking citizen—mobilizing the citizenry. Eighth, a simple solution requiring the enforcement of morality is proposed—justifying intolerant and coercive action.

Too often, symbolic politics undermines the "free marketplace of ideas" by substituting for informed discussion and government action. Moreover, production and consumption of information is dominated by market forces, with economic inequality creating political inequality. Institutional arrangements must permit all minorities, including sexual minorities, equal time to present their ideas if they are to have equal opportunity to represent their interests to the public.

IMPLICATIONS FOR PUBLIC POLICY

Although most Americans favor legal tolerance of sexual variations and lifestyles, moralistic intolerance threatens sexual freedom. Unjust and immoral laws against fornication and sodomy coercively enforce a conventional heritage of antisexual ideology. Because Americans remain confused about the application of a critical morality to sexuality, a conventional so-called moral majority too often goes unchallenged when it claims access to a God-given morality classifying all sexual contact but procreative marital coitus in the missionary position as immoral. This threat to sexual freedom stems from moralistic intolerance that instills a spiral of silence in a public that does not recognize that it is in the numerical majority and that its sexual activity, assuming it is responsible and harms no one, can be morally justified (Mosher 1989). Such moralistic intolerance is immoral precisely because it causes needless pain and the loss of freedom and pleasure. Tolerance requires merely the suspension of cruelty, cruelty that is rationalized as "moral reprobation," but which stems from irrational repugnance, disgust, and contempt.

Only a broad definition of the human good—with its respect for individual autonomy, diverse rational life plans, and the preservation of rational liberty—is consistent with the pursuit of life, liberty, and happiness in America's pluralistic society. Although diversity should ideally be respected, at a minimum, it must be tolerated.

All sexual activity should adhere to moral rules and not cause harm to others. The same moral rules apply to sexual conduct as to all human conduct. Although persons can be punished for causing harms, they can only be persuaded to pursue the good. Only sexual activity that coincides with the rational life plan of the individual, given reflective deliberation about rational desires, should be chosen. Sexual activity with a partner should respect the rational liberty of the partner, creating a dialogue that permits self-determination and respects the capacity for deliberative self-determination in the partner. Because sexual activity is a special form of human intimacy, it should encourage a duty not only not to cause harm and to prevent any harms that can be anticipated, but also to promote the partner's personal good. Impartial rational persons will want to avoid the social evils, but will not want to avoid the social goods associated with their personal sexual conduct.

Sexologists must create and expand opportunities to engage in debate in public forums on these issues of sexuality and morality, of tolerance and criminalization; they must make use of mass media to inform, educate, and persuade the public. To do this, sexologists must become better moral philosophers, clarifying their own moral concepts. To adopt a laissez-faire attitude of "anything goes sexually" between consenting adults often fails to examine what counts as an autonomous act of giving consent in a sexual situation. The risk of disability through unwanted pregnancy or sexually transmitted diseases is not gainsaid by an uninformed sexual consent. Sexual consent must be an autonomous act. Faden and Beauchamp (1986) analyze autonomous action as follows: "X acts autonomously only if X acts: (1) intentionally, (2) with understanding, and (3) without controlling influences" (p. 238). The analysis of a theory of informed consent for sexual decision making would clarify this nonspecific, often nonverbal, negotiation of a sexual contract by specifying how the moral rules apply.

Sex education must include the opportunity for young persons to present, debate, and defend their personal moral rules about sexuality. Only by examining the potential consequences of sexual activity for themselves, their partners, and society can they develop an informed opinion about what is moral sexual conduct. Freedom of speech must include the right to discuss in schools important life choices, including the making of sexual decisions.

Sexologists cannot approve of sexual conduct in which coercion causes pain and restricts freedom of choice, nor of manipulation that involves deceit, cheating, and the breaking of promises. Sexologists should advocate a justified critical morality of moral rules as a moral system for judging human conduct, including sexuality.

Advocating social tolerance, rather than criminalization, for a diversity of sexual life plans and lifestyles is consistent with the liberal claim that the harm and offense principles, duly clarified and qualified, demarcate the moral limits of the criminal law as it applies to sexuality. The liberty-limiting principles of legal paternalism and legal moralism are rejected as morally illegitimate infringements on sexual liberty. As Mill wrote, "the chief mischief of legal penalties is that they strengthen the social stigma" (p. 38). Mill recognized the evils that come from social disapproval, now justified by an unjust law as "morally legitimate intolerance."

This social tolerance must be tempered by advocating a critical morality in the form of normative moral rules. Just as neutrality of procedures in legislating, interpreting, and enforcing the law serves the public, so does advocating a normative set of moral rules as a guide to personal sexual conduct serve the public. A responsible sexuality that does not cause harm to others can be understood and publicly advocated by all impartial rational persons.

The conjunction of sexual liberty with an impartial critical morality is persuasive. A public policy of sexual liberty is best advanced by reasoned argument that is derived from data and theory. That argument must be placed within the context of a moral attitude toward sexuality that is appropriate to this diverse culture, pluralistic society, and modern historical era.

REFERENCES

Best, J., ed. (1989). *Images of Issues: Typifying Contemporary Social Problems.* New York: Aldine de Gruyter.

Best, J. (1990). *Threatened Children: Rhetoric and Concern about Child-Victims.* Chicago: University of Chicago Press.

Budziszewski, J. (1992). *True Tolerance: Liberalism and the Necessity of Judgment.* New Brunswick, N.J.: Transaction Publishers.

Devlin, P. (1965/1988). "The Enforcement of Morals." In R. M. Baird, and S. E. Rosenbaum, eds., *Morality and the Law,* pp. 15–35. Buffalo, N.Y.: Prometheus Books.

Dworkin, G. (1988). *The Theory and Practice of Autonomy.* Cambridge, England: Cambridge University Press.

Faden, R. R., and Beauchamp, T. L. (1986). *A History and Theory of Informed Consent.* New York: Oxford University Press.

Feinberg, J. (1984). *Harm to Others.* Vol. 1 of *The Moral Limits of the Criminal Law.* New York: Oxford University Press.

——— (1985). *Offense to Others.* Vol. 2 of *The Moral Limits of the Criminal Law.* New York: Oxford University Press.

——— (1986). *Harm to Self.* Vol. 3 of *The Moral Limits of the Criminal Law.* New York: Oxford University Press.

——— (1988). *Harmless Wrong-Doing.* Vol. 4 of *The Moral Limits of the Criminal Law.* New York: Oxford University Press.

Galston, W. (1991). *Liberal Purposes: Goods, Virtues, and Diversity in the Liberal State.* Cambridge: Cambridge University Press.

Gert, B. (1988). *Morality: A New Justification of the Moral Rules.* New York: Oxford University Press.

Hart, H. L. A. (1959/1988). "Immorality and Treason." In R. M. Baird and S. E. Rosenbaum, eds., *Morality and the Law,* pp. 47–53. Buffalo, N.Y.: Prometheus Books.

——— (1963/1988). "The Legal Enforcement of Morality." In R. M. Baird and S. E. Rosenbaum, eds., *Morality and the law,* pp. 37–46. Buffalo, N.Y.: Prometheus Books.

——— (1967). "Social Solidarity and the Enforcement of Morality." *University of Chicago Law Review* 35: 1–10.

Kagay, M. R. (1989). "Homosexuals Gain More Acceptance." *New York Times,* October 25, p. 13.

Larmore, C. (1987). *Patterns of Moral Complexity.* Cambridge: Cambridge University Press.

Locke, J. (1955). *A Letter concerning Toleration.* Indianapolis, Ind.: Bobbs-Merrill.

——— (1975). *An Essay concerning Human Understanding.* P. Nidditch, ed. Oxford: Clarendon Press.

Mill, J. S. (1859/1986). *On Liberty.* Buffalo, N.Y.: Prometheus Books.

Monroe, K. R. (1984). *Presidential Popularity and the Economy.* New York: Praeger.

Mosher, D. L. (1989). "The Threat to Sexual Freedom: Moralistic Intolerance Instills a Spiral of Silence." *The Journal of Sex Research* 26: 492–509.

Page, B. I., and Shapiro, R. Y. (1983). "Effects of Public Opinion on Policy." *American Political Science Review* 77: 175–90.

——— (1992). *The Rational Public: Fifty Years of Trends in American's Policy Preferences.* Chicago: University of Chicago Press.

Rawls, J. (1971). *A Theory of Justice.* Cambridge, Mass.: Harvard University Press.

Richards, D. A. J. (1986). *Toleration and the Constitution.* New York: Oxford University Press.

Russell, B. (1935). *Skeptical Essays.* London: George Allen and Unwin, Ltd.

Shklar, J. (1984). *Ordinary Vices.* Cambridge, Mass.: Harvard University Press.

Smith, R. M. (1985). *Liberalism and American Constitutional Law.* Cambridge, Mass.: Harvard University Press.

Stephen, J. F. (1873/1967). *Liberty, Equality, Fraternity.* Cambridge, England: Cambridge University Press.

17

Paraphilic Prevention: Social and Legal Implications

James J. Krivacska

INTRODUCTION

Primary prevention has been a much sought-after if not elusive goal of social science for the past thirty years. Born of an era inspired by the Kennedy and Johnson vision of a new social order, primary prevention efforts held out new hope for the eradication of a multitude of social problems from poverty and illiteracy to violence and unwanted pregnancy. Although prevention efforts over the course of this last quarter century have in many ways failed to live up to initial expectations, much has been learned in that period about the process of prevention and the development of primary prevention models which are beginning to demonstrate effectiveness. Current models still largely recognize prevention as a multitiered process.

PREVENTION MODELS

Prevention efforts targeted at populations already identified as manifesting the condition or problem to be prevented are serviced through three models: *tertiary prevention models,* whose goal is to restore the individual to a state of functioning that existed before the emergence of the target behavior or problem; *secondary prevention models,* which strive to focus energies on populations of individuals believed to be significantly at risk for the target problem, but who do not currently manifest evidence of the problem; and *primary prevention models,* which represent efforts directed at the general population with no effort at differential selection of target group, and which often involve the implementation of strategies that may appear only peripherally related to the target problem (Caplan 1964).

Each of these models has advantages and disadvantages. The primary prevention model potentially reaches a large number of recipients and generally provides training or interventions which often positively impact on areas other than the target problem (e.g., teaching of social problem solving and decision-making skills to primary level students). Reduction of the incidence of the emergence of the target problem may provide substantial savings both financially and socially. It typically requires, however, large investments of financial and human resources for effective implementation.

Secondary prevention reduces the up-front financial and human resource commitments by more selectively targeting efforts at populations believed to be at risk (e.g., a drug abuse awareness program directed at disaffected but nonabusing pre- and early adolescents). Additionally, intervention strategies may be geared more specifically to the target population and target problem. Unfortunately, current ability to identify reliably the factors or criteria by which to categorize an individual as falling within that at-risk category has not been established. Consequently, individuals may be identified as at risk inappropriately, while other individuals who are truly at risk may not be identified at all. Furthermore, under certain circumstances, by the time an individual evidences the signs to qualify for membership in the at-risk group, he or she may already be sufficiently dysfunctional, so that secondary prevention programs may be ineffective.

Tertiary prevention programs seek to reduce the levels of intensity, frequency or duration of the target problem within populations that have already been identified as evidencing the target problem (e.g., sex and contraception education for pregnant teens). The obvious disadvantage is that success rates with such individuals is relatively low while recidivism or relapse rates are relatively high. Additionally, such individuals have typically already inflicted significant costs on society prior to identification of their problem. Most current interventions designed to reduce incidence of sex offenses and paraphilias fall into the category of tertiary prevention. This model has been criticized by those who feel that secondary and tertiary prevention are actually treatment models and thus detract from a clear conceptualization of prevention (Swift & Weirich 1987; Klein & Goldston 1975).

A second paradigm for conceptualizing prevention categorizes prevention effort along a dimension that may be grossly described as encompassing the *intrapersonal* and the *environmental.* The former has, as its goal, the promotion of general psychosocial health via the enhancement of personal competence, with the expectation that individuals who interact with their environment in a confident and capable manner, and who are psychologically and socially healthy, are less at risk for mental health dysfunction (Heller et al. 1980; Meyers & Parsons 1987). Examples of this approach are current programs teaching children social problem-solving skills as a means of reducing incidence of such societal problems as substance abuse and teen pregnancy. Rather than targeting prevention efforts at a specific social problem (such as substance abuse), the focus of this approach is on teaching generic skills that will assist in prevention efforts across a number of social problems.

Environmentally oriented prevention programs seek to eliminate the causes or mediators of maladjustment through modifications of the environment. This model of prevention views poverty, for example, as an underlying social condition implicated in a wide range of social problems. Prevention programming directed at such an underlying cause (increasing economic opportunity and stability for low income families) is seen as having significant implications for the reduction or elimination of related social problems (Heller et al. 1980; Meyers & Parsons 1987).

In reality the most effective prevention approaches may be ones that incorporate the promotion of psychosocial health as well as modification of environmental variables found to be related to the social problems targeted by prevention efforts (Krivacska 1990). Models for the design and development of primary prevention programs based on either of these paradigms have been expounded elsewhere (Cowen 1980). It is beyond the scope of this chapter to provide a detailed conceptual description of a paraphilic prevention model program; however, a key aspect of Cowen's model needs to be briefly elucidated because of its importance for prospective program design and development at a conceptual level. The first step in the development of a primary prevention program, as outlined by Cowen, is identification of a program's "generative base of knowledge." According to Cowen, the generative base of knowledge consists of information, strategies and techniques with respect to a disorder or target behavior as well as any correlates such as etiology, sustaining and maintaining factors. Essentially this step calls for a cross-disciplinary analysis of the target problem.

A clear example of the importance of such a cross-disciplinary process is typified by the chaos of the current rush to develop child sexual abuse prevention programs. Most of the programs currently available on the market have been designed by individuals who have, or claim to have, specialized in the area of child sexual abuse.[1] However, sufficient consultation and collaboration has not been established with professionals in the fields of child development; learning theory; concept formation; primary prevention program development, implementation, and evaluation; sexuality and its development during childhood; and curriculum development, implementation, and evaluation. Consequently, many programs are flawed with respect to one or more of these dimensions with potential negative consequences for the ultimate goal of prevention of the sexual abuse of children (Krivacska 1990).

For example, data collected recently on a sample of elementary school children regarding how they perceived their genitals after participation in child sexual abuse prevention programs showed that 18 percent (6th graders) to 57 percent (1st graders) perceived their genitals as bad parts of their bodies. When asked to elaborate on why they perceived their genitals as either good or bad, 57 percent of the female students and 50 percent of the male students (across all grade levels) who responded, defined their genitals as bad on the basis of whether or not the genitals were touched (e.g., "Your private parts are bad if someone touches you there") (Jenson 1993).

Such data suggest that children may be confusing the vague and poorly defined concepts of "good touch/bad touch" so common in these programs, and consequently may be assigning attributes to their genitals based on the touching of the genitals by another person or, in some instances, by the children themselves. If such children are subsequently abused and believe that their genitals are now bad, the level of shame or guilt they experience may increase substantially. This may provide a strong clue as to the failure of most programs to substantially increase reporting rates of sexual abuse. It may also have implications for the development of healthy sexual functioning in adulthood, particularly for the children who have responded that they would never allow anyone to touch their genitals.

Decisions about primary prevention program development are predicated on assumptions about the target populations; the nature of the target problem; the variables which sustain or maintain the target problem; and the incidence, duration and severity of the target problem. Each of these assumptions, as well as many others, has significant implications for both the ultimate form the prevention program is to take and its likelihood for success.[2]

As noted earlier, current efforts at prevention of sex offending behavior and paraphilias are aimed primarily at identified populations of sex offenders or paraphilics. Within recent years, attempts have been made to introduce more of a primary prevention model, particularly aimed at children and adolescents (such as sexual abuse prevention programs, sexual harassment awareness programs, and rape and date rape prevention programs). The assumptions underlying these programs are highly influenced by a cultural milieu which still does not recognize sexuality as a fundamental component of healthful functioning in adults, let alone in children and adolescents. For example, there has been increased attention recently to the issue of child perpetrators of sexual abuse in which children under the age of thirteen are being labeled as sexual molesters of other children. Attempts to classify youngsters as child perpetrators have lead some authors to develop criteria by which childhood perpetrators can be identified. Although these criteria tend to distinguish between normal childhood sex play and deviant childhood sex play, they severely limit what may be considered normal sexual play, and appear even to discourage such behavior (Johnson 1988; Cantwell 1988).

One could argue that an underlying assumption of this approach is that sex and sexuality are bad and that children are best protected against it. Similarly, the current trend toward broadening the definition of sexual harassment from its original conceptualization (as the use of power in an employer/employee or student/teacher relationship to acquire sexual favors from a subordinate) to current definitions that include unwanted gestures or looks between people of equal status in any setting, further suggests an underlying assumption regarding sexuality as negative.

Current public assumptions regarding sexuality may be seen, first, as a manifestation of religious indoctrination dating back centuries and, second, as a manifestation of the phenomena known as "lay theories." Aiding and abetting the pervasiveness of these sources is the pseudoscientific model for formulating concepts about human sexuality known as social constructionism.

SEXUALITY: THE DARK FORCE

Emerging in Christendom initially with the teachings of St. Augustine and further refined philosophically by St. Thomas Aquinas, sexuality became the evil dark force for which all that was base and immoral in man could be blamed. The body and pleasures derived from it were to be subordinated to the purity of the mind or, more importantly, the soul. Sex was the Devil's road of entry into the hearts and minds of humanity; while sex was a necessary means of procreation, the itch of lust threatened constantly to lead to damnation. Consequently, only sex that had reproduction as its explicit and sole purpose could be considered morally permissible, although Augustine, for a time, struggled with the sinful nature of the act of intercourse even under these circumstances (Money 1979; Mosher 1987; Ranke-Heinemann 1988/1990).

The nineteenth century saw the introduction of "rational" science into the debate over the role of sexuality as a precursor of social problems. This period saw degeneracy theory as the scientific explanation of masturbation as the root cause of most sociologic evils (Money 1979). Elements of the religious themes as well as degeneracy theory remain as an underlying rationalization of current popular understandings of sexual behavior and sex offending. In fact, through the efforts of legislators and of social scientists expounding social constructionism, the traditional sexual morality of the religious right has been legitimized. As Money notes:

> The basic paradigm remains unchanged [since the eighteenth century]. The individual man or woman is, by definition, capable of knowing right from wrong, and is held personally responsible for choosing the path of psychosexual obedience or disobedience, conformity or heresy. Psychosexual conformity and heresy are secularized in the laws of the state. Psychosexual nonconformity is a secular heresy. (1979: 27)

SOCIAL CONSTRUCTIONISM

C. S. Vance summarizes the substantive similarities and differences between several theories of sexuality ranging from the essentialist, which views much of our sexual being as predetermined biologically, to the most radical forms of social constructionism, which holds that all of sexuality is construction within a social milieu and culture. More specifically, Vance states:

> All social construction approaches adopt the view that physically identical sexual acts may have varying social significance and subjective meaning, depending on how they are defined and understood in different cultures and historical periods. . . . A further step in social construction theory posits that even the direction of erotic interests itself, for example, object choice (heterosexuality, homosexuality, and bisexuality, as contemporary sexology would conceptualize it) is not intrinsic or inherent in the individual but is constructed from more polymorphous possibilities. . . . The most radical form of constructionist theory . . . is willing to entertain the possibility that there is no essential, undifferentiated sexual role, "impulse," "sex drive," or "lust," which resides in the body due to physiological functioning and sensation. Sexual desire, then, is itself constructed by culture and history from the energies and capacities of the body. (Vance 1991: 878)

Consequently, social constructionism claims that the culture in which a person lives and develops determines the appropriateness of a variety of forms of sexual expressions. More significantly, however, social constructionism views these expressions, including feelings, thoughts and attitudes, as originating from within that social construction. This view would be supported by many within the fields of anthropology and sexology. Social constructionism goes beyond this, however, to dispute the biological foundations of such behavior and, moreover, to view sexual behavior of the individual as infinitely socially malleable. Thus, in this paradigm, it becomes possible for an individual to deviate radically and impulsively from his or her typical pattern of sexual behavior to commit such crimes as rape, sexual abuse or ritual sexual abuse.

This has tremendous implications, of course, for social policy making, which is often linked to "lay theories" of what is normal versus abnormal sexuality. In the absence of an absolute reference for the ostensibly normal range of sexual behavior, one is left to examine current lay theories regarding sexuality and paraphilias which may themselves be sustaining sexual pathology:

Vance describes this process as follows.

> The growth of state interest in regulating sexuality (and the related decline of religious control) made legislative and public policy domains particularly attractive fields for political and intellectual struggles around sexuality in the nineteenth and twentieth centuries. Mass movements mobilized around venereal disease, prostitution, masturbation, social purity, and the double standard, employing grassroots political organizing, legislative lobbying, mass demonstrations, and cultural interventions utilizing complex symbols, rhetoric and representations. . . . Because state intervention was increasingly formulated in the language of health, physicians and scientists became important participants in the newly developing regulatory discourses. They also actively participated in elaborating these discourses as a way to legitimize their newly professionalizing specialties. (1991: 877)

Modern professional responses toward childhood sexual abuse appear to parallel, in form and strategy if not content, the response of the professional community toward sexual policy making in the later part of the nineteenth century (e.g., the treatment of masturbation as a social "problem"). In the 1980s, a conservative coalition powered the federal bureaucracy in the United States and sought to control and proscribe the boundaries of appropriate sexual behavior within a narrowly defined context. Frustrated in their pursuit of liberal causes, many mental health professionals and social scientists found child sexual abuse, sexual harassment and rape to be the areas of common ground between conservatives and liberals. Indeed, these causes represented some of the few social problems that could mobilize government resources and financial support for mental health services.

LAY THEORIES

Lay theories serve to provide a uniform, coherent, and simplistic explanation for complex, multifaceted problems. Such explanations serve multiple functions within society (Furnham 1988). These are:

1) *Establishment of a Cause-and-Effect Relationship between Phenomena Enabling One to Apportion Blame, Praise, or Responsibility.* This function of lay beliefs is frequently empowered by correlational thinking, wherein from the recognition that two variables co-vary, one draws the erroneous conclusion that one of the variables caused the other (with the assumption usually being

that the variable that appeared first caused the one that followed it). Thus lay theories about the causes of sexual violence against women are frequently based on correlational data regarding pornography and sexual violence. When confronted with a correlation that has face validity, lay theorists rarely attempt to further elaborate the presence or absence of a causal relationship. Though there is a direct positive correlation between the number of churches in a given community and the number of bars in a given community, no rational person would draw the conclusion that bars are caused by churches. When confronted with a correlation between explicit depictions of sexual activity and sexual violence in American culture, however, the presence of a cultural negativism toward sexuality sets the stage for the lay theorist to attribute sexual violence to pornography.

2) *Alleviation of Tension Engendered by a Lack of Tolerance for Ambiguity.* Any explanation is better than none at all for behaviors, problems, or conditions which create cognitive dissonance and for which responsibility or causality is not clearly established.

3) *Reduction of Cognitive Dissonance and Restoration of Balance.* This phenomenon can be observed with respect to accusations of sexual abuse of children. Such accusations compel us either to accept the truth of the accusation or to accept that the complaining child is neither innocent with respect to the concept of lying nor innocent of an awareness of or responsiveness to sexuality. That children are sexual beings creates cognitive dissonance because of the cultural demand that children are innocent and that sex is debasing. Consequently, reduction or avoidance of cognitive dissonance requires denial at all costs that accusations may be false.

Several features distinguish lay versus scientific explanations of phenomena. Scientific theories tend to be explicit and formal, derived logically with a high degree of internal consistency between conceptual components. Scientific theories are designed to be disproved or falsified, whereas lay theories are set up for verification only. The scientist tests a theory by attempting to disprove components of the theory. The lay theorist, however, seeks to verify the accuracy of a theory repeatedly, while frequently ignoring disconfirming evidence. This has been called the phenomenon of confirmatory bias. Scientific theories clearly demarcate correlations and causality, while lay theories frequently confuse the two concepts. Lay theories tend to be more descriptive of content whereas scientific theories are explanatory of process. Lay theories rely on individualistic data whereas scientific theories rely on large bodies of data from across many different individuals.

Despite their failings, lay theories serve an important role for organizing our perception of the world. We tend to notice and remember facts and events consistent with our own personal theories and to disregard contradictory information. Furthermore, we may retrospectively distort our perceptions of events based on our lay theories regarding those events.

Lay theories have enjoyed popular support through marketing strategies that make certain concepts easy to understand by reducing a big problem to a simple cause-and-effect relationship, and by linking the theory to current sociopolitical values. One example of this has been the shift of focus from physical abuse and neglect of children to sexual abuse. Public anger and interest were never fully mobilized against physical abuse since many parents too easily identified it with spanking and disciplining their own children, which in turn was not closely linked to the concept of physical abuse. However, given current cultural mores, which severely stigmatize and criminalize sexual acts with a child, public and professional condemnation and governmental response to sexual abuse of children has been swift and powerful. Despite their shortcomings, lay theories are frequently resistant to modification, particularly since empirical data appear to be much less relevant to lay persons than they are to scientists (Furnham 1988).

Much of the current national, state and local policy directed toward sex offending and paraphilias, as well as sexuality in general, is largely based on assumptions that may be viewed as lay theories. While scientific theories regarding sexuality and sex offending are still very limited, lay theories are frequently devoid of any empirical support whatsoever, or are predicated on distorted interpretations of empirical data. There are a number of lay theories which are currently popular with regard to child sexual abuse, rape, sexual harassment, pornography, treatment and punishment of sex offenders, and the full range of sexual behavior and interest as described elsewhere in this volume. Legislation, regulation and social policy at all levels of government are derived from these assumptions. Attempts at paraphilic prevention must first make these theories explicit and public, and subsequently propose and justify alternate assumptions so as to reframe and redefine public perceptions regarding these issues.

ASSUMPTIONS TO BE PROMOTED IN SUPPORT OF A BIOMEDICAL FOUNDATION FOR PARAPHILIC PREVENTION

First Assumption: Sex and sexuality are integral and inseparable components of our humanity and self-identity.

This assumption is in stark contrast with the currently popular lay theory, which holds that sexuality represents the darker side of humanity and is essentially a force destructive to the social order when practiced outside of a monogamous relationship or the prescribed reproductive function involving genital-to-genital contact within heterosexual intercourse. This currently held assumption is largely founded upon a long tradition of religious dogma about sexuality which pervades our culture and history, and which has re-emerged in certain forms, particularly with respect to male sexuality as misconstrued by some radical feminist groups. As noted by Money earlier in this volume, assumptions about degeneracy and evil as precursors to sex offending impede the acquisition of knowledge (Cowen's "generative base of knowledge") relative to paraphilias—knowledge required as part of the development of primary prevention programs mentioned earlier in this chapter.

Sex remains at its most basic level a biological function, the primary outcome of which is propagation of the species, although this view would be challenged by radical social constructionists. The evolution of sexual arousal and sexual response can be most easily understood, from a phylogenic perspective, as promoting and sustaining the sexual behavior that will allow the individual to preserve and pass on the gene pool to the next generation (Feierman 1990). While the form and object of sexual arousal and response may clearly be largely determined within the societal context, the fundamental sexual drive or impulse is an essential part of human existence; outside of a religious context, it cannot be plausibly argued to be either good or bad from a moral point of view, just as eating or drinking, as a biological function, cannot be categorized as good or bad. Moreover, despite attempts by social constructionists to diminish the relevance of biology, even those aspects of sexuality that are largely influenced by socialization processes are reflected in the neurobiological structure of the brain.

To the extent to which sexual behavior involves interpersonal interaction, moral constraints elucidated from moral precepts, outside the context of religiosity, can help to clarify the morality or immorality of various manifestations of sexual behaviors.

Second Assumption: Sexuality is a fundamental developmental process which evolves in a diverse range of expression from birth to death, and further, since sex is neither good nor bad from a moral standpoint, the concept of the child as sexually innocent is irrelevant.

There is now a substantial body of literature drawn from cross-cultural studies, historical investigations, and empirical observations at the biological and social level that documents the presence of some form of sexual drive and behavior from as early as the prenatal period. Research studies of childhood sexual experiences document the frequency and universality of a wide range of sexual behavior, including masturbation, genital exhibitionism and voyeurism, fondling, mutual masturbation, genital-genital contact, and oral-genital contact, anal-genital contact, attempted and successful sexual intercourse, all involving same- and opposite-sex peers (Calderone 1983; Constantine & Martinson 1982; Currier 1982; Gunderson et al. 1982; Haugaard & Tilly 1988; Langfeldt 1982; Langfeldt 1990; Martinson 1976; Money 1986; Spiro 1965).

Langfeldt (1990) described sexual functioning as the integration of genital activation and learning to be orgasmic. He describes genital activation as an automatic process that probably begins before birth and in boys is evidenced by penile erection. He views the variety of forms of genital activation (ranging from spontaneous erections during REM [Rapid Eye Movement] sleep to erections caused by manual or genital stimulation) as evidence of the beginning of sexual activity and the formation of healthy sexual functioning.

This concept of early sexual experiences as forming the foundation for later sexual expression has been further elaborated upon in John Money's theory of sexual development in which he hypothesizes a critical period for the normophilic development of sexuality, a period coinciding with early childhood. It is during this critical period that a child develops a "lovemap," a term by which Money refers to a type of template which describes, defines and limits the idealized lover-lover interaction that will ultimately be expressed postpubertally and in adulthood (Money 1986). The lovemap differentiates gradually throughout childhood and stores not only the image of the idealized lover, but the form and expression by which the child, as an adult, will manifest the romantic and erotic relationship with a lover. Stored in the brain, this template for sexual functioning may first be manifested in the dreams and fantasies of adolescence and eventually, through actions, feelings and behavior, with the desired love partner.

Critical to the development of a healthful sexuality in adulthood is the opportunity for sexuoerotic rehearsal play during infancy and childhood. Money states:

> [A]ge concordant, gender different, sexuoerotic rehearsal play during infancy and childhood, is prerequisite to healthy heterosexual lovemap formation. Deprivation and neglect of such play may induce pathology of lovemap formation, as also may prohibition, prevention and abusive punishment and discipline. Conversely, exposure too abruptly to socially taboo expressions of sexuoeroticism may traumatize lovemap formation. (1986: xvi)

Clearly, then, any understanding of how we might ultimately prevent the development and manifestations of paraphilias and sex offending in adults, must take into consideration the sexual development of the child. Within the theoretical framework proposed by Money, there may be a critical period during which proactive attention to the sexual development of the child may positively correlate with the emergence of healthful sexual functioning in adulthood. Conversely, distortions, traumas, or simple neglect of that sexual development may be a necessary if not sufficient precursor to paraphilic development.

Langfeldt (1990) describes four different types of interactions between the child and his/her environment which may have impacts on sexual development. He discusses how the sexual attitudes of caretakers and parents may first be transmitted to the infant based on parental responses and attitudes to such activities as toileting and bathing, and treatment of the genitals during those occasions. The second form of interaction relates to the child's sexual interest in adult sexuality. How parents respond to the child's curiosity about the genitals of the parent has implications for how the child comes to view sexuality in interpersonal relationships. The next type of interaction considers the child as a passive observer of adult sexuality and how adults transmit their own sexual perceptions. Children who are exposed to a never-ending onslaught of negative information regarding sexuality such as child sexual abuse, rape, AIDS, sexually transmitted diseases (STDs), harassment, or negative sex education may come to view sexuality in overly negative terms (Tharinger 1987). If children are not presented with a balanced view of sexuality which places such sexual activities as masturbation and intercourse in a positive light, or which fails to place sexual behavior within a broader context of sexuality that includes the expression of affection, love, and nongenital sensual touch, the normophilic development of the lovemap may be compromised. The fourth type of interaction that impacts on the formation of the child's lovemap is the sexual experience children have with other children, ranging from talking about sex to engaging in sexual games and activities.

Langfeldt (1990) describes in detail the forms of sexual response and behavior observed in children in his research, and looks at the progression that behavior takes, from clumsy forms of sexual expression to more specific and partner-cognizant behavior.

The relationship between a positive and encouraging atmosphere relative to the development of childhood sexual explorations and attitudes, on the one hand, and adult erotic adjustment on the other, can be made both empirically and logically. Although the empirical evidence is limited, there is some cross-cultural evidence from societies which promote, or do not discourage, sexual explorations and juvenile sexual rehearsal play, of low rates of sexual pathology and paraphilias in their adult populations (Currier 1982; Spiro 1965; Money 1986). Once one accepts childhood sexuality as a fundamental developmental process (as has been argued extensively elsewhere: Krivacska 1990), the importance of nurturing that development relative to promoting adult functioning becomes obvious. No rational person would deny the importance of nurturing the development of language, cognition, motor skills, sensory processing, memory and attention, or social maturation to enhance the child's ultimate functioning as a healthy adult. One knows from nearly a century of research that deprivation during certain critical periods has a profound and irretrievably harmful effect on language and cognitive development. The work of Bowlby and his associates over the last twenty years has expanded the understanding of critical developmental periods into the social/emotional, interpersonal and attachment/bonding domains as well.

It would be logically inconsistent, then, to assume that a function so critical to propagation of the species and so primitive along the phylogenic continuum would not also be both developmental in nature, and requiring exercise during a critical period. In fact, contrary to the current trend that exists in our society, the burden of proof should be on those who wish to deny sexuality as a developmental process and for whom any of its manifestations prior to adulthood is considered pathological.

Third Assumption: Children exposed to sexual contacts and the adult world of sexuality are not necessarily traumatized by those experiences.

Current cultural lay theories founded on the assumption that sex is bad and that children are asexual, concurrently view children's exposure to pornography, to the observation of sexual intercourse (especially parental intercourse), and to intergenerational sexual experiences as being necessarily and inevitably traumatic. However, when sex and sexuality are viewed in neutral terms as described under the first assumption above, and when children are understood essentially to be sexual beings, support for this premise of universal trauma erodes to some degree. There is cross-cultural as well as historical evidence of intergenerational sexual contact (Constantine & Martinson 1982; Farrell 1990; Feierman 1990; Kilpatrick 1992; Nelson, this volume; Sandfort & Everaerd 1990) which may not have had traumatizing effects on children due to the acceptance of such contacts within the cultural standards of sexual behavior. From both theoretical and empirical perspectives, it is difficult to support the conclusion that in instances of noncoercive or nonaggressive sexual contact between an older and a younger person, irrespective of age, the sexual contact per se creates trauma. Rather, whatever the trauma that might be experienced, it would appear to be engendered by the interpersonal and cultural context within which the contact occurs. Critical to the understanding and acceptance of this presumption is the acceptance of the view that how a child perceives the genitals and sexual activity is culturally determined. Given the cultural context, playing with someone's genitals might be like playing with someone's fingers. Consequently, no trauma from noncoercive, nonaggressive sex play of this type would be evoked.

Thus if the cultural context is one that supports certain types of intergenerational sexual activity as part of the sexual developmental process, then no trauma will occur. In fact, deviation from such intergenerational contact may have a stigmatizing or traumatizing effect on the child so excluded. The

Sambia of the New Guinea Highlands, for example, incorporated acts of androphilic pedophilia into their rituals of indoctrination and initiation of tribal prepubertal males. These rituals, which began at age eight and continued until the male's first ejaculation, were believed to be essential for maturation into the adult roles of warrior and heterosexual marriage partner (Herdt 1981). Similarly, childhood observations of intercourse, both directly or pictorially, need not be traumatic outside of a social milieu that defines it as traumatizing.

A fundamental premise of social constructionism as well as of anthropology demands that we consider societal norms in understanding the meaning and implications of any given sexual behavior. This is not to argue that adult-child sexual experiences should be either permitted or encouraged, but rather that the issue of how we respond to instances of such contact not only within our culture but also transculturally be confronted. A misguided response may induce trauma or magnify what has already occurred.

Yates (1990) describes how youngsters in cultures that are sexually permissive become eroticized at a young age, and consequently seek out and engage in sexual behavior in a manner not too different from that of their adult counterparts. Sexual eroticization, when it occurs within the context of socially sanctioned sexual permissiveness, does not necessarily become pervasive or intrusive in the child's overall life, but rather becomes simply another part of childhood play and social interaction. When the eroticization occurs in the context of a discrepancy between the child's sexual experiences and the norms of the society, the response of society as experienced by the child often leads to eroticized behavior with a perseveration or compulsive quality, wherein relationships with peers or adults are viewed only within the context of satisfaction of the child's sexuality. Such children may have a difficult time experiencing or expressing affection that does not have sexual satisfaction as its ultimate goal.

Fourth Assumption: Punishment is not treatment.

During the decade of the 1980s, political conservatism and the resurgence of the influence of various antisexual fundamentalist groups across the United States resurrected, as a fundamental premise underlying violent and criminal acts, the concept of the motivating force of evil. To some extent, this conceptualization can be traced to a fundamentalist Christian perspective which views man as essentially evil, with Divine intervention as the only means to redemption. Engagement in criminal, antisocial or deviant behavior is attributed to conscious choice on the part of the offender, which can be rightly answered only with retaliation, retribution, and punishment. Despite overwhelming social data that support the correlation between poverty, disenfranchisement, and dysfunctional families as a predictor of violent criminal activity in adolescence and adulthood, there has been little progress made in understanding criminal acts within a social context, as opposed to a conceptualization of good versus evil. This is even more true when dealing with sex offenders, given the presumption that sex and sexuality represent the baser forces in human nature (Miller 1991).

Those who engage in sex crimes, particularly those whose targets are children, are seen as the most evil and worthy of punishment. Even among criminals in penal confinement, child molesters are viewed as utterly despicable and often must be segregated from the rest of the prison population for their own protection. Legislatively, stiffer and stiffer penalties for sex crimes have been imposed, while constitutional safeguards afforded those accused of sex crimes, particularly against children, have been reduced. Although treatment centers for sex offenders are located in many states, treatment is typically available, if at all, only to those already convicted of sex offenses. Furthermore, treatment centers have rarely been fully staffed, and even worse, effective models of treatment, e.g., pharmacological, are rarely utilized. There are currently virtually no treatment centers available in this country for nonadjudicated sex offenders. Recent changes in the law have had another deleterious effect on self-referral treatment centers. One such center, the Sexual Disorders Clinic located at the Johns Hopkins Hospital, served self-referred pedophiles for many years, until a modification in the mandatory reporting laws in Maryland required that law enforcement agencies be informed of self-disclosed adult pedophilic clients who reported acts of sexual contact with a minor (anyone under eighteen), even if the acts were historical and no longer occurring. Berlin et al. (1991) reviewed the data on self-referrals, which went from an average of one every two months in the 1980s to none after passage of this law.

Several studies conducted in the last few years have shown that a significant proportion of psychologists, psychiatrists and other mental health professionals fail to report cases of suspected child abuse to authorities. Most of these studies criticize this behavior and seek to educate professionals about their responsibility to report. Absent from most studies is an investigation into why professionals may fail to report certain cases of abuse. In reality, many professionals recognize child protection services agencies as inadequate to meet the needs of clients referred to them, and that certain situations, particularly those involving cases of abuse that occurred in the past and are no longer going on, are left unreported in the best interests of the victim. Some adolescent victims, in particular, may be adamant about not having abuse reported, especially historical abuse. They may experience violation of the confidential client-therapist relationship as a further betrayal of trust that compounds the experience of the original victimization. Since it is the ethical responsibility of mental health professionals to specify the limits of confidentiality within the psychotherapeutic relationship, prospective clients must be told to avoid disclosures of a history of pedophilic sexual contact which will require a report to legal authorities—and which makes a mockery of therapeutic trust.

It cannot be estimated at this time how many victims have maintained the secrecy of their abuse through fear of the consequences of disclosure, and thus have not been able to receive supportive counseling necessary to deal with and integrate their experiences. Significantly, in several states, such as Maryland, the inability of a perpetrator to receive confidential treatment, other than by going through the criminal justice system, presents the prototypical example of the current preference of punishment over treatment. Out of fear of "protecting perpetrators," society has removed the one vehicle by which a pedophile can receive treatment to prevent future victimizations. In the absence of the availability of that treatment, it is only reasonable to assume that the perpetrator will, at some point, reoffend.

Conceptualizing paraphilias and other sexual dysfunctions in adulthood as manifestations of traumatized or damaged lovemaps traced to early childhood sexual development excludes "evil" as an explanation of perpetrator behavior. Scientifically, sexual offending is an issue of mental health, not of being possessed by evil or by demons. To incarcerate sex offenders but not provide treatment is irrational and counterproductive with respect to an ultimate cure as well as prevention.

Fifth Assumption: Identification does not mean prevention.

During the last decade, efforts at identification of such socially proscribed behaviors as childhood sexual abuse, date rape, and sexual harassment have been labeled as prevention efforts. Consequently, there are currently tens of millions of children exposed to child sexual abuse prevention programs where the primary purpose of the program is to get the children either to disclose abuse which they have experienced, or to interrupt and report abuse that they are experiencing, or, alas, to fabricate abuse. Note, however, that under these programs, prevention of abuse occurs after the onset of abuse. A child who successfully tells his neighbor no when the neighbor attempts to fondle the child's genitals has, within our social norms and the criminal codes of all fifty states, already been sexually abused simply by the attempt or the verbal suggestion of it. Prevention programs have not reduced the level of motivation to abuse on the part of the pedophile and, at best, may simply prompt the pedophile to be more cautious in his/her selection of opportunities. The majority of children who are presumed to have been subjected to abuse today may still not be reporting that abuse. Indeed, efforts at prevention may be doing more harm than good to the extent that the child who has been exposed to a prevention program has been unable to terminate or report the abuse and is now left to feel guilty about having failed to live up to the responsibility of reporting it (Krivacska 1990).

As in the case of sexual abuse, sexual harassment is being labeled and identified, but the fundamental societal norms and child-rearing practices which promote and sustain its existence have not been acknowledged or addressed. The issues of sexual abuse, harassment, and date rape are further compounded insofar as the current sociological trend calls for the label of "victim" to be applied to any class or group or individuals who claim to have been in any way wronged (Schultz 1980). The definition of sexual harassment, as originally derived from federal legislation, was directed at protecting individuals from unwanted sexual advances in the workplace or school, protecting them from denial of their rights to employment, advancement, compensation, or education based on their refusal of sexual advances, and protecting them from the creation of an environment either at work or school hostile to the employee or student (Williams & Cyr 1992). That definition has been broadened now to include any verbal, nonverbal or physical act that the target subjectively interprets or feels is unwanted or unwelcome, thus increasing the range of problematic behavior to unwanted gestures or glances, and to exposure to crude jokes or pinup posters (Melisurgo 1993). Recent research is now focused on documenting instances of sexual harassment among juveniles as well as those in high school environments (Williams & Cyr 1992).

Such an overly broad definition of a problem risks damaging the credibility of true victims by devaluing their experiences. It is absurd to equate the experience of being told that you must sleep with your boss in order to get a job, with being stared at from across the classroom by a peer who thinks you're good-looking. Of particular concern are attempts to broaden definitions of sexual abuse and harassment to include childhood experiences. It appears that we are failing to recognize the essential nature of socialization as one of the most critical developmental processes of childhood and adolescence. Socialization involves the navigation, mediation and negotiation of social situations and the refinement of skills so as to advance one's needs and interests while simultaneously respecting the needs and interests of others.

Children and adolescents must have an opportunity to experience experimentation in their social relations, including the opportunity to make mistakes without being labeled an abuser or a harasser. This is not to deny that some children and adolescents engage in patterns of sexual behavior and harassment which are pathological and abusive toward peers or others. However, society must do a better job of defining and categorizing that behavior so as not to be overly inclusive and thus restrict normal development.

Some fundamental changes do need to be made in societal perceptions of women and sexual relations. However, we are not being honest with ourselves if we don't recognize the confusion created within children who are given an incredibly mixed and incompatible set of messages from the media and the home with respect to the role of sexuality in their lives and interpersonal experiences. We create an environment in which date rape and sexual harassment are promoted through lack of information regarding alternative, appropriate sexual interactions and through lack of opportunities to rehearse those interactions. We present a distorted set of images and messages to our children through the media as well as through direct modeling by significant individuals in their lives. Then we expect to reeducate them, as adolescents, into politically correct behavior.

The broad definition of sexual harassment insidiously creates a negative attitude toward sex at least as much as it fosters a negative image of males as being insensitive to females. William and Cyr (1992) note that perceptions and attributions determine whether someone identifies a situation as harassing. As a result of their own and others' research, they have determined that males and females make different attributions, resulting in conflicting conclusions regarding harassing behavior. The unspoken assumption here is that the male's misperception of a situation promotes behavior which the female perceives as harassing, and that consequently the male's perceptions or attributions need to be changed—hence the need for sexual harassment awareness programs in public high schools. This assumption, however, is predicated upon the premise that sex is a patriarchal expression of power and control used to keep women subordinate and submissive.

Consider the impact of reframing the sexual harassment argument as representative of our culture's tendency to indoctrinate women into a view of sexuality which is essentially negative and which essentially denies women their sexuality by suggesting that women who enjoy and seek out sexual pleasure are impure or unchaste. A reasonable argument could then be made not only that men must become sensitized to their harassing behavior, but that women must be liberated from their sexual negativity. Such a reframing suggests that the harassing effect of telling a dirty joke in mixed company could be equally diminished by sensitizing men to avoid making such jokes and by giving women permission to enjoy such jokes.

To provide an analogy here, one needs only to take the supposedly sexually harassing situation of a group of males telling dirty jokes in the company of a woman who finds such jokes crude, and replace males and females with liberals and conservatives. Would we be arguing that the sole conservative in a crowd of liberals had been politically harassed by being exposed to the telling of liberal jokes? Hardly.

In short, then, efforts at identification of offending behavior via overly broad definitions of such behavior confounds, confuses and distracts from prevention efforts.

Sixth Assumption: Individuals (both child and adult) who experience sex offenses by a paraphilic offender do not universally experience the event as traumatic and vary considerably in the range of negative reactions manifested.

Born of investigations into the effects of child sexual abuse and rape based on evaluations of clinical populations, current dogma within the field of victimology does not allow for experience of sex offending without long-term sequelae of trauma. Those who claim no trauma may be labeled as being in repression or in denial. Certainly, many individuals, as a result of their internalization of societal norms of behavior, experience trauma and distress as a result of being exposed to sex-offending behavior. Nevertheless, the impact of those experiences is significantly mediated and affected by experiences subsequent to the event. A child who has experienced some pleasure from fondling at the hands of a familiar person may, upon disclosure of the abuse, be placed in therapy to reduce the trauma assumed to have been experienced. Wolters et al. (1985) describe the calm reactions of parents of child sexual abuse victims in the Netherlands, where a liberal climate relative to sexuality may insulate a child from iatrogenic traumatization.

If a child has not experienced trauma and is, nonetheless, exposed to therapy to uncover and express his or her "anger," trauma may be induced (Schultz 1980; Schultz & Jones 1983). The child is then repeatedly exposed to and reminded of the social abhorrence of the allegedly traumatizing activity which may heighten the perception of having been traumatized. The child may also assume the role of victim, since not to be traumatized by such allegedly abhorrent acts would imply collaboration with the abuser. When anger reduction therapy is introduced in the absence of real anger, the child may, in effect, be trained to be angry, which in itself is traumatizing (Wakefield & Underwager 1988).

The experience of the investigation, questioning, and therapy all may distort the child's perception of any ostensible event and any attitudes about it. The most significant aspect of this assumption is the failure to recognize the need for a wide range of treatment options, one of which must be the option of no treatment. There may be an incident which the child did not experience as traumatic, so that exposure to therapy may interfere with the child's natural processes for dealing with similar incidents. For such children, some guidance and education provided to the parents may be all that is necessary or appropriate. Additionally, therapy must be directed at the reality experienced by the child, rather than the assumed reality of the therapist. In the absence of clear evidence of the denial of anger, it is not appropriate to introduce anger reduction therapy since, in all likelihood, the therapist will need first to teach the child to be angry. Failure to appreciate the impact on the child of experiences subsequent to disclosure of a sex offense, may have adverse implications for subsequent sexuoerotic development.

Any time that sexual abuse has been documented, the potential impact of the abuse on the sexual development of the child must be assessed. It is not appropriate to assume that such an effect is always negative. The only effect may have been an awakening of the child's sexual awareness, without pathological consequences.

By contrast, if the effect of the sexual abuse has been to distort the child's sexuality as manifested by aggressive sexual play, obsessive masturbation, or inappropriate masturbation in public, then therapy is warranted. As described by Yates (1990), such therapy will necessitate identification and provision of an appropriate sexual outlet for the child's sexual drive, and a redirection of some of the sexual impulse into nonsexual forms of affective expression. Failure to respond in this manner may increase the likelihood that the child will become a sex offender in later life.

RECOMMENDATIONS FOR SOCIAL POLICY AND LEGAL REFORMS

When one considers current societal expectations, perceptions and norms regarding sex and sexuality, as well as popular lay theories about child sexual development and sex offending in general, it is easy to become pessimistic with respect to successful paraphilic prevention. Nevertheless, a first step in any process of change is recognition and identification of what needs to be changed. Since much of current practice in the area of sexuality and sex offending is promoted and supported by mental health professionals, a first and very important step is education of those who serve in policy making and regulatory bodies at all levels of government.

As professionals who recognize an ethical and moral responsibility to present information and data objectively, we must ourselves come to grips with and acknowledge the existence of childhood sexual development and the role and limits of juvenile sexual rehearsal play in that development. A process of education must be promoted which advocates the proactive promotion of childhood sexual development and which must, of necessity, include parents as well as children. Clearly this will not be a message that will be easy for many parents to accept. However, given the opportunity, parents do seek this information and want to engage in a discourse regarding their child's sexual development.

Currently, most children at various points in their life undergo medical evaluations by pediatricians and other physicians. In addition, a significant portion of the childhood and adolescent population have reason to be evaluated by school psychologists, social workers, psychiatrists, and other mental health professionals. The only aspect of childhood development that is routinely ignored in all of these assessments is sexuality. Sexuality assessment, such as described by Langfeldt (1990), needs to be incorporated into the protocols of psychological and medical evaluations so as to identify the early onset of pathological sexual responses, experiences or arousal patterns, but more importantly to validate sexological health as an aspect of self and identity.

Primary prevention interventions of this nature promote the development of psychosocial health and identify, through the process of promoting that health with education and training, social perceptions and environmental conditions that currently permeate our society and predispose us to high levels of sexual violence and deviancy.

Primary prevention needs to be supported by secondary and tertiary prevention efforts. Secondary and tertiary measures involve modifying the societal response to sexual offenses and require substantial restructuring of several components of current protection systems. Modification of mandatory reporting laws should be made so as to provide individuals, particularly adolescents, with opportunities to discuss and deal with experiences of sexual abuse without automatic reporting to authorities. Under many circumstances, adolescents and even some children may have compelling reasons for not wanting to disclose sexual abuse. Failure to acknowledge and respond to such reasons denies respect to the individual who may then be locked into a secret that cannot be revealed.

Tied to this issue is the need for a range of responses to reports of sex offenses, including noncriminal dispositions. One model was described by Besharov (1981) in which Belgium and the Netherlands have, since the 1940s, utilized a "confidential doctor system" to respond to and treat child abuse. Under this system, certain classes of abuse are treated by specially trained professionals and monitored with referral to the legal system only after therapeutic approaches have been unsuccessful.

Closely related to this issue is the difficulty of obtaining confidential treatment for sex offenders, particularly pedophiles. No one's interests are served, not those of the children who have been abused, or the children who might be abused in the future, or the perpetrator, or even society, when all avenues for confidential treatment without criminal referral are removed from the sex offender. Mandatory loss of confidentiality is a powerful indictment of the power of ideology over reality and strong evidence of a belief system that sees sex offenders, particularly pedophiles, as fundamentally evil in nature, and consequently in need of punishment. While it is true that many sex offenders do not seek treatment voluntarily, there is no rational reason to deny it to those who would avail themselves of it.

There has arisen in the last decade or so a new science of victimology which challenges traditional notions of human resiliency and competency. It was not long ago that social workers were cautioned against becoming enablers by engaging in what appeared to be well-meaning and compassionate responses to persons in crisis, but which in reality interfered with the promotion of a self-help and competency. Rather than helping a survivor of an abusive situation to regain social and intrapsychic equilibrium, victimology seeks to dig into the victimization experience beyond all resistance until the survivor comes to define his or her life and existence within the context of the abusive incident. The person's life is then reconstructed as that of a victim or survivor. There is no research to support the validity of this approach, and certainly nothing to support its superiority over alternative approaches. It does, however, fit within an emerging social norm in which tolerance is displaced by intolerance and offense. With sexual harassment described by some as any verbal, nonverbal or physical act which the target individuals feels is unwanted and unwelcome behavior, anything from crude jokes and bathroom graffiti, sexually explicit letters, and pin-up posters, to physical assaults, attempted rapes and rapes becomes classified as sexual harassment.

SUMMARY

Ultimately, the elimination of paraphilia and sex offenses within our culture will require a fundamental shift in cultural perceptions of sexuality in general, and childhood sexuality in particular. Removed from the tainted aura of original sin and its debasement of the human form and spirit, sexuality must be transformed into an integral and wholesome aspect of our being and daily life in which love and lust are intrapsychically integrated. Promotion of the normophilic development of childhood sexuality will be viewed as not only desirable, but also as a responsibility of parents and society, and thus not to be ignored or devalued. Children will be accepted as sexual beings and their sexual behavior considered a means toward healthful sexual expression in adulthood. Individuals who, for whatever reason, fail to develop healthful sexual functioning as adults, and who manifest a tendency toward paraphilic sexual offending, will be identified and treated as individuals in need of mental health services rather than as criminals who are voluntarily engaging in criminal activity against other members of society. Society needs to recognize that it is in its own self-interest to provide opportunities for both victims and offenders to receive help and treatment in a confidential environment, without fear of disclosure. Those who are the recipients of sexual offenses are not inevitably powerless, helpless victims whose only role in life is to enmesh themselves in their victimization, aided and abetted by well-meaning if misguided mental health professionals. There is resiliency and a capacity for healing evident in all of us, even those who have experienced sexual offenses at the highest degree of traumatization.

It is incumbent upon professionals, particularly those who have sought to practice within sexology and to serve either perpetrators or their victims, or both, to remain true to data, reason and rationality, and strive to avoid the temptation to jump on the proverbial bandwagon. To do so can only delay the emergence of a society in which sex offending and paraphilia are the subject of history books rather than front page news.

NOTES

1. Some question whether such specialty really exists given the absence of any certification, licensing or credentialing for this field as well as the absence of graduate training programs, accreditation of such programs or any agreed-upon fundamental base of knowledge which should be taught to those entering the field.

2. "Program" here is defined in its broadest manner and refers to broad-based policy decisions from a national level down to specific interventions aimed at identified target populations at a local level.

REFERENCES

Berlin, F. S.; Malin, H. M.; and Dean, S. (1991). "Effects of Statutes Requiring Psychiatrists to Report Suspected Sexual Aabuse of Children." *American Journal of Psychiatry* 148: 449–53.

Besharov, D. J. (1981). "The Third International Congress on Child Abuse and Neglect: Congress Highlights." *Child Abuse and Neglect* 5: 221–15.

Calderone, M. S. (1983). "Childhood Sexuality: Approaching the Prevention of Sexuality Disease." In G. W. Albee, S. Gordon, and H. Leitenberg, eds., *Promoting Sexual Responsibility and Preventing Sexual Problems.* Hanover, Mass.: University Press of New England.

Cantwell, H. (1988). "Child Sexual Abuse: Very Young Perpetrators." *Child Abuse and Neglect* 12: 579–82.

Caplan, G. (1964). *Principles of Preventive Psychiatry.* New York: Basic Books.

Constantine, L. L., and Martinson, F. M., eds. (1982). *Children and Sex: New Findings, New Perspectives.* Boston: Little, Brown and Co.

Cowen, E. L. (1980). "The Wooing of Primary Prevention." *American Journal of Community Psychology* 8: 258–84.

Currier, R. L. (1982). "Juvenile Sexuality in Global Perspective." In L. L. Constantine and F. M. Martinson, eds., *Children and Sex: New Findings, New Perspectives.* Boston: Little, Brown, and Co.

Farrell, W. (1990). "The Last Taboo?: The Complexities of Incest and Female Sexuality." In M. Perry, ed., *Handbook of Sexology: Childhood and Adolescent Sexology,* vol. 7, pp. 335–59. Amsterdam: Elsevier.

Feierman, J. (1990). "A Biosocial Overview of Adult Human Sexual Behavior with Children and Adolescents." In J. R. Feierman, ed., *Pedophilia: Biosocial Dimensions*. New York: Springer-Verlag.

Furnham, A. F. (1988). *Lay Theories: Everyday Understanding of Problems in the Social Sciences*. New York: Pergamon Press.

Gunderson, B. H.; Melås, P. S.; and Skår, J. E. (1982). "Sexual Behavior of Preschool Children: Teachers' Observations." In L. L. Constantine and F. M. Martinson, eds., *Children and Sex: New Findings, New Perspectives*. Boston: Little, Brown, and Co.

Haugaard, J. J., and Tilly, C. (1988). "Characteristics Predicting Children's Responses to Sexual Encounters with Other Children." *Child Abuse and Neglect* 12: 209–218.

Heller, K.; Price, R. H.; and Sher, K. J. (1980). "Research and Evaluation in Primary Prevention: Issues and Guidelines." In R. H. Price, R. F. Ketterer, B. C. Bader, and J. Monahan, eds., *Prevention in Mental Health: Research, Policy and Practice*. Beverly Hills, Calif.: Sage.

Herdt, G. H. *Guardians of the Flutes: Idioms of Masculinity*. New York: McGraw-Hill.

Jenson, G. (1993). [Children's responses to questions about their perceptions of their genitals after exposure to sexual abuse prevention program material]. Unpublished raw data.

Johnson, T. C. (1988). "Child Perpetrators—Children Who Molest Other Children: Preliminary Findings." *Child Abuse and Neglect* 12: 219–29.

Kilpatrick, A. C. (1992). *Long-Range Effects of Child and Adolescent Sexual Experiences: Myths, Mores, and Menaces*. Hillsdale, N.J.: Lawrence Erlbaum.

Klein, D. C., and Goldston, S. E. (1976). *Primary Prevention: An Idea Whose Time Has Come*. Washington, D.C.: National Institute of Mental Health.

Krivacska, J. J. (1990). *Designing Child Sexual Abuse Prevention Programs: Current Approaches and a Proposal for the Prevention, Reduction and Identification of Sexual Misuse*. Springfield, Ill.: Charles C Thomas, Pub.

Langfeldt, T. (1982). "Processes in Sexual Development." In L. L. Constantine and F. M. Martinson, eds., *Children and Sex: New Findings, New Perspectives*. Boston: Little, Brown, and Co.

——— (1990). "Early Childhood and Juvenile Sexuality, Development and Problems." In M. Perry, ed., *Handbook of Sexology: Childhood and Adolescent Sexology*, vol. 7, pp. 179–200. Amsterdam: Elsevier.

Martinson, F. M. (1976). "Eroticism in Infancy and Childhood." *The Journal of Sex Research* 12, no. 4: 251–62.

Melisurgo, L. (1993, January 14). "Researcher Calls for New Focus on Schoolgirl Sex Harassment." *The Star Ledger* (Newark, N.J.), p. 33.

Meyers, J., and Parson, R. D. (1987). "Prevention Planning in the School System." In J. Hermalin and J. A. Morell, eds., *Prevention Planning in Mental Health*. Newbury Park, Calif.: Sage.

Miller, J. G. (1991, September 24). "On Mitigating Professional Arrogance in the Treatment of Sex Offenders." Paper presented at the 2nd Annual Conference on Treating Sex Offenders, Minneapolis, Minn.

Money, J. (1979). "Ideas and Ethics of Psychosexual Determinism." *British Journal of Sexual Medicine* 6, no. 48: 27–32.

——— (1985). *The Destroying Angel: Sex, Fitness and Food in the Legacy of Degeneracy Theory, Graham Crackers, Kellogg's Corn Flakes and American Health History.* Buffalo, N.Y.: Prometheus Books.

——— (1986). *Lovemaps: Clinical Concepts of Sexual/Erotic Health and Pathology, Paraphilia, and Gender Transposition in Childhood, Adolescence, and Maturity.* New York: Irvington; Buffalo, N.Y.: Prometheus Books, 1988 (paperback).

Mosher, D. L. (1987). "Threat to Sexual Freedom: Moralistic Intolerance Instills a Spiral of Silence." *The Journal of Sex Research* 26: 492–519.

Ranke-Heinemann, U. (1990). *Eunuchs for the Kingdom of Heaven: Women, Sexuality and the Catholic Church.* Trans. P. Heinegg. New York: Doubleday. (Originally published 1988.)

Sandfort, T. G. M., and Everaerd, W. T. A. M. (1990). "Male Juvenile Partners in Pedophilia." In M. Perry, ed., *Handbook of Sexology: Childhood and Adolescent Sexology,* vol. 7, pp. 361–80. Amsterdam: Elsevier.

Schultz, L. G. (1980, August). "Victim-Helpers as Hostages to Ideology: The Case of Adult-Minor Sexual Interaction." Paper presented at the First World Congress of Victimology, Washington, D.C.

Schultz, L. G., and Jones, P. (1983). "Sexual Abuse of Children: Issues for Social Service and Health Professionals." *Child Welfare* 62: 99–108.

Spiro, M. E. (1965). *Children of the Kibbutz.* New York: Schocken Books.

Swift, M., and Weirich, T. W. (1987). "Prevention Planning as Social and Organizational Change." In J. Hermalin and J. A. Morell, eds., *Prevention Planning in Mental Health.* Newbury Park, Calif.: Sage.

Tharinger, D. J. (1987). "Children and Sexual Interest." In A. Thomas and J. Grimes, eds., *Children's Needs: Psychological Perspectives.* Washington, D.C.: National Association of School Psychologists.

Vance, C. S. (1991). "Anthropology Rediscovers Sexuality: A Theoretical Comment." *Social Science Medicine* 33: 875–84.

Wakefield, H., and Underwager, R. (1988). *Accusations of Child Sexual Abuse.* Springfield, Ill.: Charles C Thomas, Pub.

Williams, K. B., and Cyr, R. R. (1992). "Escalating Commitment to a Relationship: The Sexual Harassment Trap." *Sex Roles* 27: 47–71.

Wolters, W. H. G.; Zwaan, E. J.; Wagenaar-Schwencke, P. M.; and Deenen, A. M. (1985). "A Review of Cases of Sexually Exploited Children Reported to the Netherlands State Police." *Child Abuse and Neglect* 9: 571–74.

Yates, A. (1990). "Eroticized Children." In M. Perry, ed., *Handbook of Sexology: Childhood and Adolescent Sexology,* vol. 7, pp. 325–34. Amsterdam: Elsevier.

18

The Alleged Link between Pornography and Violence

F. M. Christensen

Charges that exposure to sexual materials in some way incites violence, notably rape, have been much debated and investigated. This chapter surveys critically the scientific investigations to date that have been either most inherently valuable or most influential; it then analyzes the theory and ideology involved in interpreting the empirical data.[1]

For purposes of this discussion, the English word "pornography" is understood in its traditional sense, as presented in standard dictionaries: "portrayal of sex for the purpose of erotic arousal," or the like. The flurry of redefinitions employed in recent years, mostly for ideological purposes, have served only to obscure the issues. Specific *types* of such portrayals—degrading or not, violent or not, aesthetic or not—can be distinguished from pornography in general, as needed. For want of space, however, this chapter must ignore the claim—debated, but to this writer plausible—that portrayals of violence, including sexual violence, can in some circumstances motivate actual violence.

I. DIRECT EMPIRICAL EVIDENCE

Generally speaking, three different types of data are appealed to as evidence for the causes or motivations of behavior: reports of individual cases, statistical samples from the general population, and experimental studies of individuals or groups. In principle, each has its strengths and weaknesses.

Anecdotal Claims

In-depth studies of individual case histories—say, the life of a serial rapist—are potentially very revealing. Their worth depends, of course, on a broad background knowledge about human nature in order to interpret the particulars of the case. The major danger is that instead, the investigator's inherent prejudice will inform both the perception and the analysis of what is discovered. In daily life, this sort of evidence degenerates into the justifiably much-maligned anecdote, with its sloppy *post hoc, ergo propter hoc* reasoning, that confuses sequence with causality.

With all the emotion surrounding the issue of pornography, this kind of thinking is rampant, even among scientifically trained investigators. We constantly hear claims about sex criminals found to own pornography, ignoring all those who do not and all the noncriminals who do. The vast and sparsely mapped terrain of human psychology being what it is, such stories can be no more than indicators of hypotheses to be pursued. Now, one can readily grant certain types of "causal connection" between pornography and violence, since nearly anything can incite a violent response from the appropriate type of sociopathic or psychotic individual. If the claim that pornography is a causal factor in eliciting violence is to have any real significance, it must be producing moral or psychological deviance in the first place, not merely triggering it, or at least doing the triggering to a degree that other such factors do not. Otherwise, when Ted Bundy reports that his desire to kill women came from repeatedly seeing pornography, it may have no more significance than when Charles Manson tells us he was inspired to his grisly murders by repeatedly reading the imprecations in the Book of Revelation—or than the fact that Bundy sought out and killed young women who looked like the first love who jilted him, with long straight hair parted in the middle.

At the very least, then, large numbers of cases involving both pornography and violence would be needed. Claims that violent sex criminals often use sexual materials are not infrequently made by law enforcement officials and therapists who treat the criminals; they are also not infrequently denied by other such officials and by a strong majority of therapists. Given the non-quantitative and even subjective nature of such claims linking sex offenses and pornography, and especially given the ideological bias pervading the emotional issue in question, it would be unwise to place much faith in them. Attempts have been made to gather pertinent data more systematically, notably by studying police reports of violent crimes. Two investigations of this type have been carried out, one for the British government's Committee on Obscenity and Film Censorship and one for the U.S. Commission on Obscenity and Pornography (Williams 1979; Thornberry & Silberman 1970). Both concluded there was very little evidence of pornography use in cases of violent crime.

In the words of the British commission report: "one can study case after case of sex crimes and murder without finding any hint at all that pornography was present in the background."

However, these studies are problematic, because we don't know to what extent the original record keepers were motivated to notice or to record that sort of information in the first place.

Another type of systematic gathering of information involves examining not the use or frequency of use of sexual materials by offenders, but their own perceptions of what has caused their behavior. In one questionnaire survey of convicted rapists, eleven out of sixty responded "yes" to the question of whether pornography had had "anything to do" with their being in prison or psychiatric hospital (Walker 1970). An even higher percentage responded affirmatively to the question whether pornography had led them at some time to commit a "sexual crime." Given the laws in the area at the time, however, that vague phrase included various noncoercive actions (consensual homosexual or heterosexual acts of oral or anal intercourse and the like). As for those eleven offenders, pornography's having "anything to do" with their being institutionalized might have been only in the same sense that any source of sexual knowledge or arousal—say, seeing women in revealing clothing—might have been involved. A much more serious doubt arises from the fact that violent criminals as a group tend to be very unaware of their own motivations—which may have much to do with their being violent in the first place—and highly prone to rationalization. They could simply have been falling back on an "explanation" they have often heard, one they might see as absolving them of blame. Other excuses that rapists commonly give, such as "she led me on," are rightly regarded with skepticism (and are often clearly false); it should be the same regarding this claim of a "necessary link" between pornography and sex crimes.

Quite apart from such doubts, however, there is positive evidence on the other side. From their extended questioning of convicted rapists and pedophiles, Goldstein and Kant (1973) concluded that "few if any" had been appreciably influenced by pornography. Instead, they decided, real persons in the environment "are far more potent sexual stimuli" for the sex criminal. In fact, many sex offenders believe that pornography has the effect of preventing sexual violence (Williams 1979; Carter et al. 1986). According to John Money, persons requesting help in a sex-offender clinic

> . . . commonly disclose in the course of counseling therapy that pornography helps them contain their abnormal sexuality within imagination only, as a fantasy. (Lynn 1986)

In the questionnaire just discussed, in fact, 39 percent of the convicts *also* agreed that pornography "provides a safety valve for antisocial impulses." All things considered, this type of evidence provides at least as much reason to believe that sexually explicit materials prevent violence as that they incite it.

Statistical Analyses

The most fundamental problem with merely collecting cases of violent crime associated with pornography is, of course, that they cannot distinguish coincidental from causal association. It would not even be helpful to know that a high percentage of such criminals use pornography; after all, a very great proportion of them drink coffee. What is needed instead is a correlation: that more pornography users than others commit rape (or, equivalently, that more rapists than nonrapists use pornography). Schematically, it isn't whether or not most As are Bs that counts, but whether a higher percentage of As than of non-As are Bs—even if both percentages are low. In such a case we have good evidence, provided the statistics are collected carefully enough to rule out biased data and coincidence, for a causal relationship of some sort between A and B. This relationship, however, could mean different things: notably that A causes B, that B causes A, or that A and B are collateral effects of some common cause, C. With the right kind of further information, we can sometimes eliminate some of the possibilities. In two obvious cases, if the A always follows the B, it clearly isn't a factor in causing B; and if we have arbitrarily produced the As ourselves (the experimental method), we know there is no common cause for both them and the Bs. In most cases, however, we simply do not know which of many possible explanations for a correlation is the right one. Consequently, though the strict absence of a correlation between them guarantees that A does not (on balance) cause B, the presence of a correlation, by itself, is very weak evidence that it does.

One important type of statistical survey that has been brought to bear on the pornography question attempts to compare the backgrounds of those who have and those who have not committed violent sex crimes, to see if they differ, on average, in their prior exposure to sexually explicit materials. Five studies of this type were performed by various researchers at the request of the U.S. Commission on Obscenity and Pornography at the end of the 1960s. Only one of them (Davis & Braucht 1970) found a greater degree of exposure to pornography in the backgrounds of those who had committed serious sex crimes than among those who had not (Cook & Fosen 1970; Goldstein et al. 1970; Walker 1970). In fact, three of them found a *smaller* amount of prior exposure among violent sex criminals than in a control group of persons not known to have committed sex crimes. The remaining investigation (Johnson et al. 1970) wasn't able to employ a quantitative analysis. In the late 1980s, another investigation of the same type found no correlation between rape and use of pornography (Condron & Nutter 1988).

This all seems to suggest that sexually explicit materials tend to prevent violence; at least it argues, if the studies are accurate, that they don't cause it. But there are various possible sources of error in studies of this kind. For one thing, they have had to depend on memory reports of what had been done in years past, which are certainly fallible, and on the answers being honest—in interviews and even anonymous questionnaires, some will not be. For another thing, there were (as there generally are) difficulties in getting control groups that were sufficiently like the groups of sex offenders in *other* respects to rule out alternative causal factors.

Two other investigations in the 1980s did in fact find a correlation between pornography use and rape. One of them claimed to be superior by virtue of work with the sex offenders over a long time, during which some of them reportedly made disclosures of pornography use which they had initially withheld (Marshall 1988). The other study avoided the problem of finding a matching control group by dealing with a single large sample from the general population in which respondents were asked to describe their exposure to pornography and also to state (anonymously) whether they had committed sexual assault. Given the great difficulties of getting accurate answers in studies of both kinds, once again, these investigations can also be challenged on various grounds. For one thing, Marshall's presentation of the scientific evidence on pornography and violence in his other writings (Marshall and Barrett 1990)—omitting all the data contrary to his own strong antiporn position—raises doubts about his objectivity. But suppose these two studies are correct; would they provide good evidence that exposure to pornography incites rape?

The answer is negative. There are a number of reasons of the "common cause" type for suspecting that sex offenders would use erotic materials more in any case. For example, these individuals often have an exceptionally high preoccupation with sex; this would tend to express itself both in acts of sexual coercion *and* in more frequent use of sex substitutes. Another study group of men who admitted having raped but who had not been prosecuted reported an appreciably greater felt need for sex than did other men, which suggests a causal influence (Kanin 1985). Secondly, rapists as a group are known to feel alienated from women; this too could be a partial cause of a greater use of pornography as a sexual substitute, and also of a greater likelihood of hostile interaction with women. Thirdly, rapists are known in general to come from social and family backgrounds that are less stable and less constrained by the prevailing standards of society (Koss 1985; Gentry 1991). That these families are more violent was confirmed by the Koss study. Being less inhibited by societal norms in general, individuals from such backgrounds might well be less inhibited about seeking out socially disapproved matter like pornography as well as more inclined to engage in sexual or nonsexual violence.

The underlying point here is this: in circumstances where a common cause for two phenomena is not only possible but known to exist, a correlation between the phenomena (in this case, sexual violence and use of pornography) is by itself useless as evidence that the one causes the other. In the same way, while there is a very strong correlation between lying down and dying, this fact is hardly evidence that the former produces the latter! Indeed, one who supposed that it did so, and tried to avoid death by always standing up, would probably hasten his own demise considerably. As this analogy also reveals, a correlation between two factors is even compatible with the one *preventing* the other. Even if it should ultimately become clear that rapists and other sex offenders do use more pornography, it would not give us grounds to believe that such use in any way causes their behavior unless all the other initially plausible explanations for the correlation could be ruled unlikely by further evidence.

A different kind of statistical approach avoids such problems as the honesty and memories of survey respondents by looking at the rates of various sex crimes and consumption of sexual materials for the population as a whole. One study of this type done in the mid-1980s did find a correlation between reported rape and sales of big-selling "soft core" magazines, by comparing the rates of both in different states of the U.S. (Baron & Straus 1984, 1986, 1989). Though there are many sources of error and considerable nonuniformity between localities in the reporting and gathering of crime statistics, the large size of the population involved makes the results look significant. On the other hand, as the authors of the study stress, there are various possible explanations for its outcome. For example, the three "common causes" enumerated above could apply here, along with various others. That one or more causal factors were responsible for both high rates of rape and higher sales of sexual materials in some states was suggested by certain other results of the same study. For example, it also found a high correlation between rates of reported rape of women and sales of various other magazines, among them the feminist periodical *Ms.* and the women's sex magazine (also read by gay men), *Playgirl.* It is certainly implausible that exposure to either of the latter somehow induces men to rape women. Also, the investigators discovered a solid correlation between sales of soft-core porn and the numerical measure of women's equality in the various states, composed of a long list of societal indicators of the status of women. This fact seems to conflict with feminist theories about *how* pornography causes rape (more on that later); in any case, the correlation between rape reports and pornography consumption no more argues for sexual materials inciting rape than soft-core pornography does for women's rights.

As to the question of what the common cause of the pornography-rape correlation (and others) might be, two further possibilities are suggested by Baron and Straus's study's correlations between the level of rape reports and both the degree of urbanization and the ratio of men to women in each state. Yet another possible common cause the researchers suggested is the degree of political liberalism in each state: where it is high, perhaps there is on average both more tolerance of sexual openness and also more sympathy for rape victims, making them more likely to report their victimization and police more likely to record it; this could also account for the higher sales of *Ms.* and *Playgirl.* Yet another common causal factor might be what the authors of the study refer to as "social disorganization": to the degree that societal structures break down, societal taboos in general are weakened. As noted earlier, that would include inhibitions against both violent crime and (in our culture) sexual openness. One more factor suggested by the authors as being the source of higher rates of both rape and porn sales is what they label a "hypermasculine culture," under which males feel compelled to express their masculinity both by violent actions and by expressing their sexuality, including the use of sexual materials.

Unlike nearly all other investigations of the "effects" of pornography to date, Baron and Straus's study employed statistical techniques going beyond mere correlation, such as multiple regression and path analysis in order to try to distinguish between cause-effect relationships and collateral-effects relationships. The authors discovered a strong correlation between rape rates and their "social disorganization" index, but the regression analysis found it inadequate as the common cause for porn sales and reported rape rates. However, when their measure for "violence approval" was factored into the analysis, the correlation between those rates disappeared, leading them to feel their "hypermasculinity" hypothesis could explain away the porn-rape correlation. Unfortunately, there are many sources of doubt concerning these further statistical tests, and many more about the particular tools with which these investigators had to work. For an example of the latter concern, there is the use of individual states of the U.S. as the basic units of measure: highly disparate in population size and heterogeneous, they are in most sociological respects artificial entities; hence they could yield (especially when merely rank-ordered) erroneous artificial results. Another concern is the degree of arbitrariness involved in deciding which statistics to compile into an aggregate measure (such as that of social disorganization or women's equality), which means that the measures themselves are suspect. In confirmation of such fears, consider what happened when the investigators proposed two different composite indexes, at different times, for gauging degree of equality for women: one of them correlated positively with rape statistics and the other, negatively.

At the time of writing, I can draw from this investigation no reasonable conclusions either way about causal connections between pornography and rape. In addition to its internal problems is the fact that subsequent studies have failed to replicate its correlation between pornography sales and reported rape, increasing the likelihood that even that result is erroneous. One such study looked at the number of "adult" book stores (where the "hard core" magazines are sold) in the United States and found no correlation to the rape rates (Scott 1985). The other focused again on sales of "soft core" porn, but used an ostensibly superior set of geographical units (i.e., not just the states) to make the comparisons—and found no correlation with the rates of reported rape at all (Gentry 1991). What it did find was a solid correlation between rates for rape and those for divorce, suggesting such causal influences as social disorganization and father absence. To have any confidence in this type of approach to the causes of rape, we would need more reliable data and more sophisticated analyses than have been employed so far.

Yet another way of examining pornography and violence looks for correlations over time rather than across space. In principle, this approach could eliminate many of the common-cause explanations for any correlation that might be found, though there remain the same problems of obtaining reliable data in the first place. The basic idea is to note whether increases or decreases in the availability of sexual materials (especially if produced by changes in the "obscenity" law, rather than by some obvious candidate for a common cause) are followed by changes in the rate of sex crimes.

Claims of this variety of evidence supporting a pornography-rape connection are often made by groups that oppose sexual materials. Given the average person's lack of scientific sophistication, such charges are very often factually in error and sometimes simply confused, that is, when they can be traced to their original source at all. But at least one researcher claims to have made a systematic attempt at gathering data of this kind from various locations, concluding that correlations of rape with availability of pornography can be found in many places (Court 1977). Unfortunately, the evidence seems clear that the claimant has been grossly irresponsible if not flatly dishonest, presenting conjecture as fact and employing hopelessly weak data at best. The British obscenity commission report published in 1979 presented some convincing evidence to discredit this researcher's claims; so when he later wrote an article (Court 1984) listing several new claims, the present writer found occasion to check out two of them: one from New Zealand, the other from Hawaii.

Concerning the New Zealand case, Court's remarks are evasively vague, and entirely speculative regarding the availability of sexual materials. Furthermore, a check of records at the time reveals no changes in the legal treatment of sexual materials. Concerning a large drop in the rate of reported rape following 1974, Court writes, "It is possible that the decline arose due to the introduction of the Auckland Task Force, established to take a tough line with crime." It is indeed very possible, but not for the reason he intimates.

Court clearly wants the reader to believe the Task Force cracked down on pornography. Yet from his only cited (but unquoted) source (Tait 1978), it is equally clear the Task Force did nothing of the sort; the effort encompassed the use of a SWAT team to deal with nighttime violence on the streets. (Revealingly, New Zealand's 1989 report by the Ministerial Committee of Inquiry into Pornography mentions Court's claims as evidence against pornography, without noting his blatantly erroneous data—even those about their own country.) In the Hawaiian case, too, Court's alleged facts are the figment of someone's imagination. There was indeed a drop in the recorded rate of rape in the two years in question. But as a review of local newspaper articles for the same period reveals, there was no crackdown on pornography; in fact, there was a glut of such materials, as well as live sex acts on stage. Rather, some legal action against sexual materials took place in earlier and later years, when rape rates were higher.

The best known, and to date still the only carefully conducted, examination of rape rates and availability of pornography over time was carried out in Denmark in the late 1960s, following a major liberalization of the obscenity laws there (Ben-Veniste 1970; Kutchinsky 1970, 1976). The fact that the resulting increase in availability of erotic materials was so large and so sudden eliminates from consideration many possible causal variables. While that increase was taking place the rate of reports of certain sex crimes dropped greatly. From questioning people about their feelings, the researchers decided that the decline in reports of some of the crimes (e.g., exhibitionism) could plausibly be accounted for by a general softening of attitudes regarding their seriousness; they likely simply weren't reported to the police as often as they had been. But no corresponding change was found in attitudes toward "peeping," still regarded as a frightening invasion of privacy, or of sex between adults and children. Yet reports of both declined drastically, by 80 percent and 69 percent, respectively, indicating that a genuine decrease in their occurrence had taken place. On the grounds that both of these offenses are often substitutes, on the part of socially maladjusted individuals, for "acceptable" sex, the researchers suggested that the new availability of erotic materials simply provided a legally safe substitute. Whatever the explanation, given that so much of today's concern over pornography stems from fears for children's safety and women's peace of mind, these statistics are highly significant.

Though the hypothesis that pornography can decrease sexual offenses thus gained support in the case of certain crimes, this was not so for violent ones. Through the period of vastly increasing amounts of pornography in Denmark, the rate at which rapes were reported remained at roughly the same level. On the same reasoning as above, then, it would appear that the psychology of rapists does not allow for any such substitution. But the claim which we are considering here is that pornography causes sexual violence;

in that regard, this is an important result. That there should have been no increase in reports of these crimes—and again, no ascertained change in attitude as regards their seriousness—under such conditions argues against that allegation. To those who suspect pornography is a major cause of rape, moreover, Denmark's continuing low rate of coercive sex crime, in spite of its liberal attitude toward sexual materials, is itself worth noting.

A number of researchers have challenged the accuracy of the data involved here (Bachy 1976), but the responses of the principal investigator have generally appeared adequate to meet them (Williams 1979; Kutchinsky 1985). Antipornography activists who don't know the scientific literature frequently repeat the charge that the rate of sex crimes in Denmark dropped only because certain acts were decriminalized at that time; that is not the case for the crimes discussed here. Kutchinsky has also compiled statistics from the U.S. and Germany—although he was unable to examine original police records or do a population survey there—and found other periods of rapid change in the availability of pornography without a corresponding change in rates of rape reports. Similar efforts were carried out for the British obscenity commission (Williams 1979), with the same result. In fact, it noted a five-year period during which the availability and explicitness of sexual materials increased but reports of sexual assault decreased; then a crackdown on hard-core pornography that greatly reduced the supply was followed by an increase in reports of sexual assault. During the first half of the 1980s, as many researchers have pointed out, the availability of pornography in the United States expanded rapidly, in the form of home videotapes; but the rate of rape remained level or even decreased.

It must be stressed again, however, that we are facing a great deal of uncertainty in all this. There may always be unrecognized social forces at work producing the net results the statistics reveal, masking the effects or lack of effects of any given factor. For instance, at the time of the big increase in sexual entertainment in Denmark, the more general "sexual revolution" was occurring and the "baby boomers" were coming of age. Beyond that, even obtaining data that are reasonably accurate and certain is in general very difficult. To mention just one difficulty involved: as judged from recent surveys, less than 50 the percent of all rapes are actually reported to police. Yet the rise in awareness of and concern about rape that has taken place in recent years has increased the percentage of rapes that are reported to and recorded by police. Thus, a climb in the police statistics during that time need not mean any actual increase in actual rapes had occurred after all. Given the often erratic variation in crime rates from year to year, in a multitude of jurisdictions, it is certainly possible to find at least short periods in at least some places where changes in the statistics for pornography sales and for various crimes either match each other or fail to, depending on which thesis one is trying to support.

What all this means is that, barring the carrying out of far more thorough statistical studies than we have yet seen, the foregoing type of investigation is also very limited in what it can tell us. As with other types of statistical data, the best evidence we currently have from crime trends over time weighs against the claim that pornography systematically induces sexual violence. But the best we have is far from conclusive. The one thing that does seem clear from available sociological data is that pornography is at most a small influence in inciting (or preventing) rape. We already know enough about the social causes of crime in general to know what some of the major ones are. In fact, variations in the rate of sexual assault over both time and space closely parallel those in the rates of aggravated assault and other violent crimes. This again argues strongly that whatever social influences produce violence in general—notably, whatever influences disinhibit the use of force against others (including men)—are by far the greatest underlying reasons for the rape of women.

Experimental Evidence

The main weakness of statistical studies in society, their lack of control over possible causal variables, leads naturally to a consideration of experimental approaches. These cannot eliminate, but can greatly reduce, the influence of extraneous factors. The most common type of experiment, repeated in a great variety of ways by different researchers, involves getting the subjects to perform acts they believe are physically painful to another person (e.g., giving supposed electric shocks as punishments of some kind). If those who have first been exposed to a certain stimulus—say, sexually explicit material—are on average likely to give more severe or less severe "punishments" than those who have not, it is concluded that something about the stimulus has been a factor in causing this result. During the 1970s and 1980s, many variations on this type of experiment were performed using pornography as the stimulus (Donnerstein et al. 1987). Eventually the following picture emerged: for experimental subjects not angered beforehand, exposure to pornography had no effect on their level of aggression. However, among angered subjects, scenes that were sexually less arousing (notably, still photos rather than movies) reduced the average level of "pain" they inflicted, and the more arousing ones increased it.

Some antisexual political activists saw in that last result evidence that pornography leads to violence in real life (though they did not draw the corollary conclusion that mildly arousing pornography prevents violence and hence should be made widely available). We may not legitimately draw any such conclusions, however. For one thing, there is the fact that the laboratory setting, with its permission to commit aggression, is highly artificial. It is not at all clear that the same results would occur outside the lab. For another, there is the serious question of whether and to what extent the mild "pain" administered in these tests can be extrapolated to the serious harm done in a real physical attack. Beyond this, the sort of portrayal found to enhance aggression is very elastic, being dependent on the experimental subjects' histories: those who are more sexually experienced, or who have already viewed large amounts of pornography in the past, were not induced to aggressiveness by highly erotic presentations in the lab.

The most important point regarding these laboratory data, however, is the one that emerges from discovering the underlying reason for them. Various experiments have made it clear that the source of the greater aggression induced by sexual presentations is nothing more than the excitement they produce. It is not a feeling of contempt for women, or a special moral nastiness, or anything of the sort; it is only a general state of heightened physiological responsivity (Zillmann 1984). Similar results of enhanced aggression have been obtained from such excitement-arousing influences as exercise and comical films, even without angering the subject first. And the greater aggressiveness lasts only as long as the state of excitement persists, a few minutes. All this raises once again the question of extrapolation beyond the laboratory, for no one would seriously suppose that the explosion of interest in exercise in recent years has increased the level of violence in our society. And even if anyone did, these results provide no more reason to oppose pornography than they do to oppose jogging. Moreover, it has been discovered that aggression is not the only type of behavior to be enhanced by a state of excitement. Experiments in which the subject is supposed to reward another person have generally found that excitement, including sexual arousal, also leads to the giving of larger rewards. It would seem that the effect of being excited is to exaggerate mildly *all* a person's responses—hardly a novel idea.

A different type of experiment tries to gauge the effects of various influences on the attitudes of subjects rather than on their immediate behavior. So far, no genuinely adverse changes in male attitudes toward females have been discovered in this way. In one test that was widely reported, some of the males who watched certain nonviolent sex films indicated afterward a higher level of belief that they might commit coercive sexual acts, if they were absolutely guaranteed they wouldn't be caught (Check 1985). That is a troubling result, but it turns out to be valueless as evidence; however, the details of this particular study sound some serious alarm bells. For one thing, the subjects were already in the habit of viewing pornographic videos in private; it is highly implausible that an hour and a half more of it would really change their attitudes. More revealingly, those shown the nonviolent sex films also reported having already, in the past, committed more sexually coercive acts than those not shown them. But since the acts preceded the experimental viewing, they could not have been caused by it. In other words, this particular experiment provided no more reason to believe pornography causes a tendency toward sexual coercion than to believe that it can change the past.

One clue concerning what went wrong lies in the way the subjects were recruited and instructed: they were told the political use to which their answers would be put. And one reasonable hypothesis is that something about the whole experimental arrangement—not only the viewing itself—made the subjects who viewed the pornography more willing to admit certain pre-existing attitudes and behaviors; but that is not at all the same thing as causing a change in those attitudes or behaviors. In any event, other experiments in which subjects viewed pornographic materials have not found changes in their self-reported likelihood of committing rape (Malamuth & Ceniti 1986), further confirming that something went awry with this one experiment.

Like the other kinds of scientific evidence, the experimental evidence that sexual materials somehow lead to rape is virtually nonexistent at this stage of inquiry; what evidence is available is once again nearly all on the other side. (There is, however, some arresting evidence that portrayals of violence, including those involving sex, can incite actual violence. See Donnerstein et al. 1987.) Given all the uncertainties, however, the overall scientific picture is still that, except on the issue of whether pornography is a major cause of violence, the direct evidence is inadequate to decide in either direction (although it is likewise true that we have no adequate grounds for deciding whether or not milk-drinking makes some people more violent.) Nevertheless, we do have some indirect evidence and general knowledge of the subject that is highly conclusive, and that is the subject of the second half of this chapter.

II. EXPLANATION AND WIDER EVIDENCE

Why should scenes of something pleasurable like sex provoke violence? After all, humans take vicarious enjoyment in portrayals involving all sorts of other needs and pleasures: friendship, love, food, skill and graceful motion—why wouldn't those presentations also be thought to have horrid effects? No genuinely adequate answer to that crucial question has been given. That is, none of the reasons so far offered as to why pornography should lead to aggression is at once both (a) remotely plausible and (b) an explanation that lays the moral blame on pornography. That being so, there is no more genuine need to pursue the kind of direct evidence discussed in Part I than there is to seek evidence that watching ballet or love stories will make people violent.

Stimulated Sexual Desire

The most obvious hypothesis might be labeled the "awakened desire" explanation: that since pornography arouses sexual feelings, in the absence of a willing partner, certain persons will be induced to use force in order to satisfy the aroused desires. In spite of its initial plausibility, this proposed explanation faces various problems. For one thing, those who believe strongly in human free will are apt to have trouble with it. Shall we say that people who drive nice cars in public are to blame for inciting car theft, or instead, that the thieves are wholly responsible for their own actions?

Even ignoring that thorny issue, two problems present themselves. First, the primary effect of pornography could plausibly be just the reverse. Though people who employ such reasoning seem reluctant to admit it, sexually explicit materials not only arouse but also satisfy sexual desires, especially (but not solely) when used as an aid to masturbation. Some seek it out as a substitute precisely because of strong sexual feelings that already exist. If it is being used as a surrogate, pornography would defuse more strong desires than it creates. This suggestion is known as the "safety valve" or substitution hypothesis. (It should not be confused, of course, with the catharsis theory concerning portrayed violence, which is in wide disrepute among psychologists.) One rapist caught carrying pornography reported that he used it as a backup, to masturbate with in case he couldn't find a victim; how many others are deterred from rape precisely because they have such an alternative?

Secondly, rapists are overwhelmingly young men; their sexual desires tend to be quite autonomous, and are continually being aroused without any help from pornography. That being so, its presence or absence would not seem to make much difference—except perhaps as a substitute way, once again, of satisfying those excited feelings. This would evidently apply even to those rapists who reportedly use sexual materials before seeking out a victim (Marshall 1988). As psychologists Goldstein and Kant (1973) expressed it after interviewing many sex criminals, "In our view erotic pictures, stories and movies simply serve as a substitute for the self-generating daydreams of the pornography user."

One could reply that sexually explicit materials may at least add to the arousal level of everyday sexual stimulation. This, the reasoning might run, would push "over the brink" certain individuals who were already predisposed toward rape. But that idea runs up against the fact that what it takes to produce strong sexual urges is highly elastic. As everyone should be aware, attempts to cool male ardor by covering more of the female body result in enhancing the power of other parts to excite, and conversely, what becomes familiar loses much of its capacity to arouse. Given the biological realities, the claim before us looks less and less reasonable.

Another version of the "stimulated desire" argument attributes the problem not to sexual arousal per se, but to the creation of feelings of deprivation. The suggestion is that sexually explicit materials can produce or heighten the sense that one is missing out on something one desires, which could lead to a willingness to take it by force. In other words, the villain this time is the frustration produced by perceiving how things might be in contrast to how they actually are. Here again, it is not at all clear that this is a genuine danger. Using pornography may be no more likely to result in violence than is seeing attractive women on the street or at the beach. But suppose there is such an effect. Would that mean sexual presentations ought to be regarded as a genuine evil? Not in the least. Consider a pair of analogies. During the career of Martin Luther King, Jr., his speeches for equality and civil rights were sometimes followed by violence among black people, in spite of his own message of nonviolence. It is a fact of human nature that raising people's hopes and expectations has the potential for inducing antisocial actions in some. In a similar vein, the women's rights movement of the past three decades might be alleged to be the cause of a rapid increase in crimes committed by women and girls; the rate of increase has been far greater than among males. It appears that the greater social freedom and assertiveness women have achieved have, in a small minority of cases, led to license and aggression. Shall we say, given these effects, that feelings such as self-confidence and self-respect, hope and desire for freedom are pernicious? Or that influences which arouse them should be prohibited? Surely no reasonable person would say this. The situation is basically no different in the case of sexual desires, and of things that awaken the hope of satisfying them.

A second plausible account of how sexual materials might conceivably lead to rape says they do so by increasing not the desire for sex, but its perceived desirability. Certainly, pornography might enhance that perception by sending the message that sex is good for its own sake. Of course, that message does not in the least justify forcing such activity on anyone. (The reverse is true, in fact, since for the victim, rape is nothing like consensual sex; it is a horrible experience.) In the twisted minds of some, unfortunately, the idea that certain behavior is desirable translates into the belief that compelling others into it is morally acceptable. Sometimes this belief is accompanied by the rationalization, "Once you're pushed into it, you'll like it after all." But that attitude can hardly be applied to other people's simple celebration of something that they consider good, sexually or otherwise.

This line of reasoning also helps to see part of what is wrong with the first "stimulated desire" argument. Suppose it is true, after all, that the existence of sexual materials results in greater amounts of sexual arousal and sexual frustration in the population at large than would otherwise exist, and that this leads, among those willing to harm others to get what they want, to greater amounts of rape than would otherwise occur. Only those who see sexual desire as bad in the first place would assign moral blame to what gives rise to such desires, rather than merely blame the willingness to harm others and whatever produces it. For a striking contrast, consider an emotion regarded as noble in this culture: romantic love. When unrequited or lost or stung by jealousy, romantic love not infrequently results in violence. However, one does not hear claims that there is too much emphasis on loving attachments these days, nor calls for the censoring of romance novels and love stories on grounds of the harms they might produce. What underlies the "awakened desire" argument, clearly, is conceiving "demon lust" as something that pollutes the soul rather than as a perfectly legitimate feeling. Otherwise, the logical conclusion would be it should be made easier for people to meet their sexual needs in noncoercive ways instead—something antipornography ideologues seldom do. If tantalizing impoverished people with scenes of delicious food and other things they long for incites some of them to theft or even violence, that is an argument for adopting social policies to end poverty, not for denouncing their perfectly human desires.

The point is made more clear when we see what else follows from the argument of repressing "demon lust." For on such a negative view of sexual desire, anything that results in increased amounts of it (or lessens repression of it) is also to be condemned: sex education, greater enjoyment of sex by women, even talk about sex in a positive way. Though they don't always admit the fact, many of those who accept the explanation of rape under discussion do indeed hold all these views. But others should be aware of its logical consequences. It leads to such conclusions as that women who dress revealingly or behave suggestively are to blame for other women (or themselves) being raped. If banning pornography on these grounds is justified, surely so is requiring women to wear clothing that covers them completely and hides the shape of their bodies, like the Iranian *chador.* And surely that is not at all justified. The consequences of this type of reasoning have been clearly perceived in the feminist movement. As will be discussed shortly, the motivations proposed by antipornography feminists to explain how pornography might lead to rape are of a very different type.

Sexual Obsession and Deviance Produced by Sexual Materials

A second major claim about how sexual materials lead to rape is that they do so by producing sexual obsessiveness and even perversion. Now, although the etiology of sexual deviance is far from fully understood, we know enough to say that the evidence is strongly against this idea (Money and Ehrhardt 1972). There is no credible evidence even that paraphilic pornography is a factor in producing actual paraphilias (any more than exposure to homosexual pornography is a cause of homosexuality), much less that the general materials under discussion here promote such behavior. As for obsession with sex, the usual charge is that "overstimulation" produced by pornographic materials has that effect. Such fears are to be expected in a culture with a long-entrenched attitude that regards the overt expression of sexuality as a dangerous force.

Obsessive desires and compulsive behaviors involving all sorts of things do exist. But it seems very clear that they are rarely if ever produced by simple overemphasis on the desire in question. Human appetites are equipped with satiation mechanisms to prevent unhealthy excess: when we get full, we lose our hunger. At least this is true of ordinary needs; chemicals to which the body has not been biologically adapted by eons of natural selection can have a very different effect from those involving natural needs and pleasures. But the scenes in nonparaphilic pornography that produce sexual arousal are exactly the same kind that would do so in real life.

What does produce obsessive desires, then? A large amount of clinical experience indicates that the compulsive search for pleasure generally begins with pain. For example, compulsive eating is often an attempt to compensate for emotional privation of some type. Typically, it is the chronically hungry or unloved who are preoccupied with food or with love, and those who are made to feel deeply guilty over their natural desires who become emotionally unbalanced regarding them. If an excessive interest in sex is in fact sometimes reflected in the use of pornography, then, the latter is a symptom rather than a cause of the former. Rather, excessive sexual interest has likely been caused by this culture's very attempts to suppress sexual feelings. This requires a lengthy explanation in itself (Christensen 1990a); the tragic irony of the antipornography campaign is that the antisexual attitudes underlying it are the real cause of many of the evils the campaign attempts to pin on pornography, including violence. For present purposes, let it merely be said that there are numerous causes of obsession and unhealthy excess in this neurotic society. Hence in those cases of sexual obsession (genuine obsession, not merely what traditional antisexualism regards as excessive) that involve use of pornography, there is no reason to regard the latter as a cause rather than merely a symptom.

To be more specific about the claim before us, it charges that use of pornography produces the desire for increasingly stronger sexual thrills, leading eventually to the wish for violent or perverted sex. (Alternatively, it says that habituation to progressively stronger stimuli makes it harder and harder to achieve sexual satisfaction, with the same result.) As a matter of fact, paraphiles are found to have developed their deviant feelings *before* exposure to normal or deviant pornography (e.g., Condron & Nutter 1988). Quite apart from such evidence, however, this theory again raises the embarrassing question—usually ignored, with the exception noted below—why engaging in real sex wouldn't produce the same obsessive quest for ever more perverse thrills. In sex, as in anything else, humans do require a certain amount of variety to prevent habituation and boredom. And *within a limited range,* the degree of arousal a stimulus provides will change if there is greater or lesser exposure to it. (Temporarily, that is: after miniskirts were out of fashion for a while, attractive thighs became more exciting to men again.) But the basic kinds of things that "turn on" normal individuals, clinicians have discovered, are remarkably stable through life, having been fixed from early childhood or youth (Money 1986).

The same is evidently the case for those whose sexuality is paraphilic. It is true that certain sadistic individuals become progressively more violent over time; but the paraphilic desire for extreme violence has been there all along. Even if that is not the case, however, to suppose that the sadist's abnormal desires are caused by exposure to pleasurable portrayals rather than by some underlying pathology is misguided. Occasionally, case histories of escalating need for sexual stimulation, involving progressively more use of pornography and then violent or deviant pornography, are presented as proof of the claim before us. But even assuming the stories are factually accurate, alternative explanations, conveniently ignored in the telling, are perfectly obvious. As fatal diseases with no known cure develop, they typically require progressively higher doses of various medicines to alleviate the symptoms; but we do not automatically blame those medicines for the disease or for its escalating level of severity.

One experiment which many have claimed gives evidence for the "stronger and stronger thrills" charge (Zillmann & Bryant 1986) actually does nothing of the sort. Subjects first shown large amounts of ordinary pornography were, when given one brief subsequent opportunity, more likely than controls to peruse "uncommon sex" videotapes (sadomasochism, bestiality, or bondage) instead. An obvious explanation for this result is simple curiosity, together with the prior disinhibition in the use of sexual materials in general and the prior satisfaction of curiosity about ordinary pornography. In other words, the subjects weren't as apprehensive about either kind after viewing the ordinary pornography, and were still inquisitive about only the more heavily tabooed type. It may also be, of course, that they were still somewhat satisfied with the softer porn. But that doesn't mean they would find hard-core pornography at all sexually arousing, or any more so than they would have in the beginning. And as the researchers themselves admitted, interest in the "uncommon" or hard-core materials also drops after sufficient exposure. One of those researchers (Zillmann 1984) has also claimed that boredom with monogamy tends to lead married couples into sadomasochism—if sexual entertainment is a threat to mental health, so is marriage! Even more so, in fact, since it is clear that the need for variety is much greater in regard to sexual partners than in regard to sexual acts. One antipornography therapist (Marshall & Barrett 1989) describes a patient whose desire for sexual variety led him into pornography and experimentation with an extreme variety of sexual acts, culminating in attempts to have sex with an underage babysitter. Yet Marshall himself notes that the man's search for sexual novelty arose from his boredom with ordinary marital sex (and with rejection of the option of having an affair). It is highly revealing that proponents of the "porn produces sexual obsession" theory do not condemn real sex, not even (in particular) monogamous sex, on grounds that it can lead to aggression against others.

Promotion of Attitudes toward Women

A very different sort of explanation for how pornography might incite rape maintains that it is not the portrayal of sex that does the harm, but the way in which most existing pornography portrays women. Such materials, it is said, routinely treat women in a callous and exploitive manner, depicting them as subservient to men and degraded in various other ways. Now, genuinely degrading portrayals certainly might have harmful consequences. Except for a very small percentage of materials, however, these charges (along with the claim that common pornography contains high levels of violence) are blatantly false (Christensen 1990a, chaps. 5–6). When the rationalizations and distortions of fact are stripped away, what is seen to underlie such charges is little but opposition to the sex itself in the portrayals—notably, to sex that is explicitly portrayed, or too adventurous, or sex that is engaged in for its own sake rather than being "redeemed" by love or monogamous commitment. There is not space here to analyze and refute those false claims about the contents of pornography, but one can look at the effects it is alleged to have on those who use it.

The rape theory based on the claim that male-oriented sexual materials are callous and exploitive basically says this "teaches" men that women are mere objects for their use, whose own desires and feelings don't matter. (In fact, once again, typical pornography no more carries such messages than typical love stories teach women that men exist only to serve them and satisfy their needs. The two sexes are usually portrayed equally in pornography, both finding satisfaction and happiness in uninhibited sex.) Usually, no attempt is even made to provide evidence for this causal claim. But one experimental study from the early 1980s is often cited in support of it. Male and female college students who had been shown many sexually explicit films were found to recommend shorter prison terms for a rapist than those who had not.

It is alleged that this study proves that such films cause insensitivity to the exploitation or abuse of women. But no such conclusion is warranted. For one thing, the average suggested prison term (five and a half years) was still longer than was usually served in the United States at the time, which in turn is longer than that usually served for other kinds of brutal assault (Bureau of Justice Statistics 1986). More fundamentally, there are explanations for the result that do not rely on reading nonexistent inequalities into the films. One of these rests on the fact, confirmed by various experiments and by clinical experience, that exposure to sexual explicitness tends to cause young people to feel more sexually tolerant (as well as to feel, for at least a short time, that others are less sexually inhibited). Evidently, the openness about sexuality reduces some of the anxiety they had been conditioned to feel in this culture. One effect of this antisexual anxiety has been that crimes involving sex are widely seen in this society as more heinous than equally violent and harmful nonsexual crimes. For example, it is quite clear that the historically heavy punishments for rape, which have even included the death penalty, were assigned not so much out of concern for the woman's trauma as out of belief that loss of her "chastity" meant the reduction of her value as a marriage partner. That being the case, the emergence of a less negative attitude toward sex itself would equate the seriousness of sexual and nonsexual assault. According to this explanation, watching pornographic films did not produce a decrease in compassion for the trauma suffered by rape victims.

This interpretation has been confirmed by other tests, in which being shown sex movies was found not to result in a rape victim being viewed as less worthy or less injured, nor to induce calloused attitudes toward such victimization. In fact, some studies of this type have even failed to assess the result of shorter assigned prison terms for rapists—which reveals how tentative such experimental findings often are (Donnerstein et al. 1987). The explanation being suggested here for the result found is also supported by the fact that in sex-positive cultures, rape is regarded as being like other, nonsexual crimes against the person; in such cultures it is also evidently much less traumatic to the victim (Marshall 1971). By way of further evidence, a later study of consumers and nonconsumers of pornography also found no greater incidence among the consumers of negative attitudes toward women (Garcia 1986).

A questionnaire purporting to reveal sexually calloused attitudes toward women was also given to the subjects in the aforementioned prison-sentence study. The result was that those who had watched the large amounts of filmed sexual behavior got scores that were a little less desirable. That questionnaire, however, was terribly flawed (Christensen 1986, 1990b). Though an affirmative answer to many of its questions would indeed indicate calloused feelings, many other questions would simply reveal a positive attitude toward sex for its own sake, while others would merely reflect factual beliefs about how inhibited or uninhibited the sexual attitudes and behavior of other people are. The unjustified interpretation of the questions was clearly influenced by the traditional view that a strong sexual interest in a female, or viewing her as having strong sexual desires, is of itself exploitive of and degrading to her. And here, too, a more plausible explanation for the experimental result is that watching sexually uninhibited behavior tends to create attitudes in the subject and beliefs about others that are more sexually liberal. (This might be especially true when sexual material is shown by authority figures such as university professors, which hints that it is not so unacceptable after all.) Although themselves strong foes of pornography, the researchers involved later admitted that the questionnaire faces such objections, and agreed to stop using it in their research (Zillmann & Bryant 1986).

A variant of the theory of pornography leading to rape by influencing attitudes toward women involves the claim that common sexual materials promote male dominance and female subservience. That, it is averred, gives men the idea that they can dominate and take what they like from women. A variant explanation based on the same claim is that it gives them the desire to "put women in their place," rape being merely a more extreme form of the sexual dominance in those materials. Once more, the premise is grossly false. Only a very small category of such materials might plausibly be said to advocate male dominance; indeed, pornography in general is less guilty of that than other media presentations are (Palys 1986). Because it treats women more as equals in matters of sexuality, it should, if anything undermine traditional attitudes, notably the "double standard," that include male dominance. What motivates the making of this false charge is unclear. It is usually put forward by people in the extremist range of feminism, whose entirely legitimate desire to eliminate male dominance has, unfortunately, turned into a tendency to see it in places where it is not—especially in situations that are found objectionable for other reasons.

Many feminists and traditionalists give yet another attitude formation explanation of the claimed causal link: that pornography leads to rape by making men feel disrespect, or even outright contempt, for women. (Extremists say it deliberately teaches such contempt.) It does this, the claim continues, by the degrading way in which it depicts women. But once more, what that means to these people is that pornography portrays women who enjoy sex for its own sake with a number of partners and through a variety of acts. The "degradation" is almost always in the eye of beholders thoroughly conditioned by our culture's venerable antisexualism. This logic could equally well lead to the premise that women who are sexually uninhibited are to blame for getting themselves or other women raped. This theory is another version of the idea that provocatively dressed women are at fault when they or others are raped: this time, it's by appearing "loose" and therefore worthy of disrespect. Of course, those who make the charge concerning pornography realize that it sounds politically incorrect these days to say that women who dress or act sexually incite rapes, so they don't usually follow their premise to its logical conclusions. Even so, the question remains: might exposure to sexually uninhibited women, real or fictional, produce loss of respect for them or for women in general?

In reply, regarding the age-group of males from which rapists come, the evidence to date is negative. Experiments designed to test attitudes after exposure to pornography have not found any decreased respect for women. As noted above, the experimental subjects have evidently been inclined to judge an unfamiliar woman—or man—to be rather more interested in sex than they otherwise would have; but only in antisexual eyes does that equate automatically with a "loss of respect." In one such test, young men who were asked thirty-two questions about a woman's character did not give a more negative assessment when she displayed uninhibited sexual attitudes; on the contrary, she was seen as being a more reasonable person (Leonard & Taylor 1983). Furthermore, as has also been noted, pornography use evidently tends to produce attitudes toward the sexual behavior of others, including that of women, that is more rather than less liberal. These facts suggest that by promoting sexual liberalism, pornography could have the opposite effect from that claimed by the argument now under discussion. After all, it is clear that there is far less hostility toward highly sexual women in sex-positive cultures than in others. Consider the attitude in Middle Eastern countries toward a "fallen woman," who may even be killed to preserve her family's "honor." The sort of society these antipornography advocates want promotes willingness to harm sexually uninhibited men and women.

The part of their claim that is true is that it is easier to bring oneself to do harmful things to someone who is considered less deserving of respect. Such feelings are very clearly involved in many crimes of violence against both men and women. There is indeed a sense, then, in which pornography might possibly lead to rape but once again, it is not one in which the moral blame is on pornography. In the eyes of a person raised to believe strong or uninhibited sexual desire is degrading, to see women as having such desires is to regard them as degraded, hence perhaps making violence against them seem more acceptable. Once a woman is "fallen," in such eyes, she no longer deserves that special deference and protection to which "pure" women are entitled. So by portraying its women as highly sexual, pornography could plausibly trigger feelings in those men who already have certain sex-negative attitudes. By way of analogy, consider the possible effect on white racists of observing scenes in which white women associate willingly with black men: it might indeed make some of them feel less respect for white women. If any such reaction does occur, however, it is clear where the blame for it lies. Similarly, the people responsible for criminalizing portrayals of sexually uninhibited women are those who preach that women who enjoy sex for its own sake are worthy of contempt. Ironically, this antipornography argument itself presupposes and advocates that very attitude.

A crucial aspect of the "loss of respect" argument must now be noted explicitly. The standard charge mentions only the sexually uninhibited *women* of pornography as being degraded. Yet such materials routinely portray men and women who are alike in their sexual disinhibition. Hence the argument takes completely for granted the sexual double standard. Yet it makes no sense to say that depictions treating men and women alike would be at fault for causing hostility solely toward women; any such differential effect would have to be blamed on the double standard of the audience, not on the egalitarian presentation of the material itself. In this way as well, then, any violence possibly stemming from the use of such pornography would have to be laid at the door of a preexisting attitude in society. In a second irony, the anti-pornography argument's tacit acceptance of that preexisting attitude helps to promote it and any violence to which it may lead. That is to say, just as the "uninhibited sex is degrading" assumption of the argument promotes disrespect and hence possibly violence, its "only women are degraded by it" assumption reinforces the sexual double standard with all of its harms to women, including violence toward women seen as not sexually "pure." It is tragic that so many feminists have been taken in by this particular objection to pornography. After all, a wider double standard underlies a traditionalist argument against feminists: that by bringing women down from their pedestal, gender equality causes violence to women. Equality is not the real cause of disrespect-engendered violence; inequality is. And, once more, respect for women or men should not be dependent on whether they are sexually "pure" but on the fact that they are human beings.

Another explanation of the cause of rape involving attitudes toward women rests on a somewhat different description of the contents of ordinary pornography: not that it involves callousness, dominance or degradation, but simply (and correctly) that the behavior portrayed is not typical of ordinary women (in this culture). But this, the argument continues, misleads men about women's real sexual desires. There is no space here to discuss such matters as the reasons for idealized or stereotypical portrayals of behavior in fiction (including pornography and women's love stories) and the extent to which it may cause misperception of real life (Christensen 1990a). However, what is most important to the present argument is the conclusion it draws from the claim of misperception: that the pornography user will be led to believe women really don't *mind* being raped. "After all, if they're so quick to engage in sex anyway, and willing to do all those other kinky things, how could they object to a little force?" (Note well that this argument is not about positive portrayals of rape, but involves pornography depicting such things as "promiscuous" behavior, consensual oral and anal sex, and masturbation.) Now, it seems clear that some rapists do in fact reason in this manner: from "doesn't mind those other sexual things" to "wouldn't mind being raped." What if it should turn out, then, that some of them have been genuinely misled concerning the desires of ordinary women? Is the portrayal of sexually uninhibited women and men morally to blame for some cases of rape? Once more, the answer is negative.

Notice first of all that this argument would have to apply equally against all other attempts—say, those "Any Woman Can" self-help books—to provide women with greater sexual enjoyment by overcoming inhibitions and experimenting sexually. The real villain, as usual, is antisexual attitudes in this society. The problem lies in the fact that various pleasurable, consensual activities have been lumped together with forcible rape in common thinking: both are "bad," in a special sexual sense of the word. (It's evidently part of the reason for the myth that only "bad" women get raped.) But the behaviors portrayed in standard nonviolent pornography, though not to everyone's taste, are perfectly healthy and wholesome; they should never have been associated in anyone's mind with genuinely evil things like rape. If they had not been so associated, there would be no special tendency to believe that a person who engaged in them would also be receptive to "other bad things." That is, there would be no more reason to suppose a sexually uninhibited woman wouldn't really object to being raped than to believe that a gourmet who likes a wide variety of foods might not mind being force-fed. In this argument as well, then, the reasoning is based on antisexual assumptions. In the minds of those who employ it, there evidently is little difference between uninhibited consensual sex and rape. But their sex-negative thinking cannot be blamed on sex-positive pornography.

It should be clear who is really responsible for such consequences, if there is any validity in this last argument. It is those who promote the view that certain kinds of sexual behavior are unclean—that only "bad" women do such things—who are morally to blame for any rapes that may occur because of portrayals of women who engage in them. They are also to blame for any rapes that may occur because of real women who are sexually uninhibited. As with earlier arguments against pornography, those who employ this one seldom follow it to the point of blaming actual women for rape. Even so, their target is not only sexual fantasy; it is quite obvious that they are promoting a repressive view of what is sexually appropriate behavior by equating uninhibited sexuality with rape and thus instilling fear of uninhibited sexuality in women. What better way to do that than by instilling fear of rape in women? "This is what happens to bad women." The message may or may not be intended, but it follows logically from their premises. The consequences of the debate over pornography, the reader must be aware, extend far beyond pornography itself.

NOTE

1. To a large degree, this chapter abridges data and argumentation given in Christensen, F. M. (1990a). *Pornography: The Other Side.* New York: Praeger.

REFERENCES

Attorney General's Commission on Pornography (1986). *Final Report.* Washington, D.C: U.S. Department of Justice.

Bachy, V. (1976). "Danish 'Permissiveness' Revisited." *Journal of Communication* 26: 40–43.

Baron, L., and Straus, M. (1984). "Sexual Stratification, Pornography, and Rape in the United States." In N. Malamuth and E. Donnerstein, eds., *Pornography and Sexual Aggression.* New York: Academic Press.

——— (1986). "Four Theories of Rape: A Macrosociological Analysis." *Social Problems* 34: 467–89.

——— (1989). *Four Theories of Rape in American Society.* New Haven, Conn.: Yale University Press.

Ben-Veniste, R. (1970). "Pornography and Sex Crime—The Danish Experience." In U.S. Commission on Obscenity and Pornography, *Technical Report,* vol. 8. Washington, D.C.: U.S. Government Printing Office.

Bureau of Justice Statistics. (1986). *Prison Admissions and Releases, 1983.* Washington, D.C.: U.S. Department of Justice.

Carter, D. L., et al. (1985). "Use of Pornography in the Criminal and Developmental Histories of Sexual Offenders." Report to the National Institute of Mental Health. Washington, D.C.: National Institute of Mental Health. (Cited in the Attorney General's Commission on Pornography [1986]. *Final Report,* p. 961. Washington, D.C: U.S. Department of Justice.)

Check, J. V. P. (1985). "The Effects of Violent and Nonviolent Pornography." Unpublished submission to the Department of Justice for Canada.

Christensen, F. M. (1986). "Sexual Callousness Reexamined." *Journal of Communication* 36: 174–84.

——— (1990a). *Pornography: The Other Side.* New York: Praeger.

——— (1990b). "Cultural and Ideological Bias in Pornography Research." *Philosophy of the Social Sciences* 20: 351–75.

Condron, M. K., and Nutter, D. E. (1988). "A Preliminary Examination of the Pornography Experience of Sex Offenders, Paraphiliacs, Sexual Dysfunction Patients, and Controls Based on Meese Commission Recommendations." *Journal of Sex and Marital Therapy* 14: 285–98.

Cook, R. F., and Fosen, R. H. (1970). "Pornography and the Sex Offender: Patterns of Exposure." In U.S. Commission on Obscenity and Pornography, *Technical Report,* vol. 8. Washington, D.C.: U.S. Government Printing Office.

Court, J. (1977). "Pornography and Sex-Crimes: A Reevaluation in Light of Recent Trends around the World." *International Journal of Criminology and Penology* 5: 129–57.

Court, J. (1984). "Sex and Violence: A Ripple Effect." In N. Malamuth and E. Donnerstein, eds., *Pornography and Sexual Aggression.* New York: Academic Press.

Davis, K. E., and Braucht, G. N. (1970). "Exposure to Pornography, Character, and Sexual Deviance: A Retrospective Survey." In U.S. Commission on Obscenity and Pornography, *Technical Report,* vol. 8. Washington, D.C.: U.S. Government Printing Office.

Donnerstein, E.; Linz, D.; and Penrod, S. (1987). *The Question of Pornography.* New York: The Free Press.

Garcia, L. T. (1986). "Exposure to Pornography and Attitudes about Women and Rape: A Correlational Study." *Journal of Sex Research* 22: 378–85.

Gentry, C. (1991). "Pornography and Rape: An Empirical Analysis." *Deviant Behavior* 12: 277–88.

Goldstein, M. J., et al. (1970). "Exposure to Pornography and Sexual Behavior in Deviant and Normal Groups." In U.S. Commission on Obscenity and Pornography, *Technical Report,* vol. 8. Washington, D.C.: U.S. Government Printing Office.

Goldstein, M. J., and Kant, H. S. (1973). *Pornography and Sexual Deviance.* Berkeley, Calif.: University of California Press.

Joint Select Committee on Video Material. (1988). *Report of the Joint Select Committee on Video Material.* Canberra: Australian Government Publishing Service.

Kanin, E. (1985). "Date Rapists—Differential Sexual Socialization and Relative Deprivation." *Archives of Sexual Behavior* 14: 219–31.

Koss, M. P. (1985). "Nonstranger Sexual Aggression: A Discriminant Analysis of the Psychological Characteristics of Undetected Offenders." *Sex Roles* 12: 981–92.

Kraus, J. (1979). "Trends in Violent Crime and Public Concern." *Australian Journal of Social Issues* 14: 175–90.

Kutchinsky, B. (1970). "Toward an Explanation of the Decrease in Registered Sex Crimes in Copenhagen." In U.S. Commission on Obscenity and Pornography, *Technical Report,* vol. 8. Washington, D.C.: U.S. Government Printing Office.

——— (1976). "Deviance and Criminality: The Case of a Voyeur in a Peeper's Paradise." *Diseases of the Nervous System* 37: 145–51.

——— (1985). "Pornography and Its Effects in Denmark and the United States: A Rejoinder and Beyond." In *Comparative Social Research: An Annual,* vol. 8. Greenwich, Conn.: JAI Press.

Leonard, K. E., and Taylor, S. P. (1983). "Exposure to Pornography, Permissive and Nonpermissive Cues, and Male Aggression towards Females." *Motivation and Emotion* 7: 291–99.

Lynn, B. (1986). *Polluting the Censorship Debate.* Washington, D.C.: American Civil Liberties Union.

Malamuth, N., and Ceniti, J. (1986). "Repeated Exposure to Violent and Nonviolent Pornography." *Aggressive Behavior* 12: 129–37.

Marshall, D. S. (1971). "Sexual Behavior on Mangaia." In D. Marshall and R. Suggs, eds., *Human Sexual Behavior—Variations in the Ethnographic Spectrum.* New York: Basic Books.

Marshall, W. (1984). "The Use of Pornography by Rapists and Child Molesters." Unpublished report to the Department of Justice for Canada.

Marshall, W. (1988). "The Use of Sexually Explicit Stimuli by Rapists, Child Molesters and Nonoffenders." *Journal of Sex Research* 25: 267–88. (Previously unpublished paper under the title "Use of Pornography by Sexual Offenders," cited in the Attorney General's Commission on Pornography [1986]. *Final Report,* p. 961. Washington, D.C: U.S. Department of Justice.)

Marshall, W., and Barrett, S. (1990). *Criminal Neglect.* Toronto: Doubleday.

Ministerial Committee of Inquiry into Pornography. (1989) *Pornography.* Wellington, New Zealand: Minister of Justice.

Money, J. (1986). *Lovemaps: Clinical Concepts of Sexual Health and Pathology, Paraphilia, and Gender Transposition in Childhood, Adolescence, and Maturity.* New York: Irvington; Buffalo, N.Y.: Prometheus Books (paperback).

Money, J., and Ehrhardt, A. (1972). *Man and Woman, Boy and Girl: The Differentiation and Dimorphism of Gender Identity from Conception to Maturity.* Baltimore: Johns Hopkins University Press.

Palys, T. S. (1986). "Testing the Common Wisdom: The Social Content of Video Pornography." *Canadian Psychology* 27: 22–35.

Scott, J. E. (1985, May). "Violence and Erotic Material—The Relationship between Adult Entertainment and Rape?" Paper presented to the Annual Meeting of the American Association for the Advancement of Science, Los Angeles.

Tait, G. (1978). *Never Back Down.* Christchurch, New Zealand: Whitcoulls.

Thornberry, T. P., and Silberman, R. A. (1970). "Exposure to Pornography and Juvenile Delinquency." In U.S. Commission on Obscenity and Pornography, *Technical Report,* vol. 8. Washington, D.C.: U.S. Government Printing Office.

U.S. Commission on Obscenity and Pornography. (1970). *Technical Report.* Washington, D.C.: U.S. Government Printing Office.

Walker, C. E. (1970). "Erotic Stimuli and the Aggressive Sexual Offender." In U.S. Commission on Obscenity and Pornography, *Technical Report,* vol. 8. Washington, D.C.: U.S. Government Printing Office.

Williams, B., et al. (1979). *Obscenity and Film Censorship.* Cambridge, England: Cambridge University Press.

Zillmann, D. (1984) *Connections between Sex and Aggression.* Hillsdale, N.J.: Lawrence Erlbaum.

Zillmann, D., and Bryant, J. (1982). "Pornography, Sexual Callousness, and the Trivialization of Rape." *Journal of Communication* 32: 10–21.

——— (1986a). "Shifting Preferences in Pornography Consumption." *Communication Research 13:* 560–78. (Previously submitted to the Attorney General's Commission on Pornography [1986]. *Final Report.* Washington, D.C: U.S. Department of Justice.)

——— (1986b). A Response. *Journal of Communication* 36: 184–88.

——— (1989). *Pornography: Recent Research, Interpretations, and Policy Considerations.* Hillsdale, N.J.: Erlbaum.

19

The Impact of Sexology on the Provision of Sex Education, Contraception, and Abortion Services

Philip Meredith

INTRODUCTION

By examining the impact of new dimensions of sexology on a generation of policy makers, political activists and educators, this chapter is an exercise in the sociology of knowledge. In western, developed societies the liberal climate which prevailed from the 1960s to the 1980s was characterized by a profound examination of sexual relations and a restatement of the nature and purpose of the sexological sciences. This account of the political evolution of sexology draws upon the development of sexuality information and education in its broadest sense as public consciousness, and specifically as the basis for school pedagogy, including the rationale for the provision of contraceptive and abortion services for the young.

In pursuit of the "facts" of human sexuality, the emergent sexological sciences have followed a more or less political agenda from the time the subject of public education on sexuality was first formalized. Partly as a response to AIDS and to liberal abortion practice, the latter part of the 1980s saw, in some countries, a conservative backlash against what was seen as the moral relativism of the essentially feminist-inspired reinterpretations of sexuality, sexual rights and relationships from a critical sexological standpoint. This has taken the form of an anti-intellectual reversion to moral imperatives which has left much social policy on sexual matters in a state of impasse.

BACKGROUND

By the mid-1970s most governments had formalized laws facilitating the provision of contraceptive and, to a lesser extent, abortion services (Population Crisis Committee 1987). Such changes were justified on "rational" and scientific rather than simply moral grounds, based as they were on public health, population planning and good economics as well as human rights. The diversity of birth control theory and practice, nevertheless, varied according to the historical circumstances of states or groups of states. For example, women in the formerly Soviet bloc of Eastern Europe had had free access to abortion services as a result of the Marxist-Leninist ideologies ("scientific socialism") adopted before or after World War II, although they did not benefit from the developments in contraceptive technology taken for granted in the West. Citizens of these countries would also remain puritan and backward in terms of the sexual freedoms emerging in Western societies, particularly in respect to attitudes regarding homosexuality (Meredith 1989a; Bach 1988).

By contrast, the Nordic countries made the greatest advances in individual sexual rights (and access to the contraceptive and abortion services underpinning these rights), partly because they were less burdened by the Victorian Protestant Puritanism which so strongly dominated social, cultural and legal attitudes to sexuality in, for example, Britain and the United States, and also because of their rational approach to the facts of sexual life.

What the Western, developed societies did share from the late 1960s was a fundamental change in attitudes toward the sexual relations and rights of young people, manifest in the widespread involvement of states in the funding of special contraceptive and abortion services and of sex education programs for schools (Meredith & Thomas 1986). This liberalization went hand in hand with political recognition of the rights of women, under the impact of the second feminist wave, along with those of ethnic and sexual minorities. The countries of southern Europe only recently providing contraceptive, abortion and sex education have adopted social policies inspired as much by feminist campaigners as by the conventional rationales of health and public safety. This has stemmed in part from the perceived need to come in line with their liberal-democratic European partners.

For two decades, the liberal and left-leaning middle classes had a profound influence on pushing forward the cause of personal freedoms in the sexual sphere and on the application of state power to realize these freedoms. Although such developments were driven by a wide range of moral platforms which had their roots in reaction to earlier conservative attitudes to women, youth, and ethnic minorities, there were also powerful intellectual and scientific bases for these developments in the expansion and popularization of the social sciences. This brief politicization of everyday life, including the sexual and personal spheres, was made possible through a widespread social scientific exposé of the political bases of social relations, feeding and being fed by the cause of feminism, and expressed in a vast outpouring of research and publications, and media interest.

It was some measure of the influence of Western liberal thinking in these times that a global United Nations endorsement of school-based sex education and contraceptive services, outside of direct parental control, was possible. Anticipating the conflict that must inevitably stem from renegotiating basic rights to educate in such a moral sphere, the United Nations' Recommendation 29 of the Mexico City Conference on Population in August 1984 was carefully worded to avoid offense:

> Governments are urged to ensure that adolescents, both boys and girls, receive adequate education, including family life and sex education, with due consideration given to the role, rights and obligations of parents, and changing individual and cultural values.. Suitable family planning information and services should be made available to adolescents within the changing sociocultural framework of each country. (E/conf 76/19)

The authority invested in the school as purveyor of "factual" knowledge awards it a status, in theory, which stands above the parent. However, the controversies resulting from this intervention of the school into this traditional sphere of parental control has meant that the authority of governments has also been required to uphold state school provision of sex education and justify the funding of contraceptive services in those countries in which they have been established. In the face of competing moral standpoints from the two extremes of the sociopolitical spectrum, the problem for liberal educators and policy makers has been to identify supramoral justifications for the kind of services they wish to be established, preferably of the scientific kind traditionally supplied by the medical profession. Conservatives such as Thomas Szasz (1981) were quick to question the wisdom of involving the state in an area believed to be outside the competence of individual parents:

> The term sex education conceals more than it reveals. It conceals the specific social, educational, and economic policies used to implement sex education, the moral values secretly encouraged and discouraged; and last but not least, the problems that derive inexorably from involving the school system—and hence the government—in defining what constitutes education in human sexuality.

Such controversies have emerged in countries with very different religious (and post-religious) traditions. All societies that have had their school systems address the subject of sexual socialization have found it necessary to deal with the struggle between "traditionalistic" and "progressive" sentiments. All such countries had found it necessary to resort to a national (or federal) government to play a part in administering services, as well as legislating and regulating the propagation of sex education. The political reactions to these developments during the 1980s and early 1990s have seen a retrenchment based on conservative thinking that has left several Western societies in discord over the future direction of sex education, abortion, and gay and lesbian rights.

FACTS AND VALUES IN SEXUALITY EDUCATION

What are teachers to present to young people as the "facts" about sexuality, and how did they come by such facts and the educational meaning derived from them? In its original common-sense usage, sex education referred to the transmission of factual knowledge to the young in appropriate ways in order to release them from problems arising from ignorance about their bodies and the nature of relationships. The assumption here was that the potential unhappiness which so often stems from sexual life can be minimized through transfer of knowledge. Controversies reported in the media largely focus upon the moral import of presentation of facts about sexuality. This has reached a point in Britain, for example, where it has been felt necessary to resort to a legislation to enforce the "correct" way of presenting facts about homosexuality. In matters of sex education, some feel that knowledge alone has the power to corrupt. As a result, parental and other forms of consultation are used to ensure that factual information is handled by teachers in acceptable ways (Rogers 1982).

While parents have a right to know how and with what effect factual information about sexuality is conveyed to their children, what prospect is there for teachers relying upon a scientifically established knowledge base for this subject without simultaneously becoming engaged in a debate over its moral import? The traditional versus progressive interpretations of sex education are built upon opposing philosophies of sexuality. Both recognize the retreat of scientific sexology from the notion of an instinctual basis of sexual identity and behavior, as it ascribes more and more to some variant of socialization or learning process of sociosexual development. However, there are fundamental differences over the significance attached to learned sexual expression. Traditionalists are more concerned with the importance of control over the sex drive, particularly during adolescence, and its ostensible rechanneling into other creative activities. The progressive sentiment, by contrast, tends more toward providing a positive basis for the sexual drive to emerge in humanizing and humanistic ways. The spiritual value attached to sexuality per se also determines opinions about the costs and benefits of contraceptives for adolescents.

The traditional and progressive tendencies do not differ with respect to their understanding of school sex education as a formal process in which moral values are addressed by means of factual instruction about reproduction and sexual behavior. However, a profound difference has emerged concerning how this process should occur.

One naive conception of traditional sex education has the teacher providing presumably objective, scientific information about sexuality and reproduction, to which desired values and moral code are attached in the home by parents. The conviction that adolescents would benefit by being permitted access to hitherto taboo and restricted details about sexuality and reproduction underlies many early professional and governmental statements on the subject. This is still perceived by many parents, as well as politicians, as the most desirable model.

A less naive version of this traditional form of sex education perceives this process as the communication of a set of pre-established moral values (e.g., about the proper time and place for sexual initiation, the form sexual activity should take, and the social systems within which it should take place, etc.), supported where necessary by appropriate "objective" information. It is not the business of the teacher to pursue his/her own preferred persuasions on these matters, but to conform with the curriculum established by those to whom the school is answerable: the parents, school board, church, etc. A yet more sophisticated version of the above would introduce scientific sexological theorizing or data that appear to support the values the education is expected to convey (e.g., the essential sociological benefits of the nuclear family structure to society, or the psychological benefits of monogamous relations).

By contrast, the most progressive variant of sex education has appeared in the form of a teacher using biological and sexological knowledge to encourage objective discussion about the range of moral values pertaining in a society, with a view to enabling pupils to arrive at their own opinion. A radical version of such education has taken the form of selective communication of existing biological-sexological knowledge to permit young people to acquire a deeper understanding of their own and others' sexuality, and to be able to evaluate for themselves the moral status quo.

As far as sex education is concerned, however, there exists no agreed-on knowledge base on which to base any of these variants. This is to say, there are as many disagreements over the "facts" of sexuality as over the values that should be so derived. Yet critics of all sex education who fail to perceive any difference between biology and "indoctrination" are ignoring the existence of extensive historical, biological, medical and social scientific analyses of sexuality. This chapter briefly reviews the knowledge—the sum of scientific sexologies beyond reproductive biology—on which our contemporary understanding of sexuality is based. How coherent and useful is this knowledge base for the purposes of formulating social policies on services for the young and for school-based sex education? To what extent can scientific knowledge about sexual behavior itself offer the means for a more standardized *moral* component of the education that is acceptable to the majority of teachers, parents, politicians and pupils in liberal, pluralist societies?

If sexuality is to be regarded as a phenomenon capable of some form of scientific analysis and explanation, then there exists the possibility of certain values being established on the basis of what is regarded as objective knowledge rather than merely sectional interests or personal persuasions. If human sexuality is amenable to biological, psychological, anthropological and sociological explanation, then the means by which values are established should depend, at least in part, on a rational examination of these scientific contributions. This is not to propose that values can, in some absolute way, be derived from or created out of scientific fact; rather, that the legitimacy of certain values over others should be increased by reference to scientific evidence.

The following section is an account of the broad range of scientific and moral bases that have been, at different times, used as a rationale for public education in sexuality (Meredith 1989b). References are principally from the emergence of the state's position on sexual matters in Britain, though equivalent references are likely to exist for the United States and other countries.

SEXOLOGY AND SEX EDUCATION

Following the period in which scientific inquiry replaced Christian theological interpretation, it is possible to identify a crude three-stage historical chronology governing our understanding of human sexuality. Following its codification as an element of individual identity, and in accordance with the principles governing science since the nineteenth century, the first stage had to do with explanations of the essence of sexuality as a fixed sociobiological human entity, as Weeks (1986) describes:

> The term [sex] refers both to an act and a category of person, to a practice and a gender. . . . The earliest usage of the term "sex," in the sixteenth century, referred precisely to the division of humanity into the male section and the female section (that is, differences of gender). The dominant meaning today, however, and one current since the early nineteenth century, refers to physical relations between the sexes, "to have sex." The extension of the meanings of these words indicates a shift in the way that "sexuality" (the

> abstract noun referring to the quality of being "sexual") is understood in our culture. (p. 13)

The contribution of Freudian psychology in the late nineteenth and early twentieth centuries paved the way for the second stage, namely, a shift in the previously unidimensional scientific understanding of the phenomenon by providing for the possibility that at least part of one's sexuality is indeterminate or unprogrammed by biological or other natural forces. The third stage has been dominated in this latter part of the twentieth century by the critical social sciences, which have provided the means for dialectical analyses of sexuality as (among other things) a necessarily social construction.

In the wake of Christian influence, the most important scientific trends that filtered into sex education did so in such a way as to permit much Western sex education to discover a further "scientific" legitimation for those dominant values relating to the status of women, the family, chastity, normality, etc., which had already been legitimized through Christian revelation. However, the social sciences, and more recently a sophisticated interpretation of Freudian psychoanalysis by feminist thinkers, have provided an alternative scientific basis for an anti-traditionalistic sex education.

Let us now examine some ways in which Christian belief has impacted on sex education, and how science has both challenged and legitimated the traditional Christian attitude toward sex and male-female relationships.

While the ancients were concerned with the question of overindulgence, dominance and passivity in sexual behavior, Christianity interpreted sexuality as first and foremost a means of reproduction, to the point of disapproving of sexual relations purely for pleasure. Christianity's regulation of the social dimension of sexuality was accomplished by the twelfth century with its elevation of marriage (and sexuality within it) to the status of a sacrament. Extramarital and nonreproductive sexual activity (e.g., homosexuality and masturbation) was therefore sinful.

In its most conservative expression, Christianity has provided a knowledge base for "anti-sexuality education": the disavowal of secular knowledge about sexuality and the refusal even to frame its definition, as if this in itself were corrupting. This is replaced by indirect references to love and reproduction through religious allusions. In less conservative forms, Christian values provide a continuing source of legitimacy for nondenominational as well as explicitly denominational sex education comprising moral codes to guide one's entry into the sexual life. Founded on the premise of a supernaturally ordained and unchanging natural order of things, Christianity perceives sexuality as potentially dangerous both for the soul and for society. The central function of sex education, in this view, is to recommend self-control over the force within, in order to ensure the survival of the marriage bond, the family, and by extension, society itself. The transmission of any factual or secular information about reproductive biology or the social reality of sexuality is subordinated to this end.

In Britain, Christian values have been proposed as the best basis for sex education because of the moral relativism characterizing "post-Christian" society. Christian standards could, therefore, be used as an "ideal" to provide order from the confusion of competing approaches (House of Lords 1976). Others reject such a mediation in a secular society because of the double standard Christianity has historically imposed on women through its attitude toward extramarital pregnancy, its heterosexual absolutism, and its generally negative perception of sexual desire.

By the nineteenth century, scientific sexology, associated with the names of Krafft-Ebing, Havelock Ellis, Hirschfeld and others, had become established, mainly through the scientific method of descriptive classification of "behaviors." Physicians began to take the place of the clergy as authorities on sexual behavior. The scientific method generated its own added form of sexual morality in the form of the stratification of sexuality into the "normal" and the "deviant," the latter interpreted as degeneracy or perversion. The positive effects this formative discipline has had in extending our knowledge of sexual behaviors has been applauded by sociologists of human sexual relations.

However, as a knowledge base for a code of sexual morality, this scientific method had a naive and inadequate theoretical foundation. Weeks (1986) has noted that in its search for the "true" meaning of sex, this tradition has contributed to the codification of a "sexual tradition":

> a more or less coherent body of assumptions, beliefs, prejudices, rules, methods of investigation and forms of moral regulation which still shape the way we live our sexualities. (p. 14)

In answer to the question, "Is sex threatening and dangerous?" the present author contends that justification may be found not only in a particular Christian tradition but in the writings of the founding father of sexology, Richard von Krafft-Ebing. Justification may equally be found in works of polemicists and scientists from the nineteenth century to the present for the contention that the liberating power of sexuality has been blocked only by the repressive force of corrupt civilization.

Making a claim to legitimacy in its affiliation with medicine (pathology and its treatment), scientific sexology reinforced the biological distinction between the sexes and the instinctual nature of sexual desire. Homosexuality could be redefined in rational-liberal fashion from being a sin to being a biosocial disposition.

It is acknowledged that Freud's theory of the dynamic unconscious made a vital contribution to the emerging science of sexuality, though aspects of psychoanalysis as therapy retain a connection with the assumptions underlying the formal nineteenth-century sexology. Thus the principal (though not only) Freudian interpretation of sexuality sees it as a "mechanical" force within the personality which needs to be controlled by cultural rules and taboos; an "instinct" which must force its way out either in direct sexual expression or, if blocked, in the form of perversions or neuroses. Moreover, Freud (preceded by Albert Moll, 1912) extended the concept of sexuality to children (the Freudian formation of the "normal" adult through the three phases of childhood sexuality), thus providing the groundwork for most subsequent child psychology. Sexuality educators influenced by psychology would henceforth have to consider the control and appropriate channeling of the "sex drive" (which appears earlier in life than had previously been believed) in such a way that it is not simply repressed at the expense of the psychological health of the adolescent. In addition, explanations and social control of homosexuality could no longer be so straightforward.

In identifying the process of sexual development as stages of childhood, Freud provided a framework by which psychosexual maladjustment could be explained in terms of arrested development. Wallis (1984) has noted that in the main use by sex educators of Freud's ideas about the family's influence on sexual development is toward a reinforcement of the status of the (nuclear) family, implying that normal development can occur only within its confines. Child psychologist John Bowlby's elevation of the mother-child relationship as the determining force on the child's healthy development has been used to uphold the virtues of family life and the mother role, as well as to provide explanations for the causes of problem families and child psychopathology in the breakdown of the mother-child bond.

This field of applied psychology, with its focus upon the significance of the mother role, appears in the field of sex education in the work of the important British educationalist, J. Newsom. His assumptions were those of the sex education thinkers of the time: that women and men have marked psychological and physical differences, which should be reflected in complementary (sexual) roles:

> The future of women's education lies not in attempting to iron out their differences from men, to reduce them to neuters, but to teach girls how to grow into women. (Newsom 1948: 109)

Education, then, should take account of the individual differences between the sexes and their social function. Moreover, the British government's Newsom Report on school education was unequivocal on the moral code which should guide sex education in its statement that "boys and girls should be offered firm guidance on sexual morality based on chastity before marriage and fidelity within it" (p. 54).

The enthusiasm with which the American "helping" professions took to post-Freudian psychological theory in the 1950s gave rise to a hugely influential trend in psycho- and other forms of therapy. This affected the direction of the psychiatric, educational, and social work professions, and even of religious pastoral care (Reiff 1966; Halmos 1965; Heraud 1970). Concerned with personal adjustment in order to achieve the (functionalist) happiness which benefits both the individual and society, the applied sciences of human and, in particular, women's sexuality became preoccupied with researching and eliminating impediments to optimal human sexual response (e.g., in the work of Masters and Johnson). This new concern with sexual well-being has been identified in British school sex education materials produced by respectable organizations, albeit aimed at older girls. Thus the National Marriage Guidance Council's pamphlet "How to Treat a Young Wife," and its successors, identified giving and receiving physical satisfaction as something as relevant to the wife as it is to the husband in cementing the marriage bond. Wallis (1984: 48) reminds us that, with the publication in 1957 of Chesser's "Love and Marriage," "the whole thrust of marriage guidance moved towards an appreciation of sex as a mode of sustaining and stabilizing the family." Davis' pamphlet, "The Sexual Responsibility of Women," notes that at no time during her formal or informal upbringing had she been impressed with the fact that marriage is a realm in which she has profound personal sexual responsibility and that women must "learn to both satisfy and be satisfied sexually" (Wallis 1984: 68).

From a quite different scientific realm, zoology and animal biology have also provided a wealth of material for educators concerned with what is both proper and natural human sexual behavior. From this discipline, descriptions of animal behavior are employed to show that apparent biological differences between male and female are universal, leading to sexual behavior that displays the same law-like (instinctual) forms. In this way, heterosexuality alone was at one time awarded the status of universal biological normality; and, by extension, sexual intercourse was understood primarily as having a reproductive purpose, in which the woman's role was to be understood by her biological design: as a repository for the male sperm. Wallis (1984) has identified two uses of zoology in the design of sex education: first, the state's recommendation of the educative function of observation of mammalian mating habits; and second, the use of the description of the sexual habits of fish, amphibia, birds and lower mammals to stress that sexuality is inherently concerned with reproduction:

> In the higher class of animals, the mammals, to which the human race belongs, male animals possess a special organ (the penis) for getting sperm cells directly into the female reproductive system. (Corner 1938)

Other zoological connections appear more recently through the use of words such as "fertilization" (Richards 1963) and "mating" (Picton 1980) to describe sexual activity.

More recently, the discipline of sociobiology has added its own scientific contributions to sexology and sex education, carrying with it somewhat similar ideological baggage as the above. Sociobiologists see all social phenomena as emanations of basic genetic material, from which scientific explanation of such phenomena must ultimately be drawn. Forms of sexual life have emerged to ensure the survival of the gene. Sociobiology seeks to explain the necessary and positive functions of not merely sexual division but conflicting interests. Males and females instinctively seek reproductive advantages. Males pursue as many sexual partners as possible in order to maximize gene transfer to the next generation. Females, by contrast, seek to ensure the best possible genetic inheritance for future generations. The ideological thrust of any education based on sociobiological theory is apparent in the contention that the most socially useful thing to do is not to eliminate or exaggerate differences but provide equal opportunity for each sex in his or her sphere. This is the least costly of choices and helps preserve the nuclear family, "the building block of nearly all human societies" (Weeks 1985: 114).

Medical biology offers further scientific material in the cause of affirming the rectitude of traditional sex roles. Here the consequences of the human biochemical makeup provide an alternative to, or underpin instinctually grounded sexual orientation. Correspondingly, sex education has drawn upon such material to justify a conformist view of gender roles where the male is dominant and the female passive. This has been ascribed to the influence of estrogen on "the mother-instinct" as the basis of women's motivation in love-making (Wallis 1984: 35).

Alternative evidence from the same scientific discipline has been used to contest the notion that the chemicals which operate in the physiological development of the sexes have a corresponding effect on gender roles also, thereby subordinating cultural socialization to biology. Reiss (1986) concluded that the evidence on human females indicates no clear increase in sexual interest during ovulation and that it cannot be logically deduced how human females will act based on how subhuman primate females behave during ovulation.

A comparable example of professional legerdemain is offered by Kirstin Luker (1984) in her examination of the emergence of abortion as a social problem in the United States in the nineteenth century, when physicians became campaigners against women acting on their own behalf. Their justification was, Luker contends, only partly moral:

> According to these physicians, women sought abortions because the doctrine of quickening led them to believe that the embryo was not alive, and therefore

> aborting it was perfectly proper. Second, they argued, they were obliged to act in order to save women from their own ignorance because only physicians were in possession of new scientific evidence which demonstrated beyond a shadow of a doubt that the embryo was a child from conception onward. (p. 21)

Luker concludes that although this claim had no basis in fact, it permitted physicians to shift the grounds of debate from moral values to empirical facts in order to strengthen their case, though this was ultimately no more than a different moral evaluation of the "facts."

THE RELEVANCE OF MEDICAL SCIENCE IN SEXOLOGY AND SEX EDUCATION

The interpretations placed on medical data remain at the center of the debate over the importance of sexual relations for human well-being. The separation of sexual intercourse from reproduction, created by the development of artificial contraceptives, has had a profound effect on the value and significance attached to sexual relations, and by extension the social structures (such as marriage) created to manage them. A byproduct of contemporary contracepting societies is the phenomenon of "recreational" sex, a subject powerfully exploited by the mass media. Consequently, much agonizing about "correct" sex education has been devoted to devising ways of salvaging a sense of sanctity for sexual relations.

One way has been to insist that teachers highlight the psychological-emotional costs of engaging lightly in sexual activity: the squandering of a whole dimension of the love relationship for the sake of short-term returns. Alternatively, traditionalist exponents of sex education call for a strategy of highlighting the greater value of long-term health over sexual enjoyment; proposing that young people be acquainted in school with medical evidence of the (potential) side effects of contraceptives, the (potential) consequences of early intercourse on later general and reproductive health, and the costs in risks of disease from successive sexual partners.

Controversies over sex education have, to a large extent, revolved around competing evaluations of the medical evidence relating to sexual relations in adolescence (e.g., the threat of cervical cancer), evaluations that have again changed according to new scientific findings or events such as the arrival of AIDS. Nevertheless, at any one time, the "evaluation" of such relations (in the moral as well as physical "cost-benefit" sense) can and should make reference to the broader "objective" processes of statistical and other scientific analysis. The debate continues in scientific and social policy circles whether the AIDS pandemic poses a serious threat to the heterosexual population in most developed societies, as it increasingly tends to do.

THE IMPACT OF SOCIOLOGY

Sociological research since the 1950s has been used to challenge the validity of scientific explanations of the fixed character of the sex roles and the status these explanations attached to a single type of sexual behavior. Moreover, critical social theory has provided the means to charge that much conventional scientific evidence is thinly disguised ideology used to legitimize one pattern of sexuality against possible alternatives.

Apart from the later radical interpretations of Freud noted below, the social scientific survey work of Alfred Kinsey et al. (1948) led to apparently incontestable conclusions which helped establish the case of liberal and even libertarian sex education. Kinsey's massive questionnaire surveys disturbed the statistical pillar of sexual normality by discovering within the United States great intracultural variation in sexual behavior, identifying heterosexual intercourse as only one of six forms of sexual outlet (including: masturbation, nocturnal emission, heterosexual petting, homosexual relations, and bestiality). Kinsey's conclusions challenged assumptions about the nature of "deviancy" and the validity of biosexual identities; for example, that there exists the genus "homosexual" rather than men who (may) express a range of homosexual tendencies. Researchers from a variety of disciplines continue to pursue answers to the question whether there is a scientific concept of "normality" which homosexuality violates (Reiss 1986). Few other subjects within the field of sex education cause so much anxiety, making the subject the test case of all sex education. Scientific theorizing and evidence will continue to play a vital political role in how this subject is dealt with at all levels of society. Social anthropology, sociology and the heritage of Kinsey's original surveys of sexual behavior established that sexuality is contingent upon the culture in which it is expressed, and therefore displays variations.

CRITICAL SOCIAL SCIENCE AND SEXOLOGY

The tradition of "critical theory," represented for much of this century in the work of the Frankfurt School of Sociology, devoted much attention to the relationship between sexuality and society. For example, the Freudo-Marxism represented in the post-war works of Wilhelm Reich and 1960s theories of Herbert Marcuse developed the notion that the liberation of sexual desire constituted a precondition of political freedom and an end to class oppression, with the corollary that sexual repression has underlying political causes (Robinson 1972). The influence of such political analyses of sexuality on educators is probably not significant, though this spirit was encapsulated in the Danish political self-help guide for the young, *The Little Red School Book,* which achieved, in Britain in the 1970s, some notoriety for its recommendation of sexual self-determination for the young (Hansen & Jensen 1971).

The later applications of critical social theory to the field of sexology produced a vast output particularly of feminist critique, whose influence on society is wide-ranging and long-lasting. Of the modern sexological sciences, Weeks observes:

> Over the past decade or so much has changed. . . . There has been a minor explosion of historical writings about sex. We now know a great deal about such topics as marriage and the family, prostitution and homosexuality, the forms of legal and medical regulation, pre-Christian and non-Christian moral codes, women's bodies and health, illegitimacy and birth control, rape and sexual violence, the evolution of sexual identities and the importance of social networks and oppositional sexualities. (Weeks 1986: 19–20)

Applied to the phenomenon of human sexuality, critical social theory embarked on a path of "de-construction" of its historical components. Michel Foucault, in particular, contributed a history of the "dea" (goddess) of sexuality in his investigation of the causes and forms of sexual behavior. It was to be viewed as a series of "meaning-giving practices," "a social apparatus" rather than a merely natural phenomenon (Foucault 1979). This being so, sexuality could be subjected to questions such as: How is it shaped and articulated with economic, social and political structures? Why is it so important in Western culture? What is the relationship between sex and power? Finally, if sex is a social construct, how can one's sexuality be changed?

Critical social theory challenged the naturalness of the dominant sex roles, the "normality" of heterosexual monogamy, and the notion of an invisible biological imperative of reproduction of the species expressed in sexual intercourse. Sexuality perceived as, in large part, a social construction has led to a reevaluation of female subordination. Feminist critical perspectives were directed in the first instance at societies and social relations; the nuclear family, in particular, has been singled out as the principal means of female economic oppression, denial of female sexuality and sexual choice, and the vehicle for the transmission of capitalist society. Necessarily, this critique has been turned upon the historical construction of scientific sexology itself. Consequently, sexual knowledge is exposed as defining sexuality in masculine terms, reflecting the (conscious and unconscious) interests of the dominant (male) scientific disciplines.

The ideology of sexuality is seen to have a material basis, taking the form of the monogamous patriarchal family. Feminists have challenged as myth the idea of sex as a purely natural rather than social phenomenon (Coote & Campbell 1982). Moving beyond the now familiar critique of "classical" Freudian psychoanalytic phallocentric bias, feminists have also returned to the psychoanalytic tradition with new interpretations, with the objective of answering certain persistent sexological problems. In particular, there remains the need to explain why one's sexual identity feels so compelling even though the de-constructionist anthropological and sociological approaches suggest that these identities are, in fact, contingent, socially organized and even changeable. It is concluded that anatomy merely predisposes the individual toward sexual identity rather than determines it. Sexuality, then, is to be explained in terms of a combination of psychic structuring and the (conscious) acquisition of pre-existing social forms. The latter component has been elaborated by reference to the learning of sexual "scripts," defined by Reiss as follows:

> I use the term cultural script to mean a shared group definition of the type of situation, type of people and type of behavior appropriate in a particular social context. There are cultural scripts aimed at producing an erotic response in the participants, and I shall call these sexual scripts. The sexual scripts derive from the shared, consensual beliefs people have about what is good and bad sexuality in their society. These sexual scripts act as guides regarding what that society believes are the proper circumstances for experiencing an erotic response. . . . The individual is constantly "editing" the sexual scripts of his or her society. (Reiss 1986: 34)

Recent history provides spectacular examples of the ways in which sexual scripts have been socially created, modified, and adopted, uniting those with common "psychic" dispositions. Ironically, the pursuit of measures of sexual normality by the positive sciences has played a hand in this by creating sexual identities through the technique of classification. The nineteenth-century sexologists chose to classify observed behaviors according to "deviations" from the "normal." Kinsey preferred the more scientifically neutral classification of sexual "diversity." Either way, this process interfered with the objects of sexology by presenting the public with a range of sexual scripts out of which new identities could be acquired to suit psychic dispositions. As science isolated the homosexual "identity" in the nineteenth century, providing a sexual script for the creation of a distinct sexual subculture, so have political changes permitted such subcultures a public voice:

> As the homosexual ways of life have become more public and self-confident, so in their wake other assertions of minority sexual identities have emerged.

> The example of homosexuality has provided a repertoire of political strategies and organizational forms for the mobilization of other erotic populations. Transvestites, transsexuals, paedophiles, sadomasochists, fetishists, bisexuals, prostitutes and others have vocally emerged, clamoring for their right to self expression and legitimacy. . . . These new sexual and social identities may have emerged on the terrain first mapped and carefully articulated by the sexologists themselves. (Weeks 1986: 77)

THE IMPLICATIONS OF "CRITICAL SEXOLOGY" FOR PUBLIC INFORMATION AND EDUCATION IN SEXUALITY

The division made by Habermas between the natural sciences and the sciences of social action, if sound, reveals the connection between the scientific method, its object and the rationale it carries with it:

> In the empirical-analytic sciences the frame of reference that prejudges the meaning of possible statements establishes rules both for the construction of theories and for their critical testing. Theories comprise hypothetico-deductive connections of propositions which permit the deduction of law like hypotheses with empirical content. The systematic sciences of social action, that is economics, sociology and political science, have the goal as do the empirical-analytic sciences of producing nomological knowledge. A critical social science, however, will not remain satisfied with this. It is concerned with going beyond this goal to determine when theoretical statements grasp invariant regularities of social action as such and when they express ideologically frozen relations of dependence that can in principle be transformed. To the extent that this is the case, the critique of ideology, as well moreover of psychoanalysis, takes into account that information about law-like connections sets off a process of reflection in the consciousness of those the laws are about. . . . [Self-reflection] releases the subject from dependence on hypostatised powers. Self-reflection is determined by an emancipatory cognitive interest. (Habermas 1978: 309–310)

The emergence of a science of sexuality since the nineteenth century has resulted in the development of competing theories of sexual orientation and behavior. It is fair to say that during this period there has been progress made in understanding how sexual identity and behavior is actively acquired rather than inherited as a form of instinctual behavior, though disagreements remain over how this learning occurs. The scientific view of sexuality as something changeable through self-reflection destabilizes the moral code that was upheld by theories of biological conditioning. The comfortable division between sexual normality and deviancy/perversity is correspondingly undermined by a recognition of sexual "diversity." Moreover, the ethics of tolerance of (and even "treatment" for) fixed sexual endowments are no longer relevant if such behaviors can potentially be acquired, enjoyed, defended or even ostensibly unlearned.

These developments have been accompanied by new approaches to public sex education, contraceptive and other services; for example, juvenile contraceptive clinics and even state-funded gay and lesbian community centers in northern European countries. Such developments represent a serious threat to defenders of traditional sexual ethics, roles and education, who are forced either to dispute the scientific basis of the feminist critique and the evidence it has brought to bear, or expound an alternative nonscientific legitimacy for their preferred sexual value-system, such as Christianity (which is indeed the basis for the anti-abortion crusades of the late 1980 and 1990s).

The emancipatory impetus of the "critical sexologies" has had a powerful impact on both progressive teachers and their traditionalist critics. Some of the former now recognize their sex education role as one dedicated to freeing their pupils as early in their lives as possible from what are seen as socially and personally destructive sex roles. Meanwhile the latter complain of the mass of conflicting ideas and ideologies imported into the classroom, and the "amoralism" that some teachers promote by encouraging sexual self-determination. Modes of teaching have evolved to accompany this shift in perception of sexuality, though the historicopolitical process appears to be approaching a full circle, as Figure 1 illustrates.

Derived from education theory (Bernstein 1977; Douglas 1973), in Figure 1, cell C (lower left), describes the emergence of the "experiential," child-centered progressivism that characterized much of Western pedagogical thinking in the 1970s. Since the 1980s, progressivism applied to sex education, as well as to many other subjects in the curriculum, has been open to attack. By the end of the 1980s, under the impact of AIDS and a conservative backlash against publicly funded abortion, the prevailing ethicoscientific thrust of public education has shifted back to models A and B, now standing in tension with C and D.

CONCLUSIONS

There are several pedagogical issues raised by this current crisis. First, there is a danger that both defenders and detractors of recent sexological theories misrepresent what these theories are proposing, for the sake of their wider moral or political interests. For example, on the right, an oversimplistic conception of sexual script-learning has appeared in the form of a pervasive anxiety that exposure to information about homosexuality during adolescence may

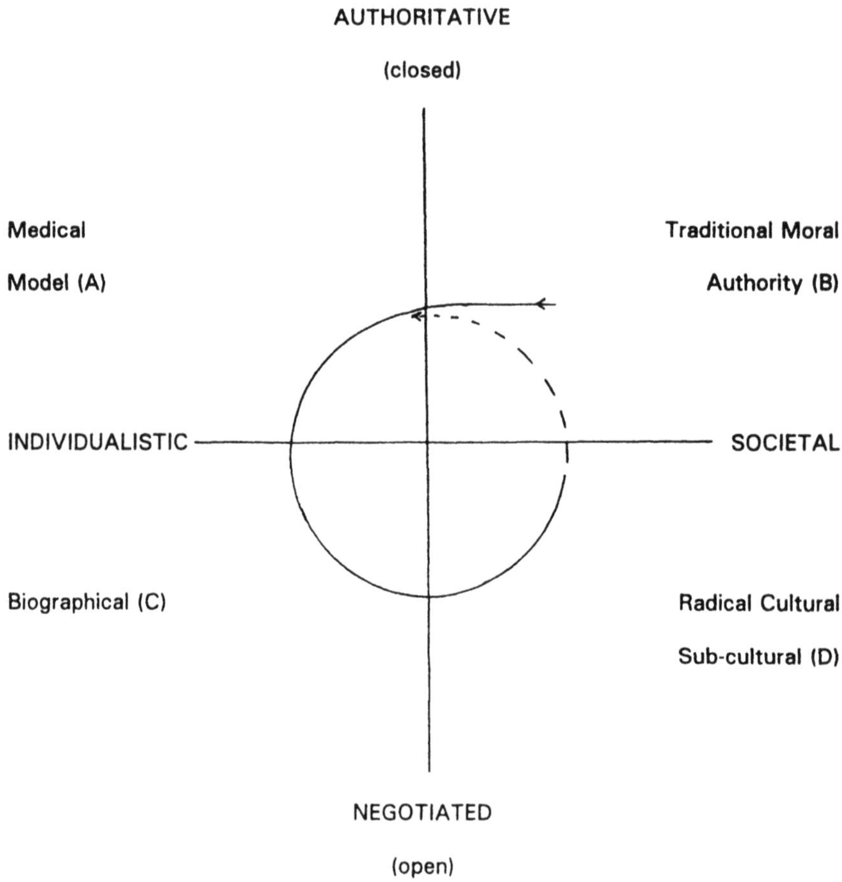

Figure 1

encourage some young people to take on this sexual orientation. Yet this is hardly the kind of learning process sexologists have in mind when they state that sexual orientation may become "fixed" through early psychic processes, rather than through a natural disposition (Mitchell 1974).

Second, there is a danger in regarding the critical sexological stance as the basis for all sexuality education, including that provided in public schools. While sex education must draw upon upon critical sexology, it can be argued that neither the classroom nor the teacher-pupil relationship are suitable vehicles to take on the full implications of this stance. For it is the task of the school to assist in the process of enabling the young person to survive in society, to recognize and absorb its higher values, and to value its more durable structures (e.g., the family). This involves as much a process of individual accommodation to the sexual status quo as the acquisition of the means to challenge what are believed to be its repressive elements.

Finally, if scientific inquiry can no longer be regarded as a "neutral" procedure, but carries with it its own constituting rationale, the moral guidelines that are the "end-product" of sex education will emerge from the social theories of which the knowledge base is comprised. They can be neither decided independently of this knowledge base nor imposed on it, even though this is what some interest groups might wish. The current clamor for the teaching of more "facts" and less "politics" is redundant insofar as the objective status of knowledge about human sexuality now depends upon whether those concerned with it are willing to concede the shift in the scientific paradigm described above. The alternative is to countenance only that knowledge which supports preferred sex roles and relations and which has no scientific basis at all, or else to ignore all criteria of a scientific nature in favor of a purely moral standpoint.

REFERENCES

Bach, K. (1988). "Sexualerziehung als Vorbereitung der Heranwachsender auf Liebe, Partnerschart, Ehe und Familie." [Sex Education in the Preparation of Adolescents for Love, Partnership, Marriage and Family.] In L. Arersin and E. Gunther, eds., *Sexualmedizin*, pp. 167–72. Berlin: VEB Verlag Volk und Gesundheit.

Bernstein, B. (1977). *Class, Codes and Control.* Vol. 1 of *Theoretical Studies towards a Sociology of Language.* London: Routledge and Kegan Paul.

Coote, A., and Campbell, B. (1982). *Sweet Freedom: The Struggle for Women's Liberation.* London: Picador.

Corner, G. W. (1938). *Attaining Manhood: A Doctor Talks to Boys about Sex.* London: Harper and Bros.

Douglas, M. (1973). *Natural Symbols.* Harmondsworth, England: Penguin.

Habermas, J. (1978). *Knowledge and Human Interests,* pp. 309–310. London: Heinemann.

Halmos, P. (1965). *The Faith of the Counsellors.* London: Constable.

Hansen, S., and Jensen, J. (1971, English trans.) *The Little Red Schoolbook. Stage 1.* London: Handyside.

Heraud, B. J. (1970). *Sociology and Social Work: Perspectives and Problems.* Oxford: Pergamon Press.

House of Lords. (1976). *Parliamentary Debates,* col. 160 ff.

Kinsey, A. C.; Pomeroy, W. B.; and Martin, C. E. (1948). *Sexual Behavior in the Human Male.* Philadelphia: W. B. Saunders.

Luker, K. (1984). *Abortion and the Politics of Motherhood.* Berkeley, Calif.: University of California Press.

Meredith, P., and Thomas, L., eds. (1986). *Planned Parenthood in Europe: A Human Rights Perspective.* London: Croom Helm.

Meredith, P., ed. (1989a). *The Other Curriculum: European Strategies for School Sex Education.* London: IPPF Europe.

Meredith, P. (1989b). *Sex Education: Political Issues in Britain and Europe.* London: Routledge.

Mitchell, J. (1974). *Psychoanalysis and Feminism.* London. Allen Lane.

Moll, A. (1912). *The Sexual Life of the Child.* Trans. Eden Paul. New York: Macmillan.

Newsom, J. (1948). *The Education of Girls.* London: Faber and Faber.

Picton, M. (1980). *Understanding Parenthood and Childcare.* London: Blackie.

Population Crisis Committee. (1987). *World Access to Birth Control.* Washington, D.C.

Reiff, P. (1966). *The Triumph of the Therapeutic.* Harmondsworth: Penguin.

Reiss, I. L. (1986). *Journey into Sexuality.* Englewood Cliffs, N.J.: Prentice-Hall.

Richards, L. (1963). *For Boys.* Oxford: Basil Blackwell.

Robinson, P. A. (1972). *The Sexual Radicals: Reich, Roheim, Marcuse.* London: Paladin.

Rogers, A. (1982, February 5). "Sex Lessons." *Times Health Supplement.*

Szasz, T. (1981). "The Case against Sex Education." *British Journal of Medicine* 8.

Wallis, G. P. (1984). "Some Ideological Issues in Sex Education in Post-War Britain," p. 48. Unpublished M.A. dissertation. London: University of London, Institute of Education.

Weeks, J. (1985). *Sexuality and Its Discontents: Meanings, Myths and Modern Sexualities.* London: Routledge and Kegan Paul.

——— (1986). *Sexuality.* London: Ellis Horwood/Tavistock Publications.

20

AIDS and Sexology

Herman N. Sno

During the 1980s, AIDS (Acquired Immune Deficiency Syndrome) emerged as a leading cause of death among young adults throughout the world. An estimated one million persons in the United States had been infected with the Human Immunodeficiency Virus (HIV) and more than 179,000 patients with AIDS had been reported to the Centers for Disease Control (CDC) as of May 31, 1991. Of these patients with AIDS, more than 113,000 (63 percent) are reported to haye died (CDC 1990, 1991). In the Netherlands, 1,912 patients had been registered as having AIDS by the December 1, 1991. More than a third of these patients have died. Between 7,500 and 9,000 patients are estimated as being HIV positive in the Netherlands (cf. Water et al. 1990). Although homosexual and bisexual men continue to account for most American and European AIDS cases, the incidence of AIDS among heterosexuals, especially women prostitutes; IV drug users; and children with perinatal HIV transmission is increasing transculturally (Postema et al. 1990; CDC 1991). Incidence figures have, at a minimum, doubled between 1991 and 1994, and the epidemic is spreading virulently in India, Southeast Asia, and Africa.

AIDS is considered to be the clinical end stage of infection with HIV. Other manifestations of HIV infection include clinically asymptomatic infection (HIV positivity), clinically acute opportunistic infection, persistent generalized lymphadenopathy (PGL) and the wasting syndrome. Until the CDC criteria were updated, a patient could be diagnosed as having AIDS only if he or she belonged to group IVB, IVC-I or IVD (see Table 1).

Nowadays virtually everyone knows that AIDS is caused by HIV infection. Most people are also aware that transmission of this virus occurs almost exclusively through body fluids during both heterosexual and homosexual activity

Table 1
Classification System for HIV Infections
[Centers for Disease Control, 1986]

Group I	Acute infection	
Group II	Asymptomatic infection	
Group III	Persistent generalized lymphadenopathy (PGL)	
Group IV	Other diseases:	
	subgroup A	: Constitutional disease*
	B	: Neurological Disease
	C–1	: Opportunistic Infections as listed in the CDC definition of AIDS
	C–2	: Other specified secondary infectious diseases
	D	: Secondary cancers as listed in the CDC definitions of AIDS
	E	: Other conditions in HIV infection

*"Wasting syndrome"—Before 1987 this subgroup was referred to as AIDS Related Complex (ARC).

(particularly anal intercourse), direct contact with infectious blood and perinatal transmission from infected mothers to their infants. Yet there are still some people who believe that AIDS can be transmitted merely by shaking hands with a patient or sharing coffee cups (Wertz et al. 1987). Not only is the public afraid, health care professionals are also fearful of AIDS and are concerned about the nosocomial risks (Gordin et al. 1987; Andre 1988; Rogers 1988). This fear and concern are not completely unfounded, as witnessed by a published personal experience of a physician with AIDS who recently died (Aoun 1989). To our knowledge, twenty-five cases of nosocomial (i.e., originating with a hospital procedure) HIV contagion have been described in the literature (CDC 1989). The nosocomial risk obviously depends on the specific occupational setting and the HIV prevalence there. The effect of the patient's clinical status in this regard remains unclear. In the Netherlands, where the Universal Precautions as recommended by the Centers for Disease Control are utilized, the risk of HIV infection for a surgeon is estimated at .0015 per professional life and in Amsterdam at .015 (Houweling & Coutinho 1987). According to Marcus et al. (1988), the nosocomial risk of HIV infection after exposure within one's own bloodstream, to the blood of a patient with HIV infection is 0.5 percent and a possible seroconversion is most likely to occur within six to twelve weeks. Twenty four months after AIDS has been diagnosed the survival rate is 28–30 percent (Hessol et al. 1989; Bindels et al. 1990).

Up to now, no curative therapy has been available. The favorable effect of the antiviral pharmaceutical zidovudine (AZT), if any, is only temporary.

HIV infection may be complicated by psychiatric disorders. HIV infection also has sexologic consequences. Discussed in this chapter are the psychiatric findings in 116 patients admitted to the Academic Medical Center (AMC) in Amsterdam between January 1, 1983, and January 1, 1990. Finally, the sexologic consequences and the role of the sex therapist in the management and care of patients with HIV infection are detailed.

PSYCHIATRIC COMPLICATIONS

The psychiatric complications can be psychogenic and/or organic. The most common psychogenic complications are: denial, anger, anxiety, hypochondriac preoccupations, depressive mood disturbances, suicidal tendencies, psychotic and obsessive-compulsive phenomena (Perry & Jacobsen 1986; Fernandez et al. 1989a). The reported incidence of these complications varies from 30 to 82.7 percent (Perry & Tross 1984; Tross et al. 1987). The most common organic psychiatric complications are delirium and the AIDS dementia complex. The organic affective syndrome and the organic personality syndrome are less common (Wolcott et al. 1985; Baer et al. 1987). The reported incidence of these complications varies between 31.3 percent and 65.4 percent (Snider et al. 1983; Perry & Tross 1984).

Obviously psychogenic complications are not always pathological. These complications are, in many ways, analogous to the reactions of other patients with life-threatening illnesses (Kübler-Ross 1969; Dilley et al. 1985; Wolcott et al. 1985).

Common psychological themes in patients with or without psychiatric disorder include uncertainty as to etiology, course, and treatment; conflicts about sexual orientation; fear of rejection by relatives and friends; feelings of guilt and self-reproach about one's previous lifestyle; and fears of disability, the loss of body control, pain, and death. The social consequences of HIV infection include necessary modifications of lifestyle, stigmatization, social isolation and loss of capacity for employment and income (Wolcott et al. 1985; Dilley et al. 1986; Ostrow & Gayle 1986; Fenton 1987).

In patients with HIV infection, denial can be expressed either by a request for a second opinion or a new HIV antibody testing or by the conviction that a cure can be achieved by sticking to a strict diet or Spartan life style. Denial can also lead to reluctance to undergo treatment or take appropriate measures (Weisman et al. 1987). As long it does not stand in the way of adequate treatment and counseling, patients' denial should be respected as much as possible (Nichols 1986).

In addition to fear as a normal reaction, there are sometimes also anxiety or panic disorders (Holland et al. 1985; Wolcott et al. 1985). Fear can be related to the prospect of death, abandonment or physical and intellectual degeneration. Visible Kaposi sarcoma skin lesions or reduced vision due to a cytomegalic virus (CMV) retinitis can intensify the fear. The fear of physical degeneration can lead to hypochondriac preoccupations, which can be reinforced by the similarity between HIV symptoms and those associated with fear such as diarrhea, perspiration, headache, and heart palpitations. In addition, fear can lead to a loss of libido and/or erectile dysfunction. Fear can become so intense that psychotic decompensations occur. Cases have been recorded of disorders resembling schizophrenia, acute paranoid disorders, short psychotic reactions, and manic episodes (Perry & Jacobsen 1986; Gabel et al. 1986). It is not uncommon for these psychotic reactions to constitute a prodrome of an organic cerebral syndrome (Buhrich et al. 1988; Fernandez et al. 1989a). Anxiety disorders can be treated with a short-effect benzodiazepin such as oxazepam, and psychotic decompensations can be minimized with a neuroleptic such as haloperidol.

As one accepts the reality of being incurably ill, there can also be hostility related to feelings of powerlessness, and uncertainty as to the disease's etiology, course, and the treatment, or the involuntary lifestyle changes that are called for (Holland et al. 1985; Dilley et al. 1985). Anger can be directed to the patient's environment and the doctors responsible for the treatment. Sometimes conflicts can escalate to the extent that the patient is deserted by friends and relatives. If the doctor is the object of the anger, the working relationship can be disturbed.

A common psychogenic complication is a depressive mood disorder, which is frequently accompanied by a loss of libido and self-reproach about one's previous lifestyle, about having infected other people, and about one's own sexuality or intravenous drug use. Usually an adjustment disorder with depressed mood is present, although sometimes a major depression and, in rare cases, a dysthymic (depressive mood) disorder is evident (Dilley et al. 1985; Toss et al. 1987).

The social withdrawal that often accompanies a depressive mood disorder can be intensified by the involuntary loss of employment and change in lifestyle, anger on the part of the patient, and the fear of negative reactions from other people. It was initially said that the suicide risk was small (Holland et al. 1985). However, there have since been indications of a growing suicide rate (Marzuk et al. 1988). In particular, patients who have experienced the death of a friend or acquaintance from AIDS are thought to be more apt to commit suicide. Not infrequently suicidal ideations among patients with an acute exacerbation of an HIV infection are difficult to assess, since these ideations can be masked by physical symptoms. During an acute exacerbation, many patients are too ill or too apathetic to talk about anything. If the exacerbation heralds the patient's death, discussing suicidality seems inappropriate or impossible. Patients who do recover often feel so relieved they wish to forget and refuse to talk about death.

Like an anxiety disorder, a depressive mood disorder may be accompanied by worrying, which can sometimes become compulsive. Compulsive worrying can also be a manifestation of a separate obsessive compulsive disorder. Compulsive acts can include the constant checking of one's own body for tiny skin lesions (Miller 1986). Compulsive thoughts are often related to death, but in some patients may also involve continually trying to remember who infected them or whom they themselves could have infected (Green 1986). In moderately severe and severe depressions, it is advisable to supplement the treatment with antidepressants (Fernandez et al. 1989a). The treatment of suicidal ideation presents the dilemma of how far one should go to prevent the suicide of an individual who is incurably ill (Marzuk et al. 1988).

The most frequent organic psychiatric complication of AIDS is the AIDS dementia complex (ADC) and delirium. The cause of ADC is attributed to cerebral infection with HIV, though it may be secondary to opportunistic infection (e.g., toxoplasmosis of brain tissue), or brain tissue lesions caused by a protozoan disease. Although ADC generally occurs in the final stage of AIDS, in rare cases it can also be the first and only symptom of HIV infection (Navia et al. 1987). ADC is clinically characterized by cognitive disorders, behavior changes and motor disturbances. Forgetfulness and concentration problems are early symptoms of ADC and are followed by slower thinking, apathy and social withdrawal. The motor disturbances consist of faulty equilibrium and weakness in the legs. The course of ADC is gradually progressive; after several weeks or months, there is severe dementia with mutism, paraplegia, incontinence, and tremors (Navia et al., 1986a; Price et al. 1986).

Neuropsychological examination reveals the impairment of sequential-alternation problem-solving and complex sequencing, slowed fine motor control and reduced verbal fluency. On the CT (computed tomography) scan, there can be signs of cerebral atrophy or focal and diffuse white matter abnormalities (Price et al. 1986). In 50 percent of the patients with ADC, the HIV-I P24 antigen is observed in the cerebrospinal fluid (Portegies et al. 1989a). Neuropathological examination reveals that the most significant abnormalities can be found in the white matter of the brain, whereas the cortex remains relatively unaffected (Navia et al. 1986).

Psychiatric treatment for ADC is the same as for dementia in the context of any other incurable illness. If dementia is accompanied by severe depression, apathy or lethargy, antidepressants or dextroamphetamine ("uppers") can be prescribed (Fernandez et al. 1989a). Early treatment with zidovudine (AZT) would seem to have a favorable effect on the course of ADC (Volberding

Table 2
HIV Infection and Delirium

therapeutic drugs
amphotericin B, trimethoprim/sulfa, vincristine, isoniazid, acyclovir, interferon, benzodiazepines, anticholinergics

nutritional deficiencies
vitamin B1 and B12 deficiency, folic acid deficiency

metabolic disorders
Liver disease (e.g., hepatitis B)
electrolyte disturbances (e.g., diarrhea, inappropriate antidiuretic hormone)
cerebral hypoxia (e.g., secondary to pneumonia)

(opportunistic) infections
pneumonia: pneumocystis carinii (PCP), cytomegalic virus
meningo-encephalitis: cryptococcosis, herpes simplex virus
toxoplasmosis, cytomegalovirus
Human Immunodeficiency Virus (HIV)

space-occupying lesions of the brain
malign lymphoma, abscess, toxoplasmosis cyst

cerebrovascular disorders
hypotension, haematoma based on thrombocytopenia (AITP)

epilepsy
intracranial space-occupying lesion, meningo-encephalitis, encephalomalacia

et al. 1990). Probably as a result of the use of zidovudine, there has been a sharp reduction in the incidence of ADC in the patient population at the Academic Medical Center in Amsterdam since mid-1987 (Portegies et al. 1989b).

In patients with HIV infection, delirium is not accompanied by symptoms specific to AIDS. In these patients, a delirium can be based on either primary or secondary cerebral disorders (Table 2). Higher dosages of zidovudine than recommended have been known to lead to side effects that are also typical of delirium, such as agitation, restlessness and insomnia (Offerhaus 1987).

The treatment of delirium in patients with HIV infection is the same as the usual therapeutic measures in other cases of delirium (Wolcott 1985; Fernandez 1989a). In general, lower dosages of neuroleptics are called for, since HIV patients seem to be highly susceptible to side effects such as orthostatic hypotension (low blood pressure), sedation and, in particular, extrapyramidal (motor incoordination) disorders (Fernandez 1989b; Seth 1991). With a delirious patient who scratches or bites, of course the utmost caution is required. It should be noted, however, that there is not a single case on record of nosocomial infection resulting from treating a patient with HIV infection complicated by psychiatric symptoms (CDC 1989).

PSYCHIATRIC CONSULTATIONS

The Academic Medical Center (AMC) is situated on the outskirts of Amsterdam. In addition to the University of Amsterdam Faculty of Medicine, it also includes a 950-bed University Hospital. As of April 1986, there has been a special ward for patients with HIV refection, initially consisting of ten beds, and later expanded to sixteen beds.

Ever since June 1987, a part-time consulting psychiatrist has been available especially for patients with HIV infection. The consultations are conducted upon the request by telephone of the attending physician. The consultant's findings, conclusions, and advice are transcribed to a special consultation form that is eventually included in the patient's chart. As of 1986, diagnoses have been made according to the *Diagnostic and Statistical Manual of Mental Disorders,* third edition, revised (*DSM-III-R*) (APA 1987). Based on the data noted on the consultation forms, diagnoses from before 1986 were reformulated in *DSM-III-R* terms.

From 1983 to 1989, the psychiatrist was consulted 116 times for 97 patients with HIV infection at the hospital (thirteen of the patients were seen by a psychiatric consultant during a previous period of hospitalization, and they were counted as separate consultations). In most of the cases (n = 87), the patients had already been diagnosed as having AIDS (Table 3). Ever since 1986 there has been a marked increase in the psychiatric consultation rate of patients with HIV infection at the AMC. This is related not only to the increased number of patients, but also to the opening of a special AIDS ward and to the participation of a psychiatrist at the weekly meetings of the multidisciplinary AIDS treatment team.

In 1988 and 1989, respectively, 355 and 321 patients with HIV infection were admitted to the AMC in Amsterdam. The consultation rate (i.e., the percentage of the total number of patients with HIV admitted to our hospital who were referred for psychiatric consultation), was 11.5 percent and 13.4 percent. The general consultation rate at the AMC (2–2.2 percent) falls within the range of 0.5–9.6 reported in the literature (Hengeveld et al. 1984). The much higher consultation rate on the AIDS ward indicates that psychiatric symptoms are probably more frequent in patients with HIV infection than in other patients in a general hospital. It would seem unlikely, however, that a consultation is requested for anywhere near all the patients with possible psychiatric complications. Consequently, not much can be concluded from

Table 3
HIV Infection and Psychiatric Referral: Number of Patients per Year

Year	AIDS	ARC (AIDS-Related Complex)	HIV negative (asymptomatic)	HIV positive (asymptomatic)	Total
1983	5	0	0	0	5
1984	2	0	0	0	2
1985	2	0	0	0	2
1986	6	1	0	1	8
1987	9	2	0	2	13
1988	32	2	2	7	43
1989	31	2	0	10	43
Total	**87**	**7**	**2**	**20**	**116**

our findings about the incidence of psychiatric complications of HIV infection.

The mean age of all the patients was 36.6 (range 23–62). The age distribution of the patients with HIV infection complicated by psychiatric symptoms corresponds to the age distribution reported by Postema et al. (1990) of all the AIDS patients registered in The Netherlands up to January 1990. Most of the patients with AIDS were homosexual or bisexual men (n = 82); there were eight female and three male intravenous drug users. Most of the patients were Dutch (n = 96) and lived in Amsterdam (n = 84). These findings are a reflection of the fact that in The Netherlands, AIDS has been mainly diagnosed among homosexual or bisexual men (83 percent); intravenous drug users constituted 8 percent of all the patients with AIDS (Postema 1989; Haastrecht et al. 1991).

The most common reasons for referral were: counseling (n = 38), evaluation of a depression (n = 27), treatment of delirium (n = 22) and diagnostic assessment (n = 15). Refusal of further medical treatment never constituted a reason to request a psychiatric consultation, though it was a topic discussed with several of the patients. The term "counseling" refers to the psychiatric help and support given to patients with psychological and/or social problems. With respect to "treatment of delirium," behavior disturbances were usually implicitly the immediate cause for the request. Behavior disturbances were explicitly the reason for referral in the case of one patient who was addicted to drugs. He continuously ignored the rules of the ward and had violent outbursts resulting in the assault of other patients. Asking for a "diagnostic assessment" implied a request for the evaluation of the patient's mental state. For example, with respect to a patient with discrete cognitive deficiencies, the question posed was whether he was still capable of driving a car. The reasons for referral of AMC patients with HIV infection appear to be nearly identical to the reasons recorded by Dilley et al. (1985) and Weisman et al. (1987). Our clinical experience is consistent with the view of Perry and Markowitz (1986), namely, that the reasons for referral in patients with HIV infection are those familiar to any psychiatrist who regularly sees patients in a general hospital.

Each patient was visited on the average of three times (range, 1–15). Forty-one patients had a history of outpatient psychiatric care and eleven patients had been admitted to a psychiatric hospital at some point in the past. In forty of the eighty-seven patients with AIDS (46 percent), some functional or psychogenic complication was assumed, including twenty-nine (33.3 percent) patients with a mood or adjustment disorder (Table 4). In one HIV positive patient, there was evidence of a psychosomatic conversion disorder with hemianesthesia, or lack of feeling on one side of the body. Because of continuous pain in the left calf, the patient had to use a wheelchair. An organic brain syndrome was observed in thirty-four (39.1 percent) of the patients with AIDS, including twenty-three (26.4 percent) patients with delirium. One patient with delirium and two patients with an organic affective syndrome exhibited manic symptoms such as elevated and irritable moods, grandiosity and psychomotor agitation.

The percentage distribution of the psychiatric diagnoses of patients with HIV infection at the AMC differs only slightly from the findings of other authors (Perry & Tross 1984; Dilley et al. 1985; O'Dowd & McKegney 1990; Seth et al. 1991). As Wolcott et al. (1985) and Detmer and Lu (1986) already emphasized, differentiation between psychogenic and organic psychiatric complications is frequently difficult. Such symptoms as anhedonia (i.e., an inability to enjoy what would normally bring pleasure), apathy and the loss of weight can be indicative of either a depression or of a malignancy or opportunistic infections. Moreover, it is not uncommon for a psychotic disorder eventually to prove to be a prodrome of an organic brain syndrome (Fernandez 1989a). We have been impressed by the prominence of apathy and anhedonia in the context of both mood disorders and AIDS dementia complex. It should be noted that ever since 1987, no AMC patients have been diagnosed as having the AIDS dementia syndrome.

All in all, our diagnostic findings reveal neither pathognomonic (i.e., related to a specific disorder) nor specific psychiatric signs or symptoms of AIDS, which is consistent with the conclusion of Dilley et al. (1986). One of the patients who was admitted with symptoms suggestive of AIDS was HIV negative. The psychiatric diagnosis was factitious disorder with physical symptoms (Munchausen syndrome*). To our knowledge, eight patients with a

*Munchausen syndrome is the repeated and convincing simulation of the symptoms of a disease for the purpose of gaining medical attention.

Table 4
HIV Infection: Psychiatric Diagnoses 1983–1989

Diagnosis (*DSM-III-[-R]*)	AIDS	ARC	seroneg	seropos	total
Adjustment Disorder depr/anx*	11	1	0	4	16
Bipolar Disorder NOS	1	0	0	0	1
Major Depression	17	2	0	3	22
Anxiety Disorder	2	0	0	1	3
Panic Disorder	0	0	0	1	1
Uncomplicated Bereavement	2	0	0	1	3
Atypical Psychosis	3	0	0	1	4
Paranoid Disorder	0	0	0	1	1
Brief Reactive Disorder	3	0	0	0	3
Delirium	23	1	0	1	25
Dementia	5	0	0	0	5
Organic Affective Syndrome	5	1	0	0	6
Organic Personality Syndrome	1	0	0	0	1
Substance Abuse	1	1	0	2	4
Anxiolytic Abuse	1	0	0	0	1
Marital Problem	0	0	0	1	1
Adjustment Disorder Conduct**	1	0	0	0	1
Factitious Dis. Physical Symptoms***	0	0	1	0	1
Conversion Disorder	0	0	0	1	1
Diagnosis Deferred on Axis I	5	0	0	1	6
No Diagnosis on Axis I	6	1	1	2	10
Totals	**87**	**7**	**2**	**20**	**116**

*Adjustment disorder with depressed or anxious mood
**Adjustment disorder with disturbance of conduct
***Chronic factitious disorder with physical symptoms

factitious disorder with HIV infection symptomotology have been described earlier (Kavalier 1989). These cases illustrate the importance of considering the possibility that when assessing patients in whom issues concerning possible HIV infection arise, part of the symptomotology at least may be psychogenically determined, or indeed frankly simulated (Sno et al. 1991).

Another patient who proved in the end to be HIV negative was afraid he had AIDS, which was why he had requested an AIDS test. He was an example of what is referred to as the "worried well" (Miller 1986). There are indications that, possibly due to the excessively ominous public information, the fear of AIDS has increasingly come to play a role in psychotic decompensations or in the delusions of chronically psychotic patients (Lawlor et al. 1987; Todd 1989; Vuorio et al. 1990).

To varying extents, twenty-three patients exhibited suicidal tendencies. In five patients, an actual suicide attempt had been the reason they were hospitalized. Eight patients had tried to commit suicide at some point in the past after the HIV infection was diagnosed. Five patients had suicidal ideations and four said they would rather be dead. One patient thought a great deal about active euthanasia. Compared with earlier findings in our population, there has been a rise in the percentage of patients exhibiting signs of suicidality (Sno et al. 1989). This tendency is in keeping with the findings of Marzuk et al. (1988). AIDS patients who have watched friends die of AIDS are thought to be a particular suicide risk (Perry & Markowitz 1986; Baer et al. 1987). In contrast, suicide appears to constitute only a small percentage of the actual causes of death among patients with HIV infection (Engelman et al. 1988). Of the first hundred AIDS patients admitted to the AMC, however, five have probably died of non-natural causes (Danner et al. 1987).

The psychiatric treatment of patients with HIV infection at the AMC almost always took place on the somatic ward. As advocated by various other authors (Dilley et al. 1985; Wolcott et al. 1985; Perry & Markowitz 1986), our patients with a major mood disorder were treated with supportive psychotherapeutic measures and antidepressants. Our experience with this type of psychopharmacological treatment in patients with HIV infection is ambiguous and requires further evaluation. Patients with a delirium generally responded to the usual psychotherapeutic and psychopharmacological interventions, e.g., frequent orientation, regulation of the volume of external stimuli, and low-dose haloperidol. Patients with AIDS dementia complex were less responsive to psychiatric interventions. In these patients low-dose haloperidol sometimes was symptomatically helpful in reducing agitation or anxiety. In eight cases, a transfer to the psychiatric ward was necessary. At discharge, one patient was referred back to a psychiatrist and five were referred to the Psychiatric Outpatient Clinic of the AMC.

SEXOLOGIC CONSEQUENCES

In addition to psychogenic and organic psychiatric complications, HIV infection also has sexual consequences, particularly as regards sexual behavior and sexual functioning. Problems with sexual functioning can consist of loss of sexual desire or pleasure, erectile dysfunction or inhibition of orgasms (Brown & Pace 1989; Brown & Rundell 1990). These consequences can be related to the psychological and psychiatric complications, but they might also be the result of neurological and systemic effects of HIV and the experimental medications used for the treatment of HIV infection (Meyer-Bahlburg et al. 1991). As regards sexual behavior, it should be kept in mind that for many gay males, sexuality is important to their sense of identity. For them, AIDS implies a critical interruption of the gay lifestyle; homosexual disclosure to relatives, colleagues, and employers; and, perhaps for the first time, an undermining of homosexuality as an increasingly acceptable social category (Miller 1986). For young adults, an age group more likely to be experimenting with sexual behavior, AIDS represents a new and increasing concern (Cochran et al. 1990).

The management and care of AIDS patients requires a biopsychosocial approach involving different disciplines. The contribution of the sex therapist includes primary prevention and sexologic care and counseling. The sex therapist is in a position to advise on the prevention of countless unnecessary deaths in the future, and the first priority should be to help stop the spread of AIDS through unprotected sexual contact (Kaplan et al. 1985). The prevention of HIV transmission should be focused on the alteration of sexual behavior and on discouraging "needle-sharing" among drug users. Risk-reduction interventions should stress the need to eliminate the exchange of body fluids during sexual encounters and to reduce the number of sexual partners. Patients should be advised about the use of condoms, reducing the numbers of sexual partners, avoiding anonymous sexual partners and the AIDS susceptibility associated with various sexual practices (Table 5). As Darro (1989) puts it: "A properly used condom will give the user at least 0.03 mm of protection, and that could be the difference between life and death."

In addition to providing information, the frequency of condom use for insertive anal intercourse can be increased by providing skills training (i.e., teaching men how to negotiate safer sexual encounters and rehearsing these imaginary encounters, Valdiserri et al. 1989). It should be emphasized that safer sex not only depends on one's partner choice, but also requires changing one's behavior with all partners. This is of even greater concern for heterosexuals, where behavioral responses such as "being careful" in partner choice are distressingly uncommon (Becker & Joseph 1988). The usefulness of a spermicide containing nonoxynol-9 in the prevention of AIDS remains a controversial alternative. Recommendation of nonoxynol-9 has been based on its record of safety in contraceptive use and on assumptions about its effectiveness as a prophylactic against other sexually transmitted diseases. However, research has not established the protective effects and the safety of nonoxynol-9-containing spermicides. Moreover, recent reports now suggest that these spermicides can cause damage to the delicate genital and rectal epithelial lining, and thus may facilitate HIV infection (Bird 1991).

Since substantial numbers of homosexual and heterosexual individuals persist in engaging in risk behavior, continued educational campaigns are needed

Table 5
Relative Degree of AIDS Susceptibility*
Associated with Various Sexual Practices
[adapted from Ostrow (1990)]

Probably Safe	Possibly Safe	Unsafe
Mutual masturbation	Anal or vaginal intercourse with a condom	Anal intercourse (male or female) without a condom
Social kissing (dry)	Fellatio interruptus	Vaginal intercourse without a condom
Body massage, hugging	Mouth-to-mouth kissing ("French" or "wet" kissing)	Fellatio to orgasm
Body-to-body rubbing (frottage)	Oral-vaginal contact (cunnilingus)	Any activities that involve bruising (heavy S&M, "fisting," etc.
Light S&M activities (without bruising, bleeding, or "fisting," etc.		
Use of sex toys		

*Because sexual contact with a partner whose serologic HIV status is unknown is associated with various degrees of susceptibility to AIDS, the risk of transmitting or contracting the disease can only be estimated in terms of the relative safety of specific sexual practices

to sustain and reinforce the changes that have been made and to encourage people who have not yet modified their sexual behavior (Becker et al. 1988; Darrow 1989; Martin et al. 1989; Meyer-Bahlburg et al. 1991). Reaching minority subgroups (e.g., Hispanic or black men), is critical since the potential for both homosexual and heterosexual transmission appears to be greater within these populations (Doll et al. 1991). The need for continued educational campaigns is emphasized by the fact that an increase in sexually transmitted diseases, which can be viewed as surrogate markers for HIV incidence, began among younger homosexual men in the late 1980s (Van Griensven et al. 1989; Van der Hoek et al. 1990). In addition, although in a recent study among young adults, self-reported condom use seemed to have increased over time, many single, sexually active young adults, particularly women, have not been insisting on condom use (Cochran et al. 1990).

Sexologic care includes pretest counseling, risk assessment, post-test counseling, assistance in partner notification, supportive psychotherapeutic and social interventions, providing information and reassurance, correcting misconceptions, clarifying psychological and social issues, and enhancing the availability of peer support. The sex therapist should provide adequate education, emotional support, and counseling not only for the patients but also for their lovers, friends and relatives (Ostrow 1990). Social support is important for people who are experiencing a terminal disease. It can act as a buffer against stress by enhancing coping effectiveness, self-esteem, motivation, and health-promoting behavior (Wolf et al. 1991).

In view of the considerable psychological and social implications and the negligible somatic consequences, patients in the Netherlands were initially advised against having themselves tested. Early intervention, including medical evaluation, antiretroviral therapies and pharmacologic prophylaxis, was once thought to delay the onset of the symptoms of AIDS in HIV-infected persons and lengthen the survival of those with AIDS (Volberding et al. 1990). That is why the policy against testing was reversed. To the disappointment of all concerned, early prophylaxis proved not to be efficacious.

Deciding whether or not to test for HIV infection remains a question of evaluating the individual benefits and drawbacks. Every test should be preceded by pretest counseling. The underlying reasons for the request for testing, the possible social, medical and legal implications of being either HIV positive or negative, the limited value of a negative result, and the advantages and disadvantages of early intervention should all be discussed with the patient. It should also be stressed that in any event, it is still necessary to take the proper precautions. The extent of knowledge the patient has about HIV infection, the risks he or she might have taken in the past, the psychological background and the social context should be addressed as well. If in the end the decision is made to perform the test, the procedure for followup care and referral to a physician should be discussed. Informing the patient of the result should be followed by post-test counseling. If the test is negative, the significance of the result can be discussed and the fact that it may be negative only for the time being. The possibility should be pointed out that the result might be pseudonegative and the test should be repeated approximately three to six months after the last risk activity. Here again, the importance of preventive measures should be stressed. If the test is positive, first and foremost the post-test counseling implies helping the patient cope with this emotionally. The medical and social repercussions should also be discussed with the patient, such as the attention to be given to physical symptoms, the monitoring of CD4-positive cells, the early intervention possibilities, the need to notify one's partner or partners, stigmatization, the effects regarding one's work, and the insurance aspect. Lastly, practical information can be provided about facilities available in the area such as psychosocial support services, support groups, telephone counseling services and so on (Anonymous 1990a, 1990b; Danner 1991; Bor et al. 1991).

The influence of the HIV test on changes in risk behavior remains uncertain. Studies of homosexual men have observed that knowledge of HIV infection status and appropriate counseling can assist persons in initiating changes in risk behavior (McCusker et al. 1988; Cates et al. 1988). In contrast, a study by van der Hoek et al. (1989) on intravenous drug users in Amsterdam demonstrated that the extent of behavioral change did not depend on learning one's infection status. Brown et al (1990) reported that, despite the awareness of their HIV status and adequate intelligence, the majority of a group of twenty middle-class, employed HIV positive women who were not IV-drug users, did not consistently follow "safe sex" guidelines.

The care of AIDS patients can be complicated by either overidentification or avoidance reactions, which may reinforce an acceleration of the "burnout" process (Douglas et al. 1985; Wallack 1989). The results of a recently held questionnaire survey among 938 doctors and 2,304 nurses confirmed the existence of these complicating factors as well as the negative influence on the doctors' and nurses' attitudes toward AIDS. Factual information alone does not seem to be sufficient to dispel the excessive concern. In training and educating medical personnel, attention should be given to emotional as well as cognitive aspects (Storosum et al. 1991).

SUMMARY

The psychiatric treatment of patients with HIV infection does not differ fundamentally from that of other medically ill patients with similar psychiatric symptoms. The sexologic consequences pertain to the risk of transmission associated with sexual behavior and functioning. Problems with sexual functioning may consist of a loss of libido, erectile dysfunction or an inhibition of orgasms. The contribution of the sex therapist in the management and care of AIDS patients includes primary prevention and sexologic care and counseling.

REFERENCES

Andre, B. C. (1988). "AIDS, Attitudes, and Infection Control." *American Journal of Infectious Control* 16: 272–73.

Anonymous. (1981). "Drugs that Cause Psychiatric Symptoms." *Medical Letter on Drugs and Therapeutics* 23: 9–12.

Anonymous. (1990a), *Vroege Medische interventie bij HIV geninfecteerde personen.* Gezondheidsraad, Gravenhage.

Anonymous. (1990b). *Guidelines for Counseling about HIV Infection and Disease.* Geneva: World Health Organization.

Aoun, H. (1989). "When a House Officer Gets AIDS." *New England Journal of Medicine* 321: 693–96.

Baer, J. W.; Hall, J. M.; Holm, K.; and Lewitter-Koehler, S. (1987). "Challenges in Developing an Inpatient Psychiatric Program for Patients with AIDS and ARC." *Hospital and Community Psychiatry* 38: 1299–1303.

Becker, M. H., and Joseph, J. G. (1988). "AIDS and Behavioral Change to Reduce Risk: A Review." *American Journal of Public Health* 78: 394–410.

Bindels, P. J. E.; Jong, J. T. L.; Poos, M. J. J. C.; Leentvaar-Kuijpers, A.; Jager, J. C.; and Coutinho, R. A. (1990). "Het epidemiologisch beloop van AIDS in Amsterdam 1982–1988." *Nederlands Tijdschrift voor Geneeskunde* 132: 806–807.

Bird, K. D. (1991). "The Use of Spermicide Containing Nonoxynol-9 in the Prevention of HIV Infection." *AIDS* 5: 791–96.

Bor, R.; Miller, R.; and Johnson, M. (1991). "A Testing Time for Doctors: Counseling Patients before an HIV Test." *British Medical Journal* 303: 905–907.

Brown, G. R., and Pace, I. (1989). "Reduced Sexual Activity in HIV Infected Gay Men." *Journal of the American Medical Association* 261: 2503.

Brown, G. R., and Rundell, J. R. (1990). "Prospective Study of Psychiatric Morbidity in HIV-Seropositive Women without AIDS." *General Hospital Psychiatry* 12: 30–35.

Buhrich, N.; Cooper, D. A.; and Freed, E. (1988). "HIV Infection Associated with Symptoms Indistinguishable from Functional Psychosis." *British Journal of Psychiatry* 152: 649–53.

Cares, W., Jr., and Handsfield, H. H. (1988). "HIV Counseling and Testing: Does It Work?" *American Journal of Public Health* 78: 1533–34.

Centers for Disease Control. (1986). "Classification System for JTLV-III/LAV Infections." *Morbidity and Mortality Weekly Report* 35: 34–339.

——— (1989). "Guidelines for Prevention of HIV Transmission and Hepatitis B Virus to Health-Care and Public-Safety Workers." *Morbidity and Mortality Weekly Report* 38: 3–33.

——— (1990). "HIV Prevalence Estimates and AIDS Case Projections for the United States: Report Bases on a Workshop." *Morbidity and Mortality Weekly Report* 39: 30.

——— (1991). "The HIV/AIDS Epidemic: The First 10 Years." *Morbidity and Mortality Weekly Report* 40: 357–69.

Cochran, S. D.; Keidan, J.; and Kalechstein, A. (1990). "Sexually Transmitted Diseases and AIDS: Changes in Risk Reduction Behaviors among Young Adults." *Sexually Transmitted Diseases* 17: 80–86.

Danner, S. A.; Eeftinck-Schattenkerk, J. K. M.; Lange, J. M. A; Van Steenwijk, R. P.; De Gans, I.; and Meinardi, T. R. A. (1987). "Ziekteverschijnselen en klinisch beloop bij de eerste honderd patiënten met AIDS." *Nederlands Tijdschrift voor Geneeskunde* 131: 1474–79.

Danner, S. A. (1991). "Advies aan patiënten met betrekking tot HIV-antistoftest." *Nederlands Tijdschrift voor Geneeskunde* 135: 404–405.

Darrow, W. W. (1989). "Condom Use and Use-Effectiveness in High-Risk Populations." *Sexually Transmitted Diseases* 16: 157–60.

Detmer, W. M., and Lu, F. U. (1986). "Neuropsychiatric Complications of AIDS: A Literature Review." *International Journal of Psychiatry in Medicine* 16: 21–29.

Dilley, J. W.; Ochitill, H. N.; Perl, M.; and Volberding, P. A. (1985). "Findings in Psychiatric Consultations with Patients with AIDS." *American Journal of Psychiatry* 142: 82–86.

Dilley, J. W.; Shelp, E. E.; and Batki, S. L. (1986). "Psychiatric and Ethical Issues in the Care of Patients with AIDS." *Psychosomatics* 27: 562–66.

Dool, L. S.; Byers, R. H.; Bolan, G.; Douglas, J. M.; Moss, P. M.; Weller, P. D.; Joy, D.; Bartholow, B. N.; and Harrison, J. S. (1991). "Homosexual Men Who Engage in High-Risk Sexual Behavior. A Multicenter Comparison." *Sexually Transmitted Diseases* 18: 170–75.

Douglas, C. J.; Kalman, C. M.; and Kalman, T. P. (1985). "Homophobia among Physicians and Nurses: An Empirical Study." *Hospital and Community Psychiatry* 36: 1309–11.

Engelman, J.; Hessol, N. A.; Lifson, A. R.; and Stephens, G. B. (1988, June). "Suicide Patterns and AIDS in San Francisco." Paper presented at the Fourth International Conference on AIDS. Stockholm, June 12–16.

Fenton, T. W. (1987). "AIDS-Related Psychiatric Disorder." *British Journal of Psychiatry* 151: 579–88.

Fernandez, F.; Holmes, V. F.; Levy, J. K.; and Ruiz, P. (1989a). "Consultation-Liaison Psychiatry and HIV-Related Disorders." *Hospital and Community Psychiatry* 40: 146–52.

Fernandez, F.; Levy, J. K.; and Mansell, P. A. (1989b). "Management of Delirium in Terminally Ill AIDS Patients." *International Journal of Psychiatry in Medicine* 19: 165–72.

Gabel, R. H.; Barnard, N.; Norko, M.; and O'Connell, R. A. (1986). "AIDS Presenting as Mania." *Comprehensive Psychiatry* 27: 251–54.

Gordin, F. M.; Willoughby, A. D.; Levine, L. A.; Gurel, L.; and Neill, K. M. (1987). "Knowledge of AIDS among Hospital Workers: Behavioral Correlates and Consequences." *AIDS* 1: 183–88.

Green, J. (1986). "Counseling HTLV-III Seropositives." In D. Miller, J. Weber, and J. Green, eds., *The Management of AIDS-Patients,* pp. 151–68. London: Macmillan Press.

Hengeveld, M. W.; Rooymans, H. G. M.; and Vecht-van den Bergh, R. (1984). "Psychiatric Consultations in a Dutch University Hospital: A Report on 1814 Referrals, Compared with a Literature Review." *General Hospital Psychiatry* 6: 271–79.

Hessol, N. A.; Lifson, A. R.; O'Malley, P. M.; Doll, L. S.; Jaffe, H. W.; and Rutherford, G. W. (1989). "Prevalence, Incidence, and Progression of HIV Infection in Homosexual and Bisexual Men in Hepatitis B Vaccine Trials, 1978–1988." *American Journal of Epidemiology* 130: 1167–75.

Holland, J. C., and Tross, S. (1985). "The Psychosocial and Neuropsychiatric Sequelae of AIDS and Related Disorders." *Annals of Internal Medicine* 103: 760–64.

Houweling, H.; Jager, J. C.; Coutinho, R.; Bijkerk, H.; and Ruitenberg, E. J. (1987). "Epidemiologie van AIDS en HIV infecties in Nederland; huidige situatie en prognose voor de periode 1987–1990." *Nederlands Tijdschrift voor Geneeskunde* 131: 818–24.

Houweling H., and Coutinho R. A. (1987). "Is AIDS een beroepsrisico voor de (para)medische beroeps groepen?" *Nederlands Tijdschrift voor Geneeskunde* 31: 1283–87.

Kavalier, F. C. (1989). "Munchausen AIDS" (letter). *Lancet* 1: 852.

Kübler-Ross, E. (1969). *On Death and Dying*. New York: Macmillan Company.

Lawlor, B. A.; and Stewart, J. T. (1987). "AIDS-Delusions: A Symptom of Our Times." *American Journal of Psychiatry* 144: 1244.

Marcus, R., and the CDC Cooperative Needlestick Surveillance Group (1988). "Surveillance of Health Care Workers Exposed to Blood from Patients Infected with the Human Immunodeficiency Virus." *New England Journal of Medicine* 319: 1118–23.

Martin, J. L.; Garci, M. A.; and Beatrice, S. T. (1989). "Sexual Behavior Changes and HIV Antibody in a Cohort of New York City Gay Men." *American Journal of Public Health* 79: 501–503.

Marzuk, P. M.; Tierney, H.; Tardiff, K.; Gross, E. M.; Morgan, E. B.; Hsu, M.; and Mann, J. J. (1988). "Increased Risk of Suicide in Persons with AIDS." *Journal of the American Medical Association* 259: 1333–37.

Meyer-Bahlburg, H. F. L.; Exner, T. M.; Lorenz, G.; Gruen, R. S.; Gorman, J. M.; and Ehrhard, A. A. (1991). "Sexual Risk Behavior, Sexual Functioning, and HIV-Disease Progression in Gay Men." *The Journal of Sex Research* 28: 3–27.

Miller, D. (1986). "Psychology, AIDS, ARC and PGL." In D. Miller, J. Weber, and J. Green, eds., *The Management of AIDS Patients*, pp. 131–49. New York: Macmillan Press.

Navia, B. A.; Jordan, B. D.; and Price, R. W. (1986a). "The AIDS Dementia Complex: I Clinical Features." *Annals of Neurology* 19: 517–24.

Navia, B. A.; Cho, E. S.; Petito, C. K.; and Price, R. W. (1986b). "The AIDS Dementia Complex: II Neuro-Pathology." *Annals of Neurology* 19: 525–35.

Navia, B. A., and Price, R. W. (1987). "The AIDS Dementia Complex as the Presenting or Sole Manifestation of HIV Infection." *Archives of Neurology* 44: 65–69.

Nichols, S. E. (1986, June). "An Overview of the Psychological and Social Reactions to AIDS." In J. C. Gluckman and E. Vilmer, eds. (1987), *AIDS: International Conference on AIDS*. Paris, June 23–25.

O'Dowd, M. A., and McKegney, F. P. (1990). "AIDS Patients Compared with Others Seen in Psychiatric Consultation." *General Hospital Psychiatry* 12: 50–55.

Offerhaus, L. (1987). "Azidothymidine en HIV infectie." *Nederlands Tijdschrift voor Geneeskunde* 131: 934–36.

Ostrow, D. G. (1990). "Psychiatric Aspects of Human Immunodeficiency Virus Infection." *Current Concepts*. Kalamazoo, Mich.: The Upjohn Company.

Ostrow, D. G., and Gayle, T. C. (1986). "Psychosocial and Ethical Issues of AIDS Health Care Programs." *Quality Review Bulletin* 12: 284–94.

Perry, S. W., and Tross, S. (1984). "Psychiatric Problems of AIDS-Inpatients at the

New York Hospital: Preliminary Report." *Public Health Report* 99: 200–205.

Perry, S. W., and Jacobsen, P. (1986). "Neuropsychiatric Manifestations of AIDS Spectrum Disorders." *Hospital and Community Psychiatry* 37: 135–42.

Portegies, P.; Epstein, L. G.; Tjong, A.; Hung, S.; de Gans, J.; and Goudsmit, J. (1989a). "Human Immunodeficiency Virus Type I Antigen in Cerebrospinal Fluid. Correlation with Clinical Neurological Status." *Archives of Neurology* 46: 261–64.

Portegies, P.; de Gans, J.; de Lange, J. M. A.; Derix, M. M. A.; Speelman, H.; Bakker, M.; Danner, S. A.; and Goudsmit, J. (1989b). "Declining Incidence of AIDS Dementia Complex after Introduction of Zidovudine Treatment." *British Medical Journal* 299: 819–21.

Postema, C. A., and Bilkert-Mooiman, M. A. J. (1990). "AIDS 1982–1989." *Nederlands Tijdschrift voor Geneeskunde* 134: 2148–50.

Price, R. W.; Navia, B. A.; Pumarola-Sune, T.; Cho, E-S.; Petito, C. K.; and Sidtis, J. J. (1986). "The AIDS Dementia Complex: Answers and Questions." In J. C. Gluckman and E. Vilmer, eds. (1987). *AIDS: International Conference on AIDS.* Paris, June 23–25.

Rogers, D. E. (1988). "Caring for the Patients with AIDS." *Journal of the American Medical Association* 259: 1368.

Seth, R.; Granville-Grossman, K.; Goldmeier, D.; and Lynch, S. (1991). "Psychiatric Illnesses in Patients with HIV Infection and AIDS Referred to the Liaison Psychiatrist." *British Journal of Psychiatry* 159: 347–50.

Snider, W. D.; Simpson, D. M.; Nielsen, S.; Gold, J. W. N.; Metroka, C. E.; and Posner, J. B. (1983). "Neurological Complications of AIDS: Analysis of 50 Patients." *Annals of Neurology* 14: 403–418.

Sno, H. N.; Storosum, J. G.; and Swinkels, J. A. (1989). "HIV Infection: Psychiatric Findings in the Netherlands." *British Journal of Psychiatry* 155: 814–17.

Sno, H. N.; Storosum, J. G.; and Wortel, C. (1991). "Psychogenic HIV Infection." *International Journal of Psychiatry in Medicine* 21: 93–98.

Storosum, J. G.; Sno, H. N.; Schalken, H. F. A.; Nahuijs, M.; Meijer, E. P.; Swinkels, J. A.; Krol, L. J.; and Danner, S. A. (1991). "Attitudes toward AIDS at Three Dutch Hospitals." *AIDS* 5: 55–60.

Todd, J. (1989). "AIDS as a Current Psychopathological Theme: A Report on Five Heterosexual Patients." *British Journal of Psychiatry* 154: 253–55.

Tross, S.; Hirsch, D. A.; Rabkin, B.; Berry, C.; and Holland, J. C. B. (1987, June). "Determinants of Current Psychiatric Disorder in AIDS Spectrum Patients." Paper presented at the Third International AIDS Conference, Washington D.C., June 1-5.

Valdiserri, R. O.; Lyter, D. W.; Leviton, L. C.; Callahan, C. M, Kingsley; L. A.; and Rinaldo, C. R. (1989). "AIDS Prevention in Homosexual and Bisexual Men: Results of a Randomized Trial Evaluating Two Risk Reduction Interventions." *AIDS* 3: 21–26.

Van den Hock, J. A. R.; van Griensven, G. J. P.; and Coutinho, R. A. (1990). "Aanwijzingen voor toenmame van onveilig seksueel gedrag bij homoseksuele mannen in Amsterdam." *Nederlands Tijdschrift voor Geneeskunde* 134: 1229–30.

Van den Hock, J. A. R.; van Haastrecht, H. J. A.; and Coutinho, R. A. (1989). "Risk

Reduction among Intravenous Drug Users in Amsterdam under the Influence of AIDS." *American Journal of Public Health* 79: 1355–57.

Van de Water, H. P. A.; Wiggers, C. C. M. C.; Bijleveld, C. C. J. H.; and Berkane, M. (1990). "Schatting van het aantal HIV-seropositieven in Nederland: Implicaties voor het toekomstige verloop van de AIDS epidemie. *Nederlands Tijdschrift voor Geneeskunde* 134: 2482–86.

Van Griensven, G. J. P.; van den Hock, J. A. R.; Leentvaar, A.; and Coutinho, R. A. (1989). "Surrogate Markers for HIV Incidence among Homosexual Men." *Journal of Infectious Diseases* 159: 1157–58.

Van Haastrecht, H. J. A.; van den Hock, J. A. R.; Bardoux, C.; Leentvaar-Kuypers, A.; and Coutinho, R. A. (1991). "The Course of the HIV Epidemic among Intravenous Drug Users in Amsterdam, The Netherlands." *American Journal of Public Health* 81: 59–62.

Volberding, P. A.; Lagakos, S. W.; and Koch. M. A. (1990). "Zidovudine in Asymptomatic Human Immunodeficiency Virus Infection. A Controlled Trial in Persons with Fewer than 500 CD4-Positive Cells per Cubic Millimeter." *New England Journal of Medicine* 322: 941–49.

Vuorio, I. C. A.; Aarela, E.; Lehtinen, V. (1990). "Eight Cases of Patients with Unfounded Fear of AIDS." *International Journal of Psychiatry in Medicine 20:* 405–411.

Wallack, J. J. (1989). "AIDS Anxiety among Health Care Professionals." *Hospital and Community Psychiatry* 40: 507–510.

Weisman, H. W.; Harvey, E.; Nienaltow, M. D.; and Eaton, D. (1987). "Psychiatric Consultation to AIDS-Patients, 1981–1986: A Consultation Liaison Perspective." Paper presented at the Third International AIDS Conference, Washington, D.C., June 1–5.

Wertz, D. C.; Scorensol, J. R.; Liebling, L.; Kessler, L.; and Heeren, T. C. (1987). "Knowledge and Attitudes of AIDS Health Care Providers before and after Education Programs." *Public Health Report* 102: 248–54.

Wolcott, D. L.; Fawzy, F. I.; and Pasnau, R. O. (1985). "AIDS and C-L Psychiatry." *General Hospital Psychiatry* 7: 280–92.

Wolf, T. M.; Dralle, P. W.; Morse, E. V.; Simon, P. M.; Balson, P. M.; Gaumer, R. H.; and Williams, M. H. (1991). "A Biopsychosocial Examination of Symptomatic and Asymptomatic HIV Infected Patients. *International Journal of Psychiatry in Medicine* 21: 263–79.

21

Sex Policy and the Law in China: Then and Now

Fang-fu Ruan

INTRODUCTION

Generally speaking, China's culture during the first 2,000 years of her recorded history was generally characterized by open and positive sexual attitudes. Then about a thousand years ago sexual attitudes began to change, gradually becoming more and more negative and repressive. The situation did not improve under the rule of the Chinese Communist Party (CCP) after 1949, although woman's liberation had been one of its slogans. Actually, contemporary mainland China may be in the most sex-repressive period of its entire history. Now, in mainland China, the only sexual behavior acknowledged to be legally and morally permissible is heterosexual intercourse within monogamous marriage.

PREMARITAL AND EXTRAMARITAL SEX

Although China has a long history of polygamy, in contemporary mainland China only monogamous marriage is legal and morally permissible. On May 1, 1950, the new Marriage Law was promulgated. It introduced a "new democratic" marriage system as follows:

The Marriage Law of the People's Republic of China (April 13, 1950)

"Article 1. The feudal marriage system which is based on arbitrary and compulsory arrangements and the superiority of man over woman and ignores the children's interests shall be abolished.

"The New-Democratic marriage system, which is based on the free choice of partners, on monogamy, on equal rights of both sexes, and on the protection of the lawful interests of women and children, shall be put into effect.

"Article 2. Bigamy, concubinage, child betrothal, interference with the remarriage of widows, and the exaction of money or gifts in connection with marriage, shall be prohibited."

In 1980, the revised marriage law followed the same principles as in 1950:

The Marriage Law of the People's Republic of China (September 10, 1980)

"Article 2. The marriage system based on the free choice of partners, on monogamy and on equal rights for the sexes, is put into effect. The lawful rights and intrests of women, children and the aged are protected. Family planning is practiced."

In *The Criminal Law of the People's Republic of China* (1980), there are some articles about behaviors against marriage and the family:

"Article 179. Whoever interferes with another person's freedom of marriage by force shall be sentenced to detention or a fixed-term imprisonment of two years or under.

"Article 180. Whoever commits bigamy or knowingly marries another person who has a spouse shall be sentenced to a fixed-term imprisonment of two years or under.

"Article 181. Whoever cohabitates with or knowingly marries the spouse of a serviceman shall be sentenced to a fixed-term imprisonment of three years or under."

Although there is no legal article to punish premarital and extramarital sex, all these behaviors could be punished as a kind of "xingzuicuo" (sexual crimes and misconduct) by government institutions. In mainland China a new phrase, "xingzuicuo," has been coined to label sexual behaviors that are illegal or officially held to be immoral. "Xingzuicuo" is comprised of three words: "xing," meaning "sex" or "sexual"; "zui," meaning crime; and "cuo," meaning "erroneous," "fault," "demerit," "wrong," or "mistaken." Thus "xingzuicuo" means either "sex crimes" or "sexual misconduct," depending on context.

The current perception in China is that both sex crimes (such as rape) and sexual misconduct (such as premarital and extramarital intercourse) have reached crisis proportions. Despite the official policy of suppressing sexual expression, and severely punishing sex crimes, the crime rate continues to rise yearly. It is difficult to assess the true extent of the crisis, since "crime" and "misconduct" are not always clearly distinguished. Rape, pedophilia, and any behavior that "subjects women to indignities or carries out other gangster activities," are all clearly illegal, according to Articles 139 and 160 of the 1980 Criminal Law of the People's Republic of China. Prostitution may be treated as a sex crime, or as sexual misconduct, depending upon the conditions; however, Article 140 of the Criminal Law states that it is illegal "to force a female to engage in prostitution." The concept of "sexual misconduct" also includes premarital sex, extramarital sex, unmarried cohabitation, group sex, homosexual behavior, and other variant sexual behaviors.

These policies are at odds with recent changes of attitude among the Chinese people. In a survey of 23,000 people in fifteen provinces conducted by the Shanghai Sex Sociology Research Center in 1989–1990, 86 percent of the respondents said they approved of premarital sex (Burton 1990). What seems to be happening is that premarital intercourse and cohabitation, irregular marriages, and unwanted pregnancies are all increasing.

Beginning in the late 1970s, the increased tolerance of nonmarital cohabitation in the West began to influence China's younger generation. College students and young intellectuals in particular were attracted to this lifestyle. Some of the younger or more open-minded sociologists also asserted the necessity of overcoming the disadvantages of traditional marriage. In actuality, practicing cohabitation was an act of courage, since these young Chinese risked arrest. In October 1987, for example, eighteen couples who were living together in the campus dormitories of Shenzen University were arrested by campus police. (Shenzhen is a special economic open city near Hong Kong.) Immediately afterward, the university administration announced that all female students living in the women's dormitories must be back in their bedrooms before midnight; otherwise they would not be allowed into the dormitory, and would be expected to give a clear explanation of their absence the following day.

In 1988, in Shanghai, 24-year-old poet Zhang Shaopo was sentenced to five years' imprisonment because he organized a sexual-freedom commune with another young man and several young women. All these young persons were living together in one apartment, and none was married. In May 1987, when Zhang was arrested, his friends feared that he would be sentenced to death. He was given a lighter sentence only because the women involved refused to accuse him of rape.

Chinese common people do not really always obey the Communist party's moral and political teachings or the government's rules. Especially after the cultural revolution, they knew that most of the party's leaders and government officers were hypocritical. People often ignore hypocritical sexual policy and law. Both premarital and extramarital sex are common in mainland China now.

A study in a major city in Kuangdong province found that of 123 young women undergoing premarital examinations, 75 (61 percent) had already experienced intercourse.

In the spring of 1991, Professor Pan at the Chinese People's University in Beijing supervised a survey in which questionnaires were distributed to a random sample of 1,003 unmarried university students in Beijing, divided nearly equally between men and women. Of 559 respondents, 106 said they had engaged in sex. Asked to guess what percentage of college students are sexually experienced, the single men's average estimate was 47 percent, while the single women's average estimate was 8 percent.

Lack of private space is a problem for young lovers. At universities, students live in cramped conditions, six to eight in a room. But the more resourceful find ways to briefly rent off-campus apartments, typically equipped with little more than a bed. These have become the local version of love hotels. Not everyone can make such comfortable arrangements, however; many young people have little choice but to meet in parks. Whereas five years ago, couples were likely to sit demurely together on a bench, it is now acceptable to hug and kiss, ignoring passersby only a few feet away. Some couples disappear into the bushes. Many parents do not approve. An architect who recently married his lover said they had kept their affair secret from their parents right up until the wedding. "If they had found out that we were having sex, they would have been angry, or at least have pretended not to know so they wouldn't have to confront it." His own parents are so conservative, he said, that they might have reported him to the police as a sexual deviant.

Abortion statistics can give an indication of premarital sexual activity, but only a partial one, because some unmarried women claim to be married when they seek abortions, and others marry when they learn they are pregnant. Thus it is highly significant that in a rural (and presumably more conservative) region of Zhejiang province, 66 percent of unmarried women have had at least one abortion. It is also significant that the proportion of admittedly unmarried women seeking abortion is increasing. For example, in Shanghai, China's most populous city, the number of abortion patients who said they were unmarried rose from 16 percent in 1986 to 40 percent in 1987; in the central hospital of a large city in Shandong province, at least 38 percent of the abortions performed in 1985, and 47 percent of those performed from January to May 1986, were done for unmarried women. Since some women who are not married claim that they are, hospital physicians estimate that the true figure may be 50 to 60 percent. This estimate is supported by additional statistics for two other cities which documented that, from 1977 through 1979, 14 to 89 percent of abortions were performed on unmarried women.

Another survey in the same city in Shandong suggested that 80 percent of the young women there engage in premarital sex. In province A, out of 2,000 members of the China Communist Youth League (CCYL) who were expelled, 85 percent of were unmarried and cohabitating and/or pregnant. In province B, 60 to 70 percent of CCYL members were punished for the same reasons (Yang 1988).

Extramarital affairs seem to occur much more than generally believed, though they are conducted in such secrecy that little statistical information is available. Perhaps the best evidence of these affairs is divorce rates: Wu (1988) found that one-third of the divorces in Beijing from 1984 to 1985 were precipitated by extramarital relationships. If this finding is at all typical, then the increasing divorce rate must reflect an increase in the number of extramarital relationships.

Although the divorce rate is not very high in China, it is increasing rapidly, as shown in Table 1.

In 1989, nationwide official statistics showed that 9,851,000 couples applied for marriage, and that 9,348,000 (about 95 percent) were granted a marriage certificate. Of the 1,307,000 couples who applied for divorce, 752,000 (58 percent) were granted a divorce certificate. The marriage rate was 16.8 per 1,000 persons, and the divorce rate 1.35 per 1,000 persons.

In one of the few surveys that have been done, Pan found that at least 10 percent of his sample of 600 couples had had extramarital sex. Perhaps most significant is the latest finding in a nationwide survey (cited in Burton 1990), namely, that 69 percent of the people surveyed did not think extramarital affairs were wrong.

Marital dissatisfaction is very common in China today. Some estimate that as many as 60 percent of the Chinese are unhappy with their marriages, and the divorce rate is rising accordingly (Burton 1988). A survey of 3,000 young people in Wuhan, the capital of Hubei Province, showed that only 20 percent of them were satisfied with their marriage. Pan's sample of 600 couples were all residents of big cities, 70 percent of whom said they were dissatisfied with their sex lives. A random survey of married couples living in Shanghai found that 45 percent were unhappy with their sexual relationships.

Sex between consenting adults is technically not illegal in China. But police have broad powers to suppress activities that they consider antisocial. Elderly women who staff local "neighborhood committees"—the grass-roots eyes and ears of the government—can also try to stop activities of which they disapprove. But a discreet affair is likely to escape interference. Means of birth control were not always available to unmarried youths, but women knew they could always get an abortion.

Table 1
Frequency of Divorces in China by Year

Year	# of divorces	Year	# of divorces
1978	170,449	1984	450,000
1979	192,894	1985	500,000
1980	180,378	1986	500,000
1981	186,891	1987	587,000
1982	210,930	1988	630,000
1983	420,000	1989	1,000,000

Regarding unmarried cohabitation, the definitions used in compiling official statistics make it difficult to estimate the popularity of unmarried cohabitation in the sense that it is understood in the West. The Chinese phrase "weihun tongju," which may be translated as "unmarried cohabitation," includes relationships between couples who are living together without benefit of both a government marriage certificate and a wedding. The phrase for couples who marry before the legal age (twenty-two for men and twenty for women), "zaohun," may refer to people who engaged in traditional wedding festivities without benefit of a marriage certificate. The official figure of 2.69 million couples in unmarried cohabitation seems low, considering that some areas report that as many as 50 percent of couples living together do so in unmarried cohabitation. As for couples marrying under the legal age, China's State Family Planning Commission reports that 6.1 million such marriages took place in 1987 alone, and that 2.5 million babies—10 percent of all births—were born to underage couples in that year; the same news article reports an estimate by the Marriage Administration Division of the national Department of Civil Administration that 30 percent of China's "married" couples are living together without having received an official marriage certificate, and that the number is growing. In short, every year there are millions of marriages that are not strictly legal. Meanwhile, one of the worst aspects of the current law is the potential for repression through selective enforcement. Obviously the government must at least hesitate to jail one-third of its youth. But it can make examples out of people, as in the cases cited above, and young people cannot fail to notice that sexual activities can be a pretext for punishing those who are "troublemakers" in other respects.

HOMOSEXUALITY

Male Homosexuality

In ancient times, male homosexuality may have been a familiar feature of Chinese life. The official Chinese historical records indicate that during the Spring-Autumn and Chin-Han Era (770 B.C.–24 A.D.), male homosexuality was considered neither criminal nor immoral, but noble. For example, during the Western Han Dynasty (206 B.C.–8 A.D.) there were eleven emperors, ten of whom had at least one homosexual lover, or expressed some homosexual proclivities. During the Western and Eastern Chin and Southern and Northern Dynasties (256 A.D.–581 A.D.), male homosexuality also seemed acceptable to upper-class society at large.

Considering the many and varied records of homosexuality in ancient China (Ruan & Tsai 1987), one would expect to find evidence of homosexuality in modern China. However, literature regarding contemporary homosexuality is scarce at best. This scarcity of literature on Chinese homosexuality is at least partly due to the prohibitions against homosexuality which are especially strong in contemporary China. Thus it was a genuine breakthrough when in 1985, through a unique and unexpected set of events, Ruan, using a pen name Jin-ma Hua, published an article titled "Homosexuality: An Unsolved Puzzle" in a widely circulated health magazine, *To Your Good Health.* The article pointed out that homosexuality has occurred in all nations, all social strata and in all eras in human history. It acknowledged that in some countries and in certain historical periods, homosexuals were severely punished and sometimes even received the death penalty, adding that such persecution was perhaps an example of how majorities subjugate minorities in human societies. The article went on to assert that homosexuals should not be persecuted for failing to reproduce; that the number of homosexuals in any society is substantial, and greater than lay people realize; that homosexuals' problems should not be ignored, and that they deserve a reasonable social status; and that homosexuals do not differ from heterosexuals in such qualities as intelligence, physical strength, and creativity, or the ability to maintain stable relationships.

The publication of this article attracted considerable attention. Many readers of *To Your Good Health,* most of them gay, wrote to the magazine's editor in response to the article. Then, five months after its first publication, the bulk of the article was reprinted in the most popular and widely read magazine in China, *The (Chinese) Reader's Digest.* By April 1986, a total of sixty letters had been received by the editor of *To Your Good Health,* and forwarded to Ruan. A striking aspect of the letters from gay men is their immense relief at having an opportunity to express their feelings.

Hua's article on homosexuality provides me with a soothing sense of relief never before experienced in my life. It also gives me hope about my life and my future. . . . (Letter #11)

I am extremely grateful for Hua's objective, humane, scientific and fair critique on homosexuality. (Letter #24)

The publication of this article is a great event in the medical field. It is a salvation of thought, a fruit of progressive advancement. To homosexuals, it is true "good news." We admire your courage and scientific attitude toward this matter. (Letter #25)

This article is truly great. It gives us, a small number of homosexuals, a spiritual uplift. It gives me the second life and takes me to the spring of my life. (Letter #28, written by a college student who had attempted suicide)

Of the two letters expressing disapproval of homosexuality, one (#57) came from a medical college in the northwest region of China, and the other (#58) came from a teacher in a factory training center in the northeastern region of China.

Hua's article is attempting to legitimize homosexual life and is not an objective treatment of the subject matter. (#57 and #58)

Homosexuality is an evil product of capitalistic society. Homosexuality brings with it a bad influence on our socialist society. It is our obligation to point out our view in stopping this product of spiritual pollution. (#57)

In a tone reminiscent of the Cultural Revolution, the writer of Letter #58 added:

We should absolutely prohibit homosexuality. . . . Widespread homosexuality will lead to epidemic deterioration of our racial spirit and destroy our society. . . . The reason that people despise, prohibit, punish and persecute homosexuals is precisely that the behavior is evil, ugly, opposed to human morality, an insult to human dignity, promotes crime among youth, ruins their mental and physical health, and leads to the destruction of our race and civilization. . . . It is imperative that we expose homosexuality lest it create a flood that sweeps away our marital, moral, legal and customary dam and destroys our socialist civilization.

Many letters expressed their writers' pain and conflicting desires for confidentiality and a chance to overcome their isolation.

I am a 29-year-old young man. . . . I am not interested in the female sex at all. I do not even want to have any physical contact with them. However,

> among the men that I have encountered, some would occupy my body and soul. . . . I am particularly interested in one man and my love for him is beyond description. He is a little smaller than I am, but I fall for him in every respect I can think of. This feeling deepens every day. It has been ten years but my feeling for him has not been changed. . . . Frequently when I thought of him I would masturbate to fulfill my sexual desire. . . . During the last ten years or so, my life had an interesting twist. When I was 25 years old, a woman fell deeply in love with me. I could not tell her about my true feelings. She insisted on marrying me no matter what. I could not do anything to discourage her. Finally I gave in and married her. I was living in a completely different world. I seldom had sexual relations with her. But on one of those very rare occasions I impregnated her. She knows nothing about my deep secret. This relationship has created pain in my heart and my life. I have been in love and devoted my love to him all this time. I think my love for him will never change for the rest of my life. However, the love is a deep secret. He would not understand nor would he be aware of this. My heart is full of contradiction and pain. (Letter #1)

> The pain that homosexuals suffer most lies not in homosexuality, but in their inability to find suitable lovers. All homosexuals lock their feelings in their hearts. They are so afraid of being discovered that it makes it impossible to live their lives. (Letter #10)

> I am longing to love others [homosexuals] and to be loved. I have met some other homosexuals but I have doubts about this type of love. With all the pressure I was afraid to reveal myself and ruin everything. As a result, we departed without showing each other homosexual love. As I am growing older my homosexual desire increases. This is too troublesome and too depressing for anyone. I thought about death many times. When you are young you cannot fall in love and when you are old you will be alone. Thinking of this makes the future absolutely hopeless. (Letter #8)

Clearly the chief source of pain for China's gay men derives from the fear of societal punishment, including arrest and possible sentence to labor reform camp or prison. The mental pressure and anguish arising from the fear that their true identity will be discovered is often unbearable.

Those who were serving prison terms for their homosexuality at the time Hua's article appeared could not possibly have read it, much less responded to it. However, Letter #22 described the testimony of one man who had been imprisoned. This man was an excellent physics teacher and had been the director of academic affairs in a high school. His homosexual relationships were voluntary and had been initiated by others. He was arrested in September 1983, and sentenced to a five-year prison term for his homosexual acts. Since the publication of Ruan's article, this man's colleagues, friends, and relatives were reported to have changed their negative attitudes toward him. His superior actually visited him in prison, but his sentence remained unaltered.

The social pressure, pain, and inner conflict homosexuals suffer can be so intense that they come to consider or even attempt suicide. Of the 56 who responded to Hua's article, fifteen, or more than 25 percent, mentioned suicide attempts.

Of all the hopes and dreams expressed in these moving letters, three types of aspirations were outstanding. The first concerned the human rights issue—the belief that society should accept gays and their right to express their sexuality without social or legal condemnation. The second concerned the issue of freedom to interact with other homosexuals—the wish that society would provide them with means to make contacts and form relationships, just as it does for heterosexuals. The third concerned the issue of knowledge—the wish that objective and scientific studies would be conducted and publicized in order to improve societal understanding.

Regarding the legal situation of homosexuals in mainland China now, although there is no specific statement concerning the status of homosexuals in the current Criminal Law of the People Republic of China, Article 106 says, "All hooliganism should be subjected to arrest and sentence." In practice, homosexual activity has been included in "hooliganism." As noted above, even the small sample of letters Ruan received contained a report of a man who received a five-year jail term for homosexuality, and additional examples will be given below.

Silence, especially a silence based on repression and enforced ignorance, must not be mistaken for approval or tolerance. When public figures do speak out on homosexuality, it is, understandably enough, usually to condemn it. For example, one of the famous attorneys in China today, Mr. Dun Li, when asked to express his opinion concerning homosexuality, said:

> Homosexuality, though it exists in different societies and cultures, with some minor exceptions is considered abnormal and disdained. It disrupts social order, invades personal privacy and rights, and leads to criminal behavior. As a result, homosexuals are more likely to be penalized administratively and criminally.

In 1987, a leading forensic psychiatrist, Dr. Zheng Zhanbei, expressed himself in similar terms, asserting that homosexuality is against social morality, interferes with social security, damages the physical and mental health of adolescents, and ought to be a crime (Wan 1988).

Another common reaction to the suggestion that homosexuality exists in China is denial. This is the stance of Mr. Z. Liu, a well-known newspaper reporter and editor of a famous magazine, who is quite familiar with the approach of Chinese authorities toward special problems. After two years of study in Chicago, Liu described his American experience in *Two Years in the Melting Pot* (1984). By his own account, his exposure to a more liberal view of homosexuality had little effect on his attitudes:

> One group on campus, calling itself the gay and lesbian Illini, met every week. . . . One of my friends argued that love between those of the same sex is natural and has existed throughout history—during the Roman Empire, it was even made legal, he said. I disagreed, saying that it wouldn't be good for society to open up this issue. In old China, homosexuality was practiced by a few rich people, but the general public didn't approve.

More evidence of the official denial of homosexuality was provided by the internationally well-known sexologist Dr. Richard Green, the Series Editor of *Perspectives in Sexuality: Behavior, Research, and Therapy*. In his "Series Editor's Comment" for Ruan's *Sex in China: Studies in Sexology in Chinese Culture,* Green wrote:

> Less than a year before the 1989 massacre in Tiananmen Square, I lectured on human sexuality at Peking Union Medical College. I described my research on the nonsexual behaviors of young boys that predicted later homosexuality. I asked the physicians in the audience whether comparable childhood behaviors were found among Chinese boys. I was told that there were no homosexuals in China. How exceptional, if true. (Ruan 1991: v)

This official attitude of denial cannot be justified. Recently officials in Shanghai recognized that there are about 10,000 homosexuals in the city. Actually, the number of homosexuals may be over 200,000. Changzheng Hospital in Tianjin, the third largest city in China, reported in a medical paper that in the past four years, out of 366 STDs (sexually transmitted diseases) cases, at least sixty-one cases of syphilis resulted from male homosexual behavior: 80 percent of the cases involved anal sex, 10 percent oral sex, and the other 10 percent anal and oral sex. Most of the patients (80 percent) had participated in sexual activity in public toilets. Most of their homosexual partners (more than 80 percent) were anonymous. Their ages ranged from sixteen to sixty, with two-thirds of the group falling between twenty and thirty years of age. Most of them were workers; some were cadres, teachers, and others.

Yet another reaction is to admit that perhaps homosexuality does exist in China, but to insist that when it occurs it is the result of Western influence. This is what was meant when, in rigid ideological fashion, Letter #57 referred to "spiritual pollution." A formal expression of this view appeared in an official newspaper, the *Beijing Daily News,* which identified homosexuality as one of the "Western social diseases," originating in "Western ideology and thoughts" (United Press International, February 4, 1987).

Finally, there are those who, when faced with undeniable evidence of homosexuality, respond by seeking to eliminate it. Thus Wan Ruixiong, a writer who, after spending considerable time conducting interviews, wrote a lengthy report on homosexuality in China, concluded that homosexuality is a crime and expressed the hope that it will some day be abolished (Wan 1988).

Even many physicians still fail to recognize homosexuality as simply one possible sexual orientation. In Harbin, one of the largest cities in northeastern China, physicians use the now discredited approach of "treating" homosexuality with aversive techniques. According to one report:

> When homosexuals are treated for what most Chinese doctors regard as their mental illness, they are sometimes given painful electric shocks to discourage erotic thoughts. An alternative approach is to offer herbal medicines that induce vomiting. In either case, the idea is to stimulate an extremely unpleasant reaction that will be associated thereafter with erotic thoughts and thus reduce the patients' ardor. Both approaches . . . are hailed by doctors in China as remarkably successful in "curing" homosexuality. (Kristof 1990)

The people subjected to this treatment had not had any criminal charges brought against them, but were sent by family members who were upset by their homosexuality.

Current unrealistic policies contribute to a number of problems. Today in mainland China there is an acute housing shortage. Since there are virtually no private rooms for anyone in the family home, many homosexuals are forced to meet elsewhere. Public restrooms are one of the few available locations for social and sexual liaisons. In these unsanitary conditions, gay men are forced to increase their risk of contracting and spreading contagious diseases—including STDs—perhaps increasing their vulnerability to AIDS. It is time—indeed, past time—for the Chinese government to change its policies. Not only must it recognize the rights of gay people and develop educational programs promoting public acceptance of their lifestyle, it must also begin promoting safe sex practices, ultimately preventing the premature deaths of perhaps millions of people (Ruan & Chong 1987).

Female Homosexuality

In ancient times, Chinese culture was characterized by a very tolerant attitude toward lesbianism. But today, lesbians in China are even more closeted than gay males. When Ruan received letters from homosexuals all over China in

1985 and 1986, not one was from a woman. Some of the women who are willing to discuss their homosexuality have already been imprisoned and have little to lose. Ruan, being an expert and leading sexologist in China, was the main speaker at the first national workshop on sex education held in Shanghai in August 1985. There he received an invitation from the Shanghai Public Security Bureau to visit the Shanghai Women Delinquents Correction Institution. As the correction officer's counselor, he was asked to interview three women. Two of them, Ms. L and Ms. Zu, were prostitutes who will be described in the section below on prostitution, and the third, Ms. Za, was a "sex criminal."

> Ms. Za was 26 years old, born into an intellectual's family. Her first sexual encounter, with a male classmate, occurred while she was still in high school. She enjoyed sex very much, and had sex with about 30 different men altogether, never taking any money. Because of her sexual "delinquency," she was jailed many times. During one jail term, Ms. Za shared a room with Ms. X, who had been arrested and jailed for lesbian behavior. Ms. Za had never even heard of homosexuality before she met Ms. X. In jail, Ms. X treated Ms. Za like a lover, touching her, petting her, and telling her that even without a man two women can have very good sex. After her initial surprise, Ms. Za greatly enjoyed receiving manual and oral sexual caresses from Ms. X. Later, Ms. Za actively seduced other women. She felt that orgasms resulting from homosexual sex were as strong as those from heterosexual sex, though she preferred male partners. Now, Ms. Za began receiving jail sentences for homosexual "sex crimes," as well as heterosexual promiscuity.

Another case, that of Ms. Jia, was reported by attorney Dun Li:

> Ms. Jia, had been deeply in love with another young woman, Ms. Yi. They were constant companions, fond of calling each other "sister," and shared a bed all night as often as they could manage. Ms. Jia had been married 6 months, reluctantly having intercourse with her husband. She only wanted to have sex with Ms. Yi. Later, Ms. Yi became engaged, but before the wedding, Jia killed her. In court, Jia confessed that she loved Yi so intensely that she wanted to divorce her husband and live with Yi forever. When Yi disagreed, Jia decided that it was better to die herself after killing her lover. (See Ruan 1985)

An exception to the usual difficulty in locating lesbians was the experience of Chinese journalists He and Fang (1989), who were actually more successful in contacting lesbians than gay males in their 1989 survey of homosexuality in China.

He and Fang encountered the usual reluctance to be interviewed among people who had every reason to fear discovery. They, too, had to rely on interviews with women who were jailed for "sex crimes," or crimes of violence inspired by sexual jealousy. Because so many investigations of female homosexuality are based on interviews with prisoners, it has been all too easy for Chinese people to develop a stereotype of lesbians as immoral, frustrated people. Thus Shui (1989), in an article in which it is impossible to separate fact from fiction, describes a secret "Lesbians' Company" of women who engage in murder and other crimes because they have been hurt and rejected by men. Unfortunately this story, one of the few publications in which homosexuality in mainland China has been discussed, is probably representative of common attitudes toward lesbianism.

It is clear that many lesbians do live painful lives, marred by fear and jealousy. But it is impossible to develop a complete and balanced picture of their lives under current conditions. No national or local statistics about homosexuals in China are available, and the kind of formal, broad survey that could develop such statistics cannot be made under prevailing repressive policies. Even anecdotal evidence must be distorted when the majority of those who supply it do so only because they are coerced by legal authorities. Given the general lack of sex information in China, and the repressive attitudes of the leadership, it will be a long time before Chinese homosexuals can hope to live normal, fulfilling lives.

It was recently reported in the official newspaper *Guizhou Ribao* (*Official Daily News of Guizhou Province*) that:

> Although two young lesbians in Wuwei County, Anhui Province, were deeply in love with each other, their parents opposed this homosexual relationship very much. At last, the angry parents reported the affair to the local police department. After several months of investigation, the police department of Wuwei County arrested these two female lovers and restrained them 15 days on charges of "misconduct." The Wuwei County police department referred the case to higher institutions until the Public Security Department of Central Government in Beijing heard the case. The Public Security Department replied and instructed the county police that since under current laws there is no article that specifies punishment for such behavior and relationship, it could not be treated as "misconduct." Therefore, the Wuwei Police Department released the two women, and let them live together as "husband" and "wife." Usually the elder one takes the role of "husband," and wears male clothing, while the younger one takes the role of "wife" and prefers to stay in the home.

If this report is true, it is a very good sign that at least some police officers, especially higher officers, have started to change their attitude toward homosexuality and other sexual variants.

TRANSSEXUALISM

Recognition of transsexualism in human society is a relatively recent phenomenon. While there have been numerous studies about transsexualism in the West, none has been conducted in China. In 1982, China's popular medical magazine, *To Your Good Health,* published a column written by Ruan titled "Psychological Counseling." It was the first column of its kind in mainland China and was very well received. Not surprisingly, a wide variety of questions about the personal problems of readers and their acquaintances were received from all over the country. By the end of 1985, seven letters had been sent by admitted transsexuals, some of whom described themselves and their problems in great detail. Two of these "men" corresponded with Ruan several times, even enclosing photographs which revealed some of their unique "female" physical characteristics. In fact, Ruan performed a medical examination on one of them (Case #1), and eventually helped him find a surgeon to conduct sex-change surgery.

Case #1 is twenty years old. Medical examination found that both his external sex organs and his sex chromosomes are those of a normal male. His parents treated him as a girl so that he would not fight or soil his clothes. He was dressed like a girl until he was about thirteen or fourteen years old, when he entered junior high school. His parents forced him to dress like a boy after that, but he did not want to. He became very quiet and isolated from his peers. He could not forget about his colorful girl's clothing. His parents made him join the army in the hope that he would become more masculine. He recalled:

> In the military, everybody ate, slept and bathed in the same open facilities. It was frightening to me. I was so afraid that I dared not go to the bathroom and could not sleep well at night.

His desire to change his identity and return to women's clothing was so strong that he threatened to commit suicide. He was finally permitted to leave the military and returned to his preferred (women's) clothing, identity and way of life. He took stilbestrol (a synthetic feminizing substance) for more than a year. As a result his breasts enlarged, and his body structure and appearance, voice and mannerisms became more feminine. His appearance was that of a beautiful, rather docile woman. His employer fell in love with him and wanted to marry him, even after he revealed his true identity. He considered himself no different from a normal woman and was strongly attracted to men. He felt he had an ordinary feminine libido. He had a strong, persistent desire to be a woman and marry a man, and said that he would rather die than live as a man.

In January 1983, with Ruan's assistance, he underwent transsexual surgery in the Plastic Surgery Department of the Third Hospital of Beijing Medical University. The surgery was a complete success. He was one of the few known successful transsexuals in modern mainland China. (Case #1's story seems to suggest that gender reversal in childhood can lead to transsexualism. However, his older brother was also raised as a girl, and had little trouble reversing his gender identity later. It may be that mistaken gender socialization alone is not sufficient to cause transsexualism.)

The greatest difficulty facing transsexuals in modern China is that of gaining the acceptance of their families and society. It is nearly impossible to obtain permission to perform transsexual surgery. The problem, however, is not a lack of appropriate surgical techniques and facilities; indeed, both general plastic surgery and such precise surgical techniques as reimplantation of severed fingers are very advanced in China. If permission were given, transsexual surgery could be performed with little difficulty in most large hospitals.

The problem is really perceptual and ideological. The absence of scientific research on the subject means that there is nothing to counteract the statements of the popular press, which describes transsexualism as not merely outlandish, but as evidence of the inroads of "decadent Western culture." This ideological tone effectively inhibits surgeons' ability to perform transsexual surgery. Anyone who performs this operation risks being labeled an embracer of Western "decadence," a social stigma that is difficult to bear. This situation is an obvious source of conflict for medical professionals, since refusing to perform transsexual surgery in order to relieve the physical and psychological suffering of their patients violates their humanitarian and moral responsibilities. Before undergoing transsexual surgery, Case #1 was examined and treated by a psychiatrist, Dr. H. Y. Yang. Dr. Yang confirmed that he had seen two transsexual patients who, after being repeatedly denied transsexual surgery, used knives to remove their penises by themselves.

PROSTITUTION

When the Chinese Communists took power, one of the first social changes they introduced was the abolition of prostitution. Only one month after the Communist army took control of Beijing (Peking) on February 3, 1949, the new municipal government announced a policy of limiting and controlling the brothels. On October 1, 1949, the founding of the People's Republic of China was declared, and less than eight weeks later, more than 2,000 Beijing policemen raided and closed all 224 of the city's brothels, arresting 1,286 prostitutes and 424 owners, procurers and pimps (Beijing Public Security Bureau

1988). Other cities soon followed suit. For example, in Shanghai there were 5,333 arrests of prostitutes between 1950 and 1955. In the 1950s it was proclaimed that there were no prostitutes in the "New China"; in the early 1960s, Communist party officials boasted that sexually transmitted diseases had disappeared from mainland China.

In October 1957, in a new attempt to maintain order, the 81st Session of the Standing Committee of the 1st National People's Congress adopted a new law titled *Rules on the Control of and Punishment concerning Public Security of the People's Republic of China.* The legislation announced the following policy on banning prostitution:

"Article 5: A person who commits any of the following acts disrupting public order shall be punished by detention of not more than ten days, a fine of not more than twenty yuan [Chinese currency unit], or a warning: . . .

"(8) Engaging in prostitution or having sexual relations with a woman secretly engaged in prostitution in violation of the government order repressing prostitution."

In 1979, at its Second Session, the 5th National People's Congress adopted the first criminal law in Red China, *The Criminal Law of the People's Republic of China,* which took effect January 1, 1980. Under this law, the punishment for prostitution is more severe:

"Chapter IV: Acts Against the Personal and Democratic Rights of Citizens

Article 140: Whoever forces a female to engage in prostitution shall be sentenced to a fixed term of imprisonment of 3 to 10 years."

This law is little more than a piece of paper. At any time, the law's provisions can be changed by the political leadership; depending on their own feelings and opinions and their political needs, they may impose harsher punishments on pimps and owners of underground brothels, who are included in Article 140, or choose to punish prostitutes and their customers, who are not listed in the Article at all.

The severe repression of prostitution did not prevent its accelerated revival in the late 1970s and throughout the 1980s and 1990s. The Public Security Department of the People's Republic of China ordered a nationwide police crackdown on prostitution in June 1981, and again in June 1982. The first official report of the recurrence and development of prostitution in mainland China appeared in March 1983. This document, which was written by the Public Security Department of the People's Republic of China and the National Association of Chinese Women, reported:

> According to the incomplete statistics from the three largest cities, Beijing, Shanghai, Tianjin, and four provinces, Kuangdong, Fujian, Zheijiang and Liaoning, from January 1982 to November 1982, more than 11,500 persons were discovered to be involved in prostitution. More than 1,200 persons were owners and pimps of underground brothels; more than 4,200 women were prostitutes; and 1,800 persons, including 223 visitors from foreign countries and Hong Kong and Macao, were customers of prostitutes. Six hundred ninety-one people were arrested, 662 were sent to labor camps, 790 were detained, and more than 1,500 were fined. More than 900 underground brothels were banned and closed. Three hundred twenty-two pornographic films and videotapes, and more than 100,000 assorted pornographic magazines, books, photos, and sex toys were confiscated. According to surveys in the provinces of Kuangdong, Fujian, Zheijiang, and Hunan, more than half the cities and counties have already discovered prostitution. According to the survey of Jiangsu and Sichuan provinces, 50–60 percent of prostitutes came from rural areas. In one village in Ho County, Guangxi Province, which has a total of 67 families, 35 women from 28 families moved to cities to engage in prostitution.

In 1985 Ruan was invited by the Shanghai Public Security Bureau to visit the Shanghai Women Delinquents Correctional Institution. This institution, founded in July 1984, began receiving prisoners in September of that year. By the time of the author's visit in August 1985, the institution had a staff of more than thirty, and 150 inmates; it is anticipated that there will be a maximum of forty staff members and 400 inmates. Of the 150 women residing in the institution, about 100 were prostitutes, and the remaining fifty women were "sexual criminals" of various kinds.

Ruan interviewed three women to investigate their frequent attacks on instructors in the institution. Two of them, Ms. L and Ms. Zu, were prostitutes. These two cases, while interesting and illustrative of the lives of prostitutes, are not necessarily representative of Chinese prostitution in general. The interviews were allowed only because the director wanted an explanation of their aggressive behavior, which occurred monthly, and was not typical of the institution's inmates. Yet these women's stories provide excellent evidence that the revival of prostitution was not necessarily the result of the open-door policy and economic reform. For example, Ms. Zu left her family and became a street prostitute as early as 1971, well in advance of the first steps toward cultural openness and economic reform in 1979.

Ms. L was thirty-seven years old, married, and lived in a semirural district of Shanghai. Her husband frequently left home to work. She engaged in sex for pay with as many as three men a day, charging from 3 to 10 yuan (at that time, about $1.50 to $5.00 U.S.). Her worst experience was with a customer who wanted vaginal-manual intercourse ("fisting"), and severely injured her vagina. Her severe premenstrual tension may have been responsible for her attacks on instructors, which usually occurred just before she menstruated.

Ms. Zu was twenty-six years old, unmarried, and lived in Zhongming county, Shanghai Province. She left home at twelve, and lived on the streets of Shanghai city for the next fourteen years, until she was arrested. She had no home, no friends, no job. What she had was a medium-sized bag which held one change of clothing. She might sleep with one man for several days, or three men in one day. She got all her food, clothing, and shelter from these men. For the most part, she did not know their names, and would not have recognized them if she met them again. By the time of interview, she estimated that she had had sexual intercourse with more than 300 men. She said that once she had genuinely fallen in love with a young soldier, and wanted to marry him. When she learned that her boyfriend's commanding officer would investigate her before granting permission to marry, she was terrified and ran away. Now she was not only homeless again but had lost hope as well. She became very anxious and nervous, and began to suffer severe premenstrual tension. She said she needed a cold shower every day "to cool her heart."

Stories like those of Ms. L and Ms. Zu represent the early, scattered beginnings of prostitution's revival in the 1970s. The very different story of the 1980s is one of rapid growth in the number of prostitutes, the profitability of the trade, and the level of its organization. The statistics given below illustrate these changes.

The growth of prostitution in Kuangzhou (Canton) alone was amazing. In 1979 only 49 pimps, prostitutes, and customers were caught. In 1985, this number had increased to approximately 2,000. In June 1987, 11,946 people were arrested for involvement in prostitution, and in both July and August the figures rose to more than 13,000 (Wen 1988a; Yi 1988).

Other statistics showed that in the twenty-two months from January 1985 to October 1987, more than 100,000 persons were found to be involved in prostitution. Prostitutes and their customers appeared everywhere, in hotels, inns, hair salons, single-family homes, apartments, dormitories, underground brothels, and taxis, in every city and every province. In the first seven months of 1987, there were 87 percent more arrests of prostitutes and their customers than in the same period of 1986 (Wen 1988a). Between July and October 1987, the rate of arrest of prostitutes and customers in all of China increased from 370 percent to 450 percent, depending on the location. Between January 1986 and July 1987, 18 prison camps for prostitutes were founded, and by December the number of camps had more than tripled, to a total of sixty-two (Du et al. 1988).

Statistics collected in 1986 in the city of Kuangzhou (Canton), in

Kuangdong Province supply some information about the men who patronize prostitutes. In 1986, of the 1,580 customers who were caught, 41 percent were from the city, 34.48 percent from the province, 15.3 percent from other provinces, 6.1 percent from Hong Kong and Macao, and 3.7 percent from other countries. Sixty-six customers were Communist party members and county officials (Yi 1988).

A typical example of the recent growth of prostitution in mainland China is the case of Changchun, the capital of Jilin Province, a city that is not as big and open as Beijing, Shanghai, or Canton, but much larger than many small cities and rural towns. A broad survey of prostitution in Changchun (which is called "C city" in the original formal publication) reported that prostitution was far more active than it had been in 1949 before the founding of the People's Republic (Huai 1989). In 1949 there were twenty-three registered brothels, seventeen known illegal brothels, and a total of 316 known prostitutes. In 1988, after forty years of the Communist government's strenuous efforts to eliminate prostitution, Changchun, with a population of 1,800,000, had an estimated total of 1,000–1,500 prostitutes. Of the city's 1,000 private hotels, at least 250 hotels were involved in the daily transactions of about 250 prostitutes. Another 300 women were expensive "call girls," typically charging 300–500 yuan (about $80–135 U.S.) a night. The highest prices were commanded by (presumed) virgins, who could charge 1,000 yuan (about $270 U.S.). It was estimated that 70 to 80 percent of Changchun's prostitutes had sexually transmitted diseases (STDs), primarily gonorrhea. The girl with the reputation of being the city's youngest prostitute was only thirteen years old.

Gargan (1988) reports that when a woman is asked why she is a prostitute, she often replies simply, "I need money." Only the high pay could motivate women in these social positions to risk prostitution. The official statistics released by the Public Security Department of the People's Republic of China showed that some prostitutes made very big money very quickly. For example, a net income of as much as 10,000 yuan in only two or three months could be earned, versus the average Chinese income of only about 100 yuan per month. A prostitute from Hunan province said that forty-five of fifty young women from her village went to Kuangdong (Canton) province to be prostitutes, and were making good money.

In the late 1980s, even harsher measures were taken in the effort to curtail prostitution, including arrests of foreign citizens. For example, in September 1987, an incident in which four Americans, one of whom was apprehended while in bed with a Chinese woman, were detained up to twelve hours by the Shanghai Police Department. Two of them were fined, one for 2,500 yuan, and the other for 4,000 yuan (at that time, $1,078 U.S.). Two days later, the same newspaper reported that a West German businessman had been fined 13,710 yuan ($3,695 U.S.) after it was found that he had entertained a Chinese prostitute in his hotel room. It was also reported that prostitutes who sold their services to foreigners would be imprisoned for two years, with even longer terms for their pimps. Similar measures were taken in other regions. In Canton, the police arrested more than 7,000 prostitutes in 1987. In June 1988, in the Shenzhen Economic Zone, which abuts Hong Kong, there was a mass arrest of 122 prostitutes and 100 customers, including Shenzhen policemen, Communist party officials and Hong Kong truckers. In the small town of Deqing, about 100 miles west of Canton, a man accused of being a pimp was executed (Gargan 1988).

There are three primary reasons for the redoubled attacks on prostitution. First, there is grave concern about the threat of STDs to public health. In particular, the fear of AIDS is so extreme that it can fairly be described as "AIDS phobia." The Chinese government sees the elimination of prostitution as a vital part of any plan for controlling and preventing AIDS and other STDs.

The second reason has to do with the opposition to prostitution on an ideological basis. In the lexicon of China's Communist leadership, "prostitution" is a very bad word. Deng Xiaoping, the top leader in China, is particularly strong in his opposition to prostitution, which he believes tarnishes his country's reputation. He advocates severe penalties.

It is also possible that China's leaders are embarrassed by the indictment of their economic policies represented by the continuing existence of prostitution. Considering that the CCP's earliest policy was to combat prostitution by offering women economic alternatives, it must be humiliating to have Chinese women tell Western sociologists that they engage in prostitution because they need the money.

Finally, vocal opposition to prostitution also results from political struggles within the Chinese Communist Party. Accusations of moral looseness are an effective means of silencing opposition, and each faction seeks not only to avoid criticism but to be the loudest in condemning "corruption." Moreover, sexual repression is an important and effective element of the general strategy for controlling the life of the common people. While neither the conservative nor reform wings openly attack other rights and freedoms, they are completely open in attacking the sexual freedom and the sexual rights of common people, especially commercial sex. Thus in the wake of the Tiananmen Square massacre on June 4, 1989, China's new leaders accused Zhao, the former General Secretary of the CCP, of supporting commercial sex and "sex liberation," and included a drive against prostitution in the general increase of repression. Mass arrests of accused prostitutes and customers were made, and, whereas before the crackdown on the democracy movement only native Chinese who patronized prostitutes were sentenced to labor camp, it was announced in September 1989 by the new leader Li Ruihuan, one of the six top leaders, a standing member of the Politburo of the Chinese Communist Party Central Committee, that foreign nationals would be subject to the same sentence. In Beijing, in the three weeks from November 25 to December 15, some 103 prostitutes were arrested. According to the formal report by Yu Lei, the vice-minister of the Department of Public Security of the People's Republic of China, during the antiprostitution, antipornography campaign initiated after the Tiananmen massacre, there were more than 79,000 arrests of prostitutes and customers. Official statistics released by the Public Security Department of the People's Republic of China show that from 1982 through July 1991 more than 580,000 prostitutes and customers were detained. A report in the government newspaper, *People's Public Security News,* showed that in the year 1991 alone, more than 200,000 prostitutes and customers were caught, and more than 30,000 prostitutes were sent to forced labor camps; 80 percent of them were streetwalkers.

Some of those arrested in the antiprostitution movement received sentences as severe as the death penalty. For example, in Wenzhou city, Zhejiang Province, a woman named Ni Pingfan and a man named Guan Wenchung were sentenced to death because from September 1988 to September 1989, they had owned several underground brothels, employing fourteen prostitutes. In Beijing a 55-year-old man named Ho Shuqi was given a death sentence because in 1988 he had allowed prostitutes to use the offices in Longtan Hospital more than twenty times. He was arrested for pandering on November 26, 1988. This procurer was sentenced more than a year after his arrest; it was obvious that the sentence was intended as a show of strength in response to the embarrassment of the events at Tiananmen Square.

Therefore, public health concerns, however valid, are not the primary basis of antiprostitution policies. From that point of view, the government-controlled prostitution of the imperial and republican eras would be more sensible. Since people will obviously not risk being sentenced to hard labor or death in order to seek medical care, the increase in sexually transmitted infections is likely to continue. To the extent that government policies toward prostitution are a measure of the sexual freedom and well-being of the people, the situation in China is probably the worst it has ever been.

PORNOGRAPHY

In China, erotic painting and literature were being produced more than one thousand years ago, i.e., in the Tang dynasty. The official prohibition on erotica started as early as about eight hundred years ago. After the founding of the People's Republic of China on October 1, 1949, a strict ban on erotic material and pornography of any kind was imposed nationwide. The *Rules on the Control of and Punishments concerning Public Security of the People's Republic of China* (October 22, 1957) contain an article regarding punishment for persons accused of involvement with pornography:

"Article 5: A person who commits any of the following acts disrupting public order shall be punished by detention of not more than ten days, a fine of not more than twenty yuan, or a warning:

"(7) putting up for sale or rent reactionary, obscene, or absurd books, periodicals, picture books, or pictures that have previously been repressed."

In the 1950s and 1960s, the policy of banning erotica was very effective. In the whole country, almost no erotic material was to be found. There were few difficulties implementing this policy until the mid-1970s. Then the legalization and wide availability of pornography in several Western countries during the late 1960s and early 1970s, coupled with China's increasing openness to the outside world, increased the supply of such material available for underground circulation. In recent years the suppression of pornography has become a very serious political and legislative concern. The number of arrests and the severity of sentences on people involved in pornography have both increased in the attempt to suppress it entirely.

To understand the current situation, it is necessary to review events during and after the "Cultural Revolution." During the late 1950s and early 1960s, the means of communication were completely nationalized; the print media, the broadcast media, and even bookstores and photographic studios, were strictly controlled; before the Cultural Revolution pornography was simply unavailable. By the middle of the Cultural Revolution, in about 1974, several hand-copied erotic short novels were secretly but broadly circulated, primarily among the youth—in high schools, colleges, and universities, and in factories. A typical example was the well-known *The Heart of a Young Girl* (also known as *The Memoir of Manna*). The CCP and the government confiscated many of these hand-copied booklets in different places across the nation by threatening to punish those who did not turn them over to authorities. In 1985, Ruan received special permission from a large urban police department to read confiscated erotic materials, among them *The Heart of a Young Girl,* a short novel consisting of about 6,000 Chinese characters. The novel, a simple love story describing the romance between the eighteen-year-old Manna and her cousin Xu, contains explicit, but not detailed, descriptions of premarital sex. The sexual behaviors mentioned includes nude petting outdoors, penile-vaginal intercourse indoors, erotic bathing, and fellatio and cunnilingus.

By the late 1970s, "X-rated" films and videotapes were being smuggled into China from Hong Kong and other countries. (In China, these are known as "yellow videos"; "yellow" refers to erotica in China). Yellow videos quickly became a fad. At first the only people who could view these tapes were rather highly placed party members and their families, since only they had access to videotape players, which were very rare and expensive in China at that time. Before long, however, "yellow videos," including the well-known American pornographic movie *Deep Throat,* were available to more people, although still very secretly and only through small underground circles. Some people used the tapes to make money; tickets for video shows were very expensive, usually 5–10 yuan per person (at that time most people's monthly salary was only about 40–50 yuan). Sometimes people who were watching these tapes engaged in sexual activity, even group sex. Because yellow videos were usually shown in small private rooms to very small audiences whose members knew each other well, a party atmosphere often prevailed. It was very easy for young people to initiate sexual activity when they were aroused by what they saw.

At about the same time, erotic photographs, reproductions of paintings, and books were also smuggled into mainland China. They, too, were sold at a great profit. One small card with a nude photo would cost as much as 5 to 10 yuan.

There was a strong reaction at the highest levels of the CCP and the government. The police were ordered to confiscate every type of pornographic material, from hand-copied books to "yellow" audiotapes and films. Severe penalties were ordered for all people involved in the showing or viewing of "yellow" videos, and, in April 1985, a new antipornography law was promulgated. This was an administrative law, "The State Council's Regulations on Severely Banning Pornography." In addition to prohibiting every imaginable type of pornography, it imposed much more severe penalties than those called for by the "Rules on . . . Public Security" of 1957. According to the new regulations:

> Pornography is very harmful, poisoning people's minds, inducing crimes . . . and must be severely banned. The items which must be severely banned include: any kind of videotape, audiotape, film, TV program, slide, photograph, painting, book, newspaper, magazine, and hand-copied material which contains explicit descriptions of sexual behavior and/or erotic pictures; any kind of toy or article with instructions for use which were printed above erotic pictures; and any kind of aphrodisiacs and sex-toys. The person who smuggled, produced, sold, or organized the showing of pornography, whether for sale or not, shall be punished according to the conditions, by imprisonment or administrative punishment.

In July 1987 The State Council enacted even stricter antipornography policies. As we will discuss below, these laws are enforced in an extremely repressive manner. Their use as an instrument of political repression is facilitated by the vagueness of the concept of "pornography." The definition is very loose and quite confusing, as the following cases illustrate.

Two state-run publishing houses, the Beijing-based Workers' Publishing House and Yanbian People's Printing House in Jilin Province, were fined 600,000 and 400,000 yuan respectively (about 150,000 and 100,000 U.S. dollars, respectively) for distributing Chinese translations of English-language editions of *Gambler* and *Fun Club.* They were printed in editions of 370,000 copies and 400,000 copies respectively. All copies were ordered destroyed, along with the printing-plates, and all profits were confiscated. The leading officials at the two publishing houses were disciplined. These two books, one by a British writer and the other by an American, were labeled as pornography by the authorities during the current nationwide drive against pornographic publications. The books were described as "full of pornographic content," "likely to encourage people to commit crimes," and "seriously harmful to young people, mentally and physically." By Western standards, these are mainstream novels that nobody would classify as "adult."

In June 1988 the head of the Central Government Department of Publications, which controls all publications in China, ordered the banning of the *Story of Chin Ping Mei* (an abridgment of the famous novel *Chin Ping Mei,* known in English as *The Golden Lotus*), which had been produced by the Writers' Publishing House, a prestigious state-run literary publisher. The original edition of *Chin Ping Mei,* published in 1617 A.D., consists of over a million characters, with about 30,000 characters (less than 3 percent) describing sexual behavior; the abridged edition, consisting of only 170,000 characters, contains no sexual descriptions at all. The decision to condemn this edition of a classic as "pornography," merely because it bears the title of a novel which originally contained explicit sex scenes, is simply ridiculous. The editor-in-chief of Writers' Publishing House, the famous author Cung Wi-xi, was so upset that he wrote a long article criticizing and protesting this absurd decision. One cannot help suspecting that the ban was motivated by some personal or professional animosity.

The suppression of materials labeled as pornographic was active and effective. In 1987, The Deputy Director of the National Publication Bureau announced that during the preceding three years 217 illegal publishers had been arrested. By the end of August 1986, forty-two publishing houses had been forced to close. Most publishers received warnings and/or fines; one who had made a profit of 600,000 yuan (about $200,000 U.S.) in three years was sentenced to three years in prison.

The nationwide crackdown on pornography led to numerous arrests and the confiscation of "pornographic" material in city after city. For example, the overseas edition of the *People's Daily* reported on July 17, 1987, that in Beijing during the previous six weeks, three publishers of pornography had been detained, and 60,000 books confiscated. Two weeks later the same publication announced that the Shanghai police had demanded the surrender of all pornographic materials, and readied a police force of thousands to arrest publishers of pornography. By October 15, 1987, the Shanghai police had confiscated 110,000 books and more than 5,000 video- and audiotapes. Also in July 1987, the Fuzhou Police and Cultural departments began confiscating materials ranging from playing cards and calendars with nude illustrations, to "yellow" videotapes; by the end of the first week of this campaign, more than 20,400 erotic pictures had been burned. Perhaps the most massive arrests of 1987 occurred in Nanchang, the capital of Jiangxi Province, where by October, forty-four dealers in pornography had been arrested, and 80,000 erotic books and magazines confiscated. It was reported that an underground publishing house with 600 salesmen had been circulating erotic materials in twenty-three of China's twenty-eight provinces, making a profit of one million yuan (in that period about $300,000 U.S.) in two years.

Two incidents are especially noteworthy. The first involved a high-ranking official, Er-fu Zhou, author of the well-known novel *The Morning of Shanghai* and the biographical novel *Doctor Norman Bethune*. Zhou also served as the former deputy minister of the Cultural Ministry of the State Council. In February 1986, he was dismissed from the position of Vice President of the Association for Foreign Friendship and expelled from the CCP for having visited a sex shop and patronized a prostitute while on an official visit to Japan in late 1985.

In the second incident, a Shanghai Railway Station employee named Qin-xiang Liang was sentenced to death. Liang and four other persons organized sex parties on nine different occasions, during which they showed pornographic videotapes and engaged in sexual activity with female viewers. The other organizers were sentenced to prison, some for life.

The climax of this wave of repression seemed to occur on January 21, 1988, when the 24th session of the Standing Committee of the Sixth National People's Congress adopted supplemental regulations imposing stiffer penalties on dealers in pornography. Under these regulations, if the total value of the pornographic materials is between 150,000 yuan and 500,000 yuan, the dealer shall be sentenced to life imprisonment. But then Deng Xiaoping went further by declaring that some publishers of erotica deserved the death penalty (*Center Daily News,* August 24, 1988). This may be one of the most severe political punishments against "pornography" suggested by a national leader anywhere in the world.

Chinese Communist leaders seek to justify their position by claiming that pornography causes crime. For example, they cite a survey finding that of 689 juvenile delinquents, 65.9 percent had read handwritten "yellow" literature (of these 454 cases, 232 were male and 222 female); 95 percent of the female delinquents had read such literature. The author of the survey, using his statistics, sought to show a connection between the reading of pornography and sexual activity.

However, the political motives for this position are obvious. Like the campaign against prostitution, the campaign against pornography was redoubled in intensity after the massacre at Tiananmen Square. At this time, leaders of the conservative faction blamed the ousted Chinese Communist Party's leader, Zhao Ziyang, for the wide circulation of pornographic works in mainland China, and the new leaders vociferously attacked pornography. The *China Daily* of September 15, 1989, reported a typical statement by Li Ruihuan, one of the six top leaders, a standing member of the Politburo of the CCP Central Committee, stating that he "pointed out that the anti-pornography drive is significant in relation to the focus on opposing bourgeois liberalization." Later, Li asserted that, "Hostile overseas forces have taken pornography, gambling and drugs as a means of corroding the fighting will of the people," intentionally "tak[ing] advantage of the development of the reform and opening to the outside world to infiltrate with pornography." This is the viewpoint of a leader widely considered to represent the reform faction.

In the latest nationwide strike against pornography, beginning on the thirty-seventh day after the Tiananmen Square massacre, 65,000 policemen and other bureaucrats were mobilized to investigate publishing houses, distributors, and booksellers. By August 21, more than 11,000,000 books and magazines had been confiscated, and about 2,000 publishing and distributing centers and one hundred private booksellers were forced out of business.

It is impossible to predict how far the CCP and the Chinese government will go in their battle against pornography. What is clear is that all Chinese political leaders, whether they belong to the reformist faction, the neutral faction, or the conservative faction, consistently oppose both pornography and prostitution, at least in public. Each group strives to outdo the others in its condemnations of "this kind of capitalist atrocity." The reformist faction is especially loud in its denunciations as it seeks to defend itself from conservative claims that the "open-door policy" is to blame for the introduction of such "rotten, decayed, corrupt, degenerating" phenomena.

The "antipornography" campaign is more dangerous than the prudery and restrictiveness of neo-Confucian laws and customs. Anyone is vulnerable to arrest if it is merely reported that he or she possesses erotic materials, and the government policy of leniency to those who confess, and harshness to those who do not, is well known. In this atmosphere of suspicion, in which the elimination of "dangerous" literature about human sexuality is a cover for suppression of personal and political freedom, nobody can feel safe. Perhaps most tragically, human sexuality, and the pleasure and intimacy it creates, can hardly be expected to flourish.

SEX EDUCATION

In line with its general policy of suppressing any discussion of sexuality, the Chinese government neglected the development of sex education courses for the general curriculum. It was not until the early 1980s that model programs were developed, and even then, discussion was usually limited to the necessity of using contraception to limit population growth.

In 1980, heartened by the end of the Cultural Revolution and inspired by the memory of Chou En-lai's support, a few authors and publishers began to produce new materials. The first effort was a new edition of a 1950s booklet *Knowledge of Sex,* published by People's Medical Publishing House. The first edition of 2.5 million copies, released in June 1980, was sold out almost immediately, and some people resold their copies at nearly double the original price. By August of 1980, there had been four reprintings of the new edition of *Knowledge of Sex,* totaling 2.3 million copies (Bullough & Ruan 1990).

From 1980 to 1984, more than ten new sex booklets were published. Two of them became best-sellers. The first, *Required Readings in Wedding Hygiene,* was originally published in September 1980, and by November 1981 had already been reprinted eight times, for a total of more than 7.5 million copies. The second, *Questions and Answers about Wedding Hygiene,* published in July 1984, was first printed in a large print run of 4.2 million copies.

To fill the need for distributing basic sex information as widely as possible, Ruan authored 84 articles which were published in fifteen magazines and seven newspapers, including the most popular magazines in China, such as *Chinese Reader's Digest* (distributing about 10 million copies per issue), *China Youth* (distributing more than 3 million copies per issue), *Popular Medicine* (more than one million copies per issue), and *Health* (more than one million copies per issue). Ruan's special series titled "Essays on Sex Education," was published in *Required Readings for Parents,* the leading national monthly magazine on child and adolescent education.

The First National Workshop on Sex Education was held in Shanghai from July 22 to August 7, 1985. This, the first such conference convened in mainland China since 1949, was an interdisciplinary workshop attended by more than eighty professionals from eighteen provinces, most of them in the fields of birth-control, sociology, urology, and high school and college education. During the workshop, the preparatory committee of the Chinese Sex Education Research Society was organized.

The first high school sex education courses were introduced in 1981 in Shanghai. In early 1986, forty Shanghai middle schools, about 10 percent of the city's total, introduced an experimental sex education course for mixed classes in the twelve-to-thirteen age group. In addition to helping students understand the physiological and psychological changes they were undergoing, the course was designed to teach hygiene and sexual morality. These experiments in sex education were so successful that six months later, on June 7, 1986, nearly 100 Shanghai middle schools gave sex education courses. By February 1988, 6,000 middle schools all over China had instituted sex education courses. Thirteen of the twenty-eight provinces, including Shanghai, Jiangsu, Tianjin, and Helongjiang, had made sex education courses part of the standard middle school curriculum. The State Council announced that sex education courses would be established soon in middle schools nationwide.

On May 23, 1988, the country's first college-level sexology course was introduced at China People's University in Beijing. This special two-week program, called "Training Workshop on Sex Science," consisted of workshops on twenty topics, conducted by seventeen professors and experts. The program was attended by 120 people from twenty-six of China's twenty-eight provinces.

The latter half of the 1980s was a time of tension between the acknowledged need for sex education and continued pressure within the government to maintain tight social control. After the Tiananmen Square massacre in 1989, the government fell into its old habit of including sexual restrictions in a wave of political repression. The most recent sign of a resurgence of repression came in July 1990, when the Vice-President of the Supreme People's Court, Lin Zhun, issued a new decree stating that the death sentence is the proper penalty for traffickers in prostitution and/or pornography. Materials for sex education have frequently been construed as pornographic in China. Therefore, it is not a surprise to see the antipornography movement having negative effects on sex education. But because of the huge pressure for population control, as well as for the prevention of STDs and teen pregnancy, the government can no longer inhibit and stop sex education. Sex education classes, exhibitions, meetings, and publications are still continuing and developing in China today. The following notice, for example, appeared in the official "Xinghuashe" Press in Nanjing on May 3, 1992:

> The 6th National Conference of the Science of Sex was held on May 3, 1992 in Nanjing. About 500 experts and scholars from all over the country attended this conference. The conference received and accepted more than 400 academic papers on the topics of sex education, sociology of sex, psychology of sex, sexual medicine, and sexually transmitted diseases.

CONCLUSION

Public policy and law relative to sexuality seriously impacts on individual and social lives. Contemporary China is a noteworthy example of the appalling effect a totalitarian government's sexually repressive policies have on the individual's life. It also exemplifies how sexually repressive policies are not effective either in inhibiting sexual desire in private lives nor in curbing the struggle for human sexual rights and freedom.

The major move toward democracy in mainland China after Mao was the "Democracy Wall" movement during 1978 and 1979. During this brief period, the government allowed young people to express their desire for personal freedom and democracy by placing "big character" posters on a wall that came to be known as "Democracy Wall." The Democracy Wall was also used for advocating sexual liberation. The author vividly recalls visiting the wall on February 20, 1979, and seeing two poems about sex written by "Sasa" and "Manman." One was titled "The Eulogy of Sexual Desire," the other "Open Sex" (Ruan 1991). By March 5, 1979, these poems had already been scrubbed away. In posters like these, China's youth first made a courageous stand on the importance of sexual openness to their country's modernization.

During the nationwide demonstration by university students in the winter of 1986–87, there were also some posters advocating sexual freedom. While sexual liberation was not a major explicit goal of the 1989 democracy movement, its importance was understood, and its value implicit in one of the loveliest events to occur at that time. During the hunger strike in Tiananmen Square, a wedding was held for one of the leaders of the demonstrators. The bride and groom, the maid of honor (the General Commander Chai Ling, now an internationally known heroine of the struggle for democracy), and the best man (Chai's husband, the Vice General Commander Feng Congde) were all fasting, as were the classmates attending the wedding. Yet all the celebrants were laughing joyously. The wedding was the ideal symbol of the connection between the longing for liberty and the desire for love, marriage, and personal happiness.

Many people believe that sexual liberation is one of the most important changes in recent years in mainland China. The major signs of this sexual liberation are the blooming of prostitution and other erotic businesses, and the open attitudes toward sex among people, especially young intellectuals (Zhao Yiheng 1992). A report in the *San Francisco Chronicle* described that:

> Interviews with dozens of young adults in Beijing reveal a society joyfully discarding taboos and simultaneously trying to define new rules of romantic and sexual conduct.
>
> . . . "I held hands with my boyfriend in college in 1986, and the director called his parents to complain," said a 24-year-old woman. "Now, we kiss in the middle of the street, and it's seen as normal."

> . . . "Five years ago, if a girl didn't go home at night, her parents went crazy," said a 33-year-old single businessman. "Now, with many girls, as long as they call home to say they're staying over, it's all right."
>
> . . . Dating is no longer seen as an awkward preliminary to marriage and has become an end in itself. . . . Dating has now expanded into married life. "The third person," as Chinese refer to the outsider in extramarital affairs, has become an important figure in the national psyche. . . . "All my friends sleep with their boyfriends," said a 24-year-old recent college graduate. "It's natural." (Price 1992)

As the tide of modernization overtakes China, sexual freedom will certainly assume its place among the vital human rights the people will enjoy in the future.

REFERENCES

(An asterisk denotes a Chinese language title.)

Beijing Public Security Bureau, ed. (1988). *The Reports on Closings of Brothels in Beijing*. Beijing: China Peace Press.*

Bullough, V. L., and Ruan, F. F. (1990). "Sex Education in Mainland China." *Health Education* 21: 16–19.

Burton, S. (1988, September). "The Sexual Revolution Hits China: Reform Has Brought a Permissiveness That Unsettles Many." *Time*, p. 65.

——— (1990, May). "Straight Talk on Sex in China." *Time*, p. 82.

Butterfield, F. (1980, January 13). "Love and Sex in China." *New York Times*, Sunday Magazine.

Cheng, L. (1991). "The March of Divorce." *China Spring*, pp. 67–72.*

Du, J. M.; Yi X.; and Xiong, H. (1988). *Watch Out: STDs Are Spreading in China*. Beijing: Zhongguo Zoyue Zuban Gongsi.*

Gargan, E. (1988, September 17). "Newest Economics Revives the Oldest Profession." *The New York Times*.

He, C., and Fang, Q. (1989, April). "The Sex-Love of Yin-Yang Inversion: An Inquiry into Homosexuality in China." *Qinghai People's Art*, pp. 2–23.*

Huai, Z. (1989). *The Yellow Sins in the Green City*. Beijing: Zhongguo Mingjian Wenyi Chubanse.*

Ji, Y. (1990). *The Revelation of Life*. Taiyuan, China: Beiyue Wenyi Chubanshe.*

Kristof, N. D. (1990, January 31). " 'Curing' Homosexuals in China." *San Francisco Chronicle*.

Liu, Y. (1988). "Marriage and the Family." *Beijing Review* 31, no. 21: 23–25.

Money, J. (1977). "Peking: The Sexual Revolution." In J. Money and H. Musaph, eds., *Handbook of Sexology*, pp. 543–50. Amsterdam: Excerpta Medica.

Price, Niko. (1992, May 26). "Young Chinese Discover Joy of Sex." *San Francisco Chronicle.*

Ruan, F. F., ed. (1985). *Handbook of Sex Knowledge.* Beijing: Scientific and Technological Literature Publishing House.*

Ruan, F. F. (1991). *Sex in China: Studies in Sexology in Chinese Culture.* New York: Plenum Press.

Ruan, F. F., and Bullough, V. L. (1988). "The First Case of Transsexual Surgery in Mainland China." *The Journal of Sex Research* 25: 546–47.

——— (1989a). "Sex in China." *Medical Aspects of Human Sexuality* 23: 59–62.

——— (1989b). "Sex Repression in Contemporary China." In P. Kurtz, ed., *Building a World Community: Humanism in the 21st century,* pp. 198–201. Buffalo, N.Y.: Prometheus Books.

Ruan, F. F., and Chong, K. R. (1987, April). "Gay Life in China." *The Advocate* 470: 28–31.

Ruan, F. F., and Tsai, Y. M. (1987). "Male Homosexuality in the Traditional Chinese Literature." *Journal of Homosexuality* 14: 21–33.

——— (1988). "Male Homosexuality in Contemporary Mainland China." *Archives of Sexual Behavior* 17: 189–99.

Ruan, F. F.; Bullough, V. L.; and Tsai, Y. M. (1989). "Male Transsexualism in Mainland China." *Archives of Sexual Behavior* 18: 517–22.

Shui, S. (1989). "Lesbians' Company." In L. Mingzu, ed., *The Love Story in the Military Tour,* pp. 66–95. Shengyang, China: Liaoning Mingzu Press.*

Wan, R. X. (1988). "The Bigger Variations of Sex and Love: About the Problems of Homosexuality in China." In B. Wen, ed., *The Ten Women's Tales,* pp. 78–109. Beijing, China: China Social Sciences Press.*

Wen, B., ed. (1988a). *The Ten Women's Tales.* Beijing, China: China Social Sciences Press.*

——— (1988b). *Marriage among the Chinese People.* Beijing, China: China Social Sciences Press.*

Wu, C. Z. (1988). *The Studies of Crimes Related to Sex, Love, and Marriage.* Beijing, China: Beijing Office of Guiding Group of Philosophy and Social Sciences Programs.*

Yang, H. X. (1988). *Psychology of Sex.* Shijiazhuang: Hebei People's Publishing House.*

Yi, N. (1988). *Pondering under a Shining Sun.* Beijing: Zhongguo Wenlian Chuban gongshi.*

Zhao Y. H. (1992). "Sexual Liberation and the Confucian Ethics of the Nineties." *Democratic China* 8: 71–78.*

22

Forensic Sexology in Russia*

A. A. Tkachenko

CULTURAL TRADITIONS AND HISTORICAL CONDITIONS

The Russian national culture includes many sexual and erotic aspects. In ancient Russia the attitude to sexuality was no less inconsistent than in Western Europe. The ancient Slavonic paganism was neither too chaste nor too free. Along with female deities it had a phallic god, Rod. The typical phallic image was mostly animal: a lion with either a long tail or a penis. You can see it still in stone ornaments on ancient temples in Vladimir and in the Church of the Protecting Veil on the river Nerl. There were also many orgies where naked men and women swam together, men symbolically fecundating the earth and the women calling the rain.

This pagan exuberance could still be seen at times after the introduction of Christianity. In Russian icons normally only the face is alive while the body is completely covered or excessively severe and ascetic. However, in some temples of the seventeenth century there are frescoes with half-naked bodies ("Baptism of Jesus") and even women bathing. Many remnants of pagan morals existed until the end of the nineteenth century and were manifested in folk customs, including "trial" marriage and orgiastic feasts. "Erotic tales"

---

*This chapter by Russian author A. A. Tkachenko provides some insight into the history of forensic sexology in Russia as well as the current legal status of sexual rights there. Time retrictions, given the delays in mail service between Russia and the United States, limited the amount of editorial intervention regarding translation. Readers may wish to contact Dr. Tkachenko at the address noted in the List of Contributors at the beginning of this volume for more information and explanation.

describe polygamy by the main characters. Sexual pranks such as the ravishment of a sleeping beauty are described sympathetically, and the rape of a maid is justified as a revenge for her refusal to marry a man.

The influence of French "libertines" in the eighteenth century did not pass by Russia unnoticed. In the palace of Gatchino belonging to Catherine the Great, there were erotic frescoes and special furniture, for instance, a table with legs shaped as penises, which were gifts from the empress to her favorite, Grigory Orlov. In the nineteenth century the younger generation of the nobility enjoyed reading both the *Immodest Treasure* by Diderot and the frivolous poems of I. S. Barkov.

In Russia, as in the West, the opponents of erotic art in the nineteenth century were political and cultural conservatives and the church. But they were especially strong in Russia because, besides having the authority of religion, they were also supported by state power. Another opponent of eroticism was represented by revolutionary democratic criticism, which influenced the attitudes of society dramatically. While the aristocrats who received secular education became, in the course of time, more detached from official hypocrisy, it was more difficult for *raznochinetzes,* i.e., intellectuals not belonging to the Russian gentry, to do so.

Conservative and religious criticism condemned eroticism because it contradicted the dogmas of faith. Revolutionary and democratic criticism found eroticism alien to the standard code of the individual, who was expected to dedicate his life to the struggle for liberation of the working people. These ideas were, in many respects, supported by traditional peasant attitudes. Marriage for them was an indispensable characteristic of adult status. In Russian villages a bachelor, irrespective of age, was not a "moujik" but a "fellow." He had no vote in family and village decisions. Attitudes to unmarried adult men are reflected in such national Russian proverbs as: "A bachelor is mad" and "A bachelor is half a man."

These attitudes had the practical effect of promoting early matrimony, and offical rejection of free sexuality. But the power of artificial barriers was gradually overcome, especially at the beginning of the twentieth century. The idea of neoplatonic Eros became connected with attempts to develop sensuality and was grounded in the work of Solovyev, Nikolai Berdyaev, Karsavin, and Visheslavtsev. They were the proponents of individual, personal love, condemning asceticism and emphasizing the connection of Eros with creativity.

Another trend, orthodox and theological, was set by Florensky, Sergey Bulgakov, and Ilyin. They adhered not to the erotic theory of antiquity but to medieval *caritas* (compassion, charity, mercy) and its relevance to the ethics of the Christian family and marriage. These two opposing trends of Russian philosophy caused a great deal of contention. Harmonious synthesis was not possible at the time, due to the very short history of a religious school of thought in Russia and the difficult conditions of its development.

The year 1917 became a real turning point. The traditional religious morality of relations between the sexes was undermined; however, a new postrevolutionary morality had not yet developed in Russia. The 1920s were characterized by heated arguments about "free love" and the necessity of sexual morals for the proletariat. Premarital and extramarital relations were widespread among students and young workers. About 85 to 95 percent of men and 48 to 62 percent of women were involved in extramarital relations. The percentage of single mothers and unwanted pregnancies was high. This situation alarmed the ruling caste: Lenin was against a simplified interpretation of the sexual drive as a purely physiological need. Philosophers, psychologists, and ethnographers seriously studied the "sexual problem." By the beginning of the 1930s, society had coped with the turmoil of the first postrevolutionary years and returned to more traditional sexual behavior and marital relations.

At this time the "administrative-command system" under Stalin showed the tendency toward total control of the personality. The necessity of de-individuation was connected with consistent extermination of eroticism. At first it was not a matter of deliberate strategy but a continuation of revolutionary asceticism. This philosophy fit both the stereotypical peasant consciousness brought up in the spirit of austere religious morals, and the ideas of the left-wing radical intellectuals who believed in the possibility and the necessity of the "alteration" of human nature.

During the *perestroika* of the 1980s the grip of censorship became less tight. The Russian public could then start reading classic erotic books and watching erotic films. Exhibitions of erotic paintings, books, and photography were opened. There was also a surge in pornography, which resulted in anti-pornographic slogans being used by conservative and chauvinistic political organizations against *glasnost* and the mass media, which were accused of spoiling the youth.

SEXUAL BEHAVIOR AND ITS LEGAL REGULATION

In comparison with today, the family legislation of 1926 looks progressive. At that time, regularized love relations were legally equated with an offical marriage. Legislation had to take into account about 80,000 to 100,000 such "marriages" (as well as 20,000 marriages that were registered officially every year). Despite active resistance by conservative men, especially in rural areas, women living in a nonofficial marriage received the right to alimony as well as the right to a share of the property in case of separation. Earlier, in December 1917, the Decree on Marriage and Divorce facilitated the procedure of divorce: the willingness of both parties was enough, the cause not needing to be mentioned. Legal divorce procedures were cancelled. Only one principle was established: the necessity to settle the issue of the children's and the former partner's support, if they had previously been provided for. The Soviet government, in this respect, was in the vanguard of other European countries.

Between 1936 and 1944, the court's divorce procedures were reestablished. In the 1930s, the demographic situation in the country became unfavorable, as the outcome of an artificially imposed famine and mass repressions. In 1936 abortions were prohibited by Stalin's order, and substantial changes were introduced in the family and matrimonial legislation.

Stalin introduced a fine for abortions, which had previously been the right of every woman. Those willing to divorce had to go to special offices under the title "Registration of Civil Status Acts." The cost of divorce was raised, and the fact of divorce was marked in one's passport with a stamp. Finally the USSR Supreme Soviet Decree of 1944 declared "free marriage" illegal. A court procedure was introduced for marriage cancellation, during which the spouses were to present their "good reasons" for divorce and the judge was to appoint a certain "conciliatory" term. The information about divorce was published in newspapers. At the same time the state began to encourage women to have more children.

The Decree of 1965 cancelled publication of divorce information. Divorce procedures became simpler, but family and marriage law was only slightly modified as compared with the legal standards of Stalin's time. For instance, couples without children could be divorced without court hearings, providing both partners agreed to it. However, in general, the order of divorce procedures was retained. Public discussion in the mass media in 1968, and the request of citizens for a facilitation of the divorce procedure accomplished nothing. The protection of marriage became state policy even though it was sometimes contrary to the interests of individual people. Thus the peasant ideology had won.

Absence of sexual civil rights and the repressive societal model are reflected in legal attempts to regulate sexual behavior. Criminal responsibility for homosexuality is especially illustrative in this respect. In Russian law, the first punishment for homosexual behavior was introduced by the military edict issued by Peter the Great in 1716. In 1832 homosexuality was discouraged by means of corporal punishment, deprivation of civil rights and exile. Homosexual violence was punished to hard labor. In 1845 it was punished by deprivation of civil rights and hard labor for four to five years. If the homosexual was a Christian, he was subjected to the church's penitential procedure. In the cases of homosexual rape of a minor or a mentally deranged person, the offender was sentenced to hard labor for ten to twelve years. In the criminal code of 1903 voluntary homosexuality was punished by imprisonment for three months to three years. If the victim was a minor or a person incapable of resistance, punishment was more severe, with confinement in a reformatory for up to three years. If the victims were boys under fourteen or if they were under the authority and power of the offender, then the latter was punished by penal servitude for eight years. The same punishment was used for non-violent as for violent homosexual behavior.

After the revolution, the punishment for homosexual behavior was preserved only in criminal codes of the Caucasus and Middle Asia. The 1922 and 1932 criminal codes of the Russian Republic did not include special mention of homosexuality. Violent homosexual behavior was included under rape, and voluntary homosexual behavior was punished only if the victim was a minor. Other variants of homosexuality were included under depraved acts committed with minors and infants.

The first special edict establishing punishment of homosexuality in the whole of the Soviet Union was issued by the Central Executive Committee (CEC) in December 1933. It provided criminal responsibility for homosexual abuse of a helpless victim, violent homosexual behavior, homosexuality in public and consenual homosexuality. Soon afterwards, in March 1934, the All-Union law by edict of the Presidium of the CEC of the USSR, "Criminal responsibility for homosexuality," was published. It increased the punishment for the mentioned actions and used only two qualifying features: violence and dependent condition of the victim. Otherwise, this edict regarded homosexuality as sexual intercourse between two men. In accordance with the All-Union standards, homosexuality was included in the criminal codes of all republics, standards still used today. The Russian criminal code, which has been used since 1961, contains the following article:

Article 121. Homosexuality

> "Sexual intercourse between men is punished by imprisonment for five years.
>
> "Homosexual acts commited with violence or threats with a minor, or with use of the dependent condition of the victim is punished by imprisonment for a period up to eight years."

Prosecution for consenual homosexuality was always subjected to criticism, both by the world community and by many Russian lawyers and medical professionals. But only now can the odious first part of this article be excluded. Meanwhile, lack of full communication between lawyers and sexologists has had an effect on the development of a new criminal code. In spite of sexologists' suggestions, the draft code contains a separate article providing criminal responsibility for violent homosexual acts. In our opinion, introduction of this article is unjustified, as it would be enough to exclude the gender concept from the article qualifying rape, thus covering responsibility for any violent sexual acts. Unfortunately many lawyers are not yet ready to acknowledge the equality of homosexual behavior; they still consider it a variant of abnormal sexuality destructive of public morals.

The new code currently being drafted is characterized in general by a moralistic approach to regulation of sexual behavior. Almost all the articles concerning sexuality are codified in Chapter IV, titled "Offenses against Sexual Immunity, Family, and Morals." It seems to us that the use of the concept of "morals" in this context is inappropriate, insofar as this concept is a reflection of stereotypes of a social consciousness which are prone to change.

The existing qualification of these offenses as "Offenses against Personal Life, Health, Freedom, and Honor" (Chapter III) seems to us preferable. This chapter includes four articles directly connected with paraphilias:

Article 117. Rape.

"Rape, i.e., sexual intercourse with physical violence, threats or with use of helpless condition of the victim is punished by imprisonment from three to seven years.

"Rape under threat of homicide or injury, or committed by a person who has previously committed a rape, is punished by imprisonment from five to ten years.

"Group rape or rape of a minor is punished by imprisonment from five to fifteen years.

"Rape committed by an especially dangerous offender or causing especially severe injury or rape of an infant is punished by imprisonment of eight to fifteen years with exile from two to five years, or without exile, or by the death penalty."

Article 118. Woman's coercion to sexual intercourse.

"Coercion of a woman to perform sexual intercourse or to satisfy sexual passion in another form by a person to whom the woman is materially or professionally dependent is punished by imprisonment up to three years."

Article 119. Sexual acts with a minor.

"Sexual intercourse with a person who has not achieved sexual maturity is punished for a period up to three years. The same actions with satisfaction of sexual passion in perverted forms is punished for a period up to six years."

Article 120. Depraved actions.

"Depraved actions with minors are punished for a period up to three years."

It should be explained that in Russia a person is legally an adult when he or she has reached eighteen years. Youngsters under fourteen are considered infants. Speaking about perverted actions, lawyers frequently mean oral and anal sex. We do not consider it justified to distinguish them as a separate *corpus delicti.*

The above-mentioned articles do not cover all possible paraphilic activities. For that reason criminal proceedings against paraphilics are possible within the framework of other articles. The most common are: Article 102: "Aggravated murder" (see point "e," associated with rape), Article 113: "Brutal Torture," included in the same chapter. In the case of fetishism it is possible to start a criminal procedure following Article 144: "Larceny," which belongs to another part of the code. These articles have been preserved almost intact in the new draft code. The only considerable change is exclusion of the death penalty in cases of rape.

It is also necessary to discuss legislative standards in cases of exhibitionism. Until recently the code did not have a separate article formulating responsibility for exhibitionism. If the object of exhibitionism is a minor, criminal proceedings are initiated according to Article 120. If the object is an adult, criminal proceedings are initiated following Article 206, Part II (deliberate actions which violate social norms with exceptional cynicism). This article provides punishment for a period of one to five years. The application of this article in cases of exhibitionism often leads to multiple convictions of offenders who are denied sexological treatment. The new formulation of this article specifies also disorderly actions such as those associated with violence or with property damage. Such formulations should exclude the use of this article in cases of exhibitionism. However the absence in the new code of a special article providing responsibility for "indecent exposure," to our mind, may lead to arbitrary use of other articles that do not imply such activity. We think it possible to include a special article about exhibitionism which would provide confinement as a measure of responsibility for exhibitionism.

As a whole, the new code draft is a step forward; it reflects the existing reality better than the present code. For example, the code currently in force ignores the problem of prostitution. This started with the declaration to eradicate prostitution in socialist society after the revolution, and was followed by cessation of the activities of the Central Council for Prostitution Prevention. Nevertheless prostitution was still included under the most severe forms of organised criminality. The new code draft does not deal with responsibility for prostitution, although it contains two articles providing punishment for "involving in prostitution" not only minors but also adult women.

A special article is expected to deal with the responsibility for transmitting AIDS. The criminal responsibility concerns the person who has knowingly spread the disease or the medical nurses or doctors who have not fulfilled their professional duties.

The new code draft provides the possibility of changing criminal responsibility for "production or sale of pornographic products." Society was not ready for the perestroika video boom. The term "pornography" was not defined clearly, which resulted in the classification of classic films by Fellini, for example, as pornographic. A check of criminal cases showed that about 60 percent of those convicted had been punished without legal grounds. The new code draft provides punishment only in cases of violation of established rules (licences) concerning manufacturing or distribution and sale of pornographic products.

The complexity of the legal regulation of sexual behavior in Russia is connected with a turning point in its history. The facts presented here help one to understand the societal situation in the past, and to get an idea of tendencies in the development of social consciousness and law. However, despite significant positive changes in legal approaches, complete reconciliation between sexologists and lawyers still remains a distant goal.

DEVELOPMENT OF SEXOLOGY AND STUDIES ON PARAPHILIA

A century ago, it was Russia that probably had the most favorable prerequisites for the development of sexology. Originally, investigations in this field were conducted within the framework of the Russian school of physiology. In 1887 I. R. Tarkhanov made a special investigation of the erection mechanism. He aroused erection in experimental animals by filling their seminal vesicles with normotonic salt solution. He also removed different organs in frogs during their sexual intercourse, but he managed to stop their erection only after the seminal vesicles had been removed. The first experimental work investigating the dependence of genital organ functioning upon cerebral cortical function was published by V. M. Bekhterev and M. A. Mislavski (1891). One of the most often cited works is that by L. M. Pussep (1912), who showed that irritation of certain areas of one hemisphere of the cerebral cortex by electric current caused erection in dogs. Ablation of these parts led to loss of sexual drive, whereas parallel ablation in the other cerebral hemisphere caused only slight and transient lessening of it.

In 1907, M. A. Chlenov (1908) performed the first extensive statistical and sociological investigation of sexual behavior. He conducted a questionnaire census of Moscow students, with 2,217 respondents. V. N. Favour (1903) similarly questioned 1,066 students in Kcharkov. Questionnaires like these became especially popular after 1917. Among the most outstanding investigations were the works by F. L. Helman (1926), S. Yu. Golosovker (1927, 1928), and D. F. Lass (1928). The results of such investigations could have served as a real basis for development of sexology.

However, such investigations soon stopped. Russian science retrogressed for a long time. Only in 1981 was it possible to raise the issue of sexology as a separate science, when the magazine *Issues of Philosophy* published an article "On the Junction of Sciences" by I. S. Kon. In 1984 this same author published another article titled "Sexology" in the *Big Medical Encyclopaedia.* Nonetheless, it was only in 1988 that Kon's book *Introduction to Sexology* was issued in the Soviet Union, much later than its appearance in Hungary and in both Germanies. In this book, sexology was defined as an interdisciplinary sphere of knowledge, covering philosophical, sociological, and judicial as well as medical, biological and psychological aspects of sexual dimorphism in its connection with various manifestations of human vital functions. To understand the significance of these works, it is sufficient to say that in 1963 the above-mentioned *Encyclopaedia* was still stating that there was no reason for singling out sexology as an independent discipline, as neither its content nor its boundaries and methods were defined, and it only mechanistically combined quite different disciplines.

On the other hand, it was also in 1963 that it became possible to create a special network of sexological regional centers and consulting rooms on issues of conjugal life. According to a decree by the USSR Health Minister, patients suffering from sexual disorders should be treated by a physician who had been specially trained in sexopathology. To coordinate research work the All-Union Research and Methodical Center in Sexopathology was established with professor G. S. Vasilchenko as its head. Vasilchenko was also editor of two manuals, the first in general and the other in special sexopathology (Vasilchenko 1979, 1983). These publications confirmed the right of sexopathology to exist as an independent discipline, being a part of sexology. Sexopathology was identified as a branch of clinical medicine, studying functional aspects of sexual disorders, including behavioral, personal, and social. Final confirmation of this right was made on May 10, 1988, when the USSR Health Ministry issued an order "On further improvement of sexopathological care of the population," and a new speciality was introduced, namely that of a "sexopathologist."

Sexopathology was created on the basis of such fundamental approaches as the systematic, the complex, and the integral; the interdisciplinary pattern of sexopathology was accepted as the principal one. Independent specific phenomenology (e.g., the concept of sexual constitution), investigation methods (various quantified scales, anthropometric methods, etc.) and terminology were developed. In classifying sexual disorders four components of the copulative cycle were distinguished, i.e.: neurohumoral, mental, erectional, and ejaculational. Each of them is characterized by its own anatomic substratum and the particular task it fulfills. To make an integral diagnosis, the method of structural analysis is used.

The dysontogenetic (i.e., "disordered development") concept of psychosexual orientation was suggested as a theory explaining paraphilic genesis.

According to this theory, paraphilia is a result of this disturbance, with fixation of early forms of the sexual drive. This hypothesis was not based on special investigations of paraphilic behavior; it reflected only an attempt to combine all existing theories. General descriptions of some paraphilias confirm the data accumulated by forensic psychiatrists about their manifestation in different mental disorders.

Early Russian work on paraphilia was conducted by V. M. Tarnavsky (1884). He substantiated the unity of origin and relationship between some forms of sexual perversions. He also suggested that patients with paraphilias should be divided into those predisposed to different nervous diseases and those relatively healthy people who developed these deflections due to their upbringing. It is noteworthy that this very dilemma of hereditary versus social influence on the formation of sexual desire turned out to be a stumbling block for subsequent investigators.

Different lines of thought and research flourished in the 1920s. At that time in sexology and the investigations of paraphilia, there were different approaches reflecting similar ideas in other countries. Thus, L. P. Sakharov (1926) and N. Sklyar (1933) shared M. Hirschfeld's views and developed the endocrinological field. B. D. Fridman (1927), N. A. Naumov (1927), and A. M. Haletsky (1927) adhered to the psychoanalytic interpretation of paraphilic etiopathogenesis. Soon, however, a firmly established administrative-command system began to show a tendency toward tightening control over all spheres of intellectual life, and that was accompanied by the political monopoly of scientific thought. In the 1930s, some books by Krafft-Ebing, Freud, and others that touched upon the issue of sexuality were removed from libraries.

Other psychiatric trends closely related to problems of sexual behavior fell victim to dogmatic political conceptions. The notorious session of the All-Union Academy of Agricultural Sciences, held in 1948, was especially infamous for dictating policy decisions in biology, natural selection and genetics. Thereafter, psychiatry realting to hereditary and brain localization was also in jeopardy. In 1950, after a joint session of the USSR Academy of Sciences and Academy of Medical Sciences, and according to orders of the Health Ministry, Dr. A. S. Shmaryan was barred from scientific activity and his clinic abolished. His investigations on clinical issues and psychopathology of local cerebral lesions (Shmaryan 1940, 1949) were characterized as "harmful, pseudoscientific, and vicious, with bourgeois-idealistic sources alien to Soviet science." Subsequently, however, Shmaryan's approach formed the basis for the neurohormonal component of the copulative cycle (Vasilchenko 1983). It also helped in the understanding of some pathogenetic links of anomalous sexuality (Blumer & Walker 1975; Blumer & Benson 1982; Money 1990; Flor-Henry 1991; and others).

Scientists were left with the only one instrument in their hands for explanation of paraphilic behavioral pathogenesis, and that was the theory of reflexes. I. P. Pavlov considered pathological desire to be a fixed system of conditioned and unconditioned reactions. When V. Bekhterev (1922) initially used a theory of combinative reflexes to explain paraphilia, he took into consideration, besides environmental influences, the innate characteristics of the nervous system. A simplified statement of Pavlov's principal theoretical postulates was passed from one book to another, despite developments and modifications contributed by more contemporary Russian physiologists.

The origin of another approach in forensic psychiatry can be detected in E. K. Krasnushkin's (1925) activity and that of the members of the Moscow Consulting Office, studying criminal personality and criminal nature. The starting point of their investigations was an interest in abnormal criminal behavior. Their multivariate approach proved to be a rather productive one, with the clinicopsychopathological method playing the leading, but not the exclusive, role. For the first time, studies in criminal behavior gained integrity. Biological and social determinants were jointly taken into account, and so, along with the psychopathological there were also sociological and psychological investigations, together with biochemical and anthropological ones. It was not by mere chance that the second collection of the Office was devoted to criminal sexual behavior as one of the top priority problems of forensic psychiatry (Krasnushkin et al. 1927). Attention to sexual crimes was probably determined by the fact that from this standpoint abnormal sexual behavior becomes a convenient and adequate pattern for studying not only sexual deviations but also common behavioral deviations.

However, objective research of paraphilia came into contradiction with the main postulates of dialectical materialism concerning the ratio of the biological and the social in a human being. Ideas on the leading role of the social were transferred into medicine and criminal law, and proved to be the main obstacle to the solution of the problem of paraphilic etiopathogenesis. Detection of biological reasons for abnormal sexual behavior contradicted the concept of criminality as caused by "deprivation, exploitation and injustice characteristic of the capitalist society" (Graham 1987). That was the reason why Krasnushkin's work was stopped, and why he was criticized for his "constitutional" approach, for his references to Lombrozo and for his overestimation of biological factors. For many years afterward multivariate investigations were impossible. Henceforth, paraphilias became a subject exclusively for psychopathological studies and have been mainly described in psychiatric manuals and textbooks devoted to psychopathology.

Sexological problems nevertheless continued to exist in forensic psychiatry and found no worthy solution. One of the first up-to-date studies of sexual perversions (Mokhov 1971) appeared in a series of works devoted to perverted desire. The most significant result of these works lies in the fact that psychopathological structure was found to be homogeneous and the dynamics of pathological desires were admitted to be natural, independent of their type, attesting to a common denominator in altered desires as a whole. Another important result of these perversion investigations was to renounce a rigid definition of "sexual psychopathy," because it turned out that typological characteristics of psychopathies apply only to superficial manifestations of sexual perversions.

Investigations of sexual perversions associated with other nosological entities were a logical continuation of the above studies. They showed the character of interaction between various mental disorders and sexual perversions, and the pathoplastic role of the main disorder in the development and clinical picture of paraphilia. However, the syndromologic approach to paraphilia used in these works does not involve the analysis of such important issues as the diverse pathogenetic links of abnormal sexual behavior, as well as the complexity of its psychopathological contents which require special consideration in solving the problem of responsibility. There is the limitation of the approach itself in that it does not regard paraphilia as an independent subject of investigation. At the same time, dynamic characteristics shown in these works testify to the absence of nosological specificity in clinical paraphilic manifestations, since similar regularities in their development are stated to be independent of the main psychiatric pathology. This independence thus indicates that paraphilia has its own peculiarly distinctive clinical feature.

It became increasingly evident that the limitations inherent in the traditional clinicopsychopathological method condemned further investigations to achieving only partial results, and could not lead to the development of criteria for expert appreciation of patients with paraphilias, nor to a solution of the problem concerning their treatment and subsequent rehabilitation and prevention of delinquency. This was because specificity of sexual pathology was ignored, whereas it demands special fields of knowledge, including data from psychiatry and other medical disciplines as well as the nonmedical sciences.

Recent investigations of paraphilia represent an attempt to perform a multidisciplinary study of abnormal sexual behavior, aimed at analysis of both psychopathological and constitutional dysontogenetic, neurobiological, and pathogenetic characteristics of perversions in their connection with forensic psychiatric and legal issues (Tkachenko 1991; Shostakovich et al. 1991; Shostakovich et al. 1992; Shostakovich & Tkachenko 1992; Kogan & Tkachenko in press; Drozdov & Kovaleva in press). Such extranosological examination of pathological desires allows one to consider the investigation of mental disorders in paraphilia to be at least as justified as the formerly prevalent investigations of sexual perversions and other variations of distorted drives within the framework of selected nosological units alone.

FORENSIC SEXOLOGY AND RUSSIAN CRIMINOLOGY

The legal concept of nonimputability (nonresponsibility) is most often used as a judicial basis for conducting forensic psychiatric evaluations and the closely connected forensic psychological and sexological evaluations. In the Russian Criminal Code, the concept of nonimputability in Part 1 of Article 11 is laid down as follows:

> A person who was in a state of nonimputability when committing a socially dangerous act—that is, when he could not be aware of his actions or could not govern them as a result of chronic mental disease, temporary mental derangement, mental deficiency or some other morbid state—is not subject to criminal responsibility. To such persons, involuntary measures of a medical nature may be applied if the court so rules.

Thus, the concept of nonimputability is defined by two criteria, namely medical and legal. The first one embraces all possible mental pathology. The second (awareness of actions committed or ability to govern them) characterizes morbid mental changes of such severity at the moment of a criminal offense as to exclude imputability. Since the 1920s, Soviet forensic psychiatry has been deprived of the opportunity to apply the concept of diminished imputability. At the same time, a number of psychiatrists considered this standard as the only just one with respect to persons with certain kinds of pathology (e.g., paraphilia). Article 15 of the draft of the criminal code introduces the concept of diminished imputability in the following manner:

> (1) A person who was in a state of diminished imputability when committing a socially dangerous act—that is, when he could not realize the full meaning of his actions or could not govern them as a result of morbid mental derangement—is not subject to criminal responsibility.
>
> (2) A state of diminished imputability can be taken into account in determining punishment and can be a basis for the application of medical measures.

It is important to note that a sharply increased interest in the problem of diminished imputability occurred at the same time as a keen interest in complex forms of expert evaluations. The valid introduction of diminished imputability in a particular case requires the elaboration of defining criteria that are successful in combining several independent forms of expert evaluation. It is through the combination of different knowledge bases of human behavior that a more complete understanding of individual behavior becomes possible, and a characterization of the different nature of his consciousness and self-regulation at the moment of the offense feasible.

Sexopathology itself is a multivariate discipline that integrates the achievements of many allied professions. However, psychiatry occupies a special place here. Sexual pathology suggests the involvement of a number of physiological systems, which result in the alteration of mental functioning or behavior. Such an interrelationship obliges a sexopathologist to acquire psychiatric knowledge, and often requires the integration of efforts of both the professions of sexology and psychiatry. Such integration is of special importance in forensic psychiatry when it is necessary to give an expert evaluation in cases connected with sexual behavior deviations. First of all, the evaluation concerns paraphilias. Such situations arise not only in cases of evident sexual deviations, but also in other pathological states in which the pathogenesis of the abnormalities of sexual and psychosexual development play a role. The participation of a sexopathologist in the process of diagnosis and evaluation is, in practice, always required in the analysis of such states.

Due to the accumulation of sexological knowledge, law-enforcement officials naturally have begun to attribute sexual offenses to morbid sexuality. Therefore, forensic psychiatrists are often questioned about the probable presence of sexual disorders in a person being evaluated, and the supposed connection to an act that has been committed. Traditional questions about other mental disorders are often ignored. However, in these cases the issue of a separate form of expert examination arises, namely the forensic sexology expert examination. In particular, it can solve specific problems unconnected with imputability. A need to solve simultaneously the problem of imputability forces the law-enforcement agencies to address such questions to forensic psychiatrists and to indicate necessary participation of a sexopathologist in the evaluation.

In the past as well as currently, a large number of questions that may be considered the purview of the sexopathologist have been taken up by other expert examiners. Thus forensic medical specialists have been inclined to consider forensic sexology as part of forensic medicine. Among the principle questions they address as part of an examination of a sexual offense are: motivation; the degree of sexual maturity; accepted sexual standards of behavior and deviations from that standard. Approached in this manner, however, such forensic medical evaluations may not use an adequate methodology, which is required for investigation of such phenomena as paraphilias that may be manifestations of both sexual and mental pathology. Therefore, the inadequacy of such an extension of the forensic medical evaluation at the expense of the inclusion of a separate forensic sexology expert evaluation is obvious.

The reason for such attempts to make extensions of forensic medicine are rooted in historical conditions of the development of sexology in Russia. The need for expert evaluations and the search for expert evidence in cases of sexual offenses existed long before sexology could be accepted in its own right as equal with other sciences and clinical disciplines. Therefore, there has traditionally existed a division of forensic medicine dealing with biomedical grounding of gender identification, sexual potency of males and females, identification of virginity and evidencies of deformation, sexual maturity, etc.

However, the performance of such examinations without the participation of psychiatrists and sexopathologists, in particular, often leads to a narrowing of the focus of these expert examinations and, not infrequently, to ungrounded conclusions. For example, in identifying true gender, forensic medicine has been oriented exclusively toward biological evidence of gender. It attaches excessive importance to the examination of "genital glands and the volume of their functional activity," meanwhile completely ignoring the multiple other variables of gender and the paramount role of gender identity, which is the principal criterion of personal gender attribution. Similar claims can be raised against other kinds of forensic medical expertise, for example, determination of a male's ability to engage in intercourse. Abnormalities of the sexual organs interfering with this ability are completely discovered by a sexological examination. However, a number of deviations, such as psychogenic disturbances and disorders caused by mental diseases or by pharmaceuticals, cannot be taken into account in the forensic medical evaluation.

Thus, the current approaches to using expert evaluations raise the issue of distinguishing the different expert examinations dealing with variable aspects of the same phenomenon. Another important issue is that of collaboration between sexopathologists and other professionals. The presence of behavioral and personality aspects in any sexual disorder stipulates the closeness of the sexological evaluation to the forensic psychiatric one, and in many cases these two types of expert examination should be combined. Such collaboration is indispensable in making a conclusion concerning imputability of a person with paraphilia and other sexual deviations, as well as in determining the medical intervention measures required.

The procedural concept of *complex expert examinations* forms the legal basis of collaboration in Russia. After heated discussions about the legality of complex expertise in the 1960s the majority of researchers and practitioners acknowledged their necessity. Complex expertise means, among other things, the application of special knowledge which constitutes the basis of professional training of experts, representing in their turn different kinds of forensic expertise. The specific methodology of a complex expert evaluation is the simultaneous examination of interrelated features (symptoms) of an object using different scientific methods, and the subsequent synthesis of the findings obtained with joint formulation of conclusions. Complex forensic psychiatric and psychologic evaluation has become one of the most well-known types of complex expert examination.

Complex forensic psychiatric and sexologic evaluation (hereinafter CFPSE) is the expertise combining special knowledge of two experts, a sexopathologist and a psychiatrist, for joint examination of psychosexual characteristics of a subject in order to reach conclusions of a forensic nature by virtue of the efforts of their joint competence.

Although the forensic sexologic evaluation can stand alone as the sole component of the CFPSE, utilizing the systematic and cross-disciplinary character of CFPSE considerably enhances the effectiveness of all the evaluations. The expert conclusions that are reached may be very different as a result of using the CFPSE approach versus the conducting of independent evaluations.

CFPSE can be used to answer forensic questions applied either to the alleged offender or to the alleged victim.

CFPSE Evaluations of the Alleged Offender

The validity of the CFPSE is derived from the questions it seeks to answer which reflect the competence of the various experts and the current state of knowledge. Critical questions with respect to the offender are:

1) determination of individual characteristics of sexual orientation;

2) how that orientation is realized or other distinctive features of the individual's sexuality;

3) determination of the effect of the sexual orientation on the offender's behavior at the moment of the criminal offense;

4) assessment of the degree of dangerousness posed by the offender;

5) selection of adequate medical measures in the event it is determined that the offender has met the legal critieria for nonimputability.

The completion of an evaluation implies a three-stage analysis of the abnormalities of sexuality within the individual: dysontogenetic, phenomenological, and syndromological.

Determination of dysontogenetic features of psychosexual development is obligatory in fulfilling any CFSPE work. Its manifestations are connected by the peculiarities of psychosexual and somatosexual development within the person as well as by deviations in any constituent of sexual maturation. Variations in sexual dysontogenesis should be identified prior to investigating the sexual behavioral disorder, and should in fact be done even if the latter is found to be absent. It may in itself provide the basis for a conclusion about the effect, more or less obvious, of sexual disorders on manifest behavior. Asynchronous sexual development greatly effects the manifestations of adult male sexuality and often influences many characteristics of sexual, including criminal, behavior. At the same time, evaluation of sexual maturation and psychosexual development allow one to observe pathogenic involvement of organic, neuroendocrine, sociopsychological and other factors in the process of sexual education and the formation of specific sexual behaviors.

The phenomenological stage consists of a specification of abnormality in the sexual drive of an individual. Perversions are polystructural formations, with each case characterized by its own combination of different paraphilias. Certain behaviors can meet different needs, while different types of sexual activity may serve the same modified drive. Therefore, identification of the leading component of a sexual disorder, especially the one that plays a role in a juridically important situation, is an essential part in the CFSPE. The specificity of sexual drive disorder differentiates it from other personality problems which serve only as a precondition of generalized illegal behavior. Paraphilias are motivational disorders and for that reason can be a direct cause of a criminal offense, which is their behavioral manifestation.

There are frequently consistent patterns of development, dynamics and clinical manifestations relative to paraphilias. The last stage of the evaluation process (syndromological) reflects an acknowledgement of these patterns. A syndromological peculiarity of paraphilias is that they may be manifested in different psychopathological states. These clinical syndromes differ in the degree of impairment in different spheres of mental functioning, as well as in the use of psychological defence mechanisms. Consequently, the syndrome may affect the ability of the individual to control his behavior. In order to define these conditions, different authors use different definitions (e.g., paraphilic fugue). We resort to a conditional subdivision of paraphilias into obsessive, compulsive, and impulsive so that we can, in each case, assess the degree of morbidity of the deviant acts. In some cases the evaluation may determine that the nature of such a condition may be sufficient to qualify the person under the criteria of nonimputability.

Because paraphilias often occur in feeble-minded persons, especially those with organic brain disorders, an analysis of the interaction of sexual abnormalities with other psychopathology is critical to a determination of culpability. Thus at the conclusion of the syndromological stage of the evaluation, the question of, first whether a sexopathological abnormality exists, and if so, second,whether the condition prevented the person from being aware of his actions or of being able to govern or control his actions when committing a criminal offense, should be answered. If the experts' decision is one that exculpates the subject, then they should also recommend appropriate medical interventions. Although voluntary treatment may be available, most frequently the recommendation is for involuntary treatment, since the subject is typically resistant to intervention. There are three degrees of involuntary treatment in hospitals, namely *strict, intensified,* or *common* observation.

At present the conditions required for treatment of imputable and sentenced persons are practically absent. However, we hope that our proposals concerning the need for such treatment will be approved by decision makers and introduced into the law as a legislative standard.

CFSPE Evaluations of the Victim

The second type of CFSPE evaluation concerns the victim of a sexual offense. Such evaluations entail determination of: (a) the victim's degree or state of helplessness and (b) the severity of the injuries constituting separate *corpus delicti.*

The determination of victim helplessness requires examination of victims' capability to properly understand the character and nature of the sexual actions with respect to them, and their ability to resist in such actions. Attainment of this capability implies a level of psychosexual development sufficient for the correct assessment of events taking place and adequate or appropriate response to them.

In case of a sexual offense, the psychogenic effect on the victim is specific in character depending on the victim's personality, level of psychophysiological development and other factors. The effects also encompass alteration of subsequent psychosexual development and any manifestations of sexuality. In sexual offenses, the assessment of psychic processes and the victim's individual characteristics, as well as immediate or remote aftereffects, requires special sexological knowledge within the framework of victimological examinations. The key evaluation issue here is the establishment of a causal relationship between the detected psychopathological phenomena and the psychic trauma. Thus, in the examination of victims of sexual offenses, the critical forensic question is whether the victim, with his or her level of psychosexual development, could properly understand the character and the nature of sexual actions and resist them at the moment of a criminal offense, taking into consideration the conditions of the actual situation. A second related question concerns the kinds of immediate and remote effects of the specific illegal actions for the victim and the degree to which those actions have resulted in severe disorders in the mental and sexual spheres.

SUMMARY

The tasks described above do not reveal the whole of CFSPE potential, but only provide a sample of the tasks related to criminal procedures. Its possibilities can be significantly extended in combination with other kinds of expert evaluations. The whole complex of forensic sexological evaluation, from theoretical to organizational aspects, should be developed in the future.

REFERENCES

Bekhterev, V. M. (1922). "Polovye uklonenija i izvrashcheija v' svete reflexologii" (Sexual Deviations and Perversions from the Point of View of Reflexology). In *Voprosy izuchenija vospitanija lichnosti* (*Issues of Investigation of Personality Upbringing*). Petrograd.

Bekhterev, V. M., and Mislavski, N. A. (1891). "O mozgovykh tsentrakh dvijenija vlagalishcha u jivotnykh" (On Brain Centers Governing Vaginal Movements in Animals). *Meditsinskoe obozrenie* (*Medical Review*) 36: 247–59.

Blumer, D., and Benson, D. F. (1982). "Psychiatric Manifestations of Epilepsy." In *Psychiatric Aspects of Neurologic Disease*, pp. 25–41. New York.

Blumer, D., and Walker, A. E. (1975). "The Neural Basis of Sexual Behavior." In *Psychiatric Aspects of Neurologic Disease*, pp. 199–215. New York.

Chlenov, E. G. (1908). *Polovaja perepis moskovskogostudechestvai ejo obshchestvennoe znachenie* (*Gender Census of Moscow Students and Its Social Significance*). Moscow.

Flor-Henry, P. (1991). "Quantitative EEG Studies of Pedophilia." *International Journal of Psychophysiology* 10: 253–58.

Graham, L. R. (1987). *Science, Philosophy, and Human Behavior in the Soviet Union.* New York: Columbia University Press.

Kogan, B. M.; Tkachenko, A. A.; Drozdov, A. Z.; and Kovaleva, I. N. (in press). "Aktivnost dofamin-b-gidroxilazy u lits s parafilijami" (Dopamine-b-Hydroxylase Activity in Paraphilic Persons). *Sotsialnaja i klinicheskaja psikhiatrija* (*Social and Clinical Psychiatry*).

Krasnushkin, E. K.; Segal, G. M.; and Fainberg, Ts. M., eds. (1925). *Izuchenie lichnosti prestupnlka v SSSR i za granitsej* (*Investigation of the Criminal Personality in the USSR and Abroad*). Moscow.

Money, J. (1990). "Forensic Sexology: Paraphilic Serial Rape and Lust Murder." *American Journal of Psychotherapy* 44: 26–36.

Pussep, L. P. (1912). "O mozgovykh tsentrakh, upravljajushchikh erektsiej polovogo chlena i semjaotdeleniem" (On Brain Centers Controlling Erection and Ejaculation). Doctoral Thesis of Medicine. Moscow.

Shmarjan, A. S. (1940). *Psikhopatologicheskie sidromy pri porazheijakh visochnykh dolej mozga* (*Psychopathological Syndromes in Temporal Lobe Brain Damage*). Moscow.

——— (1949). *Mozgovaja patologija i psikhiatrija* (*Brain Pathology and Psychiatry*). Moscow.

Shostakovich, B. V.; Smirnova, L. K.; Tkachenko, A. A.; Usjukina, M. V.; Marinina, G. P.; and Nikolaeva, T. N. (1991). "Kliniko-biokhimicheskie khrakteristiki lits s parafilijami pri khromosomnoj anomalii (XYY)" (Clinicobiochemical Characteristics of Paraphilic Persons with Chromosome Anomalies [XYY]). *Zhurnal nevropatologii i psikhiatrii imeni S. S. Korsakova* (*Korsakov's Joural of Neuropathology and Psychiatry*) 3: 24–27.

Shostakovich, B. V., and Tkachenko, A. A. (1992). *Exgibitsionizm* (*Exhibitionism*). Moscow: Taganrog.

Shostakovich, B. V.; Tkachenko, A. A.; Smirnova, L. K.; Ushakova, I. M.; Kartelishchev, A. V.; and Nikolaeva, T. N. (1992). "Sravnitelnaja otsenka biokhimicheskikh i psikhopatologicheslikh kharakteristik u lits s priznakami pedofilii" (Comparative Assessment of Biochemical and Psychopathological Characteristics in Pedophilic Persons). *Zhurnal nevropatologii i psikhiatrii imeni S. S. Korsakova* (*Korsakov's Journal of Neuropathology and Psychiatry*) 5: 83–88.

Tkachenko, A. A. (1991) "Kliniko-patogeneticheskie osobennosti exgibitsionizma" (Clinico-Pathogenetic Characteristics of Exhibitionism). *Zhurnal nevropatologii i psikhiatrii imeni S. S. Korsakova* (*Korsakov's Journal of Neuropathology and Psychiatry*) 5: 65–70.

Vasilchenko, G. S., ed. (1979). *Obshchaja sexopatologija* (*General sexopathology*). Moscow.

——— (1983). *Chastnaja sexopatologija* (*Special Sexopathology*). Moscow.

23

A Paradigm Shift for Expert Witnesses*

Ralph Underwager and Hollida Wakefield

A nation's justice system determines factual issues that cannot be settled in any other forum. In this search for truth the courts have, over the centuries, developed policies and methods for evaluating arguments and evidence. These methods and policies permit the court to deal with human events within a social, political, and historical context. While neither perfect nor totally reliable, the justice system has the virtue of being highly flexible, thus allowing the legal professionals who function within it to interpret a great deal of evidence and resolve a wide variety of questions. Consequently, no other profession has thought as much about the nature of evidence and the inferences that properly may be drawn from that evidence.

In recent years the courts have both accepted and invited greater participation in the justice system by scientists. A special category of evidence, opinion as contrasted with fact, has been developed which permits scientists to offer, as evidence, an opinion. However, across the years, the courts have been frequently troubled with resolving the question of how to determine whether or not an opinion, in a specific instance, has sufficient validity and reliability to be accepted as evidence. Although frequently criticized and understood to be unsatisfactory (e.g., Giannelli 1980; Imwinkelried 1992; McCord 1986) the *Frye* rule[1] has, since its adoption in 1923, been used by the courts to determine the evidentiary value and, therefore, the admissibility, of an expert opinion. Specifically, *Frye* requires that expert opinion must be based upon a theory or methodology that has received general acceptance within the

---

*Reprinted with permission. Originally published in *Issues in Child Abuse Accusations* 5, no. 3 (1993).

particular field in which it belongs.

Understanding how science works is the continuing effort of cliometric (cumulative, combined statistics) metatheoreticians (Meehl 1992b). This understanding is key to the effective use of science as an adjunct to the truth-seeking process of the courts. Kuhn (1962) introduced a new philosophy of science predicated upon the conceptual scheme of scientific revolutions. This view holds that within a field of science, paradigm shifts occur periodically, in which some totally new and different model suddenly emerges and becomes dominant. Before this shift, scientists continue to work out the implications of the prevailing model—what Kuhn calls "normal science." When a scientific revolution occurs and an entirely new model takes over—as when quantum physics superseded Newtonian physics—new questions and problems emerge, new discoveries are made and new techniques are developed. In legal principles, it is just such a paradigm shift—the principle of falsification proposed by Popper (1959)—that forms the basis for a new set of criteria to be applied to decisions about admissibility of scientific expert testimony. The consequence is an analogous revolution of science in the courtroom.

DAUBERT V. *MERRELL DOW PHARMACEUTICALS*

A unanimous U.S. Supreme Court decision issued on June 28, 1993, dramatically changes the expectations and roles of scientists who provide testimony as expert witnesses. The *Frye* rule is now superseded by this decision. The Court's ruling in *Daubert* v. *Merrell Dow Pharmaceuticals*[2] effectively establishes, as the law of the land, the Popperian principle of falsification as the determinant of scientific knowledge (see below). The initial reactions of the legal profession to the court's decision suggest that the full impact of this decision has not yet been perceived. Both sides in the original dispute viewed the decision as a victory. Commentators do not see that much will change although they expect more litigation over the admissibility of scientific testimony (Reuben 1993). Such an underestimation of impact is not surprising, since it would be unrealistic to expect attorneys and judges to be knowledgeable about the philosophy of science.

In one form or another, most states have adopted the Federal Rules of Evidence as the guide for determining the admissibility of evidence within court proceedings. Consequently, this Supreme Court ruling will have an effect far beyond federal trials. While it may take several years to fully integrate *Daubert* into case law and precedent, this decision will eventually change markedly what is admitted as scientific expert evidence in all trials. The result will be nothing less than a revolutionary paradigm shift that replaces a naive logical positivism with the contemporary understanding of the nature of science. The decision sets forth this momentous shift in this paragraph:

> Ordinarily, a key question to be answered in determining whether a theory or technique is scientific knowledge that will assist the trier of fact will be whether it can be (and has been) tested. "Scientific methodology today is based on generating hypotheses and testing them to see if they can be falsified; indeed, this methodology is what distinguishes science from other fields of human inquiry." Green at 645 (1992). See also C. Hempel, *Philosophy of Natural Science* 49 (1966) ("[T]he statements constituting a scientific explanation must be capable of empirical test"); K. Popper, *Conjectures and Refutations: The Growth of Scientific Knowledge* 37 (5th ed. 1989) ("[T]he criterion of the scientific status of a theory is its falsifiability, or refutability, or testability") (*Daubert*, pp. 12–13).

Falsifiability thus specifically replaces the *Frye* test as the arbiter of what kind of scientific expert witness is admissible. The opinion is based on the judgment that the Federal Rules of Evidence supersede the *Frye* test. Rule 402 is cited as establishing the baseline for what constitutes admissible evidence:

> All relevant evidence is admissible, except as otherwise provided by the Constitution of the United States, by Act of Congress, by these rules, or by other rules prescribed by the Supreme Court pursuant to statutory authority. Evidence which is not relevant is not admissible. (*Daubert*, p. 6)

The Court then specifically applies Rule 702 in its determination of the admissibility of scientific evidence in the resolution of a disputed issue.

> If scientific, technical, or other specialized knowledge will assist the trier of fact to understand the evidence or to determine a fact in issue, a witness qualified as an expert by knowledge, skill, experience, training, or education, may testify thereto in the form of an opinion or otherwise. (*Daubert*, p. 8)

The Court then states that the trial judge must initially determine that an expert is proposing to testify regarding ". . . (1) scientific knowledge that (2) will assist the trier of fact to understand or determine a fact in issue" (*Daubert*, p. 12). While the majority opinion expresses confidence that trial judges have the capacity to determine this question, the partial dissent by Chief Justice William Rehnquist concludes:

> I defer to no one in my confidence in federal judges; but I am at a loss to know what is meant when it is said that the scientific status of a theory depends on its "falsifiability," and I suspect some of them will be, too. (*Daubert*, pp. 3–4)

In this instance, Rehnquist is almost assuredly correct. Judges will neither readily understand this principle nor consistently apply it without training and education. Neither judges nor attorneys can acquire an adequate understanding of this paradigm shift in a few hours at a conference seminar. Unfortunately, many psychologists themselves have little or no understanding of falsifiability. This may be even more true of psychiatrists and social workers, few of whom will understand this principle and how it changes the rules of the game. Proper and effective assimilation of this revolutionizing construct into the justice system will require a major educational and training effort for all the players involved—scientists, attorneys, and judges.

Consequently, scientists must engage in an educational program to support understanding of this shift and what it means practically in the real world of the courtroom. One such implication is that a major role of scientific testimony may be to proffer an opinion as to the lack of credible scientific data to support a specific claim (Meehl 1989). To do this properly, the scientist must have a clear understanding of the current state of philosophy of science and be able to communicate this understanding to lay audiences.

FALSIFIABILITY

To understand the concept of falsifiability one must recognize the difference between two different meanings of the word "falsifiable" (Popper 1992: xxii). In the first meaning, falsifiable is a logical-technical term related to the criterion of falsifiability. This means that the theory or concept in question must be capable of being falsified—that is, be precise and specific enough to have something count against it. In the second meaning, falsifiable is used in the sense that the theory or concept in question can be "*definitively* or *conclusively* or *demonstrably* falsified (demonstrably falsifiable)."

The first sense refers only to the potential logical possibility of a theory or concept being falsified in principle. The second sense includes a persuasive practical demonstration using scientific procedures to produce a proof of falsity. That is, do credible research studies produce results that mean the theory cannot be maintained? There has been some discussion suggesting that final empirical proofs of falsity cannot be obtained, but Popper maintains that the potential uncertainty of falsity should not be taken too seriously (Popper 1992). Thus the principle of falsification provides two basic ways in which a judge may determine that proffered expert testimony does not meet the criterion of falsifiability. The first is whether or not it is, in principle, falsifiable and the second is whether or not it has been falsified.

The practice of blood-letting provides an example of how an understanding of the different meanings of these two uses of "falsifiable" can be promoted. For about two hundred years, physicians believed that drawing off blood cured disease. The standard treatment was to open a vein and draw a basin of blood. George Washington died from this treatment. For centuries physicians reasoned that a person who was bled and lived, was saved by the procedure. Conversely, a person who died was considered to have been so sick that nothing would have helped anyway. With this line of reasoning, it is impossible to falsify bleeding as a specific treatment for disease. This represents the first meaning of term "falsifiable." Subsequent research predicated on germ theory and other medical advances eventually proved blood letting to be a false cure, thus showing the theory was demonstrably falsifiable—the second meaning of the term.

Sir Karl Popper, who advanced the concept of falsifiability, and is specifically quoted in the *Daubert* decision, demonstrates at great length in his two-volume work, *The Open Society and Its Enemies,* that Freudian theory, like Marxism, is unfalsifiable. That Freudian theory has so pervaded psychological and psychiatric theory and thought during this century, illustrates the potential of the *Daubert* decision to fundamentally change what had been traditionally accepted with a field. Popper's critique of Freud draws heavily on the first meaning of the criterion of falsifiability. Freudian theory uses a convoluted conceptual structure that explains all human behavior after the fact. Adherents of Freudian psychoanalytic theory offer authoritative sounding explanations for all human behaviors, from individual quirks and slips of the tongue to large-scale social phenomena such as religion. It is unscientific because nothing can count against it. There is no point at which it is subject to falsification. This type of theory attempts to provide a *post hoc* explanation for every possible event, but is incapable of predicting any particular event. A successful scientific theory, by contrast, predicts outcomes from a discrete set of events with an ascertainable degree of reliability.

Although Freudian concepts may serve a purpose in psychotherapy, its lack of falsifiability means that psychiatric testimony based on Freudian psychoanalytic concepts should now be inadmissible as scientific evidence in court. It would hardly be possible for a judge—who must follow this Supreme Court decision—to rule otherwise when the *Daubert* decision specifically quotes Popper and holds that falsifiability is the determinant of what is scientific, and when that same judge is also confronted with Popper's assessment of Freudian dynamic thought as a premier example of failure to meet the criterion of falsification.

With some variations, American psychiatry is, by and large, Freudian in its orientation. The theories and concepts used by psychiatrists postulate all manner of internal processes and hidden events that cannot be falsified because they are not testable. It is also the case that wherever Freudian theory has been subjected to empirical tests, it has either failed or, at best, been inconclusive as a predictor of human behavior. It could be that the only material about which a Freudian psychiatrist should be permitted to testify is the organic assumptions of chemical imbalance as the origin and cause of emotional distress, and the subject matter of neurology. The use of the American Psychiatric Association's nosology, the *Diagnostic and Statistical Manual,* third edition, revised (*DSM-III-R*) (American Psychiatric Association 1987) may also be questioned on the grounds of its lack of reliability and testability (Kirk & Kutchins 1992).

Grand theories that are so global, indeterminate, and lacking in precision that they can be used to explain everything and anything, are ruled out as science by the principle of falsification. Theories and concepts that are developed to provide emotional security and are not meant to be changed or subjected to empirical evaluation, however comforting they may be, are not scientific and cannot be offered to the courts as such.

There is no shortage of these fuzzy, grand, cosmic explanatory systems. In an era when we are, supposedly, at least somewhat sophisticated about science, all manner of false knowledge abounds. The astrology column's daily horoscope is frequently described as the most read section of the paper. Otherwise intelligent people firmly believe in UFO alien abductions, conspiracy theories, satanic ritual abuse in day care centers, extrasensory perception, and parapsychology. Questionable taxonomic entities such as Multiple Personality Disorder—which is most likely a phenomenon generated by the procedures of the therapist (Aldridge-Morris 1989; Fahy 1988; Orne et al. 1984; Spanos et al. 1985; Weissberg 1993)—are accepted in the official nomenclature. Thought is cheap and any verbally fluent and somewhat intelligent person can come up with an unfalsifiable theory of the universe: a complex, yet untestable, description of human motivations that are plausible sounding formulations used to form postdictions or totally false accounts of prior events.

On the other hand, science is hard. It is imperfect. As Popper says, it is not an episteme, a way of knowing. Real scientists laboriously count and recount, reviewing mounds of data sheets. They do not proffer speculation because they are aware that other, junior scientists will always be collecting more data, looking to challenge the accepted wisdom. Actually producing the theories that serve as scientific explanations of observed phenomena is a difficult task. Nevertheless, the general public can be helped to understand the purpose, principles and methodology of science. It is not necessary to be a working scientist to know what science is.

Attainment of this goal of public education, however, confronts and challenges the tendency of humans to seek confirmation and support of beliefs already held and to ignore or not perceive contrary evidence (Arkes & Harkness 1980; Dawes 1992; West 1992). In an experiment comparing physical scientists, psychologists, and fundamentalist clergymen on the capacity to use falsification in reasoning, Mahoney and DeMonbreun (1977) report no differences between the groups in reasoning ability and in the generation of confirmatory rather than disconfirmatory experiences to test their hypotheses: "Both scientists and nonscientists showed marked tendencies to confirm rather than disconfirm their hypotheses and, contrary to the popular image, they did not differ in this respect" (p. 236). These findings suggest that an apparent human bias must be overcome for falsification to be understood and used.

The findings about confirmatory bias further suggest that the choice to approach a determination of scientific status by the principle of falsification must be self-consciously and structurally maintained. Even being trained as a scientist does not overcome this confirmatory bias or guarantee straight thinking (Meehl 1992b). Therefore, if the decision of the Supreme Court is to be carefully and adequately integrated into American jurisprudence, there must be an immediate effort to train judges and attorneys to understand these issues in the philosophy of science and to assimilate carefully, step by step, the import of this ruling into case law. Failure in this endeavor could be chaotic and result in a disservice to all parties involved in the resolution of disputes and application of criminal justice.

EXPERT TEXTIMONY IN CASES OF ALLEGED CHILD SEXUAL ABUSE

An area where the principle of falsifiability, testability, and degree of error may have a major impact is in the kind of testimony frequently offered by the prosecution in child sexual abuse cases. In case after case, testimony that has been offered by experts for the state presents as science conjecture and speculation of such a nature that any and every claim proves, supports, or is "consistent with" abuse, and therefore is not falsifiable.

The nature of such testimony—as unfalsifiable—becomes clear when the observations used to support allegations of abuse are delineated. Abuse is supported when the following occurs:

- The child makes any statement that may be broadly interpreted to imply abuse. Since it is assumed that children cannot lie about abuse and cannot talk about things they have not directly experienced, all such statements must be taken at face value, regardless of their face validity or incredibility.

- The child initially denies abuse but later discloses it after "disclosure therapy." The child will initially deny abuse because the child needs time to overcome shame and embarrassment, develop a trusting relationship with the therapist, and then feel safe enough to disclose the abuse. In the interval, it is perfectly proper to use leading and suggestive questioning, coercion, persuasion, and any other methods of social influence, to assist the child in disclosing the terrible secret.

- The child initially acknowledges some abuse, but then recants or retracts earlier statements. Though recanted or retracted, the abuse allegation is still true because the child is under pressure from the perpetrator or the family to recant and is scared. Recantation is described as typical of children who have been abused and, therefore, has been argued to prove abuse.
- The child "discloses" abuse years after the period encompassed by the allegation. Even given demonstrable adult social influence triggering the disclosure, the assumption is that it is typical of abused children that they will delay disclosure, even until as late as midlife.
- The child "discloses" abuse immediately after the period encompassed by the allegation. The child is viewed as overwhelmed by the abuse, or is too fearful to maintain the secret, or has found him/herself in a "safe" situation within which to disclose the abuse.
- The medical examination finds genital "trauma" indicative of sexual abuse. Medical findings of genital "trauma" may or may not take into consideration the baseline rates of similar genital findings in nonabused children.
- The medical examination finds no genital "trauma" which, given the frequency of fondling and nonpenetrative sexual contact as the predominate act of sexual abuse, is consistent with the child having been abused.
- The child is calm and cooperative during a genital examination. Such a child is viewed as experienced in having the genitals touched and examined by virtue of the abusive experience (i.e., has been desensitized to genital contact).
- The child struggles and resists the genital examination, or becomes emotionally distraught by the exam. Such a child has previously been traumatized by sexual abuse leading to his/her reluctance to have anyone else touch or examine the genitals.
- In the absence of physical findings, the adult accompanying the child to the medical exam informs the physician of the abuse history. The physician, though finding no physical evidence of sexual abuse, renders the conclusion "abuse by history" as a result of the report of abuse by the accompanying adult.

The same inability to falsify the claim of abuse may found in the interpretation of the behavior of the person accused. Thus abuse is supported when:

- The accused proclaims innocence. Such individuals are "in denial" regarding the abuse.
- The accused passes the polygraph or penile plethysmograph. Such individuals are in even greater denial regarding the abuse.
- The accused shows little or no emotion when being confronted or questioned about the abuse. The accused is thus either in denial, is sociopathic, or is a master manipulator and has little concern for society's mores and values.
- The accused becomes emotional or tearful when confronted or questioned about the abuse. The accused is overwhelmed by guilt and disgust over his/her behavior.
- The accused becomes angry or defiant when confronted or questioned about abuse. The accused is defending against his/her actions by projecting blame and responsibility onto others.
- The accused requests to speak to an attorney before questioning. If the accused had nothing to hide, an attorney would not be needed.
- The accused cooperates with the interrogator and, in attempting to identify the source of the abuse accusation, talks about innocuous or ambiguous behavior. The statements of the accused are thus viewed as confessions as he/she is struggling to admit the true nature of the abusive acts.

As this sampling of typical rationalizations illustrates, almost any circumstance, behavior or observation can be interpreted as supporting the conclusion that sexual abuse occurred. What makes such testimony, and its underlying theory, not falsifiable is the fact that there is no circumstance, behavior or observation which could be used to conclude that abuse did not occur. Consequently, there are no circumstances under which one could endeavor to prove the underlying theory false.

Widely disseminated lists of behavioral indicators, many of which are contradictory, are frequently offered as evidence to support the accusation of abuse. In testimony, all manner of behavior is declared to be typical of abused children, all without scientific evidence to support the claims. Depression or mania, hyperactivity or hypoactivity, social aggression or social withdrawal, heightened modesty or no modesty, poor hygiene or excessive concern about cleanliness, extreme compliance or opposition are all offered as evidence of abuse. This is done in spite of the fact that reasoning backward in time from observed symptoms to some prior entity or event is to commit the logical error of affirming the consequence. There are no behavioral indicators, including the absence of any problem behaviors, that can *falsify* abuse.

Consequently, in "disclosure therapy" a child may draw scribbled shapes on paper and use black or red crayons. These observations may support a therapist's testimony that these are the colors used by children who have been sexually abused and that abused children typically include phallic shapes in their drawings—despite the fact that most children's drawing include elongated shapes which might be interpreted, by one so inclined, as a phallic symbol. In hundreds of cases reviewed by the authors, there has never been an instance of a child's drawings being interpreted as supporting the *absence* of abuse. Illustrative of the extent of the rationalizations which must be offered in support of abuse inferred in the absence of evidence—and thus typifying a nonfalsifiable, unscientific theory—is the case of a young girl suspected of having been abused, who drew a picture of herself and her sister with their father. All were smiling and the two girls' arms were raised in the air. The child's description of the behavior reflected in the drawing was that they were cheering at a game. However, the therapist testified in spite of the child's explanation, that the upraised arms meant the girls were crying for help. She interpreted this as indicating that the child had, in fact, been abused, despite the fact that the child denied abuse.

Testimony of this sort is, in the truest sense, quixotic communication. Don Quixote provides an example of a theory that cannot be disconfirmed. Don Quixote, when confronted by Sancho Panza with disconfirming evidence about Mambrino's helmet, transforms the contradiction into a verification (Lee 1987). To Don Quixote the helmet is miraculous while to Sancho Panza it is an ordinary barber's basin. Don Quixote reasons to himself as follows:

> Mambrino's helmet, that object of immense value, appear[s] to everyone a barber's basin, thus protecting its owner from persecution by all those who would understand its true meaning. (Lee 1987: 555)

By this line of reasoning all contrary assertions are transformed by mental alchemy into evidence that supports Don Quixote's view and thus nothing appears unexplained, troublesome, or puzzling. Everything proves the reasoner right, and so the subjective experience is to make the erroneous belief stronger and more certain.

When the principle of falsification is properly applied to the courtroom, this quixotic kind of testimony should be declared inadmissible and not helpful to the finder of fact. It cannot assist in arriving at the most accurate decision possible. It can only increase the level and magnitude of the error generated.

SYNDROME EVIDENCE

There are a number of psychological syndromes about which experts testify in a wide variety of civil and criminal litigation which may not be testable or falsifiable when subjected to the analysis now required by *Daubert*. Myers (1993) notes that both diseases and syndromes share the medically and forensically important feature of *diagnostic value*. Both point, with varying degrees of certainty, to particular causes. However, whereas the relationship between symptoms and etiology is clear in many syndromes or diseases, this relationship is often unclear or unknown with respect to others. The certainty with which a syndrome points to a particular cause varies with the syndrome.

Myers (1993) discusses the difference between two syndromes of abuse in which expert testimony is often offered. The battered child syndrome has high certainty since a child with the symptoms of the syndrome is very likely to have suffered nonaccidental injury. In this syndrome, nonaccidental injuries typically can be distinguished from accidental injuries by the nature of the injuries. The predictions from this theory, therefore, meet the criterion of falsifiability of the *Daubert* decision and, consequently, evidence regarding this syndrome has high probative value and, in fact, has been approved by every appellate court to consider it.

This may be contrasted with the so-called child sexual abuse accommodation syndrome (CSAAS) which does not point with any certainty to sexual abuse. The fact that a child shows behaviors attributed to the CSAAS does not help determine whether the child actually was sexually abused, since observation of those behaviors does not allow one to reliably distinguish the child who has been abused from a child who has not—both may share similar behavior. The CSAAS is a nondiagnostic syndrome. Despite the lack of probative value of the CSAAS, it has been frequently offered by prosecutors as substantive evidence of sexual abuse. However, it does not meet the test of falsifiability when used to support abuse since there is nothing that can count against it. Therefore, *Daubert* should lead to the judicial decision that use of the CSAAS is inadmissible.

REPRESSION AND CLAIMS OF RECOVERED MEMORY

A careful application of the *Daubert* decision within the justice system may well also result in expert testimony supporting claims of recovered repressed memories of childhood abuse being declared inadmissible. This type of case provides an example of the second meaning of the criterion of falsifiability. Repression, a Freudian theoretical concept, cannot be proved and is widely discredited (Bower 1990; Garry & Loftus 1993; Holmes 1990; Wakefield &

Underwager 1992). Although proponents of recovered repressed memories offer three studies to support a claim of repression (Briere & Conte 1989; Herman & Schatzow 1987; Williams 1992), none of them proves repression or provides any credible scientific evidence of it.

Faced with the massive weight of over sixty years of research that discredits the concept of repression, a reasonable judge must rule that testimony based upon the concept is not scientific; it cannot be relevant or helpful to the finder of fact; and, therefore, it is not admissible. Such rulings would make it impossible for civil suits seeking monetary damages based upon a claim of recovered repressed memories to be pursued. It should result in the repeal of laws that have been passed in a number of states that essentially permit legal actions based on claims of recovered repressed memory whenever abuse is remembered or subsequent to the alleged victims' claim to have recognized that they were damaged by alleged childhood abuse. Any criminal convictions based upon evidence or testimony that derives from such a claim of a recovered repressed memory should be reversed and remanded for a new trial or else dismissed.

ISSUES IN PSYCHOLOGY AS A SCIENCE

The Popperian falsifiability principle makes psychology much more vulnerable to the impact of data falsifying its theories than, for example, physics. Meehl (1967, 1978) argues that the dominant method of assessing research in psychology, significance testing, is nothing more than statistical games and that such tests are very soft and weak measures. Meehl (1978) maintains that "the null hypothesis, taken literally, is always false" (p. 822). Furthermore, when one study may produce a .50 level of correlation and another study a .34 level, although the difference is statistically significant, it may be so small as to have very little relevance to the real world (Meehl 1978). Therefore, support for the truth of a hypothesis subjected to statistical significance testing is weak, whereas support for a falsification is much more decisive (Bowers 1977; Dar 1987). Schmidt (1992) describes the great difficulty in getting psychologists to move away from routine significance testing to a more rigorous approach. He asserts that significance testing has led to serious errors in interpreting the meaning of data and retarded the accumulation of knowledge. Meehl's basic criticism is that most journal articles reviewing an area of psychology consist of a listing of all the relevant studies located within some set of specified parameters and then a counting of those for and those against a particular proposition (Hedges & Olkin 1980). This nose counting is preposterous, according to Meehl (1978), because by the principle of falsification a single refutation is far more powerful than multitudinous corroborations:

> [T]he whole idea of simply counting noses is wrong because a theory that has seven facts for it and three facts against it is not in good shape, and it would not be considered so in any developed science. (p. 823)

This argument is essential in dealing with the courtroom advocates and judges who may be influenced by a nose counting or box score approach. That professionals are so easily influenced by this type of thinking may be due to the fact that most relatively bright and competent people have learned in school that science proceeds by the inductive method of making observations, testing them, and accepting the results as proof of the hypothesis. This naive view is no longer even partially correct as a description of science. The conceptual advance in the philosophy of science represented by the Popperian principle of falsification simply has not caught on with society.

Psychology is responding to these criticisms by developing the methods of meta-analysis and effect size. Meta-analysis (Meehl 1992a; Mullen et al. 1985) has demonstrated the weakness of individual research studies and pointed out the problems in sampling error, measurement error, and other artifacts in individual studies. Contrary to popular belief no single study can resolve an issue or answer a question. "Only meta-analytic analysis across studies can control chance and other statistical and measurement artifacts and provide a trustworthy foundation for conclusions" (Schmidt 1992: 1179–80). Effect size assesses the probability that an investigation will lead to statistically significant results. Whereas meta-analysis has been accepted and is being more widely used, effect size has been relatively ignored in the conduct of psychological research (Cohen 1992; Strube 1985). Both of these approaches to the interpretation of data will be necessary to assess the impact of the Supreme Court's decision on the admissibility of expert testimony based on the science of psychology.

When attempting to deal with scientific testimony that is counter to a proposition advanced in the courtroom, attorneys may ask if there are other studies that contradict that testimony. When the accurate answer is that there are contradictory studies, the questioning stops and the advocate thinks the witness has been impeached, and the impact of the scientific testimony lessened or removed. When a judge, who may have a naive view of scientific research, is confronted with opposing experts, the judge may come to view the process as an undesirable battle of the experts rather than as a fact-finding process. The result may be that relevant scientific testimony is not admitted since the judge may assume that all studies are on the same footing and have equal validity and reliability. Then one simply adds up the box score to see which side has the greater number of corroborative studies, and that side is the winner. This approach to science ignores the existence of both good and bad research, a fact every scientist is aware of. All studies are not equal nor does bad science meet the minimal qualifications of research design, execution and replication. The box score approach ignores the greater significance that must be given to falsification.

The Supreme Court decision in *Daubert* remedies this misunderstanding and makes the box score approach unacceptable. No matter how many corroborative studies there are, a single instance of a well-done and credible study that falsifies the theory or concept or technique, may outweigh them all and make the corroborative material inadmissible.

A review of all the briefs, motions, and amicus curiae briefs submitted to the court in this case strongly suggests that the decision is primarily based on the amicus brief submitted by the Carnegie Commission on Science, Technology, and Government as *Amicus Curiae* in Support of Neither Party (Berger et al. 1992). This is the only brief that contains reference to the principle of falsifiability, testability, and replication. It is the suggested framework of this brief as a replacement for the *Frye* Rule that is adopted by the Supreme Court in its decision.

This brief also suggests the inclusion of the degree of error as a factor for judges to consider when evaluating the scientific quality of claims for admission as testimony. The brief advises the court that a judge may have to consider study design, data collection, or error rate to determine whether the methodology used was so skewed as to justify exclusion. The decision states it as follows:

> Additionally, in the case of a particular scientific technique, the court ordinarily should consider the known or potential rate of error . . . and the existence and maintenance of standards controlling the technique's operation. (pp. 14–15)

The Supreme Court's inclusion of statistical error rate (including false positives and false negatives) as a factor in assessing the admissibility of evidence opens the door to the scientific analyses of the error rates in the entire system of child protection, law enforcement, and criminal justice in dealing with allegations of child sexual abuse. For example, if this factor is considered by judges and applied in a rational manner, much of the testimony based on a medical examination for evaluation of a child sexual abuse allegation will be inadmissible. The best scientific evidence that gives an indication of the potential error rate for medical examinations concludes that the error rate for physicians' claims that a medical examination supports penile penetration is 63 percent; for claims of digital penetration, 73 percent; and for a general conclusion of abuse, over 70 percent (Paradise 1989; Zeitlin 1987). Such a high error rate, always in the direction of false positives, can only confuse the entire process. (See chapter 10 of this volume for a more comprehensive discussion of the application of Bayes Theorem in analyzing the error rate of the decision-making process.)

This information on the error rates is established by the Supreme Court as a vital factor in assessing the scientific nature of proffered testimony. It can hardly be ruled that this is not relevant to the finder of fact in weighing and assessing the evidence presented. Even if a judge should ignore the error rate of the entire system and permit testimony by social workers, mental health professionals, and law enforcement agents, the error rate of the system is now relevant to the jury in weighing that evidence. Although we have selected psychology as the science to be discussed relative to *Daubert* decision, and have examined the effect of this decision on the evidence we are familiar with in claims of childhood sexual abuse, the same basic principles will apply to all sciences and to all trials in which scientific evidence may be a factor. The same applies to physics, biology, economics, astronomy, sociology, chemistry, and the practice of medicine.

CONCLUSION

The first step for any advocate and judge is to understand the nature of the criterion of falsifiability, which means understanding the philosophy of science. Understanding the implications of the *Daubert* decision will most likely require significant effort, since this is a revolutionary change that shifts the entire enterprise onto new and untried ground. The second step is applying the decision to specific cases. The process of working out the implications of this decision will likely take many years, countless cases, and a multitude of confused attorneys and irate judges. Change never comes easily and the justice system may be more resistant to change than many other institutions. But change it must.

One thing is certain. Scientists who offer expert testimony in the courtroom need to be knowledgeable and skilled in dealing with the philosophy of science and the issues raised by the establishment of the criterion of falsifiability as the determinant of what is scientific.

NOTES

1. *Frye* v. *United States,* 293 F. 1013, 1014, a 1923 decision of the United States Court of Appeals for the D.C. Circuit. Under the *Frye* test a scientific technique is not admissible unless the technique is "generally accepted" in the scientific community. Giannelli (1980) notes that the *Frye* rule envisions a process by which a novel technique must pass through an "experimental" stage where it is scrutinized by the scientific

community. Only after it has passed successfully through this process and has entered into the "demonstrable" stage can it be admissible. Under the *Frye* rule, it is not enough that a qualified expert or experts believe the technique to be valid and reliable: the technique must be generally accepted by the relevant scientific community.

2. *William Daubert, et ux., etc., et al., Petitioners* v. *Merrell Dow Pharmaceutical, Inc.,* Supreme Court of the United States, No. 92–102, decided on June 28, 1993.

REFERENCES

American Psychiatric Association (1987). *DSM-III-R* (*Diagnostic and Statistical Manual.* 3rd ed., rev.). Washington, D.C.: Author.

Arkes, H. R., and Harkness, A. R. (1980). "Effects of Making a Diagnosis on Subsequent Recognition of Symptoms." *Journal of Experimental Psychology: Human Learning and Memory* 6, no. 5: 568–75.

Berger, M. A.; Gallagher, S. G.; and Esty, E. H. (December 2, 1992) No. 92–102 In the Supreme Court of the United States, October term, 1992. *Daubert et al.* v. *Merrell Dow Pharmaceuticals.* Brief of the Carnegie Commission on Science, Technology, and Government as *Amicus Curiae* in Support of Neither Party.

Bower, G. H. (1990). "Awareness, the Unconscious, and Repression: An Experimental Psychologist's Perspective." In J. L. Singer, ed., *Repression and Dissociation: Implications for Personality Theory, Psychopathology and Health,* pp. 209–231. Chicago: The University of Chicago Press.

Bowers, K. S. (1977). "Science and the Limits of Logic: A Response to the Mahoney-Demonbreun Paper." *Cognitive Therapy and Research* 1, no. 3: 239–46.

Briere, J., and Conte, J. (1989, August). "Amnesia in Adults Molested as Children: Testing Theories of Repression." Paper presented at the Annual Meeting of the American Psychological Association, New Orleans, La.

Cohen, J. (1992). "A Power Primer." *Psychological Bulletin* 112, no. 1: 155–59.

Dar, R. (1987). "Another Look at Meehl, Lakatos, and the Scientific Practices of Psychologists." *American Psychologist* 42, no. 2: 145–51.

Dawes, R. M. (1992). "Why Believe That for Which There Is No Good Evidence?" *Issues in Child Abuse Accusations* 4, no. 4: 214–18.

Fahy, T. A. (1988). "The Diagnosis of Multiple Personality Disorder: A Critical Review." *British Journal of Psychiatry* 153: 597–606.

Frye v. *United States,* 293 F. 1013, 1014 (D.C. Cir. 1923).

Garry, M., and Loftus, E. F. (1993, April). "Women Who Remember Too Much." Paper presented at the False Memory Syndrome Foundation conference, Valley Forge: Penn.

Giannelli, P. C. (1980). "The Admissibility of Novel Scientific Evidence: *Frye* v. *United States,* a Half-Century Later." *Columbia Law Review* 80: 1197–1250.

Green (1992). Expert witnesses and sufficiency of evidence in toxic substances litigation: The legacy of *Agent Orange* and Bendectin litigation, 86 Nw U.L. Rev. (Cited in *William Daubert, et ux., etc., et al., Petitioners* v. *Merrell Dow Pharmaceutical, Inc.,* Supreme Court of the United States, No. 92–102, decided on 6/28/93.)

Hedges, L. V., and Olkin, I. (1980). "Vote Counting Methods in Research Synthesis." *Psychological Bulletin* 88: 359–69.

Hempel, C. (1966). *Philosophy of Natural Science.* Cited in *William Daubert, et ux., etc., et al., Petitioners* v. *Merrell Dow Pharmaceutical, Inc.*, Supreme Court of the United States, No. 92-102, decided on June 28, 1993.

Herman, J. L., and Schatzow, E. (1987). "Recovery and Verification of Memories of Childhood Sexual Trauma." *Psychoanalytic Psychology* 4, no. 1: 1–14.

Holmes, D. S. (1990). "The Evidence for Repression: An Examination of Sixty Years of Research." In J. L. Singer, ed., *Repression and Dissociation: Implications for Personality Theory, Psychopathology and Health,* pp. 85–102. Chicago: The University of Chicago Press.

Imwinkelried, E. J. (1992). "Attempts to Limit the Scope of the *Frye* Standard for the Admission of Scientific Evidence: Confronting the Real Cost of the General Acceptance Test." *Behavioral Sciences and the Law* 10, no. 4: 441–54.

Kirk, S. A., and Kutchins, H. (1992). *The Selling of DSM: The Rhetoric of Science in Psychology.* New York: Aldine De Gruyter.

Kuhn, T. S. (1962). *The Structure of Scientific Revolutions.* Chicago: The University of Chicago Press.

Lee, A. S. (1987, June). "Quixotic Communication: The Case of Expert Witness Testimony." *Knowledge: Creation, Diffusion, Utilization* 8, no. 4: 549–85.

Mahoney, M. J., and DeMonbreun, B. G. (1977). "Psychology of the Scientist: An Analysis of Problem-Solving Bias." *Cognitive Therapy and Research* 1, no. 3: 229–38.

McCord, D. (1987). "Syndromes, Profiles and Other Mental Exotica: A New Approach to the Admissibility of Nontraditional Psychological Evidence in Criminal Cases." *Oregon Law Review* 66: 19–108.

Meehl, P. E. (1967). "Theory-Testing in Psychology and Physics: A Methodological Paradox." *Philosophy of Science* 34: 103–115.

——— (1978). "Theoretical Risks and Tabular Asterisks: Sir Karl, Sir Ronald, and the Slow Progress of Soft Psychology." *Journal of Consulting and Clinical Psychology* 46, no. 4: 806–834.

——— (1989). "Law and the Fireside Inductions (with Postscript): Some Reflections of a Clinical Psychologist." *Behavioral Sciences and the Law* 7, no. 4: 521–50.

——— (1992a). "The Miracle Argument for Realism: An Important Lesson to Be Learned by Generalizing from Carrier's Counterexamples. (A Monograph)." *Study History, Philosophy, and Science* 23, no. 2: 267–82.

——— (1992b). "Cliometric Metatheory: The Actuarial Approach to Empirical, History-Based Philosophy of Science." *Psychological Reports Monographs,* 1–V71.

Mullen, B.; Atkins, J. L.; Champion, D. S.; Edwards, C.; Hardy, D.; Story, J. E.; and Vanderklok, M. (1985). "The False Consensus Effect: A Meta-Analysis of 115 Hypothesis Tests." *Journal of Experimental Social Psychology* 21: 262–83.

Myers, J. E. B. (1993). "Expert Testimony Describing Psychological Syndromes." *Pacific Law Journal* 24: 1449–64.

Orne, M. T.; Dinges, D. F.; and Orne, E. C. (1984). "On Differential Diagnosis of Multiple Personality in the Forensic Context." *International Journal of Clinical and Experimental Hypnosis* 32, no. 2: 118–69.

Paradise, J. E. (1989). "Predictive Accuracy and the Diagnosis of Sexual Abuse: A Big Issue about a Little Tissue." *Child Abuse and Neglect* 13, no. 2: 169–76.

Popper, K. (1959). *The Logic of Scientific Discovery.* London: Hutchinson.

——— (1992/1956/1983). *Realism and the Aim of Science.* New York: Routledge.

——— (1989). *Conjectures and Refutations: The Growth of Scientific Knowledge.* 5th. ed. Cited in *William Daubert, et ux., etc., et al., Petitioners* v. *Merrell Dow Pharmaceutical, Inc.,* Supreme Court of the United States, No. 92–102, decided on June 28, 1993.

——— (1966). *The Open Society and Its Enemies.* Lawrenceville, N.J.: Princeton University Press.

Reuben, R. C. (1993). "Justices Adopt New Scientific Evidence Test." *Los Angeles Daily Journal,* June 29, 1993. pp. 1, 10.

Schmidt, F. L. (1992). "What Do Data Really Mean?" *American Psychologist* 47, no. 10: 1173–81.

Spanos, N. P.; Weekes, J. R.; and Bertrand, L. D. (1985). "Multiple Personality: A Social Psychological Perspective." *Journal of Abnormal Psychology* 94, no. 3: 362–76.

Strube, M. J. (1985). "Power Analysis for Combining Significance Levels." *Psychological Bulletin* 98, no. 3: 595–99.

Wakefield, H., and Underwager, R. (1992). "Uncovering Memories of Alleged Sexual Abuse: The Therapists Who Do It." *Issues in Child Abuse Accusations* 4, no. 4: 197–213.

Weissberg, M. (1993). "Multiple Personality Disorder and Iatrogenesis: The Cautionary Tale of Anna O." *The International Journal of Clinical and Experimental Hypnosis* 41, no. 1: 15–32.

West, R. (1992). "Assessment of Evidence versus Consensus or Prejudice." *Journal of Epidemiology and Community Health* 46, no. 4: 321–22.

Williams, L. M. (1992, Summer). "Adult Memories of Childhood Abuse: Preliminary Findings from a Longitudinal Study." *APCAC Advisor,* pp. 10–21.

Zeitlin, H. (1987, October 10). "Investigation of the Sexually Abused Child." *The Lancet,* pp. 842–45.

24

"Slippage" in Research on Child Sexual Abuse: Science as Social Advocacy*

Paul Okami

INTRODUCTION

It is tacitly understood among social scientists that research in human behavior must inevitably bear the stamp of social ideology. However, the imprint of this stamp cuts more deeply and may be noticed more extensively in some academic disciplines than in others. In the field of human sexuality there has recently occurred a particularly massive "slippage" of legal, moral, and socio-political constructs and definitional criteria into scientific research ostensibly concerned with empirical phenomena. Indeed, some current sex research appears to serve less a social inquiry than a social advocacy function. This trend has hampered the development of sound professional consensus and the establishment of a coherent data base in many research areas.

For example, in the field of pornography research, the presence of scenes termed "degrading" or "demeaning" or thought by researchers to portray "subservient" females are often ascertained using operational definitions of "degrading," "demeaning," or "subservient" that do not represent a consensus view among psychologists, sociologists, or sexologists (or even feminists for that matter [Ellis et al. 1986]). Instead, these definitions reflect subjective

*Revised original English language version of " 'Intromisión Indebida' en la Investigación sobre Abuso Sexual Infantil." *La Revista Latinoamericana de Sexologia* 7 (1992): 151–73.

interpretations drawn from tenets of specific currents of cultural feminist, religious, or other sociopolitical ideologies (Garcia & Milano 1990; cf. Cowan et al. 1988; Brosius et al. 1993; Zillman & Bryant 1982).

In the area of sexual deviance, behaviors that are illegal or morally offensive, but not necessarily pathological in a psychological or sexological sense, may be treated as psychosexual pathologies by researchers simply on the basis of the legal, moral, or sex-political status of the behaviors. For example, occurrences of mutually voluntary sexual intercourse between an adult and a sexually and reproductively mature adolescent may be included in studies of "child molestation" or "pedophilia" because the younger participant, although not a child in a biological or phenomenological sense, is below the legal age of consent. Similarly, sexual behavior involving more than one partner at a time or many partners within a given month or year may be termed by researchers "sex addiction," although such behaviors may reflect little more than the flaunting of normative sexual conventions (Levine & Troiden 1988).

In studies of sexual harassment, behaviors considered by a large majority of a sample of "victims" *not* to have constituted harassment are counted as sexual harassment by researchers whose operational definitions are ideologically generated and possibly lacking discriminant validity (cf. Bremer et al. 1991; Jaschik & Fretz 1991). Even studies of rape may be similarly contaminated (cf. Koss, Dinero, & Seibel 1988). Moreover, the crime of rape continues to be studied under the presumption that "rape is not a sexual crime" but rather a crime of violent subjugation of women. This presumption is grounded in sociopolitical ideology and is not supported by empirical evidence (Palmer 1988; Symons 1979). Whereas it is true that rape is committed by men who use violence to achieve their ends and who may hold women in contempt, to ignore sexual aspects of the nature and motivation of the crime is an act of politically mediated selective attention.

Finally, unbridled slippage of legal, moral, and sex-political definitions of terms such as "attack," "assault," "aggression," "rape," "victim," "victimization," "violence," "dysfunctional," "survivor," "walking wounded," etc., into social scientific discourse has diluted the meanings of these terms to such an extent that it is often exceedingly difficult to determine in a reasonable manner the referent class of event when such terms are used in research reports. For example, it is quite typical for the author of an article to open by declaring that his or her topic is sexual "aggressions," "attacks," "assaults," or "violence" against children but to proceed to report that the large majority of the crimes under study were accomplished without the use of force or overt coercion (cf. Hall et al. 1986). If terms such as "assault" and "aggression" are used to describe sexual contacts accomplished without force or overt coercion, how then should one refer to a genuine instance of the rape of a child?

This chapter will first detail some interpretive problems that may result from failure to examine closely claims made by researchers in one area of human sexuality: child sexual abuse. This portion of the chapter is intended as a summary for those in legal, medical, and other professions of perspectives explored in greater detail in three earlier articles by the author (Okami 1990, 1992; Okami & Goldberg 1992). Possible social consequences of the slippage of legal, moral, and sociopolitical constructs and criteria into research in this field will then be discussed.

PREVALENCE OF CHILD SEXUAL ABUSE

Are 62 percent of American women victims of childhood sexual abuse? Are 16 percent of American women victims of childhood incest? These claims have been advanced in studies conducted by Wyatt (1985) and Russell (1986), respectively.

Because these studies were well funded and used probability samples, their alarming prevalence estimates are widely cited and considered credible. For example, a recent extensive review of the epidemiology of sexual abuse concluded that these studies reported the preferred prevalence estimates (Salter 1992).

However, according to the operational definitions used in the Wyatt (1985) study, an instance of an unwanted verbal proposition of one 17-year-old by another 17-year old could count as an experience of "child sexual abuse," as could an instance of an adolescent "flashing" another adolescent (exhibitionism), or the voluntary employment of a 17-year-old as a stripper or prostitute. Incidents such as these may be illegal or immoral as well as unpleasant or even harmful. Nevertheless, two mandates of science are to describe and classify phenomena. It is doubtful whether incidents such as those described above belong in the same category as, for example, the coerced sexual penetration of an eight-year-old child by an adult. Slippage of legal definitions of "child" and moral or sex-political definitions of "sexual abuse" thus compromised the validity of Wyatt's findings by creating a unitary category of pathology ("child sexual abuse") from a heterogeneous group of behaviors that were variable in type and degree of pathology.

Similarly, in Russell's (1986) study of "childhood incestuous abuse" among women, a single, voluntary, sexually motivated kiss between a 13-year-old girl and her second cousin's 19-year-old husband could be counted as an instance of "incest." That is, Russell included in her definition of "incestuous abuse" any contact or attempted contact incident of a sexual nature between a person under eighteen and a relative "no matter how distant the relationship" [including relation by marriage] (p. 59). Thus, politico-legal criteria rather than biological or anthropological criteria for definitions of kinship slip into scientific considerations of "incest." Incest is defined by Webster's *Ninth New Collegiate Dictionary* as "sexual intercourse between persons so closely related that they are forbidden by law to marry." Although it may be argued that all definitions of incest are therefore based on law, the complexity of the sexual encounter (intercourse) and the closeness of the relationship have heretofore defined incest in the scientific literature.

Moreover, sociopolitical as well as legal criteria for "abuse" supplant empirical criteria in studies such as those conducted by Russell and Wyatt. Entirely voluntary, albeit illegal, instances of sexual contact between adolescents and adults are defined as abusive if the adult's age exceeds the adolescent's by an arbitrary limit (usually five years, but sometimes ten years in the case of older adolescents). The rationales given for this judgment are (1) the sex-political principle that differential degrees of social power accorded older persons and younger persons automatically define any sexual contact between such persons as abuse (cf. Finkelhor 1984), and (2) the legal maxim (of questionable scientific validity) that no person under the age of eighteen (or sixteen) has sufficient understanding of the nature and consequences of sexual acts to be able to give informed consent to such acts. Whereas these principles may well form a solid rationale for enactment of legal restrictions on these behaviors, they do not form a defensible rationale for the use of such criteria in the context of scientific study of sexual aggression or anomalous age preference in sexual response or behavior.

Therefore, one may contrast "slipped" definitions of *child* and *sexual abuse* with those derived from empirical and phenomenological criteria. For example, a child may be defined as "a person below the age of puberty" and child sexual abuse as "physical intrusions of a sexual nature by an adult or older adolescent that are perceived by the child, or by the adult former victim in retrospect, as unwanted or unpleasant or otherwise abusive." Although the latter definition is not ideal—it would exclude an instance of coerced witnessing of a protracted sexual exhibition, theoretically would demand evidence of age of onset of puberty for each participant, would mandate the creation of a separate category of "adolescent sexual abuse," and would disallow a reasonable third party judgment of abuse where participants may have been incapable of reasonable judgment—it is still preferable from a scientific point of view to definitions that create a unitary category of pathology from a group of phenomenologically and empirically distinct behaviors.

Were one to adopt such an empirically based definition, prevalence of sexual abuse of American female children probably would more closely resemble a figure between approximately 8 percent and 13 percent. This estimate is extrapolated from studies of community samples (Badgley 1984; Finkelhor 1984; Kercher & McShane 1984; Kilpatrick 1992; Murphy, cited in Salter 1992) as well as university samples (Briere & Runtz 1988; Fritz et al. 1981;

Haugaard & Emery 1989; Reed & Kenning 1987).

However, few of these studies in fact conformed to a definition of child sexual abuse restricted to unwanted or unpleasant or otherwise abusive sexual intrusions on a prepubertal child. Most of the studies used sixteen as an upper age limit for the victim and several did not specify that the experience had to be unwanted or unpleasant or perceived as abusive. The investigations cited were chosen because they generally adhered more closely to my preferred definition than did several others and because sampling or other methodological procedures were relatively sound. In most cases I simply accepted the figures reported in these studies regardless of numerous violations of the preferred definition. Therefore, barring the possibility that large numbers of subjects were either unwilling or unable to disclose experiences of abuse (a problem facing virtually any study of sexual behavior), my 13 percent upper limit figure is probably an overestimate.

PERPETRATORS OF SEXUAL ABUSE

Pedophiles

Much of the professional literature routinely characterizes perpetrators of sexual abuse as "pedophiles." The category "pedophile" exists in sexologic and psychiatric nosology to refer to persons demonstrating or claiming primary sexual interest in prepubertal children (American Psychiatric Association 1988; Money 1990). "Pedophilia" should not be used to refer to a behavior (child molestation). Indeed, data suggest that the majority of reported acts of sexual abuse of children may not be committed by pedophiles (Okami & Goldberg 1992). It is also likely that some pedophiles may never engage in sexual conduct with a child. Because studies of "pedophiles" in virtually all cases are conducted among persons incarcerated for child molestation—and a substantial portion, if not the majority, of these crimes do not even involve prepubertal persons (cf. Gebhard et al. 1965)—studies of "pedophiles" should therefore be viewed in actuality as investigations of "adjudicated sex offenders against minors under age eighteen (or sixteen)." Reported personality and behavioral profiles of such "pedophiles" consequently are of limited utility (Okami & Goldberg 1992).

These problems have resulted directly from the slippage of legal definitions of child into investigations where empirical or phenomenological definitions are warranted, and from the unwarranted conflation of sexually criminal behavior with psychiatric or sexologic pathology. Whereas sex offenders against minors are properly termed criminal and thus socially and morally deviant, their actual psychological and sexual status may be within normal range (Langevin, Hucker, Ben-Aron, Purins, and Hook 1985; Langevin,

Hucker, Handy, Purins, and Russon 1985; see Okami & Goldberg 1992 for review).

CHILD PERPETRATORS OF SEXUAL ABUSE

Some researchers have claimed that childhood sex play frequently masks the reality of sexual abuse of children by other children (cf. Cantwell 1988; Johnson 1989). Such researchers have asserted that "explicit sexual behavior in children needs to be reported, investigated, and/or discussed," and that children should be encouraged to "tell someone if anyone, even a same-age child, approaches them initiating sexual play" (Cantwell 1988: 580–82). After having been ascertained, sexual abuse of one child by another should be adjudicated and the perpetrator punished and/or "treated" (Johnson 1989; see Okami 1992 for complete discussion).

However, this literature is seriously compromised by slippage. For example, in defining sexually abusive behaviors of children toward other children, these researchers typically use terms such as "abnormal" or "inappropriate" interchangeably with "abusive." That is, children are described as "perpetrators of sexual abuse," and recommendations are made for criminal prosecution of these "offenders" (whose ages may be as young as four years old) if they demonstrate "developmentally inappropriate" sexual behaviors that are "outside of normal limits" (Cantwell 1988: 581; Johnson 1988: 221, 1989: 194). "Child perpetrators" are diagnosed as exhibiting "sexualized behavior"—a pathology that "both boys and girls can develop," for which "medical reasons must always be ruled out through physical exams"—if they display "an unusual or excessive interest or activity in sexual matters which seems beyond the developmental norm given the child's age" (Gil 1989: 1). Gil included persons up to the age of seventeen within her definition of "sexualized child."

Compounding these definitional problems is the tendency of researchers on "child perpetrators" to use the term "abnormal" in the absence of empirically derived baseline norms. That is, behaviors considered by these researchers to be "abnormal" (i.e., "abusive") include types of childhood behaviors—for example, mutual masturbation or mock intercourse—that occur quite commonly throughout the world (Elwin 1968; Ford & Beach 1951; Marshall & Suggs 1971), including Western societies in Europe or North America (Borneman 1990; Haugaard & Tilly 1988; Kilpatrick 1992; Kinsey et al. 1948; Kinsey et al. 1953; Langfeldt 1990; Leitenberg et al. 1989; Lamb & Coakley in press; Martinson 1976; Money 1986; Reinish 1990). Such behaviors have been termed "sexual rehearsal play" by Money and Erhardt (1972) and apparently are tolerated more often than not crossculturally (Ford & Beach 1951; Gadpaille 1976). Thus, whereas it cannot be stated conclusively that these behaviors are species-typical or represent a universal human norm, there is certainly no evidence to suggest that such behaviors are in any way "abnormal."

One group of investigators (Friedrich et al. 1991) has attempted to define such behaviors as abnormal by assessing their frequency among a community sample of children aged two through twelve, these investigators "measured" such behaviors by having the children's mothers fill out questionnaires that asked them to count the occurrences of the behaviors among their children. The authors found that behaviors such as mock sexual intercourse, oral-genital contact, inserting of objects into anus or vagina, etc., were "rare." Such activities particularly were reported to have decreased in frequency as the children grew older. According to this report for example, not a single boy and virtually no girls aged seven to twelve engaged in these behaviors. The authors concluded that such behaviors were not normative, providing "evidence" for the view that the behaviors are indicative of pathology and of a possible previous history of sexual abuse.

However, asking mothers to count the frequency of behaviors that are virtually certain to be engaged in by children with the highest degree of secrecy—particularly as the children grow older and presumably become more competent at subterfuge—is not the same as measuring these activities, as the authors contend it is in their study. Indeed, it is difficult to imagine a potentially less accurate reporter of sexual behavior among older children before puberty, for example, than the children's mothers. The possible confounding effects of this methodological weakness were not mentioned in the investigators' report. Given that certain of the researchers concerned with "child perpetrators" have defined as abnormal and cause for professional intervention even behaviors such as "endless questions about sex; sexual knowledge too great for age; displays of fear or anger about babies, birthing or intercourse; painful erections; and refusal to put on clothes" (cited in Okami 1992: 113), the literature to date concerning "child perpetrators" is problematic from a scientific point of view.

SOCIAL ATTITUDES TOWARD SEXUAL ABUSE

Do Americans blame the victims, rather than the perpetrators, for sexual abuse? Broussard et al. (1991) began a recent study by claiming that both the general public and mental health professionals have tended to attribute responsibility for instances of sexual abuse to the victim rather than to the perpetrator. In order to examine public attitudes, the investigators presented university students with vignettes of sexual abuse situations while independently manipulating variables of child's response (active resistance, passive acceptance, or active encouragement), child's gender, and gender of perpetrator. The authors were interested in whether subjects considered the active encouragement condition realistic and thus to what extent people tend to "blame" the victim of sexual abuse.

However, in all vignette conditions the victim was described as "a 15-year-old child." Voluntary sexual interactions between adults and 15-year-olds are quite common and often socially sanctioned, or even socially prescribed, throughout the world (cf. Herdt 1981). Indeed, fifteen represented the average upper age limit of females for marriage in Frayser's (1965) crosscultural sample. Such liaisons are also legal in a number of the United States. Consequently, some people are unlikely to consider a 15-year-old to be a "child." It is therefore not surprising that a portion of Broussard et al.'s (1991) sample judged the "encouraging" condition realistic—just as they also judged the resisting and passive conditions realistic. Broussard et al. claimed that these results supported the view that people tend to blame the victim of child sexual abuse and minimize harm caused by sexual abuse. The authors closed their report with a call for increased funding and public education concerning sexual abuse. Apart from unintentional social advocacy concerns, however, it is difficult to understand why the authors did not manipulate the age of the victim in the vignettes. If limitations of resources or other methodological considerations made this procedure impractical, it would still seem commonsensical to have chosen an age for the victim of child sexual abuse that was more representative of childhood. It is unlikely that many subjects would have rated the "encouraging" condition as realistic or hesitated to term it harmful or abusive had the victim been described as an eight-year-old, for example.

SOME CONSEQUENCES OF SLIPPAGE

Well, so what? In the past, sociopolitical factors have tended to support a minimization of the import and prevalence of sexual abuse (Finkelhor 1984; Okami 1992; Russell 1986). What's wrong with a little affirmative action? What harm is caused by disseminating the maximum possible prevalence rates? What harm is there in presenting the worst possible sequelae as though they were intrinsic to a heterogeneous class of events, or terming a nonviolent molestation an act of "violence" if the act constitutes legal or metaphorical assault? What's wrong with stressing the destructive potential of coerced sexual experiences between peers in childhood? Who cares whether we call a child molester a "pedophile" or a "sex offender against a minor" as long as we can identify the individual and predict his or her behavior? Most important, what's wrong with morality in social science? As I mentioned earlier, values are imparted in social research regardless of investigators' attempts to remain objective—why not simply make one's values explicit and proceed from there? (cf. Vander May 1992).

The practices discussed above are counterproductive for several reasons.

They Hamper Development of Effective Treatment Models

Accurate information is essential for the development of effective models for treatment of victims of sexual abuse. Treatment models informed by research studies that employ legal definitions of a child (e.g., "person under age eighteen"), sex-political criteria for defining "abuse" (e.g., five-year age differential), and moral criteria for defining "sexual behavior" (e.g., inclusive of verbal propositions or exposure to pornography) may fail to take into account substantial differences in the needs of clients who have had widely variant experiences that are united under the rubric of "sexual abuse" only as a result of slippage.

For example, it may not be advisable to treat a victim of repeated instances of genuinely coercive or otherwise traumatic sexual abuse using strategies identical to, or even similar to, those used for the treatment of a victim of a single, relatively trivial incident or a "participant" in what he or she may have perceived to have been a voluntarily chosen sexual encounter or relationship. Indeed, treatment of the latter such client based on assumption of trauma, assignment of victim status, and insistence that he or she entirely abdicate even partial responsibility for the event ("It wasn't your fault") may prove ineffective or even iatrogenic because the victim's own sense of his or her reality is ignored by the helping professional. As Schultz (1980) observed:

> What inappropriate trauma ideology does is pit the professional (true believer) against the child or the parents who may feel differently. The risk is that a type of self-fulfilling prophecy emerges that manages to produce the problem it claims to abhor, but which it, in fact, must have in order to sustain the ideology it is based upon. (p. 40)

They Compromise Efforts at Abuse Prevention

A second reason why these practices are counterproductive is that accurate information is essential for the creation of effective programs for the prevention of child sexual abuse. Several researchers have detailed the failure of child-directed sexual abuse prevention programs that were inappropriately developed from models based on theories of sexual politics (Berrick & Gilbert 1991; Krivacska 1990; Reppucci & Haugaard 1989). Whereas such models may be applied successfully in the domain of sexual violence directed against adult women, they frequently are based on sociopolitical abstractions (e.g., "empowerment") that do not take into consideration realities of child development or children's social status.

Moreover, just as "sexual abuse" refers to a heterogeneous category of behaviors, "perpetrators of sexual abuse" also form a heterogeneous group (Langevin et al. 1985; Langevin et al. 1985; Okami & Goldberg 1992). Therefore, current personality or behavioral profiles of "pedophiles" or "child molesters" may inappropriately assume unitary psychosexual pathology where heterogeneous pathologies, or no pathologies, exist. Therefore, perpetrator-directed prevention efforts are also compromised by slippage.

They Foster Misinterpretation of Normal Childhood Sexual Development

Dissemination of exaggerated claims of prevalence or sequelae of child sexual abuse fuel the generally hysterical climate that traditionally has surrounded considerations of childhood sexuality.

Exaggerated claims of prevalence or sequelae of child sexual abuse encourage adult overreaction to the discovery of childhood sexual behavior such as masturbation or sexual rehearsal play. Overreaction and other negative messages typically imparted to American children about their own sexuality have been identified repeatedly as correlates of adult psychological or sexual dysfunctions (Money 1990; Yates 1978). I will term this type of overreaction and the imparting of negative messages to children regarding sexuality "expressive sexual abuse"—a category of abuse that probably affects a great many more children than those who are abused by adults seeking sexual gratification ("instrumental sexual abuse").

Exaggerated claims of prevalence or sequelae of sexual abuse have also contributed to a recent wholesale abandonment of the expression of physical affection toward children in childcare and public school settings in the United States. Currently, it is common policy for administrators to instruct childcare workers and teachers that they should not hug, kiss, pat, or otherwise touch a child (as in holding a child on a lap while reading). When such a policy is not specified, it is often adopted voluntarily by childcare workers in self-defense against the possibility of false allegations of sexual abuse (Okami 1990).[1]

Of greater concern is the possibility that this abandonment of physical affection may also have occurred, or will occur, to a certain extent within some family settings (Ramey 1979). A poll of mental health and legal professionals recently conducted in the State of Virginia (Haugaard & Reppucci 1988) reported that substantial numbers of these professionals expressed concern about behaviors such as a parent frequently hugging a 10-year-old child, parental kissing of a child on the lips, or the appearance of a parent nude before a child as young as five. Professional intervention was recommended for these behaviors despite the fact that no empirical evidence exists that any of these behaviors is harmful (Lewis & Janda 1988). Thus, it may be that slippage in the research is contributing to what Hyson et al. (1988) referred to as "unwarranted negative attitudes toward normal physical affection" (p. 55). It should be recalled that physical affection and parental warmth have been identified as critical factors in childhood development and subsequent adult functioning (Ainsworth et al. 1978; Franz et al. 1991).

They Divert Resources from Equally Pernicious Forms of Abuse and Neglect

Slippage contributes to inappropriate diversion of resources in sexual abuse-related research and in the application of social policy. Judicial and law enforcement as well as scientific resources have been diverted from investigations of actual abuse and neglect of children to putative problems such as allegations of conspiratorial "satanic" or "ritual" abuse. As Kenneth Lanning (1991), an FBI expert in forensic aspects of sexual abuse, and Frank Putnam (1991) of the National Institute of Mental Health have observed that no concrete evidence has been found substantiating the existence of these conspiratorial crimes, many of which grossly defy laws of probability or even possibility. Regardless of this lack of substantiating evidence, social scientists continue to study these putative crimes and their "effects" on "victims" as though the reality of the crimes had been ascertained (Nathan 1991).

The slippage discussed in the present article has also contributed to the passing into popular usage of the term "child abuse" to signify "child sexual abuse" or even "child sexuality" (Bullough 1990). This is ironically associated with a general abandonment of research and policy interest in the physical abuse of children (Okami 1990)—the reported prevalence rate of which is greater than twice that of sexual abuse—and child neglect, which accounts for considerably greater numbers of cases of reported child maltreatment than sexual and physical abuse combined (1989 American Humane Society statistics, cited in Kilpatrick 1992). Moreover, as Kilpatrick observed:

> These statistics do show that many more children and adolescents are in life-threatening situations through neglect and physical abuse than are sexually abused. In fact, many more children die from neglect than from physical abuse or from sexual abuse, which reports zero fatalities (Kadushin & Martin 1988). Not only is neglect less dramatic than physical abuse and certainly less titillating than sexual abuse, but is also more difficult to deal with. (p. xvii)

They Confabulate Real Effects of Sexual Abuse

Slippage in the literature may stimulate a backlash wherein sequelae of sexual abuse become underestimated. As investigators studying correlates and effects of sexual abuse have grown methodologically sophisticated, they have begun to report more frequently that victims of sexual abuse found in nonclinical samples generally do not differ in levels of dysfunction from those who have not been abused—or if they appear to differ, the impairment is generally related more to demographic and family background variables than to the sexual abuse itself (Beitchman et al. 1991; Beitchman et al. 1992; Fromuth 1986; Parker & Parker 1991).

However, this lack of apparent differences in impairment between abused and nonabused groups in some cases may have resulted from the failure to distinguish between cases of sexual abuse as defined using empirical and phenomenological criteria, and cases of sexual abuse as defined using moral, legal, or sociopolitical criteria. If a seemingly trivial incident of sexual contact (or noncontact) between a child and an adult, or an entirely voluntary instance of sexual contact between an adolescent and an adult, are part of the same data set as an instance of forced, coerced, or otherwise traumatic (or simply obnoxious) sexual maltreatment of a child or adolescent by an adult, it is reasonable to wonder if truly deleterious consequences of the latter type of event might be washed out when the data are analyzed.

They Promote a Sex-Negative Perspective

Slippage in the social science literature contributes indirectly to social acceptance of the sex-negative principle that human sexual behavior is singularly and intrinsically dangerous (Rubin 1986).

When sexual abuse is defined in a manner that would conflate seemingly trivial or voluntary contacts with serious instances of sexual maltreatment—and global sequelae of such "sexual abuse" are claimed—what is being proposed is the notion that any and all exposures to adult sexuality are equally dangerous for minors regardless of context, duration, subjective response, age, or other phenomenology. If this is true, then events involving sexuality do not follow psychosocial laws governing other types of human events, where it is acknowledged that the context and nature of the event in large measure determines consequences. Thus, there is something formidably dangerous about human sexuality itself quite apart from its manifestation. In my view, this notion borders on magical and paranoidal thinking.

CONCLUSION

Subjective values and ideals are undoubtedly intrinsic to the motivation of social scientists. This is desirable because values and ideals result in the asking of important research questions. However, socially committed science is not the same thing as political persuasion. While it may not be possible entirely to eradicate the biases resulting from the influence of subjective values and ideology, this does not mean that stringent efforts should not be made to contain those biases. Moreover, whereas legal statutes and social norms regarding appropriate sexual behavior serve an essential function, this does not constitute a defensible rationale for conducting scientific inquiry utilizing definitional criteria and methods that may have emerged primarily from the desire to enforce such statutes or norms. It is counterproductive to do so because accurate information is necessary for the creation of effective prevention and treatment strategies as well as for the implementation of responsible and humane social policies.

NOTE

1. Interestingly, the author's own mother, an elderly woman who recently volunteered as an assistant for the local preschool, was amazed to discover that teachers and volunteers were instructed not to hug or touch a child affectionately, even when the child was crying, as when homesick or injured. A clinician at Cedars Sinai Hospital in Los Angeles recently told me that therapists and childcare workers at the Cedars Sinai childcare center for children with developmental or psychological problems voluntarily police themselves in this respect (H. Mahmoudhi, personal communication, August 15, 1992).

REFERENCES

Ainsworth, M. D.; Blehar, M.; Waters, E.; and Wall, S. (1978). *Patterns of Attachment.* Hillsdale, N.J.: Lawrence Earlbaum.

American Psychiatric Association (1988). *Diagnostic and Statistical Manual of Mental Disorders.* 3rd ed., rev. Washington D.C.: American Psychiatric Association.

Badgley, R. F. (1984). *Sexual Offenses against Children: Report of the Committee on Sexual Offenses Against Children and Youth,* vol. I. Ottawa: Canadian Government Printing Office.

Beitchman, J. H.; Zucker, K. J.; Hood, J. E.; daCosta, G. A.; and Akman, D. (1991). "A Review of the Short-Term Effects of Child Sexual Abuse." *Child Abuse and Neglect* 15: 537–56.

Beitchman, J. H.; Zucker, K. J.; Hood, J. E.; daCosta, G. A.; Akman, D.; and Cassavia, E. (1992). "A Review of the Long-Term Effects of Child Sexual Abuse." *Child Abuse and Neglect* 16: 101–118.

Berrick, J. D., and Gilbert, N. (1991). *With the Best of Intentions: The Child Sexual Abuse Prevention Movement.* New York: Guilford.

Borneman, E. (1990). "Progress in Empirical Research on Children's Sexuality." In M. E. Perry, ed., *Childhood and Adolescent Sexology.* Vol. 7 of *Handbook of Sexology.* New York: Elsevier (Biomedical Division).

Bremer, B. A.; Moore, C. T.; and Bildersee, E. F. (1991). "Do You Have to Call

It Sexual Harassment to Feel Harassed?" *College Student Journal* 25: 258–68.

Briere, J., and Runtz, M. (1988). "Symptomatology Associated with Childhood Sexual Victimization in a Nonclinical Adult Sample." *Child Abuse and Neglect* 12: 51–59.

Brosius, H.; Weaver, J. B.; and Staab, J. F. (1993). "Exploring the Social and Sexual 'Reality' of Contemporary Pornography." *The Journal of Sex Research* 30: 161–70.

Broussard, S.; Wagner, W. G.; and Kazelskis, R. (1991). "Undergraduate Students' Perceptions of Child Sexual Abuse: The Impact of Victim Sex, Perpetrator Sex, Respondent Sex, and Victim Response." *Journal of Family Violence* 6: 267–78.

Bullough, V. (1990). "History of Adult Human Sexual Behavior with Children and Adolescents in Western Societies." In J. Feierman, ed., *Pedophilia: Biosocial Dimensions.* New York: Springer-Verlag.

Cantwell, H. (1988). "Child Sexual Abuse: Very Young Perpetrators." *Child Abuse and Neglect* 12: 579–82.

Cowan, G.; Chase, C. J.; and Stahly, G. B. (1988). "Dominance and Inequality in X-Rated Videocassettes." *Psychology of Women Quarterly* 12: 299–311.

Ellis, K.; O'Dair, B.; and Tallmer, A., eds. (1986). *Caught Looking: Feminism, Censorship and Pornography.* New York: Caught Looking, Inc.

Elwin, V. (1968). *Kingdom of the Young.* London: Oxford University Press.

Finkelhor, D. (1984). *Child Sexual Abuse: New Theory and Research.* New York: Free Press.

Ford, C. S., and Beach, F. (1951). *Patterns of Sexual Behavior.* New York: Harper and Row.

Franz, C. E.; McClelland, D. C.; and Weinberger, J. (1991). "Childhood Antecedents of Conventional Social Accomplishment in Midlife Adults: A 36-year Prospective Study." *Journal of Personality and Social Psychology* 60: 586–95.

Frayser, S. (1985). *Varieties of Sexual Experience.* New Haven: HRAF.

Friedrich, W. N.; Grambsch, P.; Broughton, D.; Kuiper, J.; and Beilke, R. L. (1991). "Normative Sexual Behavior in Children." *Pediatrics* 88: 456–64.

Fritz, G. S.; Stoll, K.; and Wagner, N. (1981). "A Comparison of Males and Females Who Were Sexually Molested as Children." *Journal of Sex and Marital Therapy* 7: 54–59.

Fromuth, M. E. (1986). "The Relationship of Childhood Sexual Abuse with Later Psychological and Sexual Adjustment in a Sample of College Women." *Child Abuse and Neglect* 10: 5–15.

Gadpaille, W. P. (1976). "The Delay of Normal Psychosexual Development." *Journal of Child Psychiatry* 15: 679–92.

Garcia, L. T., and Milano, L. (1990). "A Content Analysis of Erotic Videos." *Journal of Psychology and Human Sexuality* 3: 95–104.

Gebhard, P. H.; Gagnon, J.; Pomeroy, W.; and Christenson, C. (1965). *Sex Offenders: An Analysis of Types.* New York: Harper and Row.

Gil, E. (1989). "Children Who Molest: Responding to the Sexualized, Acting Out Child." Lecture outline. Pleasant Hill, Calif.: Gil and Associates Child Abuse Treatment and Training Programs.

Hall, G. C. N.; Maiuro, R. D.; Vitaliano, P. P.; and Proctor, W. C. (1986). "The Utility of the MMPI with Men Who Have Sexually Assaulted Children." *Journal of Consulting and Clinical Psychology* 54: 493–96.

Haugaard, J. J., and Tilly, C. (1988). "Characteristics Predicting Children's Responses to Sexual Encounters with Other Children." *Child Abuse and Neglect* 12: 209–218.

Haugaard, J. J., and Emery, R. E. (1989). "Methodological Issues in Child Sexual Abuse Research." *Child Abuse and Neglect* 13: 89–100.

Haugaard, J. J., and Reppucci, N. D. (1988). *The Sexual Abuse of Children: A Comprehensive Guide to Current Knowledge and Intervention Strategies.* San Francisco: Jossey-Bass.

Herdt, G. H. (1981). *Guardians of the Flutes: Idioms of Masculinity.* New York: McGraw Hill.

Hyson, M. C.; Whitehead, L. C.; and Prudhoe, C. M. (1988). "Influences on Attitudes toward Physical Affection between Adults and Children." *Early Childhood Research Quarterly* 3: 55–75.

Jaschik, M. L., and Fretz, B. R. (1991). "Women's Perceptions and Labeling of Sexual Harassment." *Sex Roles* 25: 19–23.

Johnson, T. C. (1988). "Child Perpetrators—Children Who Molest Other Children: Preliminary Findings." *Child Abuse and Neglect* 12: 219–29.

——— (1989). "Female Child Perpetrators: Children Who Molest Other Children." *Child Abuse and Neglect* 13: 571–85.

Johnson, T. C., and Berry, C. (1989). "Children Who Molest: A Treatment Program." *Journal of Interpersonal Violence* 4: 185–203.

Kercher, G. A., and McShane, M. (1984). "The Prevalence of Child Sexual Abuse Victimization in an Adult Sample of Texas Residents." *Child Abuse and Neglect* 8: 495–501.

Kilpatrick, A. C. (1992). *Long-Range Effects of Child and Adolescent Sexual Experiences: Myths, Mores, and Menaces.* Hillsdale, N.J.: Lawrence Erlbaum.

Kinsey, A. C.; Pomeroy, W. B.; and Martin, C. (1948). *Sexual Behavior in the Human Male.* Philadelphia: W. B. Saunders.

Kinsey, A. C.; Pomeroy, W. B.; Martin, C.; and Gebhard, P. (1953). *Sexual Behavior in the Human Female.* Philadelphia: W. B. Saunders.

Koss, M. P.; Dinero, T. E.; and Seibel, C. A. (1988). "Stranger and Acquaintance Rape: Are There Differences in the Victim's Experience?" *Psychology of Women Quarterly* 12: 1–24.

Krivacska, J. J. (1990). "Child Sexual Abuse and Its Prevention." In M. E. Perry, ed., *Childhood and Adolescent Sexuality.* Vol. 7 of *Handbook of Sexology.* Netherlands: Elsevier Science Publishers (Biomedical Division).

Lamb, S., and Coakley, M. A. (in press). " 'Normal' Childhood Sexual Play and Games: Differentiating Play from Abuse." *Child Abuse and Neglect.*

Langevin, R.; Hucker, S. J.; Ben-Aron, M. H.; Purins, J. E.; and Hook, H. J. (1985). "Why Are Pedophiles Attracted to Children? Further Studies of Erotic Preference in Heterosexual Pedophilia." In R. Langevin, ed., *Erotic Preference, Gender Identity, and Aggression in Men.* Hillsdale, N.J.: Lawrence Earlbaum.

Langevin, R.; Hucker, S. J.; Handy, L.; Purins, J. E.; and Russon, A. E. (1985). "Erotic Preference and Aggression in Pedophilia: A Comparison of Heterosexual,

Homosexual, and Bisexual Types." In R. Langevin, ed., *Erotic Preference, Gender Identity, and Aggression in Men.* Hillsdale, N.J.: Lawrence Earlbaum Associates.

Langfeldt, T. (1990). "Early Childhood and Juvenile Sexuality, Development and Problems." In M. E. Perry, ed., *Childhood and Adolescent Sexology.* Vol 17 of *Handbook of Sexology.* New York: Elsevier (Biomedical Division).

Lanning, K. V. (1991). "Ritual Abuse: A Law Enforcement View or Perspective." *Child Abuse and Neglect* 15: 171–73.

Leitenberg, H.; Greenwald, E.; and Tarran, M. (1989). "The Relationship between Sexual Activity among Children during Preadolescence and/or Early Adolescence and Sexual Behavior and Sexual Adjustment in Young Adulthood." *Archives of Sexual Behavior* 18: 299–313.

Levine, M. P., and Troiden, R. R. (1988). "The Myth of Sexual Compulsivity." *The Journal of Sex Research* 25: 347–63.

Lewis, R. J., and Janda, L. H. (1988). "The Relationship between Adult Sexual Adjustment and Childhood Experiences Regarding Exposure to Nudity, Sleeping in the Parental Bed, and Parental Attitudes toward Sexuality." *Archives of Sexual Behavior* 17: 349–62.

Marshall, D., and Suggs, R., eds. (1971). *Human Sexual Behavior: Variations in the Ethnographic Spectrum.* Englewood Cliffs, N.J.: Prentice-Hall.

Martinson, F. M. (1976). "Eroticism in Infancy and Early Childhood." *The Journal of Sex Research* 12: 251–62.

Money, J. (1986). *Venuses Penuses.* Buffalo, N.Y.: Prometheus Books.

——— (1990). "Pedophilia: A Specific Instance of New Phylism Theory as Applied to Paraphilic Lovemaps." In J. Feierman, ed., *Pedophilia: Biosocial Dimensions.* New York: Springer-Verlag.

Money, J., and Erhardt, A. (1972). *Man, Woman, Boy, Girl: The Differentiation and Dimorphism of Gender Identity from Conception to Maturity.* Baltimore: Johns Hopkins Press.

Nathan, D. (1991) "Satanism and Child Molestation: Constructing the Ritual Abuse Scare." In J. T. Richardson, J. Best, and D. Bromley, eds., *The Satanism Scare.* New York: Aldine de Gruyter.

Okami, P. (1990). "Sociopolitical Biases in the Contemporary Research on Adult Human Sexual Behavior with Children and Adolescents." In J. Feierman, ed., *Pedophilia: Biosocial Dimensions.* New York: Springer-Verlag.

——— (1992). " 'Child Perpetrators of Sexual Abuse': The Emergence of a Problematic Deviant Category." *The Journal of Sex Research* 29: 109–130.

Okami, P., and Goldberg, A. (1992). "Personality Correlates of Pedophilia: Are They Reliable Indicators?" *The Journal of Sex Research* 29: 297–328.

Palmer, C. (1988). "Twelve Reasons Why Rape Is Not Sexually Motivated: A Skeptical Examination." *The Journal of Sex Research* 25: 512–30.

Parker, S., and Parker, H. (1991). "Female Victims of Child Sexual Abuse: Adult Adjustment." *Journal of Family Violence* 6: 183–97.

Putnam, F. W. (1991). "The Satanic Ritual Abuse Controversy." *Child Abuse and Neglect* 15: 175–79.

Ramey, J. (1979) "Dealing with the Last Taboo." *SIECUS Report* 7, no. 5: 1-2, 6–7.

Reed, R. S., and Kenning, M. K. (July 1987). "The Prevalence of Child Sexual Abuse among a Midwestern College Population." Paper presented at the Third Annual Symposium on Family Violence, Durham, N.H.

Reinisch, J. M. (1990). *The Kinsey Institute New Report on Sex.* New York: St. Martins Press.

Reppucci, N. D., and Haugaard, J. J. (1989). "Prevention of Child Sexual Abuse—Myth or Reality?" *American Psychologist* 44: 1266–75.

Rubin, G. (1984). "Thinking Sex." In C. Vance, ed., *Pleasure and Danger: Exploring Female Sexuality.* Boston: Routledge and Kegan Paul.

Russell, D. (1986). *The Secret Trauma: Incest in the Lives of Girls and Women.* New York: Basic Books.

Salter, A. C. (1992). "Epidemiology of Sexual Abuse." In W. O'Donohue and J. H. Geer, eds., *The Sexual Abuse of Children: Theory and Research,* vol I. Hillsdale, N.J.: Lawrence Earlbaum Associates.

Schultz, L. (1980). "Diagnosis and Treatment—An Introduction." In L. Schultz, ed., *The Sexual Victimology of Youth.* New York: Charles C Thomas, Pub.

Symons, D. (1979). *The Evolution of Human Sexuality.* New York: Oxford University Press.

Vander May, B. J. (1992). "Theories of Incest." In W. O'Donohue and J. H. Geer, eds., *The Sexual Abuse of Children: Theory and Research,* vol 1. Hillsdale, N.J.: Lawrence Earlbaum Associates.

Wyatt, G. E. (1985). "The Sexual Abuse of Afro-American and White Women in Childhood." *Child Abuse and Neglect* 9: 507–519.

Yates, A. (1978). *Sex without Shame: Encouraging the Child's Healthy Sexual Development.* New York: Morrow.

Zillman, D., and Bryant, J. (1982). "Pornography, Sexual Callousness, and the Trivialization of Rape." *Journal of Communications* 32: 10–21.

Epilogue*

Jerome G. Miller

A number of years ago, I left clinical practice and academia at the invitation of a governor to head a large eastern state's youth corrections system. I assumed the office with an eye toward reform. Curiously, among the first "reforms" recommended by a close staff advisor was a new office and a new car. But reform didn't end there. It was also suggested that I have a two-way radio, a siren, a dome light, and perhaps carry a side-arm (something our juvenile parole counselors had sought for a decade). It was all well-meant advice to assist me in my role as chief youth corrections officer for the state.

Though I didn't succumb to the proffered embellishments, it was also true that otherwise clear-minded persons found the allure of the trappings of law enforcement particularly suited to the purposes of an agency ostensibly created to rehabilitate teenaged delinquents. It is a malady which, in recent years, has afflicted a wide segment of helping professionals in particularly ominous ways.

Helping professionals (at least, in their better moments) have traditionally marched to a different beat in societies which neglect or misuse the poor, the homeless, the errant, and the aberrant. This is no longer so. In the current national mood, psychiatrists, social workers, psychologists and others who have traditionally defined themselves as helpers, now stand in line to lend a gloss of scientific or clinical validity to criminal justice spectacles often inspired by a mélange of political winds, ambitious prosecutors, and pop psychology which plays to the worst impulses in the citizenry. It all seems more fit for

*Reprinted with permission from J. G. Miller (1992). "On Mitigating Professional Arrogance in the Treatment of Sex Offenders." *Medicine and Law* 11: 485–91.

a self-help paperback or a celebrity appearance on Geraldo Rivera than befits a thoughtful clinician.

Over it all hangs the malady of contemporary American society—characterized recently by the essayist Philip Rieff as fast becoming a culture of "moralists and busybodies." More ominously, "help" is being rooted in the false premises of the criminal justice system—that there must always be a villain to be identified and punished, and upon whom we can heap contempt and opprobrium, thereby redeeming ourselves and saving the victim.

In his marvelous treatise on the criminal justice system, written in 1917 and entitled, "The Psychology of Punitive Justice," the great American philosopher and social psychologist George Herbert Mead wrote, "Just in proportion as we organize by hostility do we suppress individuality." Mead's statement only too accurately describes the current state of affairs with reference to the diagnosis and treatment of sex offenders in the United States.

Mead specified his concerns that those who would help offenders, not trust too easy alliances with the criminal justice system.

> It is quite impossible psychologically, to hate the sin and love the sinner. We are very much given to cheating ourselves in this regard. We assume that we can detect, pursue, indict, prosecute, and punish the criminal and still retain toward him the attitude of reinstating him in the community as soon as he indicates a change in social attitude himself, that we can at the same time watch for the definite transgression of the statute to catch and overwhelm the offender, and comprehend the situation out of which the offense grows. *But the two attitudes, that of control of crime by the hostile procedure of the law and that of control through comprehension of social and psychological conditions, cannot be combined.* To understand is to forgive and the social procedure seems to deny the very responsibility which the law affirms, and on the other hand the pursuit by criminal justice inevitably awakens the hostile attitude in the offender and renders the attitude of mutual comprehension practically impossible. (Mead 1917–1918: emphasis added)

The predicament posed by Mead over seventy years ago was reiterated in the Keynote address of John Money to the attendees at the 1991 International Conference on the Treatment of Sex Offenders at the University of Minnesota. As he put it,

> . . . the adversarial principle of the law is *incompatible* with the preventive principle of biomedical science. The adversarial system for the treatment of paraphilia by means of prosecution and punishment must be pronounced an abject failure. (Money 1992, emphasis added)

It is an uncomfortable message to bring to professionals who are already much taken with their dual roles as helpers and ersatz agents of law enforcement. However, the Faustian bargain has been made and the marriage of convenience has been consummated. The criminal law has become integral to the helping contract. Indeed, those helpers who do not subscribe to this view are now systematically excluded from the process. The view is expressed succinctly in the *Prosecutor,* the journal of National Association of Prosecutors—"The mental health professional must believe that treatment and prosecution are not incompatible . . ." (Peters et al. 1990). It seems simple enough, but it's too simple. If Mead and Money are correct, the issue from this unholy alliance will be stillborn. The effect will neither minimize child abuse, nor assist society in better understanding the roots of the problem. If recent experience is any measure, it will have a decidedly deadening effect on both theory and research regarding the paraphilias. Mead summarized the dilemma succinctly, "The social worker in the court is the sentimentalist, and the legalist in the social settlement in spite of his learned doctrine is the ignoramus."

Mead's reservations concerning those who would remedy social ills through the criminal justice system were shared by others of his time. Indeed, one of the founders and pioneers of professional American social work, University of Chicago teacher and writer Charlotte Towle, expressed her opposition to professional social workers even associating themselves with the newly created juvenile courts—for fear of the corruption of casework practice if it were routinely joined to the coercive powers of the court.

It was her view that such a combination could undermine the basic values from which the new profession had been formed. Her advice was rejected—and for a while, it seemed it had been wrongheaded. However, as the number of professionals associated with courts and correctional agencies grew, the compromises mounted. Being allied with the criminal justice system is to tie one's professional identity to the shifting politics of the state or national government. As the politics of crime and punishment in the country have taken a turn toward the vicious—particularly with reference to offenders—professional theory and practice have followed in near lock-step.

A good example of this phenomenon can be found in California, where over 39,000 of the 100,000 inmates in that state's prisons in 1990 were put there by their probation officers (most supervised and managed by professional social workers and counselors). The inmates were imprisoned as "technical violators," in other words, not complying with the conditions of their supervision and counseling—such things as not keeping appointments, not attending Alcoholics Anonymous meetings, being unemployed, moving without permission, marrying without permission, having a "dirty" urine when tested for drugs, etc. None had engaged in behavior sufficient to warrant an arrest or new criminal charge. In effect, they had aggravated their helper by not complying with the conditions of their help. It is the logical and eventual byproduct of tying professional help to authority, and it makes eminently sensible the comment of social historian and civil libertarian David Rothman, that these days, any potential client should treat his or her helper, be it a social worker, psychologist or psychiatrist, as he or she would treat a policeman—with respect and civility—saying nothing.

Until recently, the distinction between help and coercion, though frequently absent in state institutional care, was still the guiding tradition among most psychiatrists, clinical psychologists, and psychiatric social workers who, even when occasionally succumbing to compromises, recognized the distinction between ethical responsibilities to the client versus allegiances to governmental entities.

But in this last decade of the twentieth century, the joining of legal authority with help is hardly an issue for discussion among contemporary helping professionals. Such arrangements are the norm and it is not uncommon to see social workers, psychiatrists and psychologists, who in the past would have been expected to be advocates for their clients, now advising prosecutorial staff (including so-called victims' assistance units) on strategies to best "get" the offender. Treating sex offenders is done on a playing field in which it is "us" versus "them" and where treatment, when grudgingly afforded, is accompanied by coercive threat or witless rejection proudly affirmed from the first interview.

It is now clear that Towle was more than a little correct. Such basic values as acceptance, client self-determination, individualization, and confidentiality have been effectively undermined by the association of the helping professions with the adversarial criminal justice system.

But it doesn't end there; the adversarial stances of criminal justice are now built into the very theories of treatment. For example, we are told that the victim will not fully recover unless he or she sees the perpetrator sent off to prison. What nonsense! To my knowledge, there is not a single controlled research study which demonstrates this bit of dogma. It does however, give a gloss of validity to countertransference feelings which too many therapists are wont to confront.

We see the enshrinement of attitudes which are antithetical to authentic therapy. In the current issue of one of the largest popular national magazines, one can read statements from putative experts in treating sex offenders such as, "The sex criminal is anything but 'sick.' He is calculating and deliberate in his actions. He just shuts off his knowledge of right and wrong long enough to commit his crimes" (Stanton Samenow, quoted in Bidinotto 1991).

Or take these comments from another proclaimed expert in treating sex offenders, "Every sex offender should do some jail time—it gives them a taste of reality." No one can gainsay the fact that some predatory offenders need to be kept in secure settings, but let's not call it "therapy." It satisfies only those with a need to feed "gut" reactions—but betrays a surprising naïveté as to the detritus of the prison experience and the outcome research on such matters.

Further characterizing those he would "treat," this expert adds, "Sexual offenders are far better at manipulation and deceit than many therapists can comprehend" (Steven Jensen, quoted in Bidinotto 1991). This is the same person who in other forums has bemoaned the lack of proper accreditation of those who would attempt to treat sex offenders, apparently to ensure they exhibit the proper degree of mistrust of their clientele before being considered qualified.

Of course, anyone who works long in this field can expect to be deceived by a client from time to time. In that event, it would seem to me that the focus should be first to question one's own suitability for coping with the problems such a client presents. I was taught that contempt for the client more likely revealed inexpertise on the part of the therapist—usually as much the result of countertransference as a response to objective reality. If indeed a client elicits anger or rejection from a therapist, the situation affords a therapeutic challenge.

As the criminal justice juggernaut plows on, we see the traditionally most bleeding of "bleeding hearts," the so-called "child protective" social workers, becoming indistinguishable from police investigators. Those who in years past would look to develop psychosocial studies and personal histories to increase understanding of the possible roots and family concomitants of aberrant and compulsive behaviors are now bent primarily on gathering evidence for making the case for prosecution. When it comes to accusations of sex abuse, "child protective services" embody what the family therapist-psychiatrist Salvador Minuchin once characterized as "family dismemberment services."

In this kind of political climate, therapists are expected to deliver one basic commodity—what the late eminent British social anthropologist Sir Edmund Leach, in speaking of "treatment" as applied to delinquents, referred to as "the imposition of discipline by force—the maintenance of the existing order against threats which might arise from its own internal contradictions" (Leach 1968).

All of this takes its toll on truth. To be effective at the tasks set forth in the criminal justice model, the professional helper must necessarily immerse himself or herself in that primal paranoid process first named by the great American psychiatrist Harry Stack Sullivan as "selective inattention." Only those facts which relate to conviction and punishment are relevant. At the same time, one must work hard at "inattending" to any realities which might otherwise dull the scent of the hunt.

One sees this mood against the backdrop of the new federal sentencing guidelines and mandatory sentencing laws being adopted by the states. The value of ignorance is proudly proclaimed—such realities as family background, physical or mental impairment, exposure to violence or abuse, are all made irrelevant and inadmissible in deciding what to do with an offender. The approach is that of the meat axe. "Do the crime, do the time." It's a great slogan for a politician on the make, but sadly, it is the ideology of the militant ignoramus. As this attitude spills over into the philosophy of help, it has produced a new generation of diagnosticians and therapists who closely resemble those functionaries whom H. G. Wells referred to in his most dystopian fantasies as "psychojusters."

Why this sea change in the ethics of professional helpers? I believe there are a number of reasons. An embarrassingly obvious one is the fact that so many are able to label themselves therapists with such a dearth of life experience and narrowness of liberal education; a couple of years of graduate school, sometimes less, and one can hang out a shingle. The focus in such a shallow world is upon technique rather than study, control rather than understanding. And though it may be crucial to assist the client in managing his or her impulses, what "works" cannot alone suffice for the thoughtful professional.

In addition, the mechanisms of insurance reimbursement have served to stunt such crucial procedures as the thoughtful gathering of a complete social history, while the static labeling schema of the *Diagnostic and Statistical Manual* of the American Psychiatric Association (1987) has drained aberrant behavior of meaning. Having been in the field for thirty-three years, I am increasingly dumbstruck at the inability of newly graduated psychiatrists to conduct a sensitive interview or take a thorough history. I fear it is less an inability than a view that such information is peripheral to the "illness" at hand.

One of the founders of the cognitive psychology movement, the eminent American psychologist Jerome Bruner, in his recent book, *Acts of Meaning,* writes:

> Now let me tell you first what I and my friends thought the (cognitive) revolution was about back there in the late 1950s. It was, we thought, an all-out effort to establish meaning as the central concept of psychology—not stimuli and responses, not overtly observable behavior, not biological drives and their transformation, but meaning. (Bruner 1990).

He goes on to recall that, "The cognitive revolution as originally conceived virtually required that psychology join forces with anthropology and linguistics, philosophy and history, even with the discipline of the law" (in discussions and theory building).

Bruner stresses above all the need for narrative, what sociologists like

Erving Golfman have referred to in another context as the individual's "career"—that strand which winds through life experiences, taking new directions, some a result of decision, others by chance, some "make-believe," some based in hard realities—always saving a substantial degree of unpredictability—the variables being so many and so complex.

Traditionally, the closest one could get to this in clinical practice was through the personal narrative—not only as a factual accounting of life's events and memories, but also as a fictive exercise—how one views oneself and creates stories accordingly. As Bruner puts it:

> In pursuit of this aim, we obviously cannot track people through life and observe or interrogate them each step of the way. Even if we could, doing so would transform the meaning of what they were up to. And, in any case, we would not know how to put the bits and pieces together at the end of the inquiry. One viable alternative is obvious—to do the inquiry retrospectively, through *autobiography.* And I do not mean an autobiography in the sense of a "record" (for there is no such thing). I mean, simply, an account of what one thinks one did in what settings in what ways for what felt reasons. It will inevitably be a narrative . . . its form will be as revealing as its substance. It does not matter whether the account conforms to what others might say who were witnesses, nor are we in pursuit of such ontologically obscure issues as whether the account is "self-deceptive" or "true." Our interest, rather, is only in what the person thought he did, what he thought he was doing it for, what kinds of plights he thought he was in, and so on. (Bruner 1990: 119–20)

In this world, the "story" is as important as the "factual" history. Indeed, it may be more important. It's why I've never been particularly distressed by a client who could not from the beginning tell the whole "truth." That usually comes later in the relationship. But reaching that point is impossible if one rejects the story out of hand, thereby demeaning the person even though he or she be self-manufactured from whole cloth.

When one gets past this point, the client's narrative often slowly begins to align itself with harsher realities. Then the clinician is positioned to both assist the client *and* contribute something of value to the society in reaching some semblance of understanding and accommodation. This also suggests that the representatives of the society must be afforded the histories and told the stories. This cannot be done easily, nor should the clinician expect it to be. Such realities are anathema to contemporary criminal justice procedure.

If we are to break confidentiality—which is now routine among helping professionals working within the criminal justice system—let it not be based in such self-defeating legal stratagems as mandatory reporting laws. Let us drag before the public something more complete than a list of putative crimes and impulses. Let us insist upon bringing into the legal arena that which is regularly ruled out as irrelevant—the life histories and experiences of our clientele—those strands of chance and meaning which have wound their destructive ways through the lives of those who threaten us.

In recent years, I have done a fair amount of death penalty work, preparing and corroborating background studies on individuals who have committed the most heinous of acts. I've never known one to fall out of the sky. The theme of the evil perpetrator who rose out of a "normal" family and background is a folk myth which serves the function of allowing us to avoid dealing with uncomfortable realities. Its purpose is to provide us reassurance, albeit false. It is much the same dynamic which plagues the field of diagnosis and treatment of sex offenders. In refusing to recognize those realities which the legal system aggressively hides, society retreats to its own storytelling, stereotypical distortions, manipulations, and self-deceptions—ultimately of much greater import than those of the offender.

So finally, we who work with sex offenders have a role well beyond whatever help we may bring to an offender in stopping his or her destructive behavior. It seems to me that we must be messengers, bringing into the public arena, virtually always over its objections, the world from which the offender arose, and in which the society had a stake from the beginning.

One could also hope that along the way, in the gathering of that narrative, we might ourselves be set astir with a more than average dose of humility in a task which will probably always be beyond our puny efforts.

REFERENCES

American Psychiatric Association (1987). *Diagnostic and Statistical Manual of Mental Disorders.* 3rd Ed., rev. Washington, D.C.: Author.

Bidinotto, R. (1991, October). "Freed to Rape Again." *Reader's Digest.*

Bruner, J. (1990). *Acts of Meaning.* Cambridge, Mass.: Harvard University Press.

Leach, E. (1968). *A Runaway World* (BBC Reith Lectures, 1967). New York: Oxford University Press.

Mead, G. H. (1917-18). "The Psychology of Punitive Justice." *American Journal of Sociology* 23: 577–602.

Money, J. (1992). "False Accusations of Nosocomial Sexual Abuse: The Hand Bitten by the Dog It Feeds May Be Your Own." *Journal of Offender Rehabilitation* 18: 225–33.

Peters, J. M.; Dinsmore, J.; and Toth, P. (1990, Winter). "Why Prosecute Child Abuse?" *The Prosecutor.* (*The Prosecutor* is the journal of the National Association of Prosecutors. The authors are staff members of the National Center for Prosecution of Child Abuse, an arm of the American Prosecutor's Research Institute.)

Subject Index

www.ingramcontent.com/pod-product-compliance
Ingram Content Group UK Ltd.
Pitfield, Milton Keynes, MK11 3LW, UK
UKHW041823100926
8556IPUK00001B/1

9 780879 758837